D1556587

Hang Your Halo in the Hall

THE SAVILE CLUB FROM 1868

Hang Your Halo in the Hall

THE SAVILE CLUB FROM 1868

by

Garrett Anderson

Published by The Savile Club

Hang Your Halo In the Hall
The Savile Club From 1968

First published 1993

© Anthony Garrett Anderson 1993

ISBN 0 9520152 0 X

The Savile Club
69 Brook Street
London W1Y 2ER

Printed and bound in Great Britain by Hartnolls Ltd, Bodmin

ACKNOWLEDGEMENTS

I would like to begin by thanking the General Committee and the House Committee of the Savile Club which in 1988 under the chairmanship of the late Neil Salmon and Clive Bingley respectively, nominated me to write this history. Flattering though this was, in the event it has turned out to be a daunting task, not least because of the vast parade – much greater than I or anyone had anticipated – of distinguished past and present members which emerged from the surviving records.

I have been assisted greatly in my research and writing during the time that has elapsed since 1988 by the many members who have written to me or otherwise sought me out to ply me with their valuable and often entertaining reminiscences of the Club's life – some of which have extended over more than half a century. There were in excess of a hundred such contributions so it is clearly impossible to acknowledge them all here; nevertheless I am profoundly grateful to them for lightening my task. Wherever possible I have ascribed the tale to the source within the text but I hope that those others who remain anonymous will accept this as my overdue thanks.

There are however, some individual members who have given much of their time and provided me with constant encouragement during my labours and at the risk of being invidious I feel I must single them out here.

First and foremost is Winston Graham, who, as well as adding distinction to the book with his foreword, read most of it in typescript and made many valuable suggestions. Sir Arthur Vick winkled out of the Club's records those unfamiliar names which – in my unpardonable ignorance of scientific matters – I might not have immediately recognized as having been such revolutionary and pioneering figures in their own particular fields.

Michael Pope with his intimate knowledge of late nineteenth and early twentieth century composers has been exceedingly generous in checking the proofs of my chapter on those Savilians who did so much to transform Britain's status as a musical nation during this period, while Gavin Henderson in his own inimitable way brought me up to date with the names and careers of more recent Savile musicians with whose work I was less familiar.

Dallas Bower, who has been a mainstay of the Club since 1944, has enlivened my work with his accounts of the Savile during the last half century as well as giving me access to his encyclopaedic knowledge of the history of film, radio and television during the period covered and in all of which he and some of his colleagues at the Savile played so prominent a part.

I am particularly indebted to Michael Meyer and his publishers, Secker and Warburg, who have been kind enough to allow me to quote so extensively from his memoirs, *Not Prince Hamlet*. Where possible I have sought permission to reproduce copyright material; however if I have anywhere unwittingly trespassed on private property I hope that the proprietors will graciously accept my apologies in advance.

I am also indebted to The National Portrait Gallery which has provided me with many of the illustrations which illuminate the text. In this respect I would like to thank Tom Griffin of Griffin Associates who has been responsible for the pictorial layout of the book. He is also responsible for the design of the dust jacket. I also wish to thank Barnet Saidman, with whose work fellow members will be familiar from his many beautiful depictions of the Club's interiors which have featured in several leading magazines over the years, some of which are reproduced here.

Colin Merton, the Club's honorary librarian, has been helpful throughout in seeking out sources on my behalf. In common with many of his kind he regards any gap in his bookshelves as a personal bereavement and I must thank him here for managing to contain *some* of his impatience with my depredation of the Monument's treasures. I have been also greatly assisted by Nigel Perryman, Michael Pater and Sally Beale Collins who undertook at various times to transfer my shaky handwriting on to computer disk. This having been done my editor, Roger Smith – most courteous and understanding of collaborators – performed sterling work in rooting out the occasional solecism and advising me on knotty points of grammer and syntax.

In preparing the typescript for the typesetters both Roger Smith and I were greatly assisted by Tom Baistow who brought his years of journalistic experience to bear to ensure that both in typescript and page proof the copy would emerge immaculate from the printers. The firm which has carried out this task is FPC International – a Pillans and Wilson Company – of which our House Committee chairman, Bill Beale Collins is a director, and more recent member, Bob Hodgson, is chairman and managing director.

The handsome product that has resulted is due in large measure to their production executive, John Clamp, whose meticulous attention to detail and miscroscopic examination of the text would make a fine-tooth comb seem in comparison to resemble a hayrake.

Before closing these acknowledgements I would like to pay tribute to Peter Aldersley, the Club's Secretary since 1977 until his retirement at the end of 1991. Without him – as every member of that period now knows – the Club's history would indeed have ended on page 408 and there would have been none of that foreseeable and prosperous future into which Peter's succesor, Nicholas Storey, is now so ably and elegantly steering us.

Finally I must thank my many friends at the Savile who sustained and encouraged me in the face of the many personal difficulties I encountered in the course of writing this book. It has also been some compensation that in researching it and in informing myself of the activities of all those men of "different professions and opinions" who have graced the club over the years, I believe I have learned more than I ever did during my years at University.

And so, with qualified awe, but unqualified affection

I dedicate this book
to my fellow members of the Savile Club.

Sodalitas Convivium

A.G.A.

Contents

LIST OF ILLUSTRATIONS

FOREWORD

by Winston Graham

Ogden Nash once said that to be an Englishman was to belong to the most exclusive club in the world. A debatable point. Please discuss.

But that London is the centre of the club culture is hardly disputed, or that a few of its clubs form, in their own particular and exclusive yet agreeable way, the nucleus of a mainly male society unique in the world.

Among these – of which there must be fewer than ten – the Savile Club has its special place. It is, in my view, the most *interesting* club in London. When I was elected forty-two years ago it seemed to me to be full of wits, wags, sages, drunks, and holy eminences in every profession; some elderly and sombre, like H.G. Wells, some elderly and effervescent, like Compton Mackenzie, some youngish and sombre, like Peter Rennel Rodd, some youngish and jolly like Monja Danischewsky and Lionel Hale. Above all – and here it is perhaps unique – it was totally classless: Walter Greenwood, who drew on his humble origins to write *Love on the Dole*, was as much at home there as that quintessential aristocrat, Eddie Sackville-West, the heir to Knole. Equally, age was no barrier to communication as, with the generation gap, it is in most of the world. I have often seen a man of about twenty-eight suddenly go across and enter into earnest discussion with a limping seventy-eight, solely because they had some subject in common.

It is also a club which has never had any religious or moral prejudice. Practising Muslims, Jews, and Christians have been as welcome as the most outspoken of atheists. Nearly forty years ago I heard two committee members discussing a potential candidate. One said: "I think he's probably been a Borstal boy." The other replied: "That should make him more interesting."

Sometimes in those days one thought of Cowper's: "Oh, to the club, the scene of savage joys, the school of coarse good-fellowship and noise." At the other extreme there could develop a tense and sober discussion on some subject close to the vital affairs of the world. This book recalls a number of such occasions when momentous decisions were taken in the Club which have affected us all.

Or one pictures Thomas Hardy writing many of his later matchless poems on the Club writing paper, late into the night.

With the enormous historical background of the eminent men who have been members, it is easy to look back – even four decades, as I can – and then look around one and wonder if the present membership is one half so good, or could ever become so good, as the muster of extraordinarily brilliant and likeable men who have been incumbents in the past. A useful antidote to this is an article about the Savile in *The Times*, written in 1923 by, it is thought, Edmund Gosse, rather regretting the quality of the present intake of younger members compared to the great achievers of his day. Not only does he appear to overlook the membership of such up-and-coming youngsters as Adrian Boult, Ernest Rutherford, J.B.S. Haldane, Arthur Bliss, Max Beerbohm and Edward Elgar, but – as a further corrective to those claiming to judge for posterity – many of the famous men cited by him among his older contemporaries have been rendered quite insignificant by the passage of the years. It is a salutary lesson.

To write a true and full and perceptive history of this unusual club it was necessary to find an unusual writer. Anthony Garrett Anderson is just that. Educated as a historian at Trinity College, Dublin, a member of the Club since 1966, he has published two acclaimed novels, and been involved in many other literary projects. This history of the Savile Club is a major book which will, I believe, distinguish him in a new way. It has taken three years to write – partly because of a disastrous fire in 1975 which destroyed many of the records and archives and so necessitated the gathering and checking of material from secondary sources – but also because of the author's consuming interest in and development of his theme. In the hands of many writers this history would have been a list of famous names, with a collection of facts and anecdotes hung on them to decorate and embellish. What Tony has done is to enlarge one's interest by following and exploring the lives of many of the Savilians far beyond the doors of the Savile, so that the history of a single club becomes a valuable record of the times in which that club has existed.

This foreword is necessarily short, for there is little one can say about the Savile which has not been fully and elegantly covered in the pages which follow. Most present-day Savilians will want this book because they are members: they will be fascinated to discover how little they know of the Club's history. I commend non-members to read the book not for its subject but for its content. They will not be disappointed.

Winston Graham

Exterior view of 69-71 Brook Street, home of the Savile Club since 1927
(Photo: Barnet Saidman)

107 Piccadilly which for nearly 50 years was regarded with such affection by Savilians as the ideal clubhouse.

INTRODUCTION

Many years ago when the world and I were young and my nerves, like my arteries, were less hardened by the toils of time, I first entered the Savile Club as a member. I had, of course, been a guest on several occasions as part of the necessary preamble; Wynford Vaughan Thomas had been my sponsor and on this, my first visit to the Club in my own right, he was late in arriving to meet me. So I sat, uncomfortably alone, envying a group in the opposite corner who had obviously lunched well and were exchanging what I felt sure must be priceless pearls of wit – after all, was not this the Club which prided itself on the scintillating conversation of its members? But there was I, a member at last, alone and speechless. I remembered from my previous visits that they seemed to be a kindly lot but this did not prevent dreadful intimations of mortality dating from non-conformist deeds during my first days at prep school. Was I, perhaps, sitting in a prefect's chair? Was I dressed in a manner forbidden to new boys? Ye gods! Should I even be smoking?

I was just about to retreat into Brook Street to wait for Wynford there, when one of the Augustan figures got up and approached the bar. He came; he stopped; he eyed me. "Are you a new member?" he barked.

"Yes," I said and just in time prevented myself from leaping to attention and adding, "I'm afraid so, sir."

"Well what on earth are you doing sitting there all on your own? Come and meet some of your fellow members. I'm Michael Ayrton. Who the devil are you?"

And so I was introduced to the group; to Malcolm Arnold, composer surely of the wittiest and most accessible of great modern English music; Arthur Cooper, the distinguished oriental scholar; Merlyn Evans, the puckish genius of a Welsh artist; and Robert Clark, perhaps the most talented yacht designer of his generation. They were the first of many friends of diverse interests, differing professions and wildly separated walks of life whom I was to meet, and whose friendship I would cherish over succeeding years in this accommodating sodality of disparate spirits.

Such a baptismal experience at the Savile is not uncommon. Nearly every member will have a similar tale to tell to demonstrate that the essential spirit with which the original founders invested the Club has remained alive and well since it was formed over 125 years ago.

The infant Savile Club was conceived in June 1868. As is usual at the outset of such happy events, the proud parents had wavered at first about the name their progeny should bear and the precise location and furnishings of the nursery in which it should be reared. But from the very first they were adamant that certain principles should be paramount throughout its existence. Central to these was that

1

it should consist in a "mixture of men of different professions and opinions" and that "it should have a careful process of election". To promote social and friendly relations between members who might not otherwise have an opportunity to mix with one another, it was also soon provided that a table d'hôte dinner should be served each night at one communal table.

This innovation was quite contrary to the usual practice in most of the established London clubs, which served food and wine to their members on the restaurant principle of separate meals at separate tables. But such insularity was anathema to the founders of the new Club. Similarly it soon became the custom that anyone looking lonely or lost in any of the public rooms should be welcomed into the general company if he so wished, irrespective of whether he was already known or not.

From the very first, also, the Club was designed to appeal to young men of promise, talent and wit who might not yet have achieved prominence in their chosen professions and might therefore be unable to afford the considerable expense of belonging to some of the more established contemporary clubs. To this end the original subscription was set at two guineas per annum with an entrance fee of the same amount. Likewise, the table d'hôte dinner was provided at a fixed price of three shillings. Times have indeed changed: the figures are now £635 and up to £500 respectively and the cheapest meal will cost four to five pounds. But the attitudes determining the selection of members have not changed. When other clubs, which might superficially seem comparable to the Savile, appear to offer their more eager embraces to those who have already achieved fame and fortune, the Savile has from the first cast its friendly eye on men of promise. Thus, although the Club leans towards the arts in its choice of members it has still contrived at one time or another to elect seventeen young men who later went on to become Nobel prize-winners, fourteen of whom were en-Nobeled for achievements in science.

Maurice Druon, one of the great contemporary cultural figures of France, gave a memorable address to the Club in April 1968 to mark his recent appointment as permanent secretary to the Académie Française, in which he flatteringly compared that association of "immortals" with the Savile, of which he has been a member since 1958:

> It is a very great honour and a very great joy for me to speak to you in this Club whose members include many of my dearest friends, and to which I am extremely proud to belong.
>
> When, in France, I am asked about the difficulties through which your country is passing, and the question is accompanied by pessimistic prophecies, I reply: "Don't worry. As long as the Savile Club exists, England is in no danger." And I go on to explain what I mean. As long as there are clubs in this country, institutions where men of different temperaments, origins and professions enjoy meeting together in a place they have chosen and a society which has chosen them, to talk around a

2

table and over a good wine, to confide their problems to each other, to help each other solve them, to express their opinions while respecting those of others, and to share their knowledge with their fellows – as long as all that endures, British civilization is not really threatened. For it is the very essence of civilization to live among one's fellows with honour and grace.

...Without the Savile, would I (for instance) have met Humphrey Hare, not only that perfect translator of my works, but also that model of some of the finest human virtues? It is with him in mind that I venture to say that the Savile Club is a place of civilization.

The French have no such thing as club-life. The few clubs that exist in Paris bear no resemblance to yours, either in the way they are run, or above all in the sort of life that is led behind their doors.

Yet there is an institution, over three hundred years old, whose members, although they don't lunch there, don't dine there, don't drink there, don't sleep there, and meet there only once a week, are still in the habit of saying about it: *"C'est notre Club."* That institution is the Académie Française...

Such an emphatic tribute might easily be discounted as Gallic hyperbole by the many who are unaware of the history of the Club and its past and present membership; for the particular distinction of the Savile and the individual contributions of its members to British and international affairs has, so far, gone largely unrecorded. Self-advertisement is not nor ever has been a Savile characteristic, nor, since its foundation, has it been regarded as acceptable for an individual member to flaunt his particular eminence or public honours within the Club. Lothar Mendes, that diminutive mid-European wit who had nevertheless been a giant of pre-war Hollywood, summed this up in his own peculiar brand of English when he rebuked any attempts at grandeur by new members with the admonition: "Here, we 'ang our haloes in the 'all", a motto which came to be an alternative, if more demotic, addendum to the more canonical *Sodalitas Convivium*.

Since its earliest days, as we shall see, the Club has faithfully maintained the principle of electing "men of different professions and opinions". It is difficult therefore, when writing about it, to mould what is essentially an amorphous collection of individuals into a conveniently coherent shape which will define the unique nature of the Savile and describe its peculiar charm. It would be easier with other clubs which provide for a specific brand of person. There are some for instance which cater for politicians of particular hues; but the Savile has contained politicians of several hues. There are clubs which cater for lawyers; the Savile has numbered a fair proportion of these also, including two Lord Chancellors and a host of others from Masters of the Rolls and judges down to the merest junior just setting out at the Bar. There are clubs which pride themselves on galleries of actors; the Savile has welcomed them too since the days of Sir Henry Irving through to the time of Esmé Percy, Sir Ralph Richardson and present luminaries such as Edward Fox, Kenneth Haigh, Brian Cox, Graham Crowden and many others. In fact, the Savile can claim men of worth, often of great distinction, from every field of human endeavour. Scientists, musicians, writers, painters have all been lured to the Club in search of relaxation and intellectual stimulus in good company; and they came there, not to "talk shop" with men of their own profession, but to extend their horizons by mixing with people of similar merit in other disciplines.

In 1935 the singer Harry Plunket Greene wrote:

> If you were to ask a member of the Savile Club to tell you the secret of its success or to define its charm, he would be hard put to it to give you an answer. It has no politics and is not affiliated to any single one of the arts or the sciences. In spite of its reputation it is innocent of snobbery; the only qualification needful in the candidate is that he should hold an honourable place in his profession, if he has one, and be recognized as having his heart in the right place.

That, perhaps, is as good a *description* as any of the Savile, though it avoids the pitfalls which would ensue in attempting any kind of *definition* of its make-up. Indeed, the impossibility of definition has been evident since the very first year of the Club's existence in 1868-9. In that year, out of 136 original members there were, in the realm of politics, 18 peers and politicians of every political persuasion, Liberal, Tory, Radical and Irish National, representing every rank from cabinet minister to back-bencher. In the greener pastures of religion there were Nonconformists, Anglicans, Anglo-Catholics, Roman-Catholics and Jews; the Rev. Mandell Creighton, Bishop of London, was an original member as was that fierce apostle of agnosticism and free-thinking, Sir Leslie Stephen. There were 16 fellows of the Royal Society, a future president of the Royal Academy, novelists and academics galore. There were three or four of the richest men in England, and several more who were hovering on the borderline of poverty. The only thing they had in common was that they enjoyed each other's company. Nothing has changed.

So, even when enumerating the several professions of members in that original year and succeeding years, no clue is to be found to explain the mystery of what brings us together and gives life to the Savile; and to complicate the matter, variety of profession in the Club's members has often been compounded by polymathy in their actual occupations. There have been medical practitioners who have gone on to shine more brightly as poets, such as the Laureate, Robert Bridges: there have been poets who have distinguished themselves as medical men like Sir Charles Sherrington, O.M., who was president of the Royal Society and winner of the Nobel Prize for medicine in 1929. There have been military men who have made their mark as musicians, like Eustace Balfour, and astro-physicists who have had illustrious army careers like Colonel "Chubby" Stratton. One could go on for the list seems as endless as it is various. The whole problem of trying to capture the essence of Savile membership by studying its individual occupations was pointedly made shortly after the war by the journalist Denzil Batchelor, who was standing at the bar one lunch-time when C.B. Fry, perhaps the most dazzling intellectual and athletic all-rounder of his generation, entered the room in a state of some excitement. He announced that he had acquired a new enthusiasm, this time for the Turf.

"Indeed?" said Batchelor, "in what capacity: breeder, trainer, jockey or horse?"

Variety of "professions" would be as nothing if it were not matched by considerable achievement in each; nor would the history of the Savile be of more than parochial interest were it not that some of its members have contributed as much, if not more, to the whole of society as they have to the life of the Savile. Arnold Toynbee, who became a member during his visits to London from the Paris Peace Conference in 1919, pronounced as a dictum in his monumental *Study of History:* "The intelligible units of historical study are not 'nations' or 'periods', but 'societies'... no portion of history is intelligible as a thing-in-itself, but only as part of a larger whole"; and the truth of this became increasingly apparent during the process of piecing together the story of the Savile. While sifting its remaining records and patching them with the memoirs of those men of "different professions" who at one time or another were its members, it gradually emerged that over the years, in the public rooms of the Club, there had taken place private discussions which had their repercussions on national and international events; from Viscount Goschen restructuring the national debt in 1888, to Herbert Agar conspiring to bring America into the war in 1940; Cockcroft and Rutherford in the Sandpit planning the exploitation of atomic energy; Robert Henriques consulting with Ben-Gurion in the library on how British Jewry might contribute to the cause of Israel's independence, together with many other such contributory examples of Toynbee's theory of the "larger whole" of history.

In short, nearly every field of activity has been explored and often enriched by men who at one stage or another in their careers have sought and found both stimulation and relaxation at the Savile. So what began as a modest account of their origins for the current membership of a small but merry West End club with no pretensions, emerged as something perhaps less than a commentary on, but certainly more than a mere footnote to, the history of England during the last 125 years. Let that be my excuse, if one is necessary, for dwelling at such length on the history of our beloved Club.

CHAPTER ONE

General History from 1868

There is a quaint sentence of Sir Herbert Stephen's which appears in *both* the previous Savile handbooks (now out of print) which may as well be given an airing for the third time if only on account of its persistence and the information it contains:

> It seems to be established, by inquiry and investigation, that the individual who did most to bring the new Club into existence, and has therefore the best right to be remembered as the founder of the Savile, was Auberon Herbert.

Quite apart from his being the great-great-uncle of Auberon Waugh, Herbert seems in other less remote ways to have been quite an extraordinary man. Widely known as "the Politician in Trouble about his Soul", he was a younger brother of the 4th Earl of Carnarvon – also a founder member of the Club – and despite his family's prominence in Conservative politics his championship of the rights of the individual led him to leave the Conservative Party and offer himself as Liberal/Radical candidate for Berkshire, to which seat he was elected in 1868. This was the same year that, together with others of like mind, he set about founding the new club. Indeed, founding clubs seems to have been something of a habit with him for he is credited with having established two others while he was an undergraduate at Oxford – the Canning and the Chatham. The new club which occupied his attentions in 1868 must, however, be deemed his masterpiece, though it was three years before it acquired the name by which it is now known.

> The Savile Club is a noteworthy instance of evolutionary growth [commented a writer in *The Times* of August 1923]. Some clubs come into existence to meet a long-felt need and others spring up suddenly owing to political disruption. The earliest physical manifestation of the Savile was not thus brought about. There is in existence a short printed memorandum showing that the Club really dates from a difference of opinion among the members of the Eclectic Club in 1868, which has arisen through the non-acceptance by this club of an offer made by the Medical Club of a good set of rooms in Spring Gardens. The acceptance of this offer would have foreshadowed a change in the character of the club of which a majority of the Eclectics disapproved, the Eclectic having hitherto been a night club on the lines of the Cosmopolitan and Century.
>
> But a minority, of whom at least two are still living, held for a change,

7

and accepted the offer. The chief mover in this enterprise was Auberon Herbert. Probably most of the new members were known to one another; the table d'hôte dinner was established from the first, and the custom of general conversation, then initiated, prevails to this day.

Sodalitas Convivium remains the motto of the Club, and upon the table d'hôte dinner, the ark of the Savilian convenant, the sacrilegious hand of the reformer has never been laid. In 1871 a move was made to 15, Savile Row, and the Savile Club appeared.

The "difference of opinion" among the members of the Eclectic Club had led to the distribution of the following undated document, probably early in May 1868:

The Medical Club having offered the Eclectic Club a pleasant and complete Set of Rooms at 9 Spring Gardens, overlooking Trafalgar Square, and the offer having been declined by a General Meeting of the Eclectic, who are at present unwilling to carry out their original design, and desire to retain their character as a Night Club only, a certain number of the Eclectic have determined to form themselves into a body for the purpose of carrying out, as a separate club, the proposal of the Medical Club. The Medical Club undertakes all expenses of service, firing, lights, etc., including rent, for £400 per annum. The members of the new Club will pay an Entrance-fee of £2 2s., and a Subscription of £2 2s. per annum; the number of the Club will be eventually raised to 300; but in order that the offer of the Medical Club may be accepted at once, and the election of Members may not take place hurriedly, Members will be asked to guarantee whatever sum they may think fit, in addition to their Subscriptions, for the next three years, for which period the lease has to be signed.

The new club will be established on the following principles:
1. A thorough simplicity in all arrangements.
2. The mixture of men of different professions and opinions; and a careful process of election.
3. Early Evening Meetings once or twice in the week.

It is also suggested that the Club should have a good selection of Foreign Newspapers, and of the best Maps.

The present Members of the new Club are:

The Rev. R. St. John Tyrrwhitt	The Earl of Carnarvon
The Rev. J. B. Payne	Godfrey Lushington, Esq
The Rev. J. Robertson	F. Mowatt, Esq
The Rev. Austen Leigh	Dr Andrew Clark
The Rev. T. W. Fowle	H. A. Hunt, Esq
John Murray, Esq	J. F. Cheetham, Esq
J. Macpherson, Esq	J. Brett, Esq
Hodgson Pratt, Esq	Graham Dakyns, Esq

C. Roundell, Esq
A. Rutson, Esq
Professor Bonamy Price
Professor Williamson
Professor Fleeming Jenkyn
Captain Helbert
Captain E. Kennard
F. Phillpotts, Esq
J. Phillpotts, Esq
R. G. Herbert, Esq
Hon. Alan Herbert
Hon. Auberon Herbert
W. E. Forster, Esq, M.P.
W. Morrison, Esq, M.P.
C. Goschen, Esq
Alexander Macmillan, Esq
H. Lee Warner, Esq
E. Levy, Esq
J. Bywater, Esq
E. Hay Currie, Esq
T. Gray, Esq
R. H. Patterson
F. Greenwood, Esq
J. Probyn, Esq

Ernest Hart, Esq
Ernest Noel, Esq
J. F. Payne, Esq
A. Sidgwick, Esq
— Wedgewood, Esq
Marwood Tucker
Thomas Woolner
Wentworth Buller
Adam Kennard, Esq
Rev. T. Fowler
Rev. J. Owen
Rev. R. Clarke
Henry Sidgwick, Esq
A. Denison, Esq
C. Appleton, Esq
Henry Hoare, Esq
E. Tebbs, Esq
John Mosley, Esq
D. Lathbury, Esq
James Corderey, Esq
John Morley, Esq
A. Storey, Esq
Captain Majendie
Rev. J. B. Phillpots

Perhaps, for the benefit of the modern reader, a sardonic footnote by Sir Herbert Stephen in the earlier memoir should be added to the above: "It will be noticed that the title of Night Club, which the Eclectic was too conservative to forgo, had not, in 1868, the same meaning for gentlemen of cultivated minds and orderly habits as it has for the police at present" – in fact it referred to institutions which assembled only periodically for the purpose of social conversation either at dinner or for drinks afterwards in various locations.

The circular reproduced above seems to have met with a speedy and satisfactory response for in June 1868 a new document was distributed:

New Club
9 Spring Gardens, SW
June 1868

The provisional Committee of the new Club have made arrangements at No. 9 Spring Gardens for the occupation of a set of very pleasant rooms on the first floor, overlooking Trafalgar Square, and for the supply on reasonable terms of breakfast, luncheon, and dinner.

It is proposed to conduct the Club on the following principles ...

The principles were then set out in nearly the same words as before, except that the "early evening meetings" were now declared to be "for the purposes of conversation" and there was no stated limitation as to their frequency. There was also included an additional "principle" that breakfasts and dinners were to be provided table d'hôte.

The notice concludes with a list of "present members of the new club" similar to that which had gone before but to which were added a further thirty-six names to bring the total founder members up to one hundred:

William P. Pattison	Harry Crompton, Esq
Edward Miall, Esq	W. H. Ashurst, Esq
Julian Goldsmith, Esq M.P.	Rev. J. Llewellyn Davies
Professor Wilson (Oxford)	Rev. W. Rogers (St. Botolph's)
Charles T. D. Acland, Esq	James Sant, Esq., A.R.A.
T. E. Cliffe-Leslie, Esq	F. A. Channing, Esq
T. H. Green, Esq	Rev. W. J. Tait
R. C. Jebb (Trinity, Camb.)	Leslie Stephen, Esq
James Heywood, Esq., F.R.S.	Professor Chandler (Oxford)
George Lillie Craik, Esq	Hon. D. Campbell
Dr. Cavafy	Walter Northcote, Esq
Dr. Pye-Smith	Lord Dufferin
Richard Harte, Esq	James Bryce, Esq
H. W. B. Davis, Esq	Sir Rowland Blennerhasset M.P.
E. J. Reed, Esq	Rev. C. K. Paul
Rev. J. Wood	Sir Samuel Baker
Hon. G. C. Brodrick	The Marquis of Lorne
Rev. W. Jowitt	Alfred Morrison, Esq

Although the above document was headed "New Club" it was not until a general meeting was held on 20 May 1869 that this title was formally adopted. That name was not destined to survive the move to Savile Row three years later. These three years, however, were important, for they established a pattern which was to be followed with very little variation throughout the history of the Club.

The custom of taking meals at a communal table was soon established and became, as it is now, a fundamental feature of the Club's existence. Furthermore, the clear statement in the original prospectus that visits to the Club were to be principally for the "purpose of conversation" – another eccentric innovation in the eyes of many contemporaries – was being greatly welcomed by the founder members who, it would seem, were generally discouraged from indulging this pleasurable art in similar institutions elsewhere.

"The careful process of election" had also been further refined. In January 1869 the committee resolved that "the names of all unelected Candidates should be reconsidered at the next meeting of the committee". Two months later it was resolved "that Candidates whose names had been passed over three times at

Committee should cease to be considered eligible ". Thus began the system of election whereby the effect of the anonymous "black ball" or the mere number of "supporters" was entirely eliminated.

The election of a candidate by the committee was then, and is now, unanimous or not at all. The process, which only very seldom fails to produce the correct result, survives to the present day. Osman Streater, a recent honorary secretary for elections and now the Club's chairman, gives the following detailed account of the procedure:

> The Savile has an election procedure which is unique amongst London clubs; it is a simple, fair, yet thoroughly searching system of establishing the suitability of a candidate. Should a friend or frequent guest of an existing member express interest in joining the club, the member, if he thinks it appropriate, will propose him by writing his name in the Candidates Book which is kept in the Morning Room. To this must be added the candidate's "description and usual address".
>
> The proposer's job is then to bring his candidate in and introduce him about in a discreet manner. It is, on the whole, not done to announce on introducing someone to a fellow member that he is a candidate; and it can be positively counter-productive to follow this up, immediately, with a request that the Savilian concerned go forthwith to the book and endorse it. Much better to see if the candidate goes down well in the course of conversation, and then later, discreetly, to inform the member that the guest is "in the book".
>
> Signing the book however, does not mean the automatic endorsement it constitutes elsewhere; at the Savile a signature simply signifies that the member concerned wishes to have a say in the candidate's election. It can be, and sometimes is, that the signatory is opposed to the candidate becoming a member. If that is the case, he cannot declare his opposition in the privacy of a letter without first publicly signing his name.
>
> About three weeks before an election meeting, the Club office sends out a stereotyped letter to each signatory. The letter requests such information as may be available on the candidate's suitability for membership. This is also when the candidate's proposer is requested to write his letter, which needs to be reasonably full.
>
> All that is required in these letters is relevant information. Length of friendship or acquaintance is a good starting point, whether it be twenty years of intimacy or ten minutes of casual conversation at the bar. Conversational abilities should follow, with other general impressions of the ability to fit in. The Honorary Secretary for Elections sorts the letters received, and in due course reads them to the General Committee at an Election Meeting.
>
> The vote in Committee on the election of a candidate must be unanimous. If one member's hand is not raised, the candidate is deferred.

Traditionally, the General Committee does not refuse to elect a candidate; instead, it defers consideration of his election. After being deferred four times, a candidate cannot be considered again for three years. In practice, in the rare event of a candidate being clearly unelectable, the Honorary Secretary for Elections has a quiet word with his proposer and advises withdrawal.

The Secretary of the Club does not attend Election Meetings, as he is not a member of the General Committee. He says that he is very glad about this, as it enables him the more effectively to deflect any furious telephone calls he may receive after an election.

* * * *

By 1870, eighteen months after its formation, the New Club was flourishing. In May of that year, at the behest of the landlord, it was shifted bodily from the first to the second floor of No. 9 Spring Gardens, where the accommodation was very slightly larger. Success had brought its attendant problems and the committee became preoccupied with schemes for further expansion. Its main purpose was to acquire more extensive premises, and one device which was considered was to amalgamate with another club. Various proposals were considered but none appeared to be entirely suitable until, in March 1871, the committee "became aware of a project entertained by members of the Anglo-American Committee for a social Club to be instituted in connection with the objects of their association". This committee, which probably also included some members of the New Club, should have been eager to grasp the immediate advantages offered by joining forces; the New Club would, at a stroke, increase its membership and would be better able to afford a house of its own, while the Anglo-American Committee would find in the New Club the accommodation which it sought.

Matters thereupon progressed rapidly. A joint sub-committee was formed to hammer out the formalities of "reconstruction" and in May 1871, in anticipation of a successful outcome from the negotiations, a recommendation was made "to make an offer to Dr Allen for the unexpired portion of his lease of No. 15, Savile Row". On 26 June twenty-three members of the Anglo-American Association were elected to the New Club; the first name on the list being Thomas Hughes Esq., M.P. Four days later the proposal to take the Savile Row house was unanimously adopted by a general meeting with Auberon Herbert in the chair. At this same meeting suggestions were invited as to a name for the Club: one was that it should be called the "Strangers' Club"; another that it be called the "Savile Club". Circulars were posted to all the members, and on 19 July it was announced that the name Savile Club had been chosen by a convincing majority.

All that now remained was to provide a legal foundation and set out in formal terms the Club's mode of administration. On 4 August a general meeting appointed Walter Morrison, M.P., Anthony John Mundella, M.P., and James

Heywood to be Trustees of the Club; the lease of 15 Savile Row, and all the other property of the Club, was to be vested in them or their successors and they were empowered to raise £3,500 by the issue to members of £20 debenture bonds, paying 5 per cent interest, or 5½ per cent if any one person held four or more of them.

During the autumn of 1871 the Club, reinforced by its new members, moved into the house at Savile Row. To tidy up some outstanding details another general meeting was held in December to discuss such matters as the number of guests a member might be allowed to entertain at the table d'hôte and "especially whether it should be lawful, and if so, under any and what restrictions, to introduce ladies as guests. The numbers for and against the latter part of the Motion under consideration were nearly equal" and that was practically the end of the matter for the next sixty years.

* * * *

At this stage in the Club's infancy when – to continue a previous analogy – it had progressed beyond the nursery stage, established an independent existence and begun to assert an individual character of its own, it might be useful to pause for a moment and take stock of its development so far.

As we have seen, one of the original intentions of its progenitors was to provide a suitable meeting place for congenial young men of promise but of slender means. Though this principle was being vigorously maintained through "the careful system of election" and the relatively modest cost of membership, it had not, by any means, prevented many who had already ascended to fame and fortune from wishing to join what seemed to be an exceedingly congenial and attractive new gathering of lively minds. It certainly was not a "poor man's substitute for a 'Gentleman's Club' "; moreover a glance at those early lists of members goes far to explain how Sir Herbert Stephen, the author of the previous account of the Club, was able to assert with a certain gloomy satisfaction that during these formative days " . . . three-quarters of the committee qualified for substantial obituary notice, [and] so did well over one-third of the Club".

Lord Carnarvon and his two brothers, Auberon and Alan Herbert, for instance, were of a wealthy family and had achieved a distinction in their own right worth several column inches of obituary. The Morrison brothers were well able to afford the two guineas subscription as they were possibly the richest men in England at that time. Walter Morrison, M.P., had been one of the original defectors from the Eclectic Club and his brother, Alfred, had joined as soon as the New Club was constituted. It was said, incidentally, that Walter was given to expressing the wish that he might outlive Alfred as he wanted to know exactly how much money his brother still had but "was in fear of doing so because he would have to look after Alfred's leavings". However, he had the first part of his wish and the "leavings" turned out to be £10 millions – or, in modern money, £300 millions. Walter lived at Malham Tarn in Yorkshire, where it was said that "Tom" of *The*

Water Babies got lost, and down the slopes of Gordale Scarr on the Malham estate that he had slithered. As the author Charles Kingsley was a close acquaintance the story is likely to be true.

There were many such Victorian grandees in those early days who graced the Club; indeed, Queen Victoria's future son-in-law, the Marquis of Lorne, became a member of the Savile before addressing himself to that more formidable challenge. Similarly, the Club possessed an impressive contingent of members who might be said to have mounted equivalent pinnacles in their respective vocations. But despite this, the election committee never lost sight, either then or later, of the need to lay in the seed corn of the Savile's future distinctive membership. Thus in 1868 we find, among all these distinguished names, others which were totally unknown outside the Club at that time; men for instance like that struggling man of letters, John Morley, who before he died in 1923 had been translated into Viscount Morley of Blackburn, P.C., O.M., D.C.L., F.R.S.

The records also show that the committee remained faithful to the principle of selecting a judicious mixture of "men of different professions". There were many politicians. Apart from Lord Carnarvon, Auberon Herbert and Walter Morrison there were also Sir Rowland Blennerhasset, M.P., Tom Hughes, Q.C., M.P. – who early demonstrated the Savilian's penchant for having a foot in several camps, by achieving alternate fame as author of *Tom Brown's Schooldays* – W.R. Anson, W.E. Forster and Julian Goldsmid.

The Savile's long association with the theatre began as early as 1874 with the election of Sir Henry Irving, although, it must be said, he never made much use of the Club, which then, as now, was not greatly frequented by members arriving later than 11 p.m. However, he must have liked it well enough, for he remained a member until his death.

Artists were already much in evidence. Thomas Woolner was the best known British sculptor of his time, while John Brett, his fellow member, was a distinguished Academician.

Academics of the scholarly kind abounded. Henry Sidgwick, one of the great moral philosophers of the age, was a member as was James Bryce of Oriel College, Oxford, whose reputation had been established with his early *Essay on the Holy Roman Empire*. The art of conversation, which was from the first a principal feature of the Club, was greatly enhanced by the presence of Sir John Pentland Mahaffey, who even wrote a book on the subject dedicated darkly "To my silent friends". He was Professor of Ancient History at Trinity College, Dublin, and renowned throughout Europe for his scholarship and wit. The year of Mahaffey's election to the Savile, 1871, incidentally was also the year when a young man signing himself Oscar Fingal O'Flahertie Wills Wilde entered Trinity as a freshman scholar, whereupon Mahaffey became his tutor. Though it is beyond doubt that Mahaffey helped set Wilde on course for the more brilliant achievements of his career, the effects of his tutelage were evidently not sufficient to steer his pupil past the Savile election committee seventeen years later when he was at the height of his fame.

In those early days, possibly because it was then a more worthily regarded profession, there were a great many clergymen members. Prominent among the first of these was the Reverend J. Llewellyn Davies, probably the best known of the London clergy at that time. His fine intellect and physical vigour were devoted to improving the lot of the working classes through the Church Militant, in which Tom Hughes also took a leading part. The Club even boasted among its several clergy the contemporary incumbent at the Vicarage of Bray – the Reverend A.H. Austen Leigh, also distinguished as a collateral descendant of Jane Austen. The Reverend W.J. Loftie was another clergyman whose membership dated from soon after the move to Savile Row; the author of some popular histories of London, he was the man who eventually but unsuccessfully proposed Oscar Wilde for membership. Sadly, and for reasons entirely unconnected, his career also came to an untimely end, as we shall see.

Literature in all its forms was, of course, well in evidence from the outset. John Murray, the publisher, was a founder member as was Leslie (later Sir Leslie) Stephen, who, apart from producing his own considerable corpus, was the guiding force behind the *Dictionary of National Biography*. There were other littérateurs then, of course, such as Tom Hughes, but it was not until three years after the move to Savile Row, when Robert Louis Stevenson was elected, that there began that great list of Savile members who, one might safely say, constitute a considerable roll-call of those who have made their mark in the world of English letters during the last hundred years.

But although the arts predominated, science, medicine, the law, engineering, the press and the civil service were also well represented by members who were either distinguished already or about to become so. The founders' intention that the membership net should be cast wide, and its tacit corollary that the "already-famous" should be amply leavened with the "up-and-coming", was remarked upon in this further quotation from the *Times* article of 1923:

> . . . in reading the lists [of past members] the names of a great number of the men who, during the last half-century, have stood prominently forth in every field of activity will be found. In 1868 Sir W. Anson, G.C. Brodrick, James Bryce, Ingram Bywater, Lord Carnarvon, Andrew Clark, Llewellyn Davies, Lord Dufferin, Thomas Fowler, Frederic Greenwood, R.H. Hutton, R.C. Jebb, John Morley, and Henry Sidgwick were elected; and in 1869 W.K. Clifford, Sidney Colvin, Mandell Creighton, Vernon Harcourt, W.H. Pater, Mark Pattison, and Ray Lankester. A comparison of these names with those of the more recent elections is likely at first sight to suggest an inquiry as to whether the newcomers can really be legitimate successors of the veteran band; but several qualifying conditions must be examined before deciding against the contemporary generation. To begin, the elected of 1868-69 were the spoil of the first cast of the net. Though the list of 1870-71 contains many illustrious names, the average is distinctly lower, and this tendency, the result of ripening time, persists throughout. Again, we must set ourselves

to regard these early giants as they appeared to their fellows, not as they appear, with all their honours thick upon them, to ourselves. In 1868 James Bryce was a clever young Scot of Balliol, the writer of the most famous of Arnold Essays, but his feats as jurist, historian, and statesman were hidden in the future. Anson's brilliant career in Parliament and as Warden of All Souls was yet to come. John Morley, out of a limited circle, was unknown. Henry Sidgwick of 1868 was certainly not the Henry Sidgwick of 1900. Mark Pattison was an essayist and reviewer and the somewhat discontented Head of Lincoln, but few knew him as the strenuous fighter to make his university a real seat of learning and research. There is no reason why the lapse of years should be less benignant in the future than in the past. Perhaps, after all, these Olympians may not have done more to preserve the Sodalitas Convivium, the vital principle of the club, than have the nameless contingent of Savilians. The learned professions, the public services, literature, science, and art can claim almost every member, care being taken to keep the numbers of each calling approximately equal. This seeking after diversity is happily exemplified by a quotation from the Spectator:

> The club of which I am a member is very luckily composed of such persons as are engaged in different ways of life and deputed, as it were, out of the most conspicuous classes of mankind; there is no rank or degree who have not their representative in the club

A handsome tribute, indeed, to the perspicacity of the forefathers. But was it shortage of editorial space or personal preference which led this writer to ignore such luminaries as Robert Louis Stevenson, Max Beerbohm, Sir Edward Elgar and many others who had been, or still were, happily ensconced at the Savile as he wrote? He was certainly correct however, in surmising that there was "no reason why the lapse of years should be less benignant in the future than in the past".

* * * *

It was in the early 1870s that the Club took to itself the motto "Sodalitas Convivium". Records are a trifle vague concerning the precise origins of this pithy encapsulation of its principles and practice but it is likely that the motto was also chosen to serve a double purpose so that the Savile Club's initials might be worked into a cipher to adorn the writing paper, napery and other property.

It is possible that the committee had in mind the Society Club founded in 1711 of which Swift was once president and whose initials, motto and purposes were so similar to the Savile's; ". . . to advance conversation and friendship, and to reward deserving persons with our interest and recommendation". But this can only be speculation. Some years ago, Brian Dowling, during the course of what was intended to be a report on the activities of the Savile's Real Tennis team of which he was then captain, embarked on one of his much appreciated "philological digressions" to investigate the "Latinity of Sodalitas Convivium":

It looks, and sounds, as though *convivium* might either be an adjective in the neuter agreeing with *Sodalitas*, or be the genitive plural of a noun; i.e. "a convivial brotherhood", or "a brotherhood of people enjoying life together".

Alas, it is not so. According to the Latin dictionary in the Morning Room, 'sodalitas' is a feminine noun, meaning (1) fellowship, companionship, brotherhood, intimacy; (2) company assembled for feasting, a club; (3) an unlawful secret society.

Convivium is a neuter noun, meaning (1) feast, entertainment, banquet; (2) company, guests.

So presumably our motto was designed as a conjunction of nouns meaning firstly that we are a fellowship, and secondly that we welcome guests.

I always thought that it meant "a convivial lot of sods", anyway.

During the ten years that it occupied the premises at No. 15 Savile Row, the Club's increasing popularity persuaded the committee to raise the maximum limit of members in several stages from 300 to 550, though the rigorous standards for selection were still strictly maintained. The entrance fee was raised to 10 guineas but the committee balked at raising the subscription to £5.00. It was also acquiring something of a reputation: "Oh, I know the Savile," a diner at one of the Inns of Court was overhead to say one evening, "it's an awful swell club. They won't elect you unless you're an atheist or have written a book."

The founders had pronounced "a thorough simplicity in all arrangements" to be one of the basic principles of the Club, not out of any puritanism but more in pursuit of their objective of keeping costs to members at the minimum. The members however were becoming increasingly restive during their days at Savile Row and the committee were constantly harassed by mutinous comments concerning the spartan nature of the furniture and the rather excessive "simplicity" of the food. Part of the difficulty with the latter was due to the system by which all meals were provided by outside caterers, whose natural desire to make a profit, despite having to conform to the stringent costings ordained by the committee, led inevitably to exceedingly short commons.

Some extracts form the Suggestions Book of the 1870s give an indication of the general dissatisfaction:

I suggest the Steward be ordered to get a better sort of bread – something fit for members to eat. Some of them like a little crust! – if that is not too much to ask. Nevill's bread is probably the best in London.

and:

That loaves be provided on Sundays that have not been cut on the previous day.

and:

I have been charged 6d for a glass of very ordinary sherry; the same at other clubs being 3d or 4d. A half-pint of the same containing three glasses is charged 10d.

In fact a slightly better system was in operation with the wine. The Club had an arrangement with selected wine merchants who stocked the cellars with their wares, which remained their property until purchased by a member. The Club then became liable to the merchant for its price which, being wholesale, provided the happy imbiber with fine wines for a very modest outlay.

However, no amount of good wine at bargain prices could compensate for the paucity of the food and in the face of a constant barrage of complaints the committee undertook the responsibility of providing all the necessary catering services under its own roof.

The economics of this evidently led to the discontinuance of the original practice of providing free tobacco as well as snuff in return for the members' subscriptions. These were the days when the use of tobacco was confined to one specific "smoking-room" and forbidden everywhere else and it was not for some years that the custom was reversed so that the habit was tolerated everywhere except in particular "no-smoking" areas such as the dining-room. But even in the opulent days when tobacco was distributed *gratis* the Suggestions Book bore its quota of complaints: "That tobacco and clay pipes be provided as well as cigars" was one, and another, rather petulant: "Could we not have wood matches in the Smoking-Room instead of wax ones which, in the present weather, stick to the fingers of members and refuse to ignite."

But by 1881 it was very evident that the Club had outgrown the house at Savile Row and plans had to be put in hand to find new premises. Various houses were inspected, until eventually, in June 1882, it was decided to make an offer for No. 107 Piccadilly. After some preliminary haggling with its owner, Lord Rosebery, during which the price of the lease was finally agreed at £11,000, the deal was struck; £9,575 was raised on debenture bonds to members, and with commendable speed and efficiency the new Clubhouse was furnished and made ready to receive the members after the usual summer closure that same year.

* * * *

This beautiful stuccoed eighteenth-century house, full of character and much beloved by members during the forty-five years in which it was to be their home, stood on the site of the present Park Lane Hotel. Lord Rosebery had come into its possession as part of a marriage settlement from his father-in-law, Baron Meyer de

Rothschild, in whose family it had been since the beginning of the nineteenth-century. It had been the home of the notorious Nathan de Rothschild who, armed with advance knowledge of the outcome of the battle of Waterloo through the superior speed of his own private courier over that of the official War Office messenger, first depressed the stock market by massive selling and then made a multi-million pound killing by buying in at the eleventh hour before Wellington's great victory became public knowledge. Something of a philistine as well as a rogue, he is reputed to have informed the great virtuoso violinist and conductor, Ludwig Spohr, who was a guest in his house, that the only music he cared for was the clink of money. The house had another connection with Waterloo, for Blücher had twice been its tenant. It was from the high entrance steps to this building (which were to prove so treacherous to future generations of well-dined Savilians) that he received the plaudits of the grateful London citizens on his first visit after the battle. This was a use which the Savile Club committee was quick to exploit as soon as it was able, for the position of the house provided an excellent view of what was then almost invariably the route of great public processions and provided an ideal grandstand for such occasions as Queen Victoria's Golden and Diamond Jubilees, her funeral and the coronations of King Edward VII and King George V and other royal occasions. Great parties were later to be held to celebrate these occasions and, perhaps because of their comparative rarity, lady guests were for the first time made welcome. In 1887 Thomas Hardy, who had then been a member for nine years and had just returned "unharmed . . . and much illuminated" from an expedition to the Mediterranean, viewed the Jubilee procession from the Savile Club with his wife Emma.

The house had been built at the end of the eighteenth century but it contained some of the remains of an earlier one, part of the façade of which could be seen in a small courtyard in the centre of the block. Although it was comparatively small by Piccadilly standards it provided ample space for the Club's requirements and very little alteration was necessary to effect the move from Savile Row.

On the ground floor, looking over Piccadilly, was a long and elegant dining room with two long tables which by all accounts were fully occupied on every day of the working week including Saturday. There was a half-crown (12½p) table d'hôte lunch with a few alternative Savile specialities such as home-made potted meat, cold apple pie, fruit cake and *mille-feuilles*. There were also the established table d'hôte dinners reinforced with two decanters of port, one vintage and one of wood port provided at each table together with snuff. Smoking was never allowed in the dining room.

Billiards and cards, always popular pastimes at the Savile, were now given adequate space in rooms of their own for the entertainment of members. Indeed that rather dour and unlikely Savilian, Herbert Spencer, was only moved to join the Club because of its excellent facilities for the former and because it was permitted to play on Sunday. The billiards-room was situated at the back of the house and for the benefit of spectators contained those long benches on raised steps which until 1988 remained a feature of the old snooker-room at Brook Street.

Apart from the serious business of billiards this room was also a main gathering point for those in search of conversation. A back room on the second floor was furnished as a card-room and this was generally occupied until 1 or 2 o'clock in the morning, drinks being served there at least until midnight and often even later. Harry Plunket Greene, the famous singer, in his biography of Stanford reminisces on these two focal points of Savilian life:

> The billiards-room at 107 Piccadilly was probably the most uncomfortable room in London. It was niblick-shaped and so small that there had to be a shuffling of knees among the gallery when a player wished to make a shot across the table. "Galley" was not a bad name for it, as the spectators were lined along a narrow dais about four feet from the ground, and followed the game from the heights. Coffee-cups and ash-trays carried their lives in their hands.
>
> It was a custom, unnamed, that conversation begun in the dining-room should be continued in the billiards-room – why it would be hard to say. The accommodation left over from the billiards-table was hopelessly inadequate, the long seats were set at a back-breaking angle and the leather was of a shininess worthy of the Rideau Slide at Ottawa. Nevertheless, it was always full. It is an understood thing at the Savile that all members are fair game in the matter of information, and that it is no breach of the conventions to ask a man to talk on his own subject. Some of the most interesting discourses I have ever heard took place in that little corner by the billiards-room fire.
>
> The card-room had no recognized customs, but made up for it in its "characters". It was a small room at the top of the house, approached by a narrow winding single-line staircase. The original architect never anticipated such crowded quarters, and what would have happened in the case of fire is awful to contemplate. In the later days a stout rope was installed in one of the windows but the wainscoting could not have withstood many descents of acrobats like Gilbert Hurst or Ray or Owen Lankester who, between them, weighed nearly 50 stone.
>
> The card-players, if few in numbers, were mostly good players. The same people turned up day after day, and each man's foibles were known to the rest who respected or exploited them for peace or diversion as the case might be. There were no conventions. Silence was sporadic and then only by accident. It was a delightful happy-go-lucky crowd, oblivious of rules, following the spirit of the Club rather than the letter of the law.

On the first floor, overlooking Green Park was an extremely handsome drawing-room. In the front part members used to read rather than talk and it is said that one of the more popular magazines supplied to the Club was *La Vie Parisienne* – which casts an interesting light on members' choice of relaxation from their more scholarly predilections. The back drawing-room, however, was yet another centre for conversation.

One of the luxuries provided by the extra space available at Piccadilly was a separate room to be used as a library. This incidentally was always known as "The Book Room", a name which survived until comparatively recently at Brook Street, where it is now generally referred to as "The Library" or just "The Monument". The room chosen for this purpose at Piccadilly was a particularly pleasant one on the second floor, looking across the Green Park to Buckingham Palace and commanding a view of a considerable length of Piccadilly in both directions. In the late 1890s the title of honorary librarian was instituted and it seems that the civilized custom of members presenting copies of their own recent works to the Club was already established by then.

The Savile was becoming more and more renowned and soon the number of candidates proposed began to exceed the number of vacancies available. To ease this situation, and because of the greater amount of space available in the new house, the committee was empowered to raise the maximum number of members from 550 to 600. But even this was not sufficient to satisfy the demand. A browse through the Candidates Books for the period reveals many distinguished names who were not elected until the second or third time of application and many more who were not elected at all. Among them were men who, one might think, would have been excellent Savile material such as Sir Arthur Quiller-Couch (1887) and, of course, Oscar Wilde in 1888. Nevertheless, the committee must have had their reasons for refusal and been satisfied to follow the principles which had served the Club so well in the past.

Any change in what had become the normal pattern was resisted unless a positive benefit could be proved. Thus it was not thought necessary until 1899 to extend the installation of electric light from the lower part of the building to the card-room on the second floor. In 1902, twenty years after its invention, the committee also dismissed the idea of installing a telephone. Professor R.W. Wood, a distinguished visitor from America who came to the Club as a guest of Sir Thomas Merton, was naive enough on his way in to ask Lawrence, the hall porter, for the use of a telephone only to receive the frosty rebuke: "Telephone, sir? This is a *gentlemen's* club."

But there was one innovation suggested in 1885 which seemed to strike at the very core of the Club's existence and which roused the committee to an unusual degree of protective fury. This was nothing less than a proposal to transfer the power of election from the committee to the members generally by a ballot with the use of a black ball, one black ball in ten to disqualify. The committee had just been defeated for the first time in its history on its proposal to raise the entrance fee from 10 guineas to 15 guineas and possibly it was this which encouraged Howard Smith, a well-known barrister and a popular member, to challenge it on this more fundamental issue. The proposal aroused great controversy and, again for the first time, the committee was forced into the agonizing dilemma of whether to maintain its lofty judicial attitude or to descend into the arena to preserve the *status quo ante*. It decided on the latter and, in the unusually emotional words of the minutes, "It was unanimously agreed to oppose these proposals *tooth and nail*."

The campaign took the form of circulars to all members stressing the appalling – if not fatal – consequences should any such proposal be adopted; the choicer phrases expressing opposition being heavily underlined individually in red ink. Such was the excitement aroused by the activity on both sides that the annual general meeting, at which these matters were to be discussed, promised to be the best attended for many years. Although the outcome appeared to be a foregone conclusion in favour of the committee, its lobbying tactics and, possibly, some of its other previous management decisions did not seem to have been receiving universal approval. Another group of members decided to seize the opportunity provided by such a large assembly to avail themselves of the rarely exercised right to nominate its own candidates for vacancies on the committee and thus challenge the virtually self-selecting process which had hitherto been the common practice.

The stage was set for an heroic encounter which, sadly, in the event, did not live up to expectations. One hundred and twenty eager members attended but the committee was put into good heart before the main business began by the election of all its nominees to the vacant places. Howard Smith, later to be a judge on the Midland circuit, then presented his case and was supported by Henry Mee Keary, the brother of Charles Keary, a fashionable novelist of the time, who was also a member.

But the committee had chosen its advocate carefully: Thiselton Dyer, later to be Sir W.T.T. Thiselton Dyer, K.C.M.G., C.I.E., LL.D., D.SC., F.R.S., his arguments, no doubt, made weightier by all these honours to come, moved as an amendment that "This meeting sees no reason for changing the mode of election." In an argument which retains its force to the present day, he reminded the assembly that the commitee had the advantage of hearing the views of a large cross-section of members before considering candidates for membership and so were better placed to make a correct judgment than individual members acting on snippets of information which might or might not even be at first hand. His persuasive powers and those of his seconder, Rowland Hamilton, won the day and his amendment was carried with only five dissensions. This was the last to be heard of this revolutionary proposal and the original system of election set down by the founding fathers continues unaltered.

* * * *

The Club returned to its customary calm, still attracting to its membership on the tried and tested method of selection a great variety of interesting men, from several professions and various walks of life. Thus the period between the move to Piccadilly and the outbreak of the First World War saw the election of many literary figures of whom some, like Rudyard Kipling, Henry James and Rider Haggard, were to become household names. In the world of art, one of the best known of contemporary painters, Sir Laurens Alma-Tadema, R.A., came to swell the ranks of the many Academicians who had already found the brief stroll down the road to No. 107 an enlivening alternative to their artistic pursuits at Burlington House. From the world of music came Sir Charles Villiers Stanford and Sir Hubert Parry. And, true to its original prospectus, the Club continued to cast its net wide by welcoming as new members men like George H. Makins, later G.C.M.G., C.B., F.R.S., Surgeon-General to the armed forces, and Herbert Cozens-Hardy, Q.C., later as Baron Cozens-Hardy, P.C., to be Master of the Rolls.

But while all this was very satisfactory, the committee suddenly woke up in 1904 to the fact that there were only five more years left to run on the lease of the clubhouse. Several meetings were held to discuss the implications and in 1909 it was empowered to surrender the existing lease and negotiate a new one with Lord Rosebery's representatives. This was done, and in 1910 a new lease was granted for a period of twenty years at an annual rent of £1,250. However, during the negotiations, the Club's advisers had recommended the formation of a new legal entity to be known as The Savile Club Limited whose main purpose would be to provide the Club with premises and to hold all the property of the Club in trust for members. It was to this new company that the lease was granted and the structure then formulated remains the basis of the Club's legal existence to the present day.

Even though the immediate future of the Club had been thus so satisfactorily assured, there were further problems to be faced. The flourishing membership and the intensive use to which the house was put created not only wear and tear but an increasing demand for better use of the existing space. Moreover, the day-to-day business of running the Club was becoming too much for part-time honorary secretaries who up till then had been chosen out of the membership – men who would naturally have their own affairs to attend to as well as those of the Club.

During the years 1908-10 a ginger group of the younger members nicknamed "the Young Turks" prepared a set of proposals to deal with all these problems. Their scheme envisaged a rearrangement of the Club's amenities to make more efficient use of available space; the addition of seven members' bedrooms, the installation of service and passenger lifts and the employment of a full-time salaried secretary. The whole of this, they suggested, might be financed by raising £6,000 in debentures and increasing the subscription from six to seven guineas.

The Extraordinary General Meeting which was called to consider these proposals in December 1909 decisively defeated them but in March of the following year at another such meeting the Club was persuaded to face up to the inevitable. It was duly decided that "there should be a paid secretary to be appointed by the committee, to act under the Honorary Secretaries, and supervise the administration of the Club".

The committee, however, took their time and were, as usual, cautious in implementing such a newfangled notion. In May 1910 they made their first tentative move by appointing a Mr W.A. Evans as the first Club secretary "in the first instance, for twelve months only". Evans was, in fact, a member and it would appear that his undoubted qualifications for the task were made even more attractive with his "kindly consenting to accept much less than the market rate of remuneration for such offices". He was to be the first of a long line; some of them good, some bad, some brilliant and some disastrous, but from now on the club's fortunes would increasingly reflect their relative merits.

Sir Herbert Stephen, writing in 1923 with his tongue (one imagines) only partially in his cheek, comments on the several secretaries he had known:

> In the selection of its secretaries . . . the Savile has been almost as fortunate as the House of Commons in the choice of its Speakers – each of whom, for as long as anyone in the Savile can remember, has been declared by the Members of Parliament of his period of office to be not only the best Speaker they ever had, but the best Speaker they can imagine.

In 1911 the committee made another tentative move to satisfy the demand of "the Young Turks" of 1908-10 by providing three "small but comfortable" bedrooms for the use of members. It was in this year, also, that the first rumblings became apparent of circumstances which were to affect the structure of the Club and lead, sixteen years later, to the move to Brook Street.

"Rumblings" there were, indeed, in the literal sense. Ten years earlier, in January 1901, the honorary secretary had been empowered by the committee to join with the landlords in opposing the construction of the Piccadilly tube lines beneath the Club's foundations. Now that, despite their opposition, it had become fully operational, subsidence was continuous; so much so that the re-hanging of the fine mahogany doors to the public rooms had become a frequent feature of the Club's maintenance. To add to the agony the houses on the western side of the clubhouse, Nos. 108-15 Piccadilly, were demolished in 1911 to make room for the building of the new Park Lane Hotel. This left the western wall of the Club unsupported and in need of constant attention to secure the safety of the house. Having got this far, however, the builders of the new hotel ran into legal difficulties and all work on the site ceased, leaving the Savile standing out, precariously on its own, like an old age pensioner's sole front tooth. But by 1912 the difficulties were overcome and the builders cast their acquisitive eyes on No. 107 so that they might build a yet larger hotel. The Club refused to entertain their advances but, in 1913, a further offer was made, one which today would be termed "an offer which could not be refused". Not only was it financially advantageous but it included as an incentive, a 22 years' lease on a much larger house in Bruton Street. The membership was torn between the obvious advantages of acceptance and sentimental attachment to the pretty house which had been its home for thirty-one years. But before such an agonizing choice could be put to the members, fate intervened. All the occupants of other houses in Bruton Street raised objections to "the establishment in their midst of a famous and popular Club". The proposal was withdrawn and there the matter rested for the time being. Twelve months later the First World War broke out.

As to every other British institution, the war brought an abrupt change in the ordered ways of the Savile. Those of its members and staff whose youth and physical fitness made them eligible were suddenly transformed into men of war, disappearing temporarily – sometimes permanently – from the scene. Fourteen members were killed on active service, as were three of the staff; many more were wounded. But there remained behind those whose age or infirmity prevented them from taking a physical part and others whose special skills were required at home for the war effort and who continued to keep the Club in regular use. Among them was the honorary secretary for elections, Hugh Elliot, of the Coldstream Guards, who boldly took upon himself the management of the Club's administration in between his time-consuming duties at the War Office. The problems he faced were formidable. Despite the shortage of food and drink supplies; the necessity of juggling whatever provisions might at any one time be available to produce such wonders as "meat-less" dinners; the chore of extracting government-issue "meat-tickets" from reluctant members; dealing with the novelty of female staff, and marshalling everyone present to places of safety during the regular air-raid warnings; typically the proudest boast made for him when it was all over was that the Savile was one of the few institutions to have survived the war without suffering the heavy fines then imposed for breaking the black-out regulations.

The end of the war saw a massive increase in prices everywhere and it became essential for the Club to raise more revenue in order to pay its way. In 1919 the subscription was raised to 10 guineas but, because of the straitened circumstances in which everyone found themselves at the time, it was not thought proper to increase the entrance fee. Several economy measures were introduced and the public rooms of the Club were rearranged in an attempt to increase their profitability. The Sodality gritted its teeth and set its face towards weathering the first of what would turn out to be many financial storms which threatened its future. Times were hard but they were not entirely devoid of compensations within the walls of 107 Piccadilly. Food and drink might be expensive and scarce for these survivors of the war; the problem of recruiting suitable staff and finding the means of paying them might exercise their ingenuity; the costs of maintaining the fabric of the building might induce nightmares; but conversation and the company of friends cost nothing and one way or another the Club soldiered on.

* * * *

By the mid-1920s the house at Piccadilly, which for nearly fifty years had been regarded with such affection as the ideal clubhouse, was beginning to give rather more than an occasional glimpse of its feet of clay – or rather, its feet of insufficient clay, for subsidence was becoming a more frequent problem. Furthermore it was too small to accommodate the number of new members which was now required to enable it to pay its way. Maintenance of the fabric at post-war prices was cripplingly expensive and, with the lease about to run out, there was a heavy liability for dilapidations, together with the likelihood of a hefty premium on any renewal.

After much soul-searching the committee was empowered, in May 1926, to

25

dispose of the lease of 107 Piccadilly and to begin the search for new premises. A "premises sub-committee" was appointed and during the next twelve months over ninety houses were inspected within the area comprising Westminster, Grosvenor Gardens, Mayfair, Piccadilly and St James's. Happily, as it was to turn out, there was one house which stood out above the rest and which was immediately available. On 31 May 1927, the Savile Club Ltd was requested by the general committee to proceed with the acquisition of a 90-year lease of No. 69 Brook Street and, once again, with admirabe expedition, the formalities were completed, the move was made and the Club was installed in its new premises by 1 November of that year.

There was a general sadness, however, at having to leave Piccadilly. Sir Compton Mackenzie, who had joined the Club in 1912, expressed a general feeling when he looked back with nostalgia to the happy times he had spent there. In an article to commemorate the Club's centenary in 1968, he wrote:

> In the autumn of 1912 the Savile occupied that beautiful house with the big bow windows looking over Green Park which had once belonged to Lord Rosebery. At that date the annual subscription was six guineas and the entrance fee the same amount. The ghost of 107 Piccadilly now haunts the Park Lane Hotel which rose about it when 107 Piccadilly was demolished.
>
> Sodalitas Convivium was the motto of the Savile, and it lived and still lives up to the spirit of that motto. From the moment the new member was elected he was expected to take part in the Club life. This was made easier by the members dining at two long tables where conversation was general; there were three tables for four apiece in the bow window. The great day was Saturday when the Club was crowded for lunch. Immediately afterwards most of the lunchers adjourned to the billiards-room either to take coffee or to play Savile volunteer snooker. I managed to discover the inventor of snooker – the late Sir Neville Chamberlain – but I never succeeded in finding out who was the inventor of the Savile game.
>
> The coffee drinkers went off soon after lunch; the billiards-players stayed on in that recess, the warmth and friendliness of which I still miss. It had a comfortable settee two steps up along one side of the recess; there was no room for any seating accommodation opposite. The frequenters of that settee were a sodality within a sodality.
>
> The drawing-room on the first floor was used more for reading than conversation, but in the recess at the back it was the custom of various senior members to sit and talk until tea-time after that Saturday lunch.
>
> Edmund Gosse used to ask me to come up with him to the drawing-room and I was privileged to sit and listen to the conversation of those seniors of whom I remember most vividly Sir Ray Lankester and Sir Herbert Stephen . . . .
>
> In those days two decanters of port, vintage and wood, and a horn of

snuff were passed round the dining-room at the end of the meal; nobody was allowed to smoke until he left the dining-room. It was a breach of etiquette to offer another member a drink; one always ordered one's own drink and paid for it oneself. The card-room was a small room on the second floor which remained sacred to whist longer than any other club card-room in England, but it had surrendered to bridge by the time I became a member of the Savile.

I seek for a phrase to express the peculiar quality of what may be called the process of Savilisation which the Club had been able to exercise over its members and still exercises, Deo Gratias, today at 69 Brook Street. Perhaps it is the conviction that, although all men may not be equal, all Savilians are equal. We have members renowned for academic, scientific, literary and artistic achievement; inside the Savile nobody would suspect it. We have had members who left us because they did not find their eminence was appreciated by their club-fellows; such unsavilised members were not missed.

I do not apologize for dwelling on the past because in commemorating a centenary the past is the present. So I am walking again along that Piccadilly of once upon a time – past Jimmy's, the St James's restaurant, the centre of rags on Boat Race night, along the wide pavement past Devonshire House, past the china cockatoo in the bow window of Lady Burdett-Coutts' house at the corner of Stratton Street, until I walk up the steps of another bow-windowed house and hear the voice of Lawrence in the hall telling me that my guest has arrived, one of those guests whom I shall never welcome again. This elegiac mood must stop, and I raise my glass to the Savilians during the next century of our beloved Club.

One great advantage of the new clubhouse at Brook Street was that it needed scarcely any alteration. In recommending the house the committee had pointed out its virtues in the annual report: it was a large private house on which much money had recently been spent so that it was in very good order; it was admirably designed on the ground and first floor for the public rooms of the Club; the accommodation for the staff was in every way an improvement on 107 Piccadilly; there were twelve to fifteen members' bedrooms as against four at 107; an automatic lift travelled from the basement to the top floor; and there was partial central heating; two garages with rooms above at the back which could be let at a good rental; the house was readily accessible by public transport, being about three minutes' walk from Bond Street tube-station and about eight minutes from that of Dover Street. In fact, the Club was acquiring a singular bargain. Carol Kennedy, in her *Social History of Mayfair*, describes it as one of the "most spectacular private houses in Mayfair to change hands during the inter-war years"; the agents described it as "one of the principal houses in Mayfair"; yet the terms of the lease which runs until the year 2017 fixed the annual rental for the whole period at the 1927 level. The capital cost of the purchase of the lease, of alterations to the fabric, and of additional furniture was estimated at £23,000. In addition the opportunity was taken to liquidate a long-standing debt of £6,000. The explanation of this debt speaks of days when paying for one's existence was easier than now:

> Members who have studied the annual accounts . . . will be aware that for some time the Club has ended each year heavily in debt to its tradesmen. This position existed before the war and was aggravated by it. The amount thus owing has for some years been nearly as much as the amount of the annual subscriptions. This system of running on the tradesmen's credit is most wasteful and in every way unsatisfactory. The committee consider it an essential part of the scheme for new premises that this long-standing debt should now be paid off. The sum required under this head is £6,000.

The total cost was therefore estimated at about £29,000 and this was to be found by obtaining a loan from The Savile Club Limited (£12,000); by a levy on the membership of £5 minimum (£4,000); and by the issue of debentures to members (£13,000). The annual subscription was raised from 10 to 12 guineas as a form of insurance against any further increase in running costs. All the skilful negotiations which these weighty matters entailed were masterminded by the honorary treasurer, Alan Barlow, and Stanley Hoare, the club's honorary solicitor.

* * * *

The house in which the Club was now established has an extremely interesting history. Although it is always addressed as "69 Brook Street", in fact it has comprised both No. 69 and No. 71 since the year 1890. It forms part of the Grosvenor Estate owned by the Dukes of Westminster whose present fortunes were founded in 1677 when the thirteen-year-old Welsh girl Mary Davies, who had inherited the Manor of Ebury from Hugh Audley, was married to Sir Thomas Grosvenor. In 1710, their son, Sir Richard, started to lay out a new square in the fields west of Tyburn brook. Number 69 Brook Street (or No. 35 Lower Brook Street as it then was) was built in 1725 by Francis Bailley, "carpenter", and No. 71, a smaller house, was built slightly later by another "carpenter", John Simmons – "carpenter" in those days having the meaning of house-builder rather than its more restricted modern definition.

The first recorded occupant of No. 69 was François de la Rochefoucauld, Marquis de Montandré, a Huguenot refugee who became a field marshal in the British Army during the reign of William III and served in Flanders with Charles Churchill, brother of the great Duke of Marlborough. His widow continued to live in the house until 1771, when it passed into the possession of the Digbys, successive generations of whom were to occupy it for more than a hundred years. The Digby family was an illustrious one in English history dating back to the time of the Conqueror and, by what now seems a remarkable coincidence, a member of it – Kenelm Digby – was one of the original band who, in 1868, were laying the foundations of the Savile Club a mile or two down the road at Spring Gardens, little realizing that fifty-nine years later his family's town house would become the home of the club he was helping to create.

The original house was built of brick in the manner of the time, and was three storeys high. But in 1850, during the Digbys' tenure, major alterations were made to No. 69 under the supervision of Thomas Grundy, surveyor to the Grosvenor London Estates. A fourth floor was added, a porch was built for the front entrance and the whole façade was stuccoed.

From 1866 to 1883 the house was occupied by the Dowager Duchess of Cleveland but in 1884 the lease was purchased by Walter Burns, a brother-in-law of that legendary financial buccaneer, J. Pierpont Morgan. It was Burns who, in 1890, purchased No. 71 and knocked the two houses together to provide his wife, Fanny, with extra space for such essential amenities as an entrance hall and grand staircase leading to a lavishly decorated ballroom in which she might exercise her yearnings for social advancement. To reinforce the impact she wished to make, the décor was conceived and carried out by the Paris firm of Bouwens van der Boijen in the dix-huitième style first introduced to London in 1830 at the Duke of Wellington's Apsley House.

Oddly, the swashbuckling brother-in-law had no hand in these arrangements. Only recently, when he had helped finance the construction of the first Protestant church to be permitted in Rome, he had demanded as a *quid pro quo* that his daunting features be represented as St Ambrose in the Burne-Jones mosaic which was intended to form one of that religious cuckoo's nest's principal attractions. Fortunately the Club was spared from inheriting such similar *jeux d'esprit*, though the exuberance of van de Boijen's décor was to prove too much for some. It might be worth mentioning in passing that Fanny's brother – another John Pierpont Morgan – managed to get into the Garrick Club a few years later without a single signature beside those of his proposer and seconder, so perhaps the Savile was spared for yet a second time.

Meantime, Fanny Burns's grandiose scale of entertaining in such glamorous surroundings had had the desired effect and in 1899 she succeeded in marrying off her daughter, Ethel May, to Lewis, later 1st Viscount Harcourt. He was Colonial Secretary under Asquith and was noted among other things for his progressive policies and for the length of his speeches. The newly married couple made 69/71 Brook Street their London home until 1922 when Lord Harcourt died. Club legend is that he committed suicide in the bath attached to the main bedroom situated on the first floor between what is now the Elgar Room and the Book Room, and members with a morbid bent and strong nerves may still derive a *frisson* by bathing there at the cost of one pound (including towel). Strict adherence to historical fact, however, compels it to be said that the official records tell a slightly different story. Harcourt had, or maybe had not, rejoiced in the nickname "Loulou" since adolescence, though he had somehow managed to maintain a more dignified public front. Private gossip persistently suggested that his sexual attentions to teenagers of both sexes extended beyond the limits of what was then

A.J. Balfour, later Earl of Balfour, a founder member
and the Club's only prime minister so far.

Edward Robert Bulwer-Lytton, 1st Earl of Lytton;
Viceroy of India and poet.

Some early members:
top left, Justin M'Carthy;
above, Sir Michael Foster;
left, Viscount Goschen
by a later member, Max
Beerbohm, demonstrating
his obsession with noses.
(See page 45.)

"Loulou" Harcourt (1st Viscount Harcourt), whose town house in
Brook Street is now the clubhouse.

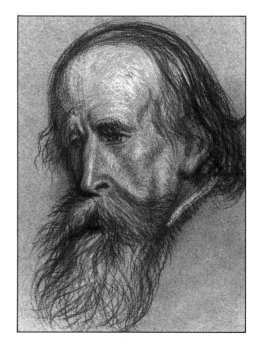

"The most elegant pair of legs in Victorian art" – Col. Frederick Gustavus Burnaby, an early member whose legendary exploits made him a national hero, depicted here in a famous portrait by his fellow member Jacques Joseph Tissot.

More early members: top left, Sir Charles Dilke, protagonist in a notorious scandal which could have divided the Club; and Herbert Spencer, who joined the Savile for the sake of its snooker but so abominated conversation that he sported ear-plugs on his visits to 107 Piccadilly; lower left, the Rt Rev. Mandell Creighton, Bishop of London, was a founder member, as was that fierce apostle of agnosticism and free-thinking, Sir Leslie Stephen (p.4.)

acceptably abnormal among his peers. It was rumoured that the mother of Edward James, a young Etonian schoolboy, was about to swear out a warrant for his arrest and the whisperings were gathering strength when he was found dead in bed by his valet on the morning of 24 February 1922. The inquest four days later at Nuneham Courtenay, Oxford, which returned a verdict of "misadventure", established that his death was due to the effect of a sleeping-draught called "Bromidia" on a "diseased heart". The coroner protested perhaps a little too much against any hint that Harcourt might have taken his own life, saying that he had lived "quite happily" with his wife, even though they had occupied separate bedrooms since Lady Harcourt had suffered a breakdown eighteen months previously. The unfortunate Edward James suffered greatly and was generally blamed for the whole affair, according to his memoirs. James, who became one of the greatest and most eccentric connoisseurs and collectors of modern art, was himself pursued by rumour; in his case the more romantic one that he was the illegitimate son of King Edward VII. Lady Harcourt appears to have survived the scandal with some resilience and her position in society seemed unaffected. Perhaps it was she whom Oscar Wilde had in mind when he remarked in one of his plays of a contemporary society lady that with the onset of widowhood "her hair turned quite gold with grief". For she continued to put the ballroom at Brook Street to regular use, entertaining the likes of Queen Mary until in 1927 the house went on the market and the Savile Club took it over.

Though it was in an excellent state of repair and well set out to adapt to its new use, a few minor alterations had to be made, mainly to expunge the rather too heady perfume left behind by the Burns/Harcourt presence. Even the imperturbable Max Beerbohm on seeing the nymphs and cupids disporting themselves on the ballroom ceiling was moved to exclaim: "Ah! 'Loulou' Quinze, I perceive". Norman Croom-Johnson in his diary entry for 1 November 1927, the day the Club opened at Brook Street for the first time, sniffs that the dining-room and ballroom "are heavily gilded and their ceilings covered with paintings of naked cupids reclining on pink and blue and white clouds – a style of decoration which may be all very well in a Venetian palace but which strikes me as incongruous in a London Club".

Other splenetic comparisons were made with certain establishments in Paris – not that any member actually admitted to having been in one – and in 1930 the committee decided that during the summer closure changes should be made, "all details as to colour, cost, etc. etc. to be left to the House Committee in conjunction with Mr Ivor Back" – a distinguished surgeon who was then chairman of the general committee. Clifford Makins was the Club's honorary architect at the time, so must also have had a hand in what transpired, the outcome of the "etc. etc." being not entirely welcomed in the way the committee had expected. The late Tom Ingram, then the Club's honorary archivist, takes up the story:

> The closure in 1930 was somewhat later than usual and it was not until the end of September that members were made aware of the great change

which had occurred. Old ones seemed content but the younger ones were angry. Robert Speaight, who at this time was playing 2nd Lieutenant Hibbert in the original production of *Journey's End*, had been a member for scarcely a year but was not thereby inhibited from giving his anger full vent in the Suggestions Book:

'May I enter my indignant protest against the act of sabotage, which has recently been committed on the Club premises? If there are any, who, like myself, sought election to the Savile not least because they believed it to possess among the most beautiful rooms in London, I have no doubt that they will share the feelings of horror and bewilderment with which I beheld the ghastly transformation which it has undergone. To mount the double staircase, carpeted in red; to admire the white and gilt splendour of Loulou Harcourt's ballroom and people it, on some May midnight, with the swaying forms of its departed revellers; to watch through the smoke of an after-luncheon cigar the pink-buttocked cherubim sporting across an empyrean of cerulean blue... these, Sir, were some of the pleasures of civilized existence. They were pleasures which I should have thought would have commended themselves to men of culture such as this Club is glad to enrol among its members. In a word the aesthetic pleasures derived from the Smoking Room, as it then was, were obtainable in no other club in London.

'It is to me a shocking thought that the Savile should prove itself incapable of safeguarding its own treasures. To what end, one may well ask, should those responsible eliminate the gilt, extinguish the colour, and reduce the white to a shade known, I believe, as parchment, but recalling the worst excesses of café au lait? To what purpose should they slavishly imitate the inconclusive "clubbery" of the majority of London clubs and seek to impose upon a room, which was the very temple of Gaiety, a reticence which it was never designed to receive? ... It were as proper, Sir, to turn the Sistine Chapel into a Skating Rink ... and let me in conclusion formally call down the curses of all cultured people upon the rape of the Rococo and hope that, when the matter of aesthetics comes up at the Day of Judgment, it will earn a severe and sevenfold retribution'.

To this the chairman of the house committee, William Wallace, replied laconically on 8 October 1930:

'The re-decoration was very carefully considered under competent advice and obviously cannot now be altered. This book is intended for practical suggestions and not for essays on the art of decoration.'

And the riposte was reinforced a week later at the meeting of the general committee when "Sir P. Chalmers Mitchell moved, and Mr Rees seconded, a vote of thanks ... to Mr Back and the House Committee for their work in re-decorating the smoking-room, and congratulations on the success of their efforts". This was carried unanimously by the eleven members present, whose average length of membership was eighteen years. The "shade" however, "... recalling the worst excesses of café au lait" remained for almost fifty years until Dennis Lennon and Bernard Wiehahn reawakened the spirit of the Rococo in Loulou Harcourt's ballroom.

Way back in 1927 there had been other rearrangements of a more practical nature to be made. The Club's dining-room was now established on the first floor as it is today. The Harcourts' old dining-room (now the bar) had its connecting doors thrown permanently open to connect with the "Sandpit" and so provide a central area for members to mix with one another "for the purpose of conversation" – the Club's *raison d'être*. The present bar area was originally used as a card-room until the beginning of the Second World War when it became apparent that the arrangements so far had failed to provide a satisfactory gathering place for members, such as there had been at Piccadilly. As an experiment a bar was set up in the corner of the Sandpit and this proved to be so popular that the card-players were reluctantly prised out of their more spacious quarters and a more commodious bar constructed in their place. It was the first time in the Club's history that drinks had been made available by any other method than individual service by a waiter. But it solved the problem of providing a proper focal point for "convivium" after members had suitably charged themselves with "sodalitas" at the long tables.

The term "Sandpit" has never been satisfactorily explained though it dates from the very earliest days at Brook Street. At first, it seems to have been known as "the cockpit", no doubt because of the vigorous conversations which took place there, and this was later adapted to "the Sandpit", perhaps because of the then rather arid décor which failed to distinguish this otherwise beautifully proportioned room whose charm therefore was forced to depend upon the people in it rather than any appeal to the eye. An early Suggestions Book, however, contains a plea that the name should revert to "cockpit". A committee member of that time later recalled that the chairman, Ivor Gunn, hesitated for a long time with the pen in his hand when "one of us suggested that he write in the reply margin: 'Surely it is better to allude to the colour of our walls than to the quality of our conversation'. But propriety prevailed." And so Sandpit it remained. Other theories for the name find its source in the kindergarten where such an amenity is provided for children of various ages to sport and socialize. Whatever its provenance, however, the room itself is an important focal point in the present house, albeit it is willy-nilly a passageway to nearly every other destination in the Club – a veritable Clapham Junction of Convivium.

Over the years other changes to the interior were made, some of which were less successful than others and have needed to be reversed. Times of acute financial hardship, now, it is to be hoped, only a memory, have sometimes led to shabbiness creeping in. Tony Marr, for instance, remembers being brought to the Club for the first time in the mid-'fifties:

> ... I was partly aware then and became fully so in the course of time of an amusing, untidy, rather neglected pretty house with a special air that one

became conscious of immediately on stepping out of Brook Street. Hideous things had been done to some of its decorations; ceilings for instance were, in some rooms, a sad khaki colour. The reason, it was said, was that someone who felt pleased to have acquired a lot of paint (in short supply during the war, of course, and officially unavailable to most people) had found what he thought was a good use for it. Blame for the consequent disfigurement of decorative features, particularly of intriguingly pretty "putti" (considered as really rather unsuitable) was laid at the door of a notable surgeon [Ivor Back]. He was not alive when I joined the Club but I happened to have known him and couldn't quite believe the story. ...

The reason why the shade recalling the "worst excesses of café au lait" had come, in Tony Marr's time, to be a "sad khaki colour" was that during the London blitz in September 1940 the Club was bombed and the damaged rooms had to be redecorated, though, sadly, in a manner which turned out to be no more aesthetically pleasing than before. This bombing, a dramatic episode in the Club's history, is rarely remembered nowadays so perhaps it is worth reproducing a breathless account of it which was set down by a member who was present at the time but whose narrative style seems to have owed more to the "penny-dreadfuls" of the day than any of the more literary influences he might have encountered at the Club.

When in the second week of September 1940, the Luftwaffe switched its raids on London to the night, the acting secretary, a member, Tindall Atkinson, had reluctantly obeyed stern orders of medical members to recuperate in the country, and with everyone on the House Committee away our Chairman, Sir Alan Barlow, asked the resident members, Professor J.M. "Chubby" Stratton by then a full Colonel of Intelligence, Judge, later Lord, Merriman and myself to do anything possible for the safety of the clubhouse and the staff. It was generally held that the dining-room was the safest against a bomb with its strong marble pillars but when, as I squeezed past the nearest to the wall and it moved easily, we were disillusioned!

However we believed that the main danger was from incendiaries and fire and that the domestics in rooms on the top floor must at once be moved to a safer place. So we decided to turn the card room (now the bar and lounge) into a dormitory for them; that they were to bring down all their clothes and belongings and that during the afternoon male staff would bring down beds and bed linen.

Then the whole top storey was to be cleared of anything inflammable: carpets, in rooms and on the landing rolled up and stored in the basement, and that all spare linens, etc., on the third and second floor be also moved down to it. A stirrup pump with buckets full of water were to be placed handy on the second and third floor and baths filled at dusk. In addition one or other of Lawrence and Keene, the hall porters, who normally lived out, was to sleep on a bed in the basement underneath the stairs to the lavatory. Finally we three would take it in turn to rest at night on a mattress and pillow in the alcove outside the dining-room, head outwards so that we could see up to the roofing.

On Sunday 22 September, it was my turn: As it was a hot night I changed into slacks and cricket shirt and dozed on the mattress until aroused at eleven thirty by air-raid alarm sirens, then the barrage of A.A. guns; the Hyde Park guns firing meant there were bombers coming over or near us. I listened to heavy thuds of exploding bombs; one between us and the Park, probably, I thought, intended to silence the battery in the Park, was unpleasantly close and the clanging of fire engines continued up Brook Street until about one a.m. A dull thud was possibly on the roof, though at first I believed I was mistaken, then came a sudden flare above as if the lights were switched on; but lights did not flicker and waver and I realised the top floor was on fire! It was a severe shock. I jumped up, ran along the balustrade, switching on in passing all lights, and down the staircase yelling to Keene to come up, that we were on fire.

Struggling into a dressing gown Keene met me in the hall. I told him to dial 999, fire emergency, then break gently to the staff in the bridge room that there was a fire on the top floor, no real danger, but to tell them to dress, pack, and go out by the back way into Three Kings Yard, until it was put out, while I went to find out if Professor Stratton in room one on the second floor was all right. I tore upstairs, saw a glow under the door of room one, pushed hard on it before it opened and was confronted by clusters of streamers, red hot and sparkling, hanging down from a gaping ceiling and saw through them that the tousled bed was unoccupied. I shut the door behind me, switched on the landing and stair lights up to the third floor, went down again to the hall and rejoined Keene with Chubby Stratton, who was sheltering and asleep in the basement. Then we heard the bell of a fire engine coming from Grosvenor Square. Quick off the mark, Keene dashed out, the first, into Brook Street and stood in the middle of the street waving and gesticulating and pointing up to the roof which had the desired effect. It pulled up at the front door, and the crew were told the seat of the fire. In no time two firemen fixed hoses to hydrants and four carried in and unrolled them into the hall and up the stairs. It transpired that they were on the way back to the station off duty! To be out of the way, we stood on the far pavement and looked up at the fire in the roof, two or three rooms on the top floor and one below them. Five minutes or so passed and the officer or Chief Fireman looked out of the front and called us in to tell us to our great relief, that the fire was well under control and that, give or take ten minutes, it would be out. He praised us that the A.R.P. instructions were carried out, (which they seldom were), in clearing the top floor, and that switched on lights facilitated the speedy carrying up of hoses. He said that the cause of the fire was an explosive incendiary oildrum that landed in the gutter between the parapet and roof and it was the first time, as far as he knew or had heard, that any house or building was not burnt down by one. We were also fortunate, according to him, that when the house was built or reconstructed asbestos sheeting was layered on steel rods reinforcing ceilings between floors thus fire-proofing all the internal walls, except for the top floor rooms.

He explained to me that the streamers I saw in the room on the second floor were composed of molten lead from the gutter, the sparking a covering of asbestos and plaster etc. off the ceiling that liquefied in the great heat. But for some charring in places the room was unharmed except by water. His forecast was almost exact. A few minutes later, the three firemen reappeared on the landing rolling up the hoses but on the way to the door warned us that a beam in the internal wall of the third floor might still be smouldering and could restart a fire, but that a stirrup pump would quell it. Keene promptly volunteered to sit on a chair in the passage and keep watch.

The crew came in to report all correct and ready but our suggestion of a pint of beer before moving on was most enthusiastically accepted. Chubby headed a procession of eight, dodging and weaving between trickles of water from the ceiling, through the lobby and down the stair to the basement to find the buttery was locked up; the firemen smilingly unsheathed and proffered axes. Chubby proposed joint action. Taking one, we clasped the handle, smashed a pane of the window and handed it back to the expert. Unanimous agreement ensued that a pint of bitter had never gone down better and another might be very welcome. A police constable materialised along the passage from the back. He pronounced that he had settled our domestics into suitable quarters for the night and, thanks, he would in the exceptional circumstances drink a pint of Bass! A cheerful, friendly party, typical of the wonderful spirit of London in the Blitz of the Autumn, Winter and Spring of 1940/41, only broke up when the firemen decided reluctantly that they must report back to their station.

Then Chubby remembered anxiously leaving rather important documents on his bedside table; the room was eerie, solidified lead covered the bedside table; lifted off, we found the documents only slightly charred at the edges.

On Keene shouting down for help with the stirrup pump and that the wall smouldered, we joined him. I pumped, Keene directed the nozzle, Chubby refilled an empty bucket from a bath, keeping up the supply. The stirrup pump was very efficient in spraying the smouldering and quelled it and we were satisfied that it was dead. We turned, speechless in surprise, at hearing behind us an irascible American declaim that "the noise in the club was intolerable and that he would stay the rest of the night at

Claridge's" whereupon an indignant Ed Murrow carrying a suitcase, strode along the passage and down the stairs. Keene was very upset, having in the excitement forgotten that at eleven last night Mr Murrow had taken Room 14, but he calmed down when told that if the fire was likely to spread it was routine for firemen to enter all rooms to ensure they were unoccupied. Both third and second floors reeked of tar so Chubby and I gathered blankets and pillows and slept uneasily on the leather settees of the Sandpit, water dripping all around. But with the roof temporarily repaired, the club was fit to re-open on the following Wednesday, minus two bedrooms and the top floor. The Staff re-occupying for a while the Bridge Room.

Ed Murrow, incidentally, as some members may recall, was the distinguished American journalist whose dramatic live broadcasts helped bring America into the war ... "This is Ed Murrow, speaking to you from London; a city ablaze, whose courageous citizens pick their way through the ruins each morning in their determination to carry on 'Business as Usual' ...etc., etc." Perhaps in the outcome it was better that our future allies should not have known that those who wished to conduct their "business as usual" were sometimes able to retire to the comfort of Claridges in order to do so.

* * * *

Dilapidations of the more usual kind continued but went mainly unrepaired for the next thirty-five years, for the less exciting reasons of austerity which followed the end of the war and the necessity of surviving the general privations and changes in social life which were to cause the demise of so many famous but less resilient London clubs than the Savile. But even at Brook Street it was often a very near thing. Matters were not helped by a succession of disastrous secretaries and "managers"; and, just as after the First World War, in similar circumstances, the skill of Sir Alan Barlow, the club's honorary treasurer, and the generosity of individual members saved the day, so also in the 'fifties, 'sixties and early 'seventies Barlow's wise advice augmented by the vigorous and often brilliant contrivances of Rupert Withers and, later, Leonard Pearce, prevented, by the merest hair's breadth, the awful prospect of the Savile disappearing out of sight for ever.

It would be tedious to enumerate the many crises which followed so relentlessly one upon another. In 1948 it had been thought for the first time that the Club might have to close its doors, and Rupert Withers forecast then that even if this could be averted it would take at least fifteen years to put the sodality on a secure financial footing.

Rupert recalls the situation then as one of almost certain impending bankruptcy:

Perhaps extinction as an identifiable and independent club would be a fairer way of describing the situation confronting the A.G.M. of that time, which revealed an appalling loss due to the irresponsible extravagance of a paid Secretary who was dismissed but, in typical Savilian fashion, was strongly supported for election to the Club. The whole episode maimed the Club financially for many years, but the generosity of a small devoted group of members enabled it to recover from a situation that might well have ended its life, and therefore its history, 40 years ago.

Winston Graham, a recent trustee, remembers his entrance to the Club in 1946:

> In spite of the magnificence of the building, the Club was a much shabbier place … Carpets were frequently threadbare; the springs of armchairs would be half collapsed; bedrooms had minimal comforts; financially we lived from hand to mouth.

Various expedients were suggested – amalgamation with another club, even selling off that half of the house which before the days of the Harcourts had been No. 71 – but all were rejected and somehow the Club staggered on, full of sodalitas and convivium but suffering, most of the time, from consumption of the purse.

One of the more cheerful notes which was struck during those days of emaciation, however, was the generosity of individual members determined that their Club should not sink into oblivion. Hugh Stewart recalls:

> For some years after the war the ballroom was a shell. Someone described it as a cross between an aircraft hangar and a cowshed. I was on the House Committee at the time, and the Chairman of Committee asked Gerald Barry if he would write an Appeal to raise some money to resuscitate the ballroom. We hoped for seven hundred pounds and to our delight and surprise got £2,300. This enabled us to refurbish the floor, get curtains, carpet, tables and other things. It effectively put a stop to a proposal from some eminent members that we should sell off No. 71 Brook Street (appalling thought!), and saw us off on the road to our full beauty.

This spirit of Sodality was no mere isolated instance. More recently, the late chairman, Neil Salmon, wrote just before he died:

> One of the endearing features of the Savile is the spontaneous generosity of members which is sometimes displayed. The bedrooms of the Savile were each refurbished at the considerable expense of a different (anonymous) member and one member when he heard about the desire to acquire a Persian carpet for the Sandpit promptly wrote out a cheque for £800. Also, when Fred Kendall thought it a good idea to buy a Henry Moore

lithograph he asked 15 members of the General Committee to contribute £10 each – and they did. I have myself experienced something similar in connection with the Stevenson Room. At the opening dinner of that room in honour of Dennis Lennon and Bernard Wiehahn, I mentioned that the redecoration had not been completed because of a shortage of funds and that another £4,000 was needed. Before the dinner broke up one member had offered to pay for the new chandelier that was wanted (£500) and 4 others had agreed to contribute £100 each if 36 further members could be found to join them. As a result I wrote to all members telling them of this and setting up a Redecoration Fund. One hundred and thirty-six members have responded and contributed over £11,000.

By 1962 The Savile Club Endowment Fund was established by Deed of Trust to provide a reserve which could be used to assist the Club if it ran into further grave financial difficulties. An earlier trust known as the "Special Fund" and intended for the assistance of members in temporary financial trouble was later incorporated. The fund had been built up over several years by annual donations, gifts and bequests from members and by the income from its investments; and by 1976 amounted to approximately £27,000. Of this, £1,000 was earmarked for the assistance of members.

Rupert Withers's forecast, gloomy enough as it was, had been slightly on the optimistic side for it was only in that year, 1976, that the tide began to turn and with the arrival of Peter Aldersley as a brilliantly efficient and boldly innovative new secretary that the unremitting efforts of the committee during previous years were brought to fruition and exploited properly in a professional way.

Peter Aldersley and the committee proceeded at first with caution, their ever-anxious gaze permanently fixed on the limitations of a realistic budget. A new system of financial control was introduced by Geoffrey Jones, the new treasurer, whereby a month-by-month examination was made of each of the club's trading activities (dining-room, bar, bedroom lettings and so on), in order that corrective action could swiftly be taken where necessary and promising activities encouraged to increase profitability. So catering for private parties at weekends was developed to make those otherwise barren periods when the Club was closed positively profitable. Rooms were rearranged so that such parties could also be accommodated during week-days at minimum inconvenience to the members. Friday evenings, when latterly it had been not uncommon for the whole of the staff to be on parade to serve one solitary diner, were transformed by the introduction of "candle-light dinners" in the ballroom when for the first time in the Club's history lady guests were welcomed on a regular basis beyond the ducking-stool in the front hall, and Friday nights became the busiest of the week.

Similarly the staff, which, with a few exceptions left over from earlier and happier days, had become a hotch-potch of itinerants with no particular interest in their work-place apart from their weekly pay-packets, were weeded out and replaced by a devoted and efficient team who for more than ten years now have demonstrated daily that their attachment to the Club is quite on a par with that of the membership itself.

Crucial to these new arrangements was the appointment of a new chef, Peter Lea, to whom Peter Aldersley gave *carte blanche* to form his own brigade and rearrange the kitchens and the serveries to suit his own style. The result has been that the standard of cuisine at the Savile can now compare with – and usually surpass – that of any other club in London.

As the increased income resulting from these innovations rolled in, so it was carefully invested in further improvements to the Club premises with a view to generating even greater profitability and hence the Club's security for the future. The bedrooms were refurbished and modernized one by one (with the help of contributions from anonymous members) so that the accommodation at Brook Street now competes with the very best to be found elsewhere in Mayfair at a quarter of the price, yet is still sufficiently profitable to provide a handsome contribution towards the upkeep of the house.

There were set-backs, of course. The ancient lift installed by Fanny Burns at the turn of the century and which had been so admired and appreciated when the members took possession in 1927 had become a potential death-trap. Huge sums had to be expended annually to prevent it from plunging unwary members to a premature doom until in 1983 the inevitable had to be faced and it was stripped out and completely renovated at a cost of £23,000. Had this, and various other afflictions, occurred earlier, they would surely have proved fatal to the club's survival. But financial prudence had won the day and the outward and visible signs of inward providence began dramatically to reveal themselves in the gradual transformation of the once shabby house into a beautiful renewal of its former glory, the like of which would have made even Fanny Burns or her daughter, Lady Harcourt, pause to take breath.

In 1978 the Club's distinguished architect members, Dennis Lennon and Bernard Wiehahn, had, at the committee's request, undertaken to restore the ballroom and redecorate it in a manner more fitting to its glorious potential. Sadly it proved impossible to retrieve more than a few fragments of the "paintings of naked cupids reclining on pink and blue and white clouds" which had caused such controversy back in 1927, for the "khaki" and "café au lait" had been laid on over them with a thorough and enthusiastic gusto. Dennis Lennon therefore started from scratch and based his new plan on the beautiful blue and silver Amalienburg Pavilion at the Nymphenburg Palace near Munich and himself mounted the scaffolding to lie horizontal, *à la* Michelangelo, to paint in the clouds on the ceiling which crown what has since been generally agreed to be a brilliant evocation of the original inspiration. Indeed, as the late Henry Threlfall, then chairman of the House Committee, remarked, "...it was probably the first time in the Club's history that 99 per cent. of the members agreed about anything".

The reopening of the room was celebrated by a crowded Club Dinner on 21 March 1979 with the then chairman, Gwynne Vevers, in the chair and since then it has been recognized by old and new members, their guests, and organizers of outside functions alike, to be one of the most spectacular and elegant rooms in London.

But the transformation of the ballroom was only the harbinger of changes, equally great, to come.

In 1987 the committee set up a working party of six consisting of the Club's chairman, Oliver Makower, Sir Thomas Barlow, Osman Streater, John Turtle, Gurdon Wattles, Tom Baistow and the secretary Peter Aldersley. By now the revenue from private functions amounted to 46 per cent of catering receipts so the working party produced – among many other recommendations on other matters – a scheme whereby the rooms in the Club would be rearranged to provide improved facilities for attracting and, indeed, increasing such vital revenue while at the same time minimizing disturbance to members going about their usual pursuits.

By April 1988 it was decided that the old morning-room off the front hall was to be renamed the Stevenson Room (after Robert Louis) and converted into a permanent venue for private functions: the old snooker-room was to become the new morning-room: the old-card room was to be named the Potter Room (after Stephen) and become the snooker-room: the offices on the second floor were to be gutted, renamed the Elgar Room (after the previous committee member, Sir Edward) and transmogrified into an elegant reception-cum-dining-room for smaller functions: the old servants' bedrooms in the Mews gutted and rearranged to provide more spacious quarters for the office.

The first three of these projects had to be carried out during the summer closure of 1988 to prevent undue disturbance to the normal functioning of the Club. In the result it was to prove a masterpiece of logistics, a further demonstration of the loyalty and devotion of the staff, and a sensational surprise to those members who had previously harboured doubts about one or other aspects of the scheme. Tom Baistow tells the story:

> With Dennis Lennon as studio master and Bernard Wiehahn in charge of logistics, supported by Peter Aldersley on the administrative front and Sid Jackson, the club's all-round maintenance man, Richard Burleton, night barman, and Peter Fitzgerald, the cellarman house supervisor, in a demanding variety of unaccustomed roles, the race against time began – the six-man team had only thirty days to complete their formidable schedule. Not only had the new Stevenson, Morning and Billiards Rooms to be completely refurbished and new carpets laid in the Dining Room, but the entire premises rewired throughout and two new boilers installed under Bernard's supervision.
>
> Dennis sums it up as a triumph of teamwork. "Peter A. was a tower of strength. Sid is a magician – you can ask him to do anything. He's a glorious handyman with few resources but every skill. Everyone was determined to get everything absolutely right. Nothing was too much trouble for them. Even the suppliers seemed inspired by the potential of our beautiful house – several provided us with the highest quality

materials at ridiculous prices. When we discovered we didn't have enough gold leaf in stock for the gilding one firm provided the extra books free."

He and Bernard also pay tribute to those members who contributed anonymously towards the cost in various ways — the handsome new chandelier in the Morning Room is just one example of their generosity. Another is the striking "Gallery" of Spy-type caricatures of celebrities of the past which adorns the new Stevenson Room. They were literally mouldering in the basement, explains Lennon, and Robin Fletcher had the whole lot treated against acid and framed at his own expense.

Apart from the triumph of achieving this remarkable feat in such a way and in such an incredibly short time, the most sensational jewel to be revealed when the Club reassembled after the Summer closure in 1988, was the new morning-room. What had seemed, by virtue of its ring-side banquettes and the central dominion of the Club's famous billiards table, to be a longitudinal room reminiscent of a faded Imperial Railway carriage, was now revealed as a beautifully proportioned rectangular saloon whose area, as only the architects concerned had realized, was identical to that of the ballroom immediately above. To those who knew it in its previous incarnation, the wonderfully realized transformation shall never cease to amaze.

The fourth and fifth components of the restructuring, that is, the removal of the offices and the creation of the new Elgar Room, had to await the summer closure of 1989, when they were similarly successfully completed.

The total cost of the operation left little change out of £100,000 but it was correctly calculated that increased revenue will have paid for this in full by the end of 1992.

The result is that, whatever, the future may hold, the Club now possesses a spectacularly beautiful house whose distinctive features have been sensitively and elegantly enhanced to create an entity finely tuned to harmonize with all the present and future needs of the membership.

So now, having arrived at the opulence of Brook Street in the 1990s from the relatively dingy lodgings at Spring Gardens in 1868, it is time to look back in detail at the membership during these years to see how and why this transformation in the Club's fortunes came about and remind ourselves of some of the reasons why the Club may anticipate so confidently an equally distinguished future.

The Club's dining-room *(Photo: Barnet Saidman)*

Two pastoral scenes on the overdoors
of the dining-room painted in the
style of Lancret and Watteau
(Photos: Barnet Saidman)

Another view of the dining-room looking into
the ballroom. The showcases contain some
of the Barlow collection of Oriental Ceramics
together with Michael Powell's and Emeric
Pressburger's Oscars.

(Photo: Barnet Saidman)

The ballroom staircase *(Photo: Barnet Saidman)*

Entrance to the ballroom from the staircase *(Photo: Barnet Saidman)*

The ballroom set out for ladies' night each friday *(Photo: Barnet Saidman)*

The morning-room
(Photo: Barnet Saidman)

CHAPTER TWO

Literary Figures

It is curious that one of the many threads which describe a teasing arabesque through the early literary history of the Savile should spin around a man who failed to be elected a member.

"Ah! The Savile Club," pronounced Oscar Wilde in one of his more extravagant fits of hubris, "a true republic of letters; not a sovereign among 'em". This little apophthegm was received with tolerant grace amongst the membership, considering that it numbered then, as it does now, a considerable proportion of the leading literary figures of the day.

Perhaps it was not – as so many of his better remarks were not – taken very seriously. After all, at a later date he was to declare blithely, "We Irish are too poetic to be really good poets", seemingly unconcerned that this particular pearl was being cast before W.B. Yeats, who was shortly to succeed – where he had failed – in becoming a member of the despised sodality.

Nevertheless it is odd that he was not permitted to join. There was, as yet, no hint of scandal; there were many members who were his friends; many more who had influenced him or been influenced by him. His tutor and guide at Trinity College, Dublin, Sir John Pentland Mahaffey, the model for Wilde's surpassing brilliance in conversation, had been elected in 1871. Mahaffey was a figure of some eminence in several European capitals as well as in his native Dublin. Like many Irishmen of his class at that time, he was a colossal snob but, unlike most of that genus, this failing did not arise from any necessity to fawn on the great in order to disguise feelings of inferiority. He was in great demand in royal circles and so famous were his powers as a conversationalist that he was regularly asked to Sandringham and Windsor by King Edward VII, who appreciated his memories of Greece and of Germany in the days of Prince Edward of Saxe-Weimar. He was proud of being on intimate terms with seven kings and seven queens and on one occasion at Windsor at the time of the Coronation of Edward VII when they were all present he came out with that famous gaffe when, intending to flatter the Queen of Spain, he paraphrased the Emperor Charles V: "Madam, Spanish is the language of kings; French is the language of diplomacy; Italian is the language of love; German I speak to my horse." Unfortunately the Kaiser overheard him and his embarrassment was only relieved when war broke out a few years later. When it did, one of his colleagues in the Common Room at Trinity chided him for his friendship with the King of Greece, who had taken sides with the Germans. The good doctor imperturbably replied: "Yes, I'm deeply disappointed in him; I shall cut him when we next meet."

But beneath the cultivated charm which was the essential stock-in-trade of a clergyman, servicing the Anglo-Irish aristocracy of the time, this well-tailored handsome young professor hid two obsessions; one for the culture of ancient and modern Greece, and the other for the social life which access to the aristocracy of a great imperial power afforded him. It was said of Mahaffey that he only lifted his eyes from Homer in order to look at invitations from the nobility, but as in his book *Rambles and Studies in Greece* he reveals great sensitivity to the beauty of the landscape, he must sometimes have lifted his eyes elsewhere. A member who in his student days was acquainted with some of Mahaffey's latter-day contemporaries recalls the pleasure with which they remembered his conversation as a perfect amalgam of Irish bravura disciplined by English formality. No one, it has been said, was better able than he to enliven a stuffy dinner party which in the peculiar social circumstances of the time might include a wide variety of guests of every conceivable hue, from dowdy dowagers through titled inarticulates to garrulous intellectuals. He was moreover a well-known figure in the hunting field, following the hounds of his friends the Duke of Leinster and Lord Carew yet equally at home at the bridge tables of their more arthritic female relations. He was made much of in a world of which the less socially mobile Wildes could only catch a glimpse. Oscar was as thrilled by the stories he brought back from Dunsany Castle as by a dissertation of Demosthenes. As one of Wilde's biographers, Philippe Jullian, records: " Oscar's phenomenal memory was of great use to Mahaffey in his work. Soon there was little else that the professor could teach him about literature, but he encouraged him to ride, to play tennis and to use a gun. Oscar's conversation, at times impetuous and a little vulgar, became polished by practice with this supreme exponent of the art."

Clearly this was a man who would have welcomed entrée to the company to be found at the Savile, and, with equal enthusiasm, would have been received into it as a worthy adornment.

But Wilde's passion for the culture of ancient Greece was matched by a similar love for that of the Renaissance. Where Mahaffey had planted the first, another member of the Savile had sown the second. No two men of such literary influence could have been more different. Walter Pater, the critic and essayist, had become a member as early as 1869. Wilde had sat among his group of pre-Raphaelites at Oxford, eagerly embracing the cult of beauty as an end in itself – a notion which Pater was to push to dangerous limits in the heady perfumed prose of his masterpiece *Marius the Epicurean*, published in 1885. How Pater coped with the Club's preoccupation with conversation is, sadly, not recorded for he spoke in little more than a whisper and tended to stammer if any of the company were particularly handsome. It is said that after one of his lectures he enquired: "I hope you heard me?" to which Wilde had replied, "We *over*heard you".

Another friend who would surely have welcomed Wilde into the sodality was Lord Lytton, elected in 1887. Edward Robert Bulwer-Lytton, 1st Earl of Lytton, was a diplomat and poet. He had been Viceroy of India and later Ambassador at

Paris, where Wilde was often his guest. Lytton wrote poetry under the pen name of "Owen Meredith", seeing himself as something of a cupbearer of the Byronic tradition. One of his better works, *Fables in Song*, had been generously reviewed by Robert Louis Stevenson in the *Fortnightly Review*, which was then edited by another Savile member, John Morley.

One of Wilde's most devoted disciples did not allow his loyalty to prevent him from joining the Club which had rejected his friend. Elected in 1893, Robert Ross was the son of a Canadian Attorney-General and grandson of the first Prime Minister of Upper Canada. Ross evidently regarded membership of the Savile as a very valuable social cachet for when he first went up to Cambridge in 1888 – the year that Wilde had been rejected – he boasted that he was himself already a member although he was not, in fact, to be elected until five years later. Admittedly he had been a guest many times of his elder brother Alex, who was elected in 1887, but it was an extremely stupid and obvious lie considering that he was surrounded by many such as Oscar Browning, a friend of Wilde's and a history fellow at Ross's own college – King's – who were genuinely members.

After coming down from Cambridge, Ross worked for another Savile member, W.E. Henley, who was then editor of the *Scots Observer*. Later he was to become much involved with the Society of Authors of which his brother Alex was honorary secretary and whose management committee included such other Savilians as Rudyard Kipling, Justin M'Carthy and Walter Besant, who had been its driving force since its inception in 1884. When Besant offered Robbie Ross the post as assistant editor of the Society's magazine, *The Author*, the salary was two shillings a quarter, which Besant kindly suggested could be drawn "weekly (weakly) if you pleased". Luckily Ross's mother was wealthy enough in her own right to provide him with a supplementary allowance. When Ross did eventually become a member of the Club he was already contributing to the *Saturday Review*, edited by another Savilian, Sir Leslie Stephen, and among his several referees was Edmund Gosse, with whom he was to sustain an enduring friendship. Apart from Ross's life-long vocation of restoring the financial fortunes of the Wilde estate and the literary reputation of its author, his main preoccupation was with art and art criticism. He established himself as a critic of wit and perception in the several journals of the time concerned with the art of painting and in 1898 he became closely associated with the Carfax Gallery in Ryder Street which had been founded by, among others, two Savile members, Edward Warren and William Rothenstein. One of the many outstanding events which he was to stage there was the first major exhibition of caricatures by his fellow member of the Savile, Max Beerbohm.

But the overriding memory of Ross at the Savile and elsewhere was of his loyal devotion to his friend Oscar Wilde, and his popularity at the Club was largely due to the brilliance of his conversation which was said at times to compare with that of the master himself. Many of the lines in Wilde's *Intentions* are taken from remarks made to him by Robert Ross.

Ross was to be Wilde's literary executor; present with him at Wilde's death-bed was Reginald Turner, who had joined the Savile a few months before in 1900. Turner was the illegitimate son of the first Lord Burnham, proprietor of the *Daily Telegraph*, who was born Edward Levy and assumed the name Lawson in 1875. When he was Levy he was a member of the Savile; when he became Burnham he joined the Garrick. Turner was extremely short of funds in his early youth but by this time was being maintained in some comfort by his half-brother, Frank Lawson, so his desire to join the Club was presumably not determined by the modesty of its subscription. To Turner the Club owes the presence among its present ranks of Sir Harold Acton, who writes:

> ...I was quite young when I became a member of the Savile, introduced by the late lamented Reginald Turner who had settled in Florence. Turner had written several light novels which enjoyed some contemporary success, though his brilliant conversation was deservedly famous; the wittiest man I have ever known, even in retrospect. His india-rubber features were intensely mobile and expressive, and he might have been a successful comedian; everything became a stage in his presence. He had been a loyal friend of Oscar Wilde, whom he visited in prison, and he shared Wilde's fantastic sense of fun. No doubt he enlivened the Savile...

The Wilde connection was even more happily compounded when his son, Vyvyan Holland, was elected in 1920.

Despite his seemingly cavalier view of Savilians' literary abilities, Wilde evidently esteemed the Club rather more than it might appear, for in September 1888 he wrote to that brilliant but quarrelsome poet, journalist and editor, W.E. Henley:

> It will give me great pleasure to lunch with you at the Savile on Saturday, though I am afraid that I shall be like a poor lion who has rashly intruded into a den of fierce Daniels. As for proposing me for the Savile that is of course one of your merry jests....

Perhaps it was; for when Wilde was proposed the following month his sponsor was the Rev. W.J. Loftie. Thirty-one other members of the Club put their names down as referees, including such "Sovereign" literary figures as Henry James, Edmund Gosse, Rider Haggard, Walter Besant, George Macmillan and R.A.M. Stevenson – Robert Louis' cousin and a distinguished critic in his own right. Henley also appended his name and this may account for Wilde's failure to be elected. Not all referees necessarily intend to support the candidate, and the highly volatile Henley, who had already fallen out noisily with his fellow member Robert Louis Stevenson, had probably taken the time to redirect his venom towards Wilde in the few short weeks which had elapsed since he had suggested proposing him.

Had Wilde pondered on his rejection and glanced at the contemporary membership list – particularly those who had supported him – he might have revised his view of the Club and seen it as "a den of literary lions" rather than a "republic of letters". Even though he had once commented that Henry James "wrote English prose as if it were a painful duty" he would surely have had to concur with the more general opinion that he was becoming a towering figure in the literary world.

James's entry to the Club had been made, as one might expect, with maidenly hesitation and fastidious caution. On 13 February 1877, just after he had moved from Paris to establish himself permanently in London, he had written to his father to describe how he was settling down and talked of the Athenaeum as "a little heaven here below". However, he then goes on to say:

> I also have temporary membership of another Club – the small and modest Savile. It is very respectably composed – supposed, I believe, to be particularly so; but after the Athenaeum it seems dreadfully caddish and I shall resort to it only when the latter fails me.

Evidently the latter did not fail him for he stayed with it and let his temporary membership of the Savile lapse and it was not until 1884 when either some greater caddishness at the Athenaeum or the increased attractions of respectability at Piccadilly drove him back to seek full membership of the Savile.

Sir Walter Besant, who was elected in 1873, was an assiduous visitor to the Club. Though modern fashion has turned against him, at the time he put his name down for Wilde he was regarded as one of the most eminent of Victorian novelists. It is said that one of his predilections was to try to persuade his friends and acquaintances to accent the second syllable of his surname instead of the first, to distinguish himself from a hated member of his family. It was, however, only at the Savile that he could be sure of being indulged in this eccentricity. Rider Haggard – another signatory for Wilde – was one of the most popular novelists of the day and novels such as *King Solomon's Mines* and *She* still have a devoted following – though perhaps his present public are more aware of him through the excruciating films they have spawned or – through a more elegant source – by "Rumpole's" apprehensive borrowing of Rider Haggard's phrase in references to his wife as "She who must be obeyed". Rider Haggard's membership of the Savile, incidentally, provides an interesting early example of how contact with fellow members has sometimes provided the inspiration for future literary or artistic products. Frederick Courtney Selous, who was elected in 1894, was the most celebrated big-game hunter of the late nineteenth century. His exploits in the African bush as hunter, naturalist and political adventurer, fulfilling as they did all the fantasies of a *Boy's Own Paper* adventure, had seized the public's imagination while his deep personal knowledge of the continent's political and physical landscapes provided him with a second career as writer and lecturer. The "Selous

Scouts" who patrol the African Game Reserves to the present day are a continuing memorial to him; Rider Haggard admired him greatly and is reputed to have used him as the model for the eponymous hero of *Allan Quatermain*. In more recent times Selous's middle name provided the popular novelist Wilbur Smith with the patronymic of the settler dynasty in southern Africa, the Courteneys, leading characters in two sequences of adventure novels.

Edmund Gosse was already the doyen of English critics when he signed the book for Wilde. He had joined the Club in 1876 and served on the committee in 1882-3. Though it was to be some years before he wrote that masterpiece of autobiography, *Father and Son*, he was already renowned for his championship of foreign literature, particularly Scandinavian and French – the last of which should have endeared him to the man he was refereeing on this occasion. Gosse had translated *Hedda Gabler* and *The Master Builder* and though this had made them immediately accessible to the British public and rightly acclaimed at the time, they have since been superseded by later and better versions, most notably by a contemporary member, Michael Meyer.

Gosse's enthusiasms for English and foreign literature did not extend to the aesthetic movement or any form of bohemianism so it is sad that there is not more record of his dealings with the artistic extravagances of some of his fellow members. Perhaps the grace and tolerance with which he imbued his critical works were extended to them: his regard for the Club was evidently reciprocated and is still commemorated in the bust by Sir William Gascombe John, R.A., presented to him by the members on his seventieth birthday, which today gazes down, perhaps a trifle sternly, on their successors from its plinth in the ballroom.

It was at the Savile that Gosse first made personal acquaintance with Robert Louis Stevenson. This happy meeting immediately blossomed into a close and enduring friendship and to it we owe a valuable addition to the literary archive in the correspondence, sadly no longer at the Savile, which passed between them.

Stevenson had been elected in 1874 and made great use of the Club while he was in London. He had been proposed by Sidney Colvin (later Sir Sidney Colvin, Litt.D), a distinguished committee member of the Savile, a literary critic, art connoisseur and, from 1873, Slade Professor of Fine Art at Cambridge. Here another thread can be discerned weaving its tortuous way through the Club's history. In 1873 Robert Louis Stevenson had fallen out with his father and had left Edinburgh to stay with a married cousin at Cuckfield in Sussex. There he met Colvin and a slightly older lady, Mrs Fanny Sitwell, who befriended him and with whom R.L.S. fell in love. His subsequent letters to her show him going through various stages from would-be lover, to worshipper from afar, and finally, son. This latter stage was perhaps as well, for Fanny became Lady Colvin. Colvin had evidently viewed the situation with equanimity, for Stevenson and he remained friends for life.

In May 1874, when Stevenson was twenty-three, he had written to Colvin:

Jenkins wrote to say he would second me in such a kind notelet. I shall go in for it (the Savile, I mean) being now a man of means. Have I told you by the way that I have now an income of £84 or as I prefer to put it for dignity's sake, two thousand one hundred francs a year?

The "Jenkins" to whom R.L.S. referred was in fact Professor Fleeming Jenkyn, F.R.S., a founder member of the Club in 1868. In that year Jenkyn had just been appointed Professor of Engineering at Edinburgh University and his wife Annie – another lively and artistic elder lady – had made the acquaintance of the then fifteen-year-old R.L.S. at the house of his parents in Edinburgh. Evidently he made a great impression on Annie Jenkyn for on her return home she had announced to her husband, "I have just met a *poet.*" She took him under her wing and R.L.S. became a regular visitor to the Jenkyns' home and later – when for a short time and against his will he was forced by his father to study engineering so that he could continue the family profession of lighthouse building and harbour works – he studied under Jenkyn at Edinburgh University. Soon, however, he was off to London for more congenial pursuits but he never lost touch with the Jenkyns and though in all his correspondence he spelled their name "Jenkins" he remained an intimate friend of both until Fleeming's early death and then his own.

Colvin's and Jenkyn's efforts on his behalf were successful and R.L.S. was duly elected to the Savile in 1874. In a letter to his mother just after his election he writes:

> I wish someone would explain to me the climate of Hampstead. To be so near London and yet to be in an atmosphere more like Peebles than any other I can think of, is surely a puzzle in meteorology. Hampstead is all my fancy painted it; it is so quiet, healthful and beautiful; and yet one can go and dine at the Club in three-quarters of an hour or thereabouts. I like my Club very much; the table d'hôte dinner is very good: it costs three bobs (sic): two soups, two fish, two entrées, two joints, two puddings; so it is not dear; and one meets agreeable people.

Stevenson's connection with the Savile was to have important literary consequences; he had already reviewed Lord Lytton's *Fables in Song* in *The Fortnightly* edited by John Morley and now he became a contributor to *The Cornhill Magazine* edited by another fellow member, Leslie Stephen. At the Savile he renewed his acquaintance with Henley, to whom Leslie Stephen had introduced him in Edinburgh while Henley was recuperating from having had his tubercular foot amputated by Sir Joseph Lister. There they joyously came together again until, in 1888, Henley made a disgraceful accusation of dishonesty against Stevenson's wife and began a feud with him which was to be fierce and unrelenting. Matters were to become worse when it became evident that Stevenson had seized on Henley's physical appearance, his one leg and penchant for rum, as the inspiration for his depiction of Long John Silver in *Treasure Island*. It must have made the Savile an exciting place to be when both were present; "Seraph in chocolate" was one of Henley's milder judgments on it when Balfour's biography of Stevenson appeared. But other members held a different view. Sir Herbert Stephen recalls the strong impression made by Stevenson in the Savile:

> He found in it some, and made others of his most intimate friends, and the various records of his life leave no possibility of doubt that when, as often happened at the Savile, he was in good spirits and in congenial company, conversation with him was an extraordinary and delightful experience. His biographer, Graham Balfour, says that from 1874 to 1879 the Savile was "the centre of his London life", and described the years 1876-9 as "the days when he most frequented the Savile Club, and the lightest and most vivacious parts of him there came to the surface. He might spend the morning in work or business, and would then come to the Club for luncheon. If he were so fortunate as to find any congenial companions disengaged, or to induce them to throw over their engagements, he would lead them off to the smoking-room, and there spend an afternoon in the highest spirits and the most brilliant talk". The Club tradition of friendliness and cheerfulness was after his own heart.

The lure of Stevenson's conversation was to have unfortunate consequences for his friend and patron, Sir Sidney Colvin. At the time Colvin was Keeper of Prints and Drawings at the British Museum he was passing the Savile Row clubhouse in a hansom cab when he remembered that R.L.S. was due back from abroad. He stopped the cab and instructed it to wait while he stepped inside but got caught up in the occasion and by the time he remembered the cab it had gone, bearing with it a priceless collection of Italian drawings that had been in his safekeeping. Restitution had to be made and it is said that he was in debt for the rest of his life.

Stevenson provides us also with another example of the fertilizing effect which encounters at the Savile were apt to produce in members prone to artistic creation. Kegan Paul had been one of the original members in 1868. He had first been in Holy Orders and later held a mastership at Eton but by 1872 had abandoned both these careers and set up the publishing house which bears his name. On one occasion, some member having expressed a particular liking for him, Robert Louis Stevenson replied: "Oh, I like Paul; he's a good fellow, a very good fellow – but every now and then Kegan looks at you out of his eyes." This idle fancy evidently lingered in the author's memory for it is from that chance remark that he is reputed to have developed the plot of *Dr Jekyll and Mr Hyde*, published in 1886.

R.L.S.'s memorable attendances at the Club, however, did not all consist of beer and conversational skittles. Finding himself in financial straits sometime in his early days as a member, he had procured a small loan from Edmund Gosse. Although this had been soon repaid he rather crassly mentioned it to a fellow Savilian with the airy comment that the sum involved would not have mattered much to Gosse. His confidant thereupon read him a stern lecture on how it really stood with Gosse financially, and how R.L.S. "should not take too light a view of the responsibility and the service". The rebuke clearly left its mark, for only two days before he died, writing to Gosse to thank him for the dedication – "To Tusitala" – of Gosse's volume of poems *In Russet and Silver*, he refers back with gratitude to the original loan. [Tusitala was the name by which RLS was known in Samoa; it means "teller of tales"].

There were other potentially hazardous encounters which were equally happily resolved. George Saintsbury, F.B.A., LL.D., the great Victorian literary man and *bon vivant* who is now chiefly remembered for his *Notes on a Cellar Book* wrote after Stevenson's death:

> The following report on how I met Robert Louis Stevenson is short, but may possibly in form be not unsweet. I was introduced to him at the Savile Club, I am not quite sure by whom, but it was almost certainly by Andrew Lang. Before I could say anything he said: "I'm told you think what I write is rot." I replied: "No: I think *some* of what you write is rot. Will you come and dine with me tonight?" Which reply, after forty years and more, I regard as in both parts not unworthy of an Englishman. So he came: and we were friends ever after. I had a pretty good notion as to who was likely to have been his teller, and probably some others may share it.

"Ah!" as some contemporaries might exclaim, "how unsweet to hear that some things have not changed".

When one considers the appalling ill-health from which R.L.S. suffered one is amazed not only by his prodigious literary output but by the vigour and cheerfulness which he brought to his very active social life at the Savile. After his death his collection of letters to his fellow member, Charles Baxter, was presented to the Club; sadly they were sold to another member, the distinguished collector, Edwin Beinecke, and now reside in Yale University Library. A further collection of letters which Stevenson wrote to Sir Sidney Colvin and others from Samoa in the years 1890-94 was compiled by Colvin and published under the title *Vailima Letters*.

One of them was written to Fleeming Jenkyn's widow, Annie, in December 1892 two years before he died, pleading with her to come and stay: "Spare us a month or two for old sake's sake, and make my wife and me happy and proud... Do, please, make a virtuous effort and take a glimpse of a new world I am sure you do not dream of and some old friends who do often dream of your arrival."

But throughout his exile he himself was dreaming of a return to England and the Savile. His stepson and collaborator, Lloyd Osbourne, wrote:

> At first (in Hawaii in 1889) he anticipated returning to England; in fact, for a while this was as good as settled; "Skerryvore" (his Bournemouth house) was still there, temporarily rented; and absence, perhaps, was endowing it with a certain glamour. But most compelling of all, I think, was R.L.S.'s desire to stroll into the Savile Club and electrify all his old

friends as the returned seafarer from the South Sea Islands. At least, he was constantly dwelling on this phase of his return, and choosing the exact hour when he could make the most dramatic entrance.

Sadly the "dramatic entrance" was never to take place, nor does the Savile still possess any of his letters except for a sad remnant of a once-promising collection – a photostat of a short note from him to his mother written on Savile writing paper: it is on lonely display in the Monument.

From 1886 to '87 Stevenson had lived with his wife at Bournemouth, whence he travelled often to see his fellow Savilian, Henry James, with whom he had developed a close friendship. Keith Piercy, in an enlightening note on the history of the Savile, recalls that during this time he also made an expedition to see that other great literary figure and fellow member, Thomas Hardy, who was living at Dorchester. The visit, says Piercy, was not a social success – but then, visiting Hardy was never guaranteed to be a rewarding social experience and Stevenson should have been warned. Much later than this, in the summer of 1923, the Prince of Wales himself was persuaded to make a detour from his annual duty visit to the Duchy of Cornwall to lunch with the reluctantly Grand Old Man of English letters. Max Beerbohm heard about this and with his usual deflatory delight composed a poem in the Hardy manner to commemorate the briskly conducted scene which he imagined had most likely ensued:

> Lift latch, step in, be welcome, Sir,
> Albeit to see you I'm unglad
> And your face is fraught with a deathly shyness
> Bleaching what pink it might have had.
> Come in, come in, Your Royal Highness.
>
> Beautiful weather? – Sir, that's true
> Though the farmers are casting rueful looks
> At tilth's and pasture's dearth of spryness –
> Yes, Sir, I've written several books –
> A little more chicken, Your Royal Highness?
>
> Lift latch, step out, your car is there,
> To bear you hence from this ancient vale.
> We are both of us aged by our strange brief nighness.
> But each of us lives to tell the tale.
> Farewell, farewell, Your Royal Highness.

Considering his eminence, Hardy seems to have made similarly small impact at the Savile. The year of his election, 1878, was the year that *The Return of the Native* was published though he had already established himself both critically and in the popular esteem with *Under the Greenwood Tree* and *Far from the Madding Crowd*. Perhaps he carried with him into the Savile the more characteristically sombre mood of his most recent novel and it was this which caused him to leave so little trace of his presence in that festive gathering place. Hardy had used the publication of *The Return of the Native* to justify his own temporary return from rural exile in Dorset to "fall into line as a London man again" and, on 18 June, the day he was elected to membership of the Savile, he "visited the west-end in hearty company". Less than seven weeks later, on 3 August, he and William Minto, critic and editor of the *Examiner*, who had proposed him for membership, were joined at the Club by Walter Herries Pollock, a "dramatic collaborator" who, like Minto, would serve on the committee in future years. After fortifying themselves with a good dinner at Piccadilly, they went off to the Lyceum, where they ended the evening drinking champagne out of tumblers with their fellow member Sir Henry Irving – who was "stripped to the waist" – in his dressing-room.

Despite his unpredictable social manner, Hardy had already many acquaintances at the Club; John Morley was one, the publishers Alexander Macmillan and Kegan Paul among others; but one of the few members who managed most successfully to pierce Hardy's protective shell and transcend mere acquaintanceship was Edmund Gosse. Perhaps it was Gosse's own experience of a restrictive childhood that enabled him to overcome Hardy's reserve and gradually to establish a friendship which, nevertheless, had to endure more than one crisis. Gosse would lure Hardy up to London for occasional week-ends – "Lord, how we would talk!" – and certainly Gosse was the first (and probably for a long time, the only) house-guest to be welcomed at Dorchester.

The first crisis in Hardy's membership of the Savile came in 1891 when *Tess of the D'Urbervilles* was published to great public and critical acclaim. There was, however, one contrary voice and it belonged to a fellow member, Andrew Lang, the critic of the *New Review*. This hurt Hardy so greatly that he considered resigning from the Savile and making his London base at the Athenaeum, which had just elected him. However, more enthusiastic responses from this other friends at the Savile prevailed upon him to recant this brief temptation to apostasy.

A more serious threat both to his friendship with Gosse and his membership of the Savile occurred towards the end of 1895 with the publication of *Jude the Obscure*. Almost with one voice the critics condemned it, most of them either members of the Savile or writing for newspapers which were edited or owned by Savilians. *The Morning Post* denounced it; the *Pall Mall Gazette* – recently edited by John Morley – found it full of "dirt, drivel and damnation", referring to it, moreover, as "Jude the Obscene". Even across the water in America, the *New York World*, owned by the Pulitzer family (Ralph Pulitzer regularly used the Savile as an honorary member during his visits to London), referred to the author as "Hardy the Degenerate".

But as Robert Gittings, in his 1978 biography *The Older Hardy*, records from other sources:

> More deeply wounding, perhaps, than all this, and nearest home, were the doubts expressed by his usually adulatory supporter, Edmund Gosse. A

week after publication, Gosse reviewed the book in the *St James's Gazette*. He wrote of "a grimy story that Mr Hardy has at last presented to his admirers". There were other cutting phrases. Hardy, though beginning a letter of 10 November by praising Gosse's article as "the most discriminating that has yet appeared", was very clearly hurt. He had an even more unpleasant shock from Gosse in December, when he and Emma paid a flying visit to London, to see both Forbes-Robertson and Mrs Patrick Campbell in *Romeo and Juliet*. At the common luncheon-table at the Savile Club, Gosse told Hardy publicly to his face that *Jude the Obscure* was the most indecent novel ever written. For the first, and, as he afterwards said, the only time in his life, Hardy became really angry with his friend. Even a more "generous view", expressed by Gosse in a new magazine *Cosmopolis* in the New Year, did not easily make up for the shock. Considering how abnormally thin-skinned Hardy was, and how much this novel of all others meant to him, it is a tribute to both men that their friendship survived.

But it can be deduced that such bristly encounters were rare and that Hardy's visits to the Club were generally of a more harmonious kind for, as Winston Graham recalls:

A few years ago when we gave a celebratory party in Hardy's memory, I was asked to be chairman, with Peggy Ashcroft as principal speaker. Shortly before this the late Michael Serpell, one of the most charming and learned members of the Club, told me that Hardy had often written his poems late at night on Savile writing paper. He also gave me a quotation from one of Hardy's lesser books (which I have ransacked my study for and cannot find) in which he compares the Savile – not by name – favourably with the Athenaeum, referring to his other and smaller club where after lunch one could sit and talk and reveal one's thoughts openly in the confident assumption that nothing said would ever be repeated beyond the four walls in which it was spoken.

No other anecdotes, however, illuminating as they might have been, are preserved in the Club's collective memory; the Savile history written five years before his death records his name only once – in the index; "Hardy, Thomas, (O.M. Litt.D., L.L.D.)." But this titan, "the last of the great Victorians", to use the words of a banal eulogy, must have received more from his membership than he gave for he remained a member for thirty-one years.

Perhaps the previous historian of the Savile shared Wilde's view of those of its members who earned their living by the pen for, with the exception of that brief memoir of Robert Louis Stevenson, he gives them only the briefest possible mention or, as in the case of Thomas Hardy, none at all in the text. The literary history of the Club would be thin indeed if, to recall again the words of *The Times* in 1923, "we set ourselves to regard these early giants as they appeared to their fellows, not as they appear, with all their honours thick upon them, to ourselves".

When Sir Herbert Stephen was writing his history in 1923 he records that "more than 170 Fellows of the Royal Society have been members of the Savile and between them *they have written a great many books....*" and that, more or less, is as far as he goes.

As his own book was being published, his fellow member W.B. Yeats was becoming the second Savilian to be awarded the Nobel Prize for Literature, the first having been Rudyard Kipling. Similarly we find "Bridges, Robert (M.B., F.R.C.P., Litt.D.)" in the index as having been elected to the Savile in 1872 and serving on the committee between the years 1879 and 1881 but nothing more. Robert Bridges did indeed practise as a physician until 1882, but by 1923 he had become rather better known as one of the finest lyric poets of his age and poet laureate to boot. Housman had said of his *Shorter Poems*, published between 1890 and 1894, that "probably no single version of English verse has ever maintained such perfection". In 1929, the year before his death, he was appointed to the Order of Merit.

Bridges was a twenty-eight-year-old medical student when he joined the Savile and, except for a gap between 1907 and 1915, he remained an active member until just before his death in 1930. If any justification is required for the Savile's principle of selecting untried young men of promise it must be well exemplified by him. Although he spent much of his time in domestic seclusion, first in Berkshire and later at Boar's Hill in Oxford, he retained a keen interest in science, art and philosophy even after he had devoted himself entirely to poetry. It was to nurture these interests and to maintain his many friendships with the leading literary figures of his day that he continued to seek the appropriate company so regularly at 107 Piccadilly.

The fifty-eight years' span of Robert Bridges' membership saw a distinguished procession of literary men into the Savile. When he joined in 1872 the Club had already sheltered the young – and then impecunious – John Morley. At the time, Morley was working as a free-lance journalist: "I was a scrawler when I first came to town", he was later to recall, "and I have scribbled many a day before now with a hungry paunch but 'twas all honest and honourable".

By the time he died in 1923, he was Viscount Morley of Bradford, a Privy Counsellor, and O.M; he had published highly regarded biographies of Burke, Voltaire, Rousseau, Cobden, Cromwell and Gladstone – this latter, incidentally, creating something of a record in its day by selling 30,000 copies in its first year and more than 100,000 during the next ten. And his ambitions had not been confined to literature only. His election to the Club had coincided with an upturn in his fortunes when he became editor of *The Fortnightly Review*, which he transformed into one of the most influential organs of liberal opinion. Shortly afterwards he was to add to that the editorship of *The Pall Mall Gazette*, and with this extension of his literary clout campaign vigorously on behalf of Joseph Chamberlain and Sir Charles Dilke for disestablishment and improved secular education. He became M.P. for Newcastle-upon-Tyne, Secretary for India and Chief Secretary for Ireland; in 1902 he was one of the first recipients of the newly created Order of Merit from King Edward VII. Solid achievement for one who had once depended on the Club's three shillings table d'hôte to assuage his "hungry paunch". It was said of him that his "charm of voice and gesture, the felicities of thought and expression, made his conversation the delight of private society" – qualities which must have earned him welcome support from the infant Savile, for it is perhaps significant that many of the men who were closely associated with him throughout his career were original members of the newly formed Club in 1868. Thus in politics he had been an ally of Arthur Balfour, Sir Charles Dilke, W.E. Forster, Viscount Goschen, and Sir William Harcourt; similarly in the academic world he had enjoyed the support and friendship of Mark Pattison, then a young don but later a famous Rector of Lincoln College, Oxford, and Thomas Fowler, later to be President of Corpus Christi; in journalism and literature he was closely connected with James Cotter Morison (who obtained for him the editorship of *The Fortnightly Review*), Herbert Spencer, and Sir Leslie Stephen, who had helped him to his first real financial independence on *The Saturday Review* and was to become a lifelong friend. (It would be interesting to know, incidentally, how any of these worthy figures reacted a year or two later when they learned that both these distinguished journals had fallen into the hands of the villainous Frank Harris.)

It is a pity also that the original Candidates Book and Minutes of the Club for 1868, the year it was founded and in which Morley became a member, have long since been lost, for they might shed light on whether he already knew so many of his later colleagues and supporters or whether these acquaintanceships stemmed from his access to the Club. (The absence of these records cannot be ascribed – as with all the others – to the famous fires of 1975 for legend had it, according to Sir Herbert Stephen, that "one of the honorary secretaries became so enamoured of these priceless relics that he could not be parted from them", and so he pinched them. Stephen, however, declared him innocent of such an outrage.)

Although the use of the Club for business purposes or any form of personal advancement is severely discouraged – indeed, forbidden – it is inevitable that men who have been drawn to it through sharing similar tastes should occasionally recognize in one or other of their fellow members inside the Club some skill or talent which can be exploited to mutual benefit outside of it. Morley, for example, was set on his way by Cotter Morison and Sir Leslie Stephen but, by the same token, he commissioned Mark Pattison and Herbert Spencer to join his other distinguished contributors like Meredith, John Stuart Mill, and Huxley, on *The Fortnightly Review*.

Sir Leslie Stephen, the editor of another influential journal, *The Cornhill Magazine*, provided a show-case for the early essays, not only of Morley and Stevenson, but also of Hardy, Gosse and Henry James. Though he is now chiefly remembered for that indispensable aid to all researchers, *The Dictionary of National Biography* – the first twenty-six volumes of which he edited as well as contributing many of its entries – he was also a pioneer in the sociological study of literature with his scholarly *English Literature and Society in the 18th Century*.

Sir Leslie made another incidental contribution to the arts – albeit at one remove. His first wife had been a daughter of Thackeray but after she died he married Julia Jackson, the widow of Herbert Duckworth, another early member of the Club, by whom he had four children of whom one was Vanessa Bell the painter, and another, Virginia Woolf the novelist.

An equally interesting though less salubrious connection between Sir Leslie Stephen, the Savile and the literary and social history of Victorian England is provided by Stephen's nephew, James Kenneth Stephen, who was elected to the Club in 1880 and remained a member until 1890, the year before he died insane in a Northampton Mental Hospital. J.K. Stephen was the tutor of Prince Albert Victor Christian Edward, Duke of Clarence and Avondale, eldest son of the future Edward VII and Queen Alexandra and great-uncle therefore of the present Queen. In the plethora of books about that famous series of murders in 1888 this royal personage has often been cited as a leading contender for the title "Jack the Ripper". The most recent work by one of America's foremost forensic scientists, Dr David Abrahamsen, claims to have proved that he was indeed involved with the Whitechapel butchery, but with the added twist that "the Ripper" was in fact two people working together in "homicidal harmony"; these two people being the Duke of Clarence and J.K. Stephen. According to Abrahamsen who has had access to documents hitherto under seal at New Scotland Yard, together with papers and information provided by the Northampton Mental Hospital, the "Ripper" murders resulted from a sado-masochistic homosexual relationship between Clarence and his Cambridge tutor. The Northampton papers disclose that from 1888 – the year of the murders – Stephen had suffered from a severe personality disorder of sexual origin which expressed itself in a violent hatred of women. Having formed an intense homosexual relationship with his royal pupil who was apparently already being treated for the syphilis which was to kill them both, Stephen embarked on the "Ripper" murders with his diseased lover "Prince Eddy" as his passive accomplice. It is an interesting conceit that all those distinguished figures who thronged the Club in the 1880s were conceivably hobnobbing with Jack the Ripper, not to mention that had the Duke of Clarence lived he would have become King Edward VIII in advance of the equally doomed Duke of Windsor.

In 1987, long before these facts become available, the late Tom Ingram, then the Club's honorary archivist, unearthed some information about Stephen's erratic behaviour in the Club which may add credence to this latest theory. He wrote:

> A recent enquiry from an American student has drawn attention to a brilliant and tragic member of the Savile Club – James Kenneth Stephen, always known as J.K.S. His father was Sir James Fitzjames Stephen, the judge and writer; he was the nephew of Sir Leslie Stephen and thus a cousin of Vanessa Bell and Virginia Woolf, and he possessed to the full the

intellectual brilliance of his family. He was born in 1859 and went as a scholar to Eton where his tutor was Oscar Browning. His uncle Leslie writes of him at this time:

"He already gave promise of unusual physical strength, and of the good looks which in later years resulted from the singular combination of power and sweetness in his features... James rowed for two years in the boats, while his weight and strength made him especially formidable at the peculiar Eton game of football 'at the wall'. The collegers, when supported by his prowess, had the rare glory of defeating the Oppidans twice in succession."

In 1878 J.K.S. won a scholarship to King's College, Cambridge, where he read history. After graduating, perhaps rather less well than expected, he was called to the Bar and travelled in France and Germany. In 1885 he was elected to a fellowship at King's, but a year later when staying at Felixstowe he was, according to his uncle's account, inspecting an engine for pumping water when he received a heavy blow upon the head. Although he seemed to recover and return to his regular writing for the St. James's Gazette and other journals his mental condition deteriorated. Periods of physical violence alternated with lucid intervals but the latter became less and less frequent and he was committed to an asylum where he died in 1892.

J.K.S. was elected to the Savile Club in June 1880. His proposer was Sir Herbert Stephen and among his supporters were Stephen Spring-Rice, Francis Balfour F.R.S. and Sidney Colvin. One imagines that he must have been a model Savilian until the effects of his accident took their toll; but it is the record of his behaviour after that tragedy which survives in the archives. The Committee met five times in November and December 1890 to consider his conduct, to enforce his resignation and to engage extra staff forcibly to prevent his re-entry into No. 107 Piccadilly. His faults seem to have been his violence to members and staff, and failure to pay his bills. At no time do the Committee Minutes show any awareness of the mental illness which, according to his uncle, brought about such change in his behaviour. That, it seems, had to wait another generation, for in February 1923 the Committee then in office authorised the Secretary to remove from the Minute Books of the Club the name of a former member referred to by name in the meetings in November and December 1890 and to destroy the correspondence bearing on the subject should it still be in existence. The Secretary, who was Geoffrey Williams, did his work thoroughly and bodily cut out every mention of the name so that the pages of the book exhibit a number of windows.

J.K.S. was the author of two volumes of light verse, *Lapsus Calami* and *Quo Musa Tendis?*, published in a collected edition in 1896. Copies inscribed by the author are in the Monument. Some of the verses – particularly the sonnets – are remarkably fine, though ironically, coming from such a source, one of the best of them is a denunciation of the evils of drink!

By 1884, Robert Louis Stevenson's friend and patron Sir Sidney Colvin had become Keeper of Prints and Drawings at the British Museum but he would have been already acquainted with Coventry Patmore (elected to the Savile in 1874), who was then working there as Assistant Librarian to supplement his income from poetry. Patmore was much involved in the pre-Raphaelite movement, being a particular friend of Dante Gabriel Rossetti and Holman Hunt. The titles of some of his poems reflect this influence: "The Angel in the House", "The Espousal", "Faithful for Ever", and, perhaps his best work, "The Unknown Eros", which can almost be described as transliterations of paintings by his friends. How he managed amid the conversational bravura of the Savile is, unfortunately, another irritating gap in the records; for in the preface to his collected works he stated: "... I have never spoken when I had nothing to say" – a form of self-denial which has never been regarded as *de rigueur* at the long table.

By contrast, Anthony Hope, the author who had created a fashion and a new literary adjective – "Ruritanian" – with his novel *The Prisoner of Zenda*, was elected a member in 1887. His full name was Anthony Hope Hawkins and his father, the Rev. Edward Comerford Hawkins, the vicar of St Dunstan's in Fleet Street, had been one of the early members, elected in 1869.

Hope, who was knighted in 1918, wrote a great deal more than the type of romance for which he is most remembered; *The Dolly Dialogues*, published in 1894, the same year as *The Prisoner of Zenda*, was of the same school of epigrammatic drawing-room comedy which had its epitome in Oscar Wilde. He also wrote some excellent serious fiction such as *The God in the Car* which is now, sadly, almost forgotten.

That master of the occult, M.R. James, was elected to the Club in 1889 when he was aged twenty-seven and yet to jolt the Victorian psyche with such works as *Ghost Stories of an Antiquary*. He had, however, already established himself as a distinguished biblical scholar, antiquary and palaeographer and was seemingly rather bashful about what he must have regarded as the more frivolous part of his literary output. He should not have feared, for the Savile had been already inured to the genre by the authors of *Dr Jekyll and Mr Hyde* and *The Turn of the Screw*. Furthermore, Algernon Blackwood was elected in 1908 so it must have been that the authors of such spine-chilling works possessed warmer qualities in their social relationships.

Rudyard Kipling had been elected to the Club in 1891 when he was just twenty-six years old. He had only recently arrived in England from India but his burgeoning literary reputation had preceded him. The year of his election was the year that *The Light that Failed* was published, confirming that a new master of fiction and supreme story-teller had arrived on the scene. His earlier work *Plain*

Tales from the Hills, originally published in India, had contained notable snatches of verse, some of which were titled *Barrack-room Ballads*, and now his new acquaintance and fellow member, Henley, reprinted them in *The National Observer*, of which by then he had become editor. These were then gathered together with his ballad "East and West" and published in 1892 as a book which established his second reputation as a considerable poet. In 1892 Kipling married Caroline Star Balestier, the sister of Wolcott Balestier his closest friend and dedicatee of the *Barrack-room Ballads*. Balestier had also been put up for the Savile, his name appearing in the candidates book immediately after Kipling's and among the signatures as referees are those of Edmund Gosse, Henry James, and Thomas Hardy. For some reason he was not elected and he died soon after. Two years later Kipling published the first *Jungle Book* and with it established a third, and some would say, his greatest reputation. He won the Nobel Prize in 1907, the second of the seventeen Savile members who have been so honoured, but the first for literature. Kipling used the Club a great deal and so long as Max Beerbohm was not also present to inhibit his enjoyment with that sardonic gaze, he took a very active part in its social life. It is said that one day he dropped a five-pound note in the card-room at Piccadilly and Frank, the greatly revered wine-waiter who served the Club throughout his working life, found it and returned it to him saying, "It's a good thing, sir, that it was not a member who found it." On another occasion Frank was asked by an inquisitive new member what Rudyard Kipling was like: "A very fiery gentleman, sir, for so small a member."

In 1894, three years after Kipling had been elected, the Club acquired another well-known writer of the time whose imperial connections were equally strong but whose literary ability was considerably less. Sir Horatio Gilbert Parker had been born into a rather dull Canadian immigrant family of which he was inexplicably very proud, and after an unsuccessful attempt to enter Holy Orders decided in 1889 to come to London and become a writer. The opening up of the Canadian North-West was his chosen subject for this ambition though it was one about which he evidently knew very little. Nevertheless, with the publication of his novel, *Pierre and His People* in 1892 he established himself as a best-selling author despite what was described as the paucity of its plot, its unbelievable characters and the hazy descriptions of a terrain which quite clearly he had never visited. The public however were entranced by the notions and phrases he coined such as "wide open spaces", "the frozen north" while the new genre he introduced into fiction of "tall guys" and "blue-blooded remittance men" battling nobly against ferocious natural elements was found particularly beguiling by a readership which had no way of comparing his yarns against the true facts. Those who could – including the critics – were less impressed. A reviewer said of him: "His industry enabled him to master a subject such as French-Canadian history and then with no great attention to verisimilitude or style he would write voluminous melodramas". At the time his novel *When Valmond Came to Pontiac* was published it was described as "the silliest of all tales about Quebec" but this did not prevent it from enhancing an already sturdy reputation. What Frederick Courtney Selous – a genuine traveller and writer who was elected to the Savile at the same committee meeting in 1894 as Parker – thought of this strange bed-fellow is unfortunately not recorded but seemingly any informed criticism would have made no matter for with the aid of a favourable marriage Parker went on to write and publish thirty-six more books. With the financial security provided from both these sources he felt able to turn his attention to politics and in 1900 entered parliament as Conservative and Imperialist member for Gravesend, in which role he campaigned vigorously for imperial unity, particularly in relation to South Africa and Egypt. In 1902 he was knighted and for two and a half years during the First World War he was deputed to publicize the British cause in America. He was made a baronet in 1915, and appointed a Privy Counsellor in 1916. Perhaps his ultimate and better deserved accolade was a *Vanity Fair* caricature by 'Spy' which can now be seen in the morning room.

In 1901 the publisher Arthur Waugh was elected. He has left few memories of his own person for present members to mull over; his bequest to the Club was, instead, the subsequent membership of his two sons, one well-remembered and the other not. Alec Waugh was elected in 1923. His first novel, *The Loom of Youth*, "had created quite a Hullabaloo", to quote the words of Sir Harold Acton, "but he was more gentle than his young brother" and was deservedly popular among his fellow members whenever he visited the Club during his infrequent returns from abroad.

Evelyn Waugh – "the less gentle" of the two brothers – was elected a member in 1930, proposed by his agent, A.D. Peters, and supported by, among others, Sir Harold Acton and the actor Robert Speaight. However he was expelled from the Club after he had indulged one of his favourite pastimes – kicking waiters – in the dining-room at Brook Street. The victim on this occasion was Frank,the self-same wine-waiter and, preferring Frank to Evelyn, the committee promptly retaliated by kicking out Waugh in return. There are, however, lingering memorials to his brief presence. In the *Collected Letters* there is a 4,000 words effusion, "AN OPEN LETTER" addressed to "HIS EMINENCE THE CARDINAL ARCHBISHOP OF WESTMINSTER" written from the Savile Club and dated May, 1933. It is an unnecessarily long and rather pompous protest at a review which had recently appeared in the Catholic intellectual journal, *The Tablet*, of his novel *Black Mischief*. It has to be said that the review in question was also unnecessarily long and pompous but Waugh excelled himself by demanding that Cardinal Bourne should dismiss the editor, "this base man", Ernest Oldmeadow, from his post for impertinence. He was not indulged and the only perceptible result must have been a large upward swing in the Club's stationery bill.

Of the passages in the novel to which *The Tablet* had so strenuously objected, one was the scene where Basil Seal is dining in bed with his wife and "a bull-terrier and a chow flirting at their feet", and another where Basil unwittingly eats the daughter of the British Minister at a cannibal feast. The character of "Basil" was based on another Savile member of whom Sir Harold Acton again recalls: "...of younger members the most ebullient was Peter Rodd, son of Sir Rennell, our

Ambassador at Rome". Sir Rennell incidentally, was later ennobled and would rebuke mis-spellers of his name by pronouncing: "I am the Lord Rennell of Rodd; two d's if you please, one is enough for God". "His son Peter", Sir Harold continues, "was married to Nancy Mitford and caricatured by Evelyn Waugh...". Peter Rodd was universally known as "Prod" and, though it was not uncommon for Waugh to exact revenge for real or imagined slights by lampooning his supposed enemies in his novels, it appears from the recollections of some of his contemporaries at the Club that there might have been some justice in Waugh's eccentric portrayal in this particular case. No one however has yet gone so far as to suggest that he indulged in cannibalism. "Prod" wrote to Waugh from the Club in some indignation to enquire whether the character of Basil Seal was, in fact, based on him and received by return a post-card on which was written the one word "yes".

Waugh obviously was aware of the poisonous incubus which possessed him and which caused him to be ejected from the Savile for he wrote to Lady Mary Lygon in September 1934 while he was engaged on his biography of the Blessed Edmund Campion:

"I am going to spend a very studious autumn writing the life of a dead beast." [the "dead beast" being Edmund Campion!] "I think I shall stay here" [his father's house at Highgate] "so that I shall not be tempted to the demon at the Savile and to go out with whores and make myself ill as I do if I am away from good parents." Evelyn's "good parent" Arthur Waugh, had, in fact, left the Club in 1915 so he was spared the embarrassment of having to witness his younger son's expulsion. But during the fourteen years he was a member he would have enjoyed the company of many, more civilized, who figured prominently in his own world of literature, publishing and scholarship.

A.A. Milne, for instance, had become a member in 1908. His connections with the Savile were already several: H.G. Wells, a member since 1903, had taught science at Henley House, a private school established by Alan Alexander's father, John Vine Milne, and had remained a close friend of all the family thereafter. At the time of his election Milne was employed as assistant editor of *Punch* under Sir Owen Seaman, who had been a member of the Club since 1893 and had served as honorary secretary for elections from 1901 to 1909. His contemporary and close associate, Edmund George Valpy Knox – who was to achieve lasting fame as "Evoe" in the pages of *Punch*, and was also to be Milne's obituarist – succeeded him both as assistant editor of the magazine and as a member of the Savile, which he joined in 1920, the year after Milne's departure. The latter's sad defection came in 1919 after he had completed his war service and had chosen to celebrate this change of life by simultaneously leaving the Savile and the offices of *Punch* to join the Garrick and embark on a new career of writing for the stage. The Savile's loss was certainly the Garrick's gain for after his widow's death the Garrick inherited 25 per cent of "The Pooh Royalties" which in a good year, so it is said, have amounted to as much as £50,000. In gratitude the Garrick now has an "A.A. Milne Room" and, sadly, the Savile can only wish that their Stevenson, Elgar and

Potter rooms were likewise so richly endowed.

H.A.L. Fisher, the great historian and statesman, had been elected in 1896 when he had just turned thirty and, like so many other Savile postulants, had still his best work to come. His monumental *History of Europe* was not published until 1935 but is still regarded as one of the best works on the subject. In the manner of so many members of that time and later, Fisher was not content with expressing his talents within one single discipline; he was later to enter Parliament and have his expert knowledge of European affairs officially recognized when he was appointed a delegate to the League of Nations in 1920. From 1925 until his death in 1940 he was Warden of New College, Oxford.

Fisher had tailored a matured learning to precise and diligently researched periods of European history. But another Savile member of the time, bereft of Fisher's early educational advantages, determined that the great mass of his fellow underprivileged should not be so similarly deprived. Among the amazingly wide range of literary works which H.G. Wells was to produce during a long lifetime was an *Outline of History* written deliberately in a style which would appeal to the general reader. The period it encompassed was nothing less than the beginning of the world until the year 1920 – the date of publication. It was also designed as a vehicle for parading his somewhat unconventional beliefs concerning economics, morals and religion. Looking back, it is odd that he concluded it even at 1920, for most of his early work had dealt in predictions of the future, and in such a convincing way that they surpassed in popularity the prognostications even of his contemporary Jules Verne. Wells was elected to the Savile in 1903 when he had already achieved a measure of fame with his first novel *The Time Machine* and the several others which he regularly produced at the rate of one a year, in all of which his fertile mind had married a painfully acquired knowledge of biology and astronomy to produce the earliest virtuoso examples of popular science fiction.

One wonders whether it was mere coincidence that just as he was about to join the Savile he abandoned such fantasy for realistic comedy of lower middle-class life: one likes to suppose it was. *Love and Mr Lewisham* had been published in 1900, *Kipps* in 1905, *Tono-Bungay* in 1909 and, perhaps his masterpiece as a novelist, *The History of Mr Polly* in 1910.

Wells was a popular member whose sometimes uncomfortable views found a complaisant home in that house of many persuasions in Piccadilly, except for one rather dramatic hiccup – as we shall see later. His son, Professor George Philip Wells, Sc.D., F.R.S., known to all as "Gip", followed him into the Club in 1929 and for many years was honorary secretary for elections. Gip was immortalized early in life by being the hero of one of his father's charming short stories, "The Magic Shop". He pursued his father's original career by becoming a biologist and then forged his own peculiar immortality by becoming the world's greatest expert on the lugworm.

Sir Henry Newbolt was elected to the Club in 1902. He had been a practising barrister until 1899 but had already an eye on a literary career. In 1892 he had published a book, *Taken from the Enemy,* and in 1895 a tragedy, *Mordred,* but it was not until 1897 with the appearance of his ballads *Admirals All* that his reputation was made. This was followed by many more volumes of stirring verse including *The Sailing of the Long Ships,* published in the year he was elected, but in true Savile tradition he continued to maintain a foot in several camps. During the First World War he was Controller of Wireless and Cables (for which he was knighted) though he continued to pour out volumes of war verse such as *Drake's Drum and other Sea Songs* and *St. George's Day and other Poems.* He was also something of an historian and among his works in this field was a *Naval History of the Great War* published in 1920.

As writers of intensely patriotic verse, both Sir Henry Newbolt and Rudyard Kipling must have been more than a little dismayed when they learned that a man whose convivial company they had shared on so many occasions at the long table had been executed for treason. Robert Erskine Childers was elected to the Savile in 1903. He was a cousin of Gladstone's colleague, Hugh Childers, and at the time of his election was a clerk in the House of Commons. In that year he had caused a stir with his great novel *The Riddle of the Sands.* In it he had married his enthusiasm for yachting and the secret service to produce not only a stirring adventure story but also a thinly disguised polemic against Britain's state of unpreparedness for war at sea against what he had already perceived to be the potential enemy, Germany. It is said that the underlying implications of this book jolted the Admiralty into action in just sufficient time to ensure the successful outcome of the First World War. In 1907 he completed Volume 5 of *"The Times" History of the War in South Africa* but in 1910 he relinquished all his other activities to devote himself entirely to the cause of Irish Home Rule. In July, 1914, he took his yacht *Asgard* into Howth harbour with a cargo of guns for the Irish Volunteers, who had been formed to meet the threat from Carson and the Unionists in the North. Present with him on the yacht was Mary Spring-Rice, the cousin of three brothers who were all Savile members, one of whom, Sir Cecil Spring-Rice ("I vow to thee, my country... "etc.) was British Ambassador to Washington at the time. This excursion into gun-running on behalf of the Irish cause did not prevent Childers, however, from immediately volunteering for active service in the Royal Naval Air Service a month later when the Great War broke out. His is a tragic example of the appalling personal dilemmas which often attend both Englishmen and Irishmen who, with honest intentions, become involved in the Irish cause, for he served in the British forces with great distinction until 1917 when he was seconded to the convention set up to evolve some form of Irish settlement by consent. His advocacy for Home Rule grew into support for an Irish Republic and in 1921 he was elected a Sinn Fein deputy for County Wicklow (when that organization was a more honest one than it is now) and was secretary to the delegation for the talks leading to the Anglo-Irish Treaty. He dissented from the terms of the eventual settlement and sided with the Republicans led by De Valera – who had himself, on a technicality, recently narrowly escaped the gallows. Civil war broke out and on 10 November 1922 Childers was arrested at his home in Co. Wicklow on a trumped-up charge of unauthorized possession of a revolver. He was court-martialled, convicted of treason and hastily executed a few days later before any – inevitably successful – appeal could be made.

On a more cheerful note, Max Beerbohm had been elected a member in 1899 and was a constant attender at Piccadilly until he retired permanently to Rapallo after the First World War. Sir Henry Maxwell Beerbohm – "the incomparable Max" as Bernard Shaw had apostrophized him – was one of those select who were as dear to the Savile's heart as the Club so evidently was to his.

In all his years of membership there was only one brief moment when it seemed his devotion might be wavering, when it was discovered that he had also joined the Athenaeum. Cedric Glover bumped into him at Piccadilly and said, "Hullo Max. We haven't seen you in the Club lately"; to which Max replied: "No. I've been thinking it may be better to be a young man at the Athenaeum than an old man at the Savile." But the mood passed and, always at the ready to be amazed by whatever was put before him, he soon discovered that the Savile provided him with a congenial perch from which he could view the picaresque in all its finery. His precise and wondering gaze focused on this entertaining pageant and from it came the inspiration for many of the brilliant caricatures in drawings and prose which provide us now with a revealing descant to the vast range of public reputations and private eccentricity assembled, as if for his special benefit, at the Savile in his time.

To be drawn by Max was to know that one had "arrived", rather in the manner of today's "Spitting Image" but more elegantly so. Like the modern travesty, such elevation had its disadvantages: when Logan Pearsall Smith was singled out for treatment his fellow member Edmund Gosse felt it necessary to comfort him: "I feel it my duty to tell you", he wrote, "that something has happened to you that sooner or later happens to us almost all. Max has got you! We don't like it, and you won't like it, but you must pretend, as we all do, that you like it. You can console yourself, at any rate, with the thought that it will give enormous pleasure to your friends."

Gosse was right. Smith went to the exhibition where his caricature was on show and confessed that he found all the drawings "laughable beyond words, – the caricature of myself I considered the only failure of the exhibition".

But even when his caricatures pierced a little too deeply into their subjects' self-esteem, the members always forgave him – or nearly always. "I shall have friends", Max had promised himself and so he had. The Savile loved him. "His friends gobbled him up," wrote a biographer, S.N. Behrman; he "inspired a peculiar devotion in people; his presence – his very existence – was a delight. It was not only that he was witty and that his speech was exquisite but also that he so evidently had, in social intercourse, no axe to grind."

To list his friends is almost to reproduce the membership list of the Savile in his time; and nearly all of them Max had unrelentingly "got". Some of them became regular targets; Henry James was one, Rudyard Kipling another; but with the exception of Kipling they all forgave him, endured it and often came to like it. One night at dinner someone asked Henry James his opinion on some topic of the day. "Ask that young man," he said pointing at Max. "He is in possession of my innermost thoughts." James's prose and conversational style were also favourite targets: in *A Book of Caricatures* published by Methuen in 1907 there are, for instance, two drawings of James with captions in Jamesian pastiche.

The first shows him groping through a London fog with his hand before his eyes as if seeking a familiar landmark. The caption reads: "...It was, therefore, not without something of a shock that he, in this to him so very congenial atmosphere, now perceived that a vision of the hand which he had, at a venture, held up within an inch or so of his eyes was, with an awful clarity, being adumbrated...".

James's conversation was likewise convoluted and so set to invite ridicule. Beerbohm compared his diction to that of a spouting whale. "One day," he told Behrman,

> ...I had heard that there was a new story by Henry James in a review that had just been started, and I thought I would go to the Savile Club to read it. Just as I was going up the rise of Piccadilly, I was hailed, I was hailed by the Master himself. A certain rumbling and circumlocutionising emerged from him. He was a great hesitator, you know, the greatest of the hesitators. He would have been a great Parliamentarian, because in the House of Commons those who hesitate are greatly valued; a fluent speaker is apt to be considered superficial, while a hesitator, they think, is hesitating because he's deeply pondering the grave issues. Balfour was a great hesitator... But that day in Piccadilly, James said he was a country cousin in town for the day and were there any exciting new pictures in any museum? I told him that indeed there was one – a new Augustus John in the Grafton Galleries. He asked me then if I couldn't take him along to see it. I don't know why, I shall never know why, but I feigned a previous engagement. Henry James walked on alone, and I made my way to the Savile to read his story. I preferred, somehow, to be with the Master's work than with the Master himself.

Arthur Balfour was another Savile victim, as was H.G. Wells. According to Thomas Hardy (also mercilessly revealed by Max) the eponymous characters in one of the stories in *Seven Men* – "Maltby and Braxton" – were based on Wells and a non-member, Arnold Bennett, but with Balfour *in propria persona* in a walk-on part. Furthermore, the setting for the story was Far Oakridge in Gloucestershire, the house of his great friend and fellow Savilian William Rothenstein. Reginald Turner, who was one of Beerbohm's greatest friends, was the subject of countless caricatures: "His face", said Max, "was part of his equipment" and his nose in particular seemed to exercise a peculiar fascination. "How does your friend Turner feel about that?" he was asked one day at the Club. "Oh, well, you know", said Max, "when you exaggerate as much as that there can be no offence in it." And nor was there, for Turner was devoted to him. So was H.G. Wells. "I walked into the Savile one day", Beerbohm told Behrman, "and saw H.G. lunching alone in the bow window. I had just finished reading *Love and Mr Lewisham* and I had been so taken by it that I felt that I must speak to H.G. about it. I went up to him and told him 'The quarrel of the young couple', I remember saying to him, 'I thought exquisite'. Do you know...do you know...H.G.'s eyes filled with tears. People used to say to me that H.G. was vindictive. I never saw that. He was always extraordinarily nice to me, perhaps because of the encounter in the bow window in the Savile." That bow window in the Savile, as we shall see, was to be the setting for a more infamous incident some time later that was to force Wells into exile at the Athenaeum for twenty-eight years until the coast was cleared and he was allowed back, crying, "Thank God for the Savile – The Athenaeum for the living!"

Meantime, Wells, Balfour, Reggie Turner, Gosse, Hardy and Henry James were all encased like butterflies for inspection in the crystalline prose and drawings of Max. Sir William Nicholson, Walter Pater, Sir John Squire, Lytton Strachey, W.B. Yeats; all Savile members, all were given the Beerbohm treatment. E.M. Forster and Beerbohm had formed a mutual admiration society in the Savile. Forster somehow escaped an impaling but it cannot only have been that which led him to say that Max's only novel, *Zuleika Dobson,* has "a beauty unattainable by serious literature...it is so funny and charming, so iridescent, yet so profound". Profundity indeed was to be discovered in even his lightest work. In the Morning Room of the Club there is Beerbohm's caricature of that distinguished member, the painter Sir William Nicholson. It shows a grim, almost surreal figure with a high choker collar which makes his eyes pop out like a strangled criminal's. When it was shown to Nicholson's wife she cried: "Oh Max, you're so good on my husband – at his worst!" Sir William naturally forgave him and turned the other cheek by painting his tormentor as the height of elegance. On his way to the Club Max took to dropping in regularly at Nicholson's studio in Appletree Yard; he used to leave his silk hat there and Nicholson stacked his paintbrushes in it.

Sometimes, maybe, he felt he might have gone too far: Professor Ray Lankester, a distinguished scientist and a burly, greatly liked member of the Savile, had been "got" and after his death, looking back on his handiwork, Beerbohm says, "Dear Ray, he was rather hurt by this. And good heavens, I don't wonder. I only wonder that he so quickly forgave me. I wish he were alive. He was one of the most delightful men I have ever known."

Kipling was the only one who couldn't take it and perhaps this was because Beerbohm could not take him; he "got" him instead. Although Beerbohm was as patriotic as the rest, Kipling's jingoism revolted him and while he admired his gifts, the exultant use to which he put them during the Boer War led to a lifelong aversion. He pursued Kipling ruthlessly and with a peculiar venom which appears nowhere else in his works or his personal relationships. Kipling's aggressive virility he regarded as spurious and he showed his contempt for it in a review of the dramatized version of *The Light that Failed* by expressing the opinion that the name Rudyard Kipling was surely the pseudonym of a woman. In *A Christmas Garland* – a book of parodies of seventeen famous contemporary authors telling a traditional Christmas story in their own style – he lampoons Kipling's arms-length truculence by writing a "Barrack-room Ballad" wherein Father Christmas comes down the chimney only to be met and arrested by a thuggish policeman on suspicion of being a German spy:

> . . . 'Ustle 'im, shake 'im till 'e's sick!
> Wot, 'e *would,* would 'e? Well,
> Then yer've got ter give 'im 'Ell,
> An' it's trunch, trunch, truncheon does the trick.

Beerbohm, in fact, claimed to admire Kipling's genius but felt it was debased by what he wrote and he could not refrain from continually saying so. He was told by mutual friends at the Club that Kipling was deeply hurt by his criticism, but to no avail. "I couldn't stop. As his publications increased, so did my derogation. He didn't stop, I couldn't stop. I meant to, I wanted to. But I couldn't." No wonder they avoided each other at the Savile and everywhere else. When they passed each other in the street they averted their eyes. It all seems so uncharacteristically petulant on Beerbohm's part; perhaps he misunderstood Kipling, though some recent biographers seem to share Beerbohm's view of him. At all events, towards the end of Beerbohm's life, he deeply regretted his persecution. He recalled an occasion when, lunching as a guest at White's, he saw Kipling at a distant table and this time caught his eye:

> I very much wanted to go over to him and to say "Mr Kipling, I admire you, I admire your very great genius. If I have written harshly of you, it is because I do not believe you are living up to the possibilities of your genius." I so much wished to do this. But I didn't. Why didn't I do it? Why didn't I unbend? Why did I go on persecuting him? And now he is dead and it is too late.

Beerbohm and his circle of friends usher us into the realm of living memory at the Savile for it is now over thirty years since he died and, happily, many present members have belonged to the Club for longer than that. Max, of course, was rarely seen in London after he retired permanently to Rapallo, though he always used the Club during his infrequent return visits, and a constant stream of secular pilgrims set out from Piccadilly and, later, Brook Street to maintain the link. It was even a Savile member, Dr Leo Rau, who witnessed the closing of the chapter in 1956 when he was summoned to Italy to treat Max during his final illness. But of all the many who went in happier times, none evoked Max's nostalgia for a departed way of life more powerfully than Sir Compton Mackenzie. He thought that of all the novels written about Oxford – not excluding his own *Zuleika Dobson* – the best by far was *Sinister Street.* "There is no book on Oxford like it," Max had said. "It gives you actual Oxford *experience.* What Mackenzie has miraculously done is to make you feel what each *term* was like; it was different in each term. Mackenzie notes the separate colour of each term. It evokes for me, more powerfully than anything else that has been written about Oxford – my own years at Merton."

68

Even in a Club that would have burst asunder at the seams had not all its members been made to adhere to the golden rule that public personae were to be firmly tethered at the hall door, Edward Montagu Compton Mackenzie stood out at once. "You're a *very* self-confident young man," expostulated H.G. Wells, pottily calling the kettle black on first meeting him and perhaps this was the opening shot in the process of "Savilization" to which Mackenzie himself referred in his later years when commenting that "although all men may not yet be equal, all Savilians are equal". Mackenzie could not help projecting himself; he came from a long line of distinguished actors; his sister was Fay Compton; and he himself could have achieved fame on the stage had not Logan Pearsall Smith fortunately persuaded him to express his talents in literature. Known universally to his friends as "Monty", he dazzled wherever he chose to settle and distinguished whatever he touched.

In 1986 that urbane journalistic guru and committee member of the Savile, Tom Baistow, paid tribute to Mackenzie at a discussion dinner:

> Monty may not have been the full-blown Renaissance man he liked to think he was, but he gave a superb impersonation of that rare breed that lingers in the memory: author of 40 novels, 25 historical and biographical works, a score of children's stories, playwright and poet, journalist and critic, spymaster in the first world war, leading figure in the old Scottish nationalist movement, gramophone pioneer, expert gardener, authority on plant palaeontology, Latinist and English grammarian, a lifelong supporter of West Bromwich Albion and an inveterate collector of islands and titles. A Fellow of the Royal Society of Literature, he was in his time President of: the Poetry Society, the Croquet Association, the Siamese Cat Club, the Songwriter's Guild and the Dickens Fellowship; Governor General of the Royal Stuart Society and Chairman of the League for Democracy for Greece.
>
> Above all, he was for sixty years a dedicated Savilian. "The Savile has been *such* an influence on my life," he declares in his monumental autobiography, *My Life and Times*, which ran, typically, to no fewer than *ten* Octaves, as he called the volumes – a total of almost one and a quarter million words ... One can only marvel at the sheer prolificity of the man. In Octave 4 he describes his entry into the Club when he was twenty-nine, in 1912, and had just published his first novel, *The Passionate Elopement*, to encouraging reviews:
>
>> For my future the most important event of that summer of 1912 was my election to the Savile Club, which has been my — well, really "home" is the only word that expresses what the Savile has meant to me for 52 years. At this date the Savile was housed in that beautiful house with the big bow windows looking over Green Park which had once belonged to Lord Rosebery ...

and so he goes on for 2,000 pages, using his amazing gift of total recall to recount his life's adventures while peppering his account throughout with tantalizing glimpses of his days of relaxation at the Savile.

Monty remained a member for the rest of his long life – sixty years in all. Whenever he was in London he would set up his headquarters at the Savile, at first in the billiards-room at Piccadilly and later in the Sandpit at Brook Street where, seemingly impervious to normal human bodily requirements such as the necessity for sleep, he would hold court to an admiring circle of acolytes until all hours of the day and the night.

Many an unwary late-comer arriving after midnight and eager for a night's rest found himself trapped into his captivating company. Michael Figgis remembers occasions when Monty was holding forth in a late night circle with that other notable raconteur, Gilbert Harding: ... "More drinks were summoned. Members returned from the theatre or wherever they might have been. The circle grew. It became almost impossible to go to bed ..." and later ... "when Monty Mackenzie was down from Edinburgh, still at work on his *Octaves*, I sat with him many times, fascinated by his reminiscences, stifling yawns and knowing that at best I should get four hours' sleep. The charming Monty seemed to hate the idea of going to bed ..." William Barnes recalls an "evening at the round table with Harold Nicholson and Compton Mackenzie sitting opposite each other and engaging in endless repartee. The rest of us were silent and spellbound: just like watching a good match at Wimbledon."

Like many such charming and talented figures, Monty had a very powerful streak of vanity. Maitland Wright returned late to the Club one night when Mackenzie was holding forth and with the usual inevitability was sucked into the conversational whirlpool. The party eventually dispersed and "going up in the lift on the way to bed I was glad to tell Compton M. that I still thought *Sinister Street* was far the best novel ever written about Oxford. I remember he patted me on the back and said: 'Thank you, dear boy, and I am glad to be able to tell you that I still get good royalties from it.' "

One of the most brilliantly funny British films of the post-war years was *Whisky Galore* based on Mackenzie's novel of the same name. Monja Danischewsky was the inspired choice of Sir Michael Balcon to be his co-producer of what was to turn out to be perhaps the greatest of the classic films emerging from Ealing Studios. Balcon had been a member of the Savile since 1945 and it seemed to him and to Monty that it would be unfair to deprive the Club of the fascinating company and coruscating wit of "Danny" who was – and still is – something of a classic in himself. Monty, at his most endearingly vainglorious, took it upon himself to effect the necessary preliminaries. Danny takes up the story of the daunting sequel:

> I became a member of the Savile in 1949, proposed by Compton Mackenzie, supported by scant referees. "Monty" Mackenzie had not done

the traditional homework of introducing candidates to members. Instead he had escaped to the Seychelles to write what he called his "Obituary of the Indian Army". I had to summon up considerable courage to visit my Club without the protection of an established member, and nearly turned back when I found myself glared at by a man I recognised as Eric Linklater. Later we became friends and I learned that he glared at everybody – to protect the shy man behind the glare. By the time Mackenzie had returned I felt at home at the Club. It was indeed a home from home.

Mackenzie did not apologise for leaving me in the lurch. Instead he said, with his customary modesty: "It wasn't necessary, dear Danny"; managing to imply that a word from him was all that was needed. He was a master of "gamesmanship" (the game invented by his fellow Savilian, Stephen Potter). He once described his train journey to his home in Edinburgh: "I hate waiting in trains. I always get to King's Cross exactly three minutes before the train is due to leave. This leaves me time for a large whisky and to complete *The Times* crossword puzzle."

Not everyone however seems to have been so willing to weigh Monty's charm and distinction so favourably against such vanity. Michael Meyer recalled his encounters with him in his autobiography *Not Prince Hamlet*:

One of the doyens of the Savile was Compton Mackenzie, who had been a member since 1912. I was anxious to meet him, since Rosamond Lehmann had named him as the most brilliant talker she had heard, as well as being a skilled mimic of the great men he had known, such as Henry James and D.H. Lawrence. Mackenzie was a vain, kindly old man, but by the time I met him, he had become a monumental bore. He no longer conversed, but held forth, and that repetitively; even if you were alone with him, he addressed you as though you were a hundred people who had paid to listen. His talk was punctuated by enormous pauses while he sniffed at and mused over a cigar before lighting it, or merely mused. Usually one can escape from aged bores because they have to go out fairly often to relieve themselves, but Mackenzie had even found a way of stopping you from doing that. Once, when I was closeted with him in an otherwise empty bar, he was in the midst of some interminable story. "And then – now this will interest you, my boy – Her Majesty ..." (enormous pause, while he savoured his drink). "What was I saying?" "Queen Alexandra, Sir Compton." "Ah, yes. Her Majesty turned to me, and said – " He touched my knee and rose. "Just a moment, my boy." And off he went to the gents. How could one not be there when he returned?

On another occasion, when staying at the Club, I returned late one night to find it empty except for Compton Mackenzie and Gilbert Harding engaged in an extraordinary dialogue. Conversation is hardly the word, for what they said could have been printed as an example of how not to write a play. One held forth at leisure while the other made no pretence of listening; then the speaker would pause, to retrieve a match from the floor or squirt some soda into his whisky, at which as though by some prearranged agreement the listener would begin speaking and the speaker fall silent, rather like "hand-out" at squash. They were still at it when I went to bed half an hour later.

Somebody told me that the secret of getting the best out of Mackenzie was to turn the conversation, or rather his monologue, from himself to the people he had known. Next time I found myself next to him at lunch, I said: "You knew Henry James well, did you not, Sir Compton?" "Indeed I did. He admired my novels." My heart sank. However, he continued: "I remember the last time I met Henry. Not long before he died, I went down to have luncheon with him at Rye. We had an excellent luncheon – he had a very good cook – and afterwards we drank coffee in the garden in the sun." This is gold, I thought; how could I have found this man boring? "And I remember, I said to him: 'Of course, Henry, the difficulty with your novels is ...' And for the next half hour he told me what he had said to Henry James, none of it remotely interesting or original. Not a word that Henry James had said, if he had got one in, was quoted.

Still, I reflected, it had been shortly before James had died, and they had been sitting in the sun after a good luncheon, so perhaps James had in fact not said anything. I tried to think of someone else Mackenzie had known who could be relied on not to have remained silent. "You also knew D.H. Lawrence well, did you not, Sir Compton?" "Ah, David was completely different." My spirits rose. This would be worth listening to. "I remember once I was staying with David and Frieda on Capri, and David and I went for a walk. David was a wonderful person to go on a country stroll with. He would talk about animals and birds, and trees and flowers, and you really felt he was closer to them than to other humans." "Yes, yes?" "Well, we were walking through an olive grove – I can see it to this day – and I said to him: "Of course, David, people are always going to say about your writing ..." And the next half hour was occupied by what he had said to Lawrence. When I at last escaped, he had not told me a single word that either James or Lawrence had uttered. I regard this as the most wasted hour of my life, when I think what he could have told me.

Others took a less severe view of the solipsism which, after all, most of his fellow members in their affection for him had helped promote. He could be extremely kind: Maitland Wright, recalling one of his 'Chimes at Midnight' experiences says "the first impression I got was of the generosity Compton Mackenzie seemed to show whenever any sort of harsh criticism was made of other people".

George Astley, whose sterling work as secretary of The Society of Authors helped lay the foundations of the present Public Lending Right and transform the

Society into a formidable lobby in support of previously vulnerable writers, was a recipient of Mackenzie's considerateness:

> In my early days at the Society of Authors [he tells us] the pay was minimal and one was on a tight string; nevertheless I scraped up the cash and invited Willie [Somerset] Maugham and Monty Mackenzie to lunch and laid on the best food and wines I could manage. During lunch a charming elderly actor with dead white hair was noticed by Maugham who asked me who he was and, on being told, remarked with his usual stutter: "A good looking young man." After lunch Maugham commented: "A good lunch, George, but I would rather have had roast beef and roly-poly as I can't get it in the south of France." Monty's eyebrows went over the top of his head and, being the kindly fellow he was, he said to me later on: "Don't worry, George, that remark was typical of the old bitch."

Mackenzie was, himself, a recipient of some of Maugham's more waspish comments. Jack Single remembers him stuttering loudly in the dining-room as Monty passed by: "I ...... *I'm* old enough to, to, to remember w', w', when that M, M, Mackenzie fellow was t', t', taken *seriously* as, a., an.. author."

For reasons probably unnecessary to explain, William Somerset Maugham was never a member though he came often as a guest of various others who were; and his more amiable brother, Frederick Herbert Maugham, K.C., later as Viscount Maugham to be Lord Chancellor, had been a devoted Savilian since 1893, serving on the committee from 1918 to 1921. It would be tempting to stray for a moment from the path of provable historical fact to wonder whether the Savile might not once again have acted as midwife to a well-known novel; whether on one of his many visits Somerset Maugham had rested those lizard-like eyes on the unlikely conjunction of Thomas Hardy and Hugh Walpole sitting at the same long table and conjured up the plot of that controversial *roman à clef, Cakes and Ale.*

Walpole, the victim of this, admittedly, highly amusing literary squib, who had proposed Compton Mackenzie for membership of the Savile, was, like his protégé, a prolific author given to occasional bouts of self-admiration, a brilliant raconteur, and a generous friend to any of his fellow writers who were suffering hard times.

Hugh Seymour Walpole was elected in 1911 when he was twenty-seven, the year that he had attracted favourable notice in literary circles with the publication of *Mr. Perrin and Mr. Traill.* Unlike his exact contemporary, however, he was unable to shuffle off criticism with the lordly panache that Monty so often was able – or required – to demonstrate. He was deeply hurt by his thinly disguised portrait in *Cakes and Ale,* as indeed he always was by any form of criticism. He had arrived in London in 1909 on the publication of his first novel *The Wooden Horse,* and came under the paternal influence of Henry James. But even this failed to please entirely, for James's benevolence towards him tended to contain a hint of mockery, feeding the self-doubt which rode in tandem throughout his life with the natural vanity which literary prominence permitted him.

Membership of the Savile so soon after his professional arrival went far to satisfy his longings to be part of London's intellectual scene but during the First World War he allowed his membership to lapse temporarily while he served with the Russian Red Cross in Galicia. He was present at the first of the two revolutions of 1917 and from his war-time experiences wrote *The Dark Forest* and *The Secret City*. By the time he returned to London and the Savile in 1919 he had become firmly established as a considerable figure in literary and artistic circles. This enabled him to undertake a series of highly successful and remunerative lecture tours in America from the proceeds of which he provided generous help to fellow authors in distress and was able to indulge his twin passions for collecting books and pictures. When he died in 1941 he had published forty-two novels and volumes of stories as well as autobiographical studies and books about Trollope and Conrad. Though some of his fellow writers underrated him, at least two generations in the present century have been brought up on works such as the four instalments of the Herries saga – *Rogue Herries, Judith Paris, The Fortress* and *Vanessa*, – and the Jeremy trilogy – *Jeremy, Jeremy and Hamlet*, and *Jeremy at Crale*. Some of his friends at the Savile and elsewhere, however, were of the opinion that his greatest gift was as a raconteur and had he but set into prose some of his brilliant recollections – particularly of writers he had known – which had provided such entertainment in the billiards room and the Sandpit, these would surely have figured among his greatest achievements. His dedication to the promotion of good literature led him to become the first chairman of The Book Society in 1929 and, later, the first chairman of The Society of Bookmen which, mainly through his efforts, was soon established as the much more powerful National Book League. He was appointed C.B.E. in 1918 and knighted in 1937.

Although their birth-dates, their careers and their membership of the Savile were to overlap during their respective lifetimes, Compton Mackenzie went on in his seemingly indestructible way to outlive Walpole by thirty-one years. During their halcyon days at Piccadilly and Brook Street, however, a formidable list of literary men assembled there to keep them company. E.M. Forster had been already installed in 1910, the year that *Howards End* was published. He had, moreover, anticipated Mackenzie's *Sinister Street* by six years with his own evocation of undergraduate life in the first chapter of *The Longest Journey*, published in 1907, which he always claimed to be his best work. Earlier, in his first novel, *Where Angels Fear to Tread*, he had revealed his knowledge and love of music through the medium of a character in it, "Philip Herriton", who was modelled on his great friend, the musicologist E.J. Dent, who had been elected to the Savile in 1905, the year that the novel was published.

Although Forster is considered by some to have been the finest novelist of his generation, his talents did not run to easy social relationships with his peers; a diffident and often melancholy man, he once said, "I warmed both hands before the fire of life – and put it out". Evidently nothing that even the Savile could do was able to rekindle it for him and as, in any case, he was much abroad at that time, he relinquished his membership in 1915.

Forster's great friend, Lytton Strachey, had preceded him into the Savile in 1909. One has to wonder, in an unworthy way, whether their common interests were purely literary though they had first encountered one another at Trinity College, Cambridge, where, along with Forster, Strachey contracted lifelong friendships with that distinguished Bloomsbury band which included Maynard Keynes, David Garnett, Leonard Woolf and Clive Bell. How Sir Leslie Stephen, the unwitting – and, one might surmise, unwilling – father and father-in-law of this literary-élitery would have reacted to the news that its most outré apostle had "interposed" his emaciated, red-bearded body into the club of which he had been an original member is, unfortunately, yet another gap in the Savile archives. Max Beerbohm, of course, fell upon him with delight to add those extraordinary features to his gallery of grotesques though, typically, this did not prevent him from expressing also his admiration for Strachey's mastery of prose style.

In the Rede lecture delivered at Cambridge in 1943, Beerbohm recalled his first sighting of Strachey:

> One day in the springtime of 1912 – a date not long ago in point of time, but infinitely long ago in point of the changes that Europe has suffered since then – I was lunching at the Savile Club. I had been living for two years in Italy; and there were some faces new to me. There was one that interested me very much; an emaciated face of ivory whiteness, above a long square-cut auburn beard, and below a head of very long sleek dark brown hair. The nose was nothing if not aquiline, and Nature had chiselled it with great delicacy. The eyes, behind a pair of gold-rimmed spectacles, eyes of an inquirer and a cogitator, were large and brown and luminous. The man to whom they belonged must, I judged, though he sat stooping low down over his table, be extremely tall. He wore a jacket of brown velveteen, a soft shirt, and a dark red tie. I greatly wondered who he was. He looked rather like one of the Twelve Apostles, and I decided that he resembled especially the doubting one, Thomas, who was also called Didymus. I learned from a friend who came in and joined me at my table that he was one of the Stracheys; Lytton Strachey; a Cambridge man: rather an authority on French literature: had written a book on French Literature in some series or other; a book said to be very good. "But why," my friend asked, "should he dress like that?" Well, we members of the Savile, Civil Servants, men of letters, clergymen, scientists, doctors, and so on, were clad respectably, passably, decently, but no more than that. And "Hang it all," I said, "why shouldn't he dress like that? He's the best-dressed man in the room!"
>
> Soon afterwards I returned to Italy, and his image faded from my mind. Two years later I was back in England, but did not again see him, and his image remained in abeyance. But it instantly and vividly recurred to me when, in 1917, I was told by Desmond MacCarthy that a friend of his,

Lytton Strachey, was writing a book about some of the Victorians; that these rather horrified the author, but that the book was sure to be a good one; and that I, though I didn't share the horror, would be sure to like it. A few months later I had the pleasure of meeting this man at dinner in the house of a gifted lady; and though I had no separate dialogue with him in the course of the meal, and though he seemed shy of general conversation, I was impressed by his mild dignity and benign good manners. Early in the following spring Desmond's prophecy that I would like the book was more than fulfilled. I did far more than like it, I rejoiced in it...

The image which had "instantly and vividly recurred" to Max was now to be set down for ever in a number of his most revealing caricatures.

H.A.L. Fisher had been the fellow member who had responded more usefully by commissioning from Strachey that first book, *Landmarks in French Literature,* for the Home University Library series to which Max referred. The success of this had led to his family and friends subscribing to make him financially independent of his previous journalism. He used this freedom, and the years of conscientious objection during the First World War, to write *Eminent Victorians,* published in 1918, after which he followed Forster's example and departed from the Club for a career which now belongs to the history of the precious who are unhappily few.

The Savile, which in every field of the arts has never allowed its feet to depart too far from *terra firma,* provided itself with a salutary antidote to Bloomsbury by electing Ernest William Hornung, the creator of "Raffles", in 1913. He was forty-seven when he joined and by then had written twenty-six highly successful popular novels. The Club, it seems, had an unusually binding effect on his creative urge for in the eight years left to him before he died he wrote only three more books.

Compton Mackenzie, then younger and less august but no less observant of enticing eccentricities, provides us with an enchanting picture of one who in some of his public posturing bid fair to be considered the greatest buffoon ever to enter the Savile but who was, at the same time, almost certainly among the most sublime poets of this or any other age in English literature.

> I was sitting in the billiards room one day in the Twenties when W.B. Yeats came in and sat down beside me [Monty records in one of his two-over-the-eight octaves]; "As a student of astrology," he said, in his most hieratic voice, "you'll be interested to know that I was born at an exact sext between the planet Venus and the Planet Mercury." Then, lowering his voice in reverence, he added "Indicating thereby the birth of a major poet."

At this moment, Monty tells us, Sir Ray Lankester, director of the Natural History Museum, lowered his massive bulk on to the bench on Monty's other side and said to him:

"I was going to see you about getting some green tree frogs for your island."

Yeats went relentlessly on: "In my sixth house is the planet Herschel, ill aspected by Saturn."

Ignoring this vital piece of information, Sir Ray explained that he had seen these "charming little creatures, bright emerald green, chirping all through dinner at a friend's place on the Riviera".

> Yeats continued [says Monty]: "In my seventh house is the moon, indicating money accruing at times but vanishing with equal rapidity." Ray Lankester prodded me. "Who is this fellow?"

> "Yeats", I whispered.
> "*Who?*"
> "W.B. Yeats"
> "*Who?*"
> "The Irish poet."
> "Never heard of him. What's he talking about?"
> "Astrology."
> "Bloody fool," ejaculated Sir Ray.

Whether Yeats, in the grip of such cosmic afflatus, actually overheard this puncturing remark remains doubtful but, at all events, he was, no matter how unwittingly, to have his revenge. Some time later Ray Lankester suffered an unfortunate accident. Like his brother, Owen, he was a man of considerable girth but, unlike his even more prodigious sibling, he was reasonably abstemious. One evening, however, leaving the Club after dinner, he had the misfortune to trip on the top step and tumble down to land heavily on the pavement below in Piccadilly. Finding himself lying like a stranded whale unable to move he bellowed for help from the hall porter who was, unfortunately, about some other business and out of earshot. A small but ribald crowd gathered to enjoy the spectacle: the inevitable cockney newsboys appeared from nowhere to offer advice: "Put more water in it next time ..." "Can't sleep here, you know, it's obstruction ..." and so on. To his relief at last the Club door opened and down the steps with dignified gait came a fellow member. It was Yeats.

"Ah! Lankester. There you are," he boomed. "Fallen down I see. How unfortunate. Tut, tut! I remember once in Dublin another acquaintance of mine suffering a similar experience on emerging from the Kildare Street Club ... Of course, the steps at the Kildare are not so steep as these but, nevertheless it was a nasty toss ..." and so he went on until the infuriated roars of the stricken biologist conveyed to him that sodality of a more practical nature was required.

Yeats was elected to the Club in 1917, when, like so many other distinguished Savile members his reputation stood high but his income remained low. Indeed, in *Autobiographies*, written in 1914, he records that he was fifty years of age before his writings earned him more than £200 a year. The time of his election, however, coincided with several important new events in his life. At the age of fifty-two he had now renounced his hopeless romantic longings for the beautiful Maud Gonne, who had been a major inspiration, and settled down to marriage with a young English girl, Georgie Lees. In that year also he published *The Wild Swans at Coole* and in an outburst of renewed inspiration and perfection of technique began to produce work of the very highest achievement.

"All changed, changed utterly:
"A terrible beauty is born"

had been his response to the shattering events which had occurred the previous year in Dublin, his beloved birthplace, and those words reflected also his new approach to life, politics, philosophy and literature. Gone were the rhythms and moods of the "Celtic Twilight" school of which he had been considered a leader and in which he had made his reputation; in came a new perception of realities in which, perhaps unfortunately, his early preoccupation with mysticism was now reinforced with more recently acquired theories of astrology and cyclical views of history. The basis of his "philosophy" or "system" was set out in his prose work *A Vision* published in 1925 but though it pervaded all the justly acclaimed work which was now to flow from his pen it did not necessarily excite universal admiration in its other manifestations, as is evidenced by Sir Ray Lankester's hearty reaction to it in the Savile billiards-room.

Max Beerbohm was one of several others who did not completely share in the reverence with which Yeats was generally regarded. He wrote a sketch in which he propounded the blasphemous notion that the poetry of Tom Moore conveyed more of Ireland than Yeats's did. When they first met, Yeats was full of the cult of Diabolism and one wonders whether Beerbohm might not have seized on this bizarre preoccupation to create Enoch Soames, the *Catholic* Diabolist who sold his soul to the Devil for a glimpse of his posthumous literary fame. Perhaps in 1997 when Soames is due to be reincarnated in the British Museum reading room a Savile reunion should be held there to ask him.

Yeats had a very commanding presence, standing over six feet tall with a great head of flowing blue-grey hair – "the living model", so it has been said, "of a poet come into his kingdom". He had also a very distinctive voice, musical but touched with Irish melancholy, "hieratic" when he wished to invoke his non-existent aristocratic "Anglo-Irish" roots. The Savile must have loved him for he was a great talker. "Everyone said that Yeats and W.J. Turner were the two best talkers in the Club," says Patric Dickinson, another distinguished Savile poet, recalling his initiation to the Savile. "This was because they talked simultaneously and never listened to one another."

Yeats agreed to be a senator in the government of the emergent Irish Free State during the final stages of the civil war in 1922, which was quite a courageous act in the circumstances of the time. But even there the bathos created by the juxtaposition of his public posturing against his noble use of language ensured that one who should have been that senate's most distinguished figure would fail to be taken wholly seriously. One of the great set pieces of rhetoric to be heard in that chamber came from Yeats when he made a speech on behalf of the Anglo-Irish minority to which he purported to belong. "I am proud to consider myself a typical man of that minority" – he declaimed. "We ... are no petty people. We are the people of Burke; we are the people of Grattan; we are the people of Swift, the people of Emmet, the people of Parnell. We have created most of the modern literature of this country. We have created the best of its political intelligence ... etc., etc.". The cause of all this eloquence was a plea to make divorce available to the Protestants and, as has often been pointed out, neither Yeats nor any of the other famous men he mentioned were strictly speaking members of the Anglo-Irish ascendancy at all.

In 1923 however, Yeats became the second member of the Savile to receive the Nobel Prize for his more genuine and considerable contribution to literature. But bathos breaks in again; in *Autobiographies* he records that he received news of the award late at night – "At half past twelve my wife and I are alone, and search the cellar for a bottle of wine, but it is empty, and as a celebration is necessary we cook sausages." Sausages! Then he went in person to Stockholm to receive the award from the King of Sweden and greatly impressed the assembled audience with his "fine manners". Thereafter his new financial independence allowed him to spend much of his time in Ireland but be made regular trips to London to maintain his literary associations with such as the Sitwells and Walter Turner, one of his great admirers at the Savile. He also began to supervise radio broadcasts of modern verse for the BBC. During these visits he was a regular attender at the Club and there is a sad little story of one of his last encounters there just before he died which Sir Victor Pritchett recounts and which is quoted in Michael Meyer's memoirs *Not Prince Hamlet*.

Some time in 1938 Sir Victor went to lunch at the Savile. He took a chair at an empty table:

> Almost immediately the place on his right was taken by W.B. Yeats and, a minute later, that on his left by H.G. Wells, who began to eat greedily with his mouth open. Yeats, who had only a few months to live, apparently hated any talk of death. Pritchett says that the following dialogue then took place across him between the two great men:
>
> Wells: Isn't it Yeats?
> Yeats: Ah. Good morning, Wells.
> Wells: You're looking very old, Yeats.
> Yeats: (goes slightly grey) None of us gets younger, Wells.
> Wells: Ah, the days we had when we were young. Do you remember how we used to walk on Hampstead Heath with X and Y?
> Yeats: Yes. I wonder what they're doing nowadays?
> Wells: (eating noisily) Dead.
> Yeats: (greys further) Both of them?
> Wells: Yes. And when we went together to the Bedford to see Dan Leno

with young Z.

Yeats: How is Z now?

Wells: Dead (Pause.) And Yeats, do you remember the time we went boating at Richmond and took those girls with us? One of them wore a pink dress and had beautiful long gold hair.

Yeats: (moved, puts down his knife and fork) Yes, I remember her. She was very beautiful. What's happened to – surely she can't be dead? She was much younger than us.

Wells: No, she isn't dead.

Yeats: Thank heavens for that.

Wells: (illustrating, graphically) Paralysed, all down one side. (To waiter) I'll have the steak.

The Savile can be a cruel place for the self-regarding: but one must deplore such an unsuitable epilogue to the membership of one of the greatest geniuses to have distinguished it.

Perhaps a happier, more rewarding memorial to Yeats's manner of comporting himself at the Club is to be found in Austin Clarke's poem, "In the Savile Club":

> I met him at four o'clock in the Savile Club
> Within the Lounge, chairs waiting for artist, savant,
> Bohemian. Smiling, all savoir-faire,
> Yeats rose to greet me, stately, cloud-grey-tweeded,
> White-haired
>   'I am in London about my book,
> *A Vision.'*
>   Holyheading back to Dublin,
> Nine years before, I saw the shadowy poet
> Stoop in a drawing-room in Kenilworth square, women
> Around him, explaining the Phases of the Moon,
> Cube, mystical circle, black disc, white dot, the Wheel
> Of Fortune, diagram of past in future,
> While, geometrically, all the Heavens
> About him, mapped the darkened walls with starlit
> Points. Week after week, I heard him astrologising
> Until a hand got up, switched on the light.
> Then I was listening in London.
>   'Many
> Will disagree with much I have written. But
> I think I have solved the Arcane Problem.'
>   Head
> Bowed low, he stood, respectful, for a few
> Moments before himself.
>   Incredulous,

A son of Nox, I waited.
                          We sat down
At a small table. The waiter brought us tea.
Then Squire came in: Sir John becoming Jack-a-napes, shook hands, then
whiskeyed under the table.
We stared. He climbed over the bar.
                                    We talked
Of poetry. I turned the unwritten pages
Of my new book, A Critical Study
Of William Butler Yeats, chapter eleven.
He interrupted. 'There are portraits of me
In Liverpool, Birmingham, Edinburgh.
And other Galleries.'
                        The pages eared
Each other.
   'Do you agree with Forest Reid,
He writes ....'
   'I have forgotten his book.'
                          My own
Remaindered, head was tumbling after it.
Soon, speaking of his plays, we leaned so close
That I could see a tiny brown eye peeping
behind his left lens cutely from the Celtic
Twilight at mine. I tried to stop the moment
I dreaded so much. Had I not promised the young
Director of the firm that I would ask him
The truth about his lyrical love affair?
I groped around the Nineties.
                                    'Mr. Yeats,
In order – as it were – to understand
The Wind among the Reeds, those exquisite
Love lyrics, can I venture to ask what is –
If I may say so – their actual basis in
Reality?'
              How could I know a married
Woman had loosened her cadent hair, taken him,
All candlestick, into her arms?
                                    A stern
Victorian replied:
                        'Sir, do you seek
To pry into my private affairs?'
                                    I paled.
The poet returned. His smile kept at a distance.
'Of course you could suggest – without offence

To any person living – that . . .'

                              I lost
His words. Maud Gonne was talking to me in that cottage,
At Glenmalure. The parrot squawked: canaries
Twittered: the wolfhound yawned. Her golden eyes
Were open to mysteries.

                              I took my hat
Leaped square and crescent at a bound,
Confused by all his gyres – and I am bound
To say I left that book, unchaptered, unbound.

The "Squire" who came in, became "Jack-a-napes", shook hands with Clarke and "then whiskeyed under the table" was, of course, Sir John Squire the notorious poet and man of letters who had been elected to the Club in 1918. He had been proposed by E.W. Hornung, the author of *Raffles,* and supported by a list of members who reflected his own increasing reputation in the literary world; among them Compton Mackenzie, Logan Pearsall Smith, Lytton Strachey and Albert Rutherston, who had the year before proposed W.B. Yeats. At the time of his election Squire was literary editor of the recently founded *New Statesman*, a job which neatly linked his literary interests with his left-wing views. But he was an expansive and witty man whose craving for amusing company had drawn him to the Savile, where he became an extremely popular member. He had published volumes of poetry and a collection of parodies which established him as a master in both these arts. The year after his election Squire established a new and beautifully produced monthly magazine, *The London Mercury*, whose eclecticism was almost a mirror image of the Club of which he was now a member. The first issue contained poems by, among others, Thomas Hardy, but also carried learned articles on scientific matters. The magazine lasted until 1934 and was a powerful influence in promoting Squire's deeply held belief in the need for an improved use of design and art in everyday life. He was made a Fellow of the Society of Arts and his enthusiastic support for better standards in architecture earned him an honorary A.R.I.B.A.

While editing *The London Mercury* he continued to produce a great number of poetical anthologies as well as his own original verse and in 1926 in collaboration with his fellow Savilian, J.L. Balderston, he dramatized Henry James's *The Sense of the Past* into a highly successful three-act play, *Berkeley Square*.

By 1933 Squire had become a considerable public figure and in that year he was knighted. But in private not all was as well as it seemed; he had offended many of his literary and intellectual acquaintances even at the Savile, not least for the difficulty many of them encountered when requesting payment for work he had commissioned. His connection with *The London Mercury* ceased in 1934, though he continued his work as a poet, reviewer and anthologist. The "Jack-a-napes" persona was taking over and his "whiskeyed" voyages "under the table" becoming more frequent. His own finances were nothing short of chaotic and by the late

Algernon Blackwood;

Sir Sidney Colvin,
proposer of Robert
Louis Stevenson and
of Sir Edward Elgar,
who dedicated his cello
concerto to Colvin.

Mr G K Chesterton.	Lord Harcourt.		Mr Maurice Baring.	Archbishop of Canterbury.	Lord Londonderry.	
Mr Pearsall Smith.	Mr George Moore.	Lord Curzon.	Lord Howard de Walden.			Mr Conrad.
Lord Beauchamp.	Mr Kipling.		Mr Arnold Bennett.	Lord Crewe.	Mr Gosse. Mr Hardy.	Lord Mo

"The Birthday Surprise"; Max Beerbohm's depiction of the Club's presentation of a portrait bust to Sir Edmund Gosse to commemorate his 70th birthday (p.48).

Lord Spencer.   Sir Frank Swettenham.   Mr Archer.   Sir E. Ray Lankester.

Mr Gosse.   Mr Ryman.   Sir A. W. Pinero.   Mr Hewlett.   Lord Balfour.

Lord Holdane.   Mr Austin Dobson.   Mr Evan Charteris.

Sir Henry Newbolt

Rudyard Kipling

W.E. Henley

Robert Louis Stevenson

Anthony Hope (Sir Anthony Hope-Hawkins)

Coventry Patmore

E.M. Forster

Andrew Lang

Robert Bridges

Edmund Gosse

William Butler Yeats, *"the living model of a poet come into his kingdom"* (pp. 76-82).

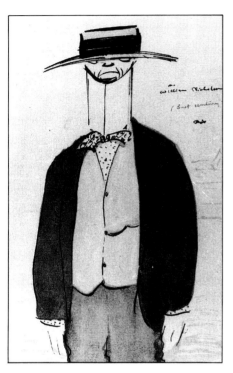

In the morning room of the Club is Beerbohm's caricature of Sir William Nicholson which inspired Lady Nicholson to exclaim: *"Oh, Max! You are so good on my husband – at his worst!"* Nicholson responded with a portrait of Max as the height of elegance (p.67).

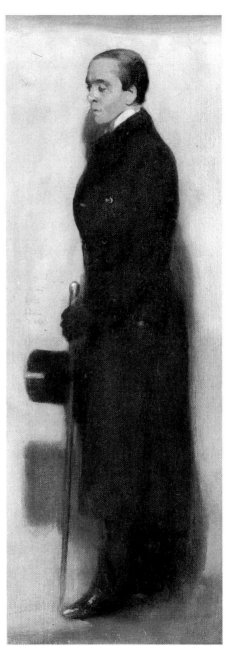

Sir Henry Rider Haggard (left) and fellow member Frederick Courtney Selous, the model of Haggard's hero Allan Quatermain.

Sir John Squire, who *"whiskeyed under the table"* at the Savile under the haughty gaze of Yeats (pp. 81-82).

Thomas Hardy

A.P. Herbert

"Jolly Jack" – J.B. Priestley by fellow member Sir David Low.

St John Ervine.

Right, H.G. Wells by his fellow Savilian David Low.

Mr. Rudyard Kipling takes a bloomin' day aht, on the blasted 'eath, along with Britannia, 'is gurl.

Beerbohm's contempt for the jingoism of his fellow member Rudyard Kipling was expressed in several caricatures, of which this is typical. It must have made the Club a tense place to be when both were present.

thirties he was increasingly dependent on his friends. However he retained his eminence as a reviewer of literature to the last, most notably in *The Illustrated London News*, and managed to preserve a certain insouciance in the face of all his problems. One night playing bridge at the Savile he found himself without any cash to cover his losses and offered to pay by cheque. His opponent shied away from the suggestion with a resounding "No, thanks", to which Squire imperturbably replied, "That's funny, they won't take my cheques at the Athenaeum either." Peter Rodd murmured, "I suppose that's what's they call forcing two clubs." His fellow member, Sidney Dark, the editor of *The Church Times*, provides a brief comment on Squire in the remorseless chronicle of Club life contained in his autobiography *Not Such a Bad Life*: ". . . [Squire] is essentially naive. He . . . pontificates about politics, on literature, on art, cricket and novels. But his pontificating is too simple to be offensive. He is more given than any other man I know to excusing the sins he has a mind to by damning those he is not inclined to" – which leads one to wonder whether despite Dark's editorial seat on the Church of England's leading newspaper he had ever heard of "motes" and "beams".

After the First World War Squire had indulged his great love of cricket by forming his own team which he named "The Invalids". Its members were mainly literary men and veterans of the recent battlefields. Among them were several Savile members such as Neville Cardus, the great music critic and cricket writer; A.D. Peters, the literary agent; A.G. Macdonell and Doctor Sidney Cusdin. The team toured country villages at weekends and bank holidays taking on local teams, though the main purpose seemed to have been to enjoy some heroic bouts of rural bacchanalia. After more than half a century these week-end odysseys remain etched on Sidney Cusdin's memory – if not his liver:

> I played in Sir John Squire's eleven in the late 'twenties and early 'thirties, mainly Sunday cricket and short tours in Sussex at the bank holidays. I was very young and precocious, and thoroughly enjoyed playing cricket in this exalted company. But I was not in their class when it came to drinking. One occasion I can recall was at Sawley Hall, the home of Sir Walter Lawrence near Sawbridgeworth: magnificent country house where we were invited to late breakfast and drinks because we could not play until after Church. The Invalids were put out to bat and we made a disastrous start and one of the old time tenants watching the game is reputed to have said "Who be these folk?" – "They be the Invalids" was the reply. "Well, they look like drunks to me!"

Possibly one of the most comic chapters ever penned in a work of recent English literature is A.G. Macdonell's description of one of Squire's cricket matches in the novel *England Their England*, published in 1933, the year he was elected to the Savile. Macdonell batted and bowled for the Invalids and was very much a man after Squire's heart: a wayward genius, fond of the bottle and despite all his problems a most sympathetic companion.

Born in Poona, India, which must have appealed to his sense of humour, Macdonell was brought back to England in 1909 and entered Winchester as a scholar. In 1914 instead of going to Oxford he enlisted in the army and was commissioned. Although about a third of his contemporaries at Winchester were killed in the war, Macdonell was "lucky" enough to be merely wounded and invalided home. He met Squire, who employed him as a reviewer and considered him to be "as good a dramatic critic as ever existed". He travelled widely abroad and from 1922-7 was on the staff of the League of Nations, part of that time as private secretary to Gilbert Murray. Returned to London, he wrote crime stories under a pseudonym until in 1933 Squire, who was at the time a reader at Macmillans, was instrumental in having *England Their England* published. Macdonell became instantly famous and in the next five years he produced five comic novels, two plays, a travel book, a biographical study and a collection of short stories. In 1940 he joined the B.B.C. to give broadcasts to "The Empire and the U.S.A." and in that year, just as he was about to concentrate on his career as a dramatist, he died.

Although their occasional lapses were, no doubt, sometimes embarrassing, Sir John Squire and his protégé A.G. Macdonell seem to have provided sufficient mirth within the Club to make themselves agreeable even to those Savilians of graver mien whose very rarity singled them out for service on the various Club committees. It is, perhaps, a tribute to the traditional broadmindedness of these more sober members that the two jesters were savoured so appreciatively and that when another humorist, A.P. Herbert, came to add to the fun in 1922 and managed to do so without causing any corresponding qualms among the more sedate, he was presently invited to bridge the gap between the two elements and serve on the general committee in 1926.

Sir Alan Patrick Herbert was thirty-two years old when he followed the example of his rather more elderly nephew, the composer Roger Quilter, who had been a member since 1906. After active service with the R.N.V.R. in France and at Gallipoli he used his convalescence from war wounds to read for the Bar and to write a book, *The Secret Battle*, on the theme of cowardice, which did much to improve courts-martial procedures in the later war. Shortly after becoming a member of the Club he was taken on the staff of *Punch*, whose figurehead of "Mr Punch" his own features came so closely to resemble towards the end of his life. There were of course several other staff members and contributors to *Punch* already at the Club, but soon the initials A.P.H. appended to any article came to be recognized as an outward and visible sign that he was using that journal to be one of the many convenient platforms from which he could conduct witty but highly effective crusades against anomalies he had detected in the English legal system. A series of articles, *Misleading Cases*, satirizing these defects was published as a book in 1927 and enlarged his reputation throughout the English-speaking world as a champion of common-sense in the application of the law. In 1935 he became Independent M.P. for Oxford University under the old University franchise and having already inveighed against the antique divorce laws in his novel *Holy Deadlock*, he was now able to achieve the distinction of having his Matrimonial Causes Act put on the statute book as a private Member's bill during his first year in parliament.

Four years after becoming a member of the Savile he began to apply himself to the theatre; *Riverside Nights*, a revue at the Lyric Theatre in Hammersmith, was his first venture, which was followed by a series of operettas, *La Vie Parisienne, Tantivy Towers* and *Derby Day*, culminating in perhaps his greatest success, *Bless the Bride*, produced in 1950. His love of sailing and life on the water – particularly the River Thames – was reflected in his novel *The Water Gipsies* published in 1930 and when at the outbreak of war in 1939 he put his converted canal boat *Water Gipsy* at the disposal of the Royal Naval Auxiliary Patrol defending the Thames he was given the rank of petty officer and the right to fly the white ensign. Meantime and subsequently he continued his crusades through every medium available to him, notably the correspondence columns of *The Times* and other influential journals. His campaign against purchase tax on books, for instance, was so vehemently expressed in a speech in the House of Commons and elsewhere that it caused the chancellor of the exchequer hastily to change his mind while his other philippics on behalf of such favourite obsessions as a public lending right for authors and passenger traffic services on the Thames achieved equally satisfactory albeit less speedy results. He received his knighthood in Sir Winston Churchill's resignation honours list of 1945 but in 1950 this 'independent Member *par excellence*' as he had been described in *The Times* was deprived of his parliamentary soap box with the abolition of the university franchise by a socialist government. In his time his various interests had been expressed as a trustee of the National Maritime Museum, president of the London Corinthian Sailing Club, president of the Inland Waterways Association, president of the Society of Authors, and vice-president of the Performing Rights Society. He was appointed a Companion of Honour in 1970. His connection with the Savile was further emphasized, if not, perhaps, reinforced, by his daughter, Crystal, who having married one member, John Pudney, decided she preferred another so took advantage of her father's Matrimonial Causes Act to become the wife of Lionel Hale.

* * * *

The Savile has provided a welcome haven for some of Britain's leading poets; Hardy, Bridges, Newbolt, Kipling and Yeats were but the forerunners of a distinguished line which continues to the present day.

Patric Dickinson, the translator of Aristophanes and himself a poet of particular worth and individual voice, was proposed for the Club by W.J. Turner – the rival monologist to Yeats. "Walter was a brilliant man", says Patric, "a fine poet, a music critic of originality, and foresight and insight. I loved his Australian accent and his formidable directness. 'Christ! It was bloody awful!' he said of a broadcast of his poems I produced. It was too. I had got the wrong reader, and knew it. He

said this to me loudly in the Sandpit which was then the bar. Nobody minded
. . ." Then, after describing Walter's conversational encounters with Yeats, Patric
recalls "...Now Yeats was dead, Walter was supreme, but he too, alas, suddenly
died. I think of Walter's dangling eyeglass that bounced a bit as he got stouter, his
marvellous spiky speech and appalling spiky handwriting" – the latter comment,
as friends of Patric might aver, being very much a case of the poet calling the
kettle black.

Turner's conversational style was not, it seems, always so rapturously regarded.
Michael Meyer in his memoirs *Not Prince Hamlet* catalogues him, along with the
elderly Compton Mackenzie, among the less captivating conversationalists in the
Savile talkathon:

> Another tedious member was the Irish poet W.J. Turner, author of the
> splendid "Romance" about Chimborazo and Cotopaxi ("when I was but
> thirteen or so..."). He was tall and spidery, and had a way of turning
> across you as he sat beside you on a sofa and grasping your lapel, so that
> there was no means of escape. My father suggested that I should have a
> special coat made with detachable lapels, so that I could slip away leaving
> him still clutching one of them in his hand. What made it worse was that
> the poor man had very bad breath. However, he was, like Mackenzie, a
> kindly man, so that one could not be brusque as one would have been had
> the offender been Major Pollard.

(Of the brusqueness-worthy Major Pollard more anon).

Patric Dickinson remembers also "talking poetry" in the Sandpit with that
enigmatic Savile writer and poet Richard Church, whose autobiography *Over the
Bridge* caused some consternation when in it he referred quite casually to his habit
as a young man of indulging in levitation to avoid traffic jams on his way to work.

> We became firm friends [says Patric]. Years later, Dick asked me, in the
> bar, what I thought was his best poem. This is a formidable question. I
> was able to answer at once and unequivocally, *The Lamp*. He blushed
> scarlet with pleasure, as old men seldom do. It is a most moving grim and
> tender narrative poem of the French Resistance, one of the least known of
> his works but for him, too, the best....

Again, in a Club of such catholic tastes there had to be a contrary view. John
Hadfield recalls:

> I was sitting in the Sandpit one hot summer's evening with my old and
> dear friend Richard Church when Gilbert Harding appeared from the bar,
> perspiring and carrying his jacket. Stopping in front of Richard Church he
> said: "I am fond of you, Richard. You are one of the very nicest members
> of this Club. It's a pity that you are not a better writer."

Sir Harold Acton, whose first recorded blow in defence of poetry was to trumpet Eliot's *The Waste Land* through a megaphone from his college rooms at Christ Church to edify a passing rowing crew (as is famously recorded in *Brideshead Revisited*), had his earliest poems published by a fellow member of the Savile. Thomas Balston of Duckworths, "a retiring bachelor of fine taste" as Sir Harold modestly admits, published *Aquarium* and *An Indian Ass*. These were followed by a series of works on Chinese poetry and drama, deriving from Sir Harold's years as a lecturer in English literature at Peking University; the classic *The Bourbons of Naples* and, perhaps his best known work, *Memoirs of an Aesthete*. Elected in 1927, Sir Harold, perhaps the most famous recent apostle of aestheticism, was made a life member in 1989.

A poet of very different kind was John Pudney, who was elected in 1949 and who died in 1977. John Sleigh Pudney was born in 1909 and in 1933 his first volume of verse, *Spring Encounter*, was published by Methuen, which brought him into the literary circle of the formidable Lady Ottoline Morrell, wife of Philip Morrell, one of the chief protagonists in a famous Savile scandal – as will be seen later – and mother-in-law to another equally notable and daunting member, the Russian aristocrat and scholar, Igor Vinogradov.

The success of this first collection encouraged Pudney to devote himself entirely to writing, though after his marriage to A.P. Herbert's daughter, Crystal, he found it necessary to take jobs at *The Listener* and as a writer-producer in the B.B.C. where he was concerned with some of the first broadcasts of music by his erstwhile schoolmate Benjamin Britten. His first novel, *Jacob's Ladder*, was published in 1938 and in 1940 he was commissioned into the R.A.F. as an Intelligence officer and later to the newly formed Air Ministry "Creative Writers' Unit". During the invasion of France he was with General Leclerc's troops when they liberated Paris but, characteristically, regarded this as merely an opportunity to be the first to visit Picasso in his studio. Although he had had no training as a fighting man he endured many hazardous encounters which inspired him to remark that he must have been the only wartime officer who "never fired a shot except in anger".

Pudney will, of course, be long remembered for one of the best-known poems of the Second World War. It was first published in the *News Chronicle* in 1941, broadcast on radio by Laurence Olivier and spoken by Michael Redgrave in the film *The Way to the Stars* directed by Anthony Asquith in 1945.

> Do not despair
> For Johnny-head-in-air;
> He sleeps as sound
> As Johnny underground.
>
> Fetch out no shroud
> For Johnny-in-the-cloud;
> And keep your tears
> For him in after years.

Better by far
For Johnny-the-bright-star;
To keep your head,
And see his children fed.

He wrote many other considerable war poems though "Johnny-head-in-air" was the one which latched on to the public's consciousness. After the war he returned to journalism and made an unsuccessful bid to be elected to Parliament as a Labour candidate at Sevenoaks in the 1945 election. He went on to publish a considerable body of verse which is now unjustifiably neglected and ten novels, of which the most successful was *The Net*, published in 1952. However, he had now succumbed to the curse whch afflicts so many of those who take up the lonely profession of writing. His addiction to "Sodality" and "Convivium" as an antidote to the solitary working hours led to what he euphemistically called "Overdrinking". As a result his marriage to Crystal Herbert was dissolved in 1955 and she proceeded to marry his fellow member, Lionel Hale, another distinguished Savile author. A nervous committee made it discreetly known that one or other – maybe even both – might feel it tactful to resign, whereupon they both met in the bar to discuss this possibility and draft a joint reply that if it was all the same to the other members they would rather stay and continue to enjoy the Club. The committee concurred; and they did. Incidentally, Michael Ayrton and Nigel Balchin had a similar problem and dealt with it in the same way.

With characteristic bravery, Pudney made up his mind in 1965 to overcome his alcoholism. This he managed to do and wrote a book about it in an effort to reduce the stigma with which the condition is generally regarded. In 1976 he developed a hideously painful cancer of the throat from which he died the following year. A writer to the last, and with the same superhuman courage, he wrote a description of the progress of the disease and the process of dying in *Thank Goodness for Cake*, published posthumously in 1978, perhaps one of the most moving works ever to have come from a Savile member's pen.

John Pudney's early acquaintance with Auden may have had only a peripheral influence on his literary career but a much stronger connection exists with a present member of the Club, Sir Stephen Spender. Indeed Auden's first book, *Poems*, published in 1928, was privately printed by Spender in an edition of 45 copies and his name, together with those of another member, Cecil Day-Lewis, Christopher Isherwood and, later, Louis MacNeice, was most commonly associated with the "new" movement in the poetry of the 'thirties which was strongly inspired by social and political motives. Stephen Spender (as he then was) was elected to the Savile in 1943 and, at the time of writing, in his eighty-second year is still maintaining a literary output which would be the despair of lesser men. "A poet of distinction and a critic of discrimination, a novelist, a full-time autobiographer and part-time dramatist, co-founder of the magazines *Horizon*, *Encounter* and *Index on Censorship*", as *The Times* explained on the occasion of his eightieth birthday, "it is hard to imagine any other literary activity in which Sir

Stephen might have busied himself, short of book binding and calligraphy."

When he was knighted in 1983 he had ruefully to remember an early "gaffe with the power to raise a ghost"; on a Channel crossing when he was seventeen he had happened to sit next to an earlier Savilian, Sir Henry Newbolt, and had discussed with him poets they admired. Spender remarked about one in particular, "Well, I can't like the work of a poet who has a title."

But literary men are not always remembered for literary matters at the Savile: Patric Dickinson, musing that "... in 1945-55 the balance of members tended more to the arts than it does now", recollects that

> in the S.E. corner of the dining-room under the window was, and still is, a table for two. One day there was John Betjeman lunching with Stephen Spender. It is not usual for dramatic events to happen in club dining rooms. Suddenly there was a crack, a crash, and there was John on the floor in the midst of a disintegrated chair. The long table was silenced, the room was loud with John's laughter and Stephen's embarrassment. But nobody at the Savile stops talking for long....

For his eightieth birthday in 1989 the Savile organized one of its more Lucullan Soirées to celebrate Sir Stephen's years of membership and, as Patric Dickinson observed on the other occasion, nobody stopped talking for long. It is a pity that one of Spender's old friends, one of the more brilliant talkers in recent times, another Savile poet, Henry Reed, could not have been present.

Like several of his lyrical colleagues at the Savile, Henry brought translations of his classical predecessors as well as his own distinctive verse to a wider public through the medium of radio, and like Spender and Pudney he had been much influenced in his youth by Auden; like Pudney too he had served in Intelligence during the war and had produced one of the most famous poems in English to come out of it – "Naming of Parts". In 1946 his fellow Savilian Edward Sackville-West persuaded him to write a dramatization for radio of *Moby Dick* which was produced a year later featuring two other Savile members, Ralph Richardson and Bernard Miles. It won the Premio della Radio Italiana and established Henry with the critics as a radio dramatist with a rare poetic gift.

In 1970 a collection of his poems, *The Lessons of War*, was published to wide acclaim and in 1971 the texts of his poetic dramas for radio were published as *The Streets of Pompeii*. *A Very Great Man* and its sequels *Hilda Tablet and Others* also appeared, between them revealing much of the man himself, a master of comedy with a deeply sombre interior. In manner and appearance he resembled a classically educated Tony Hancock, presenting a lugubrious exterior from which emanated surprising flashes of wit. Many contemporary members will retain happy memories of evenings spent in his company. On one occasion when he was suffering one of his regular bouts of financial starvation he regaled the long table with an account of his appearance that morning before the magistrates to explain his inability to pay the rates: "And what, Mr Reed, is your profession?" asked the magistrate. Diffidently, Henry admitted that he was a poet. "Yes, yes," said the magistrate testily, "but what do you do for a *living?*"

The ghost of Yeats at the Savile must be well pleased to have its chains so eloquently rattled by a contemporary member, Donald Davie, the distinguished poet, critic and academic who has on several occasions conducted the Yeats summer school at Sligo. Davie's academic career has included lectureships at Trinity College, Dublin; Cambridge, Essex, and long periods in the USA as Professor of Poetry at Stanford and Vanderbilt, where he is Emeritus Professor. There is at least one other member of the Club who, nearly forty years later, remembers that at T.C.D., where lectures were compulsory, and therefore never attended, Davie's sparkling performances were the only ones that were ever guaranteed a full house. Donald Davie was elected to the Savile in 1966 and has endowed the Monument with his several volumes of collected poems and critical essays. A new edition of his collected poems is due for publication over the next ten years and the first volume, *Under Briggflatts*, published in 1989, has already joined its fellows in the Monument.

There have been, and indeed are, many other Savilians who have written poetry of distinction but they, possibly bearing in mind the magistrate's implicit criticism of Henry Reed, have done so while earning their living otherwise.

George Buchanan, who had been a member since 1929 and who died in 1989, was an administrator who had been at one time chairman of the Town and Country Development Council of Northern Ireland but had later returned to a more congenial cultural ambience as a member of the Executive Council of the European Society, eventually becoming president of the London centre. Between whiles he wrote novels, criticism and verse. As his friend, fellow Savilian and writer, Vincent Brome, wrote in *The Guardian*:

> His forays into literature proper embraced all forms and his versatility makes him difficult to assess as a writer. The role he most respected was that of the poet, and he published several volumes of collected verse including *Bodily Responses* and *Conversations with Strangers*. Their quality varied and he only found his true "voice" in his later works, one of the most successful being *Inside Traffic*.

Brome recalled that "A great admirer of the literary salon tradition, Buchanan was a *bon vivant* and his dinner parties and poetry readings became a part of the literary London season. Gentle and benign, he presided over these with an implacable good humour capable of accommodating some of the most eccentric characters in the literary scene. Dismayed by what he regarded as the dissemination of inaccurate cultural information he once said: 'It's not so much people's ignorance that matters: it's their knowing so many things that ain't so.' "

Another Savile poet who hid his light under a different bushel was David Cleghorn-Thomson, who was tipped to be a future prime minister while he was president of the Oxford Union but at the age of twenty-nine was diverted into becoming the first Scottish Regional Director of the BBC. He published "slim volumes" of verse which deserve a wider audience and among them is to be found a wondrous evocation of his fellow member and life-long friend, Dallas Bower, in a poem which every new member should be required to learn by heart as part of the entrance fee, "Parmigiano".

David Hardman, who died in 1989, was a poet and politician whose work in the one field probably cut short his career in the other. When he was elected to the Savile in 1946 he was Parliamentary Secretary at the Ministry of Education in the recently formed Attlee administration, and he soon established for himself a prominent place in the current Saviliana. As a student at Christ's College, Cambridge he created something of a record by becoming the first avowedly socialist president of the Cambridge Union. For nearly fifty years he was secretary of the Sir Ernest Cassell Educational Trust and was closely associated with the Workers' Educational Association. He was a lecturer much in demand both here and in America for his discourses on a wide variety of subjects, from politics and local government to Shakespeare, about whom he wrote a well-received work of popular scholarship. Unfortunately for his political career he published a rather robust collection of poetry, *Poems of Love and Affairs*, just before the general election of 1951 which caused his outraged constituents at Darlington to confer upon him the doubtful distinction of being one of the only two Labour front-benchers to lose their seats.

Basil Saunders among many others has relaxed from his labours, in his case as a public relations executive and administrator for such organizations as The Wellcome Foundation, A.S.L.I.B., and the Arts Council, to produce similar personal insights in a volume entitled *Crackle of Thorns* and promises to publish more when the time is ripe. He has also, in common with other Savilians such as Kenneth Haigh, Simon Oates, Roger Braban and Charles Hodgson, been a reader at the many poetry evenings which have accompanied celebratory dinners to sing the Club's poetic heritage. Just before he died, Sir Ralph Richardson remarked that "there is almost certainly no other club in the world which could have staged so many distinguished events to honour their own members and also manage to round up so many other chaps about the house to do it so beautifully."

* * * *

But despite this poetic Pantheon, novelists still predominated, at least numerically, in the literary history of the Savile. Francis Brett Young had been elected in 1920. As a qualified doctor, practising in Devon, he began to write novels "in between epidemics" and of these early works *The Dark Tower,* published in 1915, is perhaps the best known. In the First World War he served with the R.A.M.C. in East Africa, which seriously affected his health; and during his long convalescence he wrote *The Crescent Moon* and a collection, *Poems,* published in 1919. Although it had yet to attract much public attention his literary skill had evidently been already recognized by his peers for he had been proposed for the

Savile by Sir Henry Newbolt and supported by Hugh Walpole, John Squire and the poet laureate, Robert Bridges. *Portrait of Clare*, one of his more characteristic novels, won the James Tait Black Memorial Prize in 1927 and was his first real critical success. Financial independence followed with *My Brother Jonathan* in 1928. A very English writer and by all accounts a most clubbable man.

In 1939 Francis Brett Young and his wife Jessica met two future members of the Savile, C.P. Snow and Harry Hoff, while wintering in Cap d'Antibes. This was to develop into a deep friendship and they appear as Lawrence and Mrs Knight in Snow's novels, *Time of Hope* and *Homecomings*.

That master of the atmospheric novel, Patrick Hamilton, was elected to the Club in 1930. When *Hangover Square*, one of his more disturbing accounts of mental illness, heavy boozing and seedy low-life in pre-war London, was adapted for the stage and performed in 1990, a reviewer wrote:

> If Patrick Hamilton is remembered at all today, then it is probably for his stage thrillers *Gaslight* and *Rope*, which were both turned into successful films. But before he drank himself into personal oblivion and professional obscurity in 1962, he was also well regarded as a novelist.

At Brook Street, where he is better remembered, that seems to be a less than generous judgment, for contemporaries who knew him well, such as Dallas Bower, recall him as a rewarding and engaging companion. Even the reviewer of this latest revival felt constrained to add that "J.B. Priestley described him as a 'master among the uniquely gifted minor novelists of our age' " and, as shall presently be seen, to be counted even among the "minor" novelists of the time was the equivalent of a 21-gun salute coming from that particular source.

A very English writer, but of a very different kind, was Walter Greenwood, who was elected in 1942. Certainly among the more versatile of Savile members, he had worked as a clerk, a stable-boy, a packing-case maker, a sign-writer, a driver, a warehouseman and a salesman – never earning more than 35 shillings a week – before 1933 when he published his first and best-known novel of working-class life during the slump, *Love on the Dole*. This highly successful work was, to use the hackneyed phrase properly for once, "to change the course of his life"; for after it had been adapted for the stage and made into a film he turned his attention more and more to work in those areas. Although he was to write nine more novels this introduction to the stage and the cinema led to *My Son My Son, The Cure for Love* (in which his fellow Savilian Robert Donat starred) and *Saturday Night at the Crown*, which were all highly successful plays, while from 1935 onwards he was also producing a number of film scripts. Then with the growth of television he extended his range and produced many scripts for the B.B.C., notably *The Secret Kingdom* in 1960.

Greenwood made a very distinctive figure at the Club where his broad Nothern vowels are remembered as embellishing many a lively conversation in the Sandpit and bar with such particular friends as Robert Donat and Boully Boulenger. Indeed, it was Greenwood who cared for Boully when he was taken ill at the Club, escorting him home to Cornwall and, in an atmosphere of black farce which shall be described later, ministered to him through his last illness.

Frank Swinnerton was elected in 1922. As a young man working in a junior capacity as "confidential clerk" to the publisher Hugh Dent, Swinnerton had already cast a speculative eye on some of the literary heroes of the day such as H.G. Wells, perhaps never imagining that many of them were to become his friends through his membership of the Savile. He published his own first novel, *The Merry Heart*, in 1909, and continued thereafter to produce books at the rate of one a year. His first essay into biography, a critical study of George Gissing, convinced him that "... the authors of books should ever be traced and found in their books and that all really interesting interpretation of literature – whatever the dilettanti may say – is humane". He was to use this principle to good effect in a later critical study of one of his predecessors at the Savile, Robert Louis Stevenson, and reiterate his opinion in a preface to the Everyman edition of *Angel Pavement* written by his fellow member, J.B. Priestley.

John Boynton Priestley was elected to the Club in 1945. His literary career has been fully memorialized in works by two contemporary Savile authors, *An Informal Study* by David Hughes, and the more recent official biography by Vincent Brome. In his more "relaxed" moments in the Club he certainly made his presence felt, with varying responses. An entry in Stephen Potter's diary for the 30 November 1943 reads:

> Priestley lunch – having heard that he may be able to do my suggested *Priestley on Dickens* Christmas programme, I get on to him for Savile lunch. One of those occasions when I think he really is the most understanding wise and amusing man I have ever met. When he sets out to be nice there is no-one like him. As we were leaving the dining room and I was paying – Jack had gone on – Frank (oldest and greatest of club servants) said to me "I've never enjoyed a book so much as *The Good Companions* – I did enjoy the G.C.": so I hauled Priestley back – he was extremely nice.

Michael Meyer recalls his other mood in *Not Prince Hamlet*:

> Our touchiest member, apart from Major Pollard, was probably J.B. Priestley. Behind a mask of overpowering bonhomie, he was quick to take offence, even with old friends. Ralph Richardson, with whom he had shared several considerable successes in the theatre, told me that when, after lunching together, they went to the desk to pay, the cashier asked: "Shall I charge the wine to you, Sir Ralph, or shall I split it?" At this, according to Ralph, "Jack went red in the face, didn't say a word over coffee, and I had to take him out and buy him a pound of his favourite

tobacco, which set me back eight quid". On another occasion, having purchased a new car, he invited Ralph for a drive and, once out in the countryside, asked Ralph what he thought of it. Ralph praised it highly, but ventured a small criticism of the wood used for the dashboard. Priestley said: "I asked you out to enjoy yourself, not to criticize," turned the car round and headed for home.

I once told him about my weekend with Sassoon. "I knew Sassoon," said Priestley. "He was a funny chap. A few years ago he published a book about George Meredith." "Extraordinary," I said. "I suppose he thought some people might be interested in him." "No, no, no," said Priestley angrily. "You've missed the point completely. I'd written a very good book about George Meredith." He was incredulous that anyone could regard his as anything but the last word on the subject.

Priestley had less sense of the ridiculous than anyone I have every known, with the possible exception of the actor Donald Wolfit. When my Ibsen biography won the Whitbread Award in 1971, Priestley was chairman of the judges, and on my arrival at the ceremony I was presented to him. We had not met often, and he had excusably forgotten me. The person in charge said: "Mr Priestley, this is Mr Meyer, the author of the Ibsen biography." Without any prefatory remark, Priestley said: "I did more for the art of dramatic exposition than Ibsen." Stephen Potter told me that, during the fifties, some of the Savile members were discussing in the billiards room what they would do if they got a hundred thousand pounds, at that time a small fortune. Priestley rolled in like a galleon, and Stephen said: "Jack, what would you do if you got a hundred thousand pounds?" "I've got a hundred thousand pounds." "But what would you do if you got another hundred thousand pounds?" "I've got another hundred thousand pounds".

His sense of *amour propre* was never far from the surface; a dangerous weakness at the Savile. Peter Green, who was a regular attender at the Club until his appointment as Dougherty Centennial Professor in the Department of Classics at The University of Texas, remembers the early 1960s when

among some of the best conversationalists I've ever known – Ayrton, Snow, Harry Hoff, Max Reinhardt, was John Moore who was also a superb anecdotalist: one of his best concerned J.B. Priestley, whom he once met at the bar, looking depressed, and when J.M. asked him what the trouble was, got the immortal reply: "It's me wife, she's roon off with a bloody birdwatcher". J.M. stowed this tit-bit of information away, and when he next came on Priestley at the bar, about six months later, said, cheerfully, "Hullo, Jack, and how's your bloody birdwatcher doing?" At which, John told me, J.B.P. drew himself up and replied, with some hauteur "Ah'd 'ave you know, Moore, he's the most distinguished ornithologist in England".

On another occasion, the usually ebullient Malcolm Arnold found himself alone at the bar except for Priestley and so forced into having an unwontedly solemn drink. Suddenly he was addressed:

" 'ere, Malcolm. Why does everyone in this place go round calling me 'Jolly Jack'?"

Mustering every ounce of tact in his possession, Malcolm replied:

"Well Jack, seeing as you ask, it's because you're such a gloomy old sod."

Priestley retired once more into his shell – "A tear began to gather in his eye," says Malcolm incredulously.

"Thank you Malcolm, Thank you for telling me that," he said eventually and there was another pause while he pondered a while. Then, plaintively: "Well why did none of the other boogers ever tell me?"

But for all this knockabout irreverence to which even the greatest must submit if they are to survive at the Savile, the members maintained a deep affection for this prickly master in their midst and though they might occasionally mock his foibles they admired his considerable achievements. When Priestley was awarded the O.M., filling the only vacancy in that exclusive order and thus excluding his fellow Savilian, C.P. Snow, who might reasonably have expected to receive it, Snow was among the first to send him fulsome congratulations. Priestley replied: "It is all the more generous coming from you. I feel you are more the O.M. kind of man than I am." To celebrate this honour the Club held another gastronomic soirée at which Priestley and his wife Jacquetta Hawkes were the honoured and this time more jovial guests. Sir Jack Longland, Sir Ralph Richardson, David Hardman and John Hadfield catalysed the oratorical flow which ensued.

The Savile principle of electing ". . . men of different professions and opinions" must have appealed powerfully to C.P. Snow with his own lifelong ambition himself to bestride "the two cultures", a crusade which found expression in his Rede lectures at Cambridge in 1959, *The Two Cultures and the Scientific Revolution*, which caused something of an uproar in academic circles. To have entered a Club which happily contained the likes of Sir John Cockcroft and J.B. Priestley and many other leading representatives of each culture together with some, like H.G. Wells, who had combined both, must have been balm for what was by all accounts an often tormented soul.

Snow joined the Club in 1942 when he was director of technical personnel at the Ministry of Labour under Ernest Bevin but two years earlier he had begun the *Strangers and Brothers* series of novels which was to make his name as a writer. The Club became very important to him as is evidenced in a note from his stepson, Andrew Stewart, now an overseas member:

My stepfather, the late C.P. Snow, was a regular visitor to the Savile in the 'fifties and early 'sixties, going for dinner once a week when he was in

London. He was a member of the Athenaeum too, but never went there except at times of deep depression or after receiving bad news when he said its atrocious food and morose atmosphere felt more appropriate to his mood. His family always regarded a visit to the Athenaeum as ominous. At those more usual happier times he went to the Savile and regarded it as his clubland home, often returning late. My mother (the late Pamela Hansford Johnson, also a novelist) told me that on one occasion returning from the Club after a convivial evening he wished to avoid meeting a visitor she was entertaining and, to escape being seen, crawled on hands and knees past the door of the drawing room where the visitor was sitting. Unfortunately he failed to remember that the bottom panel of the drawing room door was glazed as well as the top, so his progress took place in full view of the bemused visitor. My stepfather disliked and suffered much from the satirists of the 1960s, whom he regarded as spiteful, trivial, destructive and possessing no serious creative abilities of their own. Upon the election of one of them to the Savile he resigned his own membership. However I believe he might have taken it up again shortly before his death in 1980.

The satirist in question, in fact, did not remain long and after his departure Lord Snow did indeed resume his membership.

Like many other writers there, Snow tended to allow the atmosphere of the Club and some of the characteristics of his fellow members to creep into his novels.

I cannot recall that my stepfather ever used the Savile *explicitly* for any of the clubland venues in his novels, but likely references to it exist [says Andrew Stewart]. For example in *Last Things* (Heron 1970, p.32) Lewis Eliot says: "Round the room" [the bar in the House of Lords] one could hear a variety of accents: about as many as in the Athenaeum, which was a meritocratic club, and a good deal more than in *the other club I sometimes used*.

Certainly Savile members provided partial inspirations for some of his characters. Ones that come most directly to mind are Tom Dobell in *The Affair* (the late John Raymond, a literary journalist) and Gilbert Cooke and Sammikins in the *Strangers and Brothers* series (a particular friend the late Humphrey Hare, ex-Welsh Guards with modest private means and literary interests). Humphrey Hare's death from lung cancer is recorded in *Last Things*.

There were also, of course, Francis Brett Young and his wife Jessica in *Time of Hope* and *Homecomings*. Later in his note, Andrew Stewart recalls:

I had been taken to dinner at the Savile a few times by my stepfather when I was in my late teens. After dinner he liked to gather with friends in the bar and talk for a couple of hours on subjects of interest, often about literary matters. I was overawed at listening to what seemed to me to be the glittering conversation that took place. One of the participants once was the philosopher A.J. Ayer who, I must confess, I found garrulous and unimpressive in manner, although I am sure I had very little idea what he was talking about.

A late night participant on another occasion was Richard Adrian, now Lord Adrian, Master of Pembroke College, Cambridge. He recalls that as a newly qualified doctor doing his National Service in the R.A.M.C., and stationed near Salisbury, he "greatly enjoyed being able to spend weekends at the Club":

> I recall one such when Charles Snow confided to me in the course of a long talk after dinner (I think we were almost the only members present at dinner on a Saturday night) that his ambition was to win the Nobel Prize for Literature. Irreverently I thought it ambitious then, though I did not say so, and I have to say I still think it so.

Private Eye took a similar view. In the mid-Sixties the magazine was much given to lampooning the unfortunate Snow, who appeared in its columns variously during his several elevations as C.P. Snurd, Sir Charles Snurd and lastly Lord Snurd. In its usual way it continued to attack him after being forced to pay damages and promising to desist. The final shot was to allege that he had invited the whole Swedish Academy out to dinner in an attempt to secure the Nobel Prize. As he had not been in Sweden for ten years the accusation was not difficult to disprove and after the customary grovelling and pleas of poverty reduced damages were offered together with worthless assurances of future probity.

Using his *nom de plume*, "William Cooper", his great friend and fellow member Harry Hoff has written an account of Snow's life for the Longman's series *Writers and their work*, which is in the Monument.

Hoff had preceded Snow into the Savile, having been elected in 1946, though they had first met when Hoff was an undergraduate reading spectroscopy at Christ's College, Cambridge, and Snow was a postgraduate there. Their friendship developed and extended over nearly fifty years while their careers followed remarkably similar courses. They worked together during the war in R.A.F. administration and after Snow left the Civil Service Commission Hoff was Personnel Consultant to the Atomic Energy Authority and Central Electricity Board. But Hoff is, of course, better known to a much wider public as the novelist William Cooper. As we have seen, Snow was given to basing some of the characters in his novels on his friends and Hoff returned the compliment by including Snow in some of his. Snow is "Robert" in *Scenes from Provincial Life* and *Scenes from Married Life,* and "Swan" in *Young People.* Snow in his turn dedicated *Homecomings* to William Cooper and as a final gesture to their enduring friendship appointed him as one of his literary executors before his death in 1980. Hoff's membership of the Savile now extends to a period almost equal to that of his friendship with Snow and though their mutual influences, tastes, and performances in science and literature were evidently so similar, Harry Hoff contrives to evoke much more powerfully to present members another entirely different departed Savilian, Max Beerbohm, with the wit, precision of speech and elegant presence with which he adorns the Sandpit and the long table.

Eric Linklater, he of the terrifying stare which had so startled Monja Danischewsky on his first visit to the Club, was elected to the Savile in 1936. His appearance was, indeed, disconcertingly fierce and Danny was by no means the only new young member to contemplate flight when subjected to the awful gaze of this really kind and gentle man. In his youth, Linklater had spent some time in India as a journalist and then two years in America as a Commonwealth fellow first at Cornell and then at Berkeley. His career as a novelist was established with his third novel, *Don Juan in America,* based on his experiences there, and his reputation as a master of the picaresque was reinforced by a succession of highly entertaining works of fiction which followed it, such as *Poet's Pub.* He had been deeply affected by his experiences in both world wars, in the first of which he was wounded and left with that dramatic indentation on the great dome of his prematurely bald skull which added formidably to his fearsome appearance, while in the second he served in Italy with the 8th Army, from which came the great comic novel, *Private Angelo.*

Despite appearances, his only indulgences in aggression were reserved for his favourite rural pursuits of hunting, shooting and fishing. Some of his recollections of exploits in the field – as a student he once managed to inveigle himself into acting as a beater to that Torquemada of the butts, King George V – would probably make modern ecological fashionables blanch, but he had a great love for nature. Walking through St James's Park to the Club one day in springtime during the 'fifties he was admiring the ducks in the lake, behaving "in a mood both bridal and playful. But in the midst of them, solitary and beautiful, a lovely foreigner swam." It was a mandarin drake which caught his eye; "... his beauty made him lonely, and for his air of painted aristocracy he was ostracised... The mandarin who deserved a harem to pick and choose from was alone and unwanted.... It was an intolerable situation." The duck's enforced celibacy preyed on his mind. That night at dinner in the Club, he inveighed against the injustice of it all; in the bar afterwards his increasing eloquence moved his fellow members to agree that *something must be done.* Upstairs playing cards was a "senior official of the Zoo", (probably Gwynne Vevers) who was forced to lay down his hand and advise on the matter. Sadly, it appeared, the Zoo at that particular time possessed no female mandarins at all, never mind those minded to indulge in sexual therapy.

> We stood about the bar in a defeated silence. The plight of the mandarin –
> that I had told as a passing tale – now seemed a matter of grave
> importance. We shared responsibility for his unhappiness; and the solitude
> of the little painted drake, on a night so warm for his companions, seemed

quite intolerable. But what could be done?

Frowning and perplexed, manifestly suffering, one of our company suddenly turned and left us. His stride was long and purposeful. He had, we knew, a vested interest in such affairs, for his father had been one of the leading – indeed dominating – ornithologists of the century [probably Edmund Fisher]. With a renewal of hope, and ordering another round of drink, we awaited his return.

A little flushed with the heat of action, with a smile of pleasure half-breaking the muscular tension of resolve, he presently came back. "If all goes well", he said, "he'll have his duck tomorrow afternoon."

"How did you manage it?" we asked.

"I sent an imperative telegram to the Duke of Bedford at Woburn."

Although he was much abroad and had his home in Scotland, Linklater was a regular visitor to the Club which contained so many of his closest friends, Compton Mackenzie, Ralph Richardson and many others. Stephen Potter, in a diary entry for 25 January 1943, reveals something of Linklater's spirit and, perhaps, as much again about himself:

This evening Linklater took me and John Strachey to the shop in St James's for oysters. Phew – sherry at four shillings a glass and nine oysters each at 15 shillings a dozen. What a price! But Link is very much on top of things just now. His play, with Beaton designs, coming on at His Majesty's Theatre with Gielgud; then a Don Quixote Sunday series paid; and above all he is going to Malta with Richardson and Vincent Korda to do a drama-documentary. Now this does arouse thoughts. That, of the three, is the one job I believe I could do as well or better myself. And am I not therefore jealous of Link? I sometimes make myself so, in order to lash myself to greater efforts. But it is almost impossible to make myself personally jealous of Link, because of his modesty, my affection for him, his appreciation of myself.

That appreciation, of course, was warmly shared by the diarist but it was one that was also endorsed by many of his fellow members at the Club, who generally had an appreciative eye for egocentricity so long as it was accompanied by substance and style.

Potter had been elected to the Club in 1937. His impact there was considerable, possibly because of his surpassing skill in his own inventions, the arts of "lifemanship" and "one-upmanship". The manuals in which he had formulated these comic theories had not only provided new usages for the English language but had given their author also a literary prominence and an almost infallible process for exerting superiority over his fellows. *The Times* wrote of him:

Few writers have achieved the distinction of devising a suffix which,

99

though subject to infinite variations, has created an entirely new concept. It was in March, 1931, in a letter to Francis Meynell regarding a forthcoming tennis match against two difficult opponents, that Stephen Potter first used the word Gamesmanship. The suffix did not come into common use, however, until after the war when his dead-pan treatises and his B.B.C. programmes enlarged the concept from the Art of Winning Games Without Actually Cheating to such wider forms as Lifemanship and One-Upmanship. Thereafter it spread throughout the English-speaking world until, in the time of Foster Dulles, it achieved international status in the form of Brinkmanship.

Potter had been proposed for the Club by his uncle "Josh" Reynolds who was an extremely popular member of the Club, not least because he was manager of the newly opened branch of the Royal Bank of Scotland around the corner in Bond Street and had a particular sympathy for the financial problems which seemed to be associated with artistic endeavour. Among Potter's referees was Francis Meynell, the typographer and poet and founder of the Nonesuch Press. Meynell was to play a leading role in Potter's life both as publisher and companion in the budding author's preoccupation with "games-playing" of every kind. Indeed it was reputedly Meynell who pointed out to Potter that his general manner of conducting himself deserved a manual to itself, and so there came about the first of that stupendously successful series: *The Theory and Practice of Gamesmanship; or the Art of Winning Games without acutally Cheating.*

But before this, in 1934, Meynell had commissioned Potter to edit a "compendious" edition of Coleridge which was followed a year later by a "swank" edition of Coleridge's poems selected by Potter. Meynell recalled that as "Nonesuch was at a very low financial ebb" Potter's fee for this was £5.

From the moment he became a member, Potter's social and professional lives seemed to become intertwined with one another at the Savile. He already had many connections there; in 1929 when his first novel *The Young Man* was published, the back of its jacket contained an advertisement for Eric Linklater's *Poet's Pub*, though he was to note later than there was no reciprocal gesture on the back of Linklater's. Potter had also been augmenting his income on a free-lance basis by writing scripts for the B.B.C.'s Schools programmes (then produced by John Pudney, who was later to follow him into the Club). This work was to lead to him joining the staff at the B.B.C. as a writer-producer and during the war he worked there alongside many other Savile members such as Lawrence Gilliam, Val Gielgud, Moray McLaren, Ronald Simpson and J.B. Priestley. As most writers must, Potter had also a vigilant eye for further opportunities to add to his income. Over a round of golf he was offered the editorship of *The Leader*, a short-lived magazine from what was then the leading publishers, Hulton Press. He took the job for a short while and demonstrated that patronage was as pleasant to give as it was to receive. His fellow Savilian, Jack Hargreaves, was already on the staff, as was his biographer, Alan Jenkins, who recalls:

One cannot fail to notice how many members of the Savile Club were contributors. Indeed, there was a rumour among us underlings that the magazine was edited from the Savile where Stephen sat in state ordering articles from anyone in sight.

But it was at the Savile's snooker table that Potter exercised to the full his own mystique. His many exploits there, his practical demonstrations of the arts of lifemanship, gamesmanship and one-upmanship which he had invented and perfected shall be dealt with later in their proper place.

His devotion to the game could however yield some practical and lucrative results beyond the comparatively modest side-bets and "sweeps" which were once a feature of Savile snooker tournaments. During a game with his fellow member, Sir Frederick Hooper, the chairman of Schweppes, for instance, a famous series of advertisements for that firm's ubiquitous set of products was conceived. Based on an imaginary English county called "Schweppesshire" they poked gentle fun at various British institutions and during the fourteen years that Stephen was to write them became something of an institution in themselves, being read as eagerly as some of the editorial features they were supporting. They also contributed in no small measure to the remarkable growth of the firm they were promoting under Hooper's direction. "Schweppservescence" became as much a popular neologism in its day as "lifemanship" and its companions became, but more permanently in theirs.

This immediate post-war period – though drab in most material ways – was an impressively brilliant one in terms of the whole Savile membership – not least among those with a literary background. A glance at the reference books of that time reveals an array of influential and creative contributors to the social and intellectual life of a country struggling to return to normality after nearly six years of debilitating war.

When Stephen Potter proposed for membership that brilliant cartoonist, David Low, for instance, the referees included Richard Church; Howard Marshall (one of the best known broadcasters of the day); Robert Donat; Algernon Blackwood; Raymond Postgate; Stephen Spender; Compton Mackenzie; H.G. Wells; L.A.G. Strong; Ivor Brown, then editor of the *Observer*; Leonard Russell, the distinguished critic; Dallas Bower, fresh from his triumph as co-producer of Olivier's film of *Henry V*; Vyvyan Holland; A.D Peters; and fourteen others of equally distinguished provenance.

It was possibly to the last named of these, A.D. Peters, that the Club owed more than to any other the talented list which came to augment the literary tradition which had been established so early in the Club's history. Augustus Detlof, or "Augustus Dudley" Peters as he preferred to be named, was without doubt the most distinguished literary agent of his day. Friends, of whom there are still many in the Club, will remember him for his upright manner and almost excessive "Britishness" which was founded, perhaps perversely, on distaste for his unwelcome German origins deriving from his birth in Schleswig-Holstein in 1892 which had prevented him from taking the active part he would have wished on the English side in the First World War. From an early age he had been brought up by an aunt in Brighton and his enthusiastic embrace of his country of adoption was expressed in several ways, such as his love for cricket and his sense of "fair play". To indulge the first he had participated in Sir John Squire's "Invalids Team" so famously recorded in A.G. Macdonell's *England their England*; his sense of fair play was put to notably practical use when he put aside his own aspirations as an author to become a literary agent and operate on writers' behalf to secure square deals for them from those who were – even then – regarded as "rapacious" publishers.

He founded his agency in 1928, the same year that he was elected to the Savile. Within months his list of authors included many of the most distinguished writers in the land: Belloc, Blunden, C.S. Forester, Rebecca West and many others. Among them were notable writers who already were or were about to become members of the Savile: Sir John Squire, Cecil Day-Lewis, Alec Waugh and his brother Evelyn, Eric Linklater, and J.B. Priestley, whom he proposed in that *annus mirabilis* 1945.

In that year, also, "Pete" – as he was known to all in the Club – appended his name as referee for the candidacy of two other distinguished novelists who are now woefully neglected, Nigel Balchin and Robert Henriques. It is, perhaps, interesting that the war had so washed away awareness of their normal peace-time pursuits that Nigel Balchin lists his occupation as "Brigadier, General Staff" while Henriques was appearing in the List of Members, perhaps more aptly, as "Colonel Robert Henriques" until the end of his life.

Brian Bliss, who was elected to the Savile in 1944, anticipated Stephen Potter's theories of "one-upmanship" as he recalls in a memoir of Balchin's arrival at the Savile:

> In 1944 I had returned to a job in the War Office in a department which also included Nigel Balchin, who had recently published *The Small Back Room*, his to my mind deservedly best-selling novel about bravery and skulduggery in scientific circles. Shortly after I joined the department Nigel, whether on account of the book or not, was elevated to the post of Deputy Scientific Advisor to the Army Council with the rank of Brigadier. When he awas elected to the Savile in 1945 I was pleased, as a mere Captain on the General Staff, to be able to show off my seniority as a Savilian.

The Small Back Room was later to be made into a much-admired film by two of Balchin's fellow members, Michael Powell and Emeric Pressburger.

Balchin had a powerful physical presence; latterly bearded, dark-haired, and bulky, which combined with more than a touch of shyness to make him rather an intimidating figure to those unable to pierce his daunting carapace. He generally avoided the larger convivial groups in the bar and Sandpit, preferring to attach himself either to someone on his own or the less talkative ones when he would then sit brooding until, with a great show of carrying out a social duty, he would bark out a provoking comment on some remote subject on which, seemingly, he had been deeply pondering. If this produced a satisfactory response he would revert to silence and contented listening: if not, he would wander off in search of better fare.

Colonel Robert David Quixano Henriques, on the other hand, excelled himself in a display of Savilian versatility. He was at various times, and sometimes all at once, a writer, broadcaster, farmer, soldier and politician. His friend Compton Mackenzie thought that he remained an amateur all his life. "I once said to him, 'Robert, you must make up your mind which you want to be considered, a soldier, a novelist, a farmer or an Israeli politician'." But, if he was an amateur, he was an exceptionally gifted one. He had retired as a regular officer in the Royal Artillery before the war to take up farming at Cirencester. While there he wrote *No Arms, No Armour* which was published in 1939 and was very highly praised, but with the outbreak of war he rejoined the army to serve with one of the early commandos and later at Combined Operations H.Q. After the war he returned to farming in the Cotswolds and from a relatively modest base built up an agricultural enterprise, achieving outstanding success as a breeder of cattle. At the same time he was writing his second novel, *Through the Valley*, which was published in 1950 and won the James Tait Black Memorial Prize. This was followed in 1951 with *Red Over Green*. Meantime he had become an ardent Zionist and made frequent trips to Israel, where he acquired a small property, and was actively engaged with the Israeli army during the Suez campaign, about which he wrote a memorable short history, *100 Hours to Suez*. Edgar Duchin recalls being told by Herbert Agar that in 1947 it was Henriques who took the Jewish leader Ben-Gurion to the Club to discuss ways and means by which the British Jewish community could extend practical help to the Hagganah, the legitimate defenders of Israel. Among his more peaceable pursuits Henriques wrote many other works including two biographies and another novel set in the Cotswolds, *A Stranger Here*. He also broadcast regularly, appearing on such programmes as "Any Questions" and other television current affairs programmes. Nevertheless, many members such as Tyrrell Burgess were wont to express uneasiness about the prospects for peace in the Middle East whenever they caught sight of Henriques in earnest conversation with a guest of Levantine appearance in the dinning-room or bar.

Compton Mackenzie recalls that after what he called "The Suez mess" he was in the Sandpit with "...Colonel Robert Henriques, R.A., M.B.E., arguing with Lieutenant-Commander David Keir, M.B.E, whether the War Office or the Admiralty were more to blame over Suez. John Moore comes into the Savile Sandpit; soldier and sailor both appeal to him as an airman for a neutral opinion.

'Well,' says John Moore, 'I think the War Office and the Admiralty made an equal mess.' "

Only a compulsive and indefatigable diarist – as Monty Mackenzie was – would have found this exchange worth recording for, sadly, this is not a particularly bright example of the more sparkling remarks which made Moore stand out even in the vintage years of Savile wit and repartee. Peter Green's recollection of him as "a superb anecdotalist" and his exchanges with J.B. Priestley concerning his "bloody birdwatcher" are, perhaps, more typical. Like Henriques, Moore was also a novelist and writer on the countryside as well as a broadcaster and playwright. He became established as a novelist with *Portrait of Elmbury* which was followed by another well-received book, *Brensham Village.* His last published novel, which took him three and a half years to write, *The Waters Under the Earth,* was translated into seven languages. Among his plays were *The White Sparrow* and *The Elizabethans* and he also wrote books on angling and scripts for radio and television. During the war he served with distinction in the Fleet Air Arm – hence Monty Mackenzie's appeal to him for a verdict on Suez – and this experience featured in two subsequent novels. He also wrote a short history of the service in which his fellow Savilian, Ralph Richardson, had been an active, if sometimes hair-raising, fellow officer. In 1949 he helped inaugurate the Cheltenham Festival of Literature as a companion event to the recently well-established Festival of Music there, and he remained chairman of the Festival Committee until 1956, when he was joined as co-director by Robert Henriques. Amongst all these activities he managed to include the chairmanship of the Society of Authors from 1956-7.

Henriques and Moore are an interesting example of how many members found their careers and social lives overlapping for reasons not necessarily connected with their common membership of the Club. Another was Moray McLaren, who shared with them both an intimacy with Sir Compton Mackenzie. McLaren's connections with the Savile were being laid even before his election in 1928. A native of Edinburgh, he had come to London in the twenties to work as assistant editor to Jack Squire on the *London Mercury.* Later he was one of the staff which David Cleghorn-Thomson gathered around him when he was appointed the first Regional Director of the Scottish B.B.C. From there he was transferred to London as assistant director of talks and assistant editor of *The Listener.* During this period he travelled a great deal and indulged his particular ambition to write by producing *A Wayfarer in Poland* and *The Noblest Prospect* under the pseudonym "Michael Murray". When war broke out his experiences abroad led to his attachment to the Foreign Office as head of the Polish Region Political Intelligence Department. Afterwards he was able to return to Edinburgh and take up writing as a full-time occupation. Many of his books were devoted to studies of his native land such as *Stern and Wild* and a Pelican edition entitled *The Scots*; and like many other Savilians before him he was also seduced into writing a treatise on Robert Louis Stevenson, *Stevenson and Edinburgh.* He wrote several plays, one of which, *Heather on Fire,* won the Foyle New Play Award for 1955. "Seduced", in a less romantic connotation, is probably the correct word to describe the manner in which McLaren was persuaded by Alan Keen – the rogue librarian who had crept into the Club during the war to the eternal disadvantage of the Monument – to embark on a protracted study of Hall's *Chronicles.* Keen had discovered an annotated copy of this Shakespeare source book and wished McLaren to use his scholarship to establish its original owner as Shakespeare himself. The outcome of this bizarre quest is shrouded in mystery like many other of Keen's activities, but the thesis which he wished McLaren to make respectable was almost certainly as spurious as his own disastrous stewardship of the Savile Monument.

A fellow member at the time who might have been consulted but was not, presumably because he was so better equipped to give Keen short shrift, was Noel Blakiston, O.B.E., who spent all of his career after leaving Cambridge at the Public Record Office until his retirement as principal assistant keeper in 1970. Blakiston had won a scholarship to Eton in 1918 and became a leading figure of his generation there in the company of such luminaries as George Orwell, Steven Runciman and Cyril Connolly. As a powerful student cricketer he once distinguished himself by hitting the ball out of the ground and down the chimney of the pavilion. On another occasion he was approached on the cricket field by the young George Orwell, who evinced signs of things to come by announcing:

> "I am collecting the religions of the new boys.
> Are you Cyrenaic, Sceptic, Epicurean, Cynic, Neoplatonist, Confucian or Zoroastrian?"
> "I'm a Christian," replied Blakiston.
> "Oh," said Orwell, "we haven't had that before."

Cyril Connolly's lifelong friendship with Blakiston is recorded in the collection of letters *A Romantic Friendship* published in 1975. Eton was also to have cause to be grateful to Blakiston when he undertook the cataloguing of the archives of the College estates – more than 10,000 documents from the Middle Ages to the nineteenth century – and they recognized it by making him the first honorary fellow of the College to be appointed for more than three hundred years.

But it was for his work at the Public Record Office and his outstanding scholarship in his specialist subject, the Italian Risorgimento, that Blakiston was most renowned. His work of historical research, *The Roman Question,* has several times been reprinted and is the leading source book for this labyrinthine period of Papal history. He was as popular a figure and as equally at home in scholarly circles in Italy as he was at the Savile. In Italy he wrote and lectured in Italian, was elected fellow of the Institute for the History of the Risorgimento and was made Cavaliere dell' Ordine del Merito by the Italian Government; at home in England he managed somehow to find time from all his other activities to produce several volumes of short stories, serve on the Savile committee, and enliven the Sandpit and the long table with his wit and erudition. His characteristic panache is well remembered by some surviving members, particularly the tale of how, shortly after the outbreak of war, he set off for the country in his battered Morris 8 bearing in the boot the Domesday Book lest it should fall into the hands of the Germans, who it seemed to him were likely to invade at any moment.

A fellow member and researcher, but of a different kind, was that great lexicographer, Eric Partridge. The reference section of the Club's Monument has reason to be grateful to Philip Wilson, Stephen Potter, and several other Savilians who in 1950 coaxed him out of his "study" – seat K.I. in the British Museum Reading Room which he occupied almost as of right for more than forty years – to persuade him into membership of the Savile. That the shelves in the morning-room and the library do not bend under the number of volumes of his work which reside there as a result is perhaps as much a tribute to the lightness of manner in which he was able to wear his weightly scholarship as to the skill of the carpenter who constructed them. Among this considerable corpus are his *Dictionary of Slang and Unconventional English, Shakespeare's Bawdy,* and a work which should perhaps be on display in the public rooms of the Club as a conversational *memento mori* for members old and new, *A Dictionary of Clichés.* He also wrote works on more conventional English, and titles such as *English for Human Beings* well reflect his refreshing and accessible approach to a subject which is so often treated as dull and remote. For all this he was recognized throughout the English-speaking world as the foremost living scholar of the language; the American critic Edmund Wilson called him the "word-king". Despite the long hours of scholarly retirement and his frail and diffident appearance, Partridge was neither diffident nor retiring whenever he emerged from his labours. In the First World War he had served with the Australians in Gallipoli and Flanders; in the second he served in the R.A.F, from which experience he emerged almost inevitably with the text of *A Dictionary of R.A.F. Slang.* Likewise, if a new book was about to be published whose subject appealed to him, literary editors at the Savile and elsewhere were likely to be assailed with the forceful pronouncement: "I am the right person to review this book." Rarely did they feel able to refuse.

Food and drink have always been regarded as useful concomitants to companionship, good conversation and even, occasionally, to the more relaxed enjoyment of the higher regions of scholarship, all of which are intended to be part and parcel of life at the Savile. No recent member of the Club could be said to have assembled the knowledge and application of all these ingredients so effectively to his own use as Raymond Postgate, who was elected in 1935. For good measure he also exemplified the not uncommon political gymnastics of his kind in the 'thirties by managing to reconcile such élitist pursuits as quite intellectually compatible – if not, indeed, conducive – to his left-wing and egalitarian views.

Postgate was a considerable scholar who had published translations of the *Pervigilium Veneris* and the *Agammemnon* of Aeschylus, though this Scholar of St John's at Oxford had never taken his degree, having been sent down in 1915 after being jailed for his conscientious objection to serving in the armed forces. While still at school Postgate had become an ardent Marxian Socialist, possibly in reaction to his extremely right-wing Conservative father, and the resultant breach was widened when in 1918 he married Daisy Lansbury, the daughter of the future leader of the Labour Party.

Between the wars Postgate supported himself by writing for a variety of left-wing journals and as a departmental editor of the *Encyclopaedia Britannica;* he published studies of radicals such as Wilkes and Robert Emmet and, with his brother-in-law G.D.H. Cole, a *History of the Common People,* which was for many years a best-seller. He also wrote three detective novels, one of which, *The Verdict of Twelve*, had a considerable success.

But it was as founder and first editor of the *Good Food Guide* that Postgate is perhaps best remembered not only in the outside world but within the Savile. Even in the straitened circumstances of his early days in journalism he had refined an appetite for food and wine and in what would have seemed to anyone else the unpropitious post-war years of austerity he capitalized on these interests to launch the *Guide*. Recognition came slowly but eventually it became the most influential work of its kind not only in this country but abroad. In the mid-'fifties the vintners of St-Emilion conferred upon him the title of Grand Chancelier d'Ambassade pour la Grande-Bretagne and by 1962 the enterprise had become so large that Postgate was persuaded to merge it with the activities of the Consumers' Association, though he continued as editor until 1968.

In the early days of the *Guide*, Michael Meyer was one of the unpaid "Inspectors" whom Postgate employed to visit restaurants anonymously and report fearlessly on their findings. Apart from time off for the occasional bout of food poisoning, Michael soon found himself fully occupied in the writing and production of the *Guide*, which then boasted only two other staff members – Postgate and his wife Daisy. In his memoirs, Michael remembers him with affection:

> Raymond Postgate was an infinitely rewarding man, and to work with him daily was a liberal education. He was, I should think, unique among British authors of his generation in having had one of his books praised by Lenin. Soon after the Russian revolution, H.G. Wells, a close friend of Raymond, visited Lenin, who mentioned approvingly a pamphlet which Raymond had published in 1918 when he was only twenty-two, *The International During the War*. Wells asked Lenin if he would sign a photograph of himself for Raymond, which Lenin did, and this stood proudly framed on Raymond's desk. Unfortunately, Lenin had signed at the bottom of the photograph across his dark jacket – and perhaps the ink in Russia then was of poor quality – so that no inscription was detectable; if you looked hard, you might persuade yourself that something was there. But of course one did not dare to mention this, and no doubt Raymond, whose eyesight was not very sharp, was unaware of the deterioration.

Having established himself as such an authority on food and wine it was inevitable that Postgate should have been asked to serve on the Savile's wine committee and though his opinions did not always prevail, the cellars were certainly improved by his eclectic taste. Food, however, was beyond his control but luckily for the chef at the Savile at that time Postgate's earlier rather explosive temperament had mellowed and his appearances at the long table are remembered more for the wit and elegance of his conversation than for the death sentences he might well have pronounced on some of the dishes which appeared before the members in those less than Lucullan years.

Postgate's translations of the classics are a reminder that the Savile has harboured a number of notable practitioners in this notoriously difficult art. Charles Scott Moncrieff, the great translator of Proust, was elected in 1920. Sir Harold Acton remembers him as "garrulous" and if his sentences were as lengthy and convoluted as the master he had rendered into English he must have been a formidable companion in the Sandpit.

One of the most prestigious literary prizes in the field of translation however is now named after Scott Moncrieff and a runner-up for it just before he died in 1965 was a greatly esteemed member of the Savile, Humphrey Hare. There were many who felt that he should in fact have won it, for among scholars and critics he had gained a reputation as one of the very best translators of French literature into English. In the fifteen years before he died of cancer at the early age of fifty-six, he translated almost fifty books, including those of his great friend and fellow member – "immortal" also as a member of the French Academy – Maurice Druon. But Humphrey Hare had packed a great deal more than translation into his short life. He had written a life of Swinburne, whose poems he had also collected and edited and was a director of the publishers Barrie and Rockcliffe. He had travelled widely and during the Spanish Civil War was one of the very few Englishmen to enlist in the ranks of the Republican Army rather than join in the more politically and socially fashionable International Brigade. Again one is forced to wonder how the consequences of the Savile's principle of electing "men of different professions and opinions" can be carried off so peaceably, for in his case a notorious fellow member in his time was Major Hugh Bertie Campbell Pollard, of whom Raymond Postgate once remarked that "he had not merely flown General Franco from his base in the Canaries to take control of the Fascist cause but actually *boasted* of having done so".

When the Second World War broke out, Hare graduated to the Welsh Guards, was mentioned in dispatches, became A.D.C. to General Templer and served with him in the Anzio beach-head. Finally on a Special Service assignment he was infiltrated into one of his favourite stamping-grounds, the French Riviera, to use his local knowledge and help prepare the way for the forthcoming Allied invasion.

Hare is still well remembered by his surviving friends at the Club for his wit and individuality, while newer members can get some inkling of his distinguished but slightly sardonic appearance from the bust which stands by the doors of the morning-room at the bottom of the ballroom stairs. It is by Madge Bonham-Carter and was presented to the Club by his brother-in-law, George Astley. Hare lived always as a wealthy man of taste would wish although he was not sufficiently well-endowed to do so without the extra income which derived from his own considerable industry. When his house in Berkeley Square was about to be sold to a property developer, Edgar Duchin remembers being one of a party gathered up from the Savile to attend his grand "pre-demolition party". Maurice Druon writes from Paris, shorn of his erstwhile translator, so in his own inimitable English:

Humphrey Hare, whose memory, and bust, remain for ever in the Savile where lived and died, with an extraordinary dignity, this former officer of Guards and remarguable translator of French books – for my own benefit – a bachelor of elegance in all ways, and a smiling stoician.

Stoic, Hare certainly was, and during the last phases of his distressing illness he refused to bow to the inevitable and earned the admiration of everyone at the Club for the gallantry with which he continued to invest it with his own particular brand of wit and humour. As has been noted, C.P. Snow was moved to record this in *Last Things*.

Individual as he was, Humphrey Hare was by no means unique at the Savile in his time for the wit, elegance and talent which he seemed so casually able to display. Roger Senhouse, who was elected three years after him in 1943, was a publisher, editor, translator, and raconteur of a brilliance quite equal to Hare's but of sufficiently different kind to prevent any feeling of *embarras de richesse* in those members who had the pleasure of knowing them both. Senhouse was one of the last autumnal buds from the Bloomsbury tree. Much has been made of Lytton Strachey's early infatuation for him though even as a youth Senhouse was already too much his own man to respond to what must have been despairing blandishments from this exotic former member of the Club. Nevertheless, he had the good sense to digest the best that Bloomsbury had had to offer and he soon established himself as an editor of exceptional quality. In 1936 he was the co-founder of Secker and Warburg, where he devoted his wide knowledge of European literature to introducing such authors as Alberto Moravia, Colette and André Gide to English-speaking readers, many of whose books he himself translated. It would be interesting to know, by the way, whether Senhouse or any of his contemporaries were aware that André Gide had been granted honorary membership of the Club on a temporary basis in 1912, having been proposed for it by Edmund Gosse. The *frisson* it might cause now in this more liberal age must be nothing compared with that which it must have caused then.

A French scholar and translator of equal excellence but perhaps of more academic bent was Dr Robert Baldick, who was elected in 1966, too late to share the long table with Humphrey Hare but with just time enough to share a mutual scholarly interest for a year or two with Roger Senhouse before his own untimely death at the age of forty-four in 1972. As a student at Oxford, Baldick had come under the influence of that maverick genius, Enid – sister of an earlier member, Sir Walter – Starkie, whose wonderful Irish madness was strait-jacketed by a rigid and exact scholarship. Under her tutelage he earned his doctorate with a thesis on Huysmans, the author of that "poisonous book", *A Rebours*, which "in yellow covers" was one of the establishing features of decadence in Oscar Wilde's *Picture of Dorian Gray*. With his doctorate safely in his pocket, Baldick took himself and his thesis to Paris for further research, from which he produced a book which transformed scholarly appreciation of this previously legendary figure. In 1958 he was made a Fellow of Pembroke College, Oxford and its Tutor in French. From then on a stream of important books on French literature flowed from his pen and these included a series of excellent translations of such authors as Flaubert, Sartre, Verne, Camus and many other modern French authors. He was editor of the Oxford Library of French Classics from 1962-7 and from 1964 joint editor of Penguin Classics. He was also translator of several French theatrical productions for the English stage, most notably Jean-Louis Barrault's *Rabelais*, in London in 1971.

But like Hare and Senhouse before him, Baldick did not allow his drier academic pursuits to sap his zest for social life. He shared Postgate's love and knowledge of fine wine and was a member of the Winegrowers of Châteauneuf du Pape. Prominent among the many pleasures of life which Baldick so vigorously proclaimed was his membership of the Savile and in *The Times* obituary he was described as "the best possible dining companion, a brilliant raconteur and at the same time a good listener to others".

As joint editor of Penguin Classics, Baldick would have had a hand in the publication of that inspired translation of *Li Po and Tu Fu* of which *The Times* remarked: "few translations from Chinese are more lyrical, or so richly sensitive to rhythm and to the images and associations inherent in the script." Sadly, Baldick died just before it appeared for it was the product of his good friend, fellow member and equally engaging dining companion, Arthur Cooper.

Arthur was a brilliant linguist who taught himself Icelandic while still a schoolboy and then went on to study at the University of Stockholm. From there he entered the British Government Codes and Cypher School, where he learnt Japanese, and spent part of the war in the Far East before embarking on a long career as a cryptologist and language expert which included a six years' spell in Australia and fifteen years at G.C.H.Q. From 1953 until his death in 1988 Arthur was working on his magnum opus: *Heart and Mind: Ancient Language-Making as Recorded in the Chinese Script*. He was of Anglo-Irish stock and though, unlike most of that class of settlers of the "Ascendancy", he became fluent in Irish Gaelic, he was typical of the best kind of the breed in his courteous articulacy and gentle brand of wit. To a fellow member who was preparing a book on the Anglo-Irish he contributed some wonderful reminiscences of his Irish forebears, who included Yeats' formidable patroness, Lady Gregory, and the tale of how one summer afternoon in Ireland in the mid-'twenties when he was sitting taking tea with an aunt, a light aeroplane (piloted no doubt by someone under the influence of Yeats' poem "An Irish Airman Foresees His Death") crash-landed on the lawn beside them. The aunt, who was rather conscious of her class and not notable for hospitality to strangers, immediately invited the shaken aviator into her drawing room for a glass of whiskey to steady his nerves. When Arthur later expressed some surprise she replied: "If he can fly one of those machines at all, he must be an *educated gentleman.*" It was his delight in such eccentric notions as well as his genial approach to scholarship which made him such a valued companion in the Club, though his versatility could cause confusion. Sir Arthur Vick tells the story of how Arthur was travelling by Tube one day to the Savile when he heard two men nearby talking about him in Icelandic: "Look at that man, he is reading Chinese, but he does not look Chinese, does he?" One of the men got off at the next stop and Arthur said to the other in Icelandic; "I am sorry to disappoint you, but the book I am reading is in Japanese not Chinese, and anyway I am Irish."

Reminiscing on the characters of various friends encountered at the Savile bar, Patric Dickinson recalls sitting there one morning with "the brilliant classical scholar, poet and novelist", Rex Warner. "We were alone there (rather early) when a young man hovered in the doorway. After a bit Rex looked up and said 'Why, I think that's one of my sons' and into that line he put a kind of genuine pleasure, bewilderment and dismay which was enchanting. He was such a good writer and always laughing..."

Rex Warner was also a translator of consummate skill who further distinguished himself as a dramatist, critic, essayist and academic. Elected to the Savile in 1952, his range across the classics was phenomenal: in addition to his many books on ancient Greece he made elegant English texts from the works of Euripides, Aeschylus, Xenophon and Thucydides: negotiating the bridge between the Greek and Roman civilizations he went on to translate Plutarch as *The Fall of the Roman Republic*, which was followed by Caesar's *War Commentaries* and the *Confessions* of St Augustine. In his younger days he published a volume of poems and three novels of which the best known are *The Professor* and *The Aerodrome*, which was televised in 1983. A popular but unobtrusive member of the Club, he spent the years 1964-74 as professor at the University of Connecticut and for his services to Greek literature he was made a Commander of the Royal Order of the Phoenix by the Greek Government.

The Club's complement of classical scholars continues in the present generation with Christopher Stace, who is senior classics master at Bradfield College, where he has directed a number of their famous triennial Greek plays. A reviewer and broadcaster, he has published translations of Sophocles and Plautus which have been performed on television and the stage. Most recently he has published a stylish account of his twenty years' love affair with *Florence: City of the Lily*.

One of the great Club characters was Richard Graves, C.B.E., who was elected in 1915. Graves was the half-brother of the poet and novelist, Robert Graves, and was in his own right a distinguished Orientalist and translator of many works of German literature into English. These included the well known *Seven Years in Tibet* by Heinrich Harrer and several novels of Heinrich Böll. His extraordinary concatenation of careers included a dangerous period as Mayor of Jerusalem during the height of the conflict between Arabs and Jews in 1947-8. His immaculate appearance and dignified air, leavened with a measure of the family panache, gave rise to the sobriquet "Graves Supérieur" by which he was universally known, and he is well remembered at the Club for the cut and dash of his conversation during some of the more memorable Sandpit colloquies.

Among other members who have made their mark in literature as translators are Norman Denny, who among other projects was responsible for rendering into English the prodigious output of Georges Simenon; George Bull, who has made

111

distinguished translations of Aretino and Ariosto as well as producing a widely admired history of Venice and a best-selling biography of Machiavelli; and, of course, Michael Meyer, whose translations of Ibsen and Strindberg have distinguished the British theatre for the last thirty-five years.

According to his own account Michael Meyer's career began when, as a student at Oxford, he asked Caspar Wrede – also a contemporary member of the Savile – to direct his first play, *The Ortolan*, for O.U.D.S. In the cast, incidentally, was a talented nineteen-year-old called Margaret Smith, now perhaps better known as Maggie of the same name. After Oxford, Wrede asked Meyer to do a translation of *The Lady from the Sea* for T.V. and so began a career of translating both these Scandinavian authors, culminating in definitive biographies which have brought him recognition as this country's leading authority on their lives and work. More recently he has produced an idiosyncratic autobiography, *Not Prince Hamlet*, which throws an occasionally merciless, often amusing, but always interesting spotlight on the many famous or infamous people he has met during a long and unusual career.

Meyer's biographies of Ibsen and Strindberg are a reminder that the Savile has in every generation since the earliest days of Gosse and Morley enjoyed the membership of a considerable proportion of the leading practitioners in that art. The present generation is no exception and there are at least five members who have produced notable biographies in recent years, as we shall see.

* * * *

Setting down the literary history of the Savile is an invigorating business because of the robust variety of talent it contains and the vast body of considerable achievement it encompasses. But in contemplating the history of any institution, a contemporary is always likely to ask, "Is it now the same as it was in the good old days? Are we romanticizing a golden past to disguise a pinchbeck present? Should we not cry with the prophet Samuel, 'Ichabod'?"

The short answer to the last question must be, "No, the glory has *not* departed," but adducing evidence to deny such pessimistic questions summons up three perils for the historian; first, that it would be invidious – if not positively dangerous – to attempt to evaluate in print the work of contemporaries with whom he may shortly be spending an evening at the long table; secondly, to fail to do so might cause the casual reader to suspect that, despite all protests to the contrary, the glory *has* departed; and thirdly, an impartial recital must inevitably result in a mere catalogue of names rather than a proper historical record.

However, this celebration of the Savile could not be complete without at least a cursory glance at the contemporary membership list to reassure any doubting enquirer that the Club's literary tradition is in no danger of extinction. Out of a current membership of some 900 there are more than 60 authors, many of them household names and one current Nobel-prizewinner for literature, William Golding. This number, of course, does not include those many other members – scientists, academics and professionals of all kinds – who have contributed to the specialist literature of their own particular subject. They shall appear elsewhere. Nor is it possible here to enumerate every current member who has produced a literary work and, as a salve against the possibility of any bruised egos, those that are listed shall appear in more-or-less alphabetical order.

Nearly first in this system – only preceded by the stately Sir Harold Action – is Eric Ambler, who would surely be first on any comparable list compiled by dovotees of the intelligent, well-written modern "thriller", a genre which it could truly be said he invented and which his delighted readers have converted into a cult. Even his fellow practitioners bowed to his superiority when, in 1986, the CrimeWriters' Association, already used to awarding an annual "Gold" and "Silver Dagger" for works of outstanding merit, found it necessary in his case to institute a new category of excellence in the form of a special "Diamond Dagger" designed by Cartier. All the more impressive then that one of his fellow toilers in the killing fields whom he most admired is John le Carré, who from 1966-71 was to be found tucked away in the Savile's membership list under his real name of David John Moore Cornwell.

Cyril Barrett has the distinction of being the only Savile member who can append the initials S.J. after his name. An earlier member of the Society of Jesus was in fact elected but when the news came through to his Superior – a true descendant of St Ignatius Loyola – it was decreed that the Savile was not fertile missionary territory and he was ordered to resign at once. Luckily times have changed and the Club has now the pleasure of savouring at the long table and in the Sandpit the finely honed pronouncements of a distinguished Catholic theologian, professor of philosophy at Warwick University, and author of major works on Wittgenstein, and books and essays on Aesthetics, Ethics and religious beliefs.

In the same field, but perhaps standing in another corner of it, is Bryan Magee, who is known to a much wider public as a former Labour M.P. (from 1974 to 1982) and as broadcaster on radio and television on philosophical subjects. Notable among these have been his *Conversations with Philosophers* on Radio 3 in 1970-71; *Men of Ideas* on B.B.C.2 in 1978, and *the Great Philosophers* in 1987. He has lectured in Philosophy at Balliol and Harvard and was a visiting Fellow at All Souls in 1973-4. Maintaining the Savile's tradition of polymathy, he has published volumes of poetry, travel and one novel while among his several works on philosophy are studies of Popper and Schopenhauer. His *Aspects of Wagner* was much admired by devotees and so persuasively written as even to give the unconverted pause to reconsider.

Michael Bloch was elected to the Club in 1987, just ten years after the Duke and Duchess of Windsor's formidable lawayer, Maîitre Suzanne Blum, invited the then twenty-four-year-old to put their archives into historical perspective and produce a book which would set out their side of the now almost legendary *cause*

113

célèbre resulting from the Abdication. The book led to another and the score is now five elegantly argued and highly controversial volumes.

Vincent Brome's most recent publication at the time of writing is the monumental official biography of his former fellow member, J.B. Priestley. Brome has tilled nearly every furrow of the literary vineyard: as a journalist, critic, novelist, dramatist, and biographer. He invests his writing, his learning and his conversation with the proceeds of a continuing preoccupation with psychology – perhaps most notably in his biographies; *Jung, Man and Myth*; *Ernest Jones, Freud's Alter Ego*; and *Freud and his Disciples*.

Among Brome's fellow biographers at the Savile are Richard Huggett and Professor Norman Sherry. Huggett's picaresque career has been spent in the world of the theatre and television, where he has appeared on occasion in such memorable serials as *Doctor Finlay's Casebook* (which is perhaps best remembered at Brook Street for the accomplished performances of "Doctor Finlay" himself, the late and much mourned member, Bill Simpson). But apart from his several works as an actor and playwright, both of which he has combined in his one-man show *A Talent to Abuse*, in which he conjured an uncannily accurate reincarnation of his monstrous – if short-stayed – predecessor at the Savile, Evelyn Waugh, Huggett's recent foray into biography, *Binkie Beaumont; Eminence Grise of the West End Theatre*, won the Roger Machell prize for the best book on the performing arts in 1989.

Professor Norman Sherry, elected in 1974, has held many academic posts in the United Kingdom and abroad. A Fellow of the Royal Society of Literature, he is presently Mitchell Distinguished Professor of Literature, Trinity University, San Antonio, Texas. He has published many studies in English literature including works on Conrad, Jane Austen and Charlotte and Emily Brontë. In 1989 there appeared the first volume of his exhaustive *Life of Graham Greene* covering the years 1904-1939 which promises, when it has been completed, to stand for some time as the definitive account of one of our most outstanding English authors.

Maurice Druon's love in general for all things English and for the Savile Club in particular has already been remarked. It seems almost an impertinence to include him in any set of thumb-nail sketches of contemporary members intended to bring this chapter on Savile literary history to a chronological close, for no brief account could possibly do justice to his daunting achievements in the literary, academic and political fields. However, if only for symmetry, some attempt must be made. In England he is an honorary Commander of the British Empire; in France a Commandeur de la Légion d'Honneur and Commandeur des Arts et Lettres. In 1966 he was elected a member of the Académie Française. In 1973-4 he was Minister for Cultural Affairs, from 1978-81 a member of the French Parlement. During those years he was also a member of the Assembly of the Council of Europe and a member of the European Parliament in 1979-80. No wonder that the French journalist, Philippe Bouvard, writing a profile in 1986 when Druon was appointed lifetime secretary to the Académie Française, had to wrestle heroically with the problems of how to address him now that he was so full of distinctions:

That – in free translation – "curator of the French heritage", would probably be
an acceptable title to most of his many friends at the Savile. To list his many other
international honours is not possible here; the curious will find them catalogued in
the small print which, nevertheless, takes up ten lines of *Who's Who*.

At the Savile, Druon is perhaps best known for his literary work and the
memory of his remarkable collaboration with his translator Humphrey Hare. In
1948 Druon won the prix Goncourt for his novel *Les Grandes Familles* but perhaps
the best known of all his many works in England is *Les Rois Maudits* (The Accursed
Kings) written in six volumes between 1955 and 1960. Again, all the fruits of his
industry are too weighty to be listed here and a visit to the Monument is
recommended to see them in all their considerable glory. The complete works for
1973-9 alone consist of twenty-five volumes so it will be well understood that the
product of a literary life which has now extended over more than forty-six would
require a chapter to itself.

Since its early days the Savile has had as members historians of various and
individual voices such as John Morley, H.A.L. Fisher and H.G. Wells. The
present membership possesses equal variety and individuality in that craft. Lord
Dacre of Glanton, perhaps better known as Hugh Trevor-Roper, was elected to the
Savile in 1941. He was Regius Professor of Modern History and Fellow of Oriel
College, Oxford, from 1957 to 1980 and in that year moved to Cambridge where
he was Master of Peterhouse until 1987. His important contributions to historical
scholarship are well known and cover a wide range of British and European
religious, political and social affairs from the reformation to the present day.

Professor Michael Foot was elected to the Club in 1966. Having served with
distinction as a parachutist with the Royal Artillery during the war, for which he
was awarded the Croix de Guerre, Foot returned to academic life, lecturing first at
Oxford and later taking the chair of modern history at Manchester University.
Although his many publications include works on Gladstone and British foreign
policy in the early twentieth century, he is particularly associated with detailed
studies of military intelligence services, in particular the French resistance and the
Special Operations Executive during the Second World War.

Norman Stone, the Professor of Modern History and Fellow of Worcester
College, Oxford, since 1984, has been a member of the Savile since 1976.

This Norman Stone: is he a man or a consortium? asked *The Guardian*
recently. How, it wondered, could the professor of modern history at
Oxford University fill the centre pages of both *Mail* and *Telegraph* on the
same day (about Gorbachev) and the centre of *The Guardian* the next (on
empire), of the *Telegraph* two days later (on Wrens) and of *The Sunday Times*

books pages on Sunday? Clearly "Norman Stone" must be a pseudonym for a posse of clever young men, not one lone Scotsman at an ancient typewriter in suburban Oxford.

The occasion for this effusion in *The Sunday Times* of 15 April 1990 was the professor's appointment as that paper's senior columnist in addition to all his other activities, which had only been partially explored in that opening paragraph. A distinguished European historian and linguist – he is fluent in eight languages including Russian – he is also well known as a television commentator putting current affairs into historical perspective. Apart from his journalism and his articles in learned journals, his publications include *The Eastern Front 1914-1917*, which won the Wolfson Prize for History in 1976; and *Europe Transformed 1878-1919*, part of the *Fontana History of Europe*, which has been described as a masterpiece. He is currently writing the *Penguin History of the 20th Century* and another book on the communist take-over of central Europe.

Martyn Goff, O.B.E., was elected to the Club in 1969. He is chief executive of the Book Trust, formerly director of the National Book League of which, earlier in the century, his predecessor at the Savile, Hugh Walpole, was the first chairman. Goff's literary career has been split equally between arts administration and creative work on his own account. He has served as a member of the Arts Council Literature Panel, The New Fiction Society and many other similar associations, including the Society of Bookmen, which, again since the days of Hugh Walpole who was also its first chairman, has had close ties with the Savile. Goff's publications include several works of non-fiction and nine novels. He was appointed O.B.E. in 1977 for his services to literature.

One, perhaps the only, Savile author who would not have had an unkind word for his publisher is Michael Estorick, who was a shareholder in Duckworth's, when they published his novels *Can't Buy Me Love* and *What are Friends For?*

Sir William Golding was elected to the Savile in 1958, four years after he had made his sensational début into twentieth-century literature with *Lord of the Flies*. Such powerful beginnings usually presage a period of doldrums wherein the author must desperately attempt to out-write the auguries of critics defying him to sustain his original performance. In Golding's case this seemed not to be a problem; eleven novels, two books of essays, one play and a book of travel have followed, all of them to critical acclaim and retaining the considerable popular appeal of the original. Public recognition and academic honours have also accrued in bountiful measure to this most multi-layered of writers who describes himself simply as "a story-teller". He was elected a Fellow of the Royal Society of Literature in 1955; had the C.B.E. conferred in 1966; was made a Companion of Literature in 1984 and knighted in 1988. His novel *Darkness Visible*, published in 1979, received the James Tait Black Memorial Prize; *Rites of Passage* won the Booker McConnell Prize in 1980 and in 1983 he became the seventeenth Savile member to be a Nobel Laureate when he received the award for Literature. This "simple story-teller" is also an Honorary Fellow of Brasenose College, Oxford; an Honorary Doctor of Literature at the Universities of Sussex, Kent, Warwick, Oxford and the Sorbonne; he is also an Honorary Doctor of Laws at Bristol.

Another self-styled "simple story-teller" is Winston Graham, whose modesty and distaste for the trappings of fame (except at the Savile snooker table) is in inverse proportion to the enthusiasm of critics and readers alike for the mastery and versatility of his writing. The evidence is less modest than the author for his works have been filmed, televised, and translated into seventeen languages, and in the United States, eight of his books have been major book-club choices. Unlike most of those visitors to the Savile whose style has led to the suggestion that they might care to join it, Winston was at first most reluctant to do so:

> I first saw the Savile in 1946, when I was brought in by my dear friend, Peter Latham, whom I had met during the war and who had ideas of putting me up for membership. I rejected this. I lived in the depths of Cornwall and was the most unclubbable of men. (Or so I thought.) Benno Moiseiwitsch, the pianist, with whom I was also very friendly at this time, wanted to put me up for the Savage. When I told him I might try for the Savile he said: "Oh, that's a snob's club." He could hardly have been more wrong (unless one includes intellectual snobbery, of which there was a reasonable but not unreasonable amount.) In 1950, I was in London about a film being made from one of my books. The producer was Hugh Stewart, who became an equally dear friend, and he suggested that I might fancy belonging to "the only good club in London". Having become more receptive to the idea, I agreed that he should go into cahoots with Peter Latham, and the deed was done.

Of Hugh Stewart, more anon; the film under discussion, however, was *Night Without Stars*, which in the event was directed by another Savile member, Tony Pelissier, who had been until then unknown to Winston except by reputation. Such coincidence – or, as the Jungians would have it, "synchronicity" – persisted in two other film works of Winston Graham. In 1946 he had written the original of *Take My Life* as a film script and the director of it, appointed by the producers, was Ronald Neame, who was to be elected a member of the Club six years later in 1952 and, despite his long residence in California, retains his membership to the present day. The famous post-war partnership of Frank Launder and Sidney Gilliat – both Savilians – produced and directed *Fortune is a Woman* in 1956 from a Winston Graham novel written in 1953. That there was no element of Club nepotism in all this is demonstrated by the three other films which ensued: *Sleeping Partner*, *The Walking Stick*, and, of course, that *tour de force* of suspense, *Marnie*, directed by Alfred Hitchcock in 1963.

Like his fellow member V.S. Pritchett, Winston Graham has subsisted throughout all his working life from the products of his pen. The exact number of his works is difficult to determine, for some of his early novels are, by his own command to the publishers, "designedly out of print". Nearly all of the others, however, which have appeared at approximately annual intervals since the early 'forties, are in print and constant re-print. They cover a wide range from historical novels such as *The Grove of Eagles* (a Book Society Choice) set in the period of the Spanish Armada, to novels of mystery and suspense like *Marnie* and others on contemporary themes such as *Angel, Pearl and Little God*. There have been collections of short stories and a most remarkable and scholarly exploration of hitherto little-known aspects of a crucial period in Tudor history, *The Spanish Armadas*, published in 1972. Indeed, the meticulous research so lightly revealed in many of his works has led some of his readers to wonder whether a first class historian has not been lost to the world of fiction. His sequence of "Poldark" novels captured an immense readership from the first appearance of *Ross Poldark* in 1945. In 1975-6 the B.B.C. televised a series dramatized from the first four of these novels and this proved to be so popular that a second series consisting of the next three novels was screened in 1977. Winston's status in the world of literature was recognized when he was made a Fellow of the Royal Society of Literature and he was chairman of the Society of Authors from 1967-9. He received the O.B.E. in 1983.

It was fortunate for the Club that Hugh Stewart and Peter Latham persuaded Winston Graham to overcome his diffidence and throw in his lot with the Sodality at Brook Street in 1950, for this "unclubbable man" has been a pillar of the Savile ever since. Apart from his ability to dispel any longueurs in the Sandpit or at the long table he has served for some years on the committee, is an ex-trustee and, perhaps above all, was one of the triumvirate who transformed the fortunes of the Club in 1976 by "auditioning" Peter Aldersley for the part of secretary, one of the few of his creative inspirations he is prepared to boast about.

David Hughes, in common with his two alphabetical predecessors in this brief catalogue of current Savile authors, is also a Fellow of the Royal Society of Literature. He first became a member of the Club in 1960, two years after he had published his study of a fellow member, *J.B. Priestley; An informal Portrait*. Having previously worked as a journalist and script-writer be began his career as a novelist with *A Feeling in the Air* published in 1977. This was to be the precursor of a remarkable series of novels, notably *The Imperial German Dinner Service*, published in 1983, and *The Pork Butcher* in 1984 which won both the Welsh Arts Council Fiction Prize and the W.H. Smith Literary Award and was also made into a film.

The Club has never been less than catholic in its choice of members but even the most battle-hardened, surveying the infinite variety of pursuits indulged in by his fellows, would find it hard to reconcile the functions of an Honorary Consul to the Republic of Panama in Dublin with the activities of a son of Russian-Jewish immigrants brought up in London's East End who bestrode the literary, cinematic, theatrical and musicals world for more than three decades after he burst into prominence in the mid-fifties. But Wolf Mankowitz has managed to combine all these while adding for good measure a four-years stint as Professor of English at the University of New Mexico. To list his output in his early years is to sound a nostalgic carillon for the words and music which formed the back-drop to those exciting times when post-war austerity was giving way to the first tentative notion that "anything goes".

He was thirty when he became a member of the Savile in 1954, the year that his first two books, *Make Me an Offer* and *A Kid for Two Farthings*, were filmed. As novels they had been immediate best-sellers and were straight away followed by *Espresso Bongo*, *Casino Royale* and *The Long and the Short and the Tall*. More musicals and plays appeared; among them *Belle*, *Pickwick* and *The Passion Flower Hotel* in the 'sixties and *Casanova's Last Stand* in 1980. Wolf was so outraged by the critical reception of his musical *Belle*, whose unlikely hero was Doctor Crippen, that he had a coffin carried down Fleet Street borne by chorus girls in fish-net tights and accompanied by loudspeaker vans dispensing counter-propaganda for the show. Sadly for such an enviably robust gesture, it was to no avail; the show closed after six weeks. Meantime more novels were being written; and biographies of Edgar Allan Poe, Mazeppa and Dickens – the latter being adapted for television in 1976 – and collections of short stories and fables. He has produced histories of Wedgwood, the Portland Vase, and an *Encyclopaedia of English Pottery and Porcelain*. Altogether he has written seven plays and musicals, seventeen film scripts, eleven novels, four collection of short stories, three histories, three biographies and a collection of poems. His recreation is, not unnaturally, sleeping, though he has recently renounced the frenzied pace of yester-year and now divides his time between his house in Cork, his establishment in New Mexico and his regular visits to London and the Savile.

Gerald McKnight was for many years a journalist until he decided to devote himself exclusively to the production of carefully researched works of non-fiction on subjects of contemporary interest. He has covered a wide range, as his titles in the Monument demonstrate.

The Mind of the Terrorist in 1975 was a study of the motivations behind the various warring factions operating illegally in different parts of the world such as Cyprus, Ireland and the Middle East. He has also written on particular aspects of noteworthy figures who have included such diverse personalities as Syrie Maugham, Pablo Picasso and Andrew Lloyd Webber (who was himself a member of the Savile for a time until uxoriousness drew him away from the all-male atmosphere of Brook Street).

> I never think of myself as an 'author' [says Gerald]. True, nearly 20 volumes have appeared under my name and three or four under discreet aliases. But they are windfalls from the tree of journalism under which I have enjoyed agreeable shelter for many more years than I've been writing books.

Gerald was introduced to the Savile by his old friend and colleague, Godfrey Smith, just after the publication of his first book. "On a warm, sunny day I turned up full of myself – after all, I was now a published author – only to be served a salad in which a large slug nestled in the lettuce. This, I took it, was symbolic of clubland's reception on my budding literary career." But relations improved:

> *The Fortune Makers*, though it dealt with the world of high finance, was published by fellow-Savilian Edmund Fisher, then managing Michael Joseph. As was *Computer Crime* and *The Mind of the Terrorist*. I owe my *Syrie Maugham* biography entirely to the Savile, in that our eminent American member, Professor Paul Cranefield, inspired and encouraged its birth... the Club has been both my second home in London and a sauna for my spirits wherein writer's cramp, if it exists, can so pleasantly be assuaged at the bar.

Like Gerald McKnight, Michael Pearson came to authorship from journalism and turned the techniques of factual research to literary effect in his works of fiction and non-fiction. In the latter mode, his book on the American Revolution written from the British point of view, *Those Damned Rebels*, was extremely well received in the United Kingdom but, not unnaturally, attracted particularly controversial attention in America. *The Sealed Train*, dealing with Lenin's eight months from poverty to power, was also published in Great Britain and America and has since been translated into five other languages. *Tears of Glory* is Pearson's re-working of the legendary French Resistance story of the Vercors massacre and provided the producers of *Wish Me Luck* with the basis for the third of their recent television series: sadly, not on a par with the original "inspiration". Pearson's first novel, *The Store*, a family saga based on the development of an early department store, sold more than a million copies in seventeen different editions in seven languages; his second, *The Keys of the City*, has had similar success, having been produced in seven different editions in four languages. A third novel, *The Shadow of Elisabeth*, was published by Heinemann in September 1990.

Among the more prolific Savile authors is Allan Prior, who was elected to the Club in 1978. His own explanation for his vast output – sixteen novels, translated into many languages, some filmed or televised: "a couple of hundred television plays", ranging from *Z Cars* through *Armchair Theatre* and *Play for Today* to the more recent *The Charmer* for Nigel Havers – is that "I'm one of those writers who actually enjoy *doing* the stuff."

Sir Victor Pritchett shares with Leonard Cohen the distinction of having become a member of the Savile earlier than anyone else in the current membership list. Although the date of his election is put at 1928 he was, in fact, an honorary member for a short time in 1927 during a visit to London from Dublin where he was then working. Regarded by some as the finest writer of short stories in English, by others as the most percipient of literary critics, and, by nearly everyone who matters, as both, V.S. Pritchett – "the trade-name" with which it is said he feels most comfortable – was born in 1900. He has said that he finds it convenient to be the same age as the century in that he does not have to puzzle out how old he is, which is perhaps as well for one who has been quoted as saying, "I shall never be as old as I was between 20 and 30." As readers of his two volumes of autobiography, *A Cab at the Door* and *Midnight Oil*, will know, he grew up in poverty, the son of a father who skittered from one job to another "with the bumptiousness of a God". From an early age, therefore, he had to provide for himself, acquiring his own education and making his own living, which, apart from a brief apprenticeship in the leather trade, has derived entirely from his literary output. As Margaret Drabble wrote in a tribute to him on his eighty-fifth birthday: "Unsupported, unsalaried, he has lived as a man of letters must, by his pen, and he has done it with a freshness of interest and an infectious curiosity that has never waned."

As part of his self-education and as an apprenticeship to the profession he really hankered after, he walked across Spain to produce his first book, *Marching Spain*, which was published three years after he first entered the Club. Since then forty more books have appeared, including novels, several collections of his innumerable short stories, six volumes of literary criticism and biographies of Balzac, Turgenev and Chekhov. In his ninety-third year he maintains his prodigious output by adhering to the discipline of all his years, retiring to his study and working from 9 a.m. until 1 p.m. and again from 4 p.m. until 7 p.m. – "*Every* day, or I fear I will have forgotten how to do it". This includes week-ends and Christmas Day.

In 1978, Caroline Moorehead wrote of him: "Whenever you read anything about V.S. Pritchett you sense how much people like him, there is a universal fondness for this man...", so it is fortunate for his friends at the Savile that his rigid working regimen does not prevent his regular appearances for lunch or dinner at the long table. Nor has it prevented him from issuing from his study over the years to take up the responsibilities which attend upon such a leading literary figure. Thus he has in his time accepted lectureships and professorships at six of America's leading universities; he was president of International P.E.N. 1974-1976 and has been president of the Society of Authors since 1977. Nor has his foreshortened formal education prevented him from becoming an Honorary Doctor of Literature in the Universities of Leeds, Columbia, Sussex and Harvard. He was awarded the C.B.E. in 1968, knighted in 1975 and made a Companion of Literature in 1988.

A Savile author with an impeccably orthodox education, however, is Frederic Raphael (Charterhouse and Cambridge) and that this is also no disadvantage is demonstrated by the number of branches of literature which he has bedecked with the fruits of his early learning. Novelist – he has written sixteen; short-story writer – two collections; biographer of Somerset Maugham and Lord Byron; essayist; writer of thirteen screen-plays; translator of the poems of Catullus and the *Oresteia*; literary critic; there seems little else he can turn his hand to in the way of literature unless, as was said of Stephen Spender, he were to take up bookbinding and calligraphy.

A Fellow of the Royal Society of Literature since 1964, Raphael was elected to the Savile in 1982, the year that his biography of Byron appeared. He had published his first novel, *Obligato*, in 1956 just after coming down from Cambridge, and thereafter continued to produce an enormously popular run of successors at the rate of one a year until 1976 when *The Glittering Prizes* appeared and immediately lived up to its name by being transformed into a highly successful television series which won for him the Writer of the Year Award from the Royal Television Society. In the meantime he had produced six of his thirteen screen-plays including *Darling*, which won the Academy Award in 1967 and *A Severed Head* in 1972. Since then he has written two more novels as well as a considerable body of criticism, though his main preoccupation has been with his highly successful career as a writer of superior scripts for television and cinema.

* * * *

Such, more or less, has been the literary cavalcade which has processed through the Savile during the 125 years since the foundation in 1868 to the time of writing. Lengthy as it is, it can be by no means complete; impressive, dazzling even, as are some of the figures who have taken part in it, there have been others, and in concluding this section of the history it might be right when remembering them to recall the words of that writer in *The Times* in 1923 who, having listed some of the famous members of the day, remarked: ". . . Perhaps, after all, these Olympians may not have done more to preserve the *Sodalitas Convivium*, the vital principle of the Club, than have the nameless contingent of Savilians."

Pat Jackson, the film director whose remarkable works during and after the war such as *Western Approaches* and *White Corridors* are classics of the British cinema, provides a moving tribute to one of these, the so-called "nameless contingent", and the following extracts underline some of that ethos of the Savile expressed by Compton Mackenzie in his phrase "... although all men may not yet be equal, all Savilians are equal".

Pat writes of his friend, James Lansdale Hodson, O.B.E., who was a member of the Club from 1943 until his death in 1956:

> I had the good fortune of getting to know James early in 1943 at the Ministry of Information. We had been chosen to make a film in Rome: its premise to be the return of 'The Four Freedoms' to the first liberated capital of the Axis to fall to the Allies. It was Winston Churchill's idea, apparently, that this film should be made... James was dubious. He sensed that the last things to be found in a newly liberated city, after four years of war, would be "the four freedoms". However, it was decided that we would, with a cameraman, go out to Rome and find out for ourselves. James's forebodings were proved to be well founded. However, within a few hours of setting out on our journey, I knew that I was in the company of a remarkable man. He had been a cub reporter in 1913 on the *Guardian*

under the great C.P. Scott, before enlisting as an infantryman in the Lancashire Fusiliers. He survived the Somme, two attacks on High Wood and Passchendaele. Demobbed, he returned to the *Guardian* and scooped the story of the landing of Alcock and Brown in Ireland after their historic flight across the Atlantic. During the Second World War he became our Pepys with his seven famous war diaries which he kept during his time as a war correspondent for the Kemsley and Camrose group of papers.

He wrote ten novels and three plays, including the famous First World War play, *Red Night*. It gave John Mills his first important role in the West End and was put on by Robert Donat – fellow member of the Savile – who played the leading role. He is, perhaps, one of the most underrated novelists of recent times.

During the trip to Rome, Pat talked with Hodson about his play *Red Night*.

It had done exceptional business in the provinces to glowing notices and started brilliantly in the West End. 'The best of the World War plays,' said James Agate in his review, and this was after *Journey's End*! All looked set for a long and successful run and then King George V died. The court and the West End went into mourning for a week. Not only had the King died but almost every show died with him. That week was a killer. Agate wrote another article imploring the public to support the play. Ellen Wilkinson was so involved and interested that she wanted to try and raise money to help the play over this sticky patch.

But it was to no avail: "He had miraculously survived the First World War to build a reputation not only as a successful novelist but as a reporter of integrity and courage," says Pat, who could perhaps have added that his diaries of the Second World War were also greatly admired; Hugh Walpole declared that they were "beyond question the best books written about England in this war". H.G. Wells said of them, "It is the best reading I know of just now." Ivor Brown, Edmund Blunden, Elizabeth Bowen, Frank Swinnerton, Harold Hobson, John Betjeman and all the leading critics of the day poured praise on them as "records of immortal courage and undying humour". Yet today, together with all his novels, they are out of print and his seven plays remain unperformed. Only in the Club is he remembered for his talents and his personality. Says Pat, "He was a great man. I shall never meet a finer." It is salutary to be reminded that of such, together with all the "Olympians", is the literary history of the Savile.

CHAPTER THREE

Scientists, Public Men and Journalists

After such a lengthy list of literary men the question must now be asked, What of the founders' original intention that the Club should consist of "a mixture of men of different professions"? The answer may be found by taking a look at those who have earned their reputation in the fields of science, the fine arts and public service, when it will be seen that the Savile's electoral college has done its work nobly to preserve that first and fundamental principle.

"With 168 F.R.S.s (if my arithmetic is correct) elected between 1868 and 1900 alone, you obviously cannot comment on them all", writes Sir Arthur Vick. He then appends a list of distinguished scientists to support his gently expressed but inarguable thesis that "the common view that the Savile was primarily a literature and arts Club does not look quite correct". In addition to some of those Fellows of the Royal Society (to date, rather more than three hundred, which includes eight presidents), his list includes nine Nobel prize-winners for science. If to these are added the five laureates in science whom Professor Paul Cranefield has unearthed from the list of honorary and temporary members, we discover the rather startling equation that of the seventeen Nobel prize-winners who have distinguished the Savile, fourteen were for science as against three for literature.

Sir Arthur Vick is himself eloquent proof of Savile members' scientific distinction: a renowned physicist, president and Vice-Chancellor of Queen's University, Belfast from 1966-76 and pro-Chancellor and chairman of committee of Warwick University since 1977, he has made many notable contributions to the study and administration of science. Professor Paul Cranefield exemplifies not only the diversity of the Club generally but the polymathy of its members particularly, in that he is a distinguished cardiologist and a literary and political scholar of daunting erudition.

Nevertheless, the overriding reputation of the Savile remains that of a Club devoted to the arts and humanities. Perhaps this is because the work of successful literary men and artists tends to carry with it a higher public profile than does that of the scientist, albeit the latter may have as great – if not a greater – impact on current affairs; perhaps it is that recognition for a scientist comes necessarily from the limited number of his peers rather than from a largely uncomprehending public; maybe it is because so many Savile scientists have been of that civilized variety who have their feet firmly planted in both the "two cultures" so urgently propounded by C.P. Snow; perhaps, after all, they are just more modest.

Whatever the reason for this lack of balance in the Savile's public – and, it must be confessed, occasionally private – image, the Club in 1868 began as it meant to go on by electing among its first year's intake of 136, sixteen members who either were already, or destined to become, Fellows of the Royal Society. Of these Sir Samuel White Baker was most famous then as an explorer, having discovered Lake Albert Nyanza, so solving the mystery of the source of the White Nile before coming back to discover the joys of *Sodalitas Convivium*. His fellow pioneer as a member of the new Club was Doctor H. Charlton Bastian, who was a leader in the study of the human nervous system and became an F.R.S. in the same year that the Club was founded. On the committee of the then "New Club" was James Bryce, who is modestly described in the existing Club documents as "James Bryce, Esq., Oriel College, Oxford" but who, as an early example of Savile panache in electing "young men of promise", was to become one of the greatest jurists, historians and statesmen of his day as Viscount Bryce, P.C., O.M., G.C.V.O., D.C.L., L.L.D., M.P., F.R.S.

Another committee member of the New Club was Lord Dufferin, who was to trump Bryce's impressive collection of honours after he became the Marquess of Dufferin and Ava, by gathering a P.C., K.P., G.C.B., G.C.S.I., G.C.M.G., G.C.I.E., D.C.L., L.L.D., as well as F.R.S. His portrait is included among the sixty-four caricatures of members by Carlo Pellegrini — "Ape" of *Vanity Fair* — which have recently been splendidly reframed through the courtesy of a present member, Robin Fletcher, and are now on display in various of the Club rooms. Among them is the caricature of another founder member who was also a Fellow of the Royal Society, and a distinguished member of parliament, W.E. Forster. His contemporary and near namesake, Dr Michael Foster, was later to become an M.P. and F.R.S. also.

When the Club moved to Savile Row, adopted its new name, and formalized its constitution, one of the first trustees to be appointed was another Fellow of the Royal Society, James Heywood. J. Norman Lockyer, later Sir Norman Lockyer, F.R.S., K.C.B., was also an original member of the New Club. The rather ambivalent reference to him in the earlier history of the Club says that "he was destined to become extremely well known as an astronomer who made the results of his learning reasonably intelligible to the unlearned". In fact he made a considerable number of important discoveries which included the envelope around the sun (which he named the chromosphere), and the detection of helium in the sun's spectrum twenty-seven years before that element was discovered and isolated on earth. He also founded what is now the Science Museum at South Kensington and, in collaboration with his fellow Savile member, Alexander Macmillan, instituted the magazine *Nature* in 1869. Alexander Macmillan, brother of the famous Scottish crofter turned publisher and the great uncle of the future prime minister, was the publisher of this magazine which was to become perhaps the most influential scientific journal in the world. Lockyer continued as editor until his death in 1920. In the Monument is the recently published facsimile of Lockyer's copy of the first issue which appeared on 4 November 1869. It contained eight signed articles of which two were by Savilians and one by A.W. Bennett who was to become a member a few months later. Lockyer himself contributed a famous article "The Recent Eclipse of the Sun" and A.W. Williamson, like Lockyer and

Macmillan an original Savile member, who was also to serve on the committee from 1871-1879, contributed a eulogy of Thomas Graham. The "Notes" section contains a report by Lockyer on the election to a fellowship of Trinity College, Cambridge of another original member of the Club, W.K. Clifford, whose early death prevented wider recognition of his status as one of the greatest mathematicians, teachers and philosophers of his time. It is pleasant and perhaps not too far fetched to speculate with Paul Cranefield, who drew attention to this nugget of Club history, that some of the discussions that led to the foundation of *Nature* actually occurred in the birthplace of occasional bright ideas, the Savile.

William Kingdon Clifford, whose election to a fellowship at Trinity aged 24 Lockyer had noted in that first edition of *Nature,* had been, like many mathematicians, a precocious genius and lucky enough to be recognized early. However he was much prouder of his prowess as a gymnast and must be one of the few Fellows who is reputed to have "once hung by his toes from a crossbar of a weathercock on a college chapel". He possessed great literary ability and a gift for expressing himself with vivacity and humour which made him an extremely popular lecturer. Like a later member of the Savile, H.G. Wells, he took a great interest in popularizing scientific knowledge and regularly lectured at the Sunday Lecture Society, which had been formed for that purpose. At Cambridge he was a member of the Apostles and held very High Church views until he came under the influence of that progenitor of a famous Savile dynasty, Charles Darwin, and another brooding influence in the early days of the Club, Herbert Spencer. Two years after he had become a member of the Club he set off on the English Eclipse Expedition aboard the vessel *Psyche,* which was wrecked off the coast of Catania. However he and his equipment were saved and he returned to London to become Professor of Applied Mathematics at University College, London. His lectures and his publications attracted much admiring attention and in 1874 he was elected a Fellow of the Royal Society. His health, however, had begun to fail and he was forced to spend much time abroad in warmer climates. He died in Spain in 1879 aged thirty-four. It was said of him that his inquiring mind led him to seek out the company of people of all opinions and tastes and by all contemporary accounts he was a most stimulating and witty companion. Professor Karl Pearson, F.R.S., who became a member of the Savile thirteen years after Clifford's death, wrote of him: "As a mathematician he may be regarded as marking an epoch in the history of this Science in England", while his contribution to philosophy in works such as *The Unseen Universe* still retain their initial impact.

Clifford was but one of the first of a long line of Savilians distinguished in the science of mathematics and its associated arts, a line which continues to the present day. With him on the list of members elected in 1869 was John Venn, the great logician and man of letters. Venn belonged to a Devon family of great intellectual distinction – his grandfather, the Rev. John Venn, had been the leader of the Clapham Sect – and when he went up to Gonville and Caius College in 1853 he was the eighth generation of his family to have attended one or other of the two ancient universities. His own association with his college was to last for seventy years. He was mathematics scholar in 1854 and became a Fellow in 1857. For a short time he was in Holy Orders but in 1862 the University created for him the new post of Lecturer in Moral Science and shortly afterwards he ceased to be a priest and devoted himself entirely to the study and teaching of logic. During this time he was increasingly thrown into the company of men who like himself were to be original members of the new Club. Among them were his cousin (Sir) Leslie Stephen; Henry Sidgwick, one of the greatest moral philosophers of his time; and John Westlake, one of the most learned and authoritative writers on jurisprudence. Venn himself was producing a series of what were to become standard works, such as *The Logic of Chance* and *The Principles of Empirical Logic,* and such was his skill as a lecturer that the Moral Science Tripos began to attract an increasing number of undergraduates, among whom was another distinguished future member of the Savile, Arthur Balfour. When Venn died he had been a fellow of his college for sixty-six years and president of it for twenty. A permanent memorial to his greatest contribution to the science and form of thought embodied in logic is the Venn Diagrams, wherein he refined the diagrammatic method of illustrating the inclusive and exclusive possibilities contained in propositions.

In 1867 George John Romanes entered Caius College, Cambridge with a scholarship in science intending, like John Venn before him, to take Holy Orders. However he soon decided to devote himself to scientific research and after one of his contributions to an early issue of *Nature* was noticed by Charles Darwin, who wrote encouragingly, the two met and a friendship developed which was to make Romanes increasingly sceptical of all orthodox religion. Darwin inspired him to apply the theory of natural selection to the problems of mental evolution and the results of his work were presented to the Royal Society in 1876. In April 1879 Romanes was proposed for the Savile by one of its founder members, Sir Michael Foster, F.R.S., and later in that year became a Fellow of the Royal Society. In 1882 he was appointed Fullerian Professor of Physiology at the Royal Institution.

At this time he was writing much on science and religion and in some of his works in the Savile Monument can be seen the mingling of the poetic and the scientific with which he invested his philosophical treatises. A man of considerable inherited wealth, in 1891 he founded the Romanes Lectureship at Oxford University for which "a man of eminence was to be chosen annually to deliver a lecture on a scientific or literary subject". The first of these was given in 1892 when W.E. Gladstone lectured on Mediaeval Universities.

Although one of the attractions of the Savile is the variety of "professions and opinions" contained there, it is also true that outstanding figures in one particular field tend to lure others of their kind. As it has been with other professions so it has with mathematicians. Thus in 1911 there was elected Professor Alfred North Whitehead, Sc.D., F.R.S., the great mathematician and philosopher who was co-author with Bertrand Russell of *Principia Mathematica,* which has been described as "the greatest single contribution to logic since Aristotle".

More recently – in 1951 – Professor Sir Henry Swinnerton-Dyer, K.B.E., F.R.S., was elected. He became Professor of Mathematics at Cambridge in 1971 and later was appointed Vice-Chancellor of the University. According to his friend Colin Merton, when he was elevated to the latter position his mother was heard to remark: "I do hope he'll take this job seriously."

Sir Norman Lockyer, the founder and first editor of *Nature*, was one of several members who were to make valuable contributions to the science of astronomy. Another, whose breadth of interests, profound scholarship and gift for friendships qualified him almost as a paradigm of Savile membership was Lieutenant-Colonel Frederick John Marrian Stratton, D.S.O., whose membership of the Club from 1919 to 1960 straddled the careers of many of the other members who were to make distinguished contributions to science. Sir Arthur Vick has contributed a moving tribute to their long friendship:

> Stratton – "Chubby" to his many friends in the Savile and elsewhere, because of his general appearance and cheerful round face – was a man of wide interests and an astonishing range of activities. I first really got to know him while he was disguised as a Lt. Col. of the Royal Signals during the Second World War. Like many Savilians at that time, he kept very quiet about what he was doing, and all I know about it was that he was involved in radio communication, its security and use for intelligence purposes, for which he was awarded a D.S.O. He was also a Lt. Col. of the Signals during the First World War, when a fellow officer was another Savilian, R.A. Bagnold, brother of the novelist, Enid Bagnold.
>
> From Birmingham Stratton won an entrance scholarship to Gonville and Caius College, Cambridge (where he would have come under the influence of John Venn); in 1901 he graduated in maths and astronomy; was elected to an Isaac Newton Studentship; won a Smith's Prize, and was elected a Fellow of his College in 1906. On the way he took a London (external) B.A. in Greek, Latin and maths. He lived in College as a bachelor Fellow until his death in 1960, apart from absences during the two wars. He became Professor of Astrophysics and Director of the Solar Physics Observatory in 1928, and organized several expeditions to observe solar eclipses. On one of these, to Japan, he was accompanied by R.A. Bagnold. He was elected an F.R.S. in 1947 and was an inspiration to many generations of students and research students (especially while Senior Tutor of Caius) most of whom remained his friends for the rest of his life. To celebrate his 70th birthday some of them arranged to contribute to and publish a modest *Festschrift*. But so many wanted to contribute that it expanded to three fat volumes. Chubby often stayed in the Club. Frank, the valet, told me of his admiration for him. "He occupied the bathroom in the morning for the shortest time of any member – just jumped into the bath and jumped out again." He was a modest man and seldom spoke about his activities, such as his international involvements (he was General Secretary of the International Astronomical Union for ten years, for example), his investigations of haunted houses, his devotion to his church,

and his public work for the city and county of Cambridge where he was a Deputy Lieutenant for many years. He was always ready and willing to help whenever he felt he could be of service. Above all was his gift for cheerful and unselfish friendship, and few men have been more widely loved. He was a true Savilian for forty-one years.

Indeed, as has been already noticed, he helped save the building when it was bombed during the war, which should alone qualify him as Savilian *maximus emeritus*.

Brigadier R.A. Bagnold, O.B.E., F.R.S., to whom Sir Arthur refers, was elected to the Club in 1931 just after he had driven a Ford truck across the Baluchistan desert to Persia, and then for a thousand miles across that country, on to Damascus, through Palestine and Sinai, and eventually to Cairo. All this was before joining a party of other enthusiasts who were going to explore and study the Great Sand Sea. At that time it was thought to be impassable to motor transport until Bagnold and his friends proved otherwise.

Bagnold's exploits and several theatres of activity would seem to make him a quintessential Savilian so it is perhaps a pity that his many years of membership are not better remembered. His scientific achievements must have aroused admiration among his contemporaries at Brook Street (he was elected F.R.S. in 1944) though to the layman his published works, *Physics of Blown Sand*, etc., may have seemed rather remote. They became less remote, however, in 1939 when he was given command of the 7th Armoured Division Signals in Egypt and in 1940, under Gen. Wavell's personal sponsorship, raised and commanded the Long Range Desert Group. This "private army" operated in small independent units, penetrating hundreds of miles into enemy territory. Although its chief role was intelligence and reconnaissance, it also raided German posts and supply columns and on many occasions it co-operated with the Special Air Service – despite its main purpose being the collection of intelligence.

In 1940 Bagnold achieved further distinction when he contacted the yet undecided French Army Command in Chad, a thousand miles through enemy territory, and gained active French participation on the Allied side. At this stage he was once again mentioned in despatches. His exploits behind the lines with the Long Range Desert Group were all the more remarkable considering his age – he was born in 1896 – and the fact that he had been discharged from the army as a permanent invalid in 1934 as a result of his experiences in the First World War, in which he had served with distinction at the battles of Ypres, the Somme and Passchendaele.

In 1920, the year after Bagnold's friend Chubby Stratton had been elected to the Club, there came yet another astronomer, Sir Arthur Eddington, O.M., F.R.S. He was director of the Cambridge Observatory, a Gifford lecturer and an influential writer on astronomy. Somewhere, tucked away in the arts committee's vault, is the portrait of another Savile astronomer, Andrew Ainslie Common, F.R.S., painted as a memorial to him *post-mortem* by his fellow member, Sir

William Nicholson. According to Sir Herbert Stephen it hung over the mantelpiece in the billiards-room at 107 Piccadilly and depicts

> a fully bearded gentleman of somewhat corpulent figure, seated, as it was his habit to sit in life, on the settee on the "prompt" side of the fireplace, with a rack of private billiards cues above his head...

Common was elected in 1889 and was a conspicuous and popular figure in the Club until he died "of apoplexy" in 1902. At the time of his election he had amassed a considerable fortune as a builder and contractor but had achieved more public eminence as an astronomer, optical student and inventor. In his time he was president of the Astronomical Society and, like his fellow member, Sir William Christie, made many valuable contributions to the science from his investigations in the field of photographic astronomy.

Evidently Common endeared himself to his fellow members as well as to the staff at the Club for his amusing manners and harmless eccentricity. Because of his enormous girth he refused to entrust himself to the flimsy-looking two-wheel hansoms of the time and when going home would ask the hall porter to order "a four-wheeled cab, with the horse's head turned towards the setting sun". This led to a typical piece of Common bravura on that April evening in 1900 when the whole of London was celebrating the relief of Mafeking. Outside the Club in Piccadilly the mob was making a hideous din which promised to go on throughout the night. One member suggested that instead of passively enduring it, it might be better to join in and go to the Empire music hall where an especially patriotic entertainment was taking place. Common agreed to accompany them only on condition that a four-wheeler could be found. Miraculously, considering the teeming crowd outside, Sindon, the hall porter, managed to summon one. By this time there were fifteen members clamouring to go. The rails of the luggage rack atop the carriage were raised to form an emergency seat and Common was hoisted over the front wheel and box seat to the roof, where he majestically installed himself while the fourteen others found places for themselves wherever else they could inside and outside the vehicle. At a shilling a time – considerable money in those days – and seeing that it was Mafeking Night the cabby seemed happy to ignore the provisions of the Hackney Carriage Act. Arrived at the Empire, Common purchased a Union Jack and made a stately descent from his perch. The lack of admission tickets had then to be negotiated so his fourteen companions, trading on Common's physical presence, set up the cry "Make way for Lord Salisbury", whereupon the respectful crowd made way and they were all ushered into the auditorium free of charge.

Equally eccentric, though perhaps even more academically distinguished, was Common's contemporary at the Savile, Sir William Henry Mahoney Christie, K.C.B., D.Sc., F.R.S., who was elected to the Club in 1881, the year that he was appointed Astronomer Royal. Most of his work was based at the Greenwich Observatory, which he greatly expanded and brought to even greater international

131

prominence by his pioneering use of the then infant science of photography to record his observation of the heavens. Evidently when he came down to earth he found the carnival atmosphere of the Club extremely congenial. It is said that one evening at Piccadilly he had dined so well that another member bet him a fiver that he could not get out of the door of the billiards-room without help. This involved climbing down two hazardous high steps from his seat on the bench overlooking the billiards table, so the attendant members were treated to the sight of Her Majesty's Astronomer getting down on his hands and knees to win his bet by crawling to the door and pushing it open with his nose. As the anonymous member who witnessed this event commented later: "It is not known whether this added to the number of visible stars." Christie was also a protagonist in one of those *contretemps* which so often happen at the Club and which, while hilarious for everyone in earshot, are the stuff of embarrassing and recurring nightmares for unwary new members. The late George Vaizey in a memoir of his early days at the Club written in 1975 recalls the scene:

> A young man [probably the odious Major Pollard of whom more shall be heard later] had been recently elected and decided to make himself known at dinner. Sitting between two elderly men he determined to show that he had something to say for himself. So, to the member on his right he began to speak on astronomy, a subject which gave him much interest. His neighbour listened courteously for a while, encouraging him with nods, until at length he found it necessary to say:
> "Oh no, you're quite wrong there."
> Nettled and incautious, the new recruit replied:
> "I don't think so. The study of astronomy is a hobby of mine and I've studied it."
> "So have I," retorted the old member patiently, "I'm the Astronomer Royal."

The story, however, did not end there for as Vaizey remarks indulgently, "Alas youth and discretion are seldom partners." The disgruntled new member decided to try again, so he turned to address the dining companion on his left:

> This proved to be another elderly man with a droopy moustache who had splashed most of his earlier course of soup both over it and his waistcoat beneath. Here, for sure, the new boy decided, I am on safe ground and cannot go wrong, so he opened the talk on another subject dear to him, of how a shell left a howitzer, rose at great speed and then descended in a sudden steep curve. The calculation of these shell flights had provided, for him, much interesting calculation when engaged on laying down a barrage against the German lines in Flanders during World War I. Once again the senior member listened politely until, at length, his patience was exhausted and he exploded, less temperately than the Astronomer Royal.

132

"Rubbish, you've got your calculations all wrong."

This angered the young man and, impetuously, without recalling his recent lesson from Sir William Christie, snapped:

"With respect, Sir, you are a much older man than I am and I have first-hand experience of howitzers. Not so very long ago I was firing them in France."

"Maybe," said droopy moustache, "But I designed them."

John Morley, who has already been mentioned, was of course, an early member who was to become a fellow of the Royal Society. Doctor Philip Henry Pye-Smith was another and he has also a niche in Savile history for having served on the committee at that breathless A.G.M. in May 1884 when the motion to alter the mode of election by introducing the "black ball" system was famously defeated.

Among the last batch of members to be elected before the Club removed itself from Spring Gardens to Savile Row in 1871 was Professor John Tyndall, F.R.S., who was apostrophized in Sir Herbert Stephen's history of the Club as having "succeeded Faraday, preceded Huxley, and approximately synchronized with Darwin, as the most widely-known scientific investigator of his epoch". Such chronological athleticism might seem to have qualified him also as a precursor of "Doctor Who" or one of the Time-Lords but, at all events, his features are fixed for posterity in his proper time-slot through yet another of *Vanity Fair*'s "Spy" cartoons which is in the Club's collection.

Another entrant to the Club among that final influx to Spring Gardens was Doctor Henry Maudsley, Ph.D, M.D., F.R.C.P., L.L.D., who despite – or, perhaps, because of – his reputation as the leading authority of the time in "The study of insanity and morbid conditions of the human mind" was made cautiously welcome. Maudsley was superintendent of various mental hospitals and author of several books which anticipated the works of Freud. It was said of him that he had "a trenchant, acid exceptional mind"... "difficult to work with on account of his tart replies and scathing judgements": but he left £30,000 to the London County Council to found the Maudsley Hospital in Dulwich which, since it opened in 1923, has been probably the greatest centre of psychiatric care in Europe. Maudsley would have found rich pickings in his fellow member, Doctor George Harley, M.D., F.R.S., who was elected at the same time. Harley was a distinguished physician who practised in the street of the same name.

He was accustomed to relate with a strangely Scottish accent, in a voice of the most penetrating quality, experiences of his own which his hearers were proud of being able to believe [says Sir Herbert Stephen rather equivocally]. It was long after, in Piccadilly, that he took from his pocket and handed round the room for inspection, an object resembling a small marble, or a much desiccated bean, and challenged all beholders to guess what it was. No guess was moderately successful, and the room rang with his triumphant explanation – "It is the eye of an Aztec."

Having moved to Savile Row the Club, in the throes of that expansion which was the consequence of its growing reputation, continued to welcome promising young men from "differing professions" which, of course, included many who were scientists though not all of whom were necessarily young. The forty-eight-year-old Sir William Thomson, F.R.S., was elected in 1872. He was to be a member for twenty years and a trustee of the Club and to become better known as Baron Kelvin, P.C., O.M., G.C.V.O., L.L.D., D.C.L., President of the Royal Society and discoverer of the second law of thermodynamics, a knowledge of which his successor as a member of the Savile, C.P. Snow, was later to pronounce to be an essential part of the conversational equipment of any red-blooded literary man who wished to share his enthusiastic promotion of "the two cultures".

Kelvin was a man of wide interests who, in common with many others, was drawn to the Savile so that he might mix with men whose professions were different from his own. Like many scientists he was a great lover of music and, as an undergraduate at Cambridge, had founded the famous Cambridge University Music Society which was later to be galvanized by his great friend and fellow member, Sir Charles Villiers Stanford.

The first Savile member to be a Nobel laureate in science was Professor the Honourable Robert John Strutt, F.R.S., later to become the 3rd Baron Rayleigh. He was elected to the Club in 1903 and a year later received the Nobel prize for physics in recognition of his discovery of the inert elementary gas, argon. He had been elected an F.R.S. in 1873 at the comparatively early age of thirty-one and in 1905, the year after his Nobel award, he became the Royal Society's president. In 1902 he had become with that founder member, John Morley, one of the original recipients of the newly created Order of Merit. As a young man he had been Cavendish Professor at Cambridge but when, in 1884, he relinquished that post he was succeeded by another Savilian, Professor Sir Joseph John Thomson, O.M., Sc.D., LL.D., F.R.S. Indeed, from now on it began to seem almost *de rigueur* for any scientist having anything to do with the Cavendish to be also a member of the Savile. Thomson had been a member since 1883 so, in Club terms if not academically, he had the edge of twenty years seniority over Lord Rayleigh; his career, however, was to reflect that of the man he had succeeded at the Cavendish to quite a remarkable degree. In 1906, two years after Rayleigh's similar award, Thomson won the Nobel prize for physics to mark his pioneering experiments on the conduction of electricity through gases. He had been an F.R.S. since 1884 and in 1915, again like Rayleigh before him, he became president of the Royal Society. In 1918 he was made master of Trinity College, Cambridge, a post which he held until his death in 1940.

Thomson was the third Savilian in a row to be president of the Royal Society for, in the years which intervened between his succeeding Rayleigh, the post had been held by Sir William Crookes, who had been elected to the Club in 1888. Crookes's achievements were all the more remarkable for his origins were poor and he had left school at fifteen to be a laboratory assistant at the Royal College of Chemistry. However, by the time he was nineteen he had published his first paper on the compounds of the element selenium. Thereafter his progress was rapid and he held various teaching posts. By the time he reached the age of twenty-four he was able to devote himself entirely to independent research and journalism and in 1859, at the age of twenty-seven, he founded *Chemical News*, which rapidly became a standard work of reference in its field. In 1861 he discovered the element thalium and in recognition of this the Royal Society elected him a Fellow in 1863. Later he set up house in Kensington Park Gardens, where he installed a private laboratory to cater for the broad scope of his interests which extended from pure and applied science and their economic applications to the more arcane realms of psychical research. He was knighted in 1897, received the O.M. in 1910 and was President of the Royal Society from 1913-15, when Sir Joseph Thomson succeeded him.

In his earlier days at the Cavendish, Sir Joseph Thomson had conceived the idea of "positive rays" which opened up a new line of enquiry into isotopes. The scientist who shared his assistantship at Cambridge at that time was Francis William Aston, who was to become a member of the Savile in 1920. Aston developed Thomson's theories and through his technique of mass spectography went on to discover many new isotopes, amounting eventually to 212 out of the known total of 287. For this work he was awarded the Nobel prize for chemistry in 1922.

By this time, the Cavendish chair at Cambridge was beginning to resemble more and more a Savile fiefdom. In 1895 a twenty-four-year-old physicist called Ernest Rutherford had won an exhibition to the Cavendish, where his ability soon attracted the attention of Sir Joseph Thomson. In 1908 Rutherford was awarded the Nobel prize for chemistry as a result of work at the Cavendish which was to prove crucial for the future development of nuclear physics. In 1917 he had (one is tempted to write "almost inevitably") become a member of the Savile and in 1919, with a similar inexorability, succeeded Thomson – who in turn had succeeded Rayleigh – in the Cavendish chair. In 1925, to complete the equation, he was elected President of the Royal Society and awarded the O.M.

Sir Arthur Vick provides an interesting footnote to Rutherford's joint connections with the Cavendish and the Savile:

> His name and reputation are well-known, but his connections with the Savile Club are not. In 1919 Sir J.J. Thomson (another Savilian) resigned from the Cavendish chair of physics at Cambridge soon after being installed as Master of Trinity College. Rutherford was the obvious choice as his successor as head of the Cavendish Laboratory, but he was happily established as head of the Physics Department in Manchester University, where he had good facilities, congenial colleagues, and where he had carried out some of his best work, such as the "discovery" of the atomic nucleus. The first approach to Rutherford was made by Sir Joseph Larmor (who wrote from his home, 1 Upper Brook Street). Not wishing to compromise his position in Manchester University while discussing terms and conditions of a possible appointment in Cambridge, Rutherford wrote

personal letters to J.J. Thomson, Larmor and others from the Savile, using Club notepaper. He did move to Cambridge and stayed there until his death.

Andrew Cooper, now, unbelievably, 90 years of age, recalls an occasion when he was able to refer to Rutherford's achievements and set them against his actual motives with devastating effect against what he regarded as the pretentiousness which nowadays tends to lurk amidst the exalted circles of the scientific hierarchy. When he was appointed the first and only English president of C.I.G.R.E. (the French acronym for the International Conference on High Voltage Transmission between Countries) Cooper received warm congratulations from every participating nation – except Britain. In his presidential address at the Unesco building in Paris he equated scientific enquiry with common curiosity: "... it can lead to bad things as well as good. It was probably a scientist who insisted on opening Pandora's box. Rutherford only split the atom because he wanted to know what was inside."

Now Andrew's nephew had just been given a "Junior Carpentry Set" for Christmas and had immediately used it to saw his valuable antique rocking-horse into small pieces. "His motive was just the same as Rutherford's", said Andrew, "but the rewards were rather different. Rutherford received the Nobel prize; my nephew received a good hiding."

Cooper, who incidentally has distinguished himself also in the worlds of literature, pictorial art and broadcasting, had made his main career in the field of electrical engineering. During the war he was responsible for establishing the National Grid despite the opposition of those in authority who could not see the vital importance of this system to the nation's infrastructure. After the war he was in charge of the operation of the Central Electricity Board's nuclear power stations and it was through his friend Leonard Owen, deputy chairman of the Atomic Energy Authority, that he first became a member of the Savile in 1959.

In 1923 Rutherford had been joined at Cambridge by a young scientist, James Chadwick, who came as assistant director of the Cavendish Laboratory. In 1932 his work there resulted in the discovery of the neutron, a hitherto undetected constituent of the atom. The knowledge of its existence made possible the disintegration of the atom and for this he was awarded the Nobel prize for physics in 1935, the same year that he made what must have seemed by then the obligatory entry to membership of the Savile. He had been elected a Fellow of the Royal Society in 1927 and was knighted in 1945. After a period as head of the Atomic Research Establishment at Didcot in Berkshire he was appointed Master of Gonville and Caius College, Cambridge in 1948, as John Venn had been nearly fifty years before him.

And still the strong "family connection" between the Savile and the Cavendish persisted. At a meeting of the Royal Society on 28 April 1932 Lord Rutherford had announced that two of his workers at the Cavendish Laboratory – John Cockcroft and E.T.S. Walton – "had successfully disintegrated the nuclei of

136

lithium and other light elements by protons entirely artificially generated by high energy potentials".

Nineteen years – and seemingly centuries of compressed history – later, on 15 November 1951, the Royal Swedish Academy announced the award of the Nobel prize for physics jointly to Cockcroft and Walton for "their pioneer work on the transmutation of atomic nuclei by artificially accelerated atomic particles". One wonders whether the shade of Nobel, the inventor of dynamite, thought it a merry jest when he observed some of the uses to which this brilliant scientific discovery had already been put.

Eleven years earlier, in 1940, John Cockcroft had been elected to the Savile and remained a devoted member for the rest of his life. Sir Arthur Vick recalls that Cockcroft used to remark that thereafter he "took his acquaintances to the Athenaeum and his friends to the Savile".

Cockcroft was Jacksonian professor of natural philosophy in Cambridge from 1939 to 1946; during the war, however, he worked on air defence research and development at the Ministry of Supply. In 1946 he founded the Atomic Energy Research Establishment at Harwell and became its first director. He had been elected an F.R.S. in 1936 and knighted in 1948; created K.C.B. in 1953, and became the first Master of Churchill College, Cambridge.

> When he received his O.M. in 1957 [writes Sir Arthur Vick], about ten of his friends at the Club gave him dinner in the morning-room. C.P. Snow proposed the toast to him and Cockcroft responded with a most interesting account of the influence of the Club on his life. For example it was in the Savile that Rutherford agreed to allocate a few hundred pounds of Cavendish funds to the atom-smashing experiment. It was in the Club that a reluctant Air Minister was persuaded that the Bomber Command Aerodrome at Harwell could be given up in favour of the Atomic Energy Research Establishment. Cockcroft then associated each one of us in turn with some event in his life. My bill, including drinks, was £1-13s-1d. Cockcroft gave the talk at the first of the present series of discussion dinners, in November 1961 and I was in the chair.

Cockcroft, incidentally, was involved in another of those occasions at the long table when members – old as well as new – sometimes forget that their next-door neighbour, no matter how modestly he is comporting himself, is a likely as not the greatest authority in the country on the particular subject of discussion. Dallas Bower remembers one evening at dinner with a certain member – "a stockbroker from Budleigh Salterton, don't y'know", says Dallas, tapping his nose meaningfully – "Well, this fellow noticed the chap opposite wasn't saying much so he leaned over and said loudly: 'Been reading something in the papers about some newfangled things they've invented. Neutrons they're called. Heard anything about 'em, eh?' Cockcroft diffidently admitted that he had and relapsed into silence while the member went on expostulating that it was all a lot of nonsense: that anyone who had passed his school certificate in physics would know that the atom was the most minute and indivisible particle which could conceivably exist."

Cockcroft, forever polite as well as shy, made no comment.

George Pottinger recalls an almost identical occasion which occurred many years ago when he was dining at the long table next to the rather didactic chairman of the Royal Bank of Scotland, Sir Hamish Blair-Cunynghame. Opposite them was a member and his guest, Sir Alexander Fleming. Hamish was recovering from a throat infection and wished everyone to know the miraculous way in which this had been so swiftly cured:

> Some magic stuff they extract from mouldy cheese, or old socks or somesuch and this gets into the blood stream and stimulates the pharisees, or phagocytes, or whatever the things are called, and before the germs know what's what, they're done for. It'll be a major breakthrough, I imagine; mind you, not many people know about it yet . . .

Like Cockcroft, the discoverer of penicillin made no comment.

The Cavendish/Savile connection yields yet another of his colleagues whom Sir Arthur Vick remembers with affection:

> Dr "Big Bill" Webster was a Canadian who, after graduating in Toronto, gained a scholarship in the 1920s to carry out research in the Cavendish Laboratory. His father and his mother came from a wealthy family interested in the arts. Together they founded museums, and Bill later became senior trustee of the Webster Museums Trust. His brother John had been the only Canadian to compete in the King's Cup air race around Britain in 1930. In the early 1930s Bill felt he needed a break and spent a year or two in Africa during which he had a car built as a "safari wagon" and was, I am told, the first man to drive across the Sahara from south to north. On his return to England he studied economics at L.S.E. and, soon after the outbreak of war and on the recommendation of John Cockcroft, he was attached to my staff in the Ministry of Supply, where I became Assistant Director of Scientific Research. He became the first informal Secretary of the M.A.U.D. Committee, helping Professor G.P. Thompson, the first chairman. He was later appointed the first Secretary of the British Central Scientific Office in Washington. Much of the secret scientific and technical information passed to the U.S.A. from Britain went through his hands. When he retired from this post before the end of the war he returned to the family house in New Brunswick to be looked after by eight family retainers. When he died in 1975 he left more than $600,000 to found an education scholarship fund to be administered by the President of the University of New Brunswick. Bill was elected to the Savile in 1927 and often used the Club, for which he had a real affection.

Sir Arthur Vick recalls another distinguished Savile scientist with Cavendish connections whose professional life-span, encompassing as it did two world wars, necessarily directed much of his attention towards promoting the country's war-effort. This was Sir Geoffrey Taylor, O.M., F.R.S., elected to the Club in 1922.

> A remarkably versatile physicist whose papers originally published during more than sixty years have been reprinted in four large volumes. He worked in R.A.E. Farnborough during the first war as a member of a team which included Lindemann (Lord Cherwell) and a late fellow Savilian, George McKerrow. He learned to fly and carried out many experiments in the air. Later he and George often sailed together, and they won the Royal Cruising Club Cup in 1927. Arising from these voyages Taylor designed a radically new anchor for small boats, and McKerrow arranged for their manufacture. These C.Q.R. anchors were widely used, and were adopted for some purposes by the Navy. During the Second World War he worked on a variety of topics, including explosives. He also studied the behaviour of parachutes. After the war he returned to the Cavendish Laboratory, Cambridge, and published 47 scientific papers between the ages of 65 and 85. A modest, rather shy but truly happy man.

Despite appearances, not all the Savile's scientists and Nobel prize-winners were connected with the Cavendish. In 1918 Professor Sir Frederick Gowland Hopkins, D.Sc., F.R.C.P., F.R.S., had been elected to the Club. He had qualified in medicine from Guy's Hospital in 1894 but in 1899 had been lured to Cambridge University by that other Savile member, Sir Michael Foster, to establish a new school of Physiology there. His pioneering work in this field won him the Nobel prize for medicine in 1929. Yet another Savile member to be a president of the Royal Society, he was knighted in 1925 and awarded the Order of Merit by King George V in 1935. Hopkins's connection with the Savile was futher reinforced when his daughter, Jacquetta Hawkes, the distinguished archaeologist, married his fellow member, J.B. Priestley.

Like Gowland Hopkins, another pioneer in the related field of neurophysiology was Sir Charles Sherrington, G.B.E., M.D., D.Sc., F.R.S., F.R.C.P., F.R.C.S. He was elected to the Club in 1888 when he was just embarking on a career which was to earn him a world-wide reputation. Again, like Gowland Hopkins he was to become President of the Royal Society and have his work as a physiologist recognized in 1932 with the award of the Nobel prize for medicine. The Gifford Lectures which he had delivered were published under the title *Man on his Nature*. Like so many other Savile members he made time for activities unrelated to his own expert sphere and was, among other things, a not inconsiderable poet.

Sir Cyril Norman Hinshelwood was elected a member of the Club in 1922, the same year as Sir Geoffrey Taylor. He had already earned for himself the reputation of a "boy wonder" when, in 1916, instead of going at once to take up his Brackenbury scholarship at Balliol, he went to the Explosives Supply Factory at

Queensferry, where his outstanding gift for research immediately showed itself. After the war he went up to Oxford, where again he attracted considerable attention, having three of his research papers published by the Chemical Society. Shortly after joining the Savile he published his first book, *Kinetics of Chemical Change in Gaseous Systems*, which was regarded as a milestone in chemical literature. From 1921 he was a tutorial fellow at Trinity College, Oxford, where he established an unsurpassed reputation for his work as a supervisor of research and for the clarity of his teaching. During his years at Oxford he received many honours, which included the Davy, Royal, Leverhulme and Copley medals of the Royal Society, to which he had been elected in 1929, and of which he became president in 1955-60, the latter year being the Society's tercentenary. He was knighted in 1948, and in 1956 he shared the Nobel prize with his friend Semenov for his contribution to chemical kinetics. In 1960 he was admitted to the Order of Merit.

But Hinshelwood was a quintessential Savile all-rounder and merely to list his scientific achievements is to do him less than justice. His pithy sense of humour was much in evidence at the Club and the enormous range of his interests never ceased to amaze. He was a painter of considerable talent, a connoisseur of music and a discerning collector of Chinese porcelain and Eastern carpets. He had also a genius for languages; his eloquent use of written English prose reflecting the clarity which was so remarked upon in his spoken lectures. He was proficient in French, German, Italian and Spanish and was also able to converse in Russian and Chinese. There seemed no end to his polymathy; he was well versed in the classics and in a notable presidential address to the Classical Association he set out his philosophy of language and his strongly held belief in the essential unity of all intellectual disciplines. What is regarded as one of his finest occasional papers was far removed from his profession as a scientist, being an essay on Dante's imagery in the *Divine Comedy*, a work which had inspired him in his other preoccupation with painting. An exhibition of more than a hundred of his oils was held at the Goldsmiths' Hall after his death and these demonstrated, apart from his painterly skill, the wide range of remembered visual images which had so delighted him in life. He was a member of the Arts Council and a trustee of the British Museum; the chairman of Council of Queen Elizabeth College, London; chairman of the scientific advisory committee of the National Gallery; and chairman of the education committee of the Goldsmiths' Company, to whose court he had been elected in 1960 and to which he left most of his considerable fortune when he died in 1967.

To complete the Savile's quiverful of Nobel laureates in science it is only right to add the names of the five who were foreign nationals but found a ready welcome at the Club as honorary or temporary members during their sometimes protracted visits to England in pursuit of their scientific work.

These were the Chicago physicist Professor Edward Williams Morley, who came as a member to the Club for a year in 1899 and who was to receive the Nobel prize for physics for the work which bears his name, "the Michelson-Morley effect";

W. Wien, who was an honorary member in 1904 and who also received the prize for physics; W. Nernst and P. Zeeman, who shared the physics prize and were accommodated in the Club in 1912, and finally, the discoverer of insulin, the Canadian physiologist Professor Sir Frederick Grant Banting, who was an honorary member for twelve months in 1932.

The scientist who had been Sir Cyril Hinshelwood's tutor at Balliol, and who outlived him to be his obituarist in the 1961-70 edition of the *Dictionary of National Biography*, was Brigadier-General Sir Harold Hartley, C.B.E., M.C., F.R.S., who was elected to the Club in 1919. As his pupil Hinshelwood was to do later, Hartley had entered Balliol College, Oxford on a Brackenbury Scholarship and graduated with 1st class honours in natural science before being appointed tutorial fellow there. During the First World War he served with the 7th Leicestershire Regiment but after the German gas attacks began he was put in charge of the Chemical Warfare Department at the Ministry of Munitions. During his war service he was three times mentioned in despatches, won an M.C., was awarded the O.B.E., and rose to the rank of brigadier-general. After the war he returned to Oxford, where there had now arrived, among many other distinguished pupils, the young Cyril Hinshelwood. As a tutor, Hartley was somewhat unorthodox and it was said that he sometimes expected his students to reverse the normal process and instruct him instead. Nevertheless, his work earned him a Fellowship of the Royal Society in 1926.

In 1930 Hartley decided that his work could be of more value in industry so he resigned his academic posts and became vice-president and director of research of the L.M.S. Railway, later chairman of Railway Air Services and, after the war, chairman of British European Airways and, later still, of B.O.A.C. When a change of government brought about his removal from these posts he became the first chairman of the Electricity Council from 1949 to 1952. Again like his pupil Hinshelwood, Hartley was an active member of the Goldsmiths' Company, of which he became Prime Warden in 1941-2. There he initiated a considerable body of historical research on notable nineteenth-century chemists and himself contributed many valuable papers on such figures as Michael Faraday, Joseph Priestley, Sir Humphry Davy and many others.

In 1882 Sir Richard Tetley Glazebrook, F.R.S., who was to become Director of the National Physical Laboratory, was elected. It was something of a vintage year generally for those who were to figure in the public arena as well as in that of science. Perhaps a clue to the reason for this is to be found in the composition of the committee for that year. It included Sir Sidney Colvin; Professor Sir William Thiselton Dyer, F.R.S.; Dr Michael Foster, F.R.S.; Edmund Gosse; Professor Fleeming Jenkyn, F.R.S.; Henry Nottidge Moseley, F.R.S.; Hugo Miller, F.R.S.; Eustace Balfour and Stephen Spring-Rice. These last two are particularly interesting from another point of view in that they illustrate the practice of electing brothers and sons which had been characteristic of the Club — when individual personalities made it an attractive proposition to do so — since the days of the Morrisons and the Herberts.

There were to be eight Balfours in all as members of the Club in those early days. The first of them provided it also with its only prime minister, Arthur James (later, Earl) Balfour, K.G., P.C., O.M., F.R.S.

Despite his many considerable achievements Balfour's conduct at the Club seems by all accounts to have reflected his rather languid attitude to life. After leaving Cambridge with a second class degree and joining the infant Savile he spent his time taking up his considerable inheritance, which included a mansion at Carlton House Gardens where he installed two grand pianos which were to feature in the career of his fellow member, the composer Sir Hubert Parry. At Cambridge he had been a leading member of "The Souls" but, perhaps in a spirit of *noblesse oblige*, in 1874 he allowed himself to be elected to a constituency which, despite reforms in the franchise, still appeared to be in the pocket of his mother's family, the Cecils. However, he did not allow his new duties to become particularly burdensome; it was two years before he rose "to make a dull speech on a dull subject, delivered to an empty house", whereupon he relapsed into silence for yet another year. What would now be labelled his "laid-back" style must have impressed however, for in 1887, to everyone's surprise, he was appointed Chief Secretary for Ireland in succession to the former Savile member, John Morley. In 1891 he was made leader of the House of Commons and in 1902 he became prime minister – a distinction by the way which the previous historian of the Club was too modest to mention.

Arthur Balfour's connection with the Savile had begun in 1871 when with twenty-eight others, including Sir Charles Dilke, the Hon. Lyulph Stanley (later Lord Sheffield) and Lord Fitzmaurice from the Anglo-American Association, he was elected to the "New Club" which four days after his election moved to Savile Row and took upon itself the Savile name.

"It cannot be alleged that A.J. Balfour was ever a constant frequenter of the Club", wrote Sir Herbert Stephen in 1923, "but the Club did not wait as long as the public to discover his quality". In 1921 he was made the first and, until after his death in 1930, the Club's only life-member. One of the few reminiscences of Balfour's visits to the Club comes from Henry Jackson, who for forty years was perhaps the greatest Cambridge figure of the time. He recalled that on a boat-race day he had been sitting in the Club with Arthur Balfour discussing the race. A group of members entered, and A.J.B. anxious not to "disappoint them [and, presumably surmising they would expect the conversation in such company to have a more metaphysical edge] hastily concluded his predictions for the race by saying ". . . and so, Professor, you incline to a gloomy view of the prospects of ontology in the immediate future?" No doubt that was very sharp in the context of its day.

Arthur's younger brother, Francis Maitland Balfour, F.R.S., became a member of the Savile in 1874. He was "not only universally regarded as the right heir of Charles Darwin in the world of biological investigation", wrote Sir Herbert Stephen, "but was one of those men who exact affection from all their acquaintances and are not believed to have enemies". He was elected to the committee of the Savile in 1880 and in 1882 became a trustee of the Club. A month or two later he was killed by an avalanche while on a climbing holiday in the Alps. His eldest brother, the future prime minister, succeeded him as trustee while his youngest brother, Colonel Eustace Balfour, who had been elected in 1876, was honorary secretary of the Club, a position he held from 1881 to 1884. During his thirty-five years of membership he also became a trustee of the Club. It has been suggested, erroneously, that this Balfour was the lover of his contemporary Duchess of Marlborough, née Vanderbilt, whose vaunted Churchill connection turned out tragically. More authentic of this multi-faceted man – musician, architect, and Surveyor to the Duchy of Westminster (Balfour Street, W.1. is named after him) – was his devotion to the Club and the sterling service he provided to it, particularly during the move from Savile Row to Piccadilly.

The Balfour dynasty at the Savile continued with five more members: Professor Isaac Bayley Balfour, D.Sc., K.B.E., F.R.S., who was elected in 1883; Archibald Edward Balfour, who was elected in 1894; Frederick Robert Balfour, elected in 1897; Maxwell Balfour in 1899 and *la fin de ligne,* the Hon. Harry Robert Chichester Balfour, elected in 1910.

Sitting on that 1882 committee which had elected Sir Richard Glazebrook was Stephen Spring-Rice, C.B., then a Principal Clerk in the Treasury and another of the Savilians whose relations would find continuing favour with the election committee. Indeed his brother Cecil was elected at the very same meeting that elected Glazebrook. This was Sir Cecil Spring-Rice, P.C., G.C.V.O., K.C.M.G., a distinguished diplomat who was to serve as British Ambassador to Washington during the First World War, but who is probably better remembered these days – if at all – for those lines in his *Last Poem:*

> I vow to thee my country – all earthly things above –
> Entire and whole and perfect, the service of my love.

Another Spring-Rice, Dominick, son of one and nephew to the other, appeared in 1914.

That 1882 committee meeting, apart from electing Arthur Strachey, who in later years was to become Chief Justice, elected twelve more men of science, among them two who were already Fellows of the Royal Society and seven who would become so in future years.

Among the latter was Dr Francis Darwin, whose family's history encapsulates three of the elements dealt with in this chapter of the Savile story: scientific distinction, public service and family connections with the Club.

Sir Francis Darwin, F.R.S., as he was to become, came to join three other distinguished members of his family who were already installed at the Club and added to a line which continues to the present day. The list of Darwins comprises (at the time of writing) eleven past and present members. In 1911 the Darwins intermarried with the Barlows, another Savile family distinguished in science and public service which has had eight of its members elected since 1906. If we add in a couple of Wedgwoods for good measure (A. Wedgwood Esq., elected in 1868, and the Hon. Josiah, elected 1965), to whom the Darwins are also related by marriage, this adds up to a grand total of twenty-one members of the Savile within one family or, perhaps as they would prefer it, twenty-one members of the family in the Savile.

The three brothers whom Sir Francis Darwin came to join at the Savile were Professor Sir George Howard Darwin, K.C.B., LL.D., D.Sc., F.R.S. who was elected in 1870; Major Leonard Darwin, and William Erasmus Darwin, who were both elected in 1871. They were all sons of the great Victorian scientist Charles Darwin and it was Sir Francis who was to write the three-volume *Life and Letters of Charles Darwin* and *The Foundations of the Origin of Species.* Another Erasmus Darwin was elected to the Club in 1914 but was killed a year later at Ypres. He was followed into the Club in 1919 by Captain Sir Charles Galton Darwin, M.C., the son of Sir George, lawyer, mathematician and Plumian Professor of Astronomy at Cambridge, who had been the first of this long line of Savile members. This Charles Darwin worked with Ernest Rutherford in Manchester during the period of the discovery of the atomic nucleus. In the 1914-18 war he commanded a section in one of the R.E. units organized to detect enemy guns by sound-ranging and won the M.C. After the war he was fellow and lecturer at Christ's College, Cambridge, of which, after short spells in Edinburgh and Copenhagen, he became master. Although he was generally regarded as a warm and genial person, his fellow member of the Savile, C.P. Snow, used him as the model for the unpleasant but successful candidate in his novel *The Masters,* a travesty of the truth which his family and friends found deeply offensive.

Charles's brother William was elected to the Club shortly after him in 1922 and his son, George, thirty years later in 1952. William's sons, Philip and Erasmus are also contemporary members as is Erasmus's son Robert who was elected in 1988.

Sir Horace Darwin was the only one of the five sons of that originator of the Savile species *not* to be a member of the Club. It was his son Erasmus who was killed at Ypres before he could make his mark at the Savile but, more importantly for this history, it was his daughter Nora who began another Savile dynasty when she married Sir Alan Barlow in 1911, two years after he had been elected to the Savile, as his brother Sir Thomas Dalmahoy Barlow had been before him.

These two remarkable brothers were the sons of Sir Thomas Barlow, physician extraordinary to Queen Victoria, King Edward VII and King George V. Thomas Dalmahoy Barlow was elected in 1906. After coming down from Cambridge "Tommy Barlow" as he was generally known joined the family textile firm and rapidly became one of the most prominent figures in the Lancashire cotton spinning and weaving business. He also joined the board of the District Bank in 1922 and became its chairman in 1947. During the war he performed sterling service at the Board of Trade and when the Council of Industrial Design was created in 1944 by Sir Stafford Cripps and Hugh Dalton, he became its first chairman. His interest in beautiful things led to his forming a notable collection of early books and manuscripts which included many fine Dürer woodcuts, engravings and illustrated books. At the Club he was noted for his excellent judgment of food and wine though during the war he liked to set a patriotic example by eating at the rather elementary "British Restaurants" – which were in fact possibly preferable to what was on offer at the Club at that time. Tommy's elder brother Alan, who had married Nora Darwin, had an equally remarkable career and, probably more than any other individual member of his generation, was responsible for steering the Club through the troubled times which ensued after the First World War, for a period as honorary treasurer and subsequently as chairman. After a brilliant spell at Corpus Christi College, Oxford, where he was a scholar and later an honorary fellow, he joined the civil service as a clerk in the House of Commons, where he rose rapidly to the position of Principal Assistant Secretary in charge of the Training Department at the Ministry of Labour. In 1933 he served for an unhappy year as Principal Private Secretary to the Prime Minister, Ramsay MacDonald, before being transferred – much to his relief – to the Treasury, where he stayed until his retirement as joint Second Secretary in 1948. His financial acumen which had been so well recognized in the civil service was also put to excellent use at the Club, as has been remarked elsewhere. Similarly his strong interests in scientific and artistic matters and his wide circle of friends and acquaintances in each of these fields was put to beneficial effect in both his public life and his more private moments at the Club. In his years at the Treasury after the Second World War, Sir Alan was put in particular charge of the Government's funding of the Sciences, for Museums and Galleries, the Arts and academic institutions. At the Club, the dining room display cases were enriched with some selected pieces from the Barlow Collection of Oriental art which has been described as one of the finest private collections in the world. After his retirement he devoted more of his time to artistic pursuits and for seven years was on the board of Trustees of the National Gallery, three of them as chairman of that body.

Sir Alan's son, Captain Sir Thomas Barlow, D.S.C., R.N., who succeeded him as 3rd Baronet, was elected to the Club in 1937. During the last war he served in submarines and afterwards on the British Joint Services mission to Washington. When he retired from the navy in 1964 he was Commodore of H.M.S. *Drake* at Devonport; since then the Darwin genes have become dominant and he has devoted his time to wildlife and the conservation of the countryside, serving on many bodies connected with these aims which include the Charles Darwin Foundation for the Galapagos Islands. Both his brothers also became members, Andrew Dalmahoy Barlow, M.R.C.P., in 1943 and Doctor Erasmus Darwin Barlow in 1951. Erasmus Barlow followed in his father's footsteps by becoming chairman of the Club. However as well as being chairman of the Club, Erasmus has also been chairman of an institution founded by Sir Horace Darwin, The Cambridge Scientific Instrument Company which has featured in the careers of many other Savile members such as Peter Marshall and Leonard Pearce, an ex-treasurer of the Club, who joined the board in 1964 after thirty-seven years with the Bank of England, from which he had retired as Assistant Chief Cashier. This company, perhaps the most famous and best respected scientific instrument maker in the world, has been in the forefront of scientific development since it was founded by Sir Horace Darwin in 1878.

A history of it and an evaluation of its contributions to the development of such invaluable instruments as the seismograph and the first portable electrocardiograph is to be found in the Monument entitled Horace Darwin's Shop, and a glance through its index reveals not only a roster of most of the Savile Darwins and Barlows but a fair smattering of other members from Francis Maitland Balfour to Augustus Désiré Waller, M.B., F.R.S., one of the earlier researchers into the human heart-beat, who was elected to the Club in 1897.

Erasmus Barlow's cousin Basil, elected in 1947, recalls:

> I joined because of a strong family connection with the Club and on my first day I was greeted by someone who said, "My God! Another bloody Barlow!" I think we were seven then and the crowning triumph was a member of staff who looked after the *hors d'oeuvre* table who also bore the name.

Basil's son Nicholas was elected to the Club in 1979 and Erasmus's son Jeremy in 1960.

To do justice to all the members of these families who have distinguished themselves at the Savile and elsewhere and to include all the collaterals such as the Wedgwoods and the Keyneses would require a separate volume. Those who wish to know more could do no better than to refer to *The Intellectual Aristocracy* written by Lord Annan which appears in *Studies in Social History* edited by J.H. Plumb and gives a good account of all their interconnections.

Another Savile "dynasty" but of a less extensive span was founded in 1914 with the election of Thomas Ralph Merton, scientist, inventor and connoisseur of the fine arts. As a schoolboy Merton had equipped a room in his home as a laboratory and at Oxford he attracted much favourable attention, particularly for his work in the field of spectroscopy. During the First World War he was commissioned in the R.N.V.R. to work for the secret service, where he distinguished himself in identifying the secret ink used by German spies, for which he won a mention in despatches. After his marriage in 1912 he had set up his own spectroscopic laboratory at his home in Gilbert Street from where he issued a steady stream of scientific papers which led to his election to a fellowship of the Royal Society in 1920 at the unusually early age of thirty-two. He was to be treasurer of the society from 1939 to 1956 and vice-president from 1941 to 1956, when he had to retire owing to ill health. At the commencement of the last war Sir Henry Tizard had Merton seconded to the Air Defence Committee, where one of his earlier experiments was developed and refined to create the two-layer long-persistence radar screens which contributed so much to the successful outcome of the Battle of Britain. His other wartime inventions which are listed in the *Biographical Memoirs of Fellows of the Royal Society*, to be found in the Monument, are the black paint which reduced the proportion of light reflected from bombers caught in searchlight to less than one per cent; the use of nitrous oxide to accelerate fighter aircraft in battle; and a diffraction range-finder for fighters which was used against doodlebugs. Merton was involved in yet another invention which was to feature so prominently in the war effort, for when Sir Barnes Wallis was being fobbed off by the rather unimaginative bureaucrats at the Air Ministry it was Merton who threw his weight behind him to put into effect the "bouncing bomb" which the Dam Busters were to use with such devastating results. The energy and investment which Merton had put into his scientific enquiries and inventions was brought to bear on the world of art in 1930 when his eldest son, John, brought home the drawing prize from Eton. As a reward he took him on an extended tour of Italy to see all the great collections of Renaissance paintings and from this awakened interest began to form his own remarkable collection. The quality and extent of this can be seen in the beautifully illustrated *Catalogue of the pictures and drawings from the collection of Sir Thomas Merton, F.R.S. at Stubbings House* which is in the Savile monument and includes such incomparable masterpieces as the portrait of Giovanni di Pierfrancesco de' Medici by Botticelli and fifteenth century works by Mantegna and van der Weyden. Merton's artistic flair coupled with his scientific knowledge made him an invaluable asset and for many years he was a member of the Scientific Advisory Board and later trustee of the National Gallery and the National Portrait Gallery.

Thomas Merton had five sons who when they reached their majority were each given a share of the family fortune and enjoined to become a member of a London club. The first four chose the St James's, Brooks's, the Athenaeum and Boodle's respectively though none of them remained members for very long. Colin, the youngest, in 1947 chose the Savile where he still remains an almost daily visitor and for some years the industrious and meticulous honorary librarian. His son Simon at the newly appointed age of majority, eighteen, duly became a member also, in 1989.

So much for some of the more spectacular Savile dynasties.

In 1883, the year after Sir Francis Darwin (fourth of his line) was elected, Sir Vernon Boys, F.R.S., came to join him at the Club which had a few months earlier moved into No. 107 Piccadilly.

> Boys [writes Sir Arthur Vick] earned his living as a Gas Referee but was famous for many other things including the process for making quartz fibres. Sir Richard Paget wrote a song for Boys' eightieth birthday:
>
>> Why does Sir C.V. Boys elect
>> To do the things we least expect,
>> And always choose a task that seems
>> More suited to the land of dreams:
>> A problem other men would shirk,
>> Yet solve the task and make it work
>> By means that no one else employs?
>> The answer is: Boys will be Boys.

147

followed by five verses each describing one or more very different achievements.

One of the "other things" for which Boys was famous was a camera he devised which was used by another Savile member, Sir Basil Schonland, F.R.S., to study the physics of lightning. Elected in 1943, Schonland was yet another member who had spent some years at that Savile annexe, the Cavendish laboratory, where he began his lifelong research into the science of atmospheric electricity. He was elected a Fellow of the Royal Society in 1938 and during the war worked for a time as deputy to his fellow Savilian, Sir John Cockcroft, at the Air Defence Research and Development Establishment before becoming superintendent of the Army Operational Research Group. Later he accompanied the Allied invasion force as scientific adviser to Field Marshal Montgomery. After the war Schonland moved to Harwell to serve once again as Cockcroft's deputy at the Atomic Energy Research Establishment and succeeded him as director there in 1958.

Sir Frederick Gowland Hopkins and Sir Charles Sherrington – the Nobel prizewinners for medicine in 1929 and 1932 respectively – are representative of the ever-growing number of distinguished doctors who were being attracted to the Club as a place where they could mix with men from other spheres of interest, so it is worth a digression here to trace out a list of some from that branch of science who have made, or continue to make, their mark on the history of the Savile.

In the original intake of 1868-9 there had been only four medical doctors – that is, less than three per cent of the total membership – but, as with all the other professions to be found at the Savile, "word of mouth" soon increased the proportion. Indeed, a present member, Sam Musson, recalls that in the 'thirties and 'forties some of the members considered it a *dis*proportion when they gazed out of the morning-room and regarded Brook Street jammed with the Rolls-Royces and Bentleys of doctors who had popped over from Harley Street for a spot of lunch.

In 1928 the Committee were much concerned at the high proportion of medical members and appointed a sub-Committee of three "to consider and report on the advisability of limiting the number of members of any profession to be admitted to the membership of the Club".

The sub-Committee report was:

> Your sub-Committee met on 31 October 1928 and have to report as follows:
>
> That it is undesirable that any profession should be represented in undue proportion.
>
> That at the present time there are 108 qualified medical men in the

Club, of whom 90 are in practice, which is more than double that of any other profession.

Your sub-Committee is of the opinion that it would hardly be practicable, and would certainly be undesirable, to introduce a Rule of the Club which might fetter the liberty of the General Committee in the election of candidates.

At the same time it suggests, in order that the General Committee may be adequately apprised of the merits of medical candidates, that at the present time there should not be less than 3 (three) medical members of the General Committee, of whom one should be a consulting surgeon and one a consulting physician, both on the staff of a teaching hospital, and it submits this proposal for the consideration of the General Committee.

Murmurings, however, continued, the election committee listened, and over a period of time proportional representation was restored.

In 1900, two years after his election to the Royal Society and four years before he became Regius Professor of Medicine at Oxford, Sir William Osler, D.Sc., M.D., F.R.C.P., F.R.S., was elected after having been a "temporary member" on several occasions. Osler had graduated at McGill University in Toronto where his father had been sent as a missionary and spent much of his early professional life in North America where he became celebrated for his work as a teacher at McGill, the University of Pennsylvania and Johns Hopkins University in Baltimore. He was a great innovator and is credited with instituting the system whereby students were made to spend as much time being taught at the patient's bedside as in a remote lecture hall. At Oxford he was more able to indulge his interest in studying the humanities: apart from his medical work he became Curator of the Bodleian Library and as President of the Classical Association delivered a famous address, *The Old Humanities and the New Science*. His influence lingers on for generations of medical students who have been brought up on his magnum opus, *The Principles and Practice of Medicine*. After he died in 1919 his biographers all paid tribute to his personal magnetism as a teacher and the epigrammatic wit and charm which he brought to his social life at the Savile and elsewhere.

One of Sir Charles Sherrington's pupils at Oxford was Walter Russell Brain who as Lord Brain, F.R.S., D.M., F.R.C.P., was president of the Royal College of Physicians and one of the foremost neurologists of his generation. Brain was elected to the Club in 1953 when he was fifty-eight and had already achieved an international reputation for his work and his writings on his chosen speciality. But in 1953 the Savile and its new member seem to have established their mutual attraction on the basis of the many other qualities and interests which he possessed. Besides his professional distinction, Brain had acquired a reputation for his activities as literary critic and philosopher; for literature and philosophy were his main delights outside his work. He used his neurological and psychiatric knowledge to good effect in exploring the works and lives of such writers as Swift, Smart and Johnson, and his various publications on these subjects were gathered together in *Some Reflections on Genius and Other Essays*.

Like his mentor at Oxford and his predecessor at the Savile, Sir Charles Sherrington, Brain was no mean poet. For many years he maintained a close friendship with Walter de la Mare and in *Tea with Walter de la Mare* he recorded many of their conversations. Despite all his many other professional duties he insisted on finding time for his literary interests so that, for instance, in 1963 he was president of the Johnson Society of Lichfield. But it was as a medical man that he was known to the general public. Apart from his senior appointments at various London hospitals, his medical journalism and his presidency of the Royal College of Physicians, he was heavily involved in medical politics and was one of the senior representatives of the profession in negotiations with the Ministry of Health during the early days of the National Health Service. Among his many distinguished patients was Sir Winston Churchill and in 1966 he had cause to write to *The Times* protesting that without his knowledge Lord Moran had published in his memoirs reports on confidential consultations which had been held between them.

Among many honours Brain numbered honorary doctorates of three universities (Wales, Belfast and Newcastle) and honorary fellowships of three Royal Colleges and several overseas societies, though perhaps the honorary fellowship of his old Oxford college gave him most pleasure. He was knighted in 1952, created baronet in 1954 and elevated to the peerage in 1962. The following year he was president of the British Association.

The line of distinguished neurologists which began in the early days of the Club with Henry Maudsley and which was so brilliantly embodied in the aptly named Lord Brain continues to the present time in the person of Professor Peter Behan, who holds a personal chair at Glasgow University. Lord Adrian, M.D., F.R.S., whose encounter with C.P. Snow in his earlier days of membership was described earlier in this book, has been professor of Cell Physiology at Cambridge since 1978 and Master of Pembroke College since 1981. He has been a Trustee of the British Museum since 1979 and a member of the Council for the Royal Society since 1984. Doctor Donald Rau, whose father, in an earlier generation of Savile members, was a friend and medical adviser to Max Beerbohm, carries on his practice in Mayfair and has been, like his brother Anthony, a member since 1964.

Gordon Ostlere, F.F.A.R.C.S., was a member from 1954-1963. He was at one time an anaesthetist at Barts and assistant editor of the British Medical Journal. His only medical publication is *Anaesthetics for Medical Students* though, as Richard Gordon, he is probably better known for his novels, *Doctor in the House* and its fourteen sequels, and for the films and television serials which have been the comic – if unusual – result of his early medical training.

It may be symptomatic of a facet of character to be found at the Savile that many of its practitioners in medicine have tended to explore the by-ways, and whether in the course of clinical observation or for the relaxing balm of being surrounded by eccentricity without the responsibility for treating it, the Club has also included a considerable number of distinguished psychiatrists.

One of the fruitful by-ways was explored by Professor Wilfred Card, M.D., F.R.C.P.S., who was a pioneer in the application of computers to medical diagnosis. In 1966 the international reputation which he had acquired in this field led to Glasgow University establishing a Chair of Medicine in Relation to Mathematics and Computing for him. Card was elected to the Club in 1948 and remained a member until his death in 1985.

Leslie Elgar Gardiner, F.I.C.S., M.R.C.S., L.R.C.P., D.L.O., the world-renowned cosmetic surgeon, has been a familiar figure at the Club since his election in 1953. Leslie, having re-shaped various of their other portions, has probably done as much to shape the careers of many a "star" of stage and screen as their agents or publicists could otherwise have possibly engineered. His pithy comments on some members of the General Medical Council with which he is wont to enliven a conversation in the Sandpit may also have done something to re-shape the features of that sometimes unbeautiful body.

Another distinguished member of the Savile who could on occasion be a thorn in the side of strict orthodoxy was Doctor James Henry Cyriax, who was elected to the Club in 1969. Early in his career Cyriax took time to reconsider and redefine those complaints which were variously described as "fibrositis", "neuralgia" and by a host of other equally vague terms. He developed entirely new concepts concerning these conditions and pioneered fresh approaches to their treatment. Some of these incorporated older practices such as traction or the methods used by osteopaths and chiropractors who were regarded with suspicion by the medical establishment for operating outside the profession. So long as their methods worked Cyriax was happy to use them and though this did not endear him to some of his colleagues he was eventually to be proved right. His work, according to his friend and colleague Dr Henry Sanford – a present member of the Club – "raised the status of the whole of physiotherapy; a debt which was acknowledged by The Chartered Society of Physiotherapists who made him a Fellow in 1980. His *Text Book of Orthopaedic Medicine* in two volumes is an acknowledged classic and runs into at least eleven editions. This and other books have translations into Spanish, German and French. Between 1932 and 1978 he published thirty-four original papers."

In the course of his obituary notice recording the death of Cyriax in 1985, Henry Sandford recalled that despite the rather distant attitude of the medical establishment:

> In his own hospital (St Thomas's) he was popular. His colleagues in other fields were beguiled with his unconventional wit, extrovert generosity and sheer clinical ability. At the same time, he used to say that they found him a strange phenomenon, "whereas they turn up in their Rolls-Royce, I roll up in a No. 53 bus".

The Cyriax Foundation set up during his lifetime to promote his methods exists as his memorial as does the increasing acceptance of his methods among the present medical hierarchy.

Doctor Michael Burleigh-Carson, whose exuberant presence has been felt at the Club since 1974 and who practises in the allied field of osteopathy, was a great admirer of Cyriax's methods and still remembers with awe the visual impact of his suits at the Club and elsewhere which were always fashioned from cloth of various violent shades of green.

Cyriax had demonstrated that not all pioneering in science consists in discovering new things; that sometimes it is more a matter of resurrecting and adapting old ideas which have been left behind in the march of progress. John Bunyan, a former surgeon in the R.N.V.R. and a descendant of the author of *The Pilgrim's Progress*, who was elected to the Club in 1956, also used this principle to good effect with his creation of "The Bunyan Burn Bags". Bunyan had recollected that before the discovery of antibiotics, and particularly in the nineteenth century, burns had been treated with an antiseptic hydrochloride – similar to household bleach – as a healing, sterilizing and pain-relieving agent. It was used in Custer's Indian campaign and in the First World War until it was superseded by antibiotics. Bunyan successfully experimented with this idea and refined it by inventing a "non-friction" plastic bag to contain the fluid which could be used to replace conventional dressings. Resistance to Bunyan's treatment persisted until the Falklands War when he was suddenly asked to supply his "bags" of antiseptic at twenty-four hours' notice and his theories were thoroughly vindicated. For a time Bunyan was abroad as consultant to the Shriners Burns Hospital in Galveston, Texas, where his views had commanded more respect than they had at first in England, but many Savilians will still remember with pleasure his twinkling Chestertonian presence at the Club during his thirty years of membership.

Professor Richard Gregory was elected to the Savile in 1968.

> He is not easily pigeon-holed [bemoaned *The Sunday Times*]. He holds the chair of neuropsychology at Bristol University and is a world authority on perception – particularly the field of optical illusion. Yet he is by temperament and inclination more a philosopher than a psychologist.

He has described himself as an "experimental philosopher" and has created in Bristol a living museum cum laboratory called the Exploratory to help non-expert people find out about scientific principles through personal experience. The general purpose of this enterprise would appeal strongly to his predecessor at the Savile, H.G. Wells, while one of his other projects – a snooker-playing robot – would surely have been of particular interest to Stephen Potter, though in fact, the latter experiment has a very practical purpose in discovering mechanisms which can be applied in robotic surgery or underwater exploration where it would be dangerous for a man to go.

There is a yard of books on a Savile Monument shelf whose titles indicate that there are more dangerous places where man might go than deeply underwater:

Sexual Deviation, *Human Aggression*, *Human Destructiveness*, all proclaim the nevertheless amiable presence in the Club of Anthony Storr, whose explorations into the recesses of the human mind have not always revealed such gloomy prospects: *The Integrity of the Personality*, *The Dynamics of Creation*, and *The Art of Psychotherapy* have shown that there is hope yet for the human race, and this latter belief he has also expressed in relation to his membership of the Savile. In a booklet published to mark the centenary in 1968 Storr wrote:

> ...my life has been enriched [at the Savile]... far more than I had any right to expect. Since I have been a member I have made more friends, real friends, than I would have believed possible or indeed than I ever had before. If I am completely insolvent I shall steal enough money to keep up my membership. A former member, in a different context, put what I want to say far better than I could ever hope to do. He might equally well have been writing about the Savile:
>
>> "Think where man's glory most begins and ends,
>> And say my glory was I had such friends."

Charles Rycroft, that sane and persuasive practitioner of psychoanalysis, evidently endorses this view with the frequency of his visits to the Savile long table. Having sat on numerous committees of the British Psychoanalytical Society and – to use his own words – "held several offices and written numerous scientific papers which received polite, sincere but often uncomprehending praise", he has produced a sequence of witty and scholarly essays and books which are a condign antidote to the wilder eruptions resulting from ill-digested Freud. Packed with eloquent common sense his essays, particularly some autobiographical ones such as *Memoirs of an Old Bolshevik*, are hilarious testimonies that if more of his profession could think like him there would be a lot less madness.

Doctor Gordon Stewart Prince – "the good, kind and gentle Irishman" to quote an old companion at the Club – was elected to the Savile in 1967 and remained a devoted member until his death in 1985. Prince was consultant psychiatrist at King's College Hospital, where he specialized in the treatment of disturbed adolescents. Good and kind he was but, in fact, of Scottish ancestry having merely been brought up and educated in Dublin. He gave himself unstintingly to his work at King's and then would hasten to the Savile to sublimate the stresses of the day at the snooker table or, every Tuesday, at poker. He was a man of great charm and generosity, always prepared to take time to nurture his friendships. Sometimes, however, this could have a different effect to the one intended. A friend of long standing at the Savile found himself immured in the surgical ward at King's for several months. Prince made a point of visiting him daily bearing little gifts. Being a thoughtful person he used his position at the hospital to make these calls outside official visiting hours so as not to intrude upon the patient's family. Being also a man of infinite courtesy and *punctilio* he would make himself known each time to the staff nurse in charge of the ward and seek her permission to make his visit. The Savilian noticed that after a day or two nurses' attitude began to alter from bonhomie to a rather watchful and wary circumspection and that they ceased to visit his bed singly but only in pairs. The screens were only drawn around him in times of dire emergency. It was some time before he overheard the reason as Prince addressed the staff nurse: "Good morning, Staff. I am Doctor Prince the consultant psychiatrist at this hospital and I have come to see..."

He was the most charming of men and greatly missed at Brook Street, where his son, Alistair, still maintains the Princely presence at the snooker and poker tables.

Doctor Brian O'Connell, another habitué of the Savile poker school, has also worked for most of his professional life with disturbed adolescents and until his retirement in July 1990 was for twenty-five years Medical Director of the Northgate Clinic. Brian brought with him from Dublin, where he trained, the sobriquet "the mad doctor" – "mad in this case being a noun, not an adjective, you understand", as he is quick to explain – and now that he is retired has bought himself a snooker cue so that, like Gordon Prince before him, he can transfer his analytical skills from the consulting room couch to the Savile table.

* * * *

Among the Savile scientists there has long been a goodly proportion of naturalists and zoologists, as no doubt befits a Club containing so many Darwins. One of the first to be elected in 1870 was Professor William Thiselton-Dyer, whose achievements were soon to be recognized with a K.C.M.G., C.I.E., LL.D., D.Sc., and F.R.S. His mother was a daughter of Thomas Firminger, who had preceded Sir William Christie as assistant Astronomer Royal at Greenwich Observatory and be came to the Club armed with several other Savile connections. As an undergraduate at Oxford he had been diverted into the study of Natural Sciences by two distinguised future members of the Savile, Professor Ray Lankester and Henry Nottidge Moseley, who were to become his life-long friends. After some years as professor at the Royal Agricultural College, Cirencester, he became assistant director and later director of the Royal Botanic Gardens at Kew, where his administrative ability and botanical accomplishments greatly enhanced its world-wide reputation. Like so many other botanists and zoologists at the Savile he was greatly influenced by Darwin and his presence at the Club attracted many distinguished contemporaries in the same field. His administrative ability was not confined to Kew for he served on the Savile committee from 1874 until 1888 and was their doughty spokesman in 1884 when the proposal to introduce the "black-ball" system of election was defeated.

One of Thiselton-Dyer's great friends, professional colleague and eventually obituarist was Professor D'Arcy Wentworth Thompson, C.B., D.Litt, F.R.S., "The Scholar Naturalist" who was elected in 1886 along with eight other Fellows of the Royal Society. His early experience of the Club was, one hopes, untypical for it would certainly have daunted lesser men. In his biography it is related how:

> Early in the new year of 1886 he was elected to the Savile Club which had lately moved from Savile Row to Piccadilly, and among whose members were Robert Louis Stevenson and W.E. Henley. One day he entered the dining room of the Club where all the members dined at one long table. The only place he found empty was beside Herbert Spencer, philosopher and author of *The Principles of Ethics*. Spencer was renowned for his brusque manners and in his ears he wore little ivory plugs so that he might be spared the conversation of his fellows. On this occasion, however, D'Arcy's resonant voice must have penetrated even beyond the ivory plugs, for, shortly after, Spencer rose from his place, and, taking his plate with him, finished his meal standing at the side-board.

Only slightly less unnerving, apparently, was the experience of Winston Graham who found himself at his first dinner at the Club in 1946 "sitting next to Sir Peter Chalmers Mitchell and opposite H.G. Wells, neither of whom at that time were apostles of lightness and joy". Sir Peter had been elected to the Club in 1894; he was Secretary of the Zoological Society and responsible for the Mappin Terraces and Whipsnade. From 1922-34 he was scientific correspondent to *The Times* though, like most other Savile scientists, he displayed many wider interests and, arising out of his long residence in Spain, wrote a book describing the events leading to the civil war, *My House in Malaga*.

A contemporary of Mitchell's at the Club was the ecclesiastical journalist Sidney Dark, who remembers him thus:

> In a *galère* of what is to me unfailing interest my friend Sir Peter Chalmers Mitchell is perhaps the most interesting. After his long and distinguished direction of the Zoo, Peter had planned to spend the years of his retirement at Malaga, where he had bought a house. But the Spanish Civil War destroyed his home and his plans. Fiercely Left in his opinions, the triumph of Franco remains for him a bitter tragedy and has left him with little hope for the world in which he has played his own part with distinction and with carefully-concealed kindness. He is delightfully intemperate in his contempt of dignitaries. He carries his years with enviable courage and with an air. His candour is both devastating and bracing, and while in the Club in his opinions he is the cat that walks by himself, to a large extent he stands for the Savile spirit. "I don't much like this man," he once said to me of one of our fellow members. "He is one of those damned fools who gets annoyed when I insult him." He is a man with an acid tongue and genial smile, and he is one of the few lucky men who have retained in the 'seventies the exuberant exaggeration of the 'twenties in opinion and expression.

Among the most noticeable members of the Savile over a span of membership which ran for more than sixty years was Sir Edwin Ray Lankester, K.C.B., D.Sc., F.R.S., the eminent zoologist. It was he who had excoriated Yeats's astrological meanderings in the billiards-room at Piccadilly when they had interrupted his kindly offer of some "delightful little chirping tree frogs" to inhabit Compton Mackenzie's island home and had subsequently to suffer the poet's historical musings while he lay helpless on the Piccadilly pavement. Despite his considerable popularity, Ray Lankester could be a formidable companion:

> He was learned and deep, was apt to be dour except among his own circle of the very learned [says George Vaizey in his Savile memoir]. I never presumed to approach him, much less to engage him in conversation.

Lankester's father had been a physician and a distinquished scientist also. In his boyhood he had been accustomed to meet such eminent scientists as Charles Darwin and Huxley, so it was almost inevitable that his professional life should have taken the course it did. Having taken a 1st class honours degreee in Natural Science at Oxford he won the Radcliffe Travelling Fellowship in 1869, the same year that he became a member of the Club. This enabled him to travel to Vienna, Leipzig and Naples, where he studied marine biology with his fellow student and Savilian, Francis Maitland Balfour, brother of the future prime minister. Returned to England in 1872 he became a Fellow and Tutor at Exeter College, Oxford, and in 1875, the year he became an F.R.S., he was appointed to the Jodrell chair of zoology at University College, London. In 1891 he succeeded his fellow Savilian, Henry Moseley, as Linacre Professor of comparative anatomy at Oxford, a post which carried with it a fellowship of Merton College, at which that other less scientifically inclined member of his Club, the undergraduate Max Beerbohm, was already beginning to beguile the Victorian public with his exquisite but rather outré essays such as *A Defence of Cosmetics* ("Most women are not as young as they are painted," etc.) Max, of course, found Lankester's appearance irresistible and when they were both members of the Club produced that caricature which has been described as "the strangely disordered expanse of face, the cheeks like protoplasm in an unsettled state". While occupying the Linacre chair, Lankester was appointed director of the Natural History departments and Keeper of Zoology at the British Museum in South Kensington; he was made K.C.B., in 1907; received the Royal Medal of the Royal Society in 1885, the Copley in 1913 and was elected vice-president for the years 1882-96. Ray Lankester was undoubtedly the leading zoological authority of his day and his insatiable curiosity, wide range of interests and powerful intellect made him a commanding presence in the Club until his death in 1929.

It is of interest, incidentally, that the architect of the Natural History Museum building at South Kensington of which Lankester was director was Alfred Waterhouse, who had been a member of the Savile since 1872. He was also responsible for the design of Strangeways prison which, at the time of writing, has

Robert Bontine Cunninghame Graham, M.P., prolific author and adventurer, known throughout South America as "Don Roberto" (pp. 170-172).

Top left, Sir George Darwin, an early member and the first in a long line of Darwins at the Savile. Top right, Lord Kelvin. Bottom left, Sir Ray Lankester, founding director of the Natural History Museum and a forceful Savile character. Bottom right, Sir John Cockcroft.

Lord Rutherford, head of the Cavendish Laboratory and himself a Nobel prizewinner, whose support led to Cockcroft's winning the Nobel Prize for splitting the atom.

Kingsley Martin

Three caricatures of his fellow
members by Sir David Low: top left,
Sir Gerald Barry; right, Kingsley
Martin; and, below, a favourite
subject, H.G. Wells.

been partially demolished by its ungrateful occupants.

Lankester had two brothers who were also members: Edwin Forbes Lankester, who was a distinguished K.C., and Alfred Owen Lankester, elected in 1892, who was a highly respected physician. They were "great figures of the Savile, great in more senses than one ... Ray Lankester and his two brothers, Forbes the magistrate, and Owen, the doctor", wrote Sidney Dark, the long-time editor of the *Church Times*, who must have possessed considerable courage to have entered the Savile after publishing his unchristian opinions of some of his fellow members in his autobiography *Not Such A Bad Life*.

> They were immense men, each weighing at least eighteen stone. One of them went one day into a cheap tailor's in the Strand to order a suit at the advertised price of thirty shillings. The shopman explained that it was impossible to fit such an outsize gentlemen at this small price. "But", said Lankester, "suppose I bring my two brothers with me?" "Oh well," said the shopman, "that would of course be a very different matter." And the next day, to his consternation, the three outsizes arrived.
>
> Ray Lankester was a strange and wonderful person, and I have always regretted that his biography has not been written by someone with sufficient knowledge to estimate his importance as a scientist and sufficient imagination to appreciate his fantastic qualities as a man. Both H.G. Wells and Peter Chalmers Mitchell could have done the job admirably. Ray Lankester was an extremely rude old man, except to the few people whom he liked. I first met him when I was editing *John O'London's Weekly*, and arranged for the republication in its columns of the admirable popular scientific essays which first appeared in the *Daily Telegraph* and were published in book form with the title *Science from an Armchair*. The old man always remembered this not unprofitable transaction, and we were very good friends. When he was curator of the National History Museum he ordered one of the rooms to be repainted without consulting the trustees, who, at their next meeting, severely censured him for going outside his powers. "We don't like the new paint", said the chairman, "and we must ask you to arrange to have it taken off." "I thought you'd say that," growled Lankester, "but it won't come off". Graciousness was certainly not Lankester's characteristic. In the last months of his life, Dicky Dixon (another Savile member) offered to go to his house in Oakley Street and read to him for an hour or two in the afternoon. When he went on the first day, Lankester said to him, "My brother says that you will read to me. Let me hear the first leader in *The Times*". When Dixon had finished the leader the old man said, "You have a singularly unpleasant voice, but you have got a sense of punctuation. You can begin that Locke novel". One summer, the Savile was entertained by the Oriental Club, in Hanover Square, famous, as its name suggests, for the excellence of its curries. Lankester was brought there one day to lunch, and naturally ordered curry.

The waiter asked him if he would take chutney, and Dixon, anxious for his health, hurriedly said, "I don't think you take chutney, Sir Ray." The old man glared at him. "There is nothing", he growled, "that I hate so much as unauthorized assumptions about my personal habits. I do take chutney." Towards the end of his life his brother Owen took Sir Ray to the Zoo, and he was drawn round the ground in a bath-chair. The bath-chair man was very chatty, and of course not knowing that his passenger was a distinguished naturalist, was full of helpful information. "That's the eagle, Sir, very fierce bird," and so on. Lankester said nothing until the man was drawing him down the inclined plane for the aquarium. "Don't be afraid, Sir, I shan't upset you," he said reassuringly. "And you bloody well better not," was the reply. Forbes Lankester, the police magistrate, was as rude as his elder brother, without his distinction. Owen, the youngest, a genial mountain of a man, was a doctor, and, to Ray's disgust, a keen Churchman and one of the churchwardens at St Martin-in-the-fields. "They tell me", Ray once said, "that my brother has quite a good medical practice. God help his patients!"

Owen Lankester was in his social habits the very antithesis of his brother Ray; of even more heroic girth, this vast mountain of a man "liked to sit at the head of one of the long tables in the dining-room and his repeated bellows of laughter would drown all conversation", says George Vaizey in his memoir.

Although he was, to say the least, more partial to the pleasures of the table than his more serious brother, he nevertheless continued to avoid a tumble down the Club's steps which had so embarrassed his distinguished sibling. However, George Vaizey records that the Savile's Piccadilly portals witnessed an event involving him which was almost as equally dramatic:

After a particularly convivial evening with all too willing cronies, he negotiated the steps, but weaved unsteadily on the pavement and only the good offices of a constable who recognized him saved him from the roadway and a bus.

"Now Doctor Lankester, Sir", the young man said courteously, "I think you'd better let me call you a taxi." "Nothing of the kind! You mind your own business and I'll mind mine." Putting his massive weight behind his arm he gave the officer a mighty push and, this time, it was the awful majesty of law which narrowly escaped a bus. The eventual result was that Doctor Lankester appeared in the dock before a magistrate, accused of being both drunk and disorderly. Frank Harris, the wine-waiter, who spent all his life in service with the Savile Club, was summoned to appear in court and testify as to what he had served Doctor Lankester to drink.

"A small bottle of Apollinaris, Sir."
"Anything else, Mr Harris?"
"Another small bottle of Apollinaris, Sir."

The beak's lips twitched but he managed to say with some appearance of legal serenity:

"I must remind you Mr Harris that you are on an oath."

"Yes, Sir, thank you very much, Sir."

"Well, what else did you serve to the Doctor?"

"Another bottle of..."

"No, no, Mr Harris. According to your evidence Doctor Lankester must have been awash with Apollinaris water. But do you, on oath, seriously affirm that you served Doctor Lankester with nothing else except mineral water?"

There was a pause. The witness stroked his Dundreary moustache as if searching his memory. But the court was then shaken by a bellow from the dock:

"All right, Frank – go ahead and tell them."

"Very well, Doctor, if you say so, I will."

Always respectful, Frank Harris turned from facing him and bowed to the magistrate:

"Bottle of champagne Sir, another bottle of champagne Sir, although I should explain that the doctor had friends with him, he did not drink both himself."

"Quite so, Mr Harris, pray proceed."

"Two glasses of sherry, Sir, a bottle of claret, Sir, three glasses of port, Sir – I am not exactly sure whether Doctor Lankester chose Taylor's ninety-seven or Croft's '04, each member has his preference..."

"Nonsense, Frank," the doctor roared, "whatever the others choose I always take Crofts '04".

"We will not belabour the question of vintage," the magistrate interpolated. "Have you anything to add, Mr Harris?"

"Yes Sir. Two large brandies, Courvoisier if I remember aright, and later some whiskies and soda. I cannot say precisely whether it was four or five – I was serving other members as well."

"That will do, Mr Harris," the beak told him, "thank you for attending this court."

Apparently "the majesty of the law" decided that the entertainment value of this interchange was worth more than any fine, and the good doctor was merely admonished, told to pay the court's costs, and sent on his way back to the Savile with the faithful Frank, no doubt, to start the process all over again. Victorian values, after all, have something to be said for them.

Professor J.B.S. Haldane, F.R.S., was elected to the Club in 1920, appearing in the membership list of that time as "Captain John Burdon Saunderson Haldane", the prefix being a relic of his war service in France, Mesopotamia and

India. The year before his election to the Savile Haldane had been made a fellow of New College, Oxford, where he did research in physiology and published a number of papers in genetics. In 1922 he was appointed reader in biochemistry at Cambridge under that other Savile member, Sir Frederick Gowland Hopkins. However, he was dismissed from this post in 1925 at the instigation of the six-man disciplinary committee known as the "Sex Viri" because he was involved as co-respondent in a divorce case. He appealed and was reinstated whereupon the "Sex Viri" changed their name under the threat, so it is said, of Haldane's proposed pronunciation of their title as "sex-weary".

Like many Savile members before and after him, Haldane held rather unconventional political views. The received idea of a "Gentleman's Club" as a repository of reactionary high toryism has never been so thoroughly shattered as in the Savile and, of all the vociferously left-wing individuals that at one time or another have been found there, Haldane was – with the possible more recent exception of Robert Clark – most decibelifully the foremost. He had become a socialist when a student but his political reaction to the rise of Hitler drew him more and more towards the Communist Party, which he joined in 1942.

Haldane not only commanded the heights of British research into physiology, genetics and biochemistry between the wars, but he was also in a similar class to his fellow Savilian, H.G. Wells, as a popular writer on scientific subjects.

Wittily written books such as *Daedalus* in 1924 and *The Inequality of Man* in 1932 attracted a wide readership, as did his weekly articles in the *Daily Worker*, the editorial board of which he joined as chairman in 1940; it was a post he held until 1950 when his disenchantment with the Soviets' attitude to science caused him to resign from the Party.

Haldane had the rather dangerous habit of trying out some of his experiments on himself, and among his many writings is an essay, "On being one's own Guinea Pig". While he was researching for the Admiralty during the last war on the physiology of diving he did himself a permanent injury. In Ronald Clark's biography there is the following account:

> There were various *ad hoc* problems which were usually dealt with by Haldane himself and in one of which he suffered an injury to his spinal cord that was to give him intermittent pain for the rest of his life. This is due to a bubble of helium formed in this organ while being decompressed when testing in 1940, on behalf of the British Admiralty, a claim by an American firm that a helium-oxygen mixture is safer for divers than air, as being less likely to cause "bends" and other symptoms during a rapid ascent.
>
> He later wrote: "I was decompressed according to a time-table on which I had frequently been decompressed without harm after breathing air. I developed fairly intense pain, and have had some discomfort ever since when sitting on a hard surface. I do not complain. I have learnt to be sceptical of American salesmanship, even if I learnt it the hard way."

160

Early in the experiments Haldane discovered that while oxygen is a tasteless gas at atmospheric pressure it begins to acquire, at about five or six atmospheres, the taste of rather stale ginger beer – "a trivial discovery which, for some reason, pleases me greatly," as he described it in his Personal Note for the Royal Society.

Like many other Savile scientists Haldane was a man of many interests and among his written works is a charming collection of children's stories, *My Friend Mr Leakey*.

As may have been seen, the Savile has always reserved a special place in its affections for the fanciful or the quixotic. Of the handsome selection of members who embodied both these characteristics, Edward George Boulenger, the zoologist and ichthyologist who created the aquarium at London Zoo, must surely be counted among the fruitiest. "Boully", as he was universally known, was elected to the Club in 1913. His father was himself a leading ichthyologist and lepidopterist and a Fellow of the Royal Society. Of Huguenot extraction, he had migrated from Belgium before the First World War and taken up residence in the Strand, where the young Edward George spent his teenage years. By his own account Boully's parents were rather casual about his upbringing. He was fond of relating at the Club how they had made arrangements for him to be confirmed at St Paul's Cathedral but sent him along on his own to attend that ceremony. According to one of his intimates, Boully dutifully walked through the Strand and down Fleet Street to the foot of Ludgate Hill. The Cathedral was in sight but still there was the hill to be surmounted and the day was warm. Boully turned into the pub below the railway bridge and ordered a pint of beer; then another and another until he felt ready and able to face the bishop. However an attractive looking woman accosted him with such friendly overtures that Boully found himself on his knees at her flat rather than in the Cathedral. Three times, so he affirmed, he made the proper responses and then returned home well-satisfied to tell his parents that he had been well and truly confirmed. His style of life thereafter was to display a similar *insouciance*. During the First World War he was one of that intrepid band of "Balloonatics" who "hedge-hopped" over the German lines in Heath Robinson contraptions made up of balloons equipped with outboard motors to photograph or shoot everything in sight. Returned from the war he made such ferocious inroads into the Club's wine cellar that they made even Owen Lankester's similar depredations seem relatively modest. Warned by his doctor that he had developed a life-threatening stomach ulcer and must abjure alcohol, he responded by doubling his intake. He called this "pickling his ulcer" and as he survived until well after the Second World War – in which he served in Intelligence – there seems to have been some justification for this unorthodox therapy.

Between the wars Boulenger had found time from his social activities to pursue his professional career, of which one of the greatest achievements was his creation of that dazzling kaleidoscope of exotic fishes which is the aquarium at the London Zoo. Sadly, in view of their wildly contrasting life-styles, there is no record in the Club annals of his interchanges with the less outgoing Ray Lankester, who, among his many other accomplishments, had been founder and life president of the Marine Biological Association and its laboratory at Plymouth.

However, having missed his first appointment with a bishop, Boully's piscine expertise brought about an interesting confrontation at the Club with another, this time none less than the Archbishop of Canterbury. It was the custom during the 'twenties for the committee to hold occasional dinners at which distinguished guests connected with their respective professions might be invited. At one such, a guest was Cosmo Gordon Lang who, after the meal was over, made a point of speaking to each of his fellow diners in turn. To Boully he said:

> "Mr Boulenger, I am told that you consider yourself something of an authority on queer fish?"
>
> "Well, your Grace," said Boully, "as the founder of the aquarium at the London Zoo, I suppose I must be."
>
> "Don't you believe it," said the Archbishop, "I am the greatest. Just look at some of my clergy."

But Boully's stomach ulcer was simmering away beneath the ebullient surface and in the 'fifties he retired to Polperro in Cornwall knowing his time to be short. Making his farewell to George Vaizey he said that his only dying wish was that he should "ascend to Heavenly bliss drinking champagne out of a silver chalice". Strangely, his wish was to be granted, and moreover through the good offices of a fellow member of the Savile. Walter Greenwood, the author of *Love on the Dole*, was spending a few days with him in Polperro at the time when Boully suddenly had a haemorrhage and realized he was dying. Greenwood wanted to run and fetch a doctor but Boully roared, "Nonsense, too late for that. To the pub and get some champagne and on the way back pick up a chalice." Greenwood set off and purchased the champagne, but not even in his friend's extremity could he summon up the nerve to ask the vicar for a loan of his communion plate. However, the publican knew a village worthy who had been something of an athlete in his time and had many silver cups to show for it and so Greenwood was able to race back to let Boully ascend happily into what one hopes was "heavenly bliss" drinking champagne out of a silver cup awarded some years previously for a record-breaking mile. There is an amusing cartoon of him in the card-room drawn by his fellow member, David Low, which depicts him as a genial but evidently hard-drinking fish.

In 1928 Professor C.F.A. Pantin, F.R.S., P.P.L.S., was elected to the Club. At the time he was working in a related field to that of Boully Boulenger at the Marine Biological Association's laboratory at Plymouth, which had been the brain-child of Ray Lankester. His impressive research on the nervous systems of various marine invertebrates and his contribution to post-Darwinian scholarship led the following year to a fellowship at Trinity College, Cambridge, where in due course he became Professor of Zoology. Throughout his long and distinguished career his professional and social life overlapped with many of his colleagues at the Savile such as, for instance, Gwynne Vevers, who was vice-president of the Linnean Society during the period that Pantin was president. In his later years he was an active committee member of the Royal Society, to which he had been elected a Fellow in 1937. In 1963, six years before he died, he became chairman of the trustees of the British Museum (Natural History).

Just as in another sphere of science the Cavendish Laboratory appeared to have a disproportionate Savile contingent, so, in the study of marine biology, did the Marine Biological Association laboratory at Plymouth. Professor G.P. Wells, F.R.S., Emeritus Professor of Zoology in the University of London – known to all as "Gip" – was yet another Savilian who conducted much of his research there as well as at similar institutions at Bangor and Naples. A powerful figure in his chosen field, which he decorated with scholarship and wit, his non-professional activities were closely intertwined with the Savile, to which he was elected in 1929 and where he spent much of his week-day leisure time for the rest of his life.

Gip was the elder son of H.G. Wells, who, as we shall see, was still in exile from Brook Street at that time, but Gip was well able to establish his own niche without the aid of a famous father. An elegant summation of his career and personality was provided by his friend and colleague at the Savile, Erasmus Barlow, at the memorial held for him in 1985:

> Gip had a distinguished career as a scientist, a teacher and a broadcaster. He became Professor of Zoology at University College, London, where he spent nearly all his working life, and his scientific work was recognized by his Fellowship of the Royal Society. The research that led to these and other distinctions was carried out very largely on the biological rhythms of lug-worms, of all unlikely subjects. But that was a choice typical of his highly original and individual approach to the world around him. ... a fascinating person. He was a great communicator. This became apparent early in his career when he collaborated with his father and Julian Huxley to produce *The Science of Life,* that great pioneering work which showed how a scientific subject should be popularized. For years he chaired *Who Knows* for the B.B.C. This was an important question-and-answer programme before the days of phone-ins. Gip formed panels of experts to deal with a vast range of biological problems and would end each subject with a brilliant and lucid summary. It was that ability to say things briefly and clearly that made him such a popular member of another great B.B.C. series, the *Brains Trust.*
>
> That was all part of his professional work, done to his exacting standards. But these standards came out in his personal communications too, whether verbal, written or drawn. Gip could salvage a sticky party by bringing it to life with some original turn of conversation. Which of us

hasn't been delighted and enchanted to receive a terse and witty postcard made even better by a brilliant sketch? He could keep children and grown-ups happy for hours just with a pencil and the back of an envelope.

This was part of Gip's strong artistic streak, which showed in other ways than his brilliant sketches. For example in his unconventional garden. Great splodges of species roses and other brightly coloured plants which he enjoyed moving around, even leaving weeds for exciting new effects. Most of all, though, it showed in his love of music. His taste was yet again highly individual, Wagner to Scott Joplin, with much in between: wasn't there a strong rhythmic influence stretching through his interests, lug-worms, dancing, Scott Joplin? Meeting him in an interval at the opera was always fun; his comments were often more enjoyable than what was going on on the stage.

Whatever common threads ran through his life, he did like to keep his interests in separate compartments. His professional work was done to uncompromising standards of integrity, to which his many publications in the scientific literature will always bear witness. This was kept quite apart from his private life, which was itself divided into his London existence based on the Savile Club and his country one of Dunsmore – best of both worlds he would say. The Club owes a lot to Gip, who applied the same high standards in all he did for it as a committee member, secretary for elections, and trustee. When he had to describe candidates for membership to the committee he would present the facts fully and fairly, and with great wit, but never with malice however much the individual deserved it.

More controversial was his resistance to letting women into the Club except on rare and special occasions. Not so at Dunsmore, where many were welcome. There too his individual approach was fully evident, along with his impish sense of humour. But I know some who were definitely not amused when they discovered that a delicious stew was made from squirrels he had trapped in the garden....

Gip's sense of humour was much more greatly appreciated when it was employed to defuse potentially explosive situations, and dotted about at various relevant points in this present history will be found several examples of the skill with which he contrived peaceful solutions to heatedly argued problems. The U.C.L. Bulletin for November 1985 recalls that:

> At committee meetings Gip produced two fountain pens, one with red ink and one with black. He passed the time drawing on scraps of paper, although always with a sharp ear for the business in hand. These sketches were much collected, and some have been retained in college.

He employed the same technique at Savile committees and fortunately some have been saved for the archives, though it is likely that many more are in private hands.

Gip was greatly liked by every generation of Savilians during his fifty-six years of membership, and to this affection was added the professional respect of those many colleagues who were more able to appreciate the more serious applications of his work; men like Lankester, Pantin, Boulenger and Vevers.

When he was demobilized from the First World War, Boulenger had returned to work at the Zoo and shared a house near by with his fellow member of the Savile, the surgeon Geoffrey Marr Vevers, father of the late-lamented Gwynne and grandfather of the present Geoffrey.

The first Geoffrey Vevers had served in the R.A.M.C. during the First World War and, after being demobilized, became a Beit Research Fellow at the Gower Street School of Tropical Medicine, where he worked with Professor R.T. Leiper, F.R.S., a member of the Savile, before he was persuaded by yet another member, Sir Peter Chalmers Mitchell, to join the staff of the Zoological Society, where he eventually became Superintendent of the London Zoo. His son Gwynne was to follow him there in 1955, becoming at first Curator of the Aquarium which had been established by Edward Boulenger.

Gwynne Vevers was elected to the Club in 1949 when he was working at the Marine Biological Laboratory in Plymouth, which as we have seen had been founded by a previous Savile member, Ray Lankester. Gwynne soon showed himself to be typical of many Savile scientists in his seemingly effortless versatility: as one of the most eminent marine biologists of his day, a fluent writer and linguist, he wrote or translated over a hundred books in the eight languages of which he was a master. He also wrote a number of children's books which were a great success throughout the world.

During the Second World War he served in R.A.F. Intelligence in Iceland, where he had the ice floes photographed to discover the deepwater channels. When the German battleship *Bismarck* disappeared from the Bergen Fjord he predicted her position and confirmed it by reconnaissance aircraft and she was duly sunk. For his service in Iceland he was appointed M.B.E. (Mil.) He subsequently served in the Air Ministry, working on Enigma ciphers, and in Germany.

Like his predecessors at the Club, H.G. Wells and J.B.S. Haldane, Gwynne possessed the great gift of writing beautiful English prose in such a clear style that he could make the most complex subjects immediately comprehensible to the layman. He edited all the scientific publications of the Zoological Society of London including the *Journal of Zoology* and the *Zoological Record*.

He was vice-president of the Linnean Society and served on the councils of a number of learned societies but still managed to maintain a vast range of interests – he made many natural history programmes for wireless and television for instance, and served on the National Film Archive for many years. But, as his son Geoffrey pointed out in a memoir, the Savile Club formed a very important part of his life:

During thirty of his forty years of membership he was involved in the administration of the Club: firstly as Secretary for Elections, later as Chairman of the General Committee and latterly as Trustee. It was here that he felt most at home, enjoying the wit and bonhomie of his fellow members...

who, in turn, appreciated his immense erudition, hidden under a friendly modest manner which, as Tom Baistow wrote of him,

> put new members instantly at ease but didn't deceive old friends who were able to tempt him at the bar or over lunch into a learned dissertation on anything from Ken Livingstone's newts to the Gothic roots of Icelandic.

During his long reign as honorary secretary for elections in succession to Gip Wells, he could on occasion demonstrate the unobtrusive tact with which he was used to achieving his purposes without creating any public fuss. "Come, my dear chap," he might say to a member, "and let me have your opinion of this new picture we have in the Sandpit." And then, out of earshot of others: "This candidate of yours. Wonderfully talented, no doubt, but I wonder if we are quite ready for him yet, or whether this is quite the *right time* to put him up." Very few resisted the hint; he was rarely, if ever, wrong and the Election Committee was saved a lot of time and argument. As one of his obituarists concluded:

> He led a varied life to the full, achieving in many fields what most would have been happy to attain in one, yet he always liked to be in the background – albeit controlling events.

Lord Zuckerman, in a personal memoir written for the Zoological Society, mentions that in Gwynne Vevers's final year at Magdalen College, Oxford, he had tutored him in his special subject "secondary sexual coloration" and that it was a suggestion of his which led to Gwynne's D.Phil. thesis on the effect of the recently isolated oestrone on the sexual plumage of the Amhurst pheasant. Zuckerman records that:

> Until the onset of war in 1939 Gwynne remained in Oxford. Influenced by the colourful James Fisher, who was still around when Gwynne went up, he led an undergraduate team to the Faroes in 1937, and then to Iceland in 1939, making censuses and studying the gannet, guillemot and puffin.

Gwynne Vevers's great friend, the "colourful" James Fisher, elected to the Savile in 1942, became one of the best-known ornithologists of his generation and a prolific writer on the subject. Like the Veverses, father and son, before him, he went to work at the Zoological Society of London after graduating from Oxford, but ornithology was his major passion and in the late 'thirties he was one of the founders of the British Trust for Ornithology, of which he was honorary secretary from 1938-44. In collaboration with his fellow member, Sir Julian Huxley, he set up the Nest Record Scheme which involved for the time the properly organized co-operation of professional and amateur ornithologists.

The Times wrote of him:

> With his enthusiasm, his engaging manners and his well stored mind he was a born evangelist for ornithology. Certainly his scores of broadcasts both on sound and television must have drawn thousands of people to the study of birds which of all the postwar leisure pursuits has had the highest growth rate.

"Scores of broadcasts" was something of an understatement, for during a period of twenty-five years he made over 1,000 broadcasts of which about 200 were on television.

From his early days at Oxford and throughout his subsequent career, Fisher's especial interest in the study of Arctic seabirds, the Atlantic Gannet and the Fulmar Petrel in particular, led him to organize many expeditions of similarly minded young enthusiasts to remote sites in northern waters. After his election to the Club these took on more and more the aspect of a series of Savile outings. In May 1946, for instance, he organized a visit to the island of Skomer off the coast of Pembrokeshire. The party consisted of himself; Stephen Potter; Doctor Julian Huxley, ex-Secretary of the London Zoo and Director-General of Unesco; and Keith Piercy, chairman of Bedfordshire Natural History Society. The only non-Savilian present was a Lincolnshire postman named Reg who had apparently "remained a bachelor all his life because he feared marriage might interfere with his bird-watching". They were welcomed at Skomer by the Chief Warden, another Savile member, Ronald Lockley, who was setting up a bird observatory there. Lockley had lived on nearby Skokholm before the war, had written several books about it, and was an authority on Manx shearwaters. The party was housed in the dilapidated and sparsely furnished remains of a farm. Fisher, Piercy and Potter had to share a room containing three iron bedsteads. The only touch of colour noted by Keith Piercy was provided by two pink scarves belonging to Fisher and Potter, who were both members of Leander, having rowed for their colleges at Oxford. Julian Huxley referred to them henceforth as "Leanderthal Men".

In September 1947 another expedition under the auspices of the Royal Society, the Advisory Committee on Airborne Research Facilities, and the Air Ministry, set out in a Sunderland flying-boat with the objective of carrying out a census of young seals throughout every island in Scotland and Wales. Again under the direction of James Fisher the party included Keith Piercy and Ronald Lockley. During a stop-over at Invergordon, a further Savile Club reunion was held when Eric Linklater and his wife Mary came over from Nigg to dine with them at the Royal Hotel.

Fisher made one notable expedition without such Savilian reinforcements. In

September 1955 he was lowered on to Rockall from the helicopter of H.M.S. *Vidal*, the first professional naturalist to land on this barren islet, which became the subject of his book *Rockall* published in 1956.

Fisher left academic life due to his disappointment at not succeeding to the directorship of the Edward Grey Institute of Field Ornithology which, in common with most comtemporary experts, he felt should rightly have been his. Instead he turned to publishing; from 1946-1954 he was natural history editor at Collins – a position now held by a contemporary member of the Savile, Michael Walter – and one of the founders of their New Naturalists Library, a series of works "whereof", to quote *The Times*,

> the best volumes were truly brilliant. He himself contributed a monograph of *The Fulmar* (1952) which will long remain the definitive work.
>
> Later Fisher became a publisher in his own right. He had a great "feeling" for fine books and was much interested in the art of colour printing. Widely travelled and with an enormous acquaintance among zoologists, he placed both his knowledge of birds and his abilities as a publicist most generously at the service of the Royal Society for the Protection of Birds, being for many years on the Council of that body and receiving its gold medal for his contributions to the cause of bird protection. In 1968, he became deputy chairman of the Countryside Commission.

Two of James Fisher's sons were to follow him into the Club. Edmund, the publisher who had been managing director of Michael Joseph before, seemingly, he had cut his wisdom teeth, was elected as a "provisional" member in 1957. Later as the token "wunderkind" he was promoted to the committee shortly afterwards. His brother Crispin, who had followed in his father's professional footsteps, was elected in 1964 but sadly died untimely.

It is surprising that Sir Julian Huxley's membership of the Savile, though evidently a merry one, should have been so short and so long delayed. This eminent zoologist, philosopher and public figure was seventy years of age before he was put up for election in 1957, though throughout his career he had been constantly involved both professionally and on terms of friendship with many notable Savilians and, indeed, his own father, Leonard, had been elected a member in 1884. Huxley's career therefore belongs to other history books than this though his brief passage through the Savile is perhaps worth noting for reasons other than the escapades with James Fisher, Keith Piercy and Stephen Potter described earlier. He was, for instance, a co-author with H.G. and Gip Wells of the monumental *The Science of Life* and when he became full-time secretary of the Zoological Society of London it was in succession to another Savilian, Sir Peter Chalmers Mitchell.

James Fisher's enthusiasm for ornithology had struck oil in various other unlikely places, one of which as we have seen was in the imagination of Stephen Potter who had been his occasional companion on scientific trips and an associate in many of his B.B.C. broadcasts. Potter's biographer, Alan Jenkins, records that in 1946-7:

> Stephen's old interest in wild life, always renewed whenever he met James Fisher (who was responsible for some of the Bird-manship gambits in *One-Upmanship*) was stimulated about this time by Sir Peter Scott, yet another Savile Club friend; and the Potters were guests one year at the Wildfowl Trust dinner at the Guildhall. "Everything we ate, except the pudding, had been caught or shot," Heather (Potter's wife) remembers. In return, Stephen did some research into place-names and bird-names associated with wild life. It had all begun in a Lifemanship ploy of Peter Scott's:
>
> "One evening when we had been dining together at the Savile Club, Stephen got out a cigarette. I leant across to light it with one of the then quite new gas-filled lighters. 'I say, that's rather a good lighter,' he said. I handed it to him and he tried it a few times, 'D'you like it? Well, then it's yours,' I said. 'By all means keep it.' Stephen was clearly delighted. What he did *not* know was that I had that week given up smoking. I was not going to water down the Oneupmanship of my apparent generosity by telling him."
>
> Stephen had temporarily abandoned volume II of his autobiography for "a long book on English Natural History Words, their background etymology, etc." In this he would boldly challenge established authorities such as the *Oxford English Dictionary*. In letters to Sir Peter Scott he derived "Slimbridge", centre of the Wildfowl Trust in Gloucestershire, from "Heslinbruga", in the Domesday Book, meaning "hazel bridge"; and "duck" from an old German verb meaning "dive", through a chain of words stretching back to an Aryan root by way of Latin, and aside to a Dutch word meaning "decoy". The name "Scott" once may have meant "wanderer", and may be related to Old French *escote* = a spy. "That would mean," Stephen concludes, "that you were originally a tremendous hero or a frightful rotter, according to which side you were on".

Sir Peter Scott who was elected to the Club in 1954 could certainly lay claim to the first of that choice of descriptions, having been mentioned in despatches three times, awarded the M.B.E. and the D.S.C. and Bar for his service in the navy during the 1939-45 war. A bronze medallist for single-handed sailing in the 1936 Olympics, as painter, broadcaster and writer on the scientific observation of birds he became famous in nature conservancy circles throughout the world. The Wildfowl Trust which he founded and directed until the end of his life serves as a permanent memorial to one of the Savile's many remarkable members.

There have, of course, been many other Savilians, past and present, who have made notable contributions to the cause of nature conservancy. Sir Jack Longland, famous at the time as chairman of "Round Britain Quiz", for instance, who was elected in 1951, was a member of the Mount Everest Expedition in 1933 and two years later took part in the British East Greenland Expedition. Like his fellow member, James Fisher, he served on The Countryside Commission from 1969-1974. Dillwyn Miles, elected in 1980, has served on the Nature Conservancy Committee for Wales, has broadcast on television and radio, and written many books and articles on the history, flora and fauna of his native Pembrokeshire. A Fellow of the Royal Geographical Society since 1946, Dillwyn has also rejoiced in the title of Grand Sword Bearer to the Gorsedd of Bards of the Isle of Britain from 1959-1967, since when he has been The Herald Bard. Ian MacPhail, a member of the Club since 1948, has put his skills as a Communications Consultant for many years at the service of The World Wildlife Trust.

But of all the Savile members who have felt passionately about their heritage and used their considerable talents in several different fields to promote and preserve it, none stood out so dramatically in his day as Robert Bontine Cunninghame Graham, who was elected to the Club in 1916. Although, as a founder and first president of the Scottish Nationalist Party, he is best remembered in Britain for his efforts to promote the interests of the country of his male ancestors, he was equally revered in Spain and South America where – in the Argentine – he even had a town named after him.

To find his like, one would need to hark back to Elizabethan adventurers such as Walter Raleigh or Philip Sidney. "Traveller, poet, horseman, scholar, Scottish nationalist, laird and socialist," as the *D.N.B.* breathlessly describes him in its opening paragraph, he was a scion of two ancient Scottish families; the Cunninghams, earls of Glencairn, and the Grahams, earls of Monteith, through whom he was descended from King Robert II of Scotland. Tall and of striking appearance with flowing hair, bristling moustachios and a sharply pointed beard, he bore himself, so it was said, like a Spanish Don; and, indeed, his maternal grandmother was a high-born Spanish lady who had given birth to his mother in the admiral's cabin in a ship on the West Indies station. This aristocratic duenna, who could remember Goya, taught him Spanish and brought him up in the Spanish way so that he was as much at home in Spain, Morocco and South America (where he was to spend much of his time) as he was in Scotland or London. In his flamboyant youth he would astonish the Victorian *ton* and demonstrate his cosmopolitanism by trotting through Rotten Row on a fine English hunter but sporting an elaborate Mexican saddle. To the more sentimental "Scottish loyalists" he was the "uncrowned King of the Scots"; to the neighbours of his estates there he was simply the Laird of Gartmore; to the South Americans he was "Don Roberto" but in revolutionary circles in the London of the 'eighties he was "comrade". This came about after he was elected Liberal M.P. for North West Lanarkshire in 1886, when his work for the poorer classes and his great friendship with William Morris soon converted him into an ardent socialist. He spent some time in prison after being involved in the famous riot in Trafalgar Square on 13 November 1887 to protest against the imprisonment of the Irish leader, William Smith O'Brien. Two of the crowd were killed and the event became known as "Bloody Sunday". Another Savile member, A.J. Balfour, was Chief Secretary for Ireland at the time and his involvement on the side of authority caused him to be known as "Bloody Balfour". Cunninghame Graham also distinguished himself in Parliament by being the first M.P. to be suspended for using the word "damn" during a debate. But a great deal of his life's work was associated with the several countries of South America and the states of the North where he travelled extensively and formed many deep friendships with such agreeable figures as "Buffalo Bill". During his long and adventurous life, moreover, he managed to publish a formidable list of books, essays and sketches based on his travels and wide range of sympathies. His profound knowledge of old Spain and the Conquistadores was also set down in nine volumes of historical and biographical studies.

In his memoirs of the year 1952 – the centenary of Cunninghame Graham's birth – his friend Sir Compton Mackenzie records:

Robert Bontine Cunninghame Graham died in the Argentine in 1936 when he was attending the birth of a new town to be called Don Roberto. His body was brought back across the two Atlantics to lie beside his wife in the grave that thirty years before he had dug for her on Inchnahome, the isle in the Lake of Monteith. There on 24 May I was privileged to attend the centenary commemoration of a man whose friendship had been very dear to me. The commemoration was organized by the Young Scots National League. It was a moving occasion with prayers, psalms, pipes, songs and speeches. In my speech I quoted from the speech Don Roberto had made at Stirling on Bannockburn Day, when he unfurled for the first time the flag of the Scottish National Party.

"I lay upon you as a sacred duty that you agitate until our old Parliament is restored and once again Scotland takes her place as an Independent nationality in the family of nations…. We must have Scottish sentiment, we must have that which elevates mankind. I call upon you all here under this flag never to cease agitating until we get that autonomy for Scotland which alone can revive our ancient spirit and make real Scotsmen of us."

I was remembering that Bannockburn Day of twenty-two years earlier. Don Roberto and I were driving together in an ancient limousine at the tail of the procession through Stirling. He turned to me and said, "You know, we both ought to have ridden to the field instead of crawling along in this abominable motor-car. I suppose it would be damned hot walking up this hill."

"It would indeed," I said fervently. "And don't forget we have to do a lot of spouting."

"Yes, I suppose we'd better stay where we are, but, *caro amigo*, we do look uncommonly like the tail end of a circus procession."

In a broadcast I said: "Cunninghame Graham's knowledge of Spanish gave his prose, as it gave W.H. Hudson's prose, that Latin lucidity. I commend to young writers now under the influence of contemporary deliquescent North American prose an intensive study of W.H. Hudson and Cunninghame Graham.... We may call Don Roberto a happier knight-errant than Don Quixote, for although he did not live to see his dreams for Scotland near to fulfilment he was spared much disillusionment.... Yes, he rides now his white steed with the Mexican saddle in Elysium's Rotten Row, a happy warrior."

Among those Savile members engaged in public life in Cunninghame Graham's day there had been a greater proportion of M.P.s than there are now. Most of them demonstrated, as "Don Roberto" did, a hearty disregard for the more conventional political opinions and were also capable of expressing themselves equally well from platforms other than those provided in both houses of parliament. Moreover their interests were hardly ever exclusively political and they were as likely to be more famous in other worlds than in the rarefied sphere of pure politics.

The Club's "founder", Auberon Herbert, was typical of the Savile's generous approach to politics, embracing as he did any passing political party which happened to accord at any one particular time with his own immutable personal views. He was widely known as "the Politician in Trouble about his Soul". Sir Herbert Stephen wrote of him:

> A member of a Conservative family, and no doubt personally a Conservative, he began his political life as private secretary to Sir Stafford Northcote ... but some time in 1868 he resigned that office, and at the general election in the autumn of that year stood as a Liberal or Radical candidate for Berkshire. When first returned to the House of Commons he was regarded as an advanced Radical, but for many years before his death he was considered almost a reactionary, by reason of his uncompromising championship of the rights of the individual.

If, post-mortem, Auberon Herbert is able to scan from his celestial cross-bench the subsequent lists of Savile members, he will see that a great proportion of those who have engaged in politics since he did have adopted a similar attitude to his own. There were men like his contemporary, Sir Rowland Blennerhasset, of whom Sir Herbert Stephen also wrote:

> [he] knew everybody in Dublin amd nearly everybody at Westminster, and by the variety of his knowledge and the charm of his conversation was enough to make an attractive Club by himself.

Blennerhasset's "variety of knowledge" had been acquired at the universities of Oxford, Louvain, Munich and Berlin, and he sat first as a Liberal M.P. for Galway City and later for his native County Kerry. A prominent Roman Catholic, he was associated closely with Lord Acton in his campaign against Ultramontanism and wrote many articles in the leading journals on political and religious topics of the day. His fellow Irishman and member of Parliament at the Savile was Justin M'Carthy, who is described rather sniffily by Sir Herbert Stephen as

> ...a reputable novelist, and a maker of cheap history, [who] was at one time leader of a section of the Nationalist party in the House of Commons, and was described by Mr Parnell as "a nice old gentleman for a quiet tea-party" – praise to which, as far as it went, M'Carthy was undoubtedly entitled.

In fact M'Carthy was an extremely distinguished and effective politician in the service of the Irish cause as well as being a considerable journalist, novelist and historian. He held the Irish Nationalist Party together after the Parnell scandal and it is a significant tribute to his political skill as well as his considerable charm of manner that in all that savage controversy he succeeded in doing so without making any enemies. This must have been particularly difficult for him vis-à-vis W.E. Forster, the then chief secretary for Ireland and a relentless and bitter foe of Parnell, who had been contemporary with him at the Club.

His novels also possessed great charm and have been compared with those of Goldsmith; had he not devoted so much of his energy to politics he would undoubtedly have died rich. As it was, his health broke down, he went blind and had to leave parliament and give up writing. In 1903, his fellow-member of the Savile, Arthur Balfour, who was by then prime minister, and apparently thought better of him than Sir Herbert Stephen, arranged a Civil List pension of £300 a year for his services to literature.

The Parnell-Kitty O'Shea affair and its tragic aftermath in which Justin M'Carthy was so unhappily involved lends a certain piquancy to an enigmatic passage in Sir Herbert Stephen's account of the Club's early years when he refers to:

> ...Donald Crawford, who served in Parliament for many years, but became involuntarily famous in connection with the fortunes of another member, both of the Savile and the House of Commons – Sir Charles Dilke.

Despite the fact that Dilke had ceased to be a member by the time the scandal broke, the notorious affair in which he was involved must have caused seismic reverberations in the Club rooms, for it featured not only the wife and mother-in-law of one member but the widow of another.

Sir Charles Dilke held, like so many other Savilian M.P.s, rather unconventional views. Born into a wealthy landed family and having enjoyed a highly promising university career at Cambridge, where he was a noted scholar and sportsman, he astounded his contemporaries in 1868 by publishing a best-selling polemic entitled *Greater Britain* in which he propounded the notion that if only the English would abolish the monarchy and its consequent hierarchical society it would become the most powerful nation on earth. In that same year he entered Parliament as Radical M.P. for Chelsea, where at first he was given to expressing extremely left-wing and anti-monarchical views, although in the course of time these became less strident and a promising career seemed to beckon.

In 1869 he succeeded to the baronetcy and came into his very large inheritance. Disraeli prophesied that one day Dilke would be prime minister and by the end of Gladstone's government in June 1885 this appeared to be a distinct possibility. The following month, however, Dilke was cited as co-respondent in a sensational divorce suit. Donald Crawford's wife, Virginia, told her husband that she had been Dilke's mistress since 1882. The story was strenuously denied and when the case came to be heard in February 1886, there was adjudged to be no evidence against him, although Crawford got his divorce. A press campaign led by W.T. Stead of the *Pall Mall Gazette* continued to pursue Dilke, who appealed to the Queen's Proctor to reopen the case and clear his name. Meantime he had married Mrs Mark Pattison, the widow of a distinguished early member of the Club, whose absolute faith in him must have been severely shaken at the second hearing when, although he fiercely rebutted Virginia Crawford's allegations, he was forced to admit to having had an affair with her mother. He was never to hold public office again though six years later he was able to return to the House of Commons as member for the Forest of Dean. For most of the rest of his life he devoted all his energy to trying to clear his name, assisted by the ever-faithful ex-Mrs Mark Pattison, and though they were able to show most of Virginia Crawford's evidence to be spurious, nothing was conclusive so that the motives and the truth of the matter remain a mystery. At all events it must have provided much food for thought in the morning room at Piccadilly.

There were, of course, less exciting M.P.s to be found at the Savile in those early years. George Joachim Goschen, M.P., P.C., F.R.S., the first Viscount, was a member from 1887 until just before he died in 1907, a period which coincided with some of his greatest triumphs. He had been a director of the Bank of England at the age of twenty-seven and as an M.P. felt sufficiently confident of his own political principles to refuse Gladstone's successive offers of the vice-royalty of India, a secretaryship of state or the speakership. However when Lord Randolph Churchill made a gesture of resigning in December 1886, Goschen took his place as Chancellor of the Exchequer – "I forgot Goschen," said the rather disgruntled Churchill. Goschen set to work and, putting his banking experience to work ("he was known and trusted in the City and in the Bank Parlour," says Sir John Clapham in his history of the Bank of England) restructured the national debt in 1888 and introduced a happy era when "money was generally cheap and the country fresh and confident". Later, in Lord Salisbury's coalition he was First Lord of the Admiralty, where he supervised the expansion of the fleet which was to be so subtly and eloquently advocated by another Savile member of the time, Erskine

Childers, in his novel *Riddle of the Sands*. He retired with a viscountcy in 1900 and became chancellor of Oxford University in 1903.

Balfour, of course, is another example of the more conventional politicians who have had their representatives at the Savile throughout its history even to the present day when the contemporary list includes such stalwart figures as Lord Young and Sir Wyn Roberts.

But the maverick in politics has always seemed more typical of the Savile than the conventional. Auberon Herbert would, for instance, certainly recognize a kindred spirit in the writer and broadcaster Humphry Berkeley, who was elected to the Savile in 1971. Berkeley began his political career in the Conservative Party under whose banner he became M.P. for Lancaster from 1959-66. Then he joined the Labour Party in 1970 and contested North Fylde for them in 1974. In 1981 he joined the S.D.P., of distant memory, and contested for them the constituency of Southend East, only to re-join the Labour Party in 1988. Among his several publications is – not surprisingly – a work entitled *Crossing the Floor*, though readers generally may appreciate more his hilarious running account of one of the better practical jokes of recent years, *The Life and Death of Rochester Sneath*. This is a record of his correspondence with a number of leading figures in the world of education and their earnest responses to a variety of letters concerning totally spurious topics. This youthful indiscretion, which can be studied in the Monument, caused Berkeley to be rusticated from Cambridge for two years but the more serious side of his life has since been shown by service on several politico-social commissions and associations such as those connected with the U.N., Commonwealth affairs, and penal reform.

But the fact has to be faced: the Savile Club is not, nor ever has been, particularly associated with politics. Naturally, in a Club that insists on variety in its members' "professions and opinions" there have been many who have felt they should offer some of their time and peculiar skills to the political life of the nation. Some have already been mentioned elsewhere in this history and they have ranged from those M.P.s in the early lists such as Tom Hughes, Walter Morrison, Sir Charles Dilke, Arthur Balfour and many others to their present-day successors like Bryan Magee and David Hardman but it is interesting to notice that they – nearly all – have established sound credentials in other fields far removed from politics.

An early member of the Club who seems to have encapsulated much of the Savile's spirit in his one person, not least in its attitude to politics, was Thomas Gibson Bowles, who was elected in 1869. During his career he managed to be at various times an M.P. of somewhat uncertain allegiance, a master of several occupations totally divorced from politics and, no matter how strongly he felt, a man of great tolerance towards the opposing views of his friends and fellow members. He probably needed to be.

He was already the proprietor of that most genteel of journals, *The Lady*, but in 1868, the year before he joined the Savile, he founded the more abrasive *Vanity Fair*, which soon became one of the more popular magazines of its day with its penetrating commentaries on contemporary public figures. It is perhaps best remembered now for its series of caricatures by "Spy" and "Ape" which have become collector's items and which feature many Savile members of that period. Some of these caricatures were drawn by the great French artist, Jacques Tissot, who, as we shall see, was introduced into the Club by Bowles in 1871. In 1872 and 1873 Bowles served on the Savile Club committee. In 1892 he became Conservative M.P. for King's Lynn, and in the debate on the budget of 1894, introduced by that other Savile member, Sir William Harcourt P.C., F.R.S., (father of "Loulou") he showed himself to be a formidable member of the Opposition with his mastery of complex financial issues. However, when the Conservatives came to power in 1895 he was unaccountably passed over for office and whether out of pique or firmly held principle bitterly attacked his fellow member, Arthur Balfour, on the question of Free Trade. In 1906 he became a Liberal and having unsuccessfully contested Glasgow in 1909, returned to the House of Commons in 1910 as Liberal M.P. for King's Lynn, which he had previously held for the Conservatives. In 1911 he changed his mind once more and returned to his original party, but he was never to sit as an M.P. again. Meantime he had become something of an expert on International and Maritime Law and written several text-books on these subjects. But journalism was his major passion and, considering his incisive and sometimes uncomplimentary views on leading figures of the day – many of them members of the Savile – it is a tribute to his personality that he maintained his popularity. The abrasive side of that personality, however, clearly had its effect for *Punch* was much given to lampooning him, representing him as "Captain Tommy Bowles" with a wooden leg and a hook instead of a hand.

Bowles must have enlivened the Savile for he was in the great tradition of eccentrics; a health freak before his time, an abominator of all medicine, who would instruct his butler to stand on the roof and pour buckets of water over him as a primitive substitute for a shower. One of his daughters, Sydney, married Lord Redesdale and became immortalized as "Muv", the mother of the dazzling Mitford girls whose fey brilliance must owe more than a little to the Bowles genes. After the death of his wife he employed a governess who soon became pregnant. When she gave birth to a son he installed her in a London house and gave her a job on *The Lady*. Later she became editor and bore him three more sons but while he treated her and all the children as family, he never married her.

Bowles is also a reminder that of all the Estates of the Realm which have had their representatives in the Savile membership lists throughout its history there have also been many from that "Fourth Estate" defined by Edmund Burke when, gesturing towards the Press Gallery in the House of Commons, he dignified them by saying: "Yonder sits the Fourth Estate, more important than them all." At the time of the Club's foundation and for more than half a century afterwards, of course, the journals of the day, undiluted by wireless and television, wielded even greater influence on social and political affairs than they do now and nearly all of them had intimate connections with the Savile. A contemporary of Bowles for instance who preceded him by one year as a committee member of the Club was R.H. Hutton, who was for many years the editor of *The Spectator*. G.C. Brodrick, in the same period, was not only notable as a journalist but a distinguished academic also. Sir Herbert Stephen wrote of him:

> [he] illustrated for so many years the nickname of *Curius Dentatus*, [and] was correctly reputed to be one of the most constantly employed of the leader-writers of *The Times*, in days when an almost sacred mystery was still maintained about the identity of those really important personages, and before he came, comparatively speaking, into the limelight as Warden of Merton.

Stephen does not tell us, however, whether the undergraduates of Merton found this "fanged guardian" of *The Times* as equally a toothsome Warden of the College.

Frederick Greenwood, elected in 1869, was for many years editor of the *Pall Mall Gazette*, "an evening paper", again according to Sir Herbert Stephen, "which none of its contemporaries made any attempt to rival in political or literary knowledge and skill".

Its pages contained a stream of contributions from other Savile members both before and after Greenwood's editorship and when after many years he retired he was succeeded by John Morley, who had also edited *The Fortnightly Review*. As has been already noticed, *The Cornhill Magazine*, a purely literary publication, was being edited by Sir Leslie Stephen, who published many contributions from such once and future Savilians as John Morley, Robert Louis Stevenson, Thomas Hardy, Edmund Gosse and Henry James. Stephen also edited *The Saturday Review*.

One of the most influential dailies during the period covering the Franco-German war and afterwards until the split in the Liberal Party in 1886 was the *Daily News*, edited by F.H. Hill, who was one of the original members of the Club in 1868. Six years later William Minto, the editor of an equally influential newspaper, *The Examiner*, was elected at the same meeting which introduced Sir Henry Irving and Robert Louis Stevenson into the Club. But not all the journalism which emanated from the Savile was connected with politics or literature. One of the founder members in 1868 for example was Ernest Hart, the editor of the *British Medical Journal*; and, as might be expected from the Savile, humorous journalism – or, as some might say in this case, what passed for it – became entrenched at the Club with the election in 1893 of Sir Owen Seaman, the editor of *Punch*. Sir Owen was honorary secretary for elections from 1901-1909 but the many years of his membership began an almost unbroken line of *Punch* worthies at the Savile which continued to the present time until Stanley Reynolds as acting editor sadly and symbolically departed from the magazine taking with him the last vestiges of humour and style it might once have claimed.

Seaman had been followed into the Club in 1914 by Sidney Jerrold of the famous literary family which had included Douglas William Jerrold, one of the earliest contributors to *Punch*. Sidney's son, Douglas Francis Jerrold, also became a member in 1917. Douglas was a man of fearsomely right-wing views with, it is said "a tongue like an asp". Oddly in the circumstances, he began a career in publishing with Victor Gollancz, whose views were equally powerfully directed towards the left. Jerrold was later director and chairman of the publishers Eyre and Spottiswoode and editor of the *English Review* and the *New English Review*.

A.A. Milne was assistant editor of *Punch* under Owen Seaman at the time of his election to the Club in 1908, and he was succeeded in that post in 1920 by "Evoe" – Edmund George Valpy Knox – who joined the Savile in that same year. Knox, like his equally famous three brothers, Dillwyn, Wilfred and Monsignor Ronald Knox, had enjoyed a reputation as a considerable wit since his early days at Oxford. His nom-de-plume "Evoe" is defined as "a cry of rejoicing uttered by the followers of Bacchus" and this must have served him as well in the Savile Sandpit as at the *Punch* Table.

Evoe seems to have been on reasonably good terms with Sir Owen Seaman in their forgatherings at the Savile, though he was to write of their professional relationship:

> [he] had indeed a strong sense of vocation, and I remember him saying sadly of somebody or other "he is the kind of man who doesn't take his humour seriously."

In 1932 Knox succeeded Seaman as editor and it was said of him that under his direction the magazine "printed some of the best work that had ever appeared in *Punch*", an accolade which was only slightly marred by the sardonic addendum, "as well as some of the worst".

The drama critic in *Punch* during the 1920s was another Savile member, Joseph Thorp, who for some reason was always known as "Peter". Sidney Dark wrote of him that "he was conspicuous among the Club oddities". He had originally intended to be a Jesuit priest but lost his vocation and then turned his hand to a variety of occupations including that which he carried out for *Punch*. Apparently his threshold of boredom was low and he stuck at nothing for very long and so was nearly always short of money. Dark recalls that "once he arranged a dinner for himself at the Club, and a score of us paid for our own dinners and his in his honour!" On another occasion:

> He started a dinner club which he called Lucullus, and in a weak moment I went to one of the dinners. It was very long and elaborate, and not very good – Peter knew very little of food and drink – and my bill was four pounds, the dearest dinner for which I ever paid. I recall with a chuckle the horror of Owen Seaman, who had a guest and was notoriously careful, when he received his bill.

In the realms of those forms of journalism which were *intended* to be serious there was, of course, among others at the Savile, the aforementioned Sidney Dark, the editor of *The Church Times*. Dark had been a frequent guest of Max Beerbohm and Reggie Turner at the Savile in the pre-1914 era but it was not until 1924, the year he became editor of *The Church Times*, that he decided he had "outgrown" the Savage Club of which he was a member and which by then had "become too exuberant for a man of fifty" and, under the delusion that his social life would now be rewarded with a more proper *gravitas*, had himself proposed for the Savile by his friend Sir William Orpen. Among his referees was Robin Legge, the influential music critic of the *Daily Telegraph*. Dark was a man of strong and critical views on mankind in general and his fellow members at the Savile in particular. He regarded most of the lay readers of his newspaper as "virulently rude and stupid into the bargain", according to a journalist on the staff. Some of his acid comments on Savilians he had known have already been quoted from his chapter on the Club in his memoirs *Not Such a Bad Life* published in 1941. Nevertheless he declared that during all his years of membership it was "a happy refuge from work and worry". Certainly it was, for he is remembered at *The Church Times* as always coming back from long lunches at the Savile "in an aura of cigar smoke" and, presumably, fumes of yet another kind. His sententiousness knew no bounds; when remarking on "Peter" Thorp's "oddity", for instance, he found it necessary to add the pious ejaculation: "How grateful to God one is for His oddities!" Rupert Withers recalls that "due to an unfortunate typing error, he was described in the notice on the Club noticeboard as having died 'soddenly' – which might have been true".

During Dark's period of membership there were several other journalists of great distinction and to a few of these he gives grudging recognition in his memoirs. "Another highly competent editor", was Gerald Barry of the *News Chronicle*, who had been elected to the Club in 1948. Barry had, indeed, been the brilliant editor of the *Saturday Review* until 1930, when he resigned on a matter of political principle, taking his editorial staff with him to produce within a remarkably short time a new and at first highly successful magazine, the *Weekend Review*. Despite its distinction in the world of politics and the arts it fell into financial difficulties and in 1934 it was merged into the *New Statesman* which was then edited by a future Savile member, Kingsley Martin. Barry remained on the board of the combined journals until his death in 1968 but at the time of the merger he moved to the *News Chronicle*, of which he became editor in 1936, and remained in that position with great distinction until 1947 when he resigned and shortly after became director-general of the Festival of Britain. Later he fulfilled many other posts in public administration while maintaining a foothold in journalism as a leader writer for the *Sunday Times* and as literary editor of the *News Chronicle*. In 1958 he was asked by its founder – another Savile member, Sidney Bernstein – to be editor in charge of Granada Television's educational broadcasting. In 1965, together with his fellow members James Fisher and Sir Julian Huxley, he edited a work *Health and Wealth*.

In Barry's time at the *News Chronicle* there were several other Savile members on the staff and the connection continued until that newspaper inexplicably ceased publication in 1960. Philip Jordan, elected to the Club in 1930, was their roving foreign correspondent; described by a fellow member as having "the appearance of a sort of half Anglicized Spanish hidalgo... a revolutionist without much faith in revolution", so he must have suited that newspaper very well. David Keir, elected in 1938, was their Parliamentary correspondent and occasional leader-writer, until war broke out when he served in the R.N.V.R.

Three of the most distinguished names in journalism of recent years who were members of the Savile as well as establishing early reputations on *The News Chronicle* were (Sir) Tom Hopkinson, (Lord) Ritchie-Calder and James Cameron. Hopkinson, elected in 1949, was of course, to make his greatest impact with his remarkable use of photo-journalism as editor of *Picture Post*, which was one of the most celebrated and influential journals during the war years and for some time after. Ritchie Calder, elected in 1958, made his reputation with his famous report for the *Daily Herald* on the Jarrow March in which he took part and which presaged his increasing preoccupation with left-wing political issues, culminating in a seat in the House of Lords. He had also distinguished himself in his youth by securing a notable "scoop" for the *Daily Herald* by solving one of the most sensational mysteries of the time when he succeeded in tracking down the novelist Agatha Christie, who had unaccountably disappeared. In his later career as a political activist he performed sterling services for causes nearer to his heart such as Unesco and the World Health Organization.

James Cameron, elected in 1958, was another writer for the *News Chronicle*, though there was hardly any British journal of his time which he did not also grace with his trenchant opinions and honest reporting expressed in unique and pellucid prose. Cameron spent a great deal of time abroad on assignments:

> Without being dogmatic about it [he once wrote], I believe I may well be one of the few members of the Club who received notification of his election by way of a telegram to Peking. That wire caused some eye-brow lifting in Chinese Government circles at the time; it was not delivered to me for some days, while the bureaucrats debated as to what arcane code-message this obscure and fanciful information could contain. In the end they accepted my explanation that it was merely my initiation into a faraway English *tong*, which as far as I knew had no special designs on the People's Republic.

Despite the strength of his views on the great issues of the day he was a rather shy man in company and though he used the Club with great regularity he liked to ensure with a tentative phone-call or two beforehand that there would be some familiar faces there to shield him when he arrived. One of his particular friends at the Savile who regularly received such phone-calls was the committee member and recent editor of the Club Bulletin, Tom Baistow.

Among others from the Savile who worked at times for the *News Chronicle* and subsequently on the *New Statesman* were the writers John Pudney and Lionel Hale, who have been discussed in a previous chapter, and that fiery polemicist of varying political hues, Paul Johnson, who was a member in the late 'fifties. Barnet Saidman, the well-known photo-journalist, elected in 1966, had produced notable work for the *News Chronicle* until it folded in 1960, when he went into "private practice" with his own studios. To him we owe some of the beautiful photographs of the Club rooms which have appeared in several magazine features concerning the Club and, not least, illustrate this History.

One of the great glories of the *News Chronicle* and the *New Statesman* during the war years and after was the appearance in their pages of the cartoons of "Vicky" – Victor Weisz – who was a member of the Savile from 1953 until his tragic death in 1966. He is described elsewhere in this history but it is worth noting here that, after his arrival in England as a refugee from Nazi Germany, Gerald Barry was the first to recognize his potential and provide him with a platform from which he could develop and display his surpassing talent for satirizing personalities and policies which required to be deflated.

Tom Baistow embodies another common link between some of the Savile journalists and the publications for which they worked – that between the *News Chronicle* and the *New Statesman*, for having been foreign editor of the first he became deputy editor of the second under Paul Johnson.

Tom, with his incomparable knowledge of the history of journalism, to which he made so many notable contributions during this period, sums up the almost incestuous situation at this time:

> The Savile membership has always included a strong Grub/Fleet Street contingent, particularly of journalists of the small-l liberal tendency. A notable example has been the *New Statesman* – *News Chronicle* – Savile nexus, personified by:
>
> H.G. Wells, who helped to found the *New Statesman* in 1913; Kingsley Martin, editor of the *New Statesman* 1930-63; Sir Victor Pritchett, the doyen of English letters, former literary editor of the *New Statesman* and still writing at the age of 92; Sir John (Jack) Squire, who had earlier held the same post at the *Statesman;* Sir Gerald Barry, editor *News Chronicle* 1937-48, long a director of *New Statesman,* who created the trellis-work perspectives which adorn our garden-patio; (Lord) Ritchie Calder, *News Chronicle* and *New Statesman* director; James Cameron, *News Chronicle* and *New Statesman* contributor; Stephen Potter, literary editor *News Chronicle* and *New Statesman* writer; Vicky, *News Chronicle* and *New Statesman*; Walter Allen, literary editor of *New Statesman*; Tom Hopkinson, *Picture Post, News Chronicle*; Geoffrey Goodman, *News Chronicle* and *Mirror*; Paul Dehn, *News Chronicle* critic; Paul (later Lord) Reilly, John Pudney and Lionel Hale, all *News Chronicle;* John Morgan, *New Statesman;* ex-members Paul Johnson, editor *New Statesman*, and Anthony Sampson, *Observer* and *New Statesman*

director. And, bringing up the Lord Mayor's procession, your faithful correspondent, foreign editor *News Chronicle*, deputy editor *New Statesman*. Tom omits to mention another member, the lawyer Ben Hooberman, who was closely involved with the fortunes of this once influential journal. Ben writes:

I became a director of the *New Statesman* in 1964 and remained a director until the Spring of 1986 when I resigned.

I was appointed in the place of Gerald Gardiner who became Lord Chancellor. I remember being interviewed by Kingsley Martin, who had then retired as editor, and who was one of a group of persons who were to find out if I was a suitable candidate. I became quite friendly with Kingsley and often played chess with him during the illness which led to his death.

When I joined the Board John Freeman was editor and there was a circulation of about 95,000. I helped to preside over its decline to a circulation of about 30,000. In the 'sixties, the *New Statesman* was the only journal of the Left which was well written and authoritative. However the increase in the number of supplements of the Sunday papers and the popularity of television contributed to its decline.

Kingsley Martin, who was elected to the Savile in 1937, has been described as "the archetypal Englishman of the intellectual left" and his eccentric notions found a ready – if not always supportive – forum at the Club. In political matters he was described as "always a mixed-up Peter Pan" but as an editor he was quite brilliant. Within a few years of his appointment in 1932 he had built up the circulation of the *New Statesman* from 14,000 to 80,000 and established for it a world-wide reputation. It has to be said that the political stances adopted by the journal often seemed to be as muddled as those of the editor, who insisted on imposing his own somewhat fluctuating views on its political pages, but it was from the literary and artistic sections that the journal's outstanding reputation mostly derived, and this was because Kingsley Martin had an unerring eye for the best writers in these fields and made no attempt to interfere with the opinions they expressed. People of all political persuasions would read the *New Statesman* as much to be exasperated as to be informed and, just as "respectable" readers would buy the *News of the World* for "the excellence of its sports coverage" when they really wished to be titillated, so would many purchase the *New Statesman* for its literary pages when, in fact, they were just as fascinated by its subversive views. Kingsley Martin knew this, and shrewdly played on it. It was said of him that "he could write nothing that was unreadable" and indeed he could quite often capture the political mood of the times and provide sufficient incentive for students of politics everywhere to regard the journal as required reading despite its lack of consistent judgments.

Tom Baistow recalls some of his encounters with Kingsley Martin and others of this close-knit band at the Savile:

Kingsley Martin when he was first brought to the Club became one of the

Wells coterie. Later his Savile crony was Charles (C.P.) Snow, with whom he often dined, as well as Michael Ayrton (also *New Statesman* contributor) and occasionally myself, although I regret I can't recall any memorable *bons mots* or rare flights of rhetoric (Kingsley wasn't a sparkling conversationalist, just a brilliant writer). Cameron *was* a wit at table; but not a trencherman. When we lunched, he would order only soup or a savoury unless herring was on the menu (where are the herrings *d'antan?*), regarding time spent away from the bar as a rather crude form of indulgence. Ritchie Calder loved to rehearse his next article as he went through his three courses, and later would try out his speeches on me when he was elevated to the Lords. Barry was the best conversationalist, full of ideas, and I had the melancholy pleasure of giving him his last lunch at the Club, the week before he died, still as intellectually vigorous as when I worked for him on the *News Chronicle*. Stephen Potter was also rewarding company at the bar, full of sardonic humour and acerbic anecdotes. Although Michael Ayrton had a reputation as a non-sufferer of fools and bores, sharp to the point of rudeness, I always found him as genial as he was erudite.

Come to think of it, *sodalitas convivium* must have made quite a contribution to the thinking of the Left. . .

Another influential journal which had its representatives in the Savile membership lists throughout most of this century is the *Observer*. Perhaps its greatest editor, who brought it to national prominence in the period between the wars, was J.L. Garvin, who had become a member of the Savile in 1906. St. John Ervine, who was elected a member of the Savile in 1922, was appointed drama critic of the *Observer* at about that same time by Garvin, who was attracted by his forthright and generally good-humoured opinions on the theatre. Ervine was perhaps better known as a playwright and writer on men and matters to do with drama, though he had spent a short time managing the Abbey Theatre in Dublin in 1915. He wrote several biographies, which included an excellent study of his friend Bernard Shaw and a disgraceful and unforgiving "appraisal" of Oscar Wilde. Frank Swinnerton, his fellow member at the Savile, wrote of him: "he was observant, genial and bland but in the very moment of geniality.... he keeps his head and fails to allow his judgment to nod". From 1933-36 he was professor of dramatic literature of the Royal Society of Literature, of which he was a fellow. He was president of the League of British Dramatists in 1937 and became a member of the Irish Academy, an honorary LL.D., from St. Andrews University and D.Litt., from Queen's University, Belfast in 1945.

After St John Ervine resigned as drama critic of the *Observer* in 1929, J.L. Garvin appointed Ivor Brown in his place. Brown, who was elected to the Club in 1942, had already served his apprenticeship on the *Manchester Guardian*, where he wrote everything from editorials to pieces on sport, but he excelled in writing on the theatre, which was his major passion. He was also the drama critic for the

Saturday Review from 1923-1930. For the thirty years during which he wrote for the *Observer* he was regarded as the most knowledgeable and influential voice in British dramatic criticism, and this was recognized officially when he was made professor of drama to the Royal Society of Literature in 1939 and later, during the war, the first director of drama to the emergent Arts Council. When J.L. Garvin retired as editor of the *Observer* in 1942, Brown succeeded him and remained in that post until 1948 although he continued as drama critic until 1954. He had retired from his editorial chair in order to devote more time to writing and in all he published seventy-five books which included novels, essays, biography, auto-biography and criticism. But another of his major passions, the English language, was also indulged and, like his fellow member of the Club, Eric Partridge, he wrote many books on etymology and correct English usage, all of which were endowed with the wit and charm which made him by all accounts such a welcome companion at the Savile. Like his predecessor St. John Ervine, he was chairman of the British Drama League from 1954-1965, and a Fellow of the Royal Society of Literature. After the war he lectured regularly in Denmark and in recognition of this he had conferred on him a knighthood of the Order of Danneborg. He was appointed C.B.E. in 1957.

Yet another Savile member who distinguished himself as a journalist on the *Observer* was Edward Crankshaw, who was elected in 1944 and subsequently wrote perceptively on Russian affairs during the height of the cold-war period. Crankshaw was a regular and popular member of the Club who is now, unfortunately, most remembered at Brook Street for his perfectly innocent involvement in the notorious fracas between Gilbert Harding and Hubert Clifford, as shall be recorded later.

Edward Mace, who was elected to the Club in 1966, has worked for the *Observer* throughout this period, providing elegant accounts of his travels and whetting the appetite of his readers for far-away places.

And so the craft of journalism has been practised, through the years, to the current membership list, which includes a goodly number of contemporary figures such as Mike Molloy, the *Daily Mirror*'s former editor-in-chief, and Geoffrey Goodman, once that paper's industrial editor; Michael Peacock, the former head of BBC 1, and BBC 2, and London Weekend Television; David Bradbury, an ex-Savile committee member, who toiled for the Mirror Group, having moved from the *Sunday Mirror* to *The European*; Paul Callan, an ex-*Mirror* columnist and presenter on breakfast T.V.; Eric Jacobs, an ex-leader-writer for *Today*; and Jeremy Hornsby, another committee member, who after many years on the *Daily Express* now writes for television. Godfrey Smith's lightness of touch but weighty presence at the *Sunday Times* is also regularly enjoyed by a more exclusive audience at the Savile, while readers of its sister daily have Michael Hamlyn to thank for their elegant early morning rumbles from the old "Thunderer".

*　*　*　*

Perhaps it was not so necessary in earlier days as it is in these more litigious times, but it must always have been comforting for Savile journalists, with their trenchant views reinforced by the Club's tradition of forthright expression, to know that they had a common membership with some of the most distinguished lawyers of their day, well equipped when necessary to advise them on averting the wrath of their victims.

There are, in fact, no dazzling cases to be recorded of one member ever having had to act for another – journalist or otherwise – in a court of law, but it is certain that many a timely word of advice at the bar or the long table has been received with benefit. There have been, on the other hand, some embarrassing incidents of an adversarial kind. On one occasion, for instance, a member, fortifying himself on the eve of a long-standing appointment at Bow Street to answer for a motoring offence, enjoyed a convivial dinner with a fellow Savilian and his genial guest, only to find himself the following morning being glared at from the bench by the selfsame guest in far less genial mood. But such is the Savile: suffice it that throughout its history it has numbered a proper proportion of men at law. Among the founding members in 1868, for instance, was Walter Phillimore, who went on to be, as Baron Phillimore, P.C., D.C.L., LL.D., a Lord Justice of Appeal. Another was a celebrated writer and authority on jurisprudence, the Hon. Mr Justice Westlake. When the Club joined forces with the Anglo-American Association in 1871 it took into its membership William Shaen, who was one of the best-known London solicitors of the day, and John Macdonnell, who was to become famous as senior master of the High Court, King's Remembrancer, and a distinguished writer on legal matters. At the committee meeting in that same year which formulated the laws and constitution of the Savile, important amendments were tabled by William Donaldson Rawlins, K.C., who was a distinguished Chancery barrister, and William Rann Kennedy, who as Sir William Kennedy, P.C., F.B.A., was also to become a Lord Justice of Appeal. Rawlins was honorary secretary of the Club from 1872 to 1876 and Kennedy was a trustee from 1898 until the time of his death in 1914.

The quota of legal candidates that the committee elected in succeeding years continued in similar measure. Among the more noteworthy was a well-known and highly successful Chancery barrister, G.W. Hemming, elected in 1869, who is described by Sir Herbert Stephen as being of "rugged appearance and manners". He eventually became an official referee. He had been a senior wrangler in his time and would have endeared himself to later members such as Stephen Potter for having written a popular work on the dynamical problems involved in the game of billiards. Sir Moritz Holzmann was elected in 1870 and was apparently an assiduous member until his death in 1908; throughout most of his early career he was private secretary to the Princess of Wales, later Queen Alexandra, and subsequently became Secretary of the Duchy of Cornwall. With his customary, but in this case rather tactless ambivalence, Sir Herbert Stephen says of him:

A thoroughly patriotic Englishman, and a very popular man, he never lost his most vehement German accent, and may have escaped much trouble by dying some years before the war.

Stephen, one supposes, might have said much the same of Farrer Herschell, who was born of Jewish parents from Prussian Poland and was elected to the Club in 1872. Two years later he became Liberal M.P. for Durham; in 1880 he became Solicitor-General and was knighted. In 1886, as the first Baron Herschell, he became the first Savile member to be appointed Lord Chancellor.

However, there was one barrister at the time of whom Sir Herbert Stephen could heartily approve and this he rightly did with unstinted enthusiasm. "Henry Hood", he wrote,

> had been elected a member in 1869, his address in the new Club list being given as Brasenose College, Oxford. In 1874 he was a Chancery barrister, and within the next few years acquired a considerable chamber practice, and became known as the joint author of Hood and Challis's *Conveyancing and Settled Land Acts*. In 1878 Hood was elected to serve on the Committee. He was forthwith placed on the House Committee, and the following year became one of the Honorary Secretaries. He held this laborious office for twenty-one years, and no Club ever owed more to a man than the Savile owed to Henry Hood. For the greater number of the years of his secretaryship one member or another shared the office with him, but from very soon after his period of office began all the ordinary administration of the affairs of the Club was daily and weekly in his hands. His astonishing industry was of the unobtrusive variety. Always refined – even gentle – in manner, and deliberate in speech and action, he gave the impression that there was nothing so silly, or so impossible for anyone that had the distinction of belonging to the Savile, as to be in a hurry. He combined with a cheerfully satirical outlook on life the opinions of a Tory and the manners of a somewhat old-fashioned gentleman. He took an unaffected interest in wine, and never failed to drink port at luncheon and champagne at dinner; nor was it ever intelligible to him that a man should be capable of drinking tea at any time later than breakfast. He controlled committee meetings, and especially election meetings, in the manner of a rider endowed with perfect "hands". It is probable that he was never absent from an election meeting, and it seems to follow that every member elected between 1879 and 1900 had passed the somewhat exigent standard of his taste.

Meantime, according to Stephen, Hood was "also conducting a prosperous practice at the bar, and in later years discharging with exemplary success the duties of a Registrar in Bankruptcy"; so, despite all his "cheerfulness", a daunting presence, one would think, for members temporarily strapped for cash. In 1912 he was appointed one of the trustees of the Club and the members subscribed for his portrait to be painted by his fellow member, the distinguished portraitist of the time John Collier, which was hung over the mantelpiece in the drawing-room at 107 Piccadilly.

In 1868 one of the original members of the new Club was Sir Godfrey Lushington, for many years Permanent Under-Secretary at the Home Office. In 1875 his twin brother, Vernon, came to join him. Vernon, after holding a legal appointment at the Admiralty, became a County Court Judge and a Q.C. He and his brother so closely resembled one another, according to Sir Herbert Stephen,

> that when Vernon sustained a permanent injury to one of his hands in a shooting accident, some of his friends suggested that it was a well-meant, though inconvenient design of Providence to enable them to know one from the other. Godfrey left the Club in 1886, but Vernon became one of the Trustees in 1883, and retained that office until his death twenty-nine years later.

Charles Synge Bowen P.C., F.R.S., was elected to the Club in 1872 and remained a member until he died in 1893. In the interim he had become a judge in 1879 and later a Lord of Appeal. Lord Justice Bowen's cousin Herbert Courthope Bowen was also elected in1876 when he was a young clerk at the Bank of England. It is said that he became a regular and popular attender at the Club and, as he rose through the ranks at the Bank to become its chief cashier, the Club acquired the added cachet of having his signature "H.C. Bowen" attesting to the authenticity of the banknotes which passed into the Savile coffers. Bowen served on the committee of the Savile for many years and was honorary librarian from 1886 to 1893.

In 1883, the year after he had taken silk, Herbert Cozens-Hardy was elected to the Club. He built for himself a reputation in the Chancery Division and in 1865 was elected Liberal M.P. for North Norfolk. In 1899 he was elevated to the bench and knighted; in 1901 he became a Lord Justice of Appeal and Privy Councillor, and in 1907 he crowned his legal career when he was appointed Master of the Rolls. He is featured in one of the "Spy" Cartoons from *Vanity Fair* which are hung in the Stevenson room at Brook Street.

On the committee at that famous A.G.M. in 1884, when the proposal to alter the rules of election and embrace the "black ball" system was debated and defeated, sat a seemingly inoffensive but nevertheless eccentric lawyer named Frederick William Hayden. He was employed in the department of the Solicitor to the Treasury and was by all accounts a quiet and unassuming man, very popular at the Club and assiduous in carrying out his duties as a committee member. However he was sometimes given to demonstrating unusual flashes of spirit. On one occasion he was asked to provide the committee with a list of members who had either retired from the Club or had died so that it might be known how many vacancies would be available for the next election meeting. The names of those who had died were all properly and decently marked "deceased" except for one whom Hayden had particularly disliked; against his name was heavily inscribed "In Hell!" Nevertheless, despite such occasional eccentricities, Hayden was said to be a punctilious and highly regarded treasurer of the Club from 1891 to 1912 and seems to have served it well.

In 1893 Frederick Herbert Maugham, K.C., was elected to the Club and remained a member for the sixty-five years which were to elapse before his death in 1958. Maugham, an elder brother of W. Somerset Maugham, was born in Paris, where his grandfather and father had established a thriving legal practice, his father being also an adviser to the British Embassy. In his memoirs *At the End of the Day* written in 1954 he recalls that one of his earliest memories was the family's flight to England from the German army which was advancing on Paris during the Franco-Prussian war. At Oxford he proved himself to be an exceptional athlete as well as scholar and was regarded as the outstanding oarsman of his generation, rowing No. 7 in the Varsity boat races of 1888 and 1889. He was also a considerable rugby player, and was president of the Union. He was elected to the Savile in 1893, three years after he was called to the bar at Lincoln's Inn. Because of his lack of connections his progress was at first slow but gradually he built up one of the largest practices specializing in the Court of Chancery. In 1913 he took silk and in 1928 he was appointed a Judge in Chancery and knighted. He had acquired a reputation for being both fair and formidable and in 1934 he was elevated to the Court of Appeal and sworn in as a Privy Councillor. In 1938, despite his lack of any political experience, he succeeded the first Lord Hailsham as Lord Chancellor. In 1928, while he was still practising at the bar, Maugham made his first venture into literature with *The Case of Jean Calas*, an account of an infamous legal scandal in eighteenth-century France which Voltaire had originally exposed, and he followed this with others about the Tichborne claimant and a defence of Neville Chamberlain in *The Truth about the Munich Crisis*. After the Second World War he wrote one of the first books querying the legal justifications for the Nuremberg trials (although he sympathized with their verdicts) entitled *U.N.O. and War Crimes*.

Maugham was a regular and greatly liked member of the Club through all his years into extreme old age and, with the exception of an incident with the fearsomely unpredictable John Davenport he was generally treated with the respect and affection which his achievements and his sociable character deserved. Monja Danischewsky recalls an encounter at Brook Street in the mid-'fifties:

> Michael Pertwee and I were talking in the Hall on the occasion of a House Dinner when we were approached by Lord Maugham, then in his nineties.
>
> "Excuse me," he said. "Can you tell me if this is the Savile Club?"
>
> "Yes, Lord Maugham."
>
> "Oh, good. Do you happen to know if I am a member?"

"Yes, Sir. A life member."

"Excellent. Am I in time for a bit of food?"

"We would be delighted if you would join us."

So we dined in the company of the former Lord Chancellor and a very bright and entertaining old gentleman he was. The next day at a party Michael ran into Somerset Maugham whom he told of our meeting with his brother.

"So that's where he got to! He slipped his k-k-keeper again – t-tut-tiresome!"

Another long-lived legal member was Frank Boyd Merriman, K.C., who was elected in 1921 and was devoted to the Savile until he died with all his honours as The Right Honourable Lord Merriman, P.C., O.B.E., LL.D., a trustee of the Club.

Merriman received his O.B.E. for his service in the Manchester Regiment during the First World War, when he was three times mentioned in despatches. In 1920, the year before he became a member of the Savile, he was appointed Recorder of Wigan. In 1924 he became Conservative M.P. for the Rusholme division of Manchester and in 1928 Solicitor-General. He held this office with one short interval until 1933 when he was appointed president of the Probate Divorce and Admiralty division and was sworn in as a rivy Councillor.

One of his most noteworthy cases as a young barrister was when he had the disagreeable task of representing Captain Peter Wright in his action against Lord Gladstone – a cousin of one of his contemporaries at the Savile – arising out of defamatory statements made by Wright concerning the latter's father. A more salubrious issue was when he led the team of barristers appearing for the Palestine Zionist Executive and the Zionist Organization against the Mufti of Jerusalem and the Palestine Arab Executive, who were opposed to the policy of a Jewish National Home embodied in the Balfour Declaration of November 1917, devised by his predecessor at the Savile, the ex-prime minister who was still a fellow member of the Club at the time. Those present members who were his friends recall his great amiability and the care with which he nurtured his friendships. Sam Musson, who was elected in 1940, remembers him as a most congenial companion at the long table, where he took particular pleasure in conversing with members connected with the theatre and music. A fine portrait of him was painted by John Merton, the son of his friend and fellow member, Sir Thomas Merton, and brother of a contemporary, Colin.

Another legal light at the Savile with a keen interest in the arts – especially music – was Sir John Hazan, who had the distinction of being one of the few judges to reach the High Court from the criminal bench. Hazan was elected to the

Club in 1969, the same year that he took silk. Subsequently he served as an adviser on several committees and inquiries into such matters as Criminal Law Revision, Sexual Offences and, perhaps most notably, as Counsel for the Metropolitan Police Commissioner at Lord Scarman's inquiry into the Brixton riots. He was appointed to the High Court in January 1988 but died unexpectedly in August of that year. He is remembered at the Club for his grave good humour and for the extensive knowledge of opera with which he peppered his conversation. He was also fond of relating some of his experiences at the Bar, of which one was the occasion in his early days of comparative poverty when he was forced to accept a fee of £1.50 to defend a client who had managed to acquire legal aid. When he came to consult with the defendant he found himself being offered £500 cash for his services, which by then, of course, he had with great reluctance to refuse. Hazan was a trustee of the Savile Club, a Freeman of the City of London and a Liveryman of the Musicians Company.

His Honour, Judge David Wild, who was elected to the Club in 1969, has been a circuit judge since 1972 and is Resident Judge at Cambridge Crown Court. In some of his early experiences at the Club he came face to face with the difficulties which recur when members observe the traditional tacit injunction to "Hang your Halo in the Hall".

> One hot summer evening I arrived a little late for dinner. There was just one place at the long table. Opposite me was Raymond Postgate and for want of something better to say I asked "What is this Château Cissac that everyone is trying to sell at the moment?" Raymond turned to his left and said "Allow me to present M. Vialard. He is the proprietor of the Château Cissac!" Thereafter we had a splendid evening during which they persuaded me that the only thing to drink after dinner was champagne. Sadly I have not been able to continue the habit.

On another occasion he arrived for lunch at the long table and having exchanged greetings with his neighbour, Erasmus Darwin, was just in time to hear the latter addressed by a new member sitting opposite: "Excuse me. You won't know me. I am your cousin . . ."

That not all the Club's lawyers have made their careers at law however is typified by Sir Ernest Pooley, G.C.V.O., who was elected to the Club in 1920, and served on its committee as honorary secretary for elections from 1928-1932. Pooley was called to the bar in 1901 but – except for the period of the Great War when he fought in France and at Gallipoli – he worked as Clerk to the Drapers' Company until his retirement in 1944, when he received the unusual honour of being elected Master. During his years at the Drapers' Company he came to be recognized as one of the most important figures in the world of City companies as well as in educational and charitable circles. He had been connected with King Edward's Hospital since 1928 and like his friend and subsequent member of the Savile, Lord Brain, had to cope with the several problems which ensued from the nationalization of the hospitals when the National Health Service was introduced. His considerable interest in the arts led to his appointment as Chairman of the Arts Council in succession to Lord Keynes in 1946 and he held this position until 1953. Pooley's was a forceful presence in the Club and, as shall be seen in a later chapter of this history, he did not hesitate to make his views known if he felt that those of other members were compromising what he judged to be the best interests of the Club.

But he seems to have had a lighter side; in his autobiography Michael Meyer recalls: "On my first visit as a member I found myself urinating in the Club lavatory next to an old gentleman named Sir Ernest Pooley, whose wife's first husband had had a pass made at him by Oscar Wilde. As we stood side by side at the urinals, he turned to me and said: 'Emerson once observed that every major pleasure known to man except eating and drinking consists of one form or another of emission.' I began to think this was a place I might find congenial."

Lord (Arnold) Goodman, a lawyer similarly devoted to the arts, has been a member since 1958 though his well-known figure has rarely been seen at the Club in recent years. A glance at his entry in *Who's Who* reveals a possible reason for this in the number of time-consuming committees connected with theatre, opera and other artistic enterprises which he has listed there, though he does not make mention of his thirty-two years' membership of the Savile.

Laurence Harbottle on the other hand is regularly to be seen. He has been a member since 1959 and the Club's honorary solicitor for part of that time. Apart from being senior partner in the firm of Harbottle and Lewis, he has many close connections with the theatre. Like that Savilian of yester-year, Ivor Brown, he has served on the drama panel of the Arts Council and has been Chairman of the Central School of Speech and Drama since 1982. He has also served on the Theatres Advisory Panel, been Chairman of the Theatres Trust since 1980 and the I.C.A. since 1986.

Laurence Harbottle's predecessor as honorary solicitor of the Club was the late Edgar Duchin, who was elected in 1962. He was born Edgar Duchinsky the son of a rabbi who had intended Edgar for the rabbinate also until he chose instead to go to Oxford and study law. As an example of his own sly wit he was fond of recalling his early days in practice when the ultra left-wing advocate, Denis Pritt, the defender of Jomo Kenyatta, advised him that if he wished to prosper in his profession he would have to excise the last syllable from his name, explaining sadly that in England "the 'sky' would be the limit". Duchin, as he then became, was nevertheless extremely proud of his Jewish origins and never forgetful of them; another member, having been hopelessly snookered by him during a game some years ago, forgetfully murmured "*That* was *not* a Christian act" – to which he received the cheerful reply, "Well, what did you expect?" Nor was his connection with Pritt entirely coincidental, for his own political views in earlier days, when Fascism was a real threat, stopped just short of outright membership of the Communist Party – a stance which has been shared by a surprising number of Savile members – few of whom could have claimed kinship with the "oppressed" –

191

Humphrey Hare, Stephen Spender, Robert Clark, Michael Ayrton and J.B.S. Haldane among them. Indeed, Duchin was proposed for membership by Walter Allen, that fiery littérateur, who pursued the "capitalist classes" with all the fervour of an angry wasp, yet found no reason to disapprove of the Savile.

So we come to the end of this representative list of Savile lawyers, and to the end also of a – necessarily – incomplete survey of the many scientists, administrators, public men, politicians and journalists who have fulfilled the founders' principle of "a mixture of men of different professions and opinions". A former Savile member, Arnold Toynbee, has written: "Disinterested intellectual curiosity is the lifeblood of real civilization" and he might have added that this was to be found in ample measure among his fellow members. Diverse they may all have been, but certain common characteristics have persisted through the years; distinction in one particular field has often gone hand in hand with skill in others; political and religious beliefs, no matter how divergent, have generally been tempered by tolerance and understanding of opposing views; and, above all, no matter how grand the reputation a member may have borne with him to the Club, his halo has been firmly left hanging at the hall door.

Michael Ayrton's portrait of his fellow
member C.P. Snow – doubtless
brooding on the two cultures.

Sir Charles Sherrington, president of
the Royal Society, winner of the
Nobel Prize for medicine, and poet.

CHAPTER FOUR

Musicians

When Sir Edward Elgar was a member of the Savile committee in the early 1920s, a rather over-earnest new member attempted to persuade him into an analysis of his *Introduction and Allegro*. "Don't let's waste time talking about my string thing," said Elgar. "What I want to know is which horse to back in the 3.30 at Cheltenham." His reaction reflected a fairly common attribute of Savilians throughout the Club's history; for most, whether scientists, public men or artists, came to the Club to get away from their professional chores and refresh their leisure in the company of men whose minds were applied to other pursuits. The literary element of the Club had been a powerful attraction from an early date, but at Spring Gardens and Savile Row every other branch of the arts, from which members might select their company, was similarly represented.

It is typical of the pattern which Savile membership had soon established that the first notable musician to join was also a painter and critic of some distinction. Harry Ellis Wooldridge, who was elected in 1871, had a powerful influence on music and painting in his lifetime through his own creative output and his critical writings. Having been a protégé of Burne-Jones, his pictures were always well received by the hanging committee of the Royal Academy; and indeed the first of these was bought by Sir Frederic Leighton, regarded as one of the most discriminating of Victorian connoisseurs. A cabinet which Wooldridge decorated was also considered remarkable enough to be placed in the South Kensington Museum; but, as in artistic matters he seemed always to be something of a grasshopper, he was soon persuaded by G. F. Watts and others to divert his creative talents into the execution of wall-paintings and stained glass. The reredos in St Martin's Church, Brighton, is a notable example of his work during this phase of his career, which did not, however, detain him long, for soon he was off again, this time into the world of music. In his youth he had been an accomplished singer and at just about the time he was elected to the Savile he had begun to concentrate his energies on the study of old Italian music in the British Museum. Establishing himself almost at once as an unrivalled expert in counterpoint, he was commissioned by Chappell to produce the definitive *Old English Popular Music*, while other leading musicians of the time, among them another member of the Savile, Sir Hubert Parry, regularly sought his expert advice. His artistic career, however, once again changed course when he was recalled from music back to the plastic arts by being appointed Slade professor of fine art at Oxford in succession to that other pillar of the contemporary Savile, Sir Sidney Colvin. It was a post to which Wooldridge was re-elected twice, retiring only in 1904. It has been said that the theses he proclaimed during his tenure of this office might better have been illustrated had he expressed them in musical terms for, while he was engaged on the Slade lectures, he had already immersed himself in *The Oxford History of Music*. But even this was not the success it should have been for (as so often happens when a scholar is commissioned for a project he has longed to get his teeth into) he was led off by his enthusiasm into the by-ways of obscure antiquarian research and failed to reach the period in which he was undoubtedly and exclusively the greatest living expert. It was a defect with which some Savile members will be familiar. As a result, perhaps the most permanent monument to his scattered talents is *The Yattendon Hymnal*, which he edited in collaboration with his lifelong friend and contemporary at the Club, the future poet laureate Robert Bridges.

Like Wooldridge, John Pyke Hullah wavered between careers, interspersing his creative periods with protracted spells as a music educationalist. In 1871 when he was elected to the Savile he was serving on the management committee of the Royal Academy of Music and was the chief conductor of the academy concerts. Many years before this he had set to music a libretto by Charles Dickens, *The Village Coquettes*, which was produced at the St James's Theatre and ran for sixty nights with great success. His other forays into opera were less fortunate and he is mainly remembered now for his collections of vocal compositions, which included some beautiful madrigals such as "Wake now my Love"; songs, of which some of the more successful were "The Sands of Dee" and "The Three Fishers"; and his editorial work, which embraced a wide area of educational methods and annotated anthologies of traditional songs.

In 1877 the composer and conductor Sir Joseph Barnby was elected to the Savile. He had been a musical prodigy, teaching music from the age of 10 and becoming an organist and choirmaster at the age of 12. At the time of his election he was precentor of Eton – ie, organist and music master to Eton College – an office which he held until 1892 when he became the Second Principal of the Guildhall School of Music. During this period he composed a series of Eton songs which included the "Carmen Etonense" together with a considerable corpus of more important works, most notably the cantata *Rebekah*, and his setting of Psalm 97, "The Lord is King", which was performed at the Leeds Festival of 1883. He has left many other hymns and song-settings of which perhaps the most enduringly popular has been his melody to Tennyson's "Sweet and Low". Beside all these compositions perhaps his greatest contribution to Victorian England's musical life was his championship of such "modern" composers as Gounod and Wagner and his revival of the then lesser known Passion music of J. S. Bach. On Maundy Thursday, 1871, Barnby masterminded one of the most outstanding events in church music of that period when he performed the *St Matthew Passion* in Westminster Abbey for the first time with full orchestra and chorus, and he was to continue what was then a considerable musical novelty when, as organist and choir-master of St Anne's, Soho, he performed the *St John Passion* with orchestral accompaniment.

But these first three musical members were as "ships that pass in the night" in terms of the Club's recorded history until, in 1884, one of the most outstanding personalities both in music and Savilian folklore, (Sir) Charles Villiers Stanford, was elected. Though in fact he was aggressively Irish he has been described as "the greatest innovator in English music since Purcell", and, despite the state of neglect into which most of his *œuvre* has unjustly fallen – outside of the Church of England – his prodigious contribution as composer, conductor and teacher qualifies him as one of the most important figures in the renaissance of English musical life during the half century preceding his death in 1924. Tales of his legendary presence at the Savile card table over a period of forty years will appear later, but his influence on the musical taste of his time and the friendships he nurtured at the Savile with many of his distinguished contemporaries throughout the span of his membership provide a bracing continuo to this part of the Club's history.

Although his greatest work was yet to come, Stanford had arrived at the Savile at the age of 32 with an already formidable reputation. As a 20-year-old student at Cambridge in 1872 he became involved with the University Musical Society, which had been founded in 1843 by a later colleague of his at the Savile, the scientist William Thomson, afterwards Lord Kelvin. He seized it by the scruff, and with what was to become throughout his life a typical Irish bravura, galvanized it into one of the most influential musical forces in England. He had travelled and studied in Europe and immersed himself in the great compositional advances represented by the work of Mendelssohn and Brahms while establishing close acquaintanceships with such luminaries as the great composer and violinist, Joseph Joachim. In a paper read to the Musical Association of London in 1927, Thomas F. Dunhill (whose son, David, is a contemporary member) was able to refer to Stanford at the period he was elected to the Savile as:

> ... the youngest of the firebrands of the '70s, and unquestionably the most fiery of them all – surely to be accounted the most versatile of the composers of the latter half of the nineteenth century. There was no department of music in which he did not seek to challenge comparison with the giants of his age. Indeed there was only one contemporary composer who could have ventured to dispute this special claim to distinction – the French master, Saint-Saëns – and it is doubtful that even he succeeded in enriching the art of music in so many directions, or displayed so complete a technical mastery in every sphere. In Opera (both serious and light), in Oratorio and Cantata, Symphony and Concerto, Chamber music and Church music, unaccompanied part-songs, instrumental and vocal solos of almost every type, and music for children of all ages, Stanford has left his mark which can never be erased.

During his forty years of membership there were to be many more musicians of greater or lesser talent who were to be his confrères at the Savile, but his social and professional dealings were not confined to them alone. His fellow member, the distinguished Victorian artist Sir Laurens Alma-Tadema, had designed and mounted "an Elysian Fields scene which was truly beautiful" for a performance of Gluck's *Orpheus* which Stanford put on at the Cambridge University Musical Society in 1889, on which occasion also his biographer Harry Plunket Greene – a later member – was first to perform under his baton. Sir Henry Irving, a fellow member – though, as we have seen, more a frequenter of the Garrick – collaborated with Stanford on a production of Tennyson's *Becket*. In his diary Stanford explains how this came about:

> As Tennyson was the first to give me a helping hand in 1875 in his first theatrical venture [the incidental music for *Queen Mary* produced at the Lyceum in 1876], so his final act was to express a wish that I should be similarly connected with his last tragedy.

Irving had been invited to produce *Becket* and was delighted to hear that Stanford was to be involved, but Stanford wished to compose the music without fee as a gesture of goodwill both to Tennyson and Irving himself. Bram Stoker, the latter's man of business (although perhaps better known as the author of *Dracula*), was instructed by Irving to refuse this offer and insist on paying Stanford £200. The conversation which ensued was recorded by Harry Plunket Greene:

> *Irving:* "I am much obliged to you for agreeing to the terms Stoker suggested."
> *C.V.S.:* "They are a great deal too much."
> *Irving:* "They are not; two hundred pounds, was it? We'll make it three."
> *C.V.S.:* "You will not."
> *Irving:* "Then you shan't write the music. I mean what I say."

For once, the headstrong Stanford was out-gunned. When the music was delivered the cheque was for three, not two, hundred and for guineas not pounds.

Tennyson had originally nursed a strong prejudice against having his verse set to music and it was only his deep friendship for Stanford and admiration for his work which had gradually persuaded him otherwise. Stanford's contemporary at the Savile, Robert Bridges, however, held very different views and believed most strongly in the proper and equal union of words with music. In Plunket Greene's biography there is recorded an interesting and revealing correspondence on the subject between Bridges and Stanford dealing with his libretto for *Eden* while their work was in progress for its production at the Birmingham Festival of 1891. Sixty years later another Club composer, William Alwyn, set down his own trenchant views on the subject in his journal for 1955-56, which was published under the title *Ariel and Miranda,* and at about that time, his friend at the Savile the librettist Christopher Hassall also wrote an essay, "Music and Poetry", on this theme which drew heavily on such collaborations as that between his predecessors, Robert Bridges and Harry Wooldridge in *The Yattendon Hymnal*.

But naturally Stanford's long association with the Savile involved him both inside and out of the Club with men who were more consistently associated with his own world of music. In 1885, the year after his own election, Stanford's great admirer and colleague at the Royal College of Music, Sir Walter Parratt, was elected to the Savile. Parratt was probably the greatest organist of his day and it was said of his performances that "no term seems more adequate than 'statuesque' to which 'poetical' must be added when considering his powers as an accompanist". He had been organist at Magdalen College, Oxford, from 1872 but in 1882, three years before his election to the Savile, he was appointed by direct command of Queen Victoria to be organist of St George's Chapel, Windsor. There he continued his predecessor's traditional repertory of the great works ranging from Thomas Tallis to S. S. Wesley, but to them he now added compositions by the younger school of British Church musicians, in particular those of Stanford, many of which he performed prior to their publication. The services at St George's Chapel during his period made it a place of pilgrimage for organists from all over Great Britain. Shortly after his appointment to Windsor, Parratt was invited by Sir George Grove to become chief professor of the organ at the recently founded Royal College of Music, of which Grove was the first director. Stanford was appointed at the same time to be professor of composition together with Hubert Parry, who had meantime been elected to the Savile in 1886 – the year after Parratt. The list of pupils who were to pass through the hands of this Savilian triumvirate at the Royal College makes awesome reading, particularly those who were put through the mill by Stanford: composers and musicians of the ilk of Ralph Vaughan Williams, Frank Bridge, Walford Davies, Eugene Goossens, John Ireland, Samuel Coleridge-Taylor, and Gustav Holst; and future Savile members like Arthur Bliss, Herbert Howells, and Arthur Benjamin.

Parratt and Stanford got on well at the R.C.M. and at the Club – not always a foregone conclusion of Stanford's dealings with his fellow musicians – and Plunket Greene records that Stanford (recognizing, no doubt, a kindred spirit) was "filled with respect" for Parratt's "brain-power and caustic tongue", so "sought his advice on many matters". Despite all Parratt's onerous teaching and performing duties, to which he had added the composition of many works for religious and state occasions, he never failed to maintain his contact with Oxford University, and indeed he was to succeed his colleague at the R.C.M. and at the Savile, Sir Hubert Parry, as professor of music there in 1908.

It is an English habit to be suspicious of men of too many parts and it is possibly Hubert Parry's essential Englishness which brought about his self-deprecatory reluctance to assume the title "professional" in regard to his own musical ability, for outside of music he had the many interests of a wealthy man, particularly those concerned with outdoor activities and the sea. Sailing was one of his favourite recreations and he was an enthusiastic member of the Royal Yacht Squadron. But his overriding predilection for music had shown early. By the age of sixteen, at Eton, he had produced notebooks containing several forms of Church music, piano and organ pieces, canons, madrigals and songs, and was a stalwart of the Eton

Musical Society while placating – if not amazing – the heartier elements by being also keeper of the "School Field". During his last "half" at Eton he further surprised everyone by passing the examination for the degree of Bachelor of Music at Oxford University.

Parry is a fine exemplar of the Savile commandment which ordains that those of its distinguished members who capture public attention do so without proclaiming it within the Club or in any other way attaching their eminence to its more private collective reputation. One wonders even now, for instance, how many present members are aware that when they hymn that much-loved melody to Blake's *Jerusalem*, or rejoice in the exquisite eight-part setting, *Blest Pair of Sirens*, they are, in fact, paying tribute to this gentle, humorous past member who, in all his lifetime at the Savile, despite the evidence to the contrary which he had provided, never regarded himself as a "professional", merely because he never had to earn his living from music.

Parry had, in fact, begun work on Milton's *Blest Pair of Sirens* shortly after he was elected to the Savile and it was performed the following year (1887) by the Bach Choir, ushering in a whole series of compositions set to sacred or secular words such as *Judith*, "Ode on St Cecilia's Day", "L'Allegro ed il Penseroso" and several others which followed at approximately annual intervals.

Like many before – and after – him, Parry came to the Club with many well-established connections. It has been often said, for instance, that his musical reputation was first firmly established as a result of a concert of his chamber music staged by Arthur Balfour in 1879 at his house in Carlton House Terrace when Balfour was already a trustee of the Savile, though Parry was still seven years away from his own election. He was already acquainted with Sir Walter Parratt and Stanford through his professorship at the R.C.M., and partly because of his association with the latter had many musical encounters with the madrigalist and musical theorist William Smith Rockstro – elected to the Savile in 1886 – and the musical critic and antiquary William Barclay Squire, who had been elected in the same year. (The latter, incidentally, embraced another Savile musical connection in that he was married to the sister of the musical critic John Alexander Fuller-Maitland – elected in 1887 – who was to contribute Parry's entry in the 2nd edition of Grove's *Dictionary of Music* – which he also edited – as well as writing books on Brahms, Joachim, *Parry and Stanford,* all of whose careers were to some extent further intertwined.)

Hubert Parry was to have perhaps his most productive association at the Savile with his fellow member Robert Bridges. Bridges, whose chief claim to a musical memorial probably still lies in *The Yattendon Hymnal* produced in collaboration with Harry Wooldridge, had also written the libretto of that elaborate oratorio, *Eden*, for a musical setting by Stanford. Now he was to collaborate with Sir Hubert Parry in the creation of a similarly ambitious work, the *Ode to Music*, for the bicentenary commemoration of Henry Purcell in 1895. Bridges had used this opportunity to set out in the preface to his poem a defence of poetry against what he considered the grave perils of "declamatory music". The message evidently got home to Parry for in his setting of Milton's "At a Solemn Musick", he celebrated the "Sphere-born harmonious sisters, Voice and Verse" with a far more even hand than in *Jerusalem*, where attention to the words and their meaning tends, for some, to be obscured by the grand "declamation" of the music.

Parry's place in the history of English musical composition, his tenure as principal of the R.C.M. after he succeeded Sir George Grove in 1895, and his professorship of music at Oxford from 1900 to 1908 are recorded in other books than this, but his activities in the Club and his relations with the many friends and colleagues gathered there are less generally known. It has been said that he possessed "an abounding sense of humour which was an essential part of his genial and engaging disposition" and evidence of this can be found in some of his music, most notably his incidental music to *The Birds* of Aristophanes performed at Cambridge in 1883, and *The Frogs,* first performed at Oxford, in 1892. These more sociable traits must have made him a welcome addition to the Sodality at Piccadilly, but it has also been noted that "he could be intolerant, hasty, and even forbidding". It was inevitable, therefore, that being so prominent in the same field, and having such antipathetic personal characteristics to Stanford, there should have been more than one cause for uneasiness when both were making use of the Club rooms. Though their professional paths were to run so closely in parallel, and their names were to be so commonly associated with the renaissance of English music, the differences between them often ran deep. Stanford, for instance, had a great enthusiasm for opera and was determined to make the R.C.M. famous for it, while Parry when he was director of the college referred to this form of musical activity as "the shallowest fraud man ever achieved in the name of art . . . the appanage of the wastrels, the home of the humbugs." Undismayed, and with his indomitable enthusiasm, Stanford proceeded in his first thirty years of service at the R.C.M. to produce thirty-one operas covering an extremely wide range, from Mozart to Wagner. Parry tolerated it, but his own views on this and other matters were made quite plain. His friend at the Savile Harry Plunket Greene refers to the relations between Stanford and Parry:

> They remained strained until the latter's death in 1918. Their association at the R.C.M. was spoiled by periodic "rows" and subsequent reconciliations due, no doubt, to the clashing of opposing temperaments. Parry was that best of all administrators – a benevolent autocrat. He was responsible to his Council, but in all else saw that things were done as he wished, and, as everybody knows, he made a complete success of it. The pupils adored him; the professors and staff would have "stood on their heads" for him. It is seldom you get a dictator, and a musicial one at that, who is also a sailor, a swimmer, a rider, and had been an old cricketer and footballer and all-round athlete at Eton and Oxford. Add to this a personality which radiated charm and seemed to smooth the rough places to strong and weak alike, it was no wonder that those with whom he had to deal fell into his step unconsciously. There were many who originally

questioned the wisdom of his appointment, seeking only the bluff exterior and mistaking that heartiness for happy-go-luckiness. They were wrong. He was a great success as an administrator. Under all his warm humanity, often tender, always gentle, was a fierce fighting temperament kept firmly in leash, and with it a definite shyness which made words difficult at moments of deep feeling, when a pat on the back had to take the place of praise . . . Stanford's look-out on, and approach to, administration in general was elastic and he was liable to explode in fireworks when his suggestions were turned down. These may sometimes have been very good ones, but they made the person to whom they were addressed see red. Some would be in writing, and he never could be made to realise the inherent dangers of the *litera scripta*. These letters become almost proverbial. "I took up me pen, me boy," was the recognised prelude, among his friends to some inevitable "row" with a temporary antagonist. In spite of his long and intimate association with Hubert Parry he never realised the fundamental difference of their respective temperaments . . . Sooner or later came the inevitable explosion. This happened not once but many times and his reactions were painful to see. He had an almost dog-like devotion to Parry and it hurt him to the quick to be so ruthlessly handled as was generally the case. Parry refused to believe in this . . . he did not seem to realise that a man like Stanford did not take orders from anyone easily and that his loyal subordination in the College work had anything to do with his affection towards himself.

A more amusing description of the two men's fundamental differences in attitude, even towards the less prosaic realities of life, is given by one of Stanford's pupils, Samuel Liddle, in a letter published in *Music and Letters* after Stanford's death. Stanford, like many Irishmen of his time, had a deep appreciation of the occult:

> He evidently believed in things outside this world [wrote Liddle]. I once told him a ghost-story of my own which had happened to me in the North of Ireland. He was deeply impressed and said to me earnestly. "Was that in So-and-So? Why, me boy, that is one of the most ghost-ridden spots in the country." Parry, who was standing by, said, "What did your mother say to it?" I said, "She asked me what I'd eaten for supper." "Humph!" said Parry, "your mother's a sensible woman."

Clearly, therefore, men whose attitudes not only to life but the afterlife were very different.

Plunket Greene comments on Parry's inherent shyness as "a form of inhibition which made Clubs of no account to him and kept him a lonely man all of his life." This cannot be wholly true of his association with the Savile for he remained a devoted member of this convivial place from the day of his election in 1886 until his death of 1918, though it may explain the more muted memories of him there compared with those of the more explosive Stanford.

Stanford's dominant presence in the early days of the Savile, indeed, tends to overshadow the other prominent men of music who were rapidly gathering there to join with those other men "of different professions" who regarded them as such a welcome addition to *Sodalitas* and *Convivium*. In 1893, for instance, Sir Walter Parratt, who had by then been a member of the Savile for eight years, was appointed Master of the Queen's Musick, a post which was later to be confirmed by King Edward VII, who awarded him the MVO, and also by King George V, from whom he received the CVO in 1917 and the KCVO in 1928. Meantime, in 1908, he had succeeded Sir Hubert Parry as professor of music at Oxford. In 1886, the same year as Parry, Charles Harford Lloyd, another distinguished organist, was elected to the Savile: he was to become president of the Royal College of Organists twenty-five years later in 1912. In 1889 the violinist, organist, writer on music, and composer, Charles Adby Williams also joined the musical throng at the Club. Like Stanford he had served much of his apprenticeship to music in the Cambridge University Musical Society, and it is odd that having played the violin and the viola at its concerts and taken an active part in its management in Stanford's time, there is no record of any contact between them either in musical circles or at the Savile. Perhaps this is because Williams devoted himself mainly to the study and re-creation of ancient Greek music; and therein lies a remote connection with the contemporary Savile, for much of his work was carried out as composer and director of the famous Greek Theatre at Bradfield College, of which a contemporary Savilian, Christopher Stace, was until recently the master as head of Classics.

In 1893 the English educationalist and composer Sir Arthur Somervell was elected to the Club. Unlike Abdy Williams his connections with other leading musicians at the Savile are well recorded. At Cambridge in the 1880s he had studied music with Stanford, later entering the R.C.M., and becoming a private pupil of Parry. Just as in the sphere of science Savile members seemed for a time to exercise *droit de seigneur* at the Cavendish Laboratory, so now did the more musical of them appear to claim a similar freehold at the R.C.M., for Somervell went on to join its teaching staff in 1894. This, and his later appointment as Inspector of Music to the Board of Education – a post he held for twenty-seven years – made such inroads on his time that it severely restricted what had once appeared to be a conspicuously promising career as a composer. He had first made his name in the 1890s with a series of song-cycles, among them a setting of Tennyson's "Maud" which his fellow member of the Savile, the critic and musicologist Fuller-Maitland, described as having "a place among the classics of English song for the complete unity of feeling existing between poetry and music" – a remark which would have pleased his Club contemporary, Robert Bridges. He had also composed more ambitious works such as a Mass in C minor for the Bach Choir in 1891, but his major compositions came after his retirement from the Board of Education in 1928. These consisted of longer works; a symphony, concertos for violin, and for piano, and various chamber music. Sadly, these are all now totally neglected for reasons which are, to quote Grove's *Dictionary*, "a reflection on the superficiality or fickleness of public taste rather than a criticism of [their] musical quality".

John Alexander Fuller-Maitland had been exposed to the overpowering presence of Stanford at the Club since 1887, but he must have been well used to it for, as a student at Cambridge in the 1870s, he had entered upon what he called five or six years of "musical amateurity" under the aegis of Stanford and that other future member of the Savile, W. Barclay Squire. While contributing to, and later editing, Grove's *Dictionary of Music and Musicians*, Fuller-Maitland was invited by a founder member of the Savile, John Morley, to be musical critic of the *Pall Mall Gazette*, of which Morley was then editor. When Morley was succeeded by W. T. Stead, Fuller-Maitland was dismissed and after a period as musical critic of the *Manchester Guardian* he succeeded Francis Hueffer as musical critic of *The Times* in 1889. This post he held until his retirement in 1911, becoming a prominent, if rather conservative, figure in English musical life.

Fuller-Maitland's contemporary at Cambridge, fellow member of the Savile and subsequently brother-in-law, William Barclay Squire, was altogether a more dashing figure, and not only in the world of music. He had been a contemporary of Stanford at Cambridge and in 1885, the year he was elected to the Savile, he had been practising as a solicitor in London. In that year, however, he was appointed an assistant in the department of printed books in the British Museum, eventually becoming an assistant keeper with special charge of the printed music, and, later, honorary curator of the Sovereign's music library, which is on permanent loan there. Like so many other Savile members of that time and later, Squire was not content to practise within one particular discipline. His acquaintance with Stanford had already borne fruit four years before he joined the Savile when he took time off from the law to write the libretto of Stanford's opera *The Veiled Prophet of Khorassan*. From 1890 onwards he was successively musical critic for the *Saturday Review, Westminster Gazette, Globe,* and *Pilot*. He was a contributor to the first three editions of Grove's *Dictionary*, to the *Encyclopaedia Britannica*, and to the *Dictionary of National Biography*. His induction to the Savile probably resulted from yet another activity, his appointment in 1885 as librarian to the Royal College of Music, whence so many of his new colleagues were already finding relaxation at 107 Piccadilly. Though the bulk of his reputation lay in his antiquarian research and his cataloguing and editorial work on early printed music, these, even together with the other activities already outlined, did not represent the full extent of his boundless versatility. During the First World War he worked for the Intelligence department of the Admiralty yet found time to deliver a report on the *Tribes of Tunisia* which was officially adopted by the French government in 1916. From 1918 to 1920 he served in the historical section of the Foreign Office, which did not prevent him, however, from editing a definitive four-volume collection of Purcell's harpsichord music for the Purcell Society, of which he was then honorary secretary. He had been a fellow of the Society of Antiquaries since 1888 and, for good measure, a fellow of the Royal Geographical Society since 1894. In 1918 he became a Knight of Grace of the Order of St John of Jerusalem, and in 1926 received the CVO. Even in a Club where polymathy was then relatively commonplace, Squire's remarkable industry and wide range of achievement must have caused a few raised eyebrows.

To add to the quiverful of influential writers on music who polished their points at the Savile came Robin Legge, who was elected to the Club in 1895. Legge was a distinguished musical critic and his devotion to, and his work for, the promotion of music in his lifetime was only matched by that energy which he now applied also to the Savile. He was to serve for three separate periods on the Club's committee from 1902-5, from 1911-14, and from 1923-5, and during all his thirty-eight years of membership introduced many distinguished musicians into the Club. In addition to the many full members who were attracted to the Savile at Legge's behest, there was hardly any distinguished musical visitor to London in his time who did not find temporary hospitality at the Club as a result of his solicitude for the artistic temperament, and his firm belief that only at the Club house in Piccadilly could it be properly sustained between public performances. Among such visitors during the early years of Legge's membership were the pianists Rudolph Zwintscher and Giuseppe Aldo Raudigger; the musician Victor Beigel – who was later to become a full member; and the singers Clarence Whithill of the Royal Opera at Covent Garden, and Reinhold Von Warlick of the St Petersburg Opera. He was later to sponsor the composer Frederick Delius on many of his subsequent visits to the Club as a temporary member, though on the first occasion in 1898 Delius was proposed by Christopher Keary, a well-known novelist of the time. Because of his profession and their mutual membership of the Savile, Legge was to have many encounters of varying degrees of warmth with Stanford. As a rule they were the best of friends, but, inevitably, the volatile Irishman found an excuse to commence a testing feud which on one occasion was to last for all of six months.

Stanford had a favourite pupil called James Friskin, a talented pianist who was studying composition as a second subject at the R.C.M. One day, according to Legge, he was in the Savile and bumped into Stanford, who looked him straight in the eye and passed him by without a word. Legge knew his man and said nothing. About six months later Stanford came up to him, took him by the arm and said:

"Ye treated Friskin damned badly." (Friskin had given a piano recital.)
"I didn't," said Legge, "I wasn't there."
"Ye were – I saw ye – come and play picquet."

As Plunket Greene, who recounts this story, remarks: "Like a storm in the desert it had blown itself out and like most of them [ie. Stanford's feuds] it had been on someone else's behalf." No mention that like so many of Stanford's "feuds" it was based on a totally imaginary slight. Still Legge had adopted the Savile's attitude to Stanford, which was all-forgiving, and like so many incidents of a similar kind, it left behind no residue of bitterness.

The singer and writer Harry Plunket Greene, who has left us so many stimulating recollections of Stanford in particular and the Savile in general, was elected to the Club in 1897, two years before he made another collateral connection by marrying Gwendolen Maud, the younger daughter of his fellow member, Sir Hubert Parry. Plunket Greene came from an Anglo-Irish family of some distinction – he was a great-grandson of the first Lord Plunket, Lord Chancellor of Ireland, and his father was a distinguished barrister. These facts are not as irrelevant as they may seem to the very important place which he established for himself in English music, for he arrived on the artistic scene when it was only just ceasing to be *infra dig.* for "gentlemen of education and social position" to be concerned with the profession of music. It had been only recently, for instance, that Sir Frederick Ouseley – professor of music at Oxford in Plunket Greene's younger days – had been obliged, when a student, to defy the dean of Christ Church, who "would not permit a baronet and a gentleman commoner to read for a degree in music". It is an interesting illustration of the Club's spirit that the chief protagonists who helped spearhead this change of attitude, Sir Hubert Parry, Sir Charles Stanford, Sir Joseph Barnby, Sir Arthur Somervell, Plunket Greene and, later, Gervase Elwes, were all members of the Savile.

Not only that but it could be said that by the end of the century the Club possessed as members nearly all those men who were bringing about the great renaissance of England as a centre of musical excellence and giving the lie to the common European notion – typically expressed in German – that it was "Das Land ohne Musik". Plunket Greene stood out prominently among them. Nine years before his membership of the Savile he had made his début in England as a bass-baritone and soon established his reputation not only as a performer of German *Lieder* and Brahms' songs but as a gifted interpreter of the new generation of English composers: Stanford, Sir Arthur Somervell and Parry. He became particularly associated as a soloist with the regular series of cantatas and oratorios which the last regularly wrote for the Three Choirs festivals, especially *Job* at Gloucester in 1892. Again, the seeming inevitability of a Savile connection was apparent long before his own membership was realized, for he became famous as the "creator" of the Stanford Irish song-cycles, and was an essential element as soloist in another Club nexus, the Charles Stanford-Henry Newbolt combination of patriotic and sea songs which were applauded in their time as having "a far higher degree of merit than anything which had previously been set down". It is interesting, incidentally, that that enthusiastic seafarer, Parry, with the possible exception of a late naval ode, "The Chivalry of the Sea" (words again, by Robert Bridges), did not write any music connected with the sea, while that determined landlubber, Stanford, composed a great deal. Evidence for Plunket Greene's distinction as a writer and his wide range of interests outside of music can be found in the Monument. Apart from his biography of Stanford and his text *Interpretation in Song* there is a delightful anthem to his favourite recreation, fishing, *Where the Bright Waters Meet.* This was an obsession shared by Stanford, so that he was able to insert a long chapter on their mutual love of the sport in his biography. Plunket

Greene's obituarist, Steuart Wilson, summed him up thus:

> The effect of Greene on his generation was remarkable: it was due to his
> charm and humour combined with his magnificent presence, his perfect
> diction in speech and song, now beguiling and now commanding, and
> above all, to his fresh-air outlook which banished the hackneyed
> insincerities of the shop-ballad and raised the standard of public taste. In
> this campaign he was particularly influential as an adjudicator in the
> competition festival movement, both in this country and in Canada.

The importance of competitive festivals may have become a more controversial
issue nowadays but their influence together with that of private *salons* in
reinforcing the sometimes reluctant efforts of the more conventional concert halls
and opera houses on behalf of Victorian and Edwardian music is now often
forgotten or at least under-estimated for those years before radio and recording
techniques permitted more people in one night to hear a new work than might
have been able then to consider it in the whole of a composer's lifetime. Both of
these gathering-places were of particular relevance during the first sixty years of
the Savile's history and Savile members made distinctive contributions to their
usefulness in the promotion of living composers.

The Cambridge University Musical Society, founded by one Savile member,
Lord Kelvin, and revitalized by another, Stanford, had, as we have seen,
contributed greatly to the resurgence of music-making in England. Savile
members such as Parry, Somervell, Plunket Greene and others had made their
mark both nationally and internationally in the great spate of music festivals which
resulted from the new enthusiasm. Parry had been set on his way at a private *salon*
in Balfour's house, and he and Stanford, realizing its importance, continued the
tradition in their own etablishments until the time came when broadcasting and
recording facilities made them less necessary. Plunket Greene recalls one of the last
occasions at Stanford's house, in 1923, when the composer was already in the grip
of his last illness:

> It was a tropic night, 92 in the shade. Sybil Eaton (for whom he had
> written the *Irish Rhapsody No.6* for Violin and Orchestra) and Leonard
> Borwick played, and I sang. The room was crammed with people, and the
> old Guildhall spirit seemed to be abroad. He seemed to be rejuvenated for
> the occasion. It brought back the old days at Holland Street, where I
> remembered hearing the Joachim Quartet and seeing Lord Kelvin and Lord
> Lister listening from an ingle in the drawing-room – like most scientists
> lovers of music; and that other time when Tschaikovsky and Max Bruch
> were there, 'the one' as somebody said 'like an ambassador and the other
> like a store-keeper from the middle-west'.
>
> These parties were by no means highbrow affairs. He was not above
> playing a practical joke on the company as on the occasion when after a

Haydn quartet had came to an end Caruso's voice emerged out of the silences under the piano in '*Ah! Che la Morte*'. These were the early days of the gramophone, and it took some seconds of stunned silence before the audience realized that Jove had nodded . . .

In the '80s and '90s there was hardly a night in the London season without half a dozen musical parties; there were *salons* for the few and concerts for the many; the Opera was sold out nightly. Birmingham and Leeds packed to the doors, fought for the premiership of the great autumn festivals; Gloucester, Worcester and Hereford drew music-lovers back from their holidays . . . Not all the music was good but it was there in plenty.

The small but powerful group of musicians at the Savile had also attracted – albeit on a temporary membership basis – many visitors from abroad who were concerned with music. Some have already been listed, but perhaps the most prominent among them despite his name and French address was one of the greatest of English contemporary composers, Frederick Delius. Delius first came to the Club on a visit to London in 1898 and was to continue to use its facilities for temporary membership on subsequent visits over the next twenty years before the ravages of his distressing illness confined him to his house at Grez-sur-Loing. Although he was one of the more distinctive figures in the revival of English music at the end of the nineteenth century his work attracted more attention in Europe – particularly Germany – than it did in his native country until Sir Thomas Beecham became its powerful advocate in the 1920s. Perhaps it was this, together with the temporary nature of his membership over twenty years, which accounts for the curious omission that perhaps the greatest composer to grace the Savile until the arrival of Elgar in 1919 had no recorded dealings at the Club or elsewhere with such outstanding figures as Stanford and Parry.

Delius did, however, sustain friendships with other musical members of the Savile such as Roger Quilter, Gervase Elwes and Robin Legge, all of whom stood as his sponsors during his various visits to the Club. He also had a great personal regard for Elgar, and some explanation for his distancing from Stanford and Parry is provided in his record of a conversation he had once with Elgar, who in the course of it mentioned he was busy working on his Third Symphony and said: "My music will not interest you, Delius; you are too much of a poet for workmen like me!"

I replied that I thought there was some fine stuff in his *Introduction and Allegro* for strings, and that I admired his *Falstaff* but I thought it was a great pity that he has wasted so much time and energy in writing those long-winded oratorios.

"That" said Elgar, "is the penalty of my English environment".

"Well, anyhow, Elgar, you're not as bad as Parry," I replied. "He would have set the whole Bible to music had he lived long enough!"

Delius was evidently unaware that Parry was a lifelong agnostic.

In the ten years after Stanford's biographer Plunket Greene had been elected in 1897 there came as members to the Club: the singer Gervase Elwes; the composers, Balfour Gardiner and Roger Quilter; and the musicologists Edward Dent and Cecil Sharp.

Gervase Elwes, elected in 1904, was of that caste of Englishmen who were making the profession of music respectable at home and restoring England's musical reputation abroad. He came, like Plunket Greene, from an aristocratic Anglo-Irish family (one of whom, "Eddie" Ward, or, more formally, Viscount Bangor, is a contemporary member) and after a brief foray into the Diplomatic Service studied under a fellow member of the Savile, Victor Beigel, to become a professional singer. Under the tutelage of Beigel he rapidly became a prominent figure in the English musical world and in the year of his election, "to his great joy", was engaged by Stanford to sing "Die Preislied" from *Die Meistersinger*, and given to believe that his share in the next festival would be much larger. In her biography of him his widow records:

> Up to this time Gervase had been oddly unsettled in the way of London clubs, which seem to bulk curiously large in a man's life. Apart from the Carlton, to which he felt bound to belong, he had flitted from one to another, paying a series of extortionate entrance fees, only to find that each bored him more than the last. In a fortunate hour Harry Plunket Greene and Robin Legge put him up for the Savile, which I believe is exceptional in that the members, who are largely culled from literary and artistic callings, talk to each other freely and without restraint. Gervase really loved the Savile, with its large dining-table and its friendly and witty general conversation.

In the year of his election also, Elwes, rather diffidently so it is said, agreed to sing the title part in a performance of *The Dream of Gerontius* at the Queen's Hall. It was only its third performance in England and it proved to be a personal triumph. Weingartner conducted and Elgar himself was present to congratulate Elwes and express the wish that he would sing it many times again. Robin Legge supplemented an enthusiastic notice in *The Times* with a personal letter: ". . . I shall not forget it: it has earmarked 'Gerontius' for me . . . how beautifully, supremely beautifully you did your part . . .". The general view was expressed by Dr McNaught of Novello's, a well-known adjudicator at music festivals, who said to him, "You have made your reputation for ever; it was a supreme performance." The concert immediately established Elwes as the ideal interpreter of *Gerontius*, and Elgar was soon to have his wish. Three more performances were arranged in the same year, five in the following year and seven in 1906. In all, during the sixteen years which followed, he sang *Gerontius* one hundred and eighteen times and would undoubtedly have sung more had he not been tragically killed in a train accident during a tour of America in 1921. Elwes was a man of deep religious faith which inspired his singing and seems to have created a loving and uninhibited response from all who knew him, not only at the Club but throughout Europe and America wherever he had performed. The English and American press were filled with moving tributes to him; at his Requiem Mass at Brompton Oratory it was said that "the whole of England was mourning for him"; but perhaps the most touching tribute came in an account in the *Sunday Times* of the annual performance of *Gerontius* given at the Albert Hall by the London Choral Society for the first time in many years without Gervase Elwes. With what seems to be a most condign symmetry the two leading parts were taken by distinguished singers who were also friends of his at the Savile:

> Lovers of music said good-bye to one of their heroes yesterday afternoon . . . at the Albert Hall and all that vast place was filled with people who were thinking not so much of the steady tide of the tremendous music as of the Singer who in his time made that music his own and who will never sing to us again . . . John Coates was singing the tenor part of Elgar's great work, and singing wonderfully. But all the time one saw the figure of that other; one heard that other voice . . .
>
> > 'Jesu, Maria, I am near to death,
> > And thou art calling me'
>
> You know how the great words go. Coates sang them better, I think, than I have ever heard him sing, and the very splendour of his singing was a tribute. And presently Frederick Ranalow put our thoughts into words and music for us. 'Go forth upon thy journey, Christian soul', he sang, 'go from this world,' . . . It was hard at the last to accept with conviction the high rejoicing of the 'Praise to the Holiest' chorus, but even there Elwes was helping. For it is just what he would have said.

The year after Gervase Elwes' election, 1905, saw the arrival at the Savile of Edward J. Dent, the great musicologist, teacher, and an occasional composer. Like so many others he was already familiar with some of his fellow members; he had studied music at Eton under Charles Harford Lloyd and at Cambridge with Stanford; his admirer E. M. Forster had just published his first novel, *Where Angels Fear to Tread*, which featured him pseudonymously as "Philip Herriton"; and, while as a fellow of King's College Cambridge lecturing on the history of music, and teaching harmony, counterpoint and composition, he was beginning to incubate a hearty dislike for the works of his future confrère at the Savile, Edward Elgar. Dent contributed an article to a German publication suggesting that Elgar's music was too emotional and to some English ears perhaps even a touch vulgar. This aroused a storm of protest led by Bernard Shaw, supported by two future Savilians, the singer John Goss and the young William Walton – the latter being particularly courageous, as Dent was extremely influential while Walton had still to achieve any kind of recognition. Dent, in turn, seems to have been heartily disliked by Stanford though, typically, this had not prevented the latter from taking thorough and unstinting care in his earlier musical tuition. One is tempted to reflect that with so many discordant musical temperaments coming to rest at the house in Piccadilly it is a tribute to the Savile that it managed to remain such an harmonious place at all.

In 1906 the composers Balfour Gardiner and Roger Quilter were elected to the Club. Like several of the new generation of English musicians they came from wealthy backgrounds which enabled them to pursue their musical activities without regard for having to earn a living. Both had studied under a famous teacher of the time, Ivan Knorr, at Frankfurt, and both were to become intimate friends of Delius. Of Gardiner, Delius once said: "He is one of my oldest friends, and one of the few people I trust and admire implicitly." From 1900 until the Great War broke out Gardiner produced a steady output of compositions which were highly regarded by many of his contemporaries, but after 1924 he abandoned music altogether. He had a theory that at a certain age a man ceases to be musical and that he had reached it. "Would that many others thought the same," said Delius.

It is of passing interest, however, that Gardiner – having met Thomas Hardy at the Savile – was one of the first of a long line of composers, most notably Elgar, who were minded to make an opera out of one of his stories. He did a considerable amount of work on "The Three Strangers" but it was never completed; an extract from the music, however, "Shepherd Fennels's Dance" became very popular at the time.

Roger Quilter's music has survived better. A man of great culture, his compositions were almost entirely limited to the field of English song, and his setting of texts by Shakespeare, Herrick, Shelley, Keats and the former Savilian, R. L. Stevenson, are still firmly in the repertoire. Most of the leading singers of his day, among them Plunket Greene, John Coates, and Gervase Elwes, welcomed the opportunity to sing Quilter's songs, and Quilter regarded Elwes, with whom he formed a deep friendship, as his ideal interpreter. "He inspired me so much", wrote Quilter, "that I could never have written in quite the same way if I had not known Gervase." Delius was particularly fond of Quilter, who, in common with many other Savilians such as Balfour Gardiner and Professor Edward Dent, made regular pilgrimages to Grez-sur-Loing to cheer the stricken composer.

Although Quilter's influence on the renaissance of English music was considerable and his songs bear an unmistakable English stamp, he was not at all influenced by the contemporary folk-song revival. This must have been a disappointment to Cecil Sharp, the musician, author, and collector of English folk-songs and dances who was elected to the Savile in the same year, 1906. Although Parry had partly anticipated him in his book, *Art of Music*, in which he applied the theory of evolution to music, showing the line of succession from the simplest of folk-tunes to the most elaborate symphony, and Stanford had edited and arranged the famous Petrie collection of Irish folk-songs (not altogether successfully though it contained the beautiful "Londonderry Air" which Parry spoke of as the most beautiful tune in the world), Cecil Sharp was undoubtedly the most industrious collector and propagandist for this form of music in his time. He has left behind a vast collection – literally thousands – of regional songs, and was a pioneer in providing a form of notation for folk dances. After his death these were gathered together in Cecil Sharp House in Regent's Park, where *aficionados* can repair to extend their knowledge. On its foundation stones are inscribed the words: "This building is erected in memory of Cecil Sharp who restored to the English People the songs and dances of their country." Sadly for his undoubted claims to posterity, more musicians seem to remember Sir Thomas Beecham's immortal remark: "Everything is worth trying once, except incest and folk-dancing."

Of more general interest, perhaps, to contemporary members, is the example he is said to have provided of the relative efficiency and erudition of the contemporary postal service. While staying at a place called Seascale in Cumberland, it is claimed, he received without untoward delay a letter addressed as follows:

CUMBERLAND

Whether this *lettre à clef* emanated from a skittish member of the Savile (or whether it is true at all) is open to some doubt as the story has also been ascribed to another musician of the time, the cellist Cedric Sharp.

The teacher, musical critic, biographer of Cecil Sharp, and founder-editor of the influential *Music and Letters,* Arthur Fox Strangways, was elected to the Savile in 1911. He stood in as musical critic of *The Times* during the absence on war-service of its regular incumbent, Henry Cope Colles, who, when the war was over, also joined the Savile. Fox Strangways then joined the staff of the *Observer* as musical critic and remained there until 1939. His membership of the Club was not as lengthy for he allowed it to lapse in 1913, but his influence and his connection with the Savile remained important. The first edition of *Music and Letters,* for instance, contained Bernard Shaw's seminal article on Elgar and in common with many other members of distinction at the time, Fox Strangways' features are preserved for posterity in two pencil drawings by his contemporary at Piccadilly, Sir William Rothenstein.

The great Bach scholar Charles Sandford Terry was elected to the Club in 1914, remaining a member until he retired to Scotland in 1926; and in 1918, the violinist, composer and musical critic, Ferruccio Bonavia, came to swell the Savile's musical ranks. Although he had played violin in the Hallé orchestra under Richter for ten years, and composed some chamber music which attracted a measure of local attention, he was better known for his critical writing, first with the *Manchester Guardian* and later with the *Daily Telegraph* in which, for thirty years until his death in 1950, he wrote some fine and penetrating criticism.

Henry Cope Colles, elected to the Savile in 1919, had succeeded his fellow Savilian, J. A. Fuller-Maitland, as musical editor of *The Times* in 1911 and, with the exception of the war years when Fox Strangways substituted for him, occupied this post with great distinction until his death in 1943. As a student at the R.C.M. in the late 1890s his interest in the history of music had first been aroused by Sir Hubert Parry; and after taking a degree in music at Oxford he began his career as a teacher and writer which culminated in perhaps his greatest achievement in this field, the third and revised edition of Grove's *Dictionary of Music and Musicians*, which he edited and revised in 1927 together with its supplementary volume in 1940.

The year of Colles's election, 1919, saw also the admission of Peter Latham to the Club of which he was to remain a member until shortly before he died in 1970. At the time of his election he was a student at the Royal Academy of Music, where he gained the Charles Lucas Prize for Music and subsequently became its professor of harmony and counterpoint. Among his many associates at the Savile was Compton Mackenzie and he wrote many essays and reviews for *The Gramophone* which Mackenzie edited for many years. He succeeded Walford Davies as Gresham Professor of Music in 1946 and wrote works on Brahms and Beethoven. In 1919 also the Savile attracted to its ranks one of its classic polymaths, Walter James Redfern Turner: poet, musical critic, journalist and playwright. Turner arrived at the Savile after demobilization from the war – in which, to his surprise, he had risen to the rank of captain – with an already established reputation as a poet and was a member of a literary group led by one of his closest friends, Siegfried Sassoon. Some accounts of his literary activities and his associations at the Savile with such intimates as Yeats and Patric Dickinson have appeared earlier, but it is worth noting here that he performed sterling services to music from 1916 to 1940 when he was the influential musical critic of the *New Statesman*, which was dominated by Savile members for most of this period. He also produced more extensive studies of Beethoven, Mozart, Wagner, and Berlioz which appeared regularly in tandem with his volumes of poetry and his works for the theatre.

Once when Dallas Bower, who has a tendency on occasion to mumble, began to discuss with him one of his more recent works on music, Turner demonstrated his capacity for combining charm with blunt speaking: "I'm told that when you have something to say it can be very interesting but, alas, I can never hear a word you say."

Douglas Fox, also elected in 1919, had returned less happily from the war than Turner. Though there are more famously estimated names which spring immediately to mind when discussions occur about the Savile's connection with music – Elgar, Boult, Stanford, Parry, Walton, Alwyn, Arnold and the rest – Fox was undoubtedly one of the most remarkable members of his generation, and, except for an interval between 1957 and 1963, was a figure at the Club until his death in 1978.

In 1910 he had won an organ scholarship to the Royal College of Music where he was taught by the Savilians, Sir Walter Parratt and Sir Charles Villiers Stanford. Sir Thomas Armstrong, who succeeded him as Organ Scholar of Keble College in 1916, referred to his "brilliant technique" and how his performances on piano and organ "penetrated into the heart of the music he played". Although at first he was deferred from military service he contrived to join the 4th Gloucestershire Regiment and was serving at the front in 1917. On 4 September of that year he wrote with his left hand to a friend, Arthur Peppin, remarking laconically that this was because his right arm had been shattered and in order to save his life had had to be amputated. Sir Hubert Parry wrote a few days later to Peppin:

> I don't think anything in this atrocious war has so impressed me with the very malignity of cruelty as the utter destruction of that dear boy's splendid gifts. I can't help thinking of the thirst that will come to him to use his rare powers of interpretation and be utterly debarred. It is devilish. I can hardly bear to think of him in connection with music any more.

From the Savile Stanford also wrote to Fox's father: ". . . I am sure his art will come out somehow".

In this particular case Stanford was right and Parry wrong. Fox's friends rallied to him; when his friend Hugh Allen, the organist of New College, heard the news, he played evensong in the chapel in tribute using only his left hand and the pedals and, when Fox returned to England, invited him to become president of the Oxford University Musical Club. From there he went to Bradfield (where his fellow member, Charles Abdy Williams, had preceded him) as director of music, and remained there until 1930 when he moved to a similar position at Clifton College.

Beside the considerable brilliance as a teacher which he was now to demonstrate, Fox began building up a great repertoire for organ and piano recitals adapted to suit his physical handicap. These he performed all over the country and for the BBC; and he became especially associated with memorable interpretations of Ravel's Piano Concerto for the Left Hand. Audiences were amazed by the technical mastery which allowed him to display what Parry had called his "rare powers of interpretation" through his arrangements of many other works so they could be played by left hand alone. Even professional musicians wondered how was it done, how much had had to be omitted or rearranged? The great musicologist Sir Donald Tovey wrote to him after one concert: "Your performance was very fine. I purposely didn't look to see how it was done", adding that his companion who did, spent the evening with the balls of his eyes staring out of his head, "so I'm told has become permanently exophthalmic".

Fox was appointed OBE in 1958 and though he held many honorary doctorates of music, his doctorate from Edinburgh in 1938 was by examination. He was made a fellow of the Royal College of Music in 1973 and was also honorary R.A.M. At his memorial, the principal of the Royal Academy of Music, Sir

Thomas Armstrong, said in his address:

> Douglas stands, in a way, for the whole of that doomed generation, for all
> the men killed and maimed... We speak of them as heroes: but heroism
> manifests itself in different ways...: Sometimes it is a question of facing
> death, more often of facing life. Douglas Fox's heroism was of the latter
> kind, begun in a moment of tragedy, continued in the daily problems of
> professional life, and ended in the recognition, freely accorded him, of a
> task well done.

In 1916, Sir Adrian Boult had been elected to the Savile. At Oxford, Boult's
musical career was guided by Douglas Fox's mentor, Hugh Allen, and under his
aegis he had also become president of the University Musical Club immediately
prior to Fox's return from the war. After taking his D.Mus. degree, and spending
a year at the Leipzig Conservatoire, Boult joined the staff of the Royal College of
Music, to take classes in conducting and score-reading. A little later he succeeded
Stanford as conductor of the R.C.M. orchestra though Stanford remained
nominally in charge of the orchestra until he died. Meantime Boult was making
his reputation both at home and abroad as a conductor and promoter of English
music, giving performances of such works as Holst's *Planets*, Vaughan Williams's
Pastoral Symphony and *A Colour Symphony* by his fellow Savilian Sir Arthur Bliss of
which he had been the dedicatee. Boult became one of the front-runners of the
Savile's long association with the BBC when, in 1930, he was appointed musical
director and conductor-in-chief to the newly formed BBC Symphony Orchestra.
He held the first of these posts until he resigned it in 1942 to his fellow member of
the Savile, Sir Arthur Bliss, though he remained chief conductor until 1950. Boult
was knighted in 1937, and took part in the Coronation of King George VI as the
conductor of the music given before the ceremony, much of it written by Sir
William Walton, who was later to become a member of the Club. Fortunately for
his devotees, he worked in an era which saw the introduction of broadcasting and
recording so that succeeding generations can appreciate the talent and devotion
with which he invested his interpretations of modern English music, notably that
of his particular friends at the Savile, Bliss, Elgar, Howells and William Walton.

In 1919 – the year that the musicians Colles, Latham and Fox had become
members – Sir Sidney Colvin introduced to the Savile Sir Edward Elgar, perhaps
the first English musician of recent years whose work and reputation was already
such that it could bear comparison with even the greatest symphonic composers of
any other nation. His own countrymen had been slow to appreciate this until the
Enigma Variations was performed in 1899, and though a badly rehearsed and poor
performance of *The Dream of Gerontius* in Birmingham the following year in which
the Savilian singer Plunket Greene took part failed to ignite the same public
enthusiasm, it was properly declared a masterpiece when it was given in Germany
in 1901, moving Richard Strauss to propose a toast to "the first English
progressive musician, Meister Elgar", adding "with this work, England for the

first time becomes one of the modern musical states". That year marked the beginning of a twenty-years period of intense creative activity culminating in the violin sonata, the string quartet, the piano quintet and the 'cello concerto, the latter having been dedicated to his proposer, Sir Sidney Colvin, in the year of Elgar's election to the Savile. The music he wrote in the years between is now part of the world's heritage and needs no cataloguing here, but in 1920, the year after his election, Lady Elgar died and it was a blow from which Sir Edward never really recovered. Thereafter he produced no major works, though his reputation was such that honours continued to be heaped upon him. As Master of the King's Musick from 1924 on he wrote some occasional pieces which included No. 5 of the *Pomp and Circumstance* marches, and the *Nursery Suite*, dedicated to the present Queen Mother, the Queen and Princess Margaret. His championing by Bernard Shaw and a commission from the BBC, for his seventy-fifth birthday in 1932, however, encouraged him to commence work on a third symphony – the one to which he had referred when visiting Delius – but it remained unfinished at his death two years later.

But this creative lassitude induced by melancholy after 1920 was not so evident at the Savile. He involved himself energetically in the life of the Club and served on the committee from 1922 to 1925, some of the time as chairman of the house committee. When Dallas Bower held that position during the Second World War, he had evidence of the seriousness with which Elgar had regarded his role when Bernard Wallace, a fellow member of the committee who had also served on it in Elgar's day, accosted him with: "I say, Bower, I hear you're rather musical so I hope you won't go on about the potatoes like old Elgar did. Very fussy about the potatoes he was. Gave the kitchen a hell of a time..." Perhaps this was because the potato possessed more than a gastronomic appeal for Elgar. W.H. Reed in his *Elgar as I Knew Him* describes his working methods, and in particular his writing-table:

> Elgar's desk and writing-table were always a source of great interest to me. I was fascinated by his sheaf of pencils, all beautifully sharpened ready for instant use, his pens arranged by the inkstand and a raw potato in the place of honour in the centre.
>
> This potato was used to clean his pen. If it got in the least clogged it was at once plunged into the potato and withdrawn quite clean. I asked him why he used steel pens when he had many fountain pens which had been presented to him from time to time. His reply was, 'I use a steel pen so that I shall have to keep going forward to dip it in the ink, instead of keeping my hand in the same position the whole time, you old owl! Do you think I want to get writer's cramp – a thing I have never suffered from?'

Elgar, of course, had already many friends and acquaintances other than his proposer, Sir Sidney Colvin, when he arrived at the Savile. Harry Plunket Greene's association with him went back at least as far as 1900 when he had performed in that first disastrous performance of *The Dream of Gerontius* at Birmingham. Plunket Greene, incidently, has provided some explanation for the unhappy presentation of what was soon, despite all, to be recognized as a masterpiece:

> The Choir, audibly dragged down by a single tenor in the first chorus, had flattened by degrees until in the last number of the first part there was half a tone between them and the orchestra. I can guarantee the truth of this as I, being the bass soloist and having to sing a part above the chorus, had to choose between them and 'was not happy with either'. The greatest tribute to the work is that it survived that perilous parturition.

Elgar's relationships with Stanford and Parry at the Club and elsewhere are less clear, and much has been made of the apparent sourness between them. It all seems to have begun with an article by that arch mischief-maker, Bernard Shaw, in the first issue of *Music and Letters*, founded by Fox Strangways, in 1920. In this article, highly complimentary to Elgar, Shaw talked of:

> the effect produced at first by Elgar on the little clique of musicians who with the late Hubert Parry as its centre, stood for British music thirty-five years ago. This clique was the London section of the Clara Schumann-Joachim-Brahms clique in Germany... a little ridiculous mutual admiration gang of snobs.

Admittedly, Stanford had not liked *The Dream of Gerontius*, Elgar's setting of Newman's highly charged religious verse, nor Elgar's own Catholicism, which was repugnant to his own fierce Irish form of Protestantism, but he had always put such personal prejudice behind him in his professional dealings and, in fact, fought hard to have the piece included in the Leeds Festival of 1904. In the Savile, of course, such religious or professional differences were unmentionable even by Stanford. Moreover, both he and Parry had been "bowled over" by the *Enigma Variations*. Indeed, according to Plunket Greene, it was Parry who, on seeing the score before its publication, rushed out into "...a terrible night with a howling gale and sheets of rain" to show it to Hans Richter and extract from him a promise that it would be performed in his next concert.

That Elgar did not wholly support Shaw in his strictures against Parry (and, by implication Stanford) is made clear in a letter he sent to the next edition of *Music and Letters*. Referring to Shaw's mention of cliques, he wrote:

> ...Cliques have always existed in music and always will exist; they do not matter. All I am concerned with is the mention of Sir Hubert Parry's name with the implication that he in some way slighted me. This is quite a mistake. The moment to enumerate the many occasions on which Parry advised and encouraged me is not now; I hope to make it known all I owe

to his ungrudging kindness at some future time...

In Plunket Greene's biography of Stanford there is a chapter setting out the whole affair and from this it seems to have amounted to no more than the usual, but ephemeral, clashes of temperament between great artists; particularly when Stanford was involved in any social or professional enterprise with them. Such clashes there undoubtedly were, but Elgar seemed blissfully unperturbed, and even unaware. Certainly there are no recorded instances of such conflicts intruding on the genial ambience of the Savile.

Another of Elgar's acquaintanceships which was associated with his membership of the Club was that with Thomas Hardy. The name of Hardy, who had become a member of the Savile forty-one years earlier than Elgar in 1878, is not usually associated with music, but of all the major English poets of the time – with the possible exception of that other Savilian Robert Bridges – he had a fine appreciation of it as an influence, and the most closely related of the arts to his own.

Many clues to this are to be found in his writing; the "Mellstock Quire" singing carols in *Under the Greenwood Tree* with their accompanying string quartet of rural worthies whose profundities would surely have appealed to Elgar: "If you'd thrive in musical religion, stick to strings... . Strings be safe soul-lifters...", and the recurring underlay of his childhood memories of hymns and folk-song which pervade nearly all his other prose and poetry. It is not surprising, therefore, that many English composers were attracted by the inspiration he provided. The Savilian Balfour Gardiner, as has been observed, had already made an unsuccessful stab at setting "The Three Strangers", and Stanford's pupil Vaughan Williams longed to make an opera out of *The Dynasts,* though all that resulted from *that* was one song. Holst's tone-poem "Egdon Heath" is said to have taken its programme from the opening paragraph of *The Return of the Native,* and a more recent composer, Gerald Finzi, composed more than fifty fine settings of Hardy's poems. Benjamin Britten's sequence "Winter Words" is regarded by some as a masterpiece and possibly the nearest approach to a proper musical tribute to Hardy's genius.

What is less well known is that in 1913 Sir Sidney Colvin had arranged a meeting between Hardy and Elgar with a view to constructing an opera out of *A Pair of Blue Eyes*, Hardy's fictional account of his courtship in Cornwall of his first wife Emma. Nothing came of it, however, and though there are some who felt the conjunction would not necessarily have been a happy one, it is intriguing to speculate on that might have resulted.

When this self-taught son of a struggling music dealer and organist from Worcester, who had left school at fifteen to earn his own living, died sixty-two years later in 1934 festooned with honours, a baronetcy, the G.C.V.O., and the first musician to be appointed to the Order of Merit, it would have seemed idle to recall Sir Compton Mackenzie's pronouncement that "while men are not always equal, all Savilians are equal". No doubt within the clubhouse they are allowed to appear so but one would hazard that even the most distinguished members, then or now, would be prepared to touch their forelocks to this essential Englishman's supra-national genius. In discreet recognition of this one of the more charming new reception-rooms on the first floor of the clubhouse has been named "The Elgar Room", and in a prominent place within it is to be found the drawing of him by the Savilian Sir William Rothenstein, which was commissioned by Fox Strangways to illustrate Bernard Shaw's controversial article in that first edition of *Music and Letters*.

* * * *

Elgar was the second Savile member to be Master of the King's Musick, Sir Walter Parratt having been the first. The third to be so honoured was Sir Arthur Bliss, who had been elected to the Club in 1921. Again, like so many others within the English musical coterie of the time, Bliss arrived with many connections at the Club. Before leaving school he had developed an enthusiasm for the music of Elgar, who was later to befriend and encourage him; at Cambridge where he had taken his Mus.B degree in 1913 he had had as a mentor Edward J. Dent, and later he was to continue his studies in composition under Stanford – an experience which apparently proved to be uncongenial, though he was encourged by fellow pupils of Stanford: Vaughan Williams, Gustav Holst, and those future members of the Savile, Herbert Howells and Arthur Benjamin.

Hard as it is to believe now, Bliss's sometimes unconventional approach to the composition of music, and his occasionally eccentric but highly effective scoring of it, had earned him a somewhat "wild" reputation among the more staid sections of the musical establishment. Elgar's championship, however, secured for him a commission from the Three Choirs Festival of 1922 resulting in the exhilarating *Colour Symphony*, which was duly performed under the Savilian baton of Sir Adrian Boult. Boult, incidentally, was to play a large part in promoting the music of Bliss throughout his tours of Europe, notably *Music for Strings* with the Vienna Philharmonic at the 1935 Salzburg Festival, and the ballet *Checkmate,* written for what is now the Royal Ballet on its first visit to Paris.

Bliss was one of the many members of the Savile at that time who were exercising a profound influence on the development of the cinema as an art form. His ebullient orchestral score for *Things to Come*, based on the novel by his fellow Savilian, H.G. Wells, which is probably the first genuinely intimate collaboration between artists from these different spheres and is generally regarded as a landmark in the history of music for the cinema, created a stir which was to lead to commissions for many more, though the composer was to assume a rather detached view of this form of his art. Bliss spent some years in America, which partly accounts for the gap in his membership between the years 1926 and 1942. The year before this later date he had returned to England to serve in the war-effort, later succeeding Adrian Boult as director of music in the BBC, a task which he found creatively restricting though he continued to compose some considerable theatre and ballet music. During the war he lived for some time at the Club in what is now known as The Elgar Room. Dallas Bower remembers being invited there with Stephen Spender to hear a recording (made in America) of Bliss's piano concerto written for Solomon. Delightful though the occasion was, some embarrassment ensued when Bliss handed them the previously unseen score and neither could be sure that they were turning the pages at the appropriate time under the quizzical gaze of the composer. Bliss's interest in theatre and the ballet led him to consider opera and he proceeded to collaborate with three other Savile members at various times in writing for his medium. During the war he had planned with Stephen Spender an opera based on the *Odyssey*, but sadly this came to nothing. He had not much better fortune with *The Olympians*, libretto by J.B. Priestley. This was performed at Covent Garden in 1949 to subdued acclamation caused by the sparseness of its production, which reflected the general air of austerity at that time. Bliss was so disgusted at the dress rehearsal that he refused to attend the first night or to have any more to do with it, so the ever-tactful and obliging Dallas Bower was constrained to escort (the then) Mrs Bliss to its second performance. With *Tobias and the Angel*, however, written for television with his follow member, Christopher Hassall, he gave a convincing demonstration of his operatic gifts, and it seems a pity the work is not revived more often. He offered more evidence of his skill in settings for the human voice in the "The Enchantress" written for Kathleen Ferrier in 1951. The overlap of Bliss's profession and his social life at the Savile continued with his presidency of the Cheltenham Festival, which was so much the love-child of Robert Henriques and John Moore, whose membership and contribution to *Sodalitas Convivium* have been noted earlier. For this Festival Bliss contributed a song-cycle "A Knot of Riddles" for baritone and eleven instruments which further reinforced his reputation as a composer for this musical genre. In 1953 he was appointed Master of the Queen's Musick.

Two years earlier, in 1951, Bliss had been knighted and Winston Graham remembers him arriving to celebrate at the Savile after his investiture still dressed in all his regalia to be greeted by Monja Danischewsky who, on seeing this apparition, brought the occasion down to earth by falling to his knees in front of the new knight with pathetic cries of "Brahms; for the love of Allah!". Bliss, who had a keen sense of humour and was inured to this typical response to fame's trappings in the Club's anti-hierarchic surroundings, was fortunately able to enjoy the joke.

* * * *

In 1922 the composer and musical educationist Herbert Howells was elected to the Club. Like Elgar he was, initially, more or less self-taught but nevertheless to such good effect that in 1912 he gained a scholarship in composition to the R.C.M., where inevitably he studied under Stanford and Parry. Howells, apparently, was one of the fortunate few of whom Stanford totally approved, and Plunket Greene relates how in his rare moments of enthusiasm for a work produced by one of his pupils "... he [Stanford] became boyishly exuberant. He used to burst into my classroom at the R.C.M., dragging Herbert Howells or some other student by the collar, turn out my accompanist with a 'Listen to this, me boy' play it over, grab the genius and vanish."

By 1922, however, Howells had joined the staff of the R.C.M. to teach composition and had already achieved some prominence as a composer. As early as 1913, Stanford had conducted a performance of his C. Minor Piano Concerto at the Queen's Hall, and in the year of his election to the Savile he had works performed under Sir Henry Wood at the Promenade Concerts, and at the Gloucester Festival of that year his *Sine Nomine* for soprano, tenor, organ, and orchestra, commissioned by Sir Edward Elgar, was heard for the first time.

In common with most other Savile composers of the period, Howells's music was essentially of the reborn "English" school which was, paradoxically, so much the creation of the Irishman Charles Stanford. Like his Club contemporary, Bliss, he also experimented successfully with unusual orchestral combinations, and as had Plunket Greene, Parry, Stanford, and other musical worthies at Piccadilly and, later, Brook Street, he devoted much of his influence and skill towards the promotion of new music and young musicians by adjudicating at the several competitive festivals which were so much a part of England's musical life from the turn of the century. At his death in 1983 he had been the recipient of many honours, which included the C.H. and the C.B.E.; he was a Doctor of Music at Oxford University, President of the I.S.M. in 1952, and President of the R.C.O., from 1958-9.

In 1923, the year after Howells was elected, the distinguished singer John Coates become a member of the Savile. He came to the Club with a well-established reputation as an operatic tenor, having performed throughout Germany, and as principal tenor at Her Majesty's Theatre and at Covent Garden during Sir Thomas Beecham's operatic seasons there before the First World War. At the time of his election, however, he was putting this phase of his career behind him to concentrate on the concert hall and festival recitals where he specialized in music of the Tudor period as well as introducing new songs by more recent English composers. Coates had many links with the Club's existing band of musicians, having created the part of Claudio in Stanford's opera *Much Ado about Nothing* at Covent Garden in 1901, as well as performing in Elgar's *Dream of Gerontius* at the Worcester Festival of 1902 and at the Albert Hall tribute to Gervase Elwes.

But in 1924, the year after he took up his membership, one of these powerful social and professional connections, Sir Charles Villiers Stanford, died. From what had seemed time immemorial he had been a daily visitant to the Club, setting off from the R.C.M. in all weathers to stimulate – or infuriate – himself and others at the bridge table there. As the card table was his main battlefield it seems appropriate that it should have been his aptly named fellow composer, Frank Bridge, who has left us an account of his "bad weather starts" for the Club during

219

all those years:

> If it happened to be raining... I'm afraid I never lost the opportunity of watching C.V.S. stand on the steps of the College and ponder over the problem of getting away. The flat terrace between the Albert Hall and the R.C.M. was inadequately drained and in bad weather there would be wide patches all over it with half an inch of water on them.
>
> When the period of hesitation was over, C.V.S. would hurriedly cross the road and after going up the few low steps, halt suddenly at the edge of the flat paving, and then – for the next twenty yards or so laboriously walk through it on his heels as if on stilts! (I can't think why it amused me so much, but each succeeding time he did it the funnier it became.) Once safely across with the perils of wet feet fading from his mind he was soon inside a horse bus and off to the Savile.

And so this procedure had continued until its imminent end was signalled one evening in November 1922. On this occasion he had dined at the Club and stayed late playing bridge. When he decided to set off for home a thick fog had descended, all traffic had come to a standstill, and there was no taxi to be had. He attempted to walk home to Lower Berkeley Street and thereafter nothing is known until an hour so so later he was delivered back to the Club by a friendly stranger who had found him wandering nearby in a distressed state. It was thought he might have had a mild stroke, and that night the Savile mobilized itself to succour their ageing *enfant terrible*. All the bedrooms were occupied so the Club secretary, Major Butson, put him to bed in his own room, having first telephoned Stanford's home to inform the family of his circumstances. From that moment, however, his health deteriorated and on 17 March (St Patrick's Day) 1924 he had another stroke and twelve days later died – one week after the death of his old friend and fellow Savilian, Sir Walter Parratt. A portrait of him by another Irishman, Savilian and artist, Sir William Orpen, hangs in the hall of his *alma mater*, Trinity College, Cambridge.

* * * *

The absence of Stanford's volatile and dominating presence presaged the end of one era and the beginning of another, not only in England's musical renaissance but in the social life of the Club. New men were coming up to replace him in both spheres, though his influence would naturally linger on. In the ten years which were to elapse before the death of Elgar in 1934, several musicians came to swell the musical ranks at the Savile, though none, perhaps for some years, of a stature equivalent to these two giants.

In 1925 were elected the singer John Goss; the musical theorist teacher and distinguished organist, Professor Charles Herbert Kitson; and the well-known and

Frederick Delius

Sir William
Walton by his
fellow member
Michael Ayrton.

Top left, Sir Walter Parratt. Top right, Sir Adrian Boult, first of the three
Savilians to have been appointed Master of the Queen's/King's Musick.
Bottom left, Sir Charles Stanford, who jointly with Sir Hubert Parry (below) was
appointed first professor of composition at the newly created Royal College of Music.

Roger Quilter

Herbert Howells

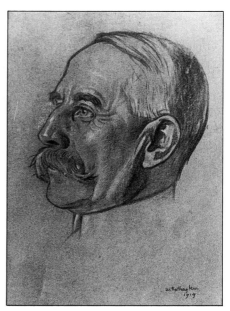

Sir Edward Elgar, the second Savilian to be appointed Master of the King's Musick.

Sir Charles Stanford, whose formidable presence in the Club for forty years is captured here in more genial mood by "Spy".

Sir Arthur Bliss, the third Savile member to be Master of the King's Musick.

influential critic of the *Morning Post*, John Francis Toye, who also composed some minor works, and wrote important biographical studies of Verdi and Rossini. In that year also were elected the famous Irish baritone of the inter-war years, Frederick Baring Ranalow ("one of the best Figaros of his generation" – though in the ebullience of his character he was more closely associated in the Club and elsewhere with the role of Captain Macheath in *The Beggar's Opera*, whch he played over 1500 times); and the musical critic and author Richard Capell. At the time of his election Capell was musical critic of the *Daily Mail*, where for many years he performed valuable service to his love for music by removing its mystique and making it accessible to a wider public. In 1933, eight years after joining the Savile, he was appointed musical critic of the *Daily Telegraph*, where he was, perhaps, better able to demonstrate the deep scholarship which informed his criticism. He also found time to write an important book on Schubert's songs and to make English translations of them as well as those of Schumann, Wolf, and Grieg. He translated Richard Strauss's opera *Friedenstag*, and published an invaluable booklet, "Opera" which was later revised, enlarged and reprinted. In 1937 when his colleague, Fox Strangways, relinquished control of the influential *Music and Letters*, Capell became its new proprietor and later its editor. His book, *Simiomata*, relating the latter part of his wartime experiences as a special correspondent for the *Daily Telegraph* in France, North Africa and Greece was published in 1946, and in that year he was awarded the O.B.E.

Wit, accessibility, profound musicianship, supported by skilful workmanship have been the most consistently prominent characteristics of Savile musicians. Whether it was possession of these qualities – particularly the first – which drew them to the Savile or whether it was an appreciation of these accomplishments which led the Club to welcome them so well is a matter for discussion. But certainly all these qualities were to be found in the Australian pianist and composer, Arthur Benjamin, who was elected to the Club in 1935. Although his music does not remain so high in the public estimation as that of some of his Savile contemporaries, it had a great vogue during his lifetime and, despite its originality, is nowadays unjustly neglected. With what must by now have seemed a remorseless inevitability for Savilian musicians, Benjamin had joined the staff of the R.C.M. soon after he had launched his own career as a composer, and among the many of his pupils there who were subsequently to make their mark was the young Benjamin Britten. His own considerable output of works in a variety of styles included three operas, a ballet, several choral and orchestral works, as well as concertos, songs and chamber music. Benjamin's operas had librettos by his cousin, great friend, and fellow member of the Savile, Cedric Cliffe. Sir Albert Sloman, the distinguished academic and, from 1963, the first vice-chancellor of the new University of Essex, who was closely associated with Cliffe for many years, has provided a revealing memoir of this multi-faceted man who, in 1952, had originally proposed him for membership of the Club. Recalling this, Sir Albert says:

I was elected a member in January 1952 on the proposal of Cedric Cliffe. I was then a Fellow of Trinity College, Dublin. The election was on the 17th by which time Cedric would have been on his way to Australia, so he wrote to me on the 12th of January: "Don't worry at all if you aren't elected this time. It is unusual for a candidate to get in the first time. But if you do, step in boldly. Sit yourself at the long table in the dining-room and chat to everyone around, irrespective of whether you've met or not."

Although I did not join the Savile until 1952 I had come to know it nearly ten years earlier. In September 1942 I was posted with some twenty or so other pilots to R.A.F. Cranfield to complete my training as a night-fighter pilot. A few days later the same number of radar observers arrived to make up the crews of the twin-seater Beaufighter. Pilots and observers were brought together that very same evening over a generous supply of drink to choose their partners. And they were obliged to leave the room in pairs, the last two in the room having their choice made for them. We were meeting for the very first time with no information whatsoever about each other. I had read Spanish at Oxford and I remember muttering quite unprompted, "Podemos hablar español", to which a tall egg-headed man, old enough to be my father, responded "Ah, but you speak the true Castilian." Within minutes we had crewed up together. Taking advantage of the R.A.F.'s decision to raise the age limit for aircrew so as to recruit people to the new job of radar observer, Cedric Cliffe had thrown up his directorship of the Latin-American Services of the BBC and, just a few months before reaching the new age limit of forty, had volunteered for flying. Cedric and I flew together, first on Beaufighters in the U.K. and in North Africa, Malta and Sicily, then on Mosquitos back in this country, until the end of the war, and we remained close friends until Cedric's death in 1969.

Cedric Cliffe was devoted to the Savile, when we were together in London we often lunched or dined there, invariably playing a game of snooker afterwards. It was at the snooker table that I saw a great deal of Chippy Kingham who was at the time living at the Club and who was a mine of information about Club lore and manners, and extremely friendly and helpful to a new boy. My memories of the Savile are associated almost exclusively with Cedric. He was quite an exceptionally gifted person. A Balliol man, he took a double first in Greats, and came first in the Civil Service examinations that year, beating both Norman Brooke and Cecil Syers. After some years in the Civil Service he joined the BBC where, after an extended tour of Latin America, he became the first director of Latin-American services.

He was an outstanding radar-observer and was twice mentioned in dispatches. But night-fighting imposed an intolerable strain on a person of his age and as soon as the war ended he suffered a severe nervous breakdown. His return to the BBC was not happy – his old post was no longer available – but he was fortunate enough to be taken back in the Civil Service by Norman Brooke. Cedric's major interest was music. The son of a professional musician, he had been prevented from studying an instrument as a child for fear that, like his father, he might make music his career. He wrote several librettos: *A Tale of Two Cities, Tartuffe* and *Prima Donna* with music by his cousin Arthur Benjamin, and just before his death an adaptation of Conrad's *Under Western Eyes* with music by John Joubert. And under a tent in North Africa, without access to a single work of reference, he wrote a book on musical recognition, in the form of a conversation between him and me. The book was accepted by Collins but, because Churchill's *History* exhausted their supply of paper, publication of the book was year after year delayed. When eventually paper was available, much of the dialogue of the book in R.A.F. slang was no longer appropriate, and it had to be completely rewritten, appearing eventually as *The Making of Music*. Cedric had a prodigious memory. When in wartime a particular R.A.F. mess had only a single copy of *The Times* he would do the crossword in his head. For many years he was, with Denis Brogan and others, a member of the London team of *Round Britain Quiz*, and Lionel Hale [another Savile member] has told how, on more than one occasion, when answering a question Cedric would compose Latin and Greek verses. And he was a man of rare personal qualities: kind, gentle, modest and very brave. I have often thought that, in his love of the arts, of good food and wine, of bridge and snooker and of good conversation, and his abhorrence of the pompous, the pretensious and the sham, he epitomized the Savile. It was, he would say – and it was the highest praise – a civilized Club.

Cedric Cliffe and his cousin Arthur Benjamin were a formidably talented creative family nexus within the Club but, as has already been observed, there was yet another musically bonded group within the Savile, that which emanated from the Royal College of Music. The musical scholar, teacher and composer, Reginald Owen Morris, elected in 1937, was another of that number. It has been said of his compositions that "they show an independence of thought which classes them among the important works of his generation", though, truth to tell, none of them has made much impression on the musical sensibilities of his time. As a teacher, and as a writer on the more esoteric by-ways of his art such as *Contrapuntal Technique in the 16th Century*, he found for himself a much more secure niche. At the Club he is remembered mostly for having assumed the daunting mantle of Stanford during the regular afternoon sessions at the bridge table, which leads one to speculate that there could be an interesting monograph to be written on the strange affinity which seemed to exist between musicians – particularly those from the R.C.M. – and the game of bridge as it was conducted at the Savile. Stanford had dominated it for the forty years of his membership and, as we shall see, was very nearly done to death there by one of his disgruntled opponents; Richard Capell, having finessed a fine grand slam, had a heart attack and promptly died at the table; Morris survived unscathed, though there are some who believe it may have been a close run thing. Certainly "contrapuntal technique" at Savile bridge seems to have owed more to its etymological origin than its musical connotations.

After Morris's election in 1937 there appears to have been a five years' rest before another musician was added to the Savile score in the person of the composer Thomas Wood. Wood was already fifty years of age when he was elected and, as he was to die untimely only eight years later, most of his work as a composer was already behind him. With what must by now have been accounted by the Savile election committee to be a necessary qualification, he had been a pupil of Stanford's at the R.C.M. and much of his choral and orchestral work shows the more benevolent aspect of that great man's influence. Wood spent some time as director of music at Tonbridge School and, later, as a lecturer at Exeter College, Oxford, having received his doctorate in Music there in 1920. Despite the comparatively short term of his membership at the Savile, his genial and courageous personality and his wide range of extra-musical activities aroused great affection, leaving pleasant memories for all those remaining who knew him. George Ivan Smith, the distinguished diplomat, political commentator, and journalist is one, and he recalls:

> Dr Thomas Wood, my sponsor to the Savile, was a courageous character. He was so blind he carried a battery of powerful lenses for various functions, to read menus, musical scores, and [to observe] the world outside. Yet he was an examiner for colleges of music and travelled the world to conduct high level examinations. It took him to my native Australia where his uncanny perceptions led him to write *Cobbers*, by far the best [literary] presentation of my country at that time. Another great contributor to the arts, Arnold Haskell, went with Ballet companies to write about performances, and, like Thomas, was entranced by the then "unknown country". [From this experience] he wrote *Waltzing Matilda* which matched Tommy's work. He often joined us at the Savile as a lunching pad for many BBC broadcasts to Australia when I was Pacific Services Director of the BBC.

Haskell, who was elected to the Savile in 1943, was one of those rare men in the twentieth century and, almost certainly, one of the only two Savile members in that time to have provided the English language with a new coinage. By coincidence these two members were approximately contemporaneous: Stephen Potter with his "Lifeman-ship" "Gamesman-ship" suffixes, and Arnold Haskell with his invention "Balletomane" deriving from the title of his first book *Balletomania*, published in 1934, which contributed so much to his lifelong work of popularizing what had hitherto been a somewhat esoteric art.

After brief flirtations with careers in the law and in publishing, Haskell devoted his life to the study and promotion of ballet. In the 'twenties and 'thirties he had been a guiding force behind the Russian Ballet under de Basil and Diaghilev, but three years after he was elected to the Savile he became director of the then struggling British Ballet School, which within the succeeding few years was – largely due to his influence – to become the Royal Ballet. Remarking on Haskell's physical appearance, the great choreographer, Massine, with whom he had many associations, christened him "Mickey Mouse" – a sobriquet, as Dallas Bower affirms, which his fellow Savilians loyally, though with great difficulty, managed to keep secret from him.

Rollo Myers, the critic and writer on music, had been elected to the Savile in 1942, a few months before Haskell. Like Thomas Wood he was already in his fiftieth year when he joined but unlike that unfortunate composer he lived to a great age, dying as recently as 1985. Undoubtedly he would have become a member many years earlier had he not spent so much of his life in Paris, where for some time he had been musical correspondent of *The Times*, and later *The Daily Telegraph*, for his father, Ernest Myers, and his two uncles, Arthur and Frederick, were all original members in 1869. According to Sir Herbert Stephen, father Ernest had a "poetic gift worthy of his family"; Uncle Frederick was a founder of the Society for Psychical Research and uncle Arthur was a distinguished doctor. With such confusing ancestry it was not surprising that Rollo should have plunged so eagerly into the artistic maelstrom of post-war Paris, before assuming a more grave demeanour at the BBC, and coming to rest at the Savile. In Paris he was much involved with the *dadaistes* during their short-lived heyday, and, more particularly with their more-enduring complementary group, *Les Six,* which was formed under the aegis of Cocteau and Erik Satie to promote the cause of modern music and whose members were Honegger, Milhaud, Poulenc, Durey, Auric, and Tailleferre. Myers, who had become an intimate of all these leading figures in the world of music and art, used his experience of them to write *Modern Music: Its Aims and Tendencies*, which was hailed as an admirable exposition of the movement for the ordinary music-lover. It was at this time too that he collected much of the material for those of his later books which were equally well received: *Erik Satie, Debussy, Emanuel Chabrier and his Circle*, and *Modern French Music*. From 1935 to 1944 Myers worked at the BBC in the music information department, though he maintained his French connection. In 1945 he returned to Paris as music officer for the British Council, though his life continued to alternate between London and Paris, where in the one he had edited *Music Today*, and, in the other, worked for the Organization for European Cooperation. He never lost his overriding love for things Parisian, however, and himself exuded a pungent Gallic flavour. Dallas Bower, and others of his friends, remember with affection his entrances to the Savile during his London period which were conducted with all the *panache* of an accomplished *boulevardier*, broad-brimmed hat, flowing cravat, spats and all.

Sir William Walton's niche in the pantheon of twentieth-century composers is securely recorded elsewhere. What is of particular interest in the history of the Savile, however, is that when he was elected to the Club in 1945 his proposer was Dallas Bower, putting the seal on the release of one of their most triumphant collaborations, the film of *Henry V*, which Dallas co-produced with Laurence

Olivier and for which Walton had written the music. Dallas Bower's promotion and patronage of so many other artists will emerge later, but his association with William Walton and the important influence he exercised on one aspect of that great composer's career belongs here, as it is less generally known.

By the mid-thirties Walton had established a reputation with such works as *Façade, Portsmouth Point* the *Sinfonia Concertante,* the Viola concerto, the First Symphony, and *Belshazzar's Feast*, but he had yet to achieve financial independence. Some of that reputation, of course, was not at first as adulatory as it might have been. Ada Leverson – Oscar Wilde's wonderful, witty "Sphinx" – invited the then nineteen-year-old Harold Acton to the first public performance of *Façade* at the Aeolian Hall in June 1923. It had been written by Walton in collaboration with his patrons the three Sitwells, and Ada Leverson recalled that: "The audience was in part hostile and the critics ferocious. The performance caused a furore and the authors were obliged to go about as if they had committed a murder." Later, however, matters improved, and Osbert Sitwell was able to write to the Sphinx from his Italian castle of Montegufoni about a recent production: "... *Façade* was a great success and Willie [Walton] has been referred to in one paper as 'il world famous wanton'!" In 1934, the British and Dominion Film Corporation was about to produce the film *Escape me Never* in which the young Margot Fonteyn was to appear with the Savile member Ralph Richardson. Dallas Bower, who was personal assistant to its director Paul Czinner, was asked to pronounce on the relative merits of various composers to provide the film score. He had not then met Walton but had conceived a great admiration for his Viola concerto, and so the choice was made. "It was the first time", says Dallas, "that a composer of such stature had been involved in film-making..." and, indeed, it was to revolutionize subsequent attitudes to the function of music in cinematic art of which Arthur Bliss was to be a subsequent, rather cynical, beneficiary. The success of this initial score was to lead to many more commissions, but it is interesting to reflect that the financial independence for Walton which ensued, and the purchase for the first time of his own house in Eaton Place, all derived from the fee of £300 for *Escape me Never*, which Dallas Bower had negotiated. Czinner was not slow to appreciate the cachet which Walton's distinguished music had added to his work, and he went on to film *As You Like It* with his wife, Elisabeth Bergner, as Rosalind, Dallas Bower again as personal directorial assistant, and Walton providing the score. Czinner was to use Walton again in his film *A Stolen Life,* released in 1939, but meantime the composer's career was burgeoning with such commissions as the symphonic march for the coronation of King George VI, *Crown Imperial,* for the entrance of Queen Mary before that ceremony at Westminster Abbey, and the Violin concerto written at the request of Jascha Heifetz. In 1937 the association between Walton and Bower was renewed when the latter, who had by then become the first producer/director of programmes for the newly created BBC Television Service, devised and directed a broadcast featuring Walton's music. *Portsmouth Point* and *Siesta* were presented as ballets with choreography by Frederic Ashton, and Walton himself conducted the BBC Television Orchestra in a performance of his Viola concerto with William Primrose as soloist.

Again, in 1942, when Dallas was working at the Ministry of Information and was asked by the BBC to provide a suitable celebration to mark the 450th anniversary of the discovery of America, he commissioned William Walton to write the score for the great epic that resulted, the circumstances of which will be described in more detail later. Relevant here, however, are the words of one of Walton's biographers, Neil Tierney:

> One of his most glorious achievements at this time was the massive and picturesque score which he created for the BBC's radio drama *Christopher Columbus*, used in a transatlantic broadcast on 12 October 1942, the 450th anniversary of the great explorer's first voyage to America.

In all, Walton was to write the film scores of fourteen films; during the war he was again part of a team which included Dallas Bower when he joined the Films Division of the Ministry of Information and wrote the music for such famous films as *The Foreman went to France* and *The First of the Few,* which, affecting as they were at the time, are now generally remembered only for his contribution to them. *The Spitfire Prelude and Fugue* which formed part of the music for the latter film is still regularly performed as a separate concert piece. But of all his film scores the best known must be his Shakespeare trilogy, *Henry V, Hamlet,* and *Richard III,* of which the first owed so much, once again, to Dallas Bower.

> My word, what an intensive piece of salesmanship I had to perform on Laurence Olivier [says Dallas]. Despite the fact that he had played Orlando to Elisabeth Bergner's Rosalind in *As You Like It*, he seemed totally unaware that much of the distinction of that film was due to William's music. Furthermore he was being influenced by another Savile member, an actor called Anthony Bushell who hated Walton's works. This was during the war, of course, and Larry was renting Noël Coward's house at Gerrards Cross. Tony Bushell and I had lunch there one Sunday and I brought records of *Portsmouth Point*, the Viola concerto and the Sinfonia Concertante. After I'd played them to Larry, Bushell turned to him and said: "Well, I call that spit and fart music." Nevertheless, I persevered, and after it was all completed Larry maintained that the film wouldn't have been the success it became if it were not for the Walton score, and I couldn't agree with him more. As you know, he went on to use William in a similar capacity for *Hamlet* and *Richard III ... .*

After the war, William Walton married and settled at the villa he had had built for himself on the island of Ischia, so his visits to the Savile were less frequent, and particularly so after 1976 when he was struggling to overcome the after-effects of his first stroke. Nevertheless he made a point of lunching or dining at the Club whenever he was in London and there are still many members who remember him well at these times for his lack of pomposity and his love of teasing. Dallas Bower recalls one of these last occasions, dining with him in the company of Rupert Withers and Sir Jack Longland. Sitting at the long table was the newly elected Andrew Lloyd-Webber, enjoying his brief period of membership before making the biblical excuse and leaving: "I have married a wife, and therefore I cannot come." At one point during the meal, Lloyd-Webber ventured that he was "working on a new piece". "Really?" said Walton. "And who is going to orchestrate it for you?" "I am," said the prodigy. "The rest", as Walton may have remembered once having had to orchestrate for himself, "was silence".

It is a curious coincidence that the three contemporary Savile musicians, Sir William Walton, Sir Adrian Boult, and Herbert Howells all died within a few days of one another in 1983, as had Sir Charles Villiers Stanford and Sir Walter Parratt nearly sixty years earlier.

The arrival of Walton and the return of Arthur Bliss from America during the last war had introduced a new theme to the musical composition of the Savile. So far, there had been certain consistent strands to it; academics and executants who generally bore with them a strong connection with the Royal College of Music, and composers who had made important contributions to the great English musical renaissance of the previous fifty years. Many of these strands were, of course, intertwined, but to them now was added a hefty proportion of serious composers in their own right who were applying their art to underpin the comparatively new media of radio, film, and television. During the forty-five years which have elapsed since Walton's election to the Club at least eleven other major contributors to the art of film music have followed his example and of these at least half are also established as major composers in the mainstream of Western music; composers of the calibre of William Alwyn, Bernard Herrman, and Malcolm Arnold. This development was perhaps mirrored by the changing pattern of Savile membership generally which had extended itself meantime to include many artists and administrators whose main professional concern was with these new media – occupations which had been unimaginable in the time of the founding fathers.

If only for the sake of symmetry, therefore, it is relevant that the first musician to be elected after Walton's arrival at the Club was Hubert Clifford, an Australian composer and conductor who wove together several of these various strands into his one career. He had studied at the Royal College of Music; through most of the war years he had been BBC Empire Music Supervisor; he had been a professor at the Royal Academy of Music where his soon-to-be-elected-to-the-Savile colleague, William Alwyn, had been professor of composition since 1927; and from 1946 – the year of his own election – he had been Musical Director to London Film Productions. In 1950 he resigned this latter post to spend more time in creative work, but most of this remained unpublished and he is now mainly remembered for a manual addressed to conductors of school orchestras and, at the Club, for his instigation of a notable *fracas* with the equally bellicose Gilbert Harding – a form of atonal behaviour which led to the instant suspension of both parties' membership, as shall presently be seen.

Neville Cardus, in his day the most elegant and influential writer on his twin passions of music and cricket, was elected to the Club twelve months after Clifford. Apart from his connection with music, Cardus had only one characteristic in common with his predecessor: a brief commission in Australia during the war years. Most of his professional life, however, was spent with the *Manchester Guardian*, on which he eventually became chief musical critic, renowned for his discernment, while also contributing brilliant and elegiac commentaries on cricket.

His friend and fellow Savilian, William Alwyn, was later to remark:

> Cricket has a peculiar fascination for musicians and poets and one can usually expect to see one's friends at Lord's. Neville Cardus writes as enchantingly about the game as he does about music. He is always to be found at the same spot in Lord's on the opposite side to the Tavern, usually with his back to the game in earnest conversation with someone or other, reporting on the match I suppose by some kind of telepathy.

Alwyn, who was elected to the Savile in 1948, was himself a passionate devotee of cricket while sharing many of the other professional concerns of the Club's more recent musical members, particularly those who were successfully seizing on the challenges offered by radio, film and television.

A writer in 1967 described him thus:

> ... one dedicated artist anxious to escape an internationally established label (a brilliant writer of music for films, including *The Way Ahead*, *Odd Man Out*, *The Magic Box*) but one whose wide and passionate curiosity outside his profession led him along the most unexpected furrows of literature and the visual arts: a cricket addict hunting for a hitherto unexpected Pre-Raphaelite, dipping into Stendhal and Nietzsche, or translating Paul Valéry... .

A candidate whose wide range would have been welcomed at the Savile, where the post-war obsession with specialization seemed sometimes to threaten the founders' original intention to cast the net wide to nurture and preserve this gathering place of men with a variety of professions and interests.

Like Walton and Bliss, Alwyn had established himself as a considerable composer long before he achieved popular fame as a craftsman of film music. His piano concerto of 1930 had attracted the attention of knowledgeable music-lovers, as had many of his subsequent concert works. But in 1936 he wrote the first of what was to become a distinguished list of more than sixty film scores, of which many – like *On Arrival*, *The Rake's Progress*, and *Odd Man Out* – were, perhaps, the most popular in the public's estimation. Like Walton he had also contributed to the war effort by providing music for such notable propaganda films as *Desert Victory* and *The Way Ahead* at the behest of the Ministry of Information, where so many of his future colleagues at the Savile such as Dallas Bower and William Walton were already heavily engaged.

Although Alwyn came relatively late to the Savile at the age of forty-three his membership was to assume a considerable importance in his social and professional life thereafter for, apart from his musical concerns, he was devoted to literature, an avid collector of paintings, and a true amateur of the pre-Raphaelites. All those interests struck a happy resonance at Brook Street and this is borne out by a journal he kept for the twelve months commencing September 1955 when he was hard at work on his third symphony. The journal was later published as *Ariel and Miranda* and, apart from demonstrating his astonishing energy (he completed two film scores as well as finishing his symphony during the period covered), it provides some fascinating insights to the work and achievements of some of his fellow members. There are, for instance, several references to his and the Club's connections with film music. On 1 October he writes:

> It must be nearly 25 years since Basil Wright's classic *Song of Ceylon* was made; the period when the documentary movement was pioneering its great contribution to the art of film and we were all fired by the energy of that remarkable man John Grierson to a visionary devotion to a cause. In the film and film music these were the fruitful years, it was then that some of us had our first chance for a new idiom and were encouragd to search for new modes of expression. In such an atmosphere an artist learns his craft. I am sure that Britten does not regret the days of *Night Mail*. I certainly do not.

Basil Wright had been elected to the Savile in 1947. Dallas Bower says of him that he was:

> far and away the most talented of documentary film producers and directors of his time, a more practical creator than Grierson, who tended to be more of a philosopher. The documentary to which Alwyn refers, *Song of Ceylon*, was the first work of what you might call "poetic realism" in this genre.

The documentary for the Post Office, *Night Mail*, with a script by Auden and music by Benjamin Britten which Wright directed, is still seen regularly as one of the great milestones in documentary film making, while his book on the art of the cinema generally, *The Long View*, is his enduring *magnum opus*.

Later in the same journal, Alwyn ruefully records:

> Committee meeting of the British Film Academy, where I learned quite by chance that all my major film scores (*Odd Man Out* etc.) and Walton's superb score for *Henry V* had been destroyed in a holocaust of tidying-up at Pinewood Studios. This was devastating news as I have not kept the

original manuscript sketches and I don't think William has either. What makes it worse is that the original sound tracks were "junked" at the same time, so all the work done on those scores is irreplaceable.

Despite his many other commitments during this period, Alwyn was collaborating with Roger Manvell and others on a text book of film. In late December he lunched with Sir Arthur Bliss, Roger Manvell, and John Huntley to discuss the project and "to get Arthur's own reactions on his own film music and his methods of work". Bliss gave a demonstration of his cynicism concerning the genre:

> Arthur was a fountain of information that bubbled over with ideas and suggestions, some sound, some outrageous, but never other than provocative. He has a prejudice against the 'film composer', feeling no doubt that it is a way of earning easy money by dubious means... . Arthur argued his point of view with good humour and infectious high spirits that swept aside opposition but left me unconvinced.

Although Alwyn's main concern was with music as an art form in its own right he evidently took his film work far more seriously. Later in his journal he comments:

> A common critical error is the confusion of film music with 'programme' music – descriptive music. No experienced film composer bothers to describe musically that which is visually obvious on the screen, nor does the intelligent director expect him to do so. Its main fascination for me is the rhythmic relationship and interplay of the *spoken* word and music; Hans Keller has been shrewd enough to notice these innovations, and has written a critical and analytical article in the *Musical Times* on my experiments in this field.

He was evidently prepared to promulgate these views with some vigour, for earlier he mentions a gathering of Savile members for a "house-warming" at David Cleghorn-Thomson's new flat in Connaught Place. On such occasions one would have expected the presence of Gilbert Harding to have been the source of potential discord but, according to Alwyn, Harding was rather subdued and looking "old and pathetic". Instead...

> The evening was enlivened by a violent argument with Bernard Herrmann the American composer and conductor, over a difference of opinion rising out of the film music book. I had written to him in America for his help and apparently he had taken exception to my choice of other composers in the States to whom I had addressed my enquiries. We parted abruptly after some heated words. However before he left he came over to me and our mutual annoyance melted under the mellowing influence of a shared enthusiasm for Liszt.

Bernard Herrmann was elected to the Club in 1960. Although American, he was a regular visitor to the Savile and very high in musicians' estimation for his scores to Orson Welles' films *Citizen Kane* and *The Magnificent Ambersons* as well as many others which included *Anna and the King of Siam*, *The Ghost and Mrs Muir*, and the film version of his fellow member Patrick Hamilton's novel *Hangover Square*. But like Alwyn, Walton, Bliss, and others of the Savile musical contingent he had already made a considerable reputation for himself outside of the film world. At the age of twenty he had formed the New Chamber Orchestra with which he gave concerts of old and new music in New York, later becoming the chief conductor of the CBS Symphony Orchestra and doing more, perhaps, than any other conductor in America to introduce new music – particularly of the British school represented by so many of his Savile friends – to American audiences. His own compositions ranged from opera to choral and orchestral works.

Another of Alwyn's many friends and professional colleagues at the Club was Muir Mathieson, whose name was almost synonymous with film music for over four decades. He had trained at that musical annexe to the Savile, the Royal College of Music, and after a period working with Sir Alexander Korda, followed by the musical directorship of the Government Navy, Army, and Air Force Film Units, he became musical director to the J. Arthur Rank Organization. Muir Mathieson's reputation as a conductor of film music soon became such that many a producer would consult him first before approaching the composer. Gavin Henderson recalls that he had an especial gift for timing the composer's music to the precise moment required to underline the relevant actions or dialogue, so that "re-takes" were rarely necessary. Alwyn had, of course, worked with him many times and records several of their meetings during the period covered by the journal when in addition to completing his symphony he was also contracted to provide the scores for two films, *Safari* at Elstree, and *Black Tent* at Pinewood – a chore which, as he comments "…does not stimulate me to much enthusiasm, but difficult to reject as I shall need the money to pay for the time that must be devoted entirely to the symphony". Alwyn completed these two scores in two months and on 19 January he began the recording session with Muir Mathieson. The journal entry is interesting for his recollections of his early days as a highly esteemed flautist:

> A full day with Muir Mathieson recording the music for the film *Safari* at Elstree. Very fine playing by the Royal Philharmonic Orchestra. Gerald Jackson, the first flute (we made our first appearance together in the LSO at that Hereford Three Choirs Festival in 1927) called me over and said that I had written an impossible passage for the flute. On picking up his flute I was delighted to find that not only could I blow the instrument after an interval of well over five years but automatically I found a good fingering for the passage at the first attempt, much to the astonishment of

the orchestra, most of whom were too young to remember that before the war I was a flute player.

I gave up the instrument because, as a well-known flautist, I was not taken seriously as a composer. The British seem to distrust versatility. Curiously enough pianistic proficiency is permissible; probably because of the long lineage of composer-pianists, from Beethoven to Chopin and Liszt to Rachmaninov. Fortunately, I am a fluent pianist and it is better that my other instrument should be forgotten. It lies coffined in its case, a memory of my salad days, and buried with it are the memories of my earlier triumphs.

Among Alwyn's many other friends at the Savile was Richard Howgill, who had been elected to the Club in 1942. Howgill had held a variety of senior positions at the BBC and as Controller of Music had commissioned or had been responsible for many of the distinguished works by English composers such as Walton's *Troilus and Cressida* which are now part of the international repertory. On 20 October Alwyn records in his journal:

Dick Howgill tonight has commissioned my symphony for the BBC, the first performance to be at the Festival Hall next October with Barbirolli conducting. This is wonderful news.

Three months later he was lunching at the Savile with Howgill, who was "singing the praises" of Edmund Rubbra's new symphony (the 6th) and trying to persuade Alwyn that this work would establish Rubbra's reputation. Alwyn disagreed, holding that the 5th Symphony was a far finer piece. But then he adds, "composers are rarely generous to one another. The two Arthurs – Bliss and Benjamin – are great exceptions always generous in their praise." Perhaps he felt this qualification necessary as they were both fellow members of the Savile, and then he sets himself to musing on his own background and that of another distinguished musician who was also to be a regular companion at the Club:

Both Rubbra and I were born at Northampton, as was also Malcolm Arnold, the youngest of the trio. It is odd that a boot manufacturing provincial town, musically isolated and unpromising ground, should have produced three composers. And it is odd that two of them are so utterly different in temperament and in their approach to their art – Rubbra, introspective and mystically serious, and Arnold, the complete extrovert to whom life is a glorious adventure and composition a delight and a joke. In physique they are also a complete contrast – Edmund bearded, slight of build and delicate-looking, Malcolm broad and exuberant and indefatigable in energy. Malcolm Arnold swept into my life like a genial tornado at a much later date. Music ws born in him, and is as irrepressible as his nature...

Malcolm had also swept *sforzando* into the life of the Savile in 1956 and for the thirty-seven years since has enlivened it with a conversational gusto which, with his gift for the unexpected can seem like verbal transpositions – now boisterous, now profound – of his musical compositions. From the time he gained a scholarship to the Royal College of Music in 1938 and received the Cobbett Composition Prize three years later he has produced what his friend Alwyn called "a prodigal output" of music which has the unusual distinction of being enjoyed and admired by the general public and academic cognoscenti alike.

To list this "prodigal output" in detail would require a chapter to itself: 9 symphonies, 18 concertos, 5 ballets (including *Homage to the Queen* in coronation year), 2 one-act operas, and 120 film scores which include the Oscar-winning *Bridge Over the River Kwai* in 1957. Likewise, his honours have come thick and fast: doctorates of music at the Universities of Exeter, Durham, and Leicester; the CBE in 1970, a fellowship of the Royal College of Music in 1983 and a knighthood in 1993. In 1985 he received the Ivor Novello Award for "outstanding services to British Music". As many Savilians will remember, his sixtieth birthday was celebrated by a concert at the Queen Elizabeth Hall where friends, admirers and a capacity audience gathered to hear the English Chamber Orchestra and the Park Lane Group pay tribute to him. His own fanfares, *Richmond* and *Fanfare for a Royal Occasion* opened each half, the first of which contained a performance of his guitar concerto with Julian Bream as soloist and the second his Sinfonietta No.1, both with the composer conducting. *The Guardian's* musical critic, Robert Henderson, recalled that as Arnold took to the podium the concert

> suddenly burst into full celebratory life. It was not just that the jokey by-play between conductor and his old friend Julian Bream introduced into the programme... an aptly affectionate air of relaxed informality... but even more pertinently that Arnold's infectiously astute direction also produced what was by far the evening's most vital, idiomatic and captivating performance.

Similarly, Henderson notes that his direction of the Sinfonietta No.1 "caught neatly that cheeky, sunny mood with which Arnold is most closely associated in the other popular imagination".

Fanfares are something of an Arnold speciality, it has been said his life has been one long fanfare, and just as the considerable list of public honours bear witness to this, so with an equal flourish do the many memorable but more private Savile occasions which have been invested with his own particular verve. For the Club's centenary celebrations in 1968 Malcolm, naturally, wrote a fanfare which was duly played before dinner by the trumpeters from Kneller Hall. It took some time in sober reflection for it to dawn on members that the rhythm of this stirring piece on the one note of C was identical to that of God Save the Queen.

Some time shortly afterwards Malcolm bought a clavichord and brought it with him to lunch at the Savile. By a happy accident, Robert Thurston Dart, a member since 1953, and perhaps the greatest musical scholar and virtuoso on early keyboard instruments of that time, happened to be lunching there too. The meal over, the clavichord was set up in the Sandpit and a merry but improving afternoon was had by all. Memories differ slightly concerning the precise contents of the impromptu programme: Gavin Henderson affirms that it consisted of selections from the monumental series on English madrigalists and the works of William Byrd which Dart had recently edited; Colin Merton (himself no mean performer) attests that as at first there was no music to hand at all, he sprinted to his flat in North Audley Street and fetched back the 48 preludes and fugues of J.S. Bach, adding rather sternly (and making no allowances for it being after lunch), that "Dart played the F minor prelude from Book 2 at a very uneven tempo".

The 'sixties saw the introduction of a series of musical evenings which continue still as a regular and welcome feature of Club "occasions". Some of the earlier ones were presented by visiting artists such as the Aeolian String Quartet but wherever possible they have been "in-house" affairs performed by musician members giving an airing either to their own or other Savilian's compositions. Among the many memorable *soirées* which have resulted was "Menu from the Orchestral Kitchen" given by that remarkable percussionist, James Blades. Blades had been elected in 1963 and on the "menu" for this notable musical occasion was the Toccata for Percussion and Piano written for him by his great friend Malcolm Arnold. An earlier Arnold work dedicated to this prince among drummers had been the Concert Piece for Percussion commissioned by the BBC in 1958. Blades was a great innovator in widening the range of his instruments, introducing, for instance, the clatter from tea-cups with such novel effect into Britten's setting for the medieval Chester morality play *Noye's Fludde*. He is also the author of the comprehensive *History of Percussion Instruments of All Ages*. One of his less publicized public performances – notwithstanding it must have been seen and heard by millions – was the sound of the great brass gong which preceded the opening credits of every Rank film for several decades. In this sequence, the massively muscled, near-naked torso of the ex-"Mister Universe", Bombardier Billy Wells, was to be seen striking the equally formidable Burmese call to prayer while the more modestly endowed James Blades, for technical reasons, was employed in a studio elsewhere to provide the actual sound.

Blade's work as a percussionist was also to form part of another notable musical event organized by Gavin Henderson in the early 'seventies, but this time with another timpanist, Robert James. The theme of the occasion was a tribute to Robert Thurston Dart, whose scholarly work on early music had already been noted. The main substance of the programme consisted of sixteenth- and seventeenth-century music collated and edited by Dart, and Sir Anthony Carey Lewis acted as chairman at the dinner beforehand. The guest harpsichordist on this occasion, incidentally, was a then unknown young student called Trevor Pinnock. Gavin Henderson's own Brass Consort performed Monteverdi with Jimmy

Edwards from the Savile ranks in unwontedly serious mood playing the tuba, and John Evans playing trombone and conducting. Robert James performed pieces for timpani by the seventeenth-century composer Phillidor which had been revived and edited by James Blades.

Sir Anthony Lewis, the chairman for this occasion, had been elected in 1958. He had shown his musical talent at an early age when he was admitted a chorister at St George's Chapel, Windsor, where he sang under the direction of that earlier Savilian, Sir Walter Parratt. At the Royal Academy of Music he studied composition under another Club member, William Alwyn, later moving to Cambridge, where he became a pupil of yet another Savilian, Edward J. Dent. Though it is said that he could have had a career as a concert pianist, Lewis elected instead to specialize in the more academic reaches of music and, after a further period studying composition with Nadia Boulanger in Paris, he returned to take his BA and Mus. B at Cambridge, where – for distinction in musical palaeography – he also won the Barclay Squire prize (founded in memory of another early Club member).

Lewis's associations with Savile members continued when in 1935 he joined the staff of the BBC under Sir Adrian Boult, where he was responsible for such long-running series as "Foundations of Music". After serving in the forces during the war he became responsible for all music for the new Third Programme, which had been anticipated (and largely motivated) by Sir Arthur Bliss in his "Musical Policy Statement" for the BBC in 1941. In this role Lewis laid down the foundations of what continues to be one of the greatest services to music since the beginning of broadcasting. As professor of music in the University of Birmingham he also founded *Musica Brittanica* as a national collection of the classics of British music. With himself as general editor and his fellow Savilian Thurston Dart as secretary to the editorial committee he had completed over fifty volumes ranging from Dunstable to Parry by the time of his death in 1983. The contemporary musician and Savilian, Michael Pope, who was Lewis's obituarist for the *Dictionary of National Biography*, remembers him as "a musician of rare accomplishment" whose imposing appearance and reserved manner only partly diguised his genial and kindly manner and his lively sense of humour at the Club and elsewhere.

The Thurston Dart tribute chaired by Lewis was only one of many musical evenings organized by Gavin Henderson during his time on the Savile's music committee in the early 'seventies. Gavin had been elected to the Club in 1968 when he was only twenty, proposed by the poet and novelist John Pudney and supported by, among others, another of his neighbours in Brighton, Lord Holford. His association with Brighton has since borne many other fruits but that with the Savile at the time would have pleased the early fathers of the Club with their twin preferences for "young men of promise" and of "differing professions and opinions". At the time of his election he was a student of sculpture at the Slade and early demonstrated his éclat to more elderly members by bringing in as guests to lunch his tutors Sir William Coldstream and Reg Butler. Shortly afterwards he was playing trumpet with the London Philharmonic Orchestra and in 1972, at the age of twenty-four, was appointed director of the York Festival. From York (where, incidentally, his assistant was a subsequent member of the Savile, the Rev. Gillian Weston Craig) he progressed to the New Philharmonia Orchestra, where he succeeded another subsequent member, Gerald Macdonald, as general manager. During his five years with the New Philharmonia, Henderson took time off in 1976 to direct the York Festival once again and in 1978 moved to Bracknell as the director of the Southill Arts Centre, where he was instrumental in the creation of the Wilde Theatre, one of the few innovative provincial theatres to be built since the war. Meantime he was keeping an eye on artistic events in his native Brighton and in 1982 was responsible for organizing the "Picasso and the Theatre" exhibition there. In 1984 he was appointed director of the Brighton Festival – a position he still holds – and since 1985, when he succeeded Sir Peter Maxwell Davies, he has also directed the annual Dartington International Summer School.

Amidst all these professional activities Gavin Henderson has found space to serve at various times on the Club's committees and, like Michael Pope, has staged several events to commemorate the musical achievements of members past and present. Some of these have been memorable for reasons other than their musical content, as will also be described elsewhere. In the mid-1970s Gavin arranged a *soirée* in honour of the distinguished American composer Virgil Thomson, who had recently been elected to the Club. It was one of the grander of such occasions and a band of players from the New Philharmonia had been assembled in the ballroom to do justice to the great man's music. At the time the Club rejoiced in the services of a porter named Brannigan, an ex-Guardsman whose liberal way of attempting to dispose of his massive thirst would have made him unemployable by any other institution than the ever-tolerant Savile. Halfway through the course of the concert, Brannigan – whose sense of time tended to be confused – awoke from wherever he had been sleeping and hazily remembered that some crates of glasses needed to be stored behind the screens at the head of the ballroom ready for a party the following day. A rapt audience was suddenly diverted in the middle of a particularly fine passage of Thomson's music by the sight of a wild Irish figure tip-toeing through the players and carefully stacking the crates he was bearing in the appropriate place. As a concession to the unexpected scene which had met his bleary eyes he had removed his boots at the doorway in an elaborate pantomime to demonstrate that he had no wish to interfere with the proceedings during his erratic progress across the parquet floor. Having completed his task it evidently began to dawn on him in a nightmarish way that perhaps he should not be there at all so he took refuge behind a pillar while the band played on. At several intervals during the quieter passages he would peek out from his hiding place and with anguished looks towards his discarded boots see if the coast was yet clear enough for him to make his escape. Members and their ladies who had assembled to savour Thomson's music found themselves treated instead to a scenario worthy of the

Marx Brothers and became increasingly convulsed. An embarrassed Gavin Henderson, peering anxiously at the guest of honour to see how he was reacting to this farcical disruption of his work, found to his relief that the GOM, having heard it all before, was fast asleep.

Virgil Thomson was elected to the Club in 1974. His considerable output of music included operas, symphonic works, concertos, and chamber music, and like many of the Savile's more recent composers distinguished in these fields he had also turned his hand to film scores, perhaps the most notable of which was his music for *The Plow that Broke the Plains,* one of Pare Lorentz's mould-breaking American documentaries which showed how the greed and ignorance of the early settlers had destroyed the natural richness and fertility of the central great plains. But, above all, he was admired and feared as the bloodthirsty musical critic of the *New York Herald Tribune,* where, in the style of his theatrical colleagues "The Butchers of Broadway", he would issue murderous dismissals of anything he considered second rate. He was not above confessing, however, that he could wield this power to further his own ends. He was anxious, for instance, that his recently composed 'cello concerto should receive a worthy first performance in a suitably prestigious location. At the same time Sir Thomas Beecham was about to embark on a series of concerts in New York and, fiery and all as he was, even this savagely self-confident conductor was a mite apprehensive about Virgil Thomson's reaction to this important tour. Thomson made his ambitions for the 'cello concerto discreetly known to Beecham; Beecham heard, and inwardly digested. Thomson awarded him rave reviews and Beecham duly reciprocated by conducting the 'cello concerto's first performance at the next Edinburgh Festival with Anthony Pini as soloist. (Pini's son, Carl, the distinguished violinist, was subsequently to become a member of the Savile, having been proposed by Gavin Henderson.)

Virgil Thomson had been proposed for the Club by Richard (Tony) Arnell who had himself become a member in 1957. Tony was an extremely popular figure at Brook Street over a period of more than twenty years, during which he would make daily pilgrimages to the Club from the Trinity College of Music in Marylebone, where he was principal lecturer in Composition. An extraordinarily generous man, he had also been in the unusual position during his early years of being able to act as financial patron to his friend Sir Thomas Beecham who was possibly more accustomed to finding himself in the reverse role. Beecham reciprocated by giving many fine performances of the five symphonies and other of Arnell's music which included two violin concertos and sundry other pieces. Arnell was "Composer of the Year" in 1966; but it was as a composer of film music that he made his reputation as a craftsman and his list of film credits is a considerable one too lengthy to be repeated here.

Tony Arnell, Virgil Thomson and others of the post-war entry of musical members to the Club had found a well-established coterie of distinguished musicians of every kind already there to greet them as they arrived. Most have been already mentioned but there were others from an earlier generation of members like John Reginald Lang-Hyde, the pianist, who had been elected in

1935 and was a life member until his death in 1989; and John Kentish, the well known tenor, elected in 1939 and happily still a member. Lang-Hyde, who performed as Lewis Hyde, was something of an infant prodigy, giving concerts from the age of eleven; after an audition for the famous Tobias Mathay Pianoforte School the principal remarked to Dame Myra Hess that he had "found a star". Having completed service in France during the First World War he continued his studies and while on a continental holiday played for Paderewski, who patted his heart and said, "You have something there that many a musician lacks." After touring Europe he went up to King's College Cambridge in 1924, where he read History and Law, and after coming down became a student at the Royal College of Music (where his tutor was his future colleague at the Savile, Sir Arthur Bliss). During a life-time of travel and performances he also composed more than three hundred songs written in English, French, German and Spanish.

John Kentish's half century as a member of the Savile has coincided with a long and rewarding career as a tenor which has included seasons as principal at the Sadler's Wells Opera Company and at Glyndebourne. He has also been director of studies at The London Opera Centre. It was he and another member of the Savile, Donald Francke (elected later in 1980), who were cast in major roles for the belated premiere of Arthur Benjamin's opera, *A Tale of Two Cities*, given at Sadler's Wells in 1957, Kentish as Charles Darnay and Donald Francke as Gabelle, although the latter was also required to sing the role of the aged Marquis at four days' notice owing to the illness of the original cast member. John Kentish's wife, Leigh Howard, herself made a graceful curtsey to a Savile member when she produced Malcolm Arnold's *The Dancing Master* in 1962 with Donald Francke and his wife Margaret Lindsay singing leading parts.

The Tale of Two Cities had been Donald Francke's professional début, although in fact he was then still a student of Herbert Howells at the Royal College of Music. This early Savile influence was reinforced by his association with Guy Warrack, who deputized for Howells during his absences. Warrack was also chairman of The Intimate Opera Company with which Donald Francke was closely involved both as performer and for a time as artistic director. Yet another Savile connection came when Francke gave his first recital at the Wigmore Hall with Gerald Moore in 1965. Like his singing predecessors at the Savile, Plunket Greene and Gervase Elwes, Francke has devoted much of his time to adjudicating at competitive festivals both in the UK and abroad and this has included three extensive tours across Canada between 1969-78 and visits to festivals at Trinidad, Hong Kong and Bermuda. Members who presently wish to sample his own skills as a singer, however, have only to queue for Andrew Lloyd Webber's *Cats* and hear him in the role of Deuteronomy, which he has made his own since 1986.

Guy Warrack, the Scottish conductor and composer who was elected in 1951, was another of the post-war musical intake to the Savile. Warrack was educated at

Magdalen College, Oxford, and at the RCM, where he studied conducting with Adrian Boult and composition with Vaughan Williams – who had, himself, been a student of Stanford. Like the later member, James Blades, he was an expert timpanist and capable of taking his place, when required, in the professional orchestras of London. On graduating from the RCM he joined its teaching staff and in 1935 became conductor of the BBC Scottish Orchestra in Edinburgh, which he soon established as a considerable musical force north of the Border. He remained in Edinburgh until 1945 when he returned to the RCM in London to take charge of the conducting class. During his time there some of his own compositions, notably his symphony of 1932, were performed, though he tended – as he had in Edinburgh – to present neglected classics from the English repertoire in those of the concerts which he himself organized. Warrack was a diligent member of the Club and served on the general committee in the late 'fifties.

At the same election meeting in 1951 which had elected Warrack, there was elected another Scotsman: pianist, conductor, organist, and writer on music, Stewart Deas. He was also a musical critic for *The Scotsman* and other journals and at the time of his election to the Savile he held the James Rossiter Hoyle Chair of Music at the University of Sheffield.

In 1954, Gerald Moore, perhaps the one musician who by his advocacy and his own superb artistry did most to raise the status of the accompanist to its proper place in the performance of chamber music, was elected to the Savile. He had cut his musical teeth at the early age of sixteen when, during a brief visit to Canada, he performed as a soloist and accompanist on a joint recital tour with the 'cellist Boris Hambourg and the tenor Redfern Hollingshead. On his return to England Sir Landon Ronald heard him and advised him to specialize in accompaniment. On taking this advice his skill was put to the ultimate test and further refined by a long association with that "exhausting and perfectionist" Savilian, the tenor John Coates. Moore regarded Coates's influence on his style to have been crucial to his development, while the pianist Solomon was also a great source of inspiration and encouragement. That their faith in him was not misplaced is indicated by the list of the great leading artists of his day who queued up to be accompanied by this most sensitive of partners: Casals and Menuhin, Dame Maggie Teyte, Kathleen Ferrier, Elisabeth Schumann, Elisabeth Schwarzkopf, Victoria de los Angeles, Hans Hotter, John McCormack, and Dietrich Fischer-Dieskau among them. In 1943 with the publication of his entertaining and instructive book *The Unashamed Accompanist* he proved himself such a lively advocate for his art that he was persuaded into a parallel career as a lecturer and as such was soon a regular performer in all the English-speaking countries and on television. His autobiography *Am I Too Loud?* published in 1962 was another entertaining but shrewd commentary on his unique approach to the musical role of an accompanist and after his retirement from the concert hall in 1967 he gave himself over to teaching, lecturing and writing while being able to spend more of his leisure time at the Savile, where his appreciative fellows could savour some of the virtuosity and wit with which he had invested his professional career.

Gerald Moore's teaching methods and his advocacy for good and proper musical performances were as gentle and persuasive as they were effective, though he could show his claws if the role of accompanist seemed in any way to be slighted. An advocate of a sterner kind and with a fiercer wit was the musical critic Peter Stadlen, who was elected to the Club in 1962, two years after he had joined the music staff of *The Daily Telegraph* and fifteen years before he became its chief musical critic. In this he was following in a Savile line which extended back through Richard Capell, Francis Toye, Ferrucio Bonavia, to Robin Legge, all of whom had held the same position, the last-mentioned having been elected as long ago as 1895. Stadlen demanded to be taken seriously for he was the antithesis of that other musical critic, Bernard Shaw's, dictum in *Maxims for Revolutionists* : "He who can, does. He who cannot, teaches." From 1934 to 1939 Stadlen had been one of the leading young pianists of Austria and Germany specializing in the Viennese classics and their more *avant-garde* successors, and in this latter mode had been personally coached by the composers Webern and Krenek for the first performances of some of their works. In 1948 he had returned to Darmstadt to give the long-delayed European premiere of Schoenberg's piano concerto: stern stuff indeed. Stadlen had come to England in 1939 and set himself to master the language, which he did with impressive speed. One of his criteria evidently was that he should be fluent enough to be able to make jokes about his chosen subject, and this he did; though some considered their lingering teutonic flavour could only be truly appreciated when they were applied to such worthy targets as, for instance, Ken Russell's awful travesty of a television film about Richard Strauss. Perhaps, too, some of this esoteric quality had crept into his social life, for while he was always a popular visitor to the Club, his conversation could be a trifle daunting for the comparatively uninformed, though for those who shared his enthusiasms it seems it could be an enlightening experience.

The flow of new musical members to the Savile had followed its more normal course with the election in 1960 of Harry Blech, the violinist and conductor whose abiding monument is the London Mozart Players, which he founded in 1949. He was also founder of the Haydn-Mozart Society, whose president for many years was another member, Sir William Walton. André Previn enjoyed a brief membership from 1972-74 while he carried out his London engagements and more recent conductors have been Jan Latham-Koenig, principal conductor of the Rome Opera, elected in 1982, and Graeme Jenkins, elected in 1986, whose work at Glyndebourne has enthused even the more jaundiced of our contemporary critics.

The Club continued to exercise its apparent attraction for writers of film music when Ron Goodwin was elected in 1969. Goodwin has composed the film scores of innumerable sagas for the cinema, including such memorable comic masterpieces as *Those Magnificent Men in Their Flying Machines,* but this aspect of his work brought him to the Savile in what could have been most inauspicious circumstances. In 1969 Sir William Walton had completed the music for the film *Battle of Britain*, which had been commissioned by United Artists Ltd. To his intense anger it was rejected, ostensibly because there was not enough material in it to fill a long-playing record. Malcolm Arnold had conducted most of the sessions during the recording of the sound track and assisted in orchestrating several sections of the music, including the "Battle of Britain March" from Walton's 3-stave short score, though the composer had himself conducted this passage. Malcolm Arnold rescored and expanded several sections of Walton's original soundtrack including the famous "Battle in the Air" sequence, the last third of which he completed. Having tried the patiences of these two Savile musicians to their utmost limits, the film company then scrapped all their work with the exception of the "Battle in the Air" sequence, which could not be removed because the film was already edited to the music, and turned to Ron Goodwin to provide an entirely new score – the one with which this rather doomed film eventually appeared. It was at this unfortunate moment that Goodwin was proposed for the Savile, and though there were some who had observed the cavalier treatment of two well-established members with dismay and were prepared to resent the arrival of the totally innocent Ron Goodwin, the matter was happily resolved when Walton marched to the morning room and appended his signature with a flourish in the candidates book.

In 1971 the composer, critic and music director Norman Kay was elected to the Savile. Like several of his musical predecessors at the Club he had studied at the Royal College of Music and had served also as music critic for such journals as *Music and Musicians* and *The Daily Telegraph.* There was to be, however, yet another and more recent close connection for he was to become part of that formidable band of Savilians who were closely concerned in the early development of Harlech Television. Wynford Vaughan Thomas had been one of the founding directors of H.T.V. in the late 'sixties and many of his companions in this enterprise had been his guests at the Club, particularly during the furious plotting stages which preceded their application for this Welsh television franchise. These colleagues of his included such well-known figures as John Morgan and Aled Vaughan, who soon revised their status from guest to member. To this "Welsh mafia" came the Lancastrian Norman Kay, who took over as music director of the company in 1976. He had already established himself as a considerable composer with such works as the Passacaglia for Orchestra of 1966 presented at the Cheltenham Festival – itself the brain-child of two previous Savilians – and with his work at the Three Choirs Festival which had so many associations with Stanford, Parry and other Savilians. Now he was to compound this creative work in collaboration with a Savile contemporary, John Morgan, who wrote the libretto for his opera, *Christmas Carol,* which won the Salzburg Opera Prize in 1980. In 1971, the year of his election, he published a masterly study of Shostakovitch. Among his other musical works are "Song Without Words" for the BBC, which won the Italia prize in 1967, and the King Herod Cantata for soloists, chorus and orchestra written for the Llandaff Festival of 1968.

The rather artificial conflict between music which is "popular" and that which is regarded as "serious" (and therefore, allegedly, the province of a select few) is one which seems particularly difficult for some music-lovers to resolve when regarding the work of modern composers. Malcolm Arnold is one who has succeeded in bridging the gap; Howard Blake, who was proposed for the Savile by Arnold and elected in 1987, is another.

Howard Blake's enchanting score to the animated film *The Snowman* (for which he also wrote the text based on a story by Raymond Briggs) has become a classic TV presentation which has dominated the screens every Christmas since it was commissioned in 1982, while his contemporary oratorio *Benedictus,* a beautiful setting of some of the poems in the Book of Psalms together with Francis Thompson's *Hound of Heaven,* is part of the regular repertoire of Sir David Willcocks and the Bach Choir. Both of these can be said to be truly "popular" in the best sense and demonstrate his masterly writing for children's voices, which possibly derives from his own early experience in Brighton as a boy soprano and organist. But his compositions have covered wider fields than these. He has produced more abstract, "non-commercial" music such as the piano quartet, the Diversions for cello, a violin sonata, a cycle of Shakespearean songs for tenor and string orchestra, and a clarinet concerto, as well as earning his living from such notable film scores as *The Duellists, Agatha,* and *The Riddle of the Sands* – the latter scripted from a novel by an earlier Savilian, Erskine Childers. Many of his works show a strong religious feeling; the longer choral work *Benedictus,* for instance, grew out of a cantata, *The Song of St Francis,* which he wrote for his monastic neighbours at Worth Abbey when he was living in Sussex. But he has written in nearly every other musical *genre;* ballet music for Sadler's Wells and the London Contemporary Dance Theatre; music for children; chamber music; music for brass ensembles; and comic opera. The eclecticism of his tastes can perhaps best be demonstrated by listing the section headings of just one of his works, his Concert Dances for piano and orchestra: Parade; Slow Ragtime; Jump; Medium Rock; Folk Ballad; Boogie; Jazz Waltz; Cha-Cha; Galop; and all this from a composer who is equally at home writing in the great classical tradition.

The Savile's musicians can therefore be seen to have moved with the times and, as with their literary confrères, a strong common theme can be discerned in the intertwining threads which have brought them together to relax in the all-embracing social and intellectual milieu provided in the Club rooms. There is also a powerful symmetry evident in their backgrounds, their achievements, and the motives which have guided them in the promotion of English music during the past one and a quarter centuries when, partly due to their efforts, "Das Land ohne Musik" has become an integral part of the great European musical tradition.

It is for this reason that though Philip Cannon was elected as long ago as 1964 he has been left to the last in this chronology, for with that same symmetry he has not only been professor of composition at the Royal College of Music since 1960 – a position shared jointly when it was first created by the two Savilians, Sir Hubert Parry and Sir Charles Villiers Stanford – but was himself a student there under Vaughan Williams and Gordon Jacob, both of whom had been Stanford's pupils.

As with so many other British composers before him – Delius, Elgar and the rest – Cannon's work was at first more greatly appreciated abroad than it was here. His string quartet performed in Paris in 1964 was hailed as "avant garde romantique" and was awarded the Grand Prix and the Critic's Prize – a singular honour in view of the usually dismissive attitude of the French towards British composers. But it was not until 1965 when his fellow Savilian, Rollo Myers, wrote of him in the *Musical Times* that here "was a fresh voice in British music" that the powers-that-be began to take proper notice. In 1972 the BBC commissioned him to provide "a symphonic work of international significance" to mark Britain's entry into Europe. The result was a choral symphony *"Son of God"* to a text by Jack Playfair adapted from the Book of Isaiah. In 1975 he was commissioned to compose a *Te Deum* to celebrate the Quincentenary of St George's Chapel, Windsor. For the same occasion Sir Arthur Bliss was also asked to contribute a work resulted in *Shield of Faith* which, sadly, he did not live to hear. Nevertheless the occasion was notable for evoking another symmetrical progression from a previous Queen's command to a Savile member, when Victoria summoned Sir Walter Parratt to be her organist there ninety-three years earlier. Cannon has also written a considerable body of other work which includes three operas, choral and chamber music and two sinfoniettas.

Thus, the roll-call of musicians who belong to the Savile unfolds and it is one of which this sometimes over-modest Club can properly be proud. It should have been no surprise, therefore, that as the last paragraphs of this section were being written the ninety-seventh season of the Henry Wood Promenade Concerts was beginning with what might almost have been described as a mini-festival of Savile composers. The opening notes on the first night came from the fanfare "Jubilant" blasted out by the costumed trumpeters of Kneller Hall in tribute to the former Savilian and Master of the Queen's Musick, Sir Arthur Bliss; the major work which it heralded was *The Dream of Gerontius* by another former Savilian and Master of the King's Musick, Sir Edward Elgar. Similarly, the first two thirds of the second night were dominated by Savilians: Bliss again, with a performance of his piano concerto and Malcolm Arnold's fine guitar concerto. And for those who might have been disappointed that the 8th Symphony of Vaughan Williams intervened to prevent the Club from boasting a royal flush of the first two nights, perhaps it was some consolation that its composer was a pupil of Stanford and a tutor of Philip Cannon.

The score of Sir Malcolm Arnold's fanfare to mark the Club's centenary.

CHAPTER FIVE

Painters and Sculptors

The Club has demonstrated its catholicity in selecting members in many ways over the years and there can be no better example of this than that to be found by glancing at the list of those painters, designers and sculptors who have been admitted to the Sodality since 1868. From Alma-Tadema to Henry Moore practitioners for every taste and in every technique have been represented, and even if to the public eye no coherent artistic attitude would be discernible, that is not unusual, for apostles of opposing styles and theories of art have always found in the Savile a compatible place in which to meet and disagree. Likewise, the exponents of these various visual arts have gone about their business in several ways and with differing degrees of success. There have been some, for instance, who from modest beginnings went on to become distinguished academicians in a conventional way, but there were others less orthodox, of whom one in particular reversed the usual process by becoming an exhibitor at the Royal Academy in his 'teens only to be reduced in later years to becoming a pavement artist and beggar in Bayswater.

In the very first intake of 1868 there were three well-known artists of the time: John Brett, Vicat Cole and Simeon Solomon.

The landscape painter John Brett like many of his contemporaries at the Savile was greatly influenced by the pre-Raphaelites d was a particular friend of John Ruskin, who used his *Val d'Aosta* as a frontispiece to his *Works*. Brett specialized in depicting Cornish scenes in a style of punctilious realism which did not always attract universal admiration. Sir Herbert Stephen wrote of him: "John Brett, both before and after he became a Royal Academician, opened the eyes of a great many of his fellow countrymen to the splendour and variety of the colours of the sea on the north coast of Cornwall", but a later obituarist commented that he "cared more for detailed veracity of record than for the creation of beauty". Although he was elected an A.R.A. in 1881 he was never raised to the rank of R.A. but, interestingly, as a Fellow of the Royal Astronomical Society with his own private observatory at Putney he demonstrated a devotion to celestial science which was shared by several of his contemporary members such as the Astronomer Royal Sir William Christie and Andrew Ainslie Common. This interest, both amateur and professional, has persisted throughout the years in the Club and is represented to the present day by the opera singer Donald Francke, who is also a Fellow of the Royal Astronomical Society.

Vicat Cole was already an A.R.A. on his election in 1868 but, unlike Brett, was later to earn the full rank of Royal Academician. He was chiefly known for his pictures of shipping and the port of London. He served on the general committee from 1883-1886.

Both Brett and Vicat Cole must have been considerably taxed later by their association at the Royal Academy and at the Club with one of the more spectacularly tragic artists of the time, Simeon Solomon, but in the year of his election as a founder member he was regarded as one of the most promising of young painters, one moreover who was possessed of considerable personal charm. With his brother Abraham and his sister Rebecca, who were also painters, he had studios in Gower Street which became famous for artistic productivity. Solomon had entered the Royal Academy schools at the age of fourteen but by 1858 at the age of eighteen he was considered sufficiently accomplished to have one of the first of his many paintings on biblical themes, *Isaac Offered*, hung in the Royal Academy exhibition. Like Brett, he was much influenced by the pre-Raphaelite movement but his paintings were much more widely admired. In the years immediately preceding his election to the Savile he came under the influence of another early member, Walter Pater, and a frequent visitor to the Club, Algernon Swinburne. At that time, too, possibly because of these connections, he abandoned biblical themes and turned to classical subjects. *Bacchus*, exhibited in 1867, had drawn great praise from Walter Pater and similarly his friend Swinburne was inspired by Solomon's drawings to write a series of poems which included *Eroticon* and *The End of the Earth*. In the year he took up membership of the Club, Solomon visited Rome with Oscar Browning, another founder member of the Savile, and from this experience ensued a new series of pictures, *Toilet of a Roman Lady*, *Love Bound and Wounded* among them, which were exhibited at the Royal Academy and added greatly to his reputation. But sadly his friendships at the Savile, instead of working to enhance his reputation, seemed more designed to bring about his downfall. The influences of Pater and Swinburne were particularly insidious; from these two, to use the words of Lionel Lambourne in a paper delivered to the Jewish Society of England in 1965 "he absorbed respectively an interest in sensuality and ritual . . . [indicating] a growing religious ambiguity which ran parallel to his departure from conventional sexual mores". To cap it all, that great Savilian and former friend of Solomon, Sir Sidney Colvin, wrote an article for the magazine *Portfolio* in 1870 praising his gifts but protesting against signs of "sentimental weakness in his paintings which too much praise has aggravated". What was undoubtedly intended as a kindly warning had a tragic sequel; having brooded on these strictures for some time Solomon sent his *Judith and Her Attendant* to the Royal Academy in 1872 and thereafter ceased exhibiting. He lapsed into alcoholism and took up another form of exhibition altogether which culminated in his arrest in 1873 for, "among other things", indecent exposure in a public urinal. He was sentenced to eighteen months' imprisonment which was subsequently suspended, but his career was effectively over. He took to the streets, where in the words of another obituarist he became "famous for his falls", although he managed some drawings of quality, such as *Medusa stung by her own Snakes*. These, however, he was able to sell for only a few shillings, deriving the main part of his income from begging and drawings on the Bayswater pavements which had become his home from home from the St Giles's workhouse that gave him occasional sanctuary. It is perhaps some compensation for the Savile's unwontedly baneful influence that it was not until 1874 that his membership was lapsed and that Robert Ross subsequently wrote an appreciative essay on his work in *Masques and Phrases*.

The public career and contributions to the life of the Savile of Sir Sidney Colvin are discussed elsewhere but his membership from its earliest days was notable not least for the number of distinguished creative artists who were drawn to the Club because of his presence there. In 1871 there came as full members (Sir) Frederic William Burton, (Sir) Edward Poynter and Rudolf Lehmann; as a "temporary" member came also the great French painter of the time, Jacques Joseph Tissot, who had fled to London after the capitulation of Paris in the Franco-Prussian war.

(Sir) Frederic Burton was at the time of his election a watercolourist of great distinction who went on to become director of the National Gallery, a post he held for twenty years until he was succeeded by Sir Edward Poynter, who was his exact contemporary at the Club. Poynter evidently shared the pre-Raphaelite tastes of his artist friends at the Savile as can be seen in the subject matter and titles of his paintings. He had spent his student years in Paris with Whistler, Du Maurier and other admirers of the French school and became a member of what was to be known as the "Trilby" Gang later to be immortalized by Du Maurier's book of that name. He first exhibited at the Royal Academy in 1861 when he was only twenty-five and thereafter exhibited every year until his death in 1919. His painting *Faithful unto Death* in the Walker Art Gallery, Liverpool, painted in 1865, first attracted admiring attention and his *Israel in Egypt* of 1867, now in the Guildhall Gallery, established his reputation as one of the foremost painters of the day. His decorative designs at this time included the mosaic of St George in the Houses of Parliament. He was elected R.A. in 1877 and shortly afterwards was appointed first Slade Professor at University College, London. His directorship of the National Gallery, which was greatly expanded under his regime, began in 1894 and in 1896 he succeeded Sir John Millais as president of the Royal Academy. His presidency coincided with what has been described as "the raucous controversy" over the Chantrey bequest but he survived it to earn a knighthood, a baronetcy and subsequently a G.C.V.O. An obituarist described him, perhaps not altogether flatteringly to modern ears, as "probably the most versatile and accomplished academic draughtsman the English school ever produced".

Another artist elected in 1871 was Rudolf Lehmann, then a well-known portrait painter, who was also a regular contributor to the Royal Academy after he settled in London in 1866, but it was yet another immigrant to the Savile in that year, Jacques Tissot, who made the greater impact on the artistic consciousness of Victorian England. Tissot, in common with several French fellow artists, had seen active service with the Garde Nationale in the siege of Paris during the winter of 1870-71. He recorded his experiences in a series of drawings and watercolours which were subsequently used to illustrate *The Defence of Paris* by the Savile member Thomas Gibson Bowles, founder and editor of *Vanity Fair*, whom Tissot had first met in 1869. The friendship which developed from that meeting was to become a valuable asset to Tissot both during the siege, when Bowles was visiting Paris as special correspondent for the *Morning Post*, and afterwards when Tissot found it expedient to lie low in London for a while as a guest of Bowles at Cleeve Lodge, Hyde Park Gate. Bowles not only provided Tissot with accommodation but also gave him a job producing caricatures for *Vanity Fair* in conjunction with those two other famous caricaturists on the magazine, Carlo Pellegrini ('Ape') and Leslie Ward ('Spy'). While in Paris Tissot had already contributed sixteen drawings, notable among them one of Napoleon III and another of the Sultan of Turkey, which had been very well received. Between the years 1871 and 1877 fifty more of his caricatures were to be published. These, however, were intended only as a sideline to enable him to earn sufficient money to pursue his main career as a painter but they had the added advantage of helping him establish his name and reputation in England as a portraitist. One of the first fruits of this, his celebrated portrait of Colonel Frederick Gustavus Burnaby, came about also through his connections at the Savile. Burnaby had been elected to the Club in 1871 at the same time as Tissot, part of an intake which was, in the words of Sir Herbert Stephen's memoir (which incidentally does not mention Tissot), to become famous in a variety of ways. "One of them", he continues, "was Captain – better known as Colonel – F. Burnaby, whose exploits and his pen both made him universally known for his adventures and his personal gallantry." Burnaby was a tall and what would then have been called "devilishly handsome" man of splendid physique; a superb horseman and shot, an athlete, boxer, gymnast and balloonist. He was also a dashingly successful officer in the Household Cavalry and an adventurer who wrote of his exploits in various journals including *Vanity Fair*, which he had helped found with his friend, partner and fellow member of the Savile, Thomas Gibson Bowles. His adventures were redolent of those to be found in the contemporary novels of Henty and similar stirring yarns in *The Boy's Own Paper* so that he was also much written about by others. It is said that he may even have been the model for the hero of Ouida's novel *Under Two Flags*. His career as an army officer, however, was to come to a mysterious if typically gallant end. One suggestion has been that, having requested leave from his regiment, he died in pursuance of his second career as a journalist and travel writer; the other is that he had gossiped to a journalist who printed his story about a fellow officer's love affair with a married woman and as a result was ostracized by his regiment to such an extent that he resigned his commission in order deliberately to seek a suitably penitential death in the Sudan. Whichever was the cause of his departure from England, the actual circumstances of his death seem to have been that during the Russian-Turkish war of 1877 he had joined his friend Valentine Baker – a man disgraced, some said unfairly, for alleged indecent assault – who was then in command of a Turkish division, and fought with distinction until his death in battle, sword in hand, at Abu Klea. One gets the impression that either of these reasons for his presence in the Sudan could equally be true. What is certain is that Tissot's famous portrait of Burnaby, depicting as someone has said "the most elegant pair of legs in Victorian art", is one of the masterpieces of portraiture in that period.

Tissot had, at the instigation and with the sponsorship of his patron Thomas Gibson Bowles, taken "temporary membership" of the Savile for twelve months in January 1871. Temporary membership was a device written early in the Club rules whereby, having been properly proposed and seconded, visitors to London might make use of the Club for periods of three, six, nine or a maximum of twelve months, paying the subscription pro rata. The rules seem to have been bent in this case for Tissot renewed his membership in 1872 and in 1873 but in September of that year he wrote to his friend Professor (later Sir) Sidney Colvin, who was treasurer of the Club at that time, resigning his membership. The reasons for this are not clear as his side of the correspondence has not survived but on September 7 Colvin wrote from 15 Savile Row: "Nous recevons avec beaucoup de regret votre démission comme membre du cercle . . ."

During his remaining years in England, however, he evidently maintained the many friendships he had made at the Savile and it may be merely that the attractions of the Arts Club in Hanover Square, which was then a kind of junior Royal Academy more particularly orientated to the world of painting, proved superior to those at the Savile. Besides, there were many men at the time who were members of both Clubs such as Cyril Flower, later Lord Battersea, who was a noted patron and collector, and Sir Laurens Alma-Tadema to whom Tissot later sold his house in St John's Wood when London became intolerable to him and he was returning to Paris after the death of his beloved mistress Kathleen Newton in 1882.

Alma-Tadema was, in fact, still a candidate for membership of the Savile at that time, not being elected until 1883, and before this took place three other distinguished figures in the worlds of Victorian painting, sculpture and architecture were to precede him as members. The first of these was that fervent evangelist and practitioner of high Victorian Gothic, the architect Alfred Waterhouse, who became a member in 1872.

"Waterhouse's work is all around us," as a contemporary member, Stanley Reynolds, reminded us in an article for *The Independent on Sunday* in April 1990; "In Holborn, London, there is the amazing redbrick palace of the Prudential Assurance Society, designed by Waterhouse in 1879. It is the capital's extreme example of the Gothic revival. In South Kensington there is the Natural History Museum, a building bursting with Waterhousian exuberance." That building, built between the years 1868-1880, would also soon be bursting – as has been noted in an earlier part of this book – with the 25-stone expanse and formidably splenetic presence of its then director, and archetypical Savilian, Sir Edwin Ray Lankester who, one suspects, may even have encouraged Waterhouse's entry to the Club so as to keep an eye on him both on and off the construction site of his new dominion. Waterhouse favoured the use of fiery red brick and terracotta for the façades of his buildings as can be seen both at the Natural History Museum and at Girton College, which he also designed and which was being expensively restored at the same time as one of his other monuments, Strangeways prison, was being destroyed by its inmates in 1990. Generations of Girton girls may have thought this process was being conducted the wrong way round but at the relevant time the style was greatly admired and much imitated. His first masterpiece, the Manchester Assize Courts, now also destroyed, made his name and led to many commissions for buildings in like style. The National Liberal Club is one of his, as are Liverpool's Lime Street Station, the Oxford Union debating hall, Tree Court at Gonville and Caius College and, what some consider to be his ultimate triumph, Manchester Town Hall.

Some of the more dramatic interior features of Waterhouse's Assize Courts in Manchester were provided by the poet and sculptor Thomas Woolner, who was elected to the Savile in 1874. This was the year also that he was elected RA and, at the height of his fame, was busily engaged in executing monumental open-air statues for several inner cities in Great Britain and abroad as well as busts of the contemporary famous, including such once and future Savilians as Professor Adam Sedgwick F.R.S. and several members of the Darwin family. Although he had been hailed as something of a young prodigy when he exhibited his first model in the Royal Academy at the age of seventeen, fortune had not always smiled on him and it was not until he made the acquaintance of Rossetti and became one of the original 'pre-Raphaelite brethren' that he achieved any kind of genuine celebrity. At this stage in his career he turned his talents to poetry, contributing two cantos, *My Beautiful Lady* and *My Lady in Death*, to that mouthpiece of the movement *The Germ*. Subsequently expanded with an illustration by Holman Hunt, it came to be regarded as a quintessential expression of pre-Raphaelitism. Through his acquaintanceship with another Savilian, Coventry Patmore, Woolner met Lord Tennyson at Coniston and this led to a commission to execute the medallion of Wordsworth in Grasmere Church. But even with such influential friends the artistic life of the time was not sufficiently rewarding financially and in 1852 he determined, like many other Englishmen in similar straits, to try his luck in the Australian goldfields. He was accompanied to the dockside by the Rossettis, Ford Madox Brown and Holman Hunt and the pathos of his departure inspired Madox Brown to use him as the model for what is undoubtedly one of the great narrative paintings of the time, *The Last of England*. The goldfields, however, turned out to be similarly unfruitful so he reverted to sculpture and had some considerable success in Australia with his portrait medallions of leading government figures, including one of William Charles Wentworth, "the father of Australian self-government". A colossal statue of Wentworth was also envisaged but never realized though Woolner had by now returned to England in the hope of obtaining this commission. On the voyage home one of his fellow passengers related a "melancholy tale" of a fisherman which Woolner on his return passed on to Tennyson, who based his poem *Enoch Arden* on it. By now the influence of Ruskin and the pre-Raphaelites had improved the status of artists in England and with his bust of Tennyson, executed in 1854, and some equally well appreciated portrait medallions of Robert Browning and Thomas Carlyle, Woolner's position was now secured. Commissions flowed in, including the massive *Moses* and other sculptures for the Manchester Assize Courts designed by Alfred Waterhouse. Woolner's works are too numerous to catalogue here but among the more remarkable are a bust of Gladstone in the Bodleian library, John Stuart Mill on the Thames embankment, Captain Cook in Sydney, Sir Stamford Raffles in Singapore and, of course, that of the Savilian professor Adam Sedgwick F.R.S. Woolner is regarded as having been particularly important at this period for reviving the art of medallion portraiture, and though his open-air statues are reckoned among the finest ornaments of the cities in which they are located, the name of Woolner is otherwise less well remembered. Perhaps, therefore, the work for which he is best known today is the enchanting little vignette of a flute player which graces the title page of Palgrave's *Golden Treasury*.

John Collier, the painter and writer on art, was elected to the Savile in 1876 and achieved the unique distinction of being appointed to the committee during his first year as a member. He was the younger son of the judge Robert Poiret Collier, afterwards the first Lord Monkswell, and after flirting with several other careers more in keeping with paternal requirements – the diplomatic service, the City and later the Foreign Office – he managed to persuade his father of his true *métier*. Monkswell, ever a seeker after the best for his son, thereupon sought the advice of that monument of Victorian art and future Savilian Sir Laurens Alma-Tadema, who advised study at the Slade, followed by periods in Paris and Munich. In the year he was elected to the Savile Collier was twenty-six and had just begun to exhibit at the Royal Academy as he was to continue to do almost without a break in every year until his death in 1934. He was particularly renowned as a portrait painter, becoming vice-president of the Royal Society of Portrait Painters, and is represented today by twelve works in the National Portrait Gallery which include his contemporaries at the Savile, Sir Michael Foster M.P. and William Kingdom Clifford, the mathematician and philosopher. There are also some portraits of other notable families of the time with strong connections at the Savile such as the Darwins and the Huxleys. Collier was to form a double connection with the latter as well as putting his advocacy of rationalism and marriage law reform to good use through his two marriages. First he married Marian, the daughter of Thomas Henry Huxley and sister of Leonard Huxley, who became a member of the Savile in 1884. Marian was herself an accomplished portraitist who has four of her works hanging in the National Portrait Gallery. After she died following the birth of their only child in 1887 Collier then married her youngest sister Ethel. This marriage had to be solemnized in Norway as it was then technically illegal in England on the grounds of incest, perhaps as a result of Henry VIII's failure to tidy up the law after his own brush with the Pope over Catherine of Aragon. Partly as a result of Collier's campaigning, the marriage was eventually regularized in England by the passing of the Deceased Wife's Sister Act of 1907. The number of Savilians who had been or were to become involved in reforming this particular aspect of the legal system – most notably, at a later date, Sir Alan Herbert – provides a curious insight into their more domestic activities outside the Savile. The Club possesses a portrait by Collier of Thomas Henry Hood, one of its most distinguished honorary secretaries, who held that position from 1879 until 1900, while Collier's own self-portrait was considered fine enough to be set alongside the flattering company to be found in the Uffizi Gallery in Florence. The vagaries of fashion, however, have dealt less kindly with his reputation. In a comment oddly reminiscent of that applied to his Savilian contemporary John Brett, an obituarist derided his work for being "concerned with accuracy rather than with truth in the artistic meaning of the word", adding that in his publications, *A Primer of Art, A Manual of Oil Painting* and the *Art of Portrait Painting*, "it is difficult to resist the conclusion that Collier had the scientific rather than the artistic habit of mind". Be that as it may, it is interesting that while Sir Laurens Alma-Tadema had been willing to advise the young Collier on the course his artistic studies should take, he had been either reluctant or unable to indulge his other wish, which was to be taken on as an apprentice in his own studios. Alma-Tadema was less diffident seven years later, however, in following his would-be pupil's example by seeking election to the Savile. An indication of how his public reputation and his personal popularity stood at that time (1883) is that he was proposed by Edmund Gosse and supported by more than forty signatures which, perhaps significantly, did not include that of the Hon. John Collier. Alma-Tadema, whatever his position in the current estimation, is surely one of the great figures in Victorian *genre* painting. At the time of his election he had just settled in his friend Tissot's "pseudo-antique style house" in St John's Wood with his wife of two years, the painter Laura Epping. Thirty years earlier he had studied in Antwerp with young men of similar tastes like his reunited fellows at the Savile, Edward Poynter and Frederick Burton, who had been drawn to the archaeology of ancient Greece, Rome and Egypt as a source of inspiration. Alma-Tadema, however, surpassed them all in his remarkably successful and beautiful depictions of idealized, permanently sunlit, and monumental locations from classical history. Despite their immense popularity at the time, titillating an appetite which was already being stimulated by novels such as Lord Lytton's *The Last Days of Pompeii*, a more recent viewing public is probably only aware of Alma-Tadema's imaginative reconstructions and interpretations through the second-hand medium of Hollywood and its early use of them as a template for biblical epics. Five representatives of the genuine article can be seen at the Tate Gallery though this is only a small fraction of his life's work, which began when he was fourteen with *Opus i: Portrait of My Sister* and ended sixty-two years later, only two months before his death, with *Opus cccviii: Preparations*. Other examples of his work can, of course, be seen in other galleries all over this country and abroad. Alma-Tadema's brilliant treatment of architecture in his paintings led to his receiving the Royal Gold Medal for the promotion of architecture on the recommendation of the Institute of British Architects. He was also much sought after by his peers in the world of music and the theatre, and his election to the Savile reinforced these connections. Henry Irving, for instance, persuaded him to design sets for his productions of *Cymbeline* and *Coriolanus* while the young Charles Stanford – already a Savile member of five years' standing – employed him to supervise the colour design and mounting of the Elysian Fields scene in Gluck's opera *Orpheus*, produced at the Cambridge University Music Society in 1889. This project must have been extremely appealing as Alma-Tadema was particularly drawn to musicians and kept a piano in his St John's Wood house, the lid of which was to become famous for the number of autographs he had persuaded visiting musicians to inscribe upon it. This "genial and attractive personality", as a contemporary described him, was elected R.A. in 1879, knighted in 1899, and awarded the O.M. in 1907.

Alma-Tadema's appreciation and affection for architecture of the classical period would have evoked a ready response from the architect and writer on historical architecture, Sir Reginald Blomfield, who was elected to the Savile in 1891. In that year he was preparing for his publisher a work entitled *The Formal Gardens of England* and this was followed in 1897 by his magisterial *History of Renaissance Architecture in England: 1500-1800*, the fame of which was to lead to many commissions from the owners of historic houses such as Apethorpe and Chequers. Less romantic but possibly more remunerative was a brief to design the warehouse in Greycoat Place, Westminster, for the Army and Navy Stores. His scholarly approach to his subject, however, continued in further writings which included a *History of French Architecture: 1494-1774*, while his wittily pungent views on the new fashions in architecture were expressed in the less academic *Memoirs of an Architect*, published in 1932, and *Modernismus* in 1934. Among his great buildings and monuments are the Usher Art Gallery, public library and water tower in Lincoln; St Paul's Cross in St Paul's churchyard; Lady Margaret Hall, Oxford; the United Universities Club; the Regent Street Quadrant, together with what was once a classic London landmark and meeting place, the old Swan and Edgar building – now the home of Tower Records. But perhaps his most affecting work is to be found in his many national and municipal war memorials. These works were to bring him into an intimate professional relationship with a fellow member of the Savile, Rudyard Kipling, through their mutual involvement with the War Graves Commission at the end of the First World War. Blomfield had been invited to design the Menin Gate at Ypres to commemorate the fallen in that savage battle of attrition and at the same time advise on how best to order the graves of those many hundreds of thousands who had perished in the rest of Flanders and the other major battlefields. It was decided to have standard headstones, not crosses, on which would be a simple carving of regimental badge, name, rank, regiment, date of death and a short inscription if required by the next of kin. Rudyard Kipling, grief stricken by the death of his own son, killed in the war, devised the phrase "A soldier of the Great War . . . Known unto God" to commemorate those many thousands without known graves. Two monuments were common to all cemeteries: a monolithic slab on three steps designed by Edwin Lutyens and a stone cross with bronze sword, designed by Sir Reginald Blomfield. Kipling chose the inscription from Ecclesiasticus that adorns Lutyens's stone: "Their name liveth for evermore". Despite the tragic overtones of this project Blomfield's and Kipling's partnership was a happy one in the fruitfulness of its results, which is perhaps surprising given their irascible temperaments:

Blomfield having been described as a controversialist of "energy, sincerity, downrightness, self-assurance, pugnacity and scholarship" while Rudyard Kipling – as we have already seen – was caught for all time in the Club's memory by Frank the wine waiter's judicial assessment of him as "a very fiery gentleman for so small a member". Perhaps, like any latent antagonisms of the battlefields they adorned and commemorated, the personal conflicts which may have arisen were for this occasion allowed a decent burial.

Robert Ross, who was elected in 1893, has already figured in this history for his literary associations with other members of the Club though professionally he was more closely associated with painters through his critical writings and his partnership in the Carfax Gallery which he and his Savilian colleague Edward Warren had acquired from a future member, William Rothenstein. The wayward course of his private life, however, caused his relations with other members such as Sidney Colvin, Edmund Gosse and Max Beerbohm, to become extremely complicated. Friendships he had formed at the Savile and elsewhere were put under severe strain, particularly during the course of prolonged libel suits which arose out of his championship of Oscar Wilde and the venomous attacks it had inspired from that arch-litigant Lord Alfred (Bosie) Douglas who, with typical hypocrisy, seized on Ross's sexual peculiarities, so similar to what had once been his own, to hound him mercilessly.

Ross's acquaintances and friends at the Club were divided; the likes of Edmund Gosse and H.G. Wells forever kindly and supportive, Beerbohm detached and neutral, Colvin exploding that anyone who consorted with "professional buggers" deserved all he got. Among his happier connections with Club members, however, were the exhibitions he mounted at the Carfax for Max Beerbohm and William Orpen.

Less controversial than Ross was Charles Wellington Furse, the English romantic painter, who was elected to the Club in 1894. Although he remained a member until his death in 1906 he seems to have been an unobtrusive presence at the Savile, for which his contemporaries, coping with the very public turmoil provided by Robert Ross, must have been heartily grateful. His reputation in the art world of that time was by all available accounts similarly muted although he regularly exhibited at the Royal Academy and his pictures such as *Cain*, *Diana of the Uplands* and *The Return from the Ride* are said to have appealed greatly to the taste of the time. He was rewarded with an A.R.A. in 1904.

A more noticeable figure in the art world who was elected to the Club in 1898 was the sculptor and craftsman Sir George James Frampton. Frampton had studied under W.S. Frith at the Lambeth School of Art and later at the Royal Academy Schools, producing all the while decorative and ornamental sculptures, using in combination a variety of materials including bronze, ivory, marble and jewels. His first exhibit at the Royal Academy, *Socrates Teaching the People in the Agora*, was shown in 1884 when he was just twenty-four years old. *An Act of Mercy*, shown in 1887, won him the Academy Gold Medal and a travelling scholarship which he spent in Paris studying under Antonin Mercié, a master of great influence during this period. By the time he was elected to the Savile Frampton had become powerfully attracted to the "arts and crafts" movement, which reflected his own predeliction for the use and admixture of several materials and techniques in the production of individual works of art. He had also brought back from Paris a strong liking for contemporary French symbolism as is demonstrated in his bas-relief *Mysteriarch*, which was awarded the *médaille d'honneur* at the Paris Exposition of 1900 and is now in the Walker Art Gallery, Liverpool. He promulgated all his views on art and craftsmanship with some vigour, and his writings on such subjects as enamelling, goldsmith's work, wood-carving and polychrome sculpture exerted considerable influence on the late nineteenth century style of decorative design, particularly in Germany where he became something of an artistic hero. Frampton was much in demand also as a sculptor of public monuments and among some considered to be his better works are those of Dame Alice Owen at Owen's School, Islington; several of Queen Victoria (Calcutta, Winnipeg, Leeds and Southport) and – an unlikely conjunction of subjects – Quintin Hogg in Langham Place and Peter Pan in Kensington Gardens. Although some of his work now seems dated and affected, if not a touch precious, he had generally an improving influence on the taste of his time so it is sad that now he should be chiefly remembered for his most visible and abysmal failure, the statue of Edith Cavell in St Martin's Lane. Members wishing to pay proper tribute to that brave woman could do no better than to avert their eyes when passing it.

Frampton's charming figure of Peter Pan in Kensington Gardens, however, must have been of particular interest to the painter, engraver, theatre designer and illustrator Sir William Newzam Prior Nicholson, who joined the Club in 1900. Four years after his election he was called upon by James Barrie to design the sets for the first production of that author's play about the little boy who refused to grow up, and by his own perpetual youthfulness which he demonstrated almost daily during most of his forty-nine years of membership, it appears that he was an inspired choice for this task. "Billy Nick", as he was known at Piccadilly and Brook Street, had already established himself in the public eye as an illustrator of *An Alphabet*, of *An Almanac of Twelve Sports* with words by Rudyard Kipling, and of *London Types* to a text by W.E. Henley. Henley also commissioned from him a woodcut of Queen Victoria for the *New Review*, which he was then editing, and this earned Nicholson even wider recognition. Indeed, Oscar Wilde, writing to Robert Ross from his exile in Dieppe, was moved to declare:

> ". . . [Nicholson's] portrait of the Queen is wonderful. I am going to hang it on the walls of the chalet. Every poet should gaze at the portrait of his Queen all day long. . . ."

And in confirmation that this rather equivocal tribute was no mere Wildean *jeu d'esprit*, André Gide (briefly a member in 1900) was later to recall that this depiction of that daunting widow did in fact gaze imperiously down on her erstwhile guest at Reading Gaol from the chalet wall for several months to come.

Throughout his life Nicholson was to show himself to be a master in several mediums. His sets for *Peter Pan* led to many other similar commissions for the theatre, and in collaboration with his brother-in-law James Pryde (styling themselves "The Beggarstaff Brothers") he produced a series of posters which were considered revolutionary in their time. These were designed to promote such diverse products as Rowntree's Cocoa and Sir Henry Irving's presentations of *Don Quixote* and *Robespierre*, both of the latter being sufficiently remarkable to be preserved at the Victoria and Albert Museum. Nicholson's skill with woodcuts, which had been encouraged by his friend Whistler and demonstrated with his portrait of Queen Victoria, has a continuing memorial in the windmill colophon which he designed at the behest of the publishers Heinemann to embellish the frontispiece and spines of their books. But it is as a landscape artist and portraitist that Nicholson is still chiefly known. The National Portrait Gallery possesses a handful of his more outstanding portraits including those of two fellow Savilians Max Beerbohm and George Saintsbury. The Club used also to possess his post-mortem picture of a much loved member, Andrew Ainslie Common, and in the Morning Room there still hangs a strange landscape — not to everyone's taste — which seems to belong to some kind of psychedelic fantasy. The explanation for this however, goes far to account for the peculiar fascination which "Billy Nick" seemed so nonchalantly to exact from his friends and acquaintances at the Savile. At once conservative and eccentric, he was always ready to sample the new. One day in the 'twenties he was invited up for a flight in a glider piloted by his son Christopher (also a member), who had a reputation as one of the foremost experts in this art of unpowered flight. Unfazed by this, to him, unique experience, he recorded several sketches of the approaching airfield as he and his son came in to land and the resulting landscape, taken from such an unusual angle and peopled by Lowry-like stick figures, is now on display to puzzle his successors taking tea or an afternoon nap in the Club's elegant new morning-room.

Nicholson's genius for friendship was given full rein at the Savile for nearly half a century and though he was physically slight his presence at the long table, in the billiards room, and the Sandpit was considerable. This, apart from his artistic renown, owed not a little to his fastidious style of dress, which became famous on account of the delicately spotted shirts, polka-dotted bow-ties, and canary waist-coats with which he adorned himself. He was known as "the dandy of English art", though his work was much more profound than that description implied, and he was a convinced opponent of "Bohemianism" while at the same time refusing to have much truck with the "Establishment", as is evidenced by his refusal to accept the title of Royal Academician. His daughter Nancy — a convinced feminist — became the first wife of Robert Graves before being replaced in that poet's affections by the farcical and pretentious American "poet", Laura Riding. Bumping into Peter Quennell near his studio one day, Nicholson complained: "It seems a pity that now the Turks have abandoned polygamy, Robert should have decided to take it up." What Graves's brother Richard, "Graves Supérieur", who was Nicholson's contemporary at the Savile, thought of the matter is unfortunately not recorded.

It was seven years before a painter of similar stature to Nicholson was entered in the Candidates' Book, but this lack of quantity in Savilian painters was soon compensated by quality when the artist Albert Rutherston (elected in 1907) encouraged his brother (Sir) William Rothenstein to follow his footsteps into the Savile in 1908. The rather confusing difference in surnames is explained by Albert's more acute consciousness of his parents' German background, which caused him to change his name on the outbreak of war in 1914 even though his family had been settled in Bradford since 1859. Rutherston's work is less well known than that of his elder brother but is, in the opinion of some, no less distinguished. In common with William he was to have some of his early work exhibited at the Carfax Gallery after he had completed his studies at the Slade. Like Sir William Nicholson, Rutherston also began to produce decorative work for the stage: posters, illustrations and theatre decorations, the latter particularly for Granville-Barker. This was to result after the war (when he served with the British Forces in Palestine) in his authorship of *Decoration in the Art of the Theatre.* Several exhibitions of his work were held in the Leicester Galleries between 1926 and 1953 and in 1930 the Soncino Press, of which his nephew and fellow Savilian Oliver Simon was a director, published a luxury edition of the Haggadah (the traditional Jewish book dealing with the celebration of the Passover and the exodus from Egypt) for which Rutherston did fourteen illustrations. His work is also represented in several public collections, including the Tate, the British Museum, the National Portrait Gallery and the Art Galleries of Bradford, Manchester, Dresden and Harvard. The Savile possesses his fine portrait in oils of a previous member, the journalist George Slythe Street, who served on the committee from 1915-1919.

Although Rutherston took an active interest in the life of the Club and successfully proposed many other distinguished figures of the time such as W.B. Yeats for membership of it, his brother "Will" Rothenstein seems to have been the more gregarious of the two and has left a deeper impression of his presence at the Savile. Certainly the list of his friends who are so entertainingly recalled in his three-volume autobiography *Men and Memories* contains a considerable number of names also to be found in the Savile's list of members. Like his friend and contemporary at the Savile, Sir William Nicholson, he was much influenced by Whistler as he was also by Fantin-Latour and Degas, who took a great interest in his early work and encouraged him while he was a student in Paris during the late 1880s. On his return to England in 1893 he made an astonishing debut into the artistic world as a result of a commission from the publisher John Lane. This required him to go to Oxford to make a series of lithographs of eminent characters. To the chagrin but eventual delight of Lane, Rothenstein ignored the implicit instruction that these should consist only of worthy dons and insisted on including some undergraduate celebrities as well. Among these was Max Beerbohm, with whom he was to forge a life-long friendship which would be continued at the Savile and elsewhere. The extraordinary success of this Oxonian venture was to be the nucleus of one of the most stunning series of portraits in the history of art, immortalising the great men of a whole era; men of such various achievements as Verlaine, Einstein, T.E. Lawrence and Elgar. Eventually it was to consist of over 750 portraits and 135 lithographs capturing the features of nearly all the figures who made their contributions to history between the years 1889-1925.

Reinforced by the respect and interest he acquired from this universally admired project, Rothenstein was able to promote his own beliefs in the importance of the arts and artists in the community and the necessity for more powerful regional teaching and creative centres for their several manifestations. In 1917 he accepted an appointment as professor of civic art at Sheffield University although at the time (from 1914-1918) he was an official war artist recording many of the battlefronts in France. In 1920 he became principal of the Royal College of Art where his success as a teacher and administrator was immense though inevitably restrictive and detrimental to his own work as an artist. From 1927-1933 he was a trustee of the Tate Gallery. He was knighted in 1931 and after delivering the Romanes Lecture at Oxford in 1934 he had conferred on him an honorary D.Litt.

Rothenstein's contribution to 20th century art, considerable as it is, is not the only aspect of this multi-faceted character which made him so memorable as an archetypical Savilian. His writings and the diversity of his friendships they revealed would alone have singled him out as remarkable in almost any generation. Like his contemporary Sir William Nicholson he seemed to have "a genius for friendship" and this, together with his admirably eclectic religious upbringing (his father had him baptized a Unitarian while his mother insisted on a Jewish regimen, Bar-Mitzvah and all, and towards the end of his life he was flirting with Catholicism) had considerable bearing on the subjects he chose for his art.

His great friend, admirer and fellow Savilian, the actor and biographer Robert Speaight, wrote of him: "One must never forget his predominantly Jewish ancestry though often he appeared to forget it himself."

In 1904 he was attracted to paint members of the Machzike Adass Synagogue, Spitalfields. He took a flat nearby and worked there for nearly three years, producing eight major paintings, including *Reading the Book of Esther*. In an interview, published by the *Jewish Chronicle* on 15th June 1906, he said: "It is not the picturesque possibilities of Tallism and Phylacteries that appeal to me. I have even left them out where I should have painted them. What appeals to me is the devotion of the Jew. It is that that I have endeavoured to put on to canvas – the spirit of Israel that animates the worshippers, not the outward trappings of the ritual." The paintings had a tremendous effect not only on the Jewish community but also on the community at large. Roger Fry was effusive with praise, describing one of the paintings as "the most serious attempt at dramatic composition that any quite modern English artist has attempted". The acquisition of *Jews Mourning in the Synagogue* by the Tate and the considerable publicity that attended it registered the arrival of William Rothenstein as a senior British artist. He also became a focal point for aspiring young artists, especially Jewish artists, seeking help and advice. Thus in 1907 he was of considerable assistance to Epstein on his arrival in England

and in 1908 he helped Gertler at the start of his career.

But Rothenstein was also to be the recipient of many other people's affectionate regard, and just as he had set down in drawings and writings the essential characteristics of his many eminent contemporaries, so too were his own to be preserved by the art of others. Through none was this effected so remorselessly yet affectionately than by his great friend and fellow Savilian Max Beerbohm.

That first meeting between them in Oxford, when Beerbohm was still an undergraduate at Merton and Rothenstein was fulfilling the commission for John Lane, might easily have turned out less well than it did, for Lane, having had his attention drawn to Max's similar talents, promptly commissioned him to produce another book of Oxford celebrities as well. Max wrote to Rothenstein apologizing for Lane's crass opportunism, adding a little bit of his own by saying that he was sure "there is room for both of us".

Rothenstein, recollecting their first meeting, described Max as being "rather tall", which only makes sense when compared with Rothenstein's own tiny physique. Beerbohm had a preference for the small and precise and a dislike for the large which he generally tended to confuse with the gross. Hence in his caricatures he was inclined to exaggerate these opposing characteristics to emphasize his point. Rothenstein's manikin-like presence gave him the opportunity to underline the former, while Viscount Goschen's and Reggie Turner's noses provided him with regular models for the latter.

In all Beerbohm's innumerable caricatures of him there is only one in which anybody is smaller than Rothenstein. This is the one in which his brother Albert Rutherston is situated under a table and Will on top of it so that he can address the recumbent and normally sized painter Wilson Steer on equally elevated terms. Beerbohm admitted that such depictions were cruel but shrugged this off with his usual detached indifference by saying: "My caricatures of him were cruel, I'm afraid. He knew they were and yet took it manfully." As has already been observed, most of his friends at the Savile, with the one exception of Rudyard Kipling, were prepared to take the same view – but in retrospect it still must seem slightly odd to modern "politically conscious" eyes. The attitude of the time is possibly best demonstrated by Rothenstein's own reaction to his appearance in Beerbohm's *Young self and old self* series. It must be mentioned that not even Rothenstein's formidable mother or any of his best friends could ever have claimed that he cut a handsome figure, but here Beerbohm went to the limit. In the drawing an appallingly ugly (and tiny) elder Rothenstein is confronted by his equally tiny and ugly younger self while he is lecturing to his students at the Royal Academy of Art. The elder, inflated by the acquisition of power and achievements, dismisses this questing apparition of his former insecurity: "Take off your hat, Sir! And leave the room!"

"How quickly he discovers the essence of each personality" was Rothenstein's forgiving assessment of Beerbohm's skills when writing of him later in *Men and Memories*. Beerbohm used often to stay with the Rothensteins at their estate in Far Oakbridge, Gloucestershire, and it was there that he completed "Maltby and

Braxton", one of the short stories in *Seven Men*. He used the Rothensteins' home there as the model for the great house in which the story is located and, as has already been observed, two Savilians also appear in the story, H.G. Wells disguised as Maltby and Arthur Balfour in a "walk-on part" as his own self.

More orthodox portraits of Rothenstein than Beerbohm's eccentric portrayals have been provided by his brother, Albert Rutherston, John Singer Sargent, Augustus John, and of course his own several self-portraits. His work is on display in many public collections including the Tate, the Imperial War Museum, the National Portrait Gallery, the Ashmolean, and the galleries of Leeds, Manchester, Sheffield, Bradford and Leicester.

In 1899 Rothenstein had married a beautiful and talented young actress, Alice Kingsley, the daughter of John Knewstub, a friend of Dante Gabriel Rossetti. Her sister married Sir William Orpen, the Irish painter who was elected to the Savile in 1909. Orpen's prodigious talent had been recognized at the early age of eleven by the Metropolitan School of Art in Dublin and at the age of seventeen he was sent on to the Slade in London where with such illustrious fellow students as Augustus John he did much to create the great reputation of that school. In 1899 at the age of twenty he won the Slade Summer Prize with a large composition, *Hamlet*, which was hailed as a remarkably mature piece of picture making rather than a mere student's exercise. By 1909 when he was elected to the Savile he had already made a name for himself with a series of precisely drawn interiors containing small figures that he exhibited at the New English Art Club, to which he had been elected in 1900. John Singer Sargent (an occasional visitor from abroad to the Savile as a "temporary member") also encouraged his ambitions as a portraitist, and Orpen's depictions of such well-known contemporaries as George Moore and Percy Wyndham added greatly to his reputation. At the time of his election to the Savile he was sharing a studio in Chelsea with Augustus John, and though it is evident that a very "good time was being had by all" who encountered this rumbustious duo at that address, he managed to produce in that year some remarkable works which included two fanciful self-portraits, *The Dead Ptarmigan* and *Myself and Venus*, as well as the even more stunning *Hommage à Manet*, now on display in the Manchester Corporation Art Gallery. By then he was also an Associate of the Royal Academy (becoming a full Academician in 1919) where his pictures came to be regarded as among the more popular features of the annual exhibitions at Burlington House. But for two years from 1917 he abandoned all private work to become, like his brother-in-law Will Rothenstein, an official war artist with the rank of major in the Royal Army Service Corps. After an exhibition at Agnew's in 1918 he presented the immense and harrowing record he had painted to the nation and most of it now resides in the Imperial War Museum. At the end of the war he was despatched, like so many other Savilians, to the Paris Peace Conference in Versailles. His own judgements on the sometimes meretricious antics of some of the participants at the Quai d'Orsay and the Hall of Mirrors were represented in some wittily executed depictions of the scenes he saw there, but his own real feelings were better expressed and more movingly in such paintings as *To an Unknown British Soldier in France*, portraying a draped coffin in the centre of an empty Hall of Mirrors, guarded by two ghost-like uniformed figures from the recent battlefields.

When, shortly afterwards, he succeeded in putting all these horrors behind him, he indulged a natural preference as a fashionable portrait painter of more elegant figures who, like himself, were attempting to expunge their recent hateful memories by immersing themselves as elegantly as they felt able in less morally taxing pursuits. Though he was to become regarded as one of the most successful British artists of his time on account of the nearly six hundred portraits together with other paintings he produced during this period, none of his work revealed the same depth of emotional involvement he was able to express both in his war pictures and his evocations of his native Ireland. His two published books, *An Onlooker in France, 1917-1919* and *Stones of Old Ireland and Myself*, reflect this as well as his consummate sense of the graphic which he further demonstrated by his artistic use of words. A member of several other clubs besides the Savile, Orpen was remembered in all of them as "an extremely entertaining companion, high spirited, droll and brim-full of songs and stories". He was therefore the natural choice as artist when a portrait of his fellow Savilian, Sir Charles Villiers Stanford, was being commissioned by that composer's old undergraduate stamping ground, Trinity College, Cambridge. It is, with the possible exception of the "Spy" cartoon in *Vanity Fair*, the best picture of this fiery but lovable Savilian, and it illustrates well the respective characteristics of both these artists.

Not all Savile artists have paid their due to the muses through their own creative work. There have been several such as Sir Sidney Colvin, whose critical writings, his encouragement of young artists and his concern for the proper conservation of the artistic heritage have been equally valuable contributions. A more recent example of this was Basil Gray C.B., O.B.E., who was elected in 1929 and, with one short break, remained a member until his death sixty years later in 1989. In the year of his election Gray had just returned from taking part in the British Academy excavations at Constantinople and in that year also he entered the Printed Book Department of the British Museum, which already had so many connections with Savile members. Twelve months later he transferred to the Sub-Department of Oriental Prints and Drawings. Here he soon established himself as one of the foremost scholars of the day in the study of oriental painting. After the war, at the outbreak of which he had organized the removal of the Museum's priceless collection to places of safety (a country house in Northamptonshire and Aldwych Tube Station!), he was made the first keeper of a truly independent Department of Oriental Antiquities. During the next twenty years he built up the collection so that it now ranks as one of the most important and comprehensive outside of the Orient itself.

A man of very similar tastes and professional pursuits to Basil Gray was Gerald Robert Reitlinger, who was elected to the Savile in 1932. Reitlinger was best known as the distinguished author of many books on the history of taste and the archaeology of Iraq. He was a frequent contributor of articles on these and other

Top, Sir David Low
(self portrait); bottom,
Sir Henry Moore by
his fellow member
Michael Ayrton.

"The Selecting Jury of the New English Art Club" (1909) by
Sir William Orpen, with his fellow member Sir William Rothenstein in the
centre professionally possessed.

Sir William Rothenstein by his
fellow member John Singer Sargent
in less frenetic mode.

subjects to the leading journals of the day, and his own important collection of European, Islamic, Chinese and Japanese ceramics can now be seen in the Ashmolean Museum, to which he donated them just before his death in 1978. Reitlinger, however, unlike Gray, was also a professional artist trained at the Slade and other leading art schools. Exhibitions of his work were held at various galleries and other locations including two of Rothenstein's old stamping-grounds, the New English Art Club and the Savile, where a recent exhibition staged by courtesy of the Bowmoore Gallery revealed, to the surprise of many members who had not appreciated that such an artist had once dwelt amongst them, some impressive examples of the "English Impressionists" school.

In a Club which is uncommonly used to observing polymathy in its midst there is still only one member's name which springs to mind when one is seeking for an artist who contrived in one relatively short career to achieve excellence as a painter, portraitist, sculptor, draughtsman, engraver, stage-designer, book-illustrator, novelist, short-story writer, essayist, critic, art historian, radio and television broadcaster and cinema and television film-maker. That name and those distinctions belong to Michael Ayrton, who was elected in 1943 and remained a familiar and enriching presence in the Club until his death in 1975. Paradoxically, his skills in all these several branches of art merely served to attract the ire of the British art establishment, which tended to dismiss him as a "Jack-of-all-trades" when, in fact, had its perception been keener, it might have observed that he was a master of all of them.

After an unconventional upbringing Ayrton had studied painting in Vienna, Paris and London, and travelled to Spain where he was present for the siege of Barcelona during the civil war. His career began when he returned to London in 1939 and had his first exhibition at the Zwemmer Gallery. On leave from the RAF in 1942, he created the designs for John Gielgud's production of *Macbeth* in collaboration with his great friend and fellow artist John Minton. In that year also he was invalided out of the RAF and shared an exhibition with Minton at the Leicester Galleries. From then on, despite his failing health and perhaps because of his realization that his life was to be short, he embarked on an artistic journey of dazzling brilliance and virtuosity which nevertheless brought him little official recognition. He was a man of great obsessions, exploring themes from classical mythology and elsewhere, and illustrating them in a variety of ingenious ways. He had travelled much in Greece and its landscapes inspired him as much as its legends, such as Daedalus, Icarus and the Minotaur, to produce some remarkable work ranging from pencil sketches to huge bronzes.

The Cretan Minotaur in particular was to find concrete expression in his reconstruction of a gigantic maze, replete with a seven-foot bronze Minotaur and equally impressive sculptures of Daedalus and Icarus which he created in Arkville, New York State, at the behest of an eccentric American millionaire. Meantime there had been exhibitions in Britain, the Continent, the USA and Canada which, while popular and successful, did little to dislodge the blinkers from the critics' eyes.

Flight, as is demonstrated in his treatments of the Daedalus and Icarus myths, was one of Ayrton's obsessions; Berlioz was another. Again this lengthy preoccupation was to find expression in many forms; sculptures, paintings, and a short story culminated in a memorable and idiosyncratic television programme for the BBC which he devised and narrated. Mirrors held another fascination for him and at the time of his death he was working on another BBC series exploring the imagery of mirrors and its applications to art, mathematics, philosophy, astronomy and life generally. Ayrton's literary output was similarly eclectic. He was art critic of *The Spectator* for a time and published many scholarly works, including *British Drawings* and *Hogarth's Drawings*, a monograph on *Giovanni Pisano, Sculptor* with a foreword by a former member, Henry Moore. As a poet he showed an equal talent in 1962 with *The Testament of Daedalus*, which was followed five years later by a novel on the same subject, *The Maze Maker*. Two years after that came another novel developing the theme in a modern setting, *The Midas Consequence*. In 1972 he published a remarkable collection of short stories, *Fabrications*, which wittily put on display the wide variety of his interests and his own philosophical conclusions from the sardonic observations he had made of life and art.

The publisher Tom Rosenthal, a friend of Ayrton's and a former member of the Savile, made particular mention in his obituary of Ayrton's devotion to the Club, where he was a much loved presence. His powerful appearance as he sat in conversation with his friends belied the ill-health from which he constantly suffered. His conversation was a delight, his beautiful enunciation reinforced by a matchless erudition. He only rarely revealed the bitterness he must have felt as a result of his treatment at the hands of philistines. A member recalls one of these occasions when, having purchased one of Ayrton's delightful early Greek paintings at a leading auction house, he proudly announced his bargain to the artist when he encountered him at the Savile bar the following day. "Yes," said Michael, "and if you'd stayed at the sale a bit longer you'd have seen the daubs by the chimpanzees at the London Zoo fetching ten times the price you had to pay for mine." But there were happier moments in the Club, where he was sure of finding many appreciative friends: Guy Nicholson, most critical yet appreciative connoisseur of good conversation, mourns his passing, and Anthony Storr, happily in possession of his own portrait by Ayrton, is proud to remember Ayrton's qualification that he would not embark on such works unless the sitter happened to be a particular personal friend. The Club thus now possesses fine Ayrton portraits of Kingsley Martin and C.P. Snow as well as an exquisite female nude. Others of his portraits appeared in the centenary booklet in 1968 and these, together with the above, were of Henry Moore and John Minton.

It has to be a peculiar distinction for an artist to have been singled out by Adolf Hitler for instant elimination when, as once seemed likely, his plans for the invasion of Britain came to fruition. But this unusual accolade was bestowed on (Sir) David Low, who was elected to the Club in 1945, the year that his would-be exterminator was gathered to his own reward. The New Zealand cartoonist and caricaturist who settled in England in 1919 earned this ultimate critical judgement by the savage lampoons with which he pricked the pretentions of those two arch-priests of fascism, Mussolini and Hitler, during their rise to power in the 'thirties. For the first eight years after his arrival in England, however, Low had worked as political cartoonist for the then leading London evening newspaper, *The Star*, from which platform he mercilessly ridiculed the coalition government of Lloyd George. In 1926 Lord Beaverbrook persuaded him to join the *Evening Standard*, which he did on the strict understanding that he could choose his own subject matter and express his own personal opinions without interference. He was by now increasingly finding much of this subject matter in affairs abroad which excelled in content the relatively tame political absurdities at home. Mussolini and Hitler were appropriate targets, constantly portrayed as dangerously aggressive little pip-squeaks strutting about the world stage. In 1933 the *Evening Standard* was banned from Germany and shortly afterwards from Italy also. During Lord Halifax's visit to Germany in 1937 he was told in no uncertain terms by Goebbels of the deep resentment felt by the Nazi hierarchy of British press criticism and particularly of the cartoons by Low. Halifax passed the information on but it made little difference and in the remaining pre-war years Low's cartoons achieved an even stronger influence by being reproduced throughout free Europe, the Commonwealth and the Americas.

After the war Low resigned from the *Evening Standard* and in 1950 joined the *Daily Herald*, where he indulged his fancy for depicting institutions he wished to mock as animals or other symbolic creatures. Just as the Lloyd George coalition had previously been embodied in *The Star* as a bad-tempered, double-headed ass, now the TUC was to be famously represented as a great big good-natured but rather clumsy cart-horse.

Churchill had described him as "the greatest of our modern cartoonists. The greatest because of the vividness of his political conceptions and because he possesses what few cartoonists have – a grand technique of draughtsmanship". He was not so pleased, however, when two other Savilians, Michael Powell and Emeric Pressburger, made a wartime film, *The Life and Death of Colonel Blimp*, based on a character created by Low in his cartoons to symbolize the inherently decent but bumbling nature of the British military command. Churchill tried to suppress this charming and innocuous work on the extraordinary ground that it might cause public "alarm and despondency" by depicting the very ineffectiveness which he had himself set out so vehemently to eradicate. Low contributed to many other journals as well as those already mentioned and his vast output included work for the *Manchester Guardian* and the *New Statesman* which had, as we have seen, displayed the talents or so many other Savile members. Anthologies of these cartoons were published which provide for the modern historian a revealing insight into social and political affairs of the last seventy years. They include *Lloyd George and Co (1921); Low's Political Parade (1936); Europe since Versailles (1940); Low's War Cartoons (1941); Years of Wrath; A Cartoon History, 1931-45 (1949);* and *Low Visibility: A Cartoon History, 1945-53 (1953)*.

Low died in 1963 and there are still many members who have happy recollections of him at snooker, at the long table, and in the Sandpit. More recent members can see evidence of his sharp eye and congenial clubbability in the several cartoons and caricatures of his contemporaries which hang on the Savile walls. There is a particularly fine one of that festive ichthyologist "Boully" Boulenger as a very hung-over fish, and another of a cosmically self-satisfied H.G. Wells, for whom on a previous occasion Low had provided the ten double-page illustrations for *The Autocracy of Mr Parham*. A further connection with Wells – although on the wrong side of the blanket from the Savile and literary associations – were his twelve double-page watercolour illustrations for *The Modern Rake's Progress* to a text by one of Wells's innumerable ex-*inamorate*, Rebecca West.

By way of the sort of contrast which the Savile seems always able to provide in its membership, Henry Moore, who is regarded as the foremost sculptor of modern times, was elected to the Savile in 1949 when he had just confirmed an international reputation with a major exhibition at the Museum of Modern Art in New York City. This was further reinforced, just after he had been proposed for the Club, by the award of the International Prize for Sculpture in Venice. His series of pictures of life in wartime London, particularly the "shelter drawings" commissioned while he was an official war artist during the London bombings, had already extended his fame far beyond its previous sculptural confines though there still remained a monumental quality to the figures in the scenes he depicted. He had many admirers at the Club, notably his fellow sculptor Michael Ayrton, who drew a fine pencil portrait of him for the centenary booklet in 1968. It is perhaps a pity that Ayrton and his other fellows at the Savile were unable to lure him more often away from his labours at Much Hadham, for his mastery of sculptural spaces and the surrealism of his massive figures, had he been persuaded to introduce them to Brook Street, would have made an admirable counterpoint to the Georgian elegance of Bidder's Yard and underlined the eclecticism of the members who, weather permitting, use it.

"Bidder's Yard", it should be explained, was the name by which the ground-level patio was known in the early days at Brook Street. There are no surviving records to confirm it but it was most likely named after George Parker Bidder Sc.D., who seems to have had some hand in its layout when the Club moved to Mayfair, though the *trompe l'œil* trellising on its walls is ascribed to a later member, Sir Gerald Barry. Bidder, incidentally, was a distinguished marine biologist who had been a pupil of that formidable Savilian, Sir Ray Lankester, later to follow in his footsteps by becoming president of the Marine Biological Association at Plymouth. An eccentric of nocturnal habits and the means evidently to indulge himself, it is said that in later life he bought Parker's Hotel in Naples merely for the power it gave him to forbid early morning calls for breakfast. Bidder, who was elected to the Club in 1897, remained a member until his death in 1953.

Sir David Low had harried the fascist dictators as soon as their grotesque ambitions became apparent to the rest of Europe in the 'thirties; Henry Moore had chronicled some of the tragic consequences of their attempts to achieve these ambitions during the 'forties; but Victor Weisz had been savaging them far more dangerously for himself in Berlin, the very heart of Nazism from its earliest beginnings in the late 'twenties. Weisz, better known as the cartoonist "Vicky", was elected to the Savile in 1953. He had been born in Berlin of Hungarian parents in 1913 and on the death of his father in 1928 he became the family's sole breadwinner as a cartoonist on a Berlin newspaper. One of his first works was a bitter anti-Hitler cartoon and his persistent criticisms in the same style inevitably aroused the wrath of the Nazis against this precocious fifteen-year-old. After the Reichstag fire he was sacked from his newspaper and came under constant harassment from the Gestapo. Only his Hungarian passport saved him and his family from the concentration camp. Friends managed to smuggle him out to England where he was given a brief trial on the *Daily Herald* which came to nothing for the simple and obvious reason that he could hardly speak English.

In a fortunate moment, however, he was introduced to Sir Gerald Barry, the editor of the *News Chronicle* and a prominent Savilian. In an article for the *Observer* at the time of Vicky's death in 1966, Sir Gerald was to recall what then transpired.

Vicky turned up in my office one day (in 1939, I think) suggesting himself through his agent as a cartoonist for the *News Chronicle*. His English was then almost as funny as the cartoons he brought under his arm; but he plainly possessed a wholly insufficient understanding of our manners and habits of thought to make a cartoonist for a popular British daily. Yet with the outstanding talent his drawings revealed it would have been a blunder to turn him away. So we paid him a retainer and started him off on a prolonged patient process of conditioning.

I remember his suggesting he should begin by reading all the plays of Shakespeare. Shakespeare, by all means, we said, but before that, Dickens; and before Dickens, *Alice in Wonderland*, and the nursery rhymes, and the back numbers of *Punch* and *Wisden*; and visits to the Derby and the dogs, and to the theatre and the Oval and White Hart Lane – and above all, hours and hours in the stupefying boredom of the gallery of the House. If he survived all this he would survive anything and perhaps turn himself into a cartoonist for a British newspaper into the bargain.

Well, we know what happened, I think it must have been almost two years before he actually joined the staff and we published his first cartoon. This is where his resilience, his persistence, his humility and his constant good humour came in. Time and time again in those early years, his first idea, and his second would be turned down; but always he would come up smiling with another, slyly insinuating himself and his drawing-board into my room with an expression half of despair and half of mischief.

For 14 years his cartoon appeared daily in the *News Chronicle*, during which time he became a great cartoonist and one of the greatest assets of our paper.

In the *New Statesman* Paul Johnson, a one-time member of the Savile, pointed out the essential characteristics which distinguished Vicky's work from all others:

> . . . the essence of Vicky's art was not literary but visual. It was his ability to drive below the surface of a politician's appearance, to get at the bones of his physical being in such a way as also to hint at his character, which made Vicky the greatest cartoonist of our time.
>
> He drew John Foster Dulles as a refrigerator, as a penguin, an iceberg, a tank, an eagle – and it still not only looked like Dulles, it *was* Dulles. De Gaulle he transformed into a hundred shapes and objects, but still the General's personality sprang from the page. I don't think Vicky ever failed to get a likeness, either in his cartoons, or in his more formal drawings.

Naturally there were many comparisons made between Vicky's work and that of Sir David Low and although the former deferred to the latter's superiority as a draughtsman it is possible that Vicky became more popular in the public's estimation. Their careers were also remarkably similar. After leaving the *News Chronicle* Vicky worked for the *Daily Mirror* then moved to the *Evening Standard* with the same guarantee of absolute freedom which had been accorded to Low, and from 1954 he also drew a regular weekly cartoon for the *New Statesman*. He made fun of friend and foe alike; Charles de Gaulle as a totem pole, Churchill as a Mr Micawber-like figure, a zither-playing Attlee, the White Rabbit Eden, street urchin Bevan, and above all Macmillan as "Supermac". Rather like Max Beerbohm before him, few of his victims seemed to harbour any resentment for long. That shrewd old bird Harold Macmillan probably realized that the "Supermac" image did him no harm at all. Certainly he was moved sufficiently when on a prime-ministerial visit to Moscow in 1966 he heard of Vicky's death to write:

> Vicky's tragic death has robbed British political and social life of the great cartoonist of our time . . . All of us who have enjoyed his creations, including not least the victims of some of these creations, mourn his passing. British public life will be the poorer for all of us.

Like David Low, Vicky was in the habit of intruding his own eccentric features into some of his cartoons as a puzzled onlooker of the events he was portraying. In these miniatures he was as revealing of himself as he was of all his other victims; tiny body, large head, bald on top with shaggy back and sides and large questing eyes made larger by the powerful spectacles he was forced to wear. Vicky was a member from 1953 and there are still some Savilians from that period who remember him for his wit and conviviality which did not, however, conceal his deep and compassionate involvement with the woes of the world. In 1966 he drew a bitter cartoon on the Labour Government's acquiesce to the Americans' war in Vietnam, took an overdose of sleeping pills, and died.

In the eight years which elapsed between 1945 and 1953 (the election dates of David Low and "Vicky" respectively) there had come to the Club two other artists of very different kinds. One, as we have seen, was the sculptor Henry Moore; the other was Bernard Venables, elected in 1950. Perhaps in Venables's case it is not quite accurate to write of "a different kind", for the diversity of his career in art and literature has overlapped the activities of many of his Savile contemporaries. Like David Low and Vicky he has been a cartoonist working for Express newspapers and the *Daily Mirror* – for the latter creating a strip cartoon *Crabtree the Fisherman*, subsequently expanded into a book which sold over two million copies; like Sir William Nicholson he has exhibited regularly at the Royal Academy as well as working as a poster designer and book illustrator; like Henry Moore and Michael Ayrton he has sculpted in wood and stone; and all in the intervals betimes he has indulged, to further creative effect, his twin passions for fishing and exploration.

A chat at the Savile bar in 1953 with his friend Howard Marshall, then a well-known broadcaster, resulted in the foundation of the hugely successful *Angling Times*. This was the first national newspaper to be devoted exclusively to what in its surprising and unobtrusive way is Britain's most popular leisure pursuit. During his nine years as editorial director of this venture he also wrote, designed, illustrated and did the typography of *The Angler's Companion* and other titles. In 1963 Venables launched a more "up-market" glossy, *Creel Magazine*, of which he was editor, sub-editor, typographer, leader writer, columnist, diarist, illustrator and designer. A mural in the Sheraton Hotel in Kathmandu is a permanent memento of a visit he made there to exhibit his watercolours, while his book *Coming down the Zambesi* is a record of his journey along all the course of that river, much of it on foot. Two seasons spent dangerously in small open boats with the primitive whalers of the Azores resulted in another book, *Baleia! The Whalers of the Azores*. In between times Venables has written nature and country scripts for BBC Radio and contributed to television on the subject of fishing. At the age of 85 and still busy, he is about to publish his autobiography.

One of the most talented and versatile artists of recent years was that effervescent and infinitely entertaining Savilian, Merlyn Evans, who was elected to the Club in 1955. Born in Wales and brought up in Scotland, he had all the creative verve of the Celt – passionate and intellectual intensity leavened by an impish sense of humour and a keen appreciation of good cheer.

Merlyn had studied at the Glasgow School of Art and, on a Royal Exhibition, at the Royal College of Art in London. He had visited Berlin, Copenhagen, and Paris on a travelling scholarship, and on regular visits to the latter had spent much time with many of the artists whose influences were to be absorbed and translated into his own unique style; in particular Mondrian, Kandinsky, Giacometti, Max Ernst, and William Hayter. In 1936 he exhibited with the London Group and at the notorious International Surrealist Exhibition in London. In 1937 he exhibited at the Salon de Mai, Paris; the Artists' International Association; the London Group and the "Surrealist Objects and Poems" exhibition at the London Gallery.

But just as his career was beginning to bloom he moved to South Africa to become lecturer in Art at Natal Technical College, and when the war intervened he served with the 8th Army in North Africa and Italy. Throughout the campaigns he contrived to continue painting and drawing, and when posted to Rome in 1945 he took the opportunity to become acquainted with Giorgio de Chirico, of whom he has left a particularly fine portrait. After the war he continued to have regular exhibitions, most notably at the Leicester Gallery and the St George's Gallery though his work was also exhibited abroad in Brazil and in several cities throughout the USA.

Evans had experimented with sculpturing in the early 'thirties and one of the later results of this is a superb black steel screen he made for Tower Hamlets Comprehensive School in 1964. This sculptural influence is also plain to be seen in many of his paintings and graphics, especially in his early works. Mel Gooding, in a perceptive introduction to the catalogue for Merlyn Evans's retrospective exhibition at the Mayor Gallery and the Redfern Gallery in 1988, wrote:

> The man behind all this creative effort was many-sided and complex . . . He had a love of convivial company, of argument and analysis and speculation. Few artists of his – or any later – generation could match the breadth and depth of his interests; in psychology, in optics, in philosophy, in politics, in the history and techniques of art; or the generosity with which he shared his enthusiasms. . . . [His] talk illuminated everything it touched and brought new and unexpected insights to play upon the matter in hand and much else besides; he could be sardonically irreverent and witty. He was imbued too with the writings of the great moderns; Kafka, Eliot, Joyce, Pound, Wyndham Lewis, Auden, and the poetry of his contemporaries, MacNeice, Day-Lewis, Dylan Thomas. He wrote a great deal of poetry, mostly for himself and his friends but much of it deserving a much wider audience. He could play the piano and the trumpet well enough to amuse himself and others with stylish pastiches and jazzy improvisations . . .

Those last remarks will strike a chord with Savilians who were his boon companions in the 'sixties. On those evenings when the "night-tray" was exhausted (then the only source of drink after the bar had closed in the dry days without a night porter) Merlyn would gather his companions together and whisk them to a decommissioned mission hall in Hampstead which he had purchased in 1963 and converted into a studio. There, apart from his artistic paraphernalia, he had installed a well-stocked bar, a slightly out-of-tune cottage piano and, of course, his trumpet; on one or other of the latter two he would perform or, as he went about replenishing glasses, spout reams of verse which sounded like Eliot or Auden and sometimes was, and the party would continue until dawn, or until the last exhausted guest had tottered back home to bed.

In 1959 C.P. Snow and Harry Hoff proposed (Sir) Sidney Nolan for temporary membership and in 1960 he proceeded to full membership. Although this great Australian artist remained a member for nearly seven years his attendances at the Club were infrequent. A more consistent visitor to Brook Street was Fred Uhlman, who was elected in 1962. Uhlman was born in Stuttgart in 1901 and took a doctorate of law at Tübingen in 1924. In 1933, as a result of the upsurge of Nazism, he was forced to flee to France where on the advice of the painter Paul Elsas he began to paint professionally. In 1936 he held his first important exhibition at Galerie Le Niveu and then left France to settle in England. In 1938 he held his first British exhibition at the Zwemmer Gallery and though at the outbreak of war in 1939 he was interned as "an enemy alien" he managed further exhibitions at the Leicester Galleries and the Redfern Gallery. After the war he went to live in Wales and continued to exhibit regularly at major galleries throughout Great Britain. His paintings thereafter owed much to the landscape surrounding the valley in Snowdonia where he had gone to live in a converted 17th century barn. Although he had travelled widely throughout Europe and elsewhere he claimed that his local terrain has as much to offer for a landscape artist as anything to be found in France, Italy, Spain, Greece, China or India. He was not alone in this, for the same valley was used during his time there for the Chinese location shots in the film *Inn of the Sixth Happiness*, which starred his fellow Savilian Robert Donat. On his regular visits to the Club from his Welsh eyrie he could, despite his diminutive size, be a daunting presence: his highly coloured weather-beaten face, topped off with a shock of wild white hair coupled with an excitable manner, gave the impression of an incensed hornet, while the churchwarden pipe, nearly as long as himself, with which he energetically gesticulated to emphasize his conversational points, seemed likely at any moment to be transformed into a particularly lethal sting. This was misleading, for he was a truly kind and modest man. He has left an autobiography, *The Making of an Englishman*, and his works are to be seen in several public collections which include the British Museum; the Victoria and Albert Museum; the art galleries of Manchester, Swansea, Newport, York and others in England, France, Germany, Australia and New Zealand.

Art patrons and gallery owners have also figured in the Savile membership over the years. Cyril Flower, later Lord Battersea, was a noted patron of the arts in the early days of the Club as was a founder member, Charles S. Roundel, of whom Sir Herbert Stephen wrote in his 1923 memoir that he was "extremely well known as a Member of Parliament and what in earlier days would have been described as a patron of the arts". The activities of many other patrons and collectors have already been mentioned and these Club connections with painting and its associated visual arts have persisted to the present day. In recent years Maurice Goldman (elected in 1951) was a notable collector while giving dedicated service to the Club's Art

Committee. Nigel Foxell has had the often thankless task of chairing that committee for as long as anyone can remember, and with his fellow committee member Robert Lewin staged many of the (often controversial) exhibitions which have been a feature of Savilian life for several decades. Robert Lewin (elected in 1979) has also been for several years the guiding force, with his wife Rena, behind the Brook Street Gallery whence have come many noteworthy exhibitions in the bar and Sandpit that engendered various emotions and enlivened press comments about activities within the Club.

Another gallery owner, Anthony d'Offay, was first elected to the Savile in 1969, seven years after he had begun dealing in modern British art. In 1977, after his marriage to a curator of modern art at the Tate, he turned his attention to modern art world-wide. In 1980 he opened his now well-known gallery in Dering Street, hard by the Savile, with an exhibition of Joseph Beuys. From this prestigious beginning he has gone on to represent many of the world's leading names in contemporary painting: Carl André, Georg Baselitz, William de Kooning, Leon Kossoff, Andy Warhol and Gilbert and George among them.

The Estoricks, *père et fils*, are also involved in the art world, both commercially and creatively. Dr Eric Elihu Estorick is now proprietor of (among others) the Grosvenor Galleries where, under previous ownership, Michael Ayrton's work was represented and regularly exhibited. His son Michael Estorick, who has been a member since 1979 (and reversed the usual sequence by proposing his father for the Club in 1985), has studied at the City and Guilds and written two novels.

George Aczel has brought to the Club something of the flavour of pre-war Vienna, where he studied art, both by his presence, which dates from his election in 1977, and in his colourful still-lifes which decorate some of the Club rooms. Known affectionately to some of his colleagues and friends throughout the international art world as "the Hungarian rhapsody", he rebukes yet absolves anyone who dares address him thus with the mock-stern rejoinder ". . . from now on you are my enemy".

In a foreword to the catalogue of an exhibition of George Aczel's pictures at the Brook Street Gallery in 1975 Nicholas Guppy spoke of Aczel's floral paintings as ". . . personal, direct evocations of a mind that is romantic and sensitive, poured out in the form of exuberant bouquets as magically fresh as the blossoms of a real springtime", adding that "Psychologists believe that we gain happiness by recreating the joys of our childhood, so perhaps these flowers are the essence of the far-off days when his mother brought narcissi and tulips, lilacs and roses straight in from the garden". That garden was in a part of Hungary which is now in Yugoslavia where George was born in 1907. Whatever the source of his inspiration it seems to come to him at all hours of the day or, more usually, the night when, if no suitable blank canvas happens to be handy, he is quite content to use old newspapers to express his creative urge. "I use anything," he avers. Many an unwary guest at the Club has therefore been startled when admiring one or other of his works to see the Stock Exchange listings from the *Financial Times* peeping out at them from behind the foliage. Such eccentricities, however, have not prevented his work from being highly regarded on the international art market and he has exhibited in many of the leading galleries throughout the UK and the Continent, including the Royal Academy, the Paris Salon, and the Petit Palais in Geneva, as well as having major exhibitions in the USA and Japan.

Aczel was educated in Hungary, France and Italy, and finally at Vienna University where as well as pursuing his own apprenticeship as a painter he studied chemistry and the history of art. These were the essential qualifications for him to continue a family tradition going back over four generations of adding the art of picture restoration to his own original creative work. As a consequence George Aczel is now recognized not only as a painter of worth but as one of the foremost picture restorers. He specializes in the Dutch and Spanish schools but his knowledge of earlier methods and materials extends far beyond them for he has restored Byzantine icons in Athens, Renaissance oils in Florence and Vienna, Impressionists in Paris, Victorian watercolours in London and much else.

Painters, as can be seen, have not been numerically prominent among the men "of different professions" who have made up the membership of the Savile over the years. Certainly their proportionate presence cannot be compared with that of artists in other spheres, but what they have lacked in numbers has been more than adequately compensated by the quality of their work. It is possible, also, that the regular exhibitions staged in the 'eighties by the Arts Committee encouraged a younger generation of painters to swell the ranks of a Club which either through default or false modesty has never sought to be identified with any single profession, particularly theirs. An indication that this might be so is provided by the experience of the most recent painter to be elected to the Savile. Alexander Sempliner was brought to Brook Street as a guest of Brian Dowling in 1990 when he was much taken with a collection of prints by the Catalan artist Joan Miro, whom he greatly admires, and which happened to be on exhibition at the time in the bar and Sandpit. On a tour of other Club rooms conducted by his host, Sempliner was again surprised to see works by Savile members such as Sir William Nicholson, Max Beerbohm, and others. Having already been advised by an acquaintance who was a member of Buck's that the Savile provided a congenial home for "arty types", and by another who was a member of Boodle's that "at the Savile one is sure to meet someone more intelligent than oneself", he readily responded to Dowling's offer to propose him for membership. He is now himself a member of the Art Committee, bent on building up a representative collection of his predecessors' work for permanent display in the Club rooms. In his own work Sempliner specializes in large "colour-field" paintings and smaller painted collages; he is represented in galleries in London, New York, Berlin and The Hague. It is good to know that sister clubs like Buck's and Boodle's are happy to recruit such members on the Savile's behalf.

Sir Henry Irving, the first actor to be knighted and the first of a large company
of actors who have been members of the Savile.

CHAPTER SIX

Radio; Television; Theatre

As the previous short history and index of Savile members was being prepared for the printers in 1923, another piece of history was being made not very far away from the Clubhouse in Piccadilly. It was one which was to produce profound reverberations within the future pattern of membership. Sir Archibald Campbell Swinton, a member of the Savile from 1904-1908, was delivering a paper to the Radio Society of Great Britain of which he was then president; it consisted of his observations on some of the practical applications of cathode-rays when conjoined to the oscillograph. Among the audience who had come to hear him were three young men who years later were to be contemporaries at the Savile and who were all to become distinguished in associated spheres: Sir Arthur Vick, Sir John Cockcroft, and the then sixteen years old Dallas Bower. Each, for his own separate reasons, had been drawn to this presentation because of the powerful reputation of the lecturer whose skill at estimating the value of new scientific discoveries and exploiting more sophisticated applications of them had already led to such diverse developments as the construction of the first steam turbine engine and the medical applications of radiography. His subject matter on this occasion, with his revelation of its implicit potential, was to expedite the inventions of television, radar and the computer screen.

Cockcroft and Vick were to go on to establish themselves in other branches of physics, as we have seen. The presence of Dallas Bower, however, presaged the manner in which he and many of his artistically oriented fellows at the Savile would be expressing themselves in future years through the new media which were to be developed as a result of the theories being outlined at that meeting.

Dallas Bower was, indeed, to become the first television producer/director in Britain's broadcasting history when, fourteen years later, on 2 November 1936, from primitive studios in Alexandra Palace he produced the opening programme that launched BBC Television as a regular service. In his own way he was following in the pioneering tradition of his Scottish ancestor, George M. Dallas, an emigrant to the United States who became American vice-president in 1845 when the newly annexed State of Texas named its capital after him. Perhaps it was as well that he could not have foreseen then the hideous use to which American television would put that location and his ancestor's name in a dire dramatic series of the future.

In those first days of British TV, all programmes had to be broadcast not only live but twice. Because of government indecision, the Baird 204-line system and the Marconi-EMI Emitron 405-line standard operated alternately, even though all involved in those early broadcasts claimed the Marconi system was the more opportunity at the BBC three years earlier. Maschwitz, who had himself been elected to the Savile in 1929, was a man of many parts, and one of that rapidly growing Savilian band who were so essential to the foundation and future development of British broadcasting.

The list of his other accomplishments, as journalist, novelist, lyricist, producer and theatrical impresario is all the more considerable in light of the enormous body of work which he contributed to the BBC. He was, as we have seen, editor of the *Radio Times* for a short period before proceeding to create a great body of light entertainment programmes for the wavelength which was throughout the war, and for many years after, entirely devoted to this morale-boosting exercise. He wrote several novels with Val Gielgud under the *nom de plume* of Holt Marvel, and adapted and produced, for radio, *Carnival* from a novel by his friend and fellow Savilian, Compton Mackenzie. As a lyricist he tugged the heart-strings of a war-time generation with songs such as *A Nightingale Sang in Berkeley Square*, and *These Foolish Things*, while as a theatrical impresario his most enduringly memorable show was probably *Goodnight Vienna*.

In the latter years of the war, about the time that Dallas Bower was elected, the influx of BBC personnel to the Club accelerated. While generally adding to the distinction of the existing membership, it caused some of the already well entrenched incumbents to wonder whether they were about to be inundated by one particular "profession" as they had so nearly been by the disproportionate medical intake in the 'thirties. This led to discontented murmuring and speculation as to whether steps should once again be taken to preserve the original principle of "different professions" in more or less equal proportions. For a time, thereafter, it became a positive disadvantage for a proposer to have to confess that his candidate was an employee of the BBC. Nevertheless the BBC bandwagon continued to roll on into Brook Street so it is perhaps all the more to the credit of those who did manage to be elected that their other personal qualities over and above their professional eminence contrived to steer them past an increasingly stringent election committee.

In 1942, for instance, the year before Dallas Bower was elected, four senior figures from different departments within the Corporation became members of the Savile: Richard Howgill, Sir Gerald Beadle, Edward Sackville-West, and Howard Marshall.

Richard Howgill has been mentioned elsewhere for his work as Controller of Music for the BBC when he commissioned his fellow Savilian William Alwyn's 3rd Symphony, and was instrumental in bringing William Walton's work to the attention of a wider public through the broadcasts of *Belshazzar's Feast* and *Troilus and Cressida*. An authority on brass bands, he was, in the words of Dallas Bower, "a fine example of the BBC 'career man' ".

Sir Gerald Beadle was yet another prime example of this new genus, the BBC career man. He had spent his professional life at the BBC, most of it in charge of the West Region in Bristol where he adopted the role of robust, no-nonsense countryman. At the Club, and later at White City, he liked to reinforce this impression by wearing suitably rustic tweeds. He must have possessed more sophisticated qualities, however, for in 1956 when the Corporation was facing increasingly stiff competition from the mushroom growth of ITV he was the man chosen to replace George Barnes as director of BBC television. According to Dallas Bower he had in fact been offered this position twice before, but had turned it down in favour of remaining in his beloved West Country where he kept his main home. When in London, he lived at the Club where, in No. 1 bedroom, he set up the first television set to be seen in Brook Street and invited any of his interested fellow members to view it if they wished. As he himself was notorious for his dislike of watching television these occasions must have been solitary vigils for the chosen few.

Although Beadle's appointment had caused some surprise, the combination of this bucolic and sturdy Savilian with the more ebullient and urbane Kenneth Adam as programme controller had the desired effect and viewing figures improved. Beadle was, for instance, a cautious but nevertheless effective supporter of a later Savilian, (Sir) Huw Wheldon, in his campaign to produce high quality programmes about the arts on a regular basis, if only – so it is said – to steal a march on the rival independent channel.

Beadle presided over a most important period of development for the television service of the BBC and his sterling work established it for many years after as the cynosure of similar organizations throughout the world. His own detached attitude to the medium evidently softened, however, for in a letter to Huw Wheldon congratulating him on his knighthood he admitted that he was watching many more programmes – now he was retired.

Second among that quartet of BBC men admitted to the Savile in 1942 (although he would never willingly have played second fiddle to anyone) was that model aristocrat, littérateur, musician, critic and wit, Edward Charles Sackville-West, fifth Baron Sackville.

Heir to Knole, one of the greatest and grandest of England's historic houses, he was a man of great sensibility who expressed himself in ways which may have seemed remote from those of the general run of great families in his time. At Eton he had displayed precocious gifts as a pianist and it was thought that had he wished he could have embarked on a highly successful musical career. His preferences, however, were literary and after studying at Oxford and travelling extensively in Europe, acquiring on the way a thorough appreciation of art and knowledge of languages, he produced his first novel whose title, significantly, was *Piano Quintet*. This was followed by *The Ruin*, a 'Gothic novel' whose settings were redolent of his upbringing at Knole; and *Simpson,* a perceptive fictional account of an English nanny which many believed would establish him as a potent force on the literary scene. Sackville-West's next book, published in 1936, was *A Flame in Sunlight*, a critical biography of De Quincey which was awarded the James Tait Black Memorial prize and remains to this day a most highly regarded work on the subject. At the outbreak of war in 1939 he joined the features and drama department of the BBC. The functions of this department were regarded as greatly 'one of Howard's boys'. Eventually he suppressed his doubts, accepted and was sent on a commentators' training course. He was given a major's uniform and to the surprise of his friends (the assignment had been kept secret) appeared in it at the Club. But within a week of this sensation, he had received a letter from the Director General forbidding him to go.

This background is necessary to appreciate fully the degree of relish behind the following 1944 entries:

31st August

Howard Marshall sent home by SHAEF!

4th September

At lunch, Savile, discussing our army Victory Week programme – and there is *Howard* back, looking a little sheepish but on the whole making a good story about his having been summoned back by SHAEF for broadcasting from Paris without censorship – he tried to cross streets under fire to find the censor, etc. The stuff was colour only... Then I tell the story at dinner to Alan Barlow, saying that after all Howard knows as much about censorship as the censor. And *of course* being the Savile a faint repetition of this last phrase from my right reminds me that I am sitting next to Col George....the censor! His version is that no secrets were given away, of course, but it was letting down the other correspondents...

Howard Marshall went on in peacetime to become one of the best known radio commentators on great state occasions and other outside broadcasts. Edward Ward, a later member (elected 1963) who succeeded to the title of Viscount Bangor in 1950, was another distinguished radio correspondent of the war years, reporting the Allied armies' victorious progress through the European campaign of liberation.

Wynford Vaughan Thomas, who is mentioned elsewhere as one of the wittier ornaments of the Savile in recent years, was yet another member who having been employed by the BBC in quite another capacity suddenly found himself in the unfamiliar role of war correspondent. He had entered the BBC in 1937, "going in by the back door" as he put it, by joining the regional office in Cardiff with the less than princely title of "Outside Broadcasts Assistant". Having arrived into what he called "the new Kingdom of Talk", however, his natural talents, eloquence, humour and intellect soon established him as a sovereign figure. Above all he was himself a fascinating and indefatigable talker, so for decades thereafter Wynford Vaughan Thomas's voice was to be heard prominently in every major outside broadcast undertaken by the BBC.

On the outbreak of war in 1939 he was moved to London and employed as a home front reporter through the blitz period and afterwards.

In 1943, with his engineer colleague Reg Pidsley, he flew in a Lancaster bomber in a night raid on Berlin, and returned with a sensational set of recordings which brought home to every listener with vivid reality the agonizing and gruelling nature of such an experience, and the perils faced by the aircrews.

Later, on the Italian front, he covered the Anzio landings – about which he wrote a book – and the Allied entry into Rome. The closing stages of the war found him giving a dramatic running commentary on the crossing of the Rhine by Montgomery's forces, and reporting on the final chase across north-west Germany. He felt that his war reporting career reached its climax on the evening when, in Hamburg, he broadcast over the BBC from a studio used up to only a day or two previously by the traitor William Joyce who – known in Britain as "Lord Haw-Haw" – had for years been pouring out Nazi propaganda in English language programmes over the air. Wynford used to say he felt in that studio that he was receiving his own symbolic surrender. His war services earned him the Croix de Guerre in 1945; perhaps it "won" him even more than that for he was fond of prefacing his reminiscences of the period after the Normandy invasion with "When I liberated Burgundy..." and his wine cellar for many years testified that there was some truth beneath the jest.

After the war he turned freelance, but maintained very close links with the BBC and broadcast extensively in a wide range of programmes reaching far beyond ordinary journalism. He covered the granting of independence to India, and some of its aftermath. "At times I was little more than an unofficial corpse-counter", he would recall. He travelled overseas with the Royal Family, reporting not so much on the day-to-day events of the tour, but giving to his audiences vivid impressions of the countries concerned.

During this period also, he broadened his activities by writing and lecturing on subjects near to his heart, particularly those to do with the history, culture, and countryside of his native Wales. In 1968, together with others of like mind, he formed the Harlech consortium which won the Independent Television contract for Wales and the West of England, and for the next three years he served as programme director for Harlech Television in Cardiff, doing much to get the new company firmly established.

Wynford was a many-faceted man as is evidenced by the variety of organizations with which he was associated after his permanent return to Wales. He served on the Welsh Arts Council, and was a director of the Welsh National Opera. He was chairman of the Council for the Preservation of Rural Wales, patron of Great Little Trains of Wales, and a member of the Gorsedd of Bards. In addition, he was president of the Contemporary Arts Society, and a governor of the British Film Institute from 1977 to 1980.

The Times in its obituary referred to Wynford as "one of the foremost raconteurs of our time" and indeed it was a dazzling experience to come into the Club when he was present and in full spate to be caught up in coruscating accounts of historical events he had attended or the wide range of people he had known.

One of Wynford's close friends and partners in setting up the Harlech TV consortium was that outstanding journalist John Morgan, who became a member of the Savile in 1977.

Like Wynford Vaughan Thomas, John Morgan had the Welshman's gift of mesmerizing eloquence. He had been a key presenter on the BBC's *Panorama*

287

Empire and Commonwealth. It was Gilliam who first brought Dylan Thomas's potential to the attention of the BBC, as he did also for Louis MacNeice whom Dallas Bower was to use so strikingly in those great wartime broadcasts of *Alexander Nevsky* and *Christopher Columbus*. Gilliam too had been instrumental in attracting Stephen Potter – already a well-established Savile member – into the BBC features department and for first employing a later member of the Savile, Geoffrey Bridson (elected 1958), as a documentary producer. Bridson is best known for his celebrated *March of the Forty Eight*, although he also wrote a well received critical work on Wyndham Lewis. Meantime there had been several key figures quietly ensconced at the Savile. Sir Lindsay Wellington, for instance, had been elected in 1946; he had made his career in radio and became Director of Sound Broadcasting, being knighted for his services.

The year after Bridson's election there came as a member George Ivan Smith, who has distinguished himself in several careers at once: as broadcaster, diplomat, political commentator and journalist, in all of these activities directing his efforts to the development and improvement of Commonwealth relations. As a broadcaster he was initially employed in this country as the first Director of BBC Overseas on loan from Australia, where he founded Radio Australia in 1939. As a diplomat he was a United Nations official in South Africa in 1965 when he was nominated by several African countries to stand for the post of secretary-general in the newly created Commonwealth. His opponent was Arnold Smith and, sadly, in the "battle of the Smiths", Arnold won.

George Ivan Smith, however, provides an intriguing memoir of life at the Savile in the immediate post-war period when some of those members and their guests who were engaged in clearing up the mess and trying to put the world to rights might be seen relaxing occasionally at the Savile.

> Dag Hammarskjold came at least three times as my guest to the Club when I had become Director of United Nations office London, but I doubt if Club members ever knew the name of that guest.
>
> It was very different when I took Danny Kaye to lunch at the Club. In 1956 Danny had been helping the UN Children's Fund with his film. He was delighted by the wonderful British sense of reserve used by our Club members when his well-known person appeared. I suppose I was a little stuffily formal myself. To Lindsay Wellington I said . . . "May I introduce my guest Danny Kaye?" Lindsay: "How do you do, Mr. Kaye . . . a visitor to London?" I suppose Lindsay had tongue in cheek too but Danny loved it and also when as we were leaving, Denzil Batchelor, a wonderful, jovial brilliant man, came quickly across our tiled front hall and almost from a hidden corner of his mouth said, "May I have your autograph sir? If I am seen asking for it I may be blown out of the Club, but if I do not get it my son will cut me out of his will." He got it. We had looked in at the library. It was a moment when a few members had closed their eyes in armchairs. Danny mimed his tip-toed exit as though

leaving a funeral parlour and brought the scene back to life again a few nights later when we were guests at a particularly stiff dinner given by about a dozen rigid Dutch politicians at the Hague. Everyone bowed and coughed quietly behind hands. Halfway through Danny called aloud to me at the far end of the table . . . "George. Isn't this just a lovely atmosphere? . . . just like the library at the Savile Club".

The most moving event of its kind was when Garfield Todd made his first return visit to London after he had been kept under house arrest in Rhodesia because of the courageous stand he had taken against Ian Smith's UDI and long before that against the treatment of Africans by a minority of Europeans who abused human rights. I had known Garfield when I was UN roving Ambassador in Southern Africa 1960-64 and covered the ever-erupting Rhodesians too. On his second day Garfield came to the Club. We were sitting at the Sandpit, James Cameron, one of the greatest journalists of this century, came through, took a quick double-take, came and stood before Garfield and said "It is an honour to have you in this Club". Garfield was visibly moved and told me later how much this meant because he had long regarded James as the greatest champion of human freedom and never before had met him.

I had a visiting American whose first love happened to be theatre. We sat alone at one large round table at the Savile. Two others joined us and I saw my guest go white when one newcomer, as is our habit introduced his guest and I mine. In a booming voice heard so clearly from world stages Sir Ralph Richardson announced his guest, Sir John Gielgud. I had to help my guest to his car.

But such is the Savile.

Given the eclecticism of the membership and the BBC's enormous requirements from such a variety of "different professions" it is not surprising that the two institutions have maintained a fairly close connection since the earliest days of broadcasting. A glance at the present membership list reveals that the relationship still remains a rewarding one. Names such as Michael Peacock, John Turtle, Aubrey Singer, Alan Protheroe and many others, speak of the influence Club members have exerted – and still exert – on the fortunes of what is probably the most widely admired broadcasting institution in the world.

Michael Peacock, for instance, has been successively editor of *Panorama,* editor of BBC television news, and controller of BBC 1. When he was elected to the Savile in 1968 he had changed channels to become managing director of Weekend Television Ltd and is now in charge of his own production company. He has also made himself felt on other channels and wavelengths by consistently winning races with his yacht *Juno.*

John Turtle (elected 1979) has been a senior producer and editor of consumer affairs programmes, particularly of the investigative kind which the BBC pioneered, and after a period with the television service became head of the BBC's radio training department and is currently presenter of *Learning World* on the World Service. Aubrey Singer (elected 1985) has exerted a powerful influence during a long career at the BBC. This has encompassed periods as head of the features department, controller of BBC 2, managing director of BBC radio, deputy director general, and managing director BBC television. He was awarded the C.B.E. for his services and is currently chairman and managing director of White City Films.

Alan Protheroe (elected 1986) began as a reporter with BBC News and has been successively editor of news and current affairs and assistant director general while producing, directing, and presenting a wide variety of films and radio programmes.

Savile members' influence on sound and television broadcasting, however, has not been confined to the BBC alone. There have been many others who have profoundly affected the development of the independent sector. Wynford Vaughan Thomas and those associated with the foundation of Harlech television have already been mentioned but other names spring out when combing through the lists of past and present members: Sidney Bernstein (elected in 1946) for instance, was one of the founders of Granada Television, and Sir Denis Forman (elected 1949) under whose direction this company established itself as one of Britain's leading broadcasters whose high quality productions established through the national network an enviable reputation far beyond its own original northern territory.

Graham Benson (elected 1981) has been controller of drama at TVS where, under his aegis, several notable plays and series have also been enjoyed by a wider audience through the networking system. He has added to this the chairmanship of the British Academy of Film and Television Arts (BAFTA), whose present incumbent is Richard Price, elected to the Club in 1980.

But it is another member, the late Sir Huw Wheldon, elected in 1950, who comes to mind when one seeks to summarize the achievements of Savile members. Wheldon not only had a profound influence on British television which set a high tone of excellence for a generation but through such standard-bearing arts programmes as *Monitor* he also paid tribute to the work of many other Savilians: Arthur Bliss, Michael Ayrton, William Alwyn, and E.M. Forster among them. Although Sir David Attenborough referred to Wheldon as "the best director general the BBC never had", his achievements nevertheless were remarkable.

It was not until two years after he was elected to the Savile that Wheldon made a late entry to the BBC. Previously he had been Arts Council Director for Wales where his work with the Festival of Britain (masterminded by another Savilian, Sir Gerald Barry), earned him an O.B.E. In this period immediately after the war television was being brought to life again after nearly six years of blank screens. Wheldon's interest in film drew him towards television and in 1952 he joined the publicity department of the BBC in the hope of "jumping sideways into programmes".

As in the case of Wynford Vaughan Thomas and John Morgan, Wheldon's Welsh eloquence served him well and soon he had his wish and was making a name for himself as a presenter. He first attracted attention with *All Your Own,* a programme for children in which his pleasing personality established an instant *rapport* with interviewees and viewers alike. But it was with *Monitor* in the years between 1958 and 1964 that he consolidated his position and made his name. Since 1957 there had been talk of creating a new magazine for late-night viewing and the concept slowly developed into an arts format which it was suggested should be "highly sophisticated but appealing to a wider audience than third programme types". Several presenters were considered before Huw Wheldon was finally chosen but it was not until Sir Gerald Beadle became interested that this talk was translated into action. Beadle's motive was undoubtedly to compete more strenuously with the newly created independent television stations but his decision to go ahead resulted in the creation of some of the most distinguished programmes ever to be seen on television, the success of which was due not least to the skill and style of their presenter. Among the several Savilians whose work was featured in those early trail-blazing programmes was Sir Arthur Bliss, who afterwards suggested to Wheldon that a documentary on the life and work of Elgar might be made. This resulted in a fine film directed by Ken Russell, who followed this up with one about another Savilian composer, Frederic Delius.

Wheldon's talents were not expressed through *Monitor* alone. He "invented" *Civilization,* that notable series presented by Lord Clark, and was involved as producer and presenter in a sequence of productions over the years. Among them were *Men in Battle, Portraits of Power, Orson Welles, Sketch Book* and, after his retirement, *Royal Heritage* and *Destination D-Day.*

In combination with managerial capacity, his gifts had marked him for advancement. In 1962 he became Head of Documentary Programmes, a post enlarged to Head of Music and Documentary Programmes the following year. From 1965 to 1968 he was Controller of Programmes, and in the latter year he succeeded Kenneth Adam – an early admirer – as director of BBC Television, a post later re-designated as managing director.

Wheldon was now in command of one of the largest broadcasting enterprises in the world and he set himself to preserve it and enhance it as the one which would have also the highest and most exacting standards. He was sometimes referred to as "the last of the great actor/managers" but he was much more than that. His brilliance as a performer was matched by his skill as an administrator, which was reminiscent, some said, of his military experience when during the war he had served with the Royal Welsh Fusiliers in North Africa, Western Europe, and the Middle East, winning the MC and being with the Airborne Division at Arnhem. On retirement, he presided over the Court of Governors of his *alma mater,* the London School of Economics.

The Royal Television Society awarded him its Gold Medal for services to television in 1976. The next year saw the screening of the series *Royal Heritage,* which he presented, and in 1978 the Society awarded him its Silver Medal for creative achievement in front of the camera. From 1979 to 1985 he was President of the Society.

Beyond broadcasting Wheldon's interests spread wide, embracing trusteeships of the National Portrait Gallery and of the Royal Botanic Gardens, Kew. In retirement he did much work in connection with educational and communications bodies on both sides of the Atlantic. He was awarded an International Emmy in 1981.

The social life of the Club has thus been enhanced over the years by men who have put their various professional skills to use developing and enhancing the art of broadcasting in Britain. Sir Huw Wheldon is only a more recent example of those who have contributed so greatly to its present excellence for as we have seen there have been many others who had been responsible for notable developments in the years preceding his election: Sir Adrian Boult, who, as director of music at the BBC in the 'thirties, was responsible for forming the world-famous BBC Symphony Orchestra, of which many years he was principal conductor; Sir Arthur Bliss who laid out the blueprint for the Third Programme (Radio 3) which another Savilian, Sir Anthony Lewis, was later to realize. Indeed, an examination of the history of nearly every branch of broadcasting yields up the names of many Savilians who have played a crucial part in either its creation or development and a glance at the present membership list provides a hint that in the future there may be many more.

With so many broadcasters, writers and artists of several kinds being drawn to the Club over the years it is not surprising that there came to complement them many members concerned with the theatre or cinema either as producers, directors, or actors.

The Savile's connection with the theatre began sonorously with the election in 1875 of Sir Henry Irving, fresh from his triumphant season at the Lyceum with *The Bells*. Sir Herbert Stephen in his 1923 memoir of the Club states: "He never made much use of the Club which indeed has at no time been greatly frequented by members arriving later than 11pm, but he continued to be a member until his death in 1906." Irving made much more use of the Garrick, which catered particularly for the needs of actors, but nevertheless he maintained close connections with many friends and acquaintances at the Savile who figured more prominently in his professional and domestic life than they did at the Club. Edmund Gosse was a great admirer though Irving's distaste for the plays of Ibsen which Gosse had translated may have strained their friendship. Irving had said that he understood from one authority that "one of the qualifications for playing Ibsen is to have no fear of making yourself 'acutely ridiculous' ", and he had no intention of going along with the prevailing fashion. In his own effort to combat the craze for this gloomy Scandinavian which seemed to be sweeping London he sought everywhere for plays more suitable to his own temperament which he might put on at the Lyceum. In 1891 his fellow Savilian Thomas Hardy sent him an adaptation of one of his novels, eager for his opinion but diffidently suggesting that perhaps "there is too much actuality in it for the romantic Lyceum". Irving evidently agreed but turned it down more probably because it did not contain a sufficiently meaty part for him to play. The rejection must have been gentle, however, for Hardy wrote to thank him saying "...it was all the more kind of you to consider it so carefully". W.E. Henley and Robert Louis Stevenson, before the dramatic rift in their friendship, had collaborated on the new version of the play *Robert Macaire* but for similar reasons when Irving revived it he played it in Lemaître's original version. Hardy's friend, fellow Savilian and man of the theatre, Walter Pollock, went along to see it and thought it very fine and impressive, though other critics and more crucially the public took a different view. A critic who harboured a great aversion to Irving's style of acting in *any* play was Henry James, whose blistering attacks on it must have made their encounters at the Club quite memorable. Shortly after James had made his stately progress from Paris to London and subsequently the Savile in 1875 he began to contribute unsigned articles on the state of the theatre in both capitals to American journals and newspapers. Like many Americans he became besotted with the cultural life of Paris, particularly with the grace and polish of the Comédie Française, which, unusually for his class of transatlantic snob, had the effect of souring his opinions of what was on offer in London. In a splendid comment, Irving's son and biographer records: "...he approached the London theatre in the frame of mind of a man, who having dined exquisitely at Lapérouse is forced to eat a cut off the joint with the appropriate vegetables in a London coffee house. 'There is a want of delicacy', [James] said, 'in speaking of the first theatre in the world one day and of the London stage the next ... if you talk about one you forfeit the right to talk about the other.' " He was perplexed by Irving's method and though he purported to be objective his reviews were scathing. To an American paper, *The Nation*, he contributed the following typical response to Irving's performance of *Macbeth*:

> ...Mr. Irving's acting is, to my mind, not of a kind to provoke enthusiasm, and I can best describe it by saying that it strikes me as the acting of a very superior amateur. If Mr. Irving were somewhat younger, and if there existed in England any such school of dramatic training as the Conservatoire of Paris, any such exemplary stage as the Théâtre Français, a discriminating critic might say of him: "Here is an aspirant with the instincts of an artist, and who, with the proper instruction, may become an actor." But thanks to the absence of a school and of any formidable competition, success has come easily to Mr. Irving and he has remained, as the first tragic actor in England, decidedly incomplete and amateurish. His personal gifts — face, figure, voice, enunciation — are rather meagre; his strong points are intellectual. He is ingenious, intelligent, and fanciful; imaginative he can hardly be called, for he signally fails to give their great imaginative value to many of the superb speeches he has to utter. In declamation he is decidedly flat; his voice is without charm, and his utterance without subtlety....

and much else besides.

philosopher revelling in a foolish world. I was sure that when he alighted on the platform of Paddington his bearing would be more than ever grave and stately with even the usual touch of bohemianism obliterated now in honour of the honour that was to befall him.... That day when I saw him on his way to Windsor and tried to imagine just what impression he would make on Queen Victoria, I found myself thinking of the impression made there by Disraeli; and I fancied that the two impressions might be rather similar...

"The honour that was to befall" Irving was, of course, a knighthood, making him the first English actor to be so honoured. Max Beerbohm's conjectures turned out to be fairly accurate. The Queen on these occasions was notoriously rather taciturn, saying no more than the traditional words of the ceremony, but on this occasion, as she laid the sword on Irving's shoulder she was heard to murmur: "We are so very, very pleased."

Artistic circles in England which were only just beginning to be officially recognized in this way must have been slightly muted in their response to this novel royal gesture, for the day that Irving's impending honour was announced was also the day that Oscar Wilde was convicted at the Old Bailey and sentenced to two years' hard labour for his homosexual practices. Irving did not know Wilde well and though their styles were at opposite ends of the theatrical spectrum they evidently possessed a certain admiration for one another. No doubt Irving was relieved that he had no professional dealings with Wilde as his contemporary the actor manager Sir George Alexander did and who, on that day, behaved disgracefully by removing the newly convicted "felon's" name from all his theatre posters. Irving, it is thought, nursed a certain sympathy for Wilde and when he was miserably awaiting his second trial at his Chelsea home, a "veiled woman", reputed to be Irving's leading lady Ellen Terry, called and left a bouquet of violets with a message of sympathy. The choice of violets – Irving's favourite flower – suggest that he had a hand in this humane gesture. Moreover, when Wilde was released from prison two years later one of the few messages of encouragement he received was from Irving. It is also fairly certain that Irving felt a profound contempt for the philistines, among them many of his profession, who had rallied to the Marquess of Queensberry's cause to bring about the downfall of Wilde and who openly exulted in his eventual degradation. This must have posed him with a particular problem close to home, for chief among them was Charles Brookfield, an actor in his own company and a fellow member of the Savile.

Just as George Alexander had had no scruples about continuing to profit from the disgraced author while distancing himself from any other association with him, so did Brookfield willingly accept the bountiful opportunities with which Wilde provided him in the good days while at the same time he was plotting his destruction. Actors are, as generations of Savilians have had cause to know, by their nature generally a sensitive bunch. Brookfield seems to have been particularly prickly. Wilde affected perhaps a too hearty superiority in his treatment of actors who – with Irving's example before them – were beginning to see themselves as distinguished figures in London society, careful of their reputations and with an eye to the possibility of yet another dramatic knighthood. There were several touchy encounters between Wilde and Brookfield in which the latter, with his overweening sense of *amour propre*, inevitably came off worse. Wilde, it is thought, sowed the seeds of what was to become an almost insane campaign of vengeance when he once rebuked Brookfield for being unsuitably dressed off stage. As Brookfield's parents moved in Court circles he was furious at being given lessons in propriety by someone whom he probably regarded as an Irish upstart. When *Lady Windermere's Fan* had been running for some weeks Wilde heard that Brookfield was collaborating with Jimmy Glover – a fellow Irishman and director of music at Drury Lane Theatre – to compose a musical skit on his play entitled *The Poet and the Puppets*. As the 'Poet' was called 'Oscar' in the skit, the Lord Chamberlain withheld a licence for its performance until the real Oscar had had the libretto read to him for approval. When this was done Wilde infuriated his enemy even further by punctuating the reading with such exclamations as "Delightful!", "Charming, my old friends!", "Exquisite!" and the like. The only change he asked for was that "O'Flaherty" (one of his middle names) should be substituted for the more immediately recognizable "Oscar". Despite the presence of Charles Hawtrey in the leading part, however, the skit turned out to be a flop. More agreeable than many of Wilde's other connections with the Savile is that when after its successful run of 156 performances it was published in book form the dedication was to an earlier Savilian: "To the dear memory of Robert Earl of Lytton in Affection and Admiration".

Brookfield was elected to the Savile in 1877. Sir Herbert Stephen refers to the 'Spy' cartoon of him which the Club possesses, describing him as "actor, author, and ultimately examiner of plays" – the latter being rather ironic in that a predecessor had advised the Lord Chamberlain to modify his own skit on Wilde. Though Brookfield was evidently a man of some culture, Sir Herbert Stephen could have added that he was also a vindictive gossip and a consorter with blackmailers when it suited him in his relentless quest to gather evidence for Queensberry to bring down Wilde. It was Brookfield who procured the incriminating letters from the rent boys who had previously tried to blackmail Wilde, it was Brookfield who scoured the streets to provide the prosecution with their lethal evidence, and it was Brookfield who conducted a whispering campaign around the clubs of London – of which the Savile was his principal base – in order to create an atmosphere in which Wilde could hardly defend himself. Now that the scandal had broken the Club must have been relieved that seven years earlier, long before there had been any hint of it, they had "deferred" Wilde's application for membership. Nevertheless opinion within the walls of the Piccadilly Clubhouse must have been passionately divided. The likes of W.E. Henley (who was shortly to resign for reasons unconnected) would have been delighted; Robert Ross dismayed. At all events, Brookfield seems to have kept his head held high in the atmosphere he had done so much to create, though one surmises there were many members who must have shunned him.

Brookfield's hatred of Wilde had not prevented him from making use of his enemy whenever he could. Only a few months before the tragic sequence of events began to reach a climax, Brookfield had felt no compunction in accepting the small part of Lord Goring's servant in a production of *An Ideal Husband* at the Haymarket Theatre. Wilde did not make any objection either but there was a small incident which gave a clue to how matters really stood between them. To everyone's annoyance Wilde insisted on having a rehearsal on Christmas Day and then added to it by keeping them waiting about a cold stage for over an hour before making his own appearance.

> "Don't you keep Christmas, Oscar?" Brookfield asked angrily.
> "No, Brookfield," replied Wilde blandly. "The only festival of the Church I keep is Septuagesima. Do you keep Septuagesima, Brookfield?"
> "Not since I was a boy."
> "Ah then, be a boy again."

In that production of *An Ideal Husband* was an actor named Lewis Waller who, as well as playing the part of Sir Robert Chiltern, had just taken over the running of the Haymarket Theatre from Beerbohm Tree, who was about to embark on a tour of America.

Waller, who had also acted in Irving's company, was only briefly a member of the Savile. In the 1968 Centenary booklet Sir Ralph Richardson provided an amusing explanation for this:

> Lewis Waller of the Edwardian stage, hero of the "K.O.W" (Keen on Waller) club, was taken one day as a guest to luncheon at the old Savile in Piccadilly. He much enjoyed the occasion; he had an excellent meal, and met a group of gay and amusing clubmen. He expressed an earnest wish that he might become a member, and his joy was complete when later on he came to be elected.
>
> Always well-dressed, Waller took particular care with his clothes on the day he decided to lunch at the club for the first time as a member. But this lunch was a disappointment compared with the time when he had gone to the club as a guest. The meal was as good, but the men he had met were not there and he didn't seem to know anyone.
>
> "Never mind", he said to himself. "It takes time to make acquaintances. I shall go every week to the club and I must always try to look my best." Months went by; Waller continued to go to the club, but he never seemed to feel at home. Perhaps he'd arrive as the table was emptying, and soon find himself sitting alone. If he went to the billiards room, it was either crowded or completely empty. Perhaps he grew a little shy, and would shelter behind a copy of the *Spectator*. Somehow he never chanced to gain entry to the little groups and circles that buzzed with life and

semi-private fun.

Disappointed and dispirited, when the month of January came he did not renew his subscription. Some time afterwards, one Savilian remarked to another, "I say, that new chap, you know, Waller, I hear he's resigned." "A good thing too," his friend replied. "Conceited actor. Never spoke to a soul."

Perhaps Richardson was providing a lesson for all new members.

Richardson was proposed for the Club in 1933 by Robert Speaight, whose own election in 1929 seems to have been among the first for a member of his profession in over a decade. Speaight's arrival marked the beginning of a small resurgence in the number of actors seeking membership of the Savile, particularly those who preferred a less theatrical ambience in which to spend their leisure and wished to take advantage of the founders' first principle of providing a meeting place for "men of different professions". This was almost certainly the reason for Speaight's desire to join the Savile (as it was later with Ralph Richardson) and it coincided with the Club's removal into its new premises at Brook Street. As was noted earlier in a different context, Speaight's election took place while he was enjoying his first West End success in that famous drama of the First World War, *Journey's End* by R.C. Sherriff. In this production, which featured Laurence Olivier in the leading role for most of its eighteen months' run, Speaight played the equally crucial part of the cowardly 2nd lieutenant Hibbert and consolidated an already burgeoning reputation. After this success there followed a long list of Shakespearian roles in productions such as Gielgud's *King Lear* in 1931, and the 1931-2 season at the Old Vic, where he shared leading roles and a dressing room with Ralph Richardson, playing Hamlet, King John, Cassius and – his favourite minor part – Fluellen. Speaight's election to the Savile coincided also with a great broadening of his interests outside the theatre, which encompassed some revelatory forays into literary scholarship. In 1932 he began a distinguished writing career with the publication of the first of his four novels, *Mutinous Wind* but before this – in 1930 – he had converted to Catholicism, an event which was to influence and inform both his literary and theatrical careers thereafter. He was, for instance, said to be the first to discover how to recite the poems of Gerard Manley Hopkins in such a way as to bring out both their full meaning and their sprung rhythms, and when T.S. Eliot wrote *Murder in the Cathedral* for the Canterbury Festival Speaight was regarded as the "natural choice" to play Thomas à Becket. It was a performance he was to repeat over one thousand times throughout Britain and North America. His obituarist, the former Savilian Paul Johnson, records a characteristically wry compliment to Speaight from another Club member, W.B. Yeats: "Long before I saw you act I divined that you were important – because your acting was derided by all the people I most dislike." But from now on his style of acting and his mode of life made him somewhat type-cast. In 1941 he was given the much sought after part of Christ in Dorothy L. Sayers's *The Man Born to be King*, performed on the radio by the BBC, and thenceforth he found it difficult to get parts which were

Sir Ralph Richardson, photographed by Snowdon ". . . both as an actor and as a Savilian he was quite simply incomparable".

Michael Powell, the Oscar winning film director.

not either saints or clerics. He played Christian in *The Pilgrim's Progress* at Covent Garden, Gerontius in Newman's *The Dream of Gerontius*, St Peter at Westminster Abbey, and Cardinal Pole at Canterbury. He also played St Thomas More in Robert Bolt's *A Man for All Seasons* in an Australian production, although for reasons which then seemed inexplicable he was not asked to play it in England.

Meantime his literary work was being strongly influenced by his twin preoccupation with religion and the theatre. He wrote many books on Shakespeare, particularly in context of the proper staging of his plays, and as well as publishing three further novels he began to write on matters to do with France. Like his friend Hilaire Belloc (whose official biography he was commissioned to write) he enjoyed exploring the French countryside, which complemented his devotion to French literature and the contemporary school of continental religious philosophers – with many of whom he was intimately acqainted. The fruits of all these interests were rich: *A Companion Guide to Burgundy*; a study of *Teilhard de Chardin*; and books on *Georges Bernanos* and *François Mauriac*. When not himself on stage he extended his theatrical work to include adjudication at drama festivals and by writing on the art of stagecraft. He was, moreover, a brilliant linguist, capable of performing in German or of directing a French version of *Antony and Cleopatra*. Such gifts must have made him a welcome addition to the Savile membership although, as has been observed in a previous section of this history, his reaction to the ruination of the ballroom's décor during his first few weeks of membership was not wholly appreciated by a committee less aesthetically minded than he. Members of a later period, however, will discern from his elegant autobiography *The Property Basket* that even if the role of *A Man for All Seasons* eluded him in his own country, he could justly claim to have been indeed a man of many parts.

When Robert Speaight proposed Ralph Richardson for membership in 1933, one of the names appearing in the candidates book as a referee was that of Victor Clinton-Baddeley, who had been elected in 1928. Clinton-Baddeley was a well known broadcaster at the time but he had had an extremely varied career as university don, historian, editor, actor, playwright and author. He first appeared with Ben Greet's company in 1922, but later left it to return to Cambridge, and shortly after was appointed Modern History editor of the *Encyclopaedia Britannica*. He had a long career in broadcasting but is now chiefly remembered for his books on the theatre, which include *Words for Music*; *The Burlesque Tradition in the English Theatre after 1660*; and *All Right on the Night*, an entertaining study of the Georgian theatre.

Ralph Richardson's appearance on the Savile scene in 1933 tended to overshadow the presence of other actors who at various times during the fifty years of his own membership belonged to the Club. This was not due merely to his theatrical eminence, and certainly not to any overbearing displays of *amour propre* – of which, anyway, he was incapable – but solely to his delightful presence and unaffected eccentricity which inspired innumerable Club legends, as we shall see. Nevertheless, the theatrical "names" who came to the Savile during this period would have been impressive enough in any company. The well-known actor of the time, Esmé Percy, for instance, was elected to the Club in 1939, the golden-voiced Robert Donat in 1942, and that most versatile man of the threatre, Bernard Miles, in 1943.

Esmé Percy had made his London début as Romeo in 1905 after studying in Paris, where he acted with Sarah Bernhardt. Although Michael Meyer remembers Percy as "rewarding to listen to" he also recalls a rather embarrassing though poignant encounter at the Club:

> Once I asked him if he had seen Edith Evans's legendary début as Cressida for the Elizabethan Stage Society in 1912, when she was still a milliner, "See her, my boy? I acted opposite her". "Were you Pandarus?" I asked without thinking, for in his old age Esmé's appearance was slightly grotesque. There was a slight pause. "I was Troilus," he at length replied, "I was rather beautiful then".

During a long and distinguished career Esmé Percy had appeared on more than one occasion with Robert Donat, notably in Antoine Bibesco's *The Heir* and in the 1943 revival (only the second since 1895) of Wilde's *An Ideal Husband*, in which Percy played Lord Caversham. Donat had only recently joined the Savile, having been introduced to it as a guest of Dallas Bower during his BBC production of *Alexander Nevsky*.

Although Donat died as long ago as 1958 his reputation remains fresh through the number of classic films he made during the post-war years, a time which some regard as the "golden age" of the British cinema. These included René Clair's *The Ghost Goes West*, Hitchcock's *The Thirty-nine Steps* (for which he received an Oscar nomination), *The Citadel*, and his best-loved film *Goodbye Mr Chips*, for which he did eventually receive the Oscar award. Other roles to which he lent distinction were *Pitt the Younger*, *The Count of Monte Cristo*, the barrister in Rattigan's *The Winslow Boy*, and the founder of the cinema in *The Magic Box*. His work in the legitimate theatre, which included tours with Sir Frank Benson's company, was equally distinguished and culminated in his final stage appearance as Becket in *Murder in the Cathedral* which his friend and fellow Savilian, Robert Speaight, had made so much his own. Throughout his life he was racked with chronic asthma which made the excellence of his performances even more triumphant. Few who have seen it will forget the poignancy of the final scene in *The Inn of the Sixth Happiness*, which was his final film performance before his early death at the age of fifty-three. In his role of a Chinese mandarin, looking old and frail, he takes leave of Ingrid Bergman, who is playing the part of the missionary Gladys Aylward: *"It is time to see old friends. Stay here … for a little. It will comfort me as I leave to know it. We shall not see each other again I think. Farewell."* A few weeks later he was dead.

In happier times Donat was by all accounts a familiar and welcome presence at the Club. Indeed for some time during the war years he lived in the mews flat belonging to the Club in Three Kings Yard where by coincidence Peter Aldersley, who had in his theatrical days taken over Donat's role in the touring version of

Goodbye Mr Chips, also lived after he became secretary of the Savile. Michael Meyer remembers Donat as "delightful and very accessible" and remarks that Donat was fond of recalling how his father had tried to dissuade him from speaking in a thick Manchester accent, leading him to transpose his voice into the beautifully modulated instrument it became. In the Club one day . . .

> I was chatting with Walter Greenwood, the author of *Love on the Dole*, that fine working-class novel about the depression of the 1930's. Walter had the broadest of Manchester accents. Donat came in, and was talking at the bar in his usual aristocratic voice when Walter spotted him and said "Ullo, Robert." Robert turned round, cried "Ullo, Walter!", sat down with us and without affectation dropped into his own natural accent which was identical with Walter's, and equally broad. I could barely understand much of what they said.

In 1943, the year after Donat's election, Bernard Miles became a member of the Savile. He has been described by a leading theatre critic as "arguably a more complete man of the theatre than any other of the thespian knights and barons of his time – an actor, writer, director, producer and, pre-eminently, a manager". Be that as it may he will be long remembered for his creation against fearful odds of the Mermaid Theatre, which for twenty years delighted London audiences with its stylish but inexpensive productions. These included some memorable performances of the classic Greek tragedies; celebrations of Noël Coward (*Cowardy Custard*) and of Cole Porter (*Cole*); musicals like *Side by Side with Sondheim*; and old war horses like *Journey's End*, so closely associated with his fellow Savilian Robert Speaight. There were also new discoveries like the immensely successful *Hadrian the Seventh* and Brecht's *Life of Galileo*. One of his first triumphs was his own adaptation of Stevenson's *Treasure Island*, repeated regularly at Christmas, in which he delivered a powerful performance as Long John Silver. One wonders whether it occurred to him that this character was based on W.E. Henley – an earlier Savilian – and whether, if it had, it would have made his interpretation less beguiling. Miles was appointed C.B.E. in 1953, knighted in 1969 and created a life peer as Baron Miles ten years later in 1979.

Sadly, Miles's career as an actor had been constantly overshadowed and hampered by his need to raise funds to keep his remarkable theatre alive. When Miles founded the Mermaid at Puddle Dock after the war it became the first playhouse in the City for the 300 years since the Puritan City Councillors of the 17th century had decreed that "rogues and vagabonds" should be kept out of the Square Mile. The theatre he created, a kind of social centre embodying restaurants, bookstalls and facilities designed to appeal to family audiences, became the model for the number of provincial theatres that were to open in the 1960s and 1970s.

Before the Mermaid was constructed at Puddle Dock, Miles had rehearsed his theatrical theories and innovations first in a mock-up of an Elizabethan theatre in the garden of his house in St John's Wood and later at the Royal Exchange in the

City for a three-month season of Shakespeare, Jonson and Purcell. By coincidence the Royal Exchange of another city – Manchester – was also to become associated with theatre rather than commerce but in this case more permanently, more successfully, and with a much greater input from the Savile.

Laurence Harbottle, the Club's honorary solicitor who has – as noted earlier – been involved with many theatre companies and was a member of the Arts Council, serving for a long time on its Drama Panel, writes: "Most relevant to the Club was the fact that the 69 Theatre Company of Manchester was established by two Club members, Caspar Wrede [elected 1957], and Michael Elliott, [elected 1958] with my help. Michael Meyer was closely involved in its inception too. As the 69 Theatre Company was established in 1968 it was probably the number of the Clubhouse which decided its title. Later it grew into the Royal Exchange Theatre, Manchester." Another member, Braham Murray (elected 1965), was also closely associated with the running of the Royal Exchange, which rapidly became the most distinguished and widely acclaimed theatre outside London, superior in the opinion of some to any in London including the National.

In 1967 Michael Croft, the founder of the National Youth Theatre, was elected to the Savile. This nursery for what were to turn out to be some of the great acting talents of the time had begun in a small way in 1956. In that year Croft was a teacher at Alleyn's School in Dulwich, sharing his keen interest in the theatre with a group of boys who included Simon Ward, John Stride and Derek Jacobi. When he gave up teaching in 1956 with the intention of becoming a writer the boys pleaded with him to put on plays with them in their holidays and from these "theatrical summer schools" developed the project which eventually was attracting nearly 600 pupils from schools all over the country. The list of "names" who began their careers at the National Youth Theatre (as it soon became) is impressive. Apart from those already mentioned there were Michael York, Martin Jarvis, Ben Kingsley, Ian McShane, Helen Mirren, Paula Wilcox, Diana Quick and the future Savilian Hywel Bennett. When Croft was forced to retire through ill health in 1986 a leading national newspaper wrote:

> Michael Croft is not a name as famous as Lord Olivier or Sir Peter Hall. It is not heard with any great pleasure in the environs of the Arts Council. Yet few would disagree that Michael Croft has done more to maintain the traditional high standards of creative excellence in British Theatre than anyone else.

Croft's regular visits to the Club could be jolly affairs but his occasional gloomy aspect reflected his constant fights with the Arts Council and other bodies to raise the necessary finance to keep this unique theatre project alive. That he managed to do so was something of a small miracle but it took a terrible toll on his health and shortly after his retirement he died.

The year of Michael Croft's election (1967) was also the year that another much mourned member, the Scottish actor Bill Simpson, was elected. Although he had

had a notable career in repertory and pantomime he will be chiefly remembered for his at once craggy yet polished performances as the eponymous hero of the long running BBC television serial *Doctor Finlay's Casebook* produced by his fellow Savilian, the late Royston Morley, who had been elected in 1962.

There have been other distinguished actors in the interim years who briefly came and subsequently went either through commitments elsewhere or because there were other meeting places more specific to their private and professional interests. Notable amongst these were those fine actors Freddie Jones and Timothy Dalton who, despite their brief tenure of membership, are well remembered.

Nevertheless the present list of Savile members contains perhaps the greatest number of actors and others concerned with the theatre that has ever congregated together in *sodalitas convivium* at one and the same time since the Club was founded in 1868. These actors' achievements need no embellishment here for much of their work is there forever for all to see on film and video-tape. Nevertheless a dip into the list provides a taste of the theatrical quality presently to be found at Brook Street. To follow theatrical precedent these *dramatis personae* shall therefore be listed "in order of appearance".

First to enter comes Graham Crowden (elected 1968) whose rich and fruity Scottish presence both on and off the stage lends charm and distinction to his professional work as well as to his regular appearances at the Club. In addition to his work for the live theatre there have been those popular television series woven about his powerful projections of eccentricity which include *A Very Peculiar Practice* and *Waiting for God*.

Next to take the stage comes Zia Moyheddin (elected 1969), doyen of that band of accomplished actors of Asian origin who have inspired the English theatre in recent years and whose appearances in films such as *My Beautiful Laundrette* and *A Passage to India* (from the novel by that former Savilian, E.M. Forster) has added a new dimension to the British cinema.

Kenneth Haigh (elected 1972) as is well known had already established a reputation as an up-and-coming talent worth watching as he played classical roles in repertory throughout the United Kingdom and Ireland, when in 1956 he was called upon to create the part of Jimmy Porter, the central character in that iconoclastic whirlwind of words, woe-wailing and wit which has entered the theatrical history books under the title of *Look Back in Anger*.

The éclat with which he invested this part has since been addressed to many other theatrical roles both in Great Britain and America, where he is a visiting professor of drama at New York University and Vassar. Haigh's "ambassadorial" forays to the Savile's sister clubs – The Players and The Coffee House – during his visits to the States have enticed several of their members to seek full election to the Savile rather than merely exercising their visiting rights, while home grown Savilians have had many opportunities to enjoy his art in the poetry readings of past and present members' work which are an occasional alternative to the Club's discussion dinners.

The year of Kenneth Haigh's election was the forerunner of another excellent theatrical vintage when in 1973 there were elected to the Savile Hywel Bennett, Brian Cox, and Edward Fox.

Hywel Bennett had been set on his career by Michael Croft's National Youth Theatre during the early 'sixties to such effect that a profile of him in *The Times* in 1986 was moved to record that "Everything that happens to Hywel Bennett has a fictional air – as if he were a figure created solely to reflect cultural change. From the zany 'sixties to the solid 'eighties, from Virgin Soldier to James Shelley, he always seems to be there busily exemplifying his age." This theory was supported by a list of credits which had ensued since his career took off in the 1966 Boulting Brothers film *All in Good Time*, in which he co-starred with Hayley Mills. (Coincidentally, Roy Boulting had been elected to the Savile twenty-two years earlier in 1944, but had ceased membership by the year of Bennett's election in 1973.) More films – for example *Loot* – followed together with stage appearances, all of which reflected contemporary *mores*. In the 'seventies came the part of the Pimp in Dennis Potter's *Pennies from Heaven*, Dr Bickleigh in *Malice Aforethought* and Ricky Tarr in *Tinker, Tailor, Soldier, Spy* (adapted from the novel by the former member John le Carré). This led him into the 'eighties with the creation of the immortal *Shelley*, that most literate of situation comedies about a well-educated "drop-out", which achieved massive popularity and is still running at the time of writing. What his future impersonations will reveal about the state of society during the rest of the 'nineties remains to be seen; a remake of Walter Greenwood's *Love on the Dole* perhaps?

Next in that theatrical trio elected in 1973 comes a master of the classical roles and award-winning actor, Brian Cox, though in some ways Cox's connections with the Savile had begun six years earlier: in 1967, still young and relatively unknown, he was playing the lead in Michael Meyer's translation of *Peer Gynt:* "Cox, at twenty-one, was a remarkable Peer," wrote Meyer afterwards, "the best with Leo McKern that I have ever seen". Such was Meyer's enthusiasm that shortly afterwards he took his fellow Savilian Michael Elliott, with whom he was associated at the Royal Exchange Theatre, to see Cox playing Iago to Michael Gambon's Othello. "This was the beginning of a fruitful relationship between Cox and Elliott," writes Meyer in his memoirs, "culminating eighteen years later in Cox's magnificent Captain Ahab in Elliott's last theatre production, *Moby Dick*".

Meyer calls Cox "a natural Ibsen actor" but would be the first to confirm that his range has been demonstrably much wider. His work at the Royal Shakespeare Company and the National is testimony to this while his performance as *Tamburlaine the Great* is one of the great landmarks of recent theatrical history. Cox also demonstrates the Savilian penchant for even-handedness for, just as Kenneth Haigh regularly exports his skills as actor, director, and lecturer on drama to New York, so also has Cox transported his – but in his case to Moscow.

"Bennett, Cox, and Fox" – the election of this theatrical trinity in 1973 surely calls out for a Gilbertian stanza or two to celebrate it and a Malcolm Arnold melody to underline it. Edward Fox had already some connections with the Club when he was elected to the Savile. He had been briefly married to Anthony

Pelissier's daughter, the actress Tracy Reed, and his uncle by marriage is the ex-house committee chairman Guy Nicholson. Fox's career is too well known to need rehearsing here; from the cuckolded fiancé in *The Go-Between* to the eponymous "hero" in the *Day of the Jackal*, and from *The Admirable Crichton* to Edward VIII he has brought his own particular brand of distinction to a multitude of roles. Fox's skills at impersonation evidently linger convincingly on long after the cameras have stopped rolling. A member recalls an occasion at the Club at about the time *Edward and Mrs Simpson* was achieving massive viewing figures on television. In the morning room two guests were sitting waiting for their host to arrive. As is sometimes the case when people find themselves in unfamiliar surroundings they were showing signs of unease. While they sat murmuring nervously to one another against the oppressive silence, Edward Fox strolled in in search of an evening newspaper. Both visitors immediately leapt to their feet and stood to courtier-like attention. "Pray sit down, gentlemen," said Fox with a princely wave and, in a modest expression of their humble duty, they did.

Simon Oates was elected a member of the Club in 1976. He remembers with a shudder that as a young man setting out on his theatrical career he was minded to replace his given name with the stage style of Titus. Luckily he was dissuaded and achieved national renown in the long running series *Doomwatch* during the 'seventies, simply as Simon rather than in the denomination of that much reviled professional perjurer. As an actor-director since then he has travelled extensively in the Americas with his own touring company staging such popular "two-handers" as *The Owl and the Pussy Cat* and *Two on a Seasaw* as well as making many appearances in cabaret. He has been a committee member of the Club since 1991. And so to complete the current theatrical cast list at the Savile come the two latest arrivals, Richard Gibson (elected 1982), known most recently as the mock-sinister gestapo officer in the long-running play and television series *'Allo, 'Allo*, and Norman Rodway (elected 1988) whose mellifluous Anglo-Irish tones have lent distinction to so many theatrical and radio dramas.

* * * *

Figures from the world of film production were late arrivals at the Savile. The first film producer-director of note to be elected was Dallas Bower in 1943, as we have seen, but from then on the pace quickened, and in 1945 there came two leading producers of the time (Sir) Michael Balcon and Roy Boulting. Basil Wright in his exhaustive history of the cinema, *The Long View*, notes that his fellow member Balcon together with Alexander Korda "turned out to be Britain's *only* producers in the American sense . . . men who had spent their lives in films, and were capable of guiding and directing a group of film directors in the same way that directors themselves guide the actors". Balcon had many professional associations with other members of the Club; it was he, for instance, who imported René Clair to make *The Ghost Goes West* starring that great Savilian and actor, Robert Donat. It turned out to be one of the many delightful films produced in the post-war

British Studios whose excellence Balcon himself had been so instrumental in creating. It was he too who had commissioned the charmingly malapropic Savilian mascot, Lothar Mendes, a refugee from Hitler's Germany, to direct *Jew Süss*, a remarkably brilliant piece of film-making which is unfortunately almost forgotten except in the history books. Balcon's heyday at Ealing Studios was to see the creation of some outstanding wartime films, one at least of which was to lampoon mercilessly the pretensions of the fascist dictators who brought about the Second World War. Very much in the manner of those two contemporary satirists at the Savile, the cartoonists David Low and "Vicky", Balcon had produced in 1941 a savage and sarcastic compilation film, *Yellow Caesar*, to mock Mussolini's gimcrack empire. This was followed by a feature film from an idea by Graham Greene, *Went the Day Well?* which aroused considerable controversy not least because it posited the unthinkable notion that some British citizens might not behave well in the event of a successful German invasion. Not for the only time was the wartime leader Winston Churchill moved to fire an indignant salvo towards Brook Street, where members like Michael Powell – for all their patriotism – occasionally uttered disaffected noises. Balcon's policy at Ealing Studios was moreover different from his exact contemporaries, Carol Reed and David Lean. He had determined to give prominence to teams of writers and "ideas men" and as a result he reaped a spectacular reward. Chief amongst these collaborators was "the White Russian with a Red Face" to quote the title of Monja Danischewsky's hilarious biography, who began as his publicist and went on to produce one of Balcon's greatest successes, *Whisky Galore*, from the novel by another Savilian, Compton Mackenzie. "Danny", as shall be seen later, has been one of the wittiest stand-bys of the Club and his erudition and humour have enlivened several generations of Savilians since his election in 1949.

Roy Boulting was one of the twin Boulting Brothers whose names were attached to so many distinguished films of the post-war period, *Fame is the Spur*, *Brighton Rock*, and *Seven Days to Noon* among them. Purely coincidentally (one supposes) shortly after his election Roy and his brother John settled down to producing highly successful but less intellectually demanding comedies "sending up" one or another of Britain's more cherished institutions. Of these, *Privates Progress* and *Brothers-in-Law* were notably superior to most of the home-produced films of their time.

Roy Boulting had entered the film industry, and subsequently the Savile, after wartime service in the Army Film Unit. By coincidence the commander of the Army Film and Photographic Unit (to give it its full title) in North Africa and later in Normandy for the duration of the European campaign leading to the final German surrender in 1945 was Hugh Stewart, who was elected to the Savile a year later in 1946.

In North Africa Hugh Stewart had been co-producer with that prince among American film-makers, Frank Capra, of a propaganda film, *Tunisian Victory*, designed particularly to establish closer co-operation with America. To this end it became the first film to open with credit titles announcing: "The Governments of the United States and Great Britain present...". The rather decisive full stop to the continuation of the war provided by the dropping of the atom bomb (made possible by another contemporary Savilian, Sir John Cockcroft) prevented Hugh Stewart from taking up his appointment to a similar role in the far East for which Lord Louis Mountbatten had personally singled him out. The war over, Hugh Stewart turned away from historical record and in comic mode produced the series of films featuring Norman Wisdom, and one with Morecambe and Wise. On a more serious level he was also the producer who brought the work of two other Savile members to the screen in the film *Night Without Stars* from a novel by Winston Graham which was directed by Anthony Pelissier. He has also produced a number of films for the Children's Film Foundation but his most recent productions, of which he is equally and justifiably proud, are the series of admirable "Discussion Dinners" and musical evenings which, as "honorary impresario", he has masterminded at the Savile over the last several years.

Anthony Pelissier, the director of *Night Without Stars*, was yet another Savilian with a web of family connections weaving through the Club, most notable of which perhaps were through his mother, that great lady of the theatre and sister of Sir Compton Mackenzie, Fay Compton, and also through his marriage to the actress Ursula Howells, who was the daughter of the composer Herbert Howells. Elected in 1945, Pelissier was Savilian in his versatility, taking on every role with equal aplomb, whether as actor, scriptwriter, set designer, producer or director, and equally at home in the theatre, film or television.

His début as actor was in the musical *Follow Through* at London's Dominion Theatre. It was an engagement, however, which ended in disaster when he and three other members of the cast went for an afternoon's sail in the Thames estuary and became stuck on a mudbank for two days and two nights, missing their performances. On being rescued they were immediately dismissed. His habitual charm evidently earned him absolution from what in the acting profession is regarded as the unforgivable sin of missing a performance, for after a brief period of penance he was back in the West End creating the part of Lord ("Chubby") Martlett in Noël Coward's *Cavalcade* at Drury Lane. But he was probably best known for his association with the actor John Mills, whom he introduced to his future wife, the playwright Mary Hayley Bell, later directing him in her play *Duet for Two Hands*. Mills also appeared in Pelissier's 1937 play *Talk of the Devil* at the Piccadilly and in Pelissier's *Follies of 1938* at the old Saville.

After the war the two collaborated on the films of H.G. Wells's *The History of Mr Polly* (produced by and starring Mills, written and directed by Pelissier) and D.H. Lawrence's *The Rocking Horse Winner*, for which Pelissier again wrote the screenplay as well as directing. Among his other films were *Encore, Night Without Stars, Meet Me Tonight, Personal Affairs* and *Meet Mr Lucifer*. He was also much in demand as a theatre director in the West End in the 1950s, when among his productions were the controversial homosexual drama *The Green Bay Tree* at the Playhouse and Frederick Lonsdale's *The Way Things Go* at the Phoenix.

In 1959 he founded the Langham Group at the BBC, working on

experimental films. Five years later he won the Screenwriters' Guild Award for outstanding British documentary with his *Suspects All*.

Tony Pelissier spent a large part of his leisure time at the Savile, where his wit and humour were as much appreciated as his professional achievements. It is perhaps a pity that this appreciation was not more general for sometimes his conversation could take on the bitter edge of a disappointed man. "Oh, I'm just a Jack-of-all-trades," he would sometimes exclaim, though other members took a different view; that great historian of the cinema, Basil Wright, for instance, recording that *The Rocking Horse Winner* was one of the best but most underestimated films of the time.

In 1951 Sidney Gilliat was elected to the Savile. With his partner Frank Launder he sought to reflect the mood of the later wartime years in a series of down-market films such as *Millions Like Us* and *Waterloo Road*, extolling the yearnings of the so-called "little man" towards a new and better life. In this he was at one with a surprising number of his fellow Savilians, though no doubt the comparative opulence – shabby and all as it was in those days – of the Club rooms provided some escape from his somewhat dingy scenarios. Nevertheless there were some pundits at the time who believed that in expressing these themes so eloquently he contributed in part to the post-war electorate's rejection of Churchill in favour of a Labour government.

The effects of the war and its immediate aftermath were naturally reflected in the activities of nearly every category of member elected to the Savile during those years. This was particularly noticeable among the film-makers whose talents had often been employed either in propaganda or morale-boosting productions as part of the war effort. The list is impressive: Dallas Bower with his incomparable *Henry V*, Hugh Stewart with *Tunisian Victory* have already been noted, but there were others working then who came later to the Club.

Ronald Neame was one of the two young and then unknown directors (David Lean was the other) who were chosen by Noël Coward to be his colleagues in the making of that great wartime film *In Which we Serve*. As the perilous national situation then demanded, it was a highly successful combination of patriotic uplift and good entertainment which for nearly half a century since has continued to attract large audiences whenever it is repeated on television. When Neame was elected to the Savile in 1952 he was still collaborating with David Lean and Noël Coward on those other notable films of the time, *This Happy Breed* and *Blithe Spirit*. The connection with David Lean continued with those other oft-repeated classics *Great Expectations* and *Oliver Twist*. After this partnership was severed Neame went on to reinforce his considerable reputation with another film with a military theme, *Tunes of Glory*, which dealt however with the seemingly greater stresses involved in peacetime soldiering.

One of the great classics of wartime documentay, *Western Approaches*, came from yet another film director who in the postwar years was to become a staple of the Savile. Pat Jackson was elected to the Club in 1958, the year that he had briefly allowed himself a holiday from documentary to produce *Virgin Island*, which was also to be perhaps the most orthodox of all his films. This delightful real-life tale of a honeymoon couple who set up house on an uninhabited West Indian island was, under Jackson's direction, among the first to draw attention to the acting potential of John Cassavetes, Virginia Maskell, and Sidney Poitier. But it was Jackson's skilful and deliberate use of amateur actors which put the seal on his earlier masterpiece, *Western Approaches*. This remarkable film, which caused a sensation in its time and is still occasionally shown on television in tribute to its status as a landmark in documentary film-making, was written, cast, and directed by Jackson. The result was an intensely moving disquisition on the hazardous life of the merchant seaman in wartime having to contend not only with the natural elements but also the perils of enemy action while he strove to keep the nation's life-lines open.

The making of this film was almost as hazardous as the scenario it was representing. It was shot in colour, which had been almost unheard of in a documentary of its kind until then. The unsophisticated colour cameras of the time were about the size of a large commercial refrigerator and as they had to be located in small boats in sometimes heavy seas it was as well that though the protagonists were all amateur as actors they were all in fact professional seamen. To those other professionals who protested that to make a film involving over fifty speaking parts – eight of them major ones – with a cast of amateurs was sheer lunacy, Jackson replied that his intention was to represent the spirit of the nation and reveal the true backbone of its people. Who better to do it with than the actual men involved? That his direction succeeded in overcoming any artistic deficiencies is indicated by the film's nomination for an Oscar. Pat Jackson was to repeat this technique – though with variations – in *White Corridors*. This "semi-documentary" made for the commercial cinema was a forerunner of the spate of hospital dramas which ensued and still continues. In pursuit of his aim to present a realistic image of national character Jackson again made extensive use of amateur actors, though this time they were supported by a handful of professionals which included Basil Radford and Googie Withers. Chief Petty Officer Hills, a veteran of Jutland who had taken a prominent part in *Western Approaches,* appeared again but (though this time in a less familiar role) according to Pat he stole every scene in which he was matched against the professionals. The film was an enormous success and Pat became the first British documentary producer to be invited to Hollywood. There he made *Shadow on the Wall,* which among its many other distinctions featured a young actress ("not too bad a one, either", says Pat) called Nancy Davies who was later to achieve wider exposure as Nancy Reagan, America's "First Lady".

Jackson's preferences always tended towards the documentary style, as it had done with his proposer for the Savile, Basil Wright, and so many other Savilian film-makers, even if their work was of sufficient interest to achieve wider acclaim when put on general release in the nation's commercial cinemas. But there were still other film producers at the Savile who have distinquished themselves by providing pure entertainment; members such as George Brown (elected 1953) whose productions included classic comedies like *Hotel Sahara* starring Peter Ustinov and *The Chiltern Hundreds* featuring nearly every comic actor of the post-war years who made English film comedy a by-word throughout the English-speaking world. In a different genre Euan Lloyd (elected 1966) has filmed such stirring adventures as *Wild Geese I, Wild Geese II* and *Who Dares Wins.*

But as it has been with so many Savile membes in all their "different professions" over the years, the Club's film-makers have sometimes seemed to express rather radical views in their work, swimming strongly against the current of contemporary received opinions. It is a tradition which goes back to the founding fathers like Auberon Herbert and Sir Charles Dilke and has marked out the Savile as unique among West End clubs by giving the lie to the popular notion that all such clubs are bastions of privilege and upholders of the established order. No one represented this maverick tradition more eloquently than Michael Powell who with his partner Emeric Pressburger produced an astonishing range of fine films, many of which – to paraphrase Samuel Butler – "set some of the folks who govern us/Together by the ears".

Michael Powell was elected to the Club in 1952 and though his partner Emeric Pressburger was often his guest during the next few years it was not until 1970, after the partnership had been dissolved, that the latter sought his own election to the Savile.

Like so many of the film-making contingent at Brook Street some of the partners' best early work was devoted to promoting the war effort but, as that doyenne of film critics, Dilys Powell (no relation), has observed, whereas "others made propaganda from cinema, Michael Powell made propaganda into cinema". It was the war that brought the Englishman Powell together with the Hungarian Pressburger to form a production team called The Archers and from this source came a spate of uplifting films to do with the war: *One of Our Aircraft is Missing, 49th Parallel, The Life and Death of Colonel Blimp* among them.

Powell's emergence as one of the most creative forces in Britain's film industry had begun, however, some years before the war broke out. He had entered the industry as a scriptwriter but only began to be noticed when in 1936 he directed his first film, *The Edge of the World.* This was followed in 1938 with *The Spy in Black,* which brought him to the notice of Alexander Korda, who, recognizing Powell's potential, hired him to direct his 1939 Anglo-American production, *The Thief of Baghdad.* By then war had broken out and Powell was on his way with the sequence of films combining high entertainment value with the subtle propaganda which was to make his name.

Not all of these were received with the same enthusiasm from on high as was accorded to them by the ordinary cinema-going public. Powell's fellow Club member Basil Wright makes the wry comment in his book *The Long View* that Powell's and Pressburger's films "always beautifully made, seldom failed to raise ideological storms of considerable magnitude". He goes on:

Their first main wartime film, *49th Parallel* (1941), was about six members of an escaped U-Boat crew on the run in Canada, who are one by one pursued and captured. The first feature film to be partly financed by the Ministry of Information, it was criticised in some quarters for having a negative propaganda slant... It was also complained that Leslie Howard, as a rather defeatist English intellectual, was a less sympathetic character than the ruthless, dedicated U-Boat commander played by Eric Portman.

Against all this it was claimed that Powell and Pressburger were doing no more than express general criticisms of the British attitude to the rest of the world and, by showing these to be essentially false, aiming to shock the Americans and Canadians into treating apparent dilettantism with more respect. The whole story and motivation of the film was, indeed, very carefully calculated. In the course of their flight the Nazis met a French-Canadian trapper (Laurence Olivier), a German Hutterite settler (Anton Walbrook), a toughly cynical Canadian soldier (Raymond Massey), and an assortment of Red Indians and Eskimos as well as Leslie Howard's aforesaid dilettante. All this was planned to indicate that in the British Commonwealth there was room for all, regardless of race, language or creed; and the story-line is such that in each confrontation the Nazis come off worst, even when, as an added anti-Hitler stroke, the U-Boat commander commits a typically cold-blooded murder. Finally, it is the 'typical' Englishman, apparently so weak and cynical, who gives the knockout to the Nazis.

49th Parallel brought into sharp focus, and quite early in the war, the hair-trigger differences of emphasis in the world of propaganda. In this case I think the balance tipped the right way, and the superiority of the democratic over the totalitarian view point was satisfactorily demonstrated.

Another controversial Archer film was *The Life and Death of Colonel Blimp* based on the reactionary but lovable cartoon character invented by another Savile member, David Low. Like all the Powell and Pressburger films it was superbly made but its ideological conceptions which seem perfectly proper now aroused howls of rage from the war cabinet headed by Winston Churchill. Again Basil Wright points our attention to the nub of the matter:

> ...I think one of the reasons why criticism of the content or motive in these films was always exceptionally violent was exactly because they were tremendously good entertainment and therefore very convincing. Blimp himself – based of course on the figure invented by the cartoonist David Low to symbolise all that was most reactionary in Britain – was here transformed into a real human being as we watched his reactions to the war. He was in fact shown as a sincere though misguided reactionary with a heart of gold; and Powell and Pressburger chose to reveal his behaviour and development through the eyes of a Prussian.

The result was certainly a fascinating if over-long film, but its fatal flaw, as I pointed out at the time, was this very Prussian. By including him as, in the event, a sort of *deus ex machina,* the Archers created a situation in which the English represented what people from the mainland of Europe (and especially Germany) thought they would like them to be – stupid, brave, amiable kind to animals and domestics and, *au fond,* eminently amenable to reason, particularly from someone of another nationality.

...So for all their efforts the Archers in this case misjudged the fire-power of their thesis; despite a number of very fine performances – not least from Roger Livesey as Blimp in a love-hate relationship with Anton Walbrook as the Prussian – the film gently but firmly backfired.

In 1944 Powell made a curious film called *A Canterbury Tale* which displayed for the first time that element of "kinkiness" which was later to destroy his reputation for some time when he gave it free rein in *Peeping Tom.* This first glimpse of his Achilles heel dealt with a fictional psychotic Justice of the Peace in Kent whose extra war-effort involved him in lecturing to the locally stationed American troops on archaeology and other more peaceable pursuits. Alarmed at the thought of the men being seduced from these delights by the wiles of the local girls, he takes to going around in the black-out and pouring glue on their hair. Repentance for these psychotic excesses is eventually achieved by the J.P. through a sort of pilgrimage to Canterbury Cathedral in the company of a sweet kind girl, a British soldier and an American ditto. The intention of the film-makers remains highly mysterious even now and not surprisingly the authorities showed some reluctance to export this picture of British administrators of justice to our American allies.

Less controversial was his 1946 film *A Matter of Life and Death.* It still was redolent of the recent war but it contained a more acceptable and appealing message for the American public. Dilys Powell recalled it as "a daring fantasy, a venture before its time":

> An airman (David Niven) miraculously spared from death in the Channel is tried by a celestial American court; his judges remember their wrongs at the hands of the British. But what we all saw in 1946, and see now, is a happy blending of realism and the imagined, a love-story wrapped in the fabric of drama.

The Archers went on to display another facet of their talents with the triumphant cinematic success *The Red Shoes,* which appeared in 1948, and followed this up with *The Tales of Hoffman* in the early 'fifties. Meantime they had made (in 1949) what was perhaps their last masterpiece together, *The Small Back Room,* based on the novel of that name by another Savile member, Nigel Balchin.

But the partnership was beginning to falter; they made two more reasonably acceptable war films, *The Battle of the River Plate* and a treatment of the real-life adventure of the kidnapping of a German general in Crete, *Ill Met by Moonlight,* and shortly afterwards, for reasons which have never been fully explained, the partnership of Powell with Pressburger was ended, although their friendship survived.

Neither man's subsequent work would ever match the quality or achieve the critical and popular success of what they had created together. From Powell's extensive memoirs *A Life in Movies* it is evident that he was deeply wounded by the obloquy which was hurled upon him after his admittedly appalling film *Peeping Tom,* and by the rejection and enforced obscurity which ensued. One of his difficulties was that he had always been – both professionally and socially – unable to suffer fools either gladly or otherwise, and the multitude of would-be backers or collaborators whom he had insulted and snubbed in the days of his strength were only too happy to see him now as a spent force. But even in adversity he refused to compromise. In the year before he died he walked out on a Swiss banker because he thought him "ignorant", and this rigidity was often demonstrated during his forays into the Club. He could be the most charming and entertaining of companions unless one of the company was tempted to make an ill-considered remark for the sake of a well-turned phrase. An uneasy chill would ensue fuelled by a caustic interrogation for further enlightenment. Few transgressors were ever able to survive. This ruthlessness was particularly unfair for, as Lindsay Anderson pointed out in his review of the second volume of Powell's memoirs, he himself had a preoccupation with style – often at the expense of content. Nevertheless it was this flaw which paradoxically brought about a dramatic revival in his fortunes in the late 'seventies. During the 'fifties, when films for showing on television were still scarce, a series of retrospectives were shown on New York's Channel 9. The series, which was called *The Million Dollar Movie,* included some of the best work of Michael Powell, notably *The Red Shoes* and *The Tales of Hoffman.* Among the youngsters who were watching in amazement were the budding film directors Francis Ford Coppola, Martin Scorsese and George Romero, all of whom would subsequently admit their debt to his pioneering work. Powell's reputation and his mastery of style became an underground phenomenon. Bertolucci recalled that before his marriage his future wife made him study all the Powell films he had not already seen.

Later, when Scorsese was well established, he came to England in search of Powell and found him living in a caravan in the country trying to set up a production of *The Tempest.* It was the beginning of a friendship which transformed Powell's fortunes in more ways than one; he was to meet Scorsese's editor, Thelma Schoonmaker, and marry her (as his third wife) and be invited over to California to work with Francis Ford Coppola. Powell had always dreamed of having a studio where the creators could get on with it without tiresome interference from businessmen and financiers and Coppola tried to create it for him in the same Hollywood lot where his maverick rediscovery had once made *Thief of Baghdad.* The project failed but Powell's reputation remained safely restored. So apparently did his penchant for unconventional behaviour; Bertolucci recalled that Powell once arrived unannounced at his house with Robert De Niro, "a most unpredictable couple, I didn't know what do do". Bertolucci brought lobsters and set them on the floor, so they raced "with a strange sound towards Powell and De Niro. It was the Charge of the Light Brigade with crustaceans". It was a scene which might very well have been enacted at the Savile when Powell was present, though the only animal incursion associated with him at Brook Street was the occasional presence of an elderly and most lugubrious spaniel called Mr Johnson, which, contrary to all the rules, he was allowed to keep in his bedroom on his rare overnight visits to the Club. In his later years Powell divided his time between his new-found work place in California and his country home in Gloucestershire. It is an indication of the affection and respect in which for all his acerbity he was held by the younger generation of American film directors that when death was imminent after a hideously prolonged fight against cancer, and when the commercial airlines refused to accept him as a passenger, one of his devoted Hollywood disciples put his private aeroplane at his disposal so that he might have his final wish to die in the English countryside, which next to film-making was one of the great passions of his life.

Powell was only one of the great men of the theatre and cinema who have distinguished the Savile membership list but for all the talented cast which has been reviewed in the foregoing pages, the Club's contribution to the world of theatre and cinema would not be complete without proper mention of Sir Ralph Richardson, who has so far only been noticed in passing. His professional career is well recorded elsewhere and his impact on twentieth-century drama is now a matter for the history books. It is only fitting however, that his delightfully fey attendances at the Savile over a period of more than half a century should be set down here, as a supplement to his more solid legacy to British theatre.

It is no disrespect to all the other talented figures from his own profession who thronged the Savile during Richardson's period of membership to say that while he was by far the most distinguished Savilian actor since Sir Henry Irving he was also the best loved and most rewarding companion to be encountered at the long table, snooker room or bar. Part of the joy of being with him was the knowledge that beneath his unassuming exterior there lurked an extremely eccentric imp bursting to be let out. Given a suitable opportunity it *was* let out, and these excursions gave rise to a host of stories which have become permanently engraved into Club legend. To see his Rolls-Royce drawing up to the door at Brook Street or to see his motor-bike parked outside and his massive crash helmet hanging in the cloak-room was to know that rare entertainment was likely to ensue. There is, for instance, the legend that once at the long table when, the conversation having taken some bizarre turn to do with monkeys on a stick or the Indian rope trick, Richardson challenged the company to bet him he could not perform similar feats. The bet was taken and an astonished dining room was treated to the sight of one of our elderly theatrical knights shinning up the pillar next to the cash desk like a youthful acrobat.

317

Richardson's powerful motor-bike which he still insisted on riding until just before he died at the age of eighty-one also took its place in Club lore. His arrivals and departures kitted out like an astronaut preparing for a space walk were, as one might expect, moments of high drama. When he was in his seventies there was one occasion when he realized he was going to be late for an appointment; he abruptly left his company to tog himself out for a high-speed trip across London. Some of his companions followed him to the door to see him off. He emerged into Brook Street totally encased in space-invader garb, mounted his machine and roared off the wrong way down Gilbert Street which he had decided was a useful short-cut. A passing policeman having failed to take his number addressed the Savilians gathered at the door with a mournful shake of his head: "These young tearaways nowadays! But what can you do?"

Michael Meyer in his memoirs *Not Prince Hamlet* alludes to Richardson's strange love affair with what in anybody's estimation must be regarded as an unconventional mode of transport for an elderly gentleman of such distinction:

> His devotion to his motor cycle sometimes caused his friends embarrassment. He would offer other members of the Savile lifts home, and they, thinking he meant his Rolls-Royce, would accept, only to be led round the corner and find Ralph's fingers pointing at the pillion. The eminent American Milton Waldman told me that when aged around eighty, he mentioned to Ralph at lunch that he was going for a heart check-up, was offered a lift and a few minutes later found himself in the predicament described. Waldman protested that he could not possibly ride pillion in his condition, but somehow he found himself on it with his arms around Ralph's waist and his face pressed into Ralph's tweedy back. 'I think we can just make it.' said Ralph, and weaved through the Oxford Street traffic to deposit Waldman on his specialist's doorstep. But Waldman's embarrassment had only just begun. The specialist greeted him, looked at him thoughtfully, took his pulse and asked: 'Did you walk here?' 'No.' 'Taxi?' 'No.' 'How did you come?' 'By motor cycle.' 'You drove here on a motor cycle? At eighty, with a heart condition?' Feeling, he told me, more foolish than he had done for sixty years, Waldman had to reply: 'Actually, I rode pillion.' The specialist said it was no use examining him in his present condition and told him to return in a week, by taxi.

Michael Meyer was one of Richardson's particular friends at the Club and was also associated with him professionally. His memoirs are studded with references to this most blithe of theatrical spirits and after retailing the terrorizing of the unfortunate Milton Waldman he goes on to recall another famous occasion at the Savile when the great creator of illusion found the intrusion of reality too much of a puzzle for easy digestion:

318

Like most actors of his generation, Ralph could not sustain any accent but his own for more than a few sentences except as a caricature. Apart from its disadvantages on stage, this also meant that when he told stories, which he did very well, all the characters spoke like Ralph, sometimes with ludicrous effect. Once I was about to pay my lunch bill at the Savile. I saw Ralph standing by the cashier's desk with a pained expression. Before I could ask if anything was wrong, he turned his great eyes on me and with his customary lack of prelude, said: 'There isn't anything particularly odd about a jam omelette, is there?' He continued: 'I had a fine steak, and thought: 'I'll end with a jam omelette'. I told the waitress: 'Bring me a jam omelette, my dear'. She came back and [Irish waitress speaking like Ralph]: 'Sorry, sir, we have ham, cheese and herb, but no jam'. I said: 'Would you ask if they could make a jam one for me?' She came back and said: 'They want to know who it's for.' I gave her my name and she came back the third time and said: 'Sorry, sir, no jam omelette.' What I want to know is, who would I have had to be to get a jam omelette?'

There can have been few people in recent years who could have constructed a three act tragi-comedy from such a trivial incident. No doubt the Club will continue to attract like men of talent and wit from the theatrical as well as all the other professions but it is a reasonable assumption that when the history of the Club is updated one and a quarter century hence it is unlikely to record the subsequent presence of a spirit so rare as Richardson's; for both as an actor and as a Savilian he was quite simply incomparable.

CHAPTER SEVEN

Scandals

Every institution is distinguished by its own peculiar scandals and the way in which it deals with them. Clubs are no exception. The Athenaeum, one surmises, might be wakened from its slumbers by a member denying one of the Thirty-nine Articles; White's and Boodle's inflamed by an opponent of primogeniture; Pratt's by one who presented himself as a small "p" and one "t" and so on, but all of them reveal something of themselves in the nature of the sins they find unforgivable.

Perhaps because of the "careful process of election" there are few unforgivable sins committed at the Savile except being boring, which is why the few generators of tedium who have managed to creep through the election committee's sieve are included here; for to be boring at the Savile is properly accounted scandalous. Moreover, with one or two unfortunate exceptions most of the Savile "scandals" have turned out to be rather jolly affairs and together with many of the "Club bores" have provided excellent material for subsequent joyful anecdote so that Tennyson might almost have been describing the Savile's long table when he wrote:

> You'll have no scandal while you dine,
> But honest talk and wholesome wine.

One of the first sensational events to disturb the normal equilibrium of the Club was provided by the Rev. W.J. Loftie, the clergyman who had proposed Oscar Wilde for membership after Henley had failed to carry out his original offer to do so. It is odd, incidentally, that just as the rejected presence of that great Irish wit permeated the early literary history of the Club at second hand, so it did also in the primordial scandal, albeit in this case a heterosexual one.

Loftie was an assistant chaplain at the Chapel Royal, Savoy, and had published, among his other works, a book with the incredible title: *A plea for Art in the House with special reference to the economy of collecting works of Art and the importance of Taste in Education and Morals*. He was also an expert on Egyptian scarabs and a world authority on *gravel*. Max Beerbohm, in his inimitable way, provides a potted version of his sad history in which we can also hear something of the exquisite cadences of that great satirist's conversational style:

> There was a man in London, a clergyman, the Reverend W.J. Loftie who wrote a book about scarabs – two books I believe... He was a great authority on gravel. He liked scarabs, but his great passion was gravel. He was a chaplain somewhere, but he lived for gravel. He was constantly

excavating the substrata of old buildings and old churches to find out what was beneath them. He was on the *Saturday Review* for a time. He published articles and even, I believe, a book about gravel. But there was a still greater authority in London on gravel than even the Rev. W.J. Loftie. He was the acknowledged master of gravel, and Loftie knew, as everyone interested in gravel knew, that his great work was coming from the publishers soon. For this, the Rev. W.J. Loftie waited, hoping, praying that his own more modest endeavours would be noticed in it. One day the book arrived. Loftie was knee deep in an excavation beneath some church, but he had arranged that the master's book be delivered to him, no matter where. He opened the volume with trembling hands, at the index. There it was, his name – "Loftie, the Rev. W.J." His heart leapt – and then sank. Because after his name was written, in smaller type, "Strange error of...."

He looked up the page where his name appeared in the body of the book and found that, according to the author, he had made a wrong deduction from certain of his observations about London gravel. At the Savile Club, of which he and I were both members, there was nothing we could do to alleviate this disaster to his pride.

Do you know, [continued Max, when recounting this story] I wonder whether the rest of Loftie's career, its deterioration, did not stem from this disappointment?

Years passed. One day, the Savile Club reverberated with scandal. The Reverend W.J. Loftie had been diverted from his interest in gravel long enough to seduce a parlour maid and he had found it expedient to give up the Church. He was left alone with his major passion. Alec Ross came into the Club and was told the shattering news: "Oh," he said. "Poor Loftie, W.J. – the strange error of...."

A more enigmatic figure in those early days was one Alexander James Duffield, of whom Sir Herbert Stephen wrote:

Few of the members were more conspicuous from a strictly internal point of view, for the greater part of the Savile Row period, and a few years afterwards, than A.J. Duffield, who had been elected in 1869. He was an odd-looking man of rather squat figure and rugged appearance, with an untidy beard and a most impressively broken nose, of both of which features he seemed to be proud, who recounted with singular deliberation the most incredible adventures, of which he said he had been the hero, in all parts of the world. He did not habitually boast of the fact, but he let it be known that he had been in prison in Australia, and he apparently wished it to be believed that this misfortune was the climax of a spirited attempt on his part to introduce the South American alpaca among the Australian fauna, which was to be a commercial enterprise of the first order of importance. The attempt failed, because private jealousies and official pedantry kept Duffield's ship outside its intended port of arrival until all the alpacas were dead. His life was mysterious. For months together he would live in the Club as constantly as its constitution allowed, and then for months he would disappear absolutely, and no one would know anything of his whereabouts. In 1875 two members of the Club prosecuted a man named Slade at Bow Street for unlawful spiritualistic imposture. It happened that Duffield was a witness, and when at the beginning of his cross-examination Slade's solicitor asked him what he was, the crowd of members who made up a great part of the audience waited with passionate anxiety for his answer. Duffield looked round with full appreciation of the situation, paused with the weightiest deliberation, and then answered with immense dignity, and as slowly as he could, "I am an Analytical Chemist." The Savilians found this answer exceedingly entertaining, and signified the same in the usual manner. What the magistrate or the public thought of it is not known nor was anything further ever discovered about Duffield's pursuits or alleged pursuits. It ultimately became possible to find his discourse tedious, especially if you were in haste to be gone, but no one ever disliked him....

A more likable figure despite his habitual crustiness was the distinguished Irish composer, Sir Charles Villiers Stanford. He was an inveterate cards-player, a notoriously bad loser but nevertheless an extremely popular presence about whose exploits in the card-room legendary tales abounded. Most of them were very amusing but one incident might well have ended in tragedy. Harry Plunket Greene, the biographer of Stanford, recounts the story:

> There was a well-known *habitué* of the card-room, now deceased, who was a typical "character". He was a short, stocky, grey-bearded man, hide-bound by his self-imposed rules, and, except that he was very much from Ireland, might have come straight out of a Dickens novel. He followed a daily fixed routine which was known off by heart by all the members. Punctually at 5.45 p.m. the card-room door would open half-way and a copy of the *St James's Gazette* would appear with puffs of smoke coming out of the top; this being followed by the top of a head, the rest immersed in the paper. He came slowly into the room, reading and puffing his pipe, walked to a chair reading and puffing, and kept on reading and puffing until a table was up. The time of arrival and the subsequent technique never varied a hair's breadth from one day to another. His conversation at play consisted of one monosyllable, one dissyllable and one trisyllable – "hearts" – "two clubs" and "I'll doubl'um." (These were the days before "Auction.") There he sat, unmoved, inscrutable, the very puffs of his pipe following one another at regular (*allegro*) intervals. His smoking technique reminded one of the jets of steam from a factory blow-pipe.

To Stanford he was irresistible. His inscrutability intrigued him and the fact that he came from Ireland gave a peculiar zest to the chase. He pursued him day after day with relentless fervour, casting fly after fly on the head of the old trout in the dark under the mill-pool arch – all in vain. And suddenly one afternoon he rose. He seized the heavy brass match-box and hurled it at Stanford's head, providentially missing him, and walked out of the room – the whole thing without a word. He turned up again next day at the appointed time quite unconcerned and followed the usual routine. Only once in living memory was he thrown out of his stride, and that was not his fault. The *St James's Gazette* ceased publication and he ceased to appear. It took him a week to re-arrange the scattered pieces of his being; then the door opened at 5.45 and an apologetic *Pall Mall* walked slowly into the card-room, picked up the old technique and carried on as usual.

Such violence is fortunately rare at the Savile as indeed it should be but there have been occasional outbreaks as well as some near-misses. One *very* near-miss was when a consequence of H.G. Wells's exuberant philandering insinuated itself into the Club. Tom Baistow recounted the story during an H.G. Wells Discussion dinner in 1987.

Wells had not only made a fellow Savilian's daughter pregnant but had had the bad manners to use their scandalous affair as the plot of a *roman à clef*. The girl was Amber Reeves, the book was *Ann Veronica*, and in case the reader could not find *la clef*, St Loe Strachey, editor of the *Spectator*, attacked it furiously and condemned the easily identifiable heroine as a whore. This was too much for her father, Pember Reeves, a fellow Fabian who had actually introduced Wells to the Savile in 1903. Every day Reeves, the very respectable director of the London School of Economics, sat in the bow window of the Club, then in Piccadilly, with a revolver on the table, waiting for H.G. to appear. It was also too much for the Savile. The committee asked Wells to resign and he disappeared from the Club. But the Savile is nothing if not broadminded. Twenty-eight years later, in 1937, after the outraged Reeves had died, the prodigal member was welcomed back with open arms, to resume his role as conversationalist extraordinary as if nothing had happened.

He had spent the intervening years at the Athenaeum and on his return to Brook Street declared blithely, "Ah! The Savile. The Athenaeum for the living."

In his memoirs *Not Prince Hamlet,* Michael Meyer recalls two incidents which are now part of Club legend involving not only violence but the participation of two of the most notorious Club bores at the time.
As he so rightly begins:

The Savile was unlike other London clubs in its informality and its willingness to include mavericks. The level of tolerance was high, and I can recall only two instances in which serious action had to be taken. The most notorious occurred during the war and concerned John Davenport, a choleric and sometimes violent writer who was the more dangerous by reason of his having won a boxing Blue while at Oxford. He had been, and may still have been, a Communist at the time. On this occasion he drank heavily at the bar for some time before proceeding upstairs to dinner. As he sat drinking his tomato soup, his eye was caught by a white waistcoat and tails worn by an old and eminent gentleman dining opposite him. "You're dressed up," said Davenport, to which the old gentleman replied that his granddaughter was celebrating her twenty-first birthday and he was going to her party. "Drinking champagne, I suppose?" said Davenport. The old gentleman beamed and nodded. "You bloody swine," said Davenport. "People are being killed all over the world and you doll up and drink champagne," and he threw the remains of his tomato soup over the white waistcoat. For this he was ordered out of the dining-room.

Davenport returned to the bar and drank for a further hour. Then, needing to visit the lavatory, he walked through the Sandpit in which several elderly members were listening to the news on a wireless set. The main item concerned an advance by the Russians, prompting one member to remark that these Reds had something in them. Davenport halted in his tracks. "You bloody old bastards! When they were trying to build a decent country you did all you could to stop them, and now they're dying for your sake all you can say is they've got something in them. You're not worthy to listen to the news of their victories," and he yanked the flex out of its plug so fiercely that it broke and the transmission could be heard no more. Davenport then proceeded to the hall, where the third and most controversial event of the evening took place.

The Savile members were in general a liberal-minded lot, but we included one dreadful Fascist, a Major Pollard, of whom Raymond Postgate once remarked that he had not merely flown Franco into Spain in 1936, but boasted of having done so. Major Pollard was an expert in ballistics. If anything was fired up, he was the man to tell you where it would come down. His intolerance knew few bounds; years later, on being asked where he lived, he named some suburb, adding: "It's not the most convenient, but it has one advantage. There aren't any niggers there," and when his questioner said: "Don't you like black people?" Major Pollard shouted for the whole room to hear: "I hate 'em." Nobody in the Club could stand him, but he had been elected long before anyone had heard of Fascism, and we had to put up with him.

During the war Major Pollard worked at some ministry, from which he would patriotically walk each evening after work (we were all exhorted not to use public transport if we could avoid it), take up a position against the mantelpiece in the bar and deliver a detailed and boring account of his day's work, with many a reminder of how secret it was ("You'll understand I can't go into details about this"). On this occasion, he happened to enter the Club at the precise moment when John Davenport was passing through the hall on his way to the lavatory. Unpopular as Major Pollard was in the Savile, by no one was he hated more than by John Davenport. As Major Pollard came through the door, no doubt looking forward to describing his day to the members eagerly awaiting his appearance, he was confronted by the gorilla-like figure of Davenport, who said: "You're the worst of the bloody lot", advanced on him and threw him out into the night.

But Major Pollard had not been a soldier for nothing. He carried a swordstick, in case he should be attacked in the black-out. This he now unsheathed, and the porter was treated to the unusual sight of a member entering the Club with a drawn sword and advancing on a fellow-member who disarmed him easily, broke the sword over his knee and threw him a second time into the night. Major Pollard did not attempt to force a third entry. This action of Davenport's was generally approved, but his earlier behaviour was not, and he was asked to resign.

Monja Danischewsky reminds us that Davenport was also a protagonist in one other legendary incident:

> In the Savile Club bar there is a massive marble sideboard. It was used at Christmas time to support the traditional boar's head. Apart from that it seems to have no purpose, except for one memorable evening when it supported a precious burden. A convivial group included Lord Maugham, the Lord Chancellor, and John Davenport, a writer of considerable talent and a man of extraordinary strength. It is now lost in the mists of time what triggered the event. Lord Maugham was holding forth on the subject of punctuality. He prided himself that a clock could be set by his own time-keeping. "You *are* a clock," cried Davenport. Whereupon he lifted the eminent member bodily and sat him up on the marble slab.
> "Now go tick-tock, tick-tock."
> Details of the aftermath are not to hand. Like the Indian rope-trick, nobody has actually seen it but everyone knew it had happened. Mr Davenport was not seen afterwards at the Savile, which saddened his contemporaries. Lord Maugham continued to be punctual.

In general, however, although Savile members may consume drink in quantity they show a healthy respect for quality, as can be seen from the wine list. "Danny" adds a further anecdote to illustrate this – though perhaps at a less exalted end of the scale:

> The late Herbert Agar, distinguished American historian, was made a

Special Assistant during the war years to Ambassador Winant. A great anglophile and an enthusiastic member of the Savile, Agar became Chairman of the Club, a unique honour (as he would put it) for an American visitor. He had made England his home, and it was our way of saying thank you for his efforts to help America into the war.

He was a fastidious man, as the following story should demonstrate. He had been a friend from their college days of Scott Fitzgerald, and Agar was asked at what age could Fitzgerald have become an alcoholic.

"Scott was already a pretty hard drinker when I first knew him. But you must remember that we are talking about the time of Prohibition. I suppose we all drank too much in those days and of course we all drank bad liquor." Herbert hastened to correct himself: "I should add that I was luckier than most. My whisky was fixed for me by a friend at Princeton who later won a Nobel Prize for chemistry."

Strangely enough, drink has only rarely been the cause of unpleasantness at the Club; more often it has been the source of comedy. Winston Graham, most abstemious but tolerant of men (worth mentioning for the two so rarely go together) was bemused by what met his eyes when first he became a member in the mid-'forties.

There was (I *think*, and I speak now with little recent knowledge of evenings at the Club) a great deal more drinking. Many of my friends and most admired companions were huge drinkers. (I am referring, I would emphasize, to the evenings.) A few, like John Raymond, who went to sleep every night at the dinner table and had to be asked to resign, became incapable; most stayed on their feet staggering but indomitable. My film agent, Alan Grogan, though sometimes hardly able to focus, would play better and better snooker the more he drank. There was one occasion when Norman Crump emerged from the billiards room intent on spending a penny. But in the Sandpit he met a waiter bearing a tray of drinks for the billiards room. The waiter stepped to one side – and so did Norman. They then each stepped the other way. This went on in Chaplinesque style until in the end Norman was facing back the way he had come. He followed the waiter back into the billiards room, having forgotten what he came out for; three minutes later he re-emerged in great haste.

Then there was Ted Liveing, who used to drink himself into a state of glazed happiness not warranted by his circumstances and wander round the billiards table urging his partner to "hit it like bloody hell, partner!" And Ralph Wightman, famous on the B.B.C. on the Brains Trust and like programmes for his agricultural wisdom, who would wander into the billiards room and go to sleep on the settee, occasionally waking and raising his head to remark: "Jesus Chroist, ef Oi could'n play berrer'n tha-at." And then go to sleep again.

While the not infrequent sight of members in their cups is regarded at the Club with a tolerance which most probably defuses any explosive potential this condition might cause elsewhere, it is certainly not seen as acceptable behaviour in a guest, particularly one who is being presented as a candidate. This attitude – not so hypocritical as it appears – seems to be based on the theory that at least a *glimpse* of a candidate's best behaviour is a useful prelude to acceptance of whatever he is capable of performing after, if ever, he is elected. Sadly, George Brown, the once deputy prime minister, failed this elementary test in 1971. Lord George-Brown, as he then was, had been proposed by his life-long friend and one time political colleague, David Hardman. Members with their extraordinary range of political views but common appreciation of eccentricity rushed to fill the Candidates Book with their signatures so they might have a say one way or another in the committee's forthcoming grave decision. Then, after several preliminary appearances in the company of David Hardman, the great day arrived when George Brown was invited to a House Dinner where, along with a few others in the same pre-confirmational state, he could be covertly examined by all and sundry as to his state of grace. He began well by arriving seemingly sober. At that time the Savile possessed a barmaid of magnificent presence called Barbara Curtis, known to all at the Club as "The Duchess of Portsmouth" on account of her legendary reign at the "Admiral Keppel" – in the home of the British navy – during the early days of her dazzling youth, which are undoubtedly still remembered fondly by many contemporary Lords of the Admiralty. Hardman had not yet arrived but had left instructions that his guest should be given whatever he required. George Brown at first ordered a small brown sherry which Barbara served with a mixture of disappointment and disbelief. It was early and the bar was relatively empty. George Brown ordered another; then he began to weave from side to side. He ordered a large brandy to steady himself and fixed the redoubtable Barbara with a fearsome eye:

"I'm up for membership of this place, you know."

"So I've heard, sir."

"I suppose you're with all those other capitalist lackeys who don't want an honest socialist to pollute a Mayfair Club?"

"My Lord, I am a barmaid in this Club. My living depends upon it. I should be *delighted* to see you become a member."

Brown was enchanted by this, but as the bar began to fill and more brandies were pressed upon him his condition deteriorated into that which *Private Eye* has immortally associated with him: "tired and emotional".

It is the custom at House Dinners that no speeches are made; Brown insisted on making one. "I know that most of you don't want me... I'm as good as any of you... If you won't have me, I'll form my own club, it'll be better than this... then you'll be sorry... etc., etc." Having delivered himself of this he marched from the dining-table, tumbled down the ball-room stairs and landed insensible at the bottom.

Despite the years of friendship, his proposer felt constrained to remove his name from the Candidates Book and although the whole affair was regarded as highly comical it caused some regret among the members. If only it had happened a week or two later and Brown had been elected, he would have been quietly told to shut up, rescued from the bottom of the stairs, revived, escorted home and remembered for a particularly juicy piece of native eccentricity. Dear Jack Packard mournfully summed it up: "Oh Damn!" he said, "now I'll *still* be the biggest loud-mouth in the Club."

Apparently Brown's rejection continued to rankle. Years later, in 1981, Edgar Duchin was a member of the Savile Club Chess team in their biennial tournament against the Metropolitan Club of Washington D.C. As part of the hospitality arranged by the organizer, Captain Belin, a high official in the U.S. Navy Department, a reception was held at which, of course, Edgar and his wife were present. They were talking to their hostess, a striking lady in a beautiful Dior dress, when Lord George-Brown appeared and accosted her:

"May I kiss you on the lips?"

"No."

At this, George Brown seized Betty Duchin and kissed her instead. Having thus introduced himself to his own satisfaction, Brown enquired the reason for the Duchins' presence in Washington and on being told they were part of the Savile's chess team, Brown gloomily replied, "Ah yes. That's the bloody Club that wouldn't have me."

Mention of Barbara Curtis's imperturbability behind the bar recalls an earlier occasion, when, all the other members having gone up to dine, she found herself alone with a *very* distinguished member indeed. The thoroughness with which this pillar of the arts had laced himself with aperitifs, together with the statuesque charms of her who had been serving them, had banished all thoughts of dinner from his mind and replaced them instead with an overpowering passion. Summoned from the pantry behind the bar to serve him, as she thought with yet another glass, Barbara was treated to the sight and sound of this portly member with his trousers around his ankles and the optimistic query:

"What do you think of this, then?"

Naturally, no one else was there to witness it but later when the other diners returned and asked the reason for the Duchess's unwonted skittishness they were horrified.

"Whatever did you do then?" one of them anxiously enquired.

"Well sir," she replied, "I said to him, 'If my memory serves me correctly, you're a boy'."

Excess of drink was, however, undoubtedly the cause of one of the less pleasant occurrences which happened in the Club although, perhaps, its postscript can be seen as faintly comic after the passage of so many years. It concerned Gilbert Harding, now almost forgotten, but at the time one of the best known men in Britain by virtue of his emergence as one of the first "T.V. personalities" in the early days of post-war broadcasting.

Gilbert, indeed, possessed an overpowering personality, even in private, and people who met him reacted in one of only two ways: enormous affection or absolute detestation. This was no doubt because, depending on the mood he was in, he could be either lovable or detestable. Compton Mackenzie esteemed him greatly through many years of friendship, and thirty or more years after his death Winston Graham still remembers him kindly and misses him greatly. Depending on which camp you were in he was either a great wit or an intolerable bore. Winston considers him to have been one of the greatest of the Savile raconteurs but Peter Green writes that "one of the most stunning bores" he ever encountered at the Savile was "the late Gilbert Harding, who used to lie in wait for the unwary like the roadside lion in *Pilgrim's Progress* [and] as Michael Ayrton said, if they'd made it a competitive sport he'd have bored for England…"

Perhaps there were elements of truth in both judgements. At all events he was involved in a most unseemly fracas with another member, Hubert Clifford, late one night at the Savile. Once again, Michael Meyer records some of this incident in his memoirs:

> Harding was homosexual but, as he explained to everyone, impotent. He was an unhappy, impossible, yet often endearing man. One evening he came to the Club with two young male guests, one of them an American, and sat drinking with them in the bar. Hubert Clifford, a portly red-haired Australian of about Gilbert's age, who was head of music for the B.B.C. Light Programme and was fairly drunk, took it into his head to walk up and down in front of Gilbert and his guests with a glass of brandy in his hand, saying loudly: "I am normal." Gilbert, who for once was not drunk, endured this for a while, then said: "By normal, I take it you mean pacing the pavements of Piccadilly pawing the soiled smalls of prostitutes." At this, Clifford threw his brandy into Gilbert's face and rushed at him, and the two grossly overweight men rolled locked on the Club floor.
>
> An ex-colonel named Edward Crankshaw, who wrote with distinction

330

for the *Observer* on military and other matters, tried to separate them but, being small, failed, and was rolled by them on to the brandy glass, which broke and cut him badly so that he bled on to the carpet. At this the young American panicked, ran to the phone, dialled 999 and asked for the police. When he got them, he said: "Come quickly. There's a terrible fight." "Where?" "It's a club." "What club?" "I think it's called the Savage." The police promptly sent a carload of constables to the Savage Club in Carlton House Terrace, which proved to be empty except for four elderly members playing bridge.

By way of postscript: when the police finally arrived at Brook Street having exercised some time-consuming detective work in estabishing their correct destination, the two unlikely pugilists had been separated and sent on their respective ways: Edward Crankshaw was discovered by them, public-spiritedly mopping up the pools of blood which had by then extended to the hall door, but somehow managed to convince them that this was a perfectly normal and innocent occupation for an elderly member to be engaged in at midnight outside a gentlemen's club. The Savage took more convincing and a much longer time to forgive.

A more gentle form of blood-letting can usually be found in the Savile's treatment of bores. As Winston Graham remarks:

> The Savile was not without bores, but considering the size of the membership they have always been mercifully few. Norman Crump was generally to be avoided on the subject of trains, and there was an American called Evarts Scudder who took a great fancy to me and would corner me at the bar telling me how much superior in every way the Americans were to the British. Later he took to inviting me back to his home to dinner, where he would pressure me into reading his own poetry aloud, punctuating my reading with comments like: "Isn't that fine!" "Isn't that superb! I've never done anything better than that!"
>
> Years later, when he died, the wickedly caustic Denys Kilham Roberts wrote him an epitaph.
>
>> "Stop, passer by, and spare a shudder,
>> Here lie the bones of Evarts Scudder.
>>
>> "Now Greek meets Greek on equal terms.
>> The worms bore him; he bores the worms."

There have also been four-letter men of less agreeable aspect, such as Wilfred Evill, who during the war, I am told, always ate at Claridge's Causerie (fixed price) before coming on to the Savile to dinner, and often managed to talk in a loud voice about the food he'd eaten in the hearing of some member who had recently lost a son or a brother. He was a great art collector, and one of the last things I heard him say was: "I'm going to buy more Stanley Spencers. I hear he's got cancer." A few years later I used him as a character in one of the novels and got a letter of protest from one of his lady friends, who clearly saw much more good in him than I had ever been able to. She hadn't read the novel but recognized the likeness from the review in *The Times*.

The novel, incidentally, is *Angel, Pearl and Little God*, a wonderful example of how art can improve on ill-nature.

Poor Wilfred Evill! Hardly anyone who knew him has had a good word to say for him and it can only have been an extremely thick skin and the tolerance through gritted teeth of his fellow members which allowed him to remain in the Club at all. "Chippy" Kingham, who was secretary for elections and himself a member of somewhat explosive views who lived in the Club during his later years, hated him.

Stephen Morland remembers (albeit with some reluctance) the long antipathy between "Chippy" Kingham and Wilfred Evill, described as the "most private-spirited member of the Club".

> He had decided as a very young man that he would travel through life First Class, and in this he had been successful. Was he a conscientious objector during the first war because he thought that prison would be more comfortable than the trenches? When he was nominated for the Club committee, "Chippy" organised his defeat. As a solicitor, he advised clients on evasion of Income Tax, and left behind him a collection of modern art, Graham Sutherland etc., which he had accepted in lieu of fees (to evade his own income tax). When he died he left the Club £500, which would have been £5,000 if he had been elected to the Committee!

During his lifetime when it became known at the Club that on a visit to Seville, Evill had accidently fallen into the Guadalquivir, William Barnes recalls Chippy growling that it was "bad luck on the river" and Sam Musson tells of a macabre incident when this mutual antipathy caused *Sodalitas Convivium* to fly out of the window. One Christmas day in those more expansive times when the Club remained open for those who had no other place to celebrate, only two members turned up – Wilfred Evill and Chippy Kingham. There they sat at opposite ends of the long table wearing paper hats in a seasonable – if unsociable – frosty silence surrounded by a great mass of redundant festive paraphernalia, the only sound of gaiety and mirth coming from the Club's kitchens.

Ralph Richardson, with his appetite for the grotesque, was one of the few members who claimed to be "fond" of Evill. He wrote of one of his encounters:

> Those who knew Wilfred Evill are unlikely to have forgotten him – a mini-Falstaff, a Sidney Greenstreet, blue-eyed and bland. He came into the Sandpit one evening, carrying in his capacious bosom the smallest imaginable dog. Of course, however small, 'NO DOGS' is a rule of the Sandpit. Evill stood with his back to the fire and smiled blandly.
>
> > "What," asked Eric Linklater, "what, Evill, is that?"
>
> > "This," beamed Evill, "is my little Fifi."
>
> > Out of silence I think I ventured to say, "Indeed?" I was fond of Wilfred.
>
> > "A perfect miniature," exhibited Evill, "and a perfect dear – aren't you, Fifi?"
>
> Fifi did not reply, and neither did anyone else. The silence lengthened.
>
> One does not know what was in Evill's mind, but he set Fifi down on the hearthrug and, rubbing his hands genially, he took a step or two towards the hall.
>
> > "Fifi – Fifi," he called.
>
> Fifi started in the direction of her master. Malcolm Sommerset said, "Follows you like a dog."

Evill's flamboyant and unabashed mean-spiritedness was not appreciated at the Club and even now he is long gone the motto when his name is mentioned seems to be *De mortuis nil nisi Evill*, but there were others whose financial caution was able to arouse mirth rather than opprobrium. Ernest Franklin, a wealthy banker who was elected in 1929, came into the Club one day in expansive mood after a game of golf and approached the crowded bar.

"For the first time in my life," he announced, "I have just holed in one. Have a drink..." and then seeing the array of gaping brandy glasses expectantly waiting, paused and hastily amended his sentence, "... one of you."

The Club has experienced – admittedly in small measure – some miserliness, some violence, some drunkenness, and some sexual misdemeanours of both kinds, so one must ask what further outrages remain other than sacrilege, cheating at cards, theft and arson? But true to its founders' original principle that the Club should consist in "a mixture of men of different professions" it is indeed able to claim acquaintance with practitioners in all of these black arts.

Sacrilege has been successfully committed only once; the other occasion of it being narrowly averted at the last moment. The first, and successful, sacrilege is recalled by Dr John Fisher Stokes, who was elected in 1947 and subsequently served on the committee:

> Doyne Bell, who, was Chairman for some time, became a close friend and led to my serving happily on the committee for a number of quite eventful years. My clearest memory at this time is of the occasion on which two club servants had been found in *flagrante delicto* on the billiards table. The normal relaxed and often witty committee exchanges were submerged in a wave of high moral tone and demand for punitive action, spearheaded by Charles Snow; I recall Herbert Agar getting quite upset as the argument sharpened, until a perfectly timed interjection from G.P. Wells – "The trouble with young people nowadays is that they show insufficient respect for the cloth" – brought the debate cheerfully down to earth.

Clearly this was a variation of "Savile Snooker" which even the ingeniously fertile mind of Stephen Potter had failed to envisage; propriety forbids speculation on which prefix he would have attached to it in his "- - - - manship" series of satirical manuals on social intercourse.

The other potentially sacrilegious occasion was when Sir Ernest Pooley, presiding at a Club dinner, realized that the ultra left-wing cleric, Canon Collins of St Paul's, who had been a member for some years, was about to rise and start the proceedings by saying Grace. This was too much for Pooley, who considered it tantamount to inviting a divine thunderbolt to burst through the ballroom ceiling. He leapt to his feet to silence the hated apostle of C.N.D. with a stentorian roar of "Thank God! Let's eat. Amen".

Cheating at cards is equally rare – perhaps because, particularly at poker, no one seems to know the rules, which apparently change at the whim of each dealer. However, in 1935, at the more irascibly pedantic bridge table, a situation arose which bid fair to rival even that of Tranby Croft. In the autumn of 1934 a bridge club called the Wellington had to be wound up and as a gesture of sympathy the Savile committee issued an invitation to some of its members – up to a limit of a hundred – to move into Brook Street without entrance fee or subscription until the end of the year, with the provision that if they wished to remain after that they must be proposed and seconded in the usual way and pay the appropriate fees. One of the members of the Wellington who availed himself of this generous offer was a barrister-at-law called Stanley Harris who had, in fact, previously worked as an electrical engineer and been blinded in an accident. He was a devoted bridge player who managed to pursue this hobby by the use of special packs of cards which had Braille marks imprinted on them. Before becoming a member of the Wellington Club he had been a member of another famous bridge club, Almacks, which had also had to close its doors in 1928, but not before his extraordinarily skilful play had attracted a certain amount of jealousy and whispered allegations that he had profited by being able "to read" the cards while dealing. The members of the Wellington, however, discounted this rumour and he had made a great many friends there. At the Savile he proved to be equally popular and in due course he was put up for election, proposed by Dr T. Watts Eden, a member for twenty-five years, and supported by twenty-one other signatories, who included "Chippy" Kingham, the honorary secretary for elections; Peter Rodd ("Prod"); Vyvyan Holland, the son of Oscar Wilde; J.A. Barlow, Tom Barlow's father, who was chairman of the Club for more than twenty-five years; Sidney Dark, the editor of the *Church Times*; W.R. Darwin, father of Erasmus; Sir John Squire, Norman Croom-Johnson and Philip Morrell, who had been a member for thirty-eight years. It was extremely strong support, much greater than that for any of the other Wellington Club candidates, but Harris was the only one of them not to be elected. This infuriated Philip Morrell, who began a bitter and relentless campaign which nearly split the Club while he tried to remedy what he believed to be an intolerable injustice.

Morrell was not a man to be trifled with; he was head of the Oxfordshire brewing family and also "Keeper" of the Oxford University "Chest". He was married to the formidable *éminence grise* of the Bloomsbury Group, Lady Ottoline Morrell, and father-in-law to his fellow Savilian, Igor Vinogradov, the kindly and scholarly Russian aristocrat who could, nevertheless, paralyse the brash at twenty paces.

Morrell, a committee member, had arrived late to the relevant election meeting and found to his astonishment that "the member whom I had believed to be his principal supporter" was in the middle of a speech giving reasons why Harris should not be elected. Apparently the rumours which had emanated from Almacks six years earlier had been resurrected and furthermore there were suggestions that his manners at the bridge table were bad. Despite Morrell's protestations, the committee made up its mind "to defer" him. At the next election meeting, and without further consultation with the individuals concerned, his name was marked in the Candidates Book as "Withdrawn by request".

Morrell in the meantime had had to go abroad, but on his return he began a campaign which consisted of obtaining sufficient evidence to prove that allegations of cheating at Almacks were "absurd and impossible" and that "far from being a disagreeable man at the card table" Harris was "an extremely good player... and a pleasant and easy man to play with".

To this end he began a vigorous correspondence with people who could provide expert evidence from personal experience in favour of Harris on both counts.

Among the mass of correspondence which ensued were letters from Captain Sir Beachcroft Towse, V.C., K.C.V.O., C.B.E. of the National Institute for the Blind, on the 16 May 1935:

> MY DEAR HARRIS... I am writing to you to say that from my own personal experience I am strongly of opinion that it is quite impossible for a blind man to read braille dots on his cards whilst he is dealing them

either to himself or to the other players at the table...

... It is most regrettable that some people, without knowing anything about braille, are so ready to accuse us of doing the impossible.

And, from a former member of the committee of the Wellington, on 19 May 1935:

I have known Stanley Harris well. Speaking as a committee-man I can assure you he was a perfect member. Speaking as a fellow member, and seeing a good deal of him, I should like to tell you he was very popular.... a very good player. In the card room, he was always very affable.

... Being blind, he had to use braille cards. Members did not seem to mind this. He was, at one time, a member of Almacks. There was, I believe, some trouble about these cards, and certain members, who did not like Harris, made some unfriendly remarks about him. I took the trouble to ask several members of Almacks about it, and they have all told me the allegations were quite untrue, and only made by worse players than himself, who were likely to lose their money to a better player.

Yours sincerely,

Spencer Thornton.

Meantime, while he was gathering all his evidence, Morrell was conducting a brisk correspondence with the equally implacable "Chippy" Kingham.

3 April 1935

MY DEAR KINGHAM,

I was greatly disappointed on my return from abroad on Saturday to hear that Stanley Harris's candidature had again been rejected. The news was all the more distressing because I gathered from some members with whom I talked the matter over that there is an impression that there must be some serious reason to account for a candidate who has received such unusually strong support, including the support of five members of the Committee, being twice rejected. I am therefore writing to ask you as one of his principal opponents to tell me quite frankly whether you know of anything that reflects on his honour or character and would make him unfit to be a member of the Club. As both our names appear in the candidates' book amongst his supporters and yours in fact is at the head of the list I think I am fairly entitled to ask what has led you to change your views about him.

I am,

Yours sincerely,

Philip Morrell.

SAVILE CLUB

5 April 1935

DEAR MORRELL

Thank you for your letter.

I think you have failed to notice that the candidature to which you refer has been withdrawn.

Yours sincerely,

A. KINGHAM.

10, GOWER STREET,

8 April 1935.

DEAR KINGHAM,

The fact that Harris's candidature was withdrawn by the proposer does not seem to me to affect the question of the injury to his reputation caused by his previous rejection, more especially as the withdrawal was arranged by Eden without Harris's consent. I hope therefore that you will be good enough to let me have an answer to the questions I put to you in my letter of the 3rd. At present I find there are a great many people who suppose that there must be some serious objection to Harris's *character* to account for the emphatic rejection of a candidate who was so strongly supported. If you know of no such objection it would be fair to say so. On the other hand if there is some charge against him of which his friends are unaware it would be fair to us to indicate what that is, so that at least we may have enquiries made.

Yours sincerely,

PHILIP MORRELL.

9 April 1935.

DEAR MORRELL

I'm sorry, but I'm afraid I am not prepared to discuss the Committee's reasons for failing to elect a candidate.

Yours sincerely,

(Signed) A. KINGHAM.

10, GOWER STREET,

10 April 1935.

DEAR KINGHAM

I don't suppose it is much use continuing our correspondence but I should like to point out that what I asked you to discuss was not the Committee's reasons for failing to elect a candidate but your own for proposing his rejection and especially whether you know of any serious charge against him. In my first letter of 3 April I wrote "As both our names appear in the candidates' book amongst his supporters I think I am fairly entitled to ask what has led you to change your views about him," but I gather you prefer not to say.

Yours sincerely,

PHILIP MORRELL.

10, GOWER STREET

11 April 1935.

DEAR KINGHAM

You will remember that at the Committee Meeting yesterday you leant forward and pointing to a sentence in my letter to you which you had evidently just received said something which I thought was "The answer is I did not." If I heard you correctly this must mean I suppose that you did not propose Harris's rejection. If not it is a little difficult for me to understand what exactly happened. I came to the Election Meeting as you will remember on 31 December while you were speaking and from what I then heard I gathered that you were giving reasons why in your opinion Harris should not be elected as a member of the Club. Can you tell me if this is a fair statement of the case or it not what happened? I am really anxious to know.

Yours sincerely,

PHILIP MORRELL.

SAVILE CLUB,

13 April 1935.

DEAR MORRELL

I'm so sorry but I simply can't carry on this correspondence.

Yours sincerely,

A. KINGHAM.

By 23 May 1935 Morrell had privately printed a 56-page booklet outlining all the facts of the case and reproducing the considerable evidence he had amassed together with the relevant correspondence which he distributed at his own expense to every member of the Savile. But the committee refused to budge and Morrell felt so strongly that, after thirty-eight years of membership, he decided to resign. Before doing so, however, he made one last defiant gesture by hosting a grand

"Farewell Dinner" in the morning room of the Club on 24 July. The invitation cards read pointedly that "the pleasure of your company" was confined to "*some* of his friends". What happened to Harris is lost in the mists of time.

Theft has not featured greatly among the list of Savile "scandals". There has been, of course the usual crop of "misplaced" umbrellas and someone has recently walked off with the counters belonging to the backgammon board, though in this case an "outside job" is suspected. All in all, with one major exception, those thefts which have occurred have been relatively minor. Dallas Bower remembers one such which did not however seem so trivial to its hapless victim, whose very anguish invested his loss with a grandeur it would not normally possess. Dallas, with his inimitable delivery and gift for seemingly irrelevant asides, recounts it as a masterprice of tragi-comedy of which from memory a prose version can only provide a faint echo:

> There was this dear man, Alison Phillips; *Professor* Alison Phillips, don't you know. He was an historian. By all accounts, a *very fine* historian. One of his more notable contributions to history was a *Life of Elizabeth of Austria*. Now, when this dreadful incident took place he was a man of some age; getting on in years, you understand; not to put too fine a point on it, he was *very old indeed*. Well, one day, Norman Edwards and I were sitting in the Sandpit when Phillips began to shuffle through; he was something of a shuffler, you realize – particularly in his later years. As he passed us by he was muttering – he was something of a mutterer as well as a shuffler, you see – he was muttering: "It's too bad! It's just too bad!", so Norman and I felt rather alarmed for him and enquired the cause of his quite evident misery. I mean to say, the man was quite *distraught*. "somebody has stolen my cardigan!" he replied; "It's gone! Gone! The most disgraceful thing. Not at all what you'd expect to happen in a place of this distinction. Gone, I say. Stolen! My cardigan!"
>
> So we duly commiserated and followed him into the bar to support him while he strove to face up to his grievous loss. After some while he seemed to become more reconciled to the situation and felt able to talk about it in a more resigned fashion: "Well there it is; gone! Gone for ever, I suppose. The last time I had a cardigan stolen it was taken by the Abbé Liszt. I'd known him well. Frightful man with the women of course, but he played the piano beautifully: liked him well until I discovered he'd stolen my cardigan...."

Theft, or rather, a series of thefts, of more truly tragic proportions occurred during and immediately after the war when a considerable number of the valuable signed first editions which constitute the unique Savile Monument began gradually and at first imperceptibly to disappear.

In 1941, when the exigencies of war had made election to the Savile rather less of "a careful process" than it would have been in more normal times, a man called

Gordon Alan Keen was elected. He was proposed by Moray McLaren and there was only one other signature in the Candidates Book, N. Harcourt-Preston. Keen's occupation was entered in the book – ironically as it turned out – as "Dealer in Manuscripts". He was evidently a man of some charm but then, as Rupert Withers, who knew him, remarks, "to get away with the sort of things he did, he would need to be". Dallas Bower provides some insight into his style. In 1945, Dallas had recently completed the co-production of his masterpiece of Shakespearean cinema, *Henry V*, with Laurence Olivier. One of the opening scenes is a brilliant realization of Tudor London based faithfully on a contemporary print by Fisher. In the foreground is the Globe Theatre; in the distant background are several ships moored in the Thames. "When the film was completed," says Dallas, "Keen pestered me to obtain for him one of the model ships used in this shot. I told him they were worthless. As they were so far in the background of the shot they had been simply made out of deal and were not even constructed to scale. But Keen persisted and so I telephoned the prop-master at Denham Studios and arranged for one to be sent to him, whereupon I put the matter from my mind."

Some months later Dallas was invited to dinner by his old friend and fellow member, Val Gielgud, who was Head of Drama at the BBC. Val asked Dallas to arrive at his house in advance of his other guests, and when he did so, handed him a small parcel which he said he had been asked to pass on as a gift from Alan Keen. Inside was a 4th Folio of *Henry V* beautifully bound in leather. Apparently Keen had managed to sell the worthless model ship to a gullible American for some vast sum and this was Dallas's reward for his unsuspecting role in the confidence trick.

The Savile, however, was not so lucky. When it was discovered that Keen, by then the honorary librarian of the Club, was himself responsible for the decimation of the Monument it was already too late. The works of such earlier members as Rider Haggard, Kipling, Hardy and many others, all personally inscribed to the Club, were gone forever and only Keen, who by now had disappeared, would ever know where. Many other public-spirited members, such as Peter Rodd and Humphrey Hare, rallied round to replace them with similar editions, but the inscriptions with their more personal associations could not be replaced and the Monument shall never be the same.

After such tragedy, arson should not come as light relief, but when it happens at the Savile, can farce be far behind?

Apart from the Nazi incendiaries in 1941 there were, in fact, five deliberate acts of fire-raising in rapid succession during the autumn of 1975, of which the fifth and final occasion was by far the funniest and the most dramatic – if only in the sense that that term would be used in an Ealing comedy. There must have been well over a hundred people present to witness this event, most of whom will have their own cherished memories of it; but of all accounts, that of Tyrrell Burgess must take the prize for appreciation of the comic undertones.

By way of prologue Tyrrell has preserved a copy of the document which was posted on the Club notice board in the middle of all the excitement. It demonstrates, in its dead-pan way, the true "Dunkirk spirit" adopted by the

341

committee while all their world was falling about them:

> Members have already been advised that our former Secretary relinquished his position with the Club with effect from Wednesday, 22 October.
>
> Our Chef, Mr Wall, was admitted to Hospital and may not return for several weeks.
>
> On Thursday last, 30 October, our Breakfast Chef had to be dismissed.
>
> Our Valet gave one week's notice. There will be no valet service for the week commencing 3 November.
>
> THERE WAS A SERIOUS FIRE AT 0200 HOURS IN THE REAR OF THE CLUB ON SATURDAY MORNING. The police and Fire Brigade were called and the fire was contained.
>
> We hope for the forbearance of our Members and ask them to help the staff wherever they can. In particular it may be difficult (perhaps impossible) to provide hot meals after 1340 hours and 2040 hours.
> We welcome from today our new Manager Mr Peter Aldersley and wish him every success.
>
> SODALITAS CONVIVIUM
>
> > Guy Nicholson
> >
> > Chairman, House Committee
> >
> > 3 November 1975.

With upper lips suitably stiffened the members looked forward to the forthcoming week when a dinner party and concert to celebrate William Alwyn's seventieth birthday was due to take place. Tyrrell Burgess takes up the story:

> One of the traditions of the Savile Club is to treat itself periodically to performances of the works of its members who are composers. It is thus probably the only secular institution in which one can hear the work of Charles Villiers Stanford. It was decided to celebrate the seventieth birthday of William Alwyn with a dinner, for members and guests, followed by a recital of songs by Schubert, Wolf, and Alwyn. The singer was Benjamin Luxon.
>
> For the formally dressed ladies and gentlemen, the evening provided two additional incidents. The first was provided by the chairman of the dinner, another distinguished composer who had been celebrating William Alwyn's seventieth birthday for most of the day. He had firmly

grasped the idea that after one of the courses at the dinner, he had to get up and make a speech, but he plainly couldn't remember which course it was. So he got up after each one. He would stand, looking glassily at the chandeliers and utter a few words connected only by long pauses. "Happy" he would say... "old friend"... "m-u-u-u-u-si"... "Bill here".... At some point he would sit down, either in one of the pauses, or in one of the words. He failed to rise only at the point where speeches are normally made, indeed at this point the diners discovered that he was no longer in sight.

Tyrrell here omits to mention that Michael Pope, the distinguished musicologist and authority on nineteenth and twentieth century English music who had masterminded the evening, seeing all his carefully laid plans disintegrating before his eyes, handed the notes he had prepared for the chairman to the guest of honour, who now seemed to be the only competent substitute for the chairman, who was in fact snoozing beneath the table. Bill Alwyn, the most modest and obliging of men, agreed to deliver the prepared speech and had got as far as some such sentence as; "... William Alwyn is undoubtedly one of the greatest and most lyrical of living English composers...", before he realized what it was he was reading and broke off with, "My God! I can't say all this... . This is about me!" and sat down again. Back to Tyrrell for the real excitement of the evening, which was yet to come:

The second incident came during the songs, in the cycle by Wolf with which the evening was to end. At one moment the listeners heard faintly in the distance the bee-barp, bee-barp of an emergency service, and a flicker of irritation crossed one or two faces as people feared that it would intrude into the music. In fact it stopped, and people gave themselves up to art.

Some minutes later, a faint wisp of smoke was seen curling round the door from the dining room. People noticed, but pretended not to. Another wisp appeared, and then another. People sat on. The singer continued. The smoke began to be not so much a series of wisps as a settled mist. Nobody stirred. It was clear that people had begun to think of the *Titanic*. By the time Benjamin Luxon had brought the Wolf song cycle to a triumphant conclusion the room was quite thick with smoke. People clapped and then, not quite slowly, got up from the table and went down stairs.

There had indeed been a fire. A breakfast chef who had been dismissed some weeks earlier had formed a grudge against the Club on this account, and had got into the habit of returning now and again to set fire to it. He had done this during dinner.

The fire had been discovered and the fire brigade called. The member of staff who had done so had been considerate. Because there was a musical

343

evening going on, would the fire brigade please turn off their klaxon as they approached and make as little noise as possible? The brigade were pleased to help. Indeed, as the diners came down the front stairs they were confronted by a uniformed fireman standing in his stockinged feet. He had removed his boots so as not to make too much noise. He too was celebrating William Alwyn's seventieth birthday.

Let us hope that all, if any, future scandalous occasions at the Savile can be celebrated so discreetly, with such mirth, and with the immortal imperturbability of Guy Nicholson may the cry be heard "Sodalitas Convivium"!

Frank, the legendary and much-loved wine-waiter who served the Club throughout his long adult life.

Stephen Potter, whose theory of gamesmanship often expressed itself at the Savile snooker table, by his fellow member Sir David Low.

Merlyn Evans's impressionistic view of Savile snooker contributed for the centenary booklet.

CHAPTER EIGHT

Club Life (ambience and anecdotes)

"There can be no doubt that of all the accomplishments prized in modern society that of being agreeable in conversation is the very first," wrote Sir John Pentland Mahaffey, perhaps one of the greatest wits to grace the Savile, in his paradoxically boring primer, *The Principles of the Art of Conversation*. What he said may have been universally true in civilized circles when his fellow member, Alexander Macmillan, published his book in 1888 but sadly it no longer seems so. Nevertheless, one of the few outposts where Mahaffey's writ still runs is the Savile. When a member repairs to Brook Street to refresh his mind he knows that on any day of the week he can stroll into the Club to find at least a handful of people out of the many present with whom he can spend an hour or two in pleasurable resuscitation. This may take several forms – food, drink, snooker, cards or conversation – but of these by far the most important and all-consuming will be conversation, partly because it can be continued and sometimes even enhanced while indulging in any one or more of the others.

It does not matter that on these occasions he may not know or will have forgotten the names of those with whom he has chosen to spend his time; any embarrassment he is likely to feel shall soon be dissipated by the realization that his companions may not know or will have forgotten his. There are very few – if any – clubs in London like the Savile where nearly all the members are in fact *known* to one another, but known in the sense of having shared episodes of congenial social intercourse in a kind of mingling which demands no knowledge of names or personal backgrounds. At the Savile such details are irrelevant. When the late Gwynne Vevers was a young new member in the 'forties, for instance, he found himself engaged in an energetic conversation with some distinguished figure who had evidently been a member for some considerable time. When he left the table, Vevers asked his father who the man was and what did he do? "I don't know," said his father, "he's just a Savilian." So far as he was concerned that was enough.

Such informality takes some getting used to, as Patric Dickinson remembers: "For a new member going up to lunch for the first time alone was an ordeal. On my right was a spry natty small old chap. He was wearing a white bow-tie with pink polka dots. He soon broke into what I'm sure he could see was my nervousness. 'What do you do?' 'I'm a poet.' 'I'm a painter.' So we talked and talked. He never asked me my name; I dared not ask him his. It was Sir William Nicholson."

This sort of experience is by no means uncommon; indeed, at the Savile it seems almost commonplace. Michael Figgis recalls his own introduction to the Club:

... my proposer introduced me to several members, a number by the wrong name. Not being particularly clever at remembering names, this took years to put right although, much to my delight, I realised that names, identities and qualifications never seemed to matter very much. What did matter was what a man had to say for himself on any subject and how he said it. Once in the early 'sixties I happened to be sitting with a man who engaged my interest despite my ignorance of nuclear physics. He scribbled diagrams. He was lucid. When he moved to leave the table I, in an un-Savilian way, asked his name. John Cockcroft, he told me. Once, too, at the long table at lunch, I began to replenish my neighbour's glass. "I think not," he firmly said. "In fifteen minutes I shall be operating on a brain and hope to finish the job by eight o'clock. I don't think any more will help."

Perhaps this disregard for "names" is because there is no hierarchy at the Savile, where, as Andrew Cooper remarks:

everybody was somebody, nobody was anybody, and every member who walked in was expected to hang up his halo with his hat. I felt ill at ease in this new environment for I knew scarcely anyone. I did not like butting into conversations and if I were told the names of different members they were forgotten or wrongly attributed almost immediately. Gradually things changed. The first person to greet me with Savilian warmth was Dallas Bower and we talked for hours about the technicalities of film production and of the personalities who flitted in and out of this glamorous world. I shall never forget Dallas.

I was not an easy mixer for apart from forgetting names or getting them wrong I was not a drinking man. My early life was spent in a mining community where the "Demon Drink" flourished. Total abstinence was the rule for the family and it was not until I was in my early twenties that, one Christmas, we were each given a tiny glass of sherry. We thought we were going to the Devil. This attitude prevented my mixing freely with the jovial discussions in the bar and I must have seemed to be a stiff neck to my associates.

Things changed but I still had problems in meeting certain people. Pat Jackson for example, who became a close personal friend. For years I could not remember whether his name was Pat Jackson or Jack Patman. Sometimes I would call him Jack at others Pat. But now I know. Discussing this problem in the Sandpit one day I was told that the simple answer was to call everyone Michael. Nobody cared anyway.

Perhaps that is not *entirely* true: every Savilian accepts that the meaningful pause before introducing an old friend *may* be due to forgetfulness of that friend's name, but they do not always like to admit it. The late chairman of the Club, Neil

346

Salmon, recalled:

> On one occasion, before I was a member, I attended a cocktail party in a
> friend's home and two fellow guests whom I knew (Joe Links and John
> Arkell) each saw me talking to the other and each asked me shortly
> afterwards if I would tell him the name of the person to whom I had been
> speaking as they were members of the same Club. I later found them
> talking to each other and could not resist telling them what had happened;
> I thought they would both find this amusing; not at all, they said I had
> behaved most improperly in disclosing to each of them that the other could
> not name him!

This seemingly cavalier disregard of names may appear perverse or even
downright rude to a stranger, particularly if, as is often the case, the person mis-
addressed happens to be a considerable public figure, but in fact it is only the
logical corollary of the tradition in the Savile that a man must stand on his own
two feet rather than his dignity. One of the amusing consequences, of course, is
the series of innocent but nightmarish gaffes which sometimes occur when one
member unwisely pontificates on a subject to an audience which may include the
world's greatest authority on it. Some examples of this have already been given,
but, for another instance, there is a member (who wishes to remain anonymous)
who still wakes up at three in the morning with the memory of an enthusiastic
description of the joys of Florence culminating in his polite enquiry to a
companion at the bar, "Have you ever been there?" – only to discover he was
addressing Sir Harold Acton.

William Barnes had a similar experience:

> I was sitting next to a wizened man and remarked that I had just come
> from the Chelsea Antiques Fair where there was a terrible lot of enormous
> oak furniture. "Oh," he said, "we have quite a lot of that at home."
> Plunging in, I replied, "It must be a pretty big house." Shyly, he did not
> want to tell me, but he proved to be Eddie Sackville-West and his home
> was Knole. Egg on the face.

Andrew Stewart, the son of Pamela Hansford Johnson and stepson of C.P.
Snow, was sitting at the long table one night next to a member who was holding
forth on contemporary literature:

> "C.P. Snow's novels are not so good," he said. "The books of Pamela
> Hansford Johnson, his wife, are much better, have you read them?" I
> assured him that I had but made no further comment on his pontifications.
> Of course he had no idea of my relationship to them.

This aspect of *Sodalitas* can be equally unnerving for guests or candidates for membership until they grow used to it. On one of his first visits to the Club as a guest of Andrew Robertson, Basil Saunders came down from lunch in mellow mood: "Ah!" he said to Andrew with an expansive gesture to embrace his surroundings, "I feel as if I have lunched within the setting of a William Cooper or C.P. Snow novel." "Well," said Andrew, "Snow is just upstairs paying his bill, and that's William Cooper's coffee you've just knocked over."

But this is the stuff of life at the Savile and though the person concerned may not enjoy it he can be sure that all his friends and fellow members will rejoice. Moreover, Andrew Cooper should not have been afeared of "butting into conversations" as so many new members are; at the Savile it is the accepted thing for a member seeing (or hearing) a promising group to join them without ceremonial and take part if he so wishes. By the process of "Savilization" he will soon know if his contribution is welcome and it usually is, otherwise he would not have been elected in the first place.

On a similar principle any member of a group of talkers feels free to wander off at a whim for, as Winston Graham discovered to his astonishment on joining, "Men would move away from men, breaking a conversation without apology, because they happened to have lost interest." Basil Davidson provides some explanation for this when recalling conversational groups of the 1950s:

> There were, of course, a few dangers to be noticed, some shoals and rocks to be steered past, and how could it be otherwise? The seas of talk cast up their perils. Monologue is the death of talk, and even the Savile could never be entirely safe from the member who comes not to listen and converse but to hold forth and impose; and since the Savile is a civilized arena the answer then, as I suppose it is now, had to lie in tactful choosing of one's route and means of escape. Or else there could be the case of A and B and C for whom a club within a club was their ideal, as though in need of some visible self-promotion in being separate and special, sodalitas being not enough; and that could be another kind of bore requiring treatment of another sort.

But perhaps the occasional Club bore – in small doses – should not be underestimated for he is a great stimulus to lively conversation . . . after he has gone; and it seems also, sometimes, that one man's hellebore is not necessarily another man's poison. Professor John Waterlow recalls that he was first brought into the Club by a friend's uncle, Colonel Charles Waley-Cohen, who had the reputation of being the Club bore, or one of them:

> However, I found him a most interesting old man. He used to start a conversation off with a phrase like "When I was leading the retreat from Yugoslavia (in World War I) . . ." and I used to listen with fascination, although never quite certain how much was true. He had another very good trick, of saying, for example "There are three things about

electricity . . .", and of course you couldn't interrupt him until he had got through all three. I missed him very much when he died.

Conversational ability, not professional eminence, is the criterion at the Savile, which must be unique among London clubs in the way it prizes good talk and expects every member to throw his hat – if not his halo – into the conversational ring. That this is certainly not the case elsewhere can become painfully obvious when members go visiting.

As an undergraduate of Cambridge in the 'forties William Barnes had joined another club and later, when he came to London to work, used it frequently.

> In those days a young bachelor could afford to dine frequently at his Club, [he says] but I found it a lonely experience: no-one ever spoke to me ... There was a story of a member who was found in tears in the lavatory: when asked what was wrong, he whimpered, "I have just been spoken to by another member."

Ben trovato, no doubt, as Barnes himself admits, but the story carried the essential element of truth and so, in search of human contact and civilized conversation, he packed his bags and under the auspices of St John Ervine and Professor Sir Frank Adcock, who had lectured him in Roman history at Cambridge ("Caesar went to Egypt in pursuit of Pompey and stayed in pursuit of Cleopatra"), became a member of the Savile in 1949.

It was within a few weeks of the Club's inauguration in 1868 that the founding fathers decreed the principle that meetings were to be "for the purposes of conversation", and nothing since has stemmed the flow. The essentially ephemeral nature of this otherwise absorbing activity poses a problem for the commentator attempting to set down what is, after all, the Club's chief *raison d'être,* for verbal wit and conversational felicities are notoriously the most difficult of human skills to capture and contain on the printed page; so much depends on the timing, the contributory gesture, the facial expression of the speaker, the tone of his voice, and the mood of his company. Furthermore, a mere recital of other men's *mots* can, paradoxically, become more tedious than a well-turned account of quite ordinary, or even boring, exchanges.

It was possibly for this reason that when Edmund Gosse wrote an appreciation of the kind of conversation to be found at the Savile when he joined in the 1870s he jibbed at trying to set down samples of it. His recollections are interesting, however, for providing yet another example of the baleful presence of the great philosopher Herbert Spencer, probably the only member ever elected who positively hated conversation and used ear-plugs to protect himself from contamination.

Gosse was writing in 1923:

> In its present house in Piccadilly the double drawing-room on the first floor runs through the whole breadth of the building. At least thirty years ago I happened to be alone between the divisions of the room, and saw a pleasing sight. In the front room Mr Herbert Spencer was sitting at the fireplace, reading a book; in the back room a young writer, already celebrated – whom I will not name, since he has left us – was regaling a circle of admirers with stories. At the close of each story there was a burst of laughter, at which Herbert Spencer lifted a pale face, tortured with disapprobation. At last a supreme story provoked in the back room a more explosive hilarity than ever. The philosopher, hurriedly feeling in his pockets, produced two padded ear-protectors; these he clapped to the two sides of his head, and fixed them; and then calmly resumed his book.
>
> There was a popular song in those days, "The Old Obadiah and the Young Obadiah," and this was an illustration of it.
>
> The conversations in the 'seventies and 'eighties in which the two Stevensons – R. L. S. and his wonderful cousin R. A. M. S. – took the predominant part, were not so vociferous nor so purely anecdotal. Day after day, these met at the luncheon-table with, to name only the dead, Andrew Lang, W. E. Henley, William Minto, H. J. Hood, sometimes Coventry Patmore and Austin Dobson. Cambridge sent its occasional contingent, A. W. Verral, Frank Balfour, A. G. Dew-Smith, W. Robertson Smith. The talk was not noisy when these men met in the absolute liberty of 15, Savile Row, but it was worthy of the finest traditions of eager, cultivated conversation.

Robert Louis Stevenson based the first of his famous essays entitled "Talk and Talkers" on these heroic encounters at the Savile. They appeared in 1882 in *The Cornhill Magazine* edited by his fellow member, Sir Leslie Stephen, and for some reason he felt it necessary to disguise his fellows with pseudonyms; his cousin Robert Alan Mowbray Stevenson he calls "Spring-Heel'd Jack"; Fleeming Jenkyn (one of his supporters) "Cockshot"; Sir Walter Grindlay Simpson is "Athelred"; Sir Edmund Gosse is "Purcel", and W. E. Henley is "Burly". (It was not until 1888, by the way, that the dramatic rift occurred between the latter and R. L. S. which must account for the kindly tone of his reminiscence.)

Stevenson commences this essay with a bold affirmation of his own approach to conversation, which also happened to be a perfect reflection of that which had drawn him to the Savile and which had already been enunciated by Mahaffey:

> There can be no fairer ambition than to excel in talk... the first duty of a man is to speak; that is his chief business in this world; and talk, which is the harmonious speech of two or more, is by far the most accessible of

pleasures. It costs nothing in money; it is all profit; it completes our education, founds and fosters our friendships, and can be enjoyed at any age and in almost any state of health . . . Talk is, indeed, both the scene and instrument of friendship. It is in talk alone that the friends can measure strength, and enjoy that amicable counter-assertion of personality which is the gauge of relations and the sport of life.

By way of example he cites first his cousin R. A. M. Stevenson, elected to the Club in 1886, twelve years after his own entry:

The very best talker, with me, is one whom I shall call Spring-Heel'd Jack. I say so, because I never knew anyone who mingled so largely the possible ingredients of converse. In the Spanish proverb, the fourth man necessary to compound a salad, is a madman to mix it; Jack is that madman. I know not which is more remarkable; the insane lucidity of his conclusions, the humorous eloquence of his language, or his power of method, bringing the whole of life into the focus of the subject treated, mixing the conversational salad like a drunken god. He doubles like the serpent, changes and flashes like the shaken kaleidoscope, transmigrates bodily into the views of others, and so, in the twinkling of an eye and with a heady rapture, turns questions inside out and flings them empty before you on the ground, like a triumphant conjuror. It is my common practice when a piece of conduct puzzles me, to attack it in the presence of Jack with such grossness, such partiality and such wearing iteration, as at length shall spur him up in its defence. In a moment he transmigrates, dons the required character, and with moonstruck philosophy justifies the act in question. I can fancy nothing to compare with the *vim* of these impersonations, the strange scale of language, flying from Shakespeare to Kant, and from Kant to Major Dyngwell –

"As fast as a musician scatters sounds
Out of an instrument –"

the sudden, sweeping generalisations, the absurd irrelevant particularities, the wit, wisdom, folly, humour, eloquence and bathos, each startling in its kind, and yet all luminous in the admired disorder of their combination. A talker of a different calibre, though belonging to the same school, is Burly [W. E. Henley]. Burly is a man of great presence; he commands a larger atmosphere, gives the impression of a grosser mass of character than most men. It has been said of him that his presence could be felt in a room you entered blindfold; and the same, I think, has been said of other powerful constitutions condemned to much physical inaction. There is something boisterous and piratic in Burly's manner of talk which suits well enough with this impression. He will roar you down, he will

351

bury his face in his hands, he will undergo passions of revolt and agony; and meanwhile his attitude of mind is really both conciliatory and receptive; and after Pistol has been out-Pistol'd, and the welkin rung for hours, you begin to perceive a certain subsidence in these spring torrents, points of agreement issue, and you end arm-in-arm, and in a glow of mutual admiration. The outcry only serves to make your final union the more unexpected and precious. Throughout there has been perfect sincerity, perfect intelligence, a desire to hear although not always to listen, and an unaffected eagerness to meet concessions. You have, with Burly, none of the dangers that attend debate with Spring-Heel'd Jack; who may at any moment turn his powers of transmigration on yourself, create for you a view you never held, and then furiously fall on you for holding it. These, at least, are my two favourites, and both are loud, copious, intolerant talkers.

How little has changed at the Club in the hundred years since these lines were written, and as Stevenson goes on to describe his companions long dead we could almost be looking at and hearing their mirror-images performing in the Sandpit at the very moment these later words are written.

Cockshot [i.e. Fleeming Jenkyn] is a different article but vastly entertaining and has been meat and drink to me for many a long evening [says Stevenson]. His manner is dry, brisk and pertinacious, and the choice of words not much. The point about him is his extraordinary readiness and spirit. You can propound nothing but he has either a theory about it ready-made, or will have one instantly on the stocks, and proceed to lay its timbers and launch it in your presence. "Let me see," he will say. "Give me a moment, I *should* have some theory for that." A blither spectacle than the vigour with which he sets about the task, it were hard to fancy... Cockshot is bottled effervescency, the sworn foe of sleep. Three-in-the-morning Cockshot, says a victim. His talk is like the driest of all imaginable dry champagnes. Sleight of hand and inimitable quickness are the qualities by which he lives.

Could Compton Mackenzie have had a previous incarnation? And then again:

Athelred [Sir Walter Grindlay Simpson], on the other hand, presents you with the spectacle of a sincere and somewhat slow nature thinking aloud. He is the most unready man I ever knew to shine in conversation. You may see him sometimes wrestle with a refractory jest for a minute or two together, and perhaps fail to throw it in the end. And there is something singularly engaging, often instructive, in the simplicity with which he thus exposes the process as well as the result, the works as well as the dial of the clock. Withal he has his hours of inspiration. Apt words come to him as if by accident, and, coming from deeper down, they smack the more personally, they have the more of fine old crusted humanity, rich in sediment and humour. There are sayings of his in which he has stamped himself into the very grain of the language; you would think he must have worn the words next his skin and slept with them.

Dallas Bower, perhaps? Later in the essay Sir Edmund Gosse himself appears in all his glory:

Purcel is in another class from any I have mentioned. He is no debater but appears in conversation, as occasion rises, in two distinct characters, one of which I admire and fear, and the other love. In the first, he is radiantly civil and rather silent, sits on a high, courtly hilltop, and from that vantage-ground drops you his remarks like favours. He seems not to share in our sublunary contentions; he wears no sign of interest; when on a sudden there falls in a crystal of wit, so polished that the dull do not perceive it, but so right that the sensitive are silenced. True talk should have more body and blood, should be louder, vainer and more declaratory of the man; the true talker should not hold so steady an advantage over whom he speaks with; and that is one reason out of a score why I prefer my Purcel in his second character, when he unbends into a strain of graceful gossip, singing like the fireside kettle. In these moods he has an elegant homeliness that rings of the true Queen Anne.

Like Edmund Gosse before him, Winston Graham remembers the Savile in his early days (the 'fifties) as being:

. . . much noisier, more extrovert. Although a vast majority of its members were, no doubt, quite ordinary, it *seemed* to be chock-full of wits and eccentrics, and this was probably true of the nucleus of the regular attenders who made up the core of the Club day-in, day-out... Although a friendly Club it was also intimidating. People like Chippy Kingham and Richard Graves – known to the wits as *Graves Supérieur* – did not give their approval lightly, nor many others whose names alas have faded.

. . . the Club seemed also to be full of raconteurs, with a leavening of wit. Genuine wit is one of the rarest of commodities. Gilbert Harding was the finest raconteur of his day but he was not witty. (I do remember him saying once about a man and a woman who had been caught in some collusive malpractice: "Oh well, we all know he's been hand-in-blouse with her for years." And I think it was spontaneous.) Compton Mackenzie was in the same category. Both had encyclopaedic memories and a tremendous instinctive sense of how to present a story to the best advantage. To sit with either of them for an evening was a great experience.

One thing that was early borne in was the difference between a funny story and an anecdote. At the Savile anecdote was all: that is, a story about real people, not invention. To tell a funny story was simply not on. And a *dirty* funny story was too jejune to be tolerated. (Sometimes late at night Gilbert Harding, when still surrounded by a laughing group and his store of anecdotes exhausted, would come down to a funny story of a normal kind.) It's a remarkable fact that I hardly ever heard Gilbert or Monty tell the same anecdote twice.

One of the best raconteurs is still with us: Jack Hargreaves. But there were good talkers in plenty, of varying excellence. Michael Ayrton on his day could coruscate; Jack Lambert, in stimulating company; Lionel Hale, St John Ervine, Wynford Vaughan Thomas, Eric Maschwitz. It is invidious to try to name them all.

The two wittiest men I knew were Malcolm Baker Smith and Monja Danischewsky. Malcolm – a BBC executive who died young – was perhaps the sharpest of them all, but usually his wit was so quick that it splintered off and was forgotten as soon as uttered. Paradoxically, I remember him for two of his less memorable remarks: "In my opinion, psycho-analysis is all my I," and – of a visitor to the Club – "He looks the sort of man who has spent his life supporting the flag in British West Hampstead." Danny, with perhaps a greater sense of theatre, made his points in a way that was more easily recallable.

The Club also had a fair smattering of aesthetes. The first time I saw Eddie Sackville-West he was leaning elegantly against the bar talking to another man, and I heard him say: "My dear fellow, I'm sure you appreciate the social nausea of meeting one's friends' friends." And another man I heard explaining to a companion the difficulty of compressing his poetic thoughts "within the corset of the ballade".

As to wit . . . At a round table at lunch one day a conversation broke out about various mild perversions, until Humphrey Hare said loudly: "What d'you expect me to do? Go to bed with a horse?" A little man at the table who had not previously spoken said: "I thought the Age of Cavalry was past."

Joe Compton invited me to go with him to a gala performance of "Swan Lake" at the Opera House. When I got back to the Savile someone asked me who was there. I said I recognised Sir John Anderson in the next row, and there was Sir Somebody here and Sir Somebody else there. Danischewsky said: "My word, you *were* rubbing garters with the knights." Another of Danny's pronouncements was when I wanted to leave a bouquet of red roses at Claridge's for a Russian lady I had met in Paris and I asked him to tell me the Russian word for "Welcome". He drew himself up to his full 5 feet 5 inches in height and said: "In my contry der iss no soch vord."

Winston Graham himself claims not to be a witty man, properly preferring, as a good author should, to listen rather than waste his substance in the ephemeral moment but he has shown himself more than capable of holding his own. Returning to the Savile from a performance of *Titus Andronicus* with a cast that included Olivier and Ashcroft he was heard to declare for instance that it had been "money for old rape".

Hugh Stewart was responsible for a similar *mot*. Towards the end of the war when the Allies were preparing to land in Sicily, the General Staff formed Allied Military Government Occupied Territories – or A.M.G.O.T. for short. Peter Rodd and his brother, Lord Rennel of Rodd, were appointed to *be* A.M.G.O.T. The acronym turned out to be the Turkish word for goat dung and so it rapidly faded away into the nitrogen-cycle of disuse. As Hugh Stewart remarked, it was the "Amgötterdämmerung of the Rodds".

But Winston Graham's point that the pertinent anecdote concerning *real* people is paramount at the Savile is a sharp one. Witticisms there are a-plenty in the Sandpit and bar while the long table on a good night can be a very Cape Canaveral for well crafted flights of fancy. These are, however, regarded as isolated verbal missiles which merely decorate a conversation as grace-notes do a piece of music. The illuminating anecdote arises out of – and adds to – the substance of the conversation; Savilians seem to have a rich supply of these too.

One of the greatest pleasures in life must be to have the appropriate anecdote or illustration ready to trip off the tongue at a relevant moment in a conversation. Peter Gorb remembers one such blissful moment in his early days at Brook Street:

> It happened to me in the Savile twenty or more years ago; after '65 when I became a member, but not long after. It is my contribution to Savile history, and my own personal and entirely accidental vainglory. I came down from lunch to the Sandpit to find myself in a most illustrious group. Stephen Potter, Jimmy Edwards, Val Gielgud, Wynford Vaughan Thomas and some others – equally star-spangled – were discussing how to reply courteously to a letter from a son whilst also correcting his grammatical errors. "Perhaps by making a spelling mistake myself and thus showing how frail a father can be," suggested one.
>
> "Never do that," said another. "I once missed two letters from the word squirrel in writing to my son, and he pronounced it squirl for years."
>
> "Oh," I interjected (my eyes glazing over with fear and pleasure) as I reeled off the following; the only bit of Ogden Nash I knew my heart, and still remember, perhaps a little imperfectly:
>
> "Some call a squirrel a squirrel
> And some call a squirrel a squirl.
> In order to unfold this riddle
> A terrible tale I'll unfurl.
> A virile young squirrel named Cyril,

355

                    In an argument over a girl,
            Was lambasted from here to the Tyrol
                By a churl of a squirl named Earl."

There was an awesome silence. I sat in false modesty, my eyes cast down knowing that never again would life provide such serendipity; and in such company! Eventually Stephen Potter broke the silence. "Do we know you?" he ventured. "I am a very new member," I replied. "In that case we are glad to know you," he said. He paused, thought, sighed and turned to Wynford Vaughan Thomas who was leaning glass in hand over the back of the Sandpit bench. "Can you cap that, Wynford?" he said. "No," said Wynford Vaughan Thomas waving his glass, "my muse is very blotto voce" – which I thought was capping it quite well.

A week or two later Gwynne Vevers took me by the arm and asked me in his kindly confidential manner if I would like to join the committee. Was there a connection? I like to think so.

Peter Green, who now lives in Texas but remains an overseas member, remembers with nostalgia similar encounters:

The Club was a civilized haven where you could be certain, when you dropped in for a drink, that you'd find yourself talking, if not to a known friend, quite certainly to someone of charm and interest who was likely to become a friend. The famous team of Frank Muir and Denis Norden, much to my astonishment, regularly put on an *ad hoc* show in the bar that was at least as funny as their public routine . . .

But brilliant and greatly appreciated as they are, such "double-acts", whenever they occur, lack the comity which is the more usual mark of the sodality's conversation. Wynford Vaughan Thomas was an exemplar of that verbal dexterity which has always been so much preferred at the Savile. In full flight his entrancing stories and reminiscences might occasionally take on some of the nature of a performance, though there was never any hint – as there sometimes is in the private moments of a professional talker – that his effects had been rehearsed or his jests re-cycled. Part of the joy of listening to him, indeed, was in the realization that his wilder fancies were totally impromptu, surprising and delighting himself as much as his listeners. But he was not a monologuist; he always deferred. As someone said of Oscar Wilde, he would take the dullest of remarks from one of the company, polish it until it shone like a gem, and then hand it back with a bow. He had all the equipment of a great conversationalist: courtesy, a well-stocked and scholarly mind, knowledge lightly worn, a career packed with vivid experiences, a prodigious memory, a circle of friends and acquaintances ranging from Dylan Thomas to Lord Mountbatten, all of which provided him with a brimming reservoir of anecdote to supply his lively wit. At the Club he was not alone in this, but in his time, in the opinion of many, he was supreme.

Style is very much a part of conversational equipment and with such a diverse membership it is not surprising that the Club should possess a wide capacity to bemuse. There can be encounters like those so well-remembered with Wynford Vaughan Thomas which are all crackling pyrotechnics, and others which will be as dry and rewarding as a pre-prandial *fino* or as elaborate and rococo as the Sandpit decor. Part of the pleasure is often the manner in which a participant launches his particular squib; Monja Danischewsky, master of the sly murmur; Dallas Bower's devastating parentheses; or Peter Aldersley's seriously appalling puns. Eccentricity of utterance can also add spice. That extraordinary character, Igor Vinogradov, was wont to get lost in one of many remote trains of thought during the progress of a conversation and would go into a semi-trance uttering the word "yes" at steady intervals. It was alleged that seventeen was his record. One day he came into the Club full of excitement and announced that he had met a man who knew more about the Czar Paul 1st than he had thought possible. He added that the man would be lunching with him at the Club the following Friday. He was told that that would not be possible, as it was Good Friday and the Club would be shut. Igor, being a member of the Russian Orthodox Church which has a different date for Easter, went into one of his meditations. "Yes... yes... yes... yes... yes... yes... yes... poor fellow."

Lothar Mendes, one of whose fractured aphorisms has given this history its title, would daily sit like Scylla to Dallas Bower's Charybdis, guarding the entrance to the bar from the Sandpit. There the two of them would reminisce about the great days of Hollywood and Pinewood and accost the passers-by with suitable pleasantries. These would often include Lotharisms which owed more than a little to his early collaborations with Sam Goldwyn. "Now then! Easy come, go easy!" said Lothar once to a member hastening towards the bar. "No, No," said the member, patiently pausing to explain, "The phrase is 'easy come, easy go'." "That's what I said," roared Lothar, contorting his face as if to screw an imaginary monocle into an outraged eye. "Easy come, go easy"; and then to Dallas, when the discomfited member had crept away: "That petarded him with his own hoist."

Another of Lothar's great pronouncements concerned a member who was "ready to pontificate on anything and anybody with a smattering of ignorance". Inevitably, the Club possesses more than one member who might fit that description though Sir David Milne's theory that "you can pick up more inaccurate information on more subjects at the Savile than anywhere else in London" is probably carrying the notion too far. It takes no account of the corrective expert – equally tiresome in the opinion of some – who is almost certainly present and ready to pounce and put matters right.

Nevertheless, the searcher after the remote or the arcane is sure to have his quest satisfied at the Savile. Keith Piercy provides a sample:

> Ralph Richardson was seated opposite to me at one of the round tables; next to him was an American guest, who remarked how much he had

enjoyed *The School for Scandal* which had been produced in New York in 1962. Richardson then said that there was one word in the play which none of the touring company could understand. The word was "avadavats" which occurs in Act V when Joseph Surface complains that his rich uncle in the West Indies never sent him anything of value, but only "a few presents now and then, china, shawls, congou tea, avadavats and Indian crackers". "What are 'avadavats'?" asked Richardson. None of us knew but James Fisher at once answered, "Indian Birds".

Over the years Tyrrell Burgess has amused himself by collecting similar unconsidered trifles which have been served at the Savile long table. Thus, Gwynne Vevers:

> It is now generally accepted by those best qualified to judge that the function of the tonsils was to act as a resonating device for the mating call when as a species we went on all fours. A comparative decline in success in mating on all fours has accompanied the practice of removing the tonsils in childhood.

And Teddy Cusdin:

> The dimensions of the common or domestic stair are such that the tread plus twice the riser is equal to 23 inches. A normal stair has a 9-inch tread and a 7-inch riser. The theory behind this is that it takes twice as much effort to go up as to go along – and 23 inches is the length of the average pace. This theory was first published, as something universally accepted, by Batty Langley in 1702.

And an unlikely contribution from a pillar of the Bank of England, Leonard Pearce, which one hopes was not inspired by the sort of food on offer all those years ago:

> Pigs, unlike horses or cows, can spit. When pigs are fed on swill from hotel kitchens, they not only avoid the inevitable knives, forks and spoons which come with it, but they also carefully spit out pieces of broken glass and crockery. The well-emptied troughs of pigs fed on such swill tend to have a neat row of broken glass left along the bottom.

An eavesdropping stranger trying to assess the nature of the membership would therefore find it most confusing to pass around the dinner table picking up such crumbs of information or earthier pronouncements from, for instance, Gip Wells winding up some zoological discussion with: "... the fact is that all male mammals are buggers at bottom". Conversation at dinner does indeed take some untypical, if not peculiar, turns; "What is the principal religion in Ulan Bator?" was a recent enquiry from a member at table who seemed genuinely keen to find out and, perhaps not entirely to his surprise, immediately received a ten-minutes tutorial on the particular forms of Mongolian Buddhism to be found there.

> The long table, then as now, was the heart and soul of the place [says Basil Davidson recalling his early days of membership in the 'fifties], and seats were chosen by the wise in relation to whomever was in full spate and voice. Was there more politics discussed? I rather think there was, but that is perhaps no more than a misleading trick of aged memory, or else an outcome of the fact of politics having become so boringly authoritarian in these latter times; and perhaps if I came up from the country more often than I do, I should hear grand declaimings and disclaimings on behalf of X or Y, more sendings to the devil of he-and-she, and more bestridings of the mighty Globe. No doubt I should, since talk remains the Savile *raison d'être:* good talk, and therefore the more outrageous the better. "I may be eighty," Francis Meynell remarked to me very many years after standing as a guarantor of my worthiness, "but I still feel tête-à-têtey".

Basil Davidson's *aperçu* that the long table was the "heart and soul of the place" is borne out by all the many references to it throughout the Club's history. In a witty *résumé* in the August 1975 Bulletin entitled "1067 and all that" the then House-Committee chairman, Guy Nicholson, recalled Sir Herbert Stephen's explanation for the Savile's survival when, all around it, wealthier clubs were being driven to amalgamate or disappear. This was due, said Stephen:

> ... primarily to the fact that it offers a kind of society which wins the abiding affection and loyalty of its members. The Motto *SODALITAS CONVIVIUM* implies that sharing the pleasure of friendship together with the pleasures of the table is the chief purpose. By the pleasures of the table is not meant that the Savile Club is a Club for gourmets. The first intention was to establish a modest and economical 'convivium' whereat the conversation along and around the tables would be not the least of the attractions.

Guy Nicholson then continued with a dissertation on the table itself rather than the members it accommodated:

> It is true that round tables of reasonable size are attractive and encourage "convivium" and that rectangular tables vary in width between too narrow and too wide. Some time after our arrival at 69 Brook Street, it was decided that we needed a table to replace one which was too big. We wanted one which would be wide enough conveniently to take all the plates, glasses and wine carafes – a refectory table, for instance, being too narrow for this purpose; but we also needed one which would not be so

wide as to prevent easy conversation across the table.

Measurements were taken and experiments were made; and the combined wisdom of the Members and of the Committee arrived at the exact width necessary for our purpose; and this proved to be just 1067 millimetres, or about 42 inches.

We have never been a rich Club but we have always been extremely fortunate in having members who show their affection for the Club in their generosity when any call is made on them for some purpose at the time beyond our financial resources. (The re-decoration of the ballroom and also the card room are relatively recent examples.) On this occasion the wood to make the table was provided as a gift by a timber merchant member, the cost of making it coming from the proceeds of the sale of the old table – now, incidentally, in use in Freshfield's boardroom.

No: for our purposes ten sixty-seven is not a date but a measurement; and for the Club an interesting and important measure of width.

The table is the long table in the main dining-room by the window and its width *is* 1067 millimetres. The length is quite immaterial unless one regards it as being infinite.

While many members are to be seen at various times both at the lunch and dinner tables, the attenders at these meals exhibit separate characteristics which seem to inspire different forms of conversation.

Dinner, perhaps because it comes towards the end of the day, tends to be a more contemplative affair, when speculation can hover about the remoter issues secure in the knowledge that it can overlap afterwards into the bar downstairs. Conversation at lunch is for matters of more immediate moment as befits men who may (or may only wish to appear to) have business to transact once they have completed their meal.

But not all members at lunch require to seem so brisk. Maurice Druon writes from Paris of a sub-division in the 'fifties, a group of "late lunchers" which – with different members – continues to the present day.

> We used to call "the late lunchers", at the end of the 'fifties and during the 'sixties, a group of members who entered the dining-room between five to two and two o'clock, because, up to two, we were able to order our lunch and, after two, allowed to light our cigarettes. The group was led by the tall Herbert Agar, eagle profile, great essayist, nourished with Greek and Latin literature, with Gibbon prose also, an example of cultural symbiosis of English and American culture, perfectly representative of the best of New England, with a very high moral conscience, and who, for several years, had been chairman of the Savile. It was Herbert Agar, in fact, who decided to introduce me to the Club. Amongst the late lunchers were also Michael Ayrton, sculptor, painter and writer of vast knowledge, bitter temperament and genial talent . . . Anthony Pélissier,

360

distinguished stage and film author, too distinguished perhaps, seducing mind and unhappy life; later, Robert Baldick, a young and splendid Oxonian scholar, who looked like the King François 1er and knew everything of French and English literature of the 19th century. He died much too early, when he was forty years old.

The only remainders of the group are, today, Monja Danischewsky, "the white Russian with a red face", film director and producer, always laughing at the troubles he met in his life, and our dear George Astley, marvellous friend, who administered and animated so perfectly the Society of Authors during many years and for the sake of all writers. Famous and modest Winston Graham joined sometimes. All three can complete my souvenirs of this happy period, when I used to come to London four or five times a year, partly for the pleasure of enjoying these Savilian encounters. The conversation was a real pleasure of mind, and gave a rare feeling of civilization. No question on history, art, politics, ethics, but also on galleries, publishers, or even on the address of a book-shop or an antique dealer, which could not find an immediate answer. The judgments on people, known or unknown, famous or not, were moderate and sharp... I add that a rule, established by Herbert Agar for the "late lunchers", was: "No less than half bottle of claret for each table companion". The Club cellar was, as it remains, excellent.

Breakfast, however, was another matter. Since the morning of 28 June 1868 when that meal was first served at Spring Gardens, silence was sacred except for whispered requests for the salt. Like many an excellent custom its origins are obscure; perhaps it was felt that the effort of restoring the gastric processes to some semblance of normality after the abandon of the night before left little time or inclination for idle badinage; maybe such prodigious talkers needed a mute period to recoup their strength. Whatever its provenance, the relaxation of this (dare one say, "unspoken") rule in 1989 caused an even greater *furore* outside the Club than it did within. Word got out to the press that "The General Committee has agreed to a trial period of Conversation at Breakfast". It was a very limited indulgence; those wishing to take advantage of it were asked to book in advance and be prepared to retire behind a *cordon sanitaire* at the terrace end of the dining-room, but the newspapers took little notice of that. The *Sunday Telegraph* led the way in its issue of 5 November 1989 by devoting ten column inches of its front page to "the death-knell" of one of the Savile Club's "most cherished traditions". *Today*, despite its name, lumbered along twenty-four hours later to engage its readers by comparing the Club's tentative flirtation with modernity to the "Retreat from Mons" and "the decision to give away India". The *Daily Mirror* obliged also with a screaming headline: "POSH CLUB GOES CHAT CRACKLE AND POP" and managed with typical ingenuity to insert a titillating cross-head "NOOKIE", which on closer examination turned out to be a disappointing quotation from some obscure comedian concerning his wife's disinclination for any kind of intercourse in the morning. Seething noises from various other clubs were quoted in the *Evening Standard* a day or two later, indicative, no doubt, of the garrulous breakfasts they were trying to digest while the bandwagon churned on. The Club's chairman, Osman Streater, was awakened at home and, before he could tackle even a modest poached egg, asked to enlarge on the issue for the BBC. Peter Aldersley, who had, perhaps unwisely, castigated "business breakfasts" as "an American custom" unsuitable for the Savile, found himself the following Tuesday explaining this heresy to C.B.S. coast-to-coast in the U.S.A., the Public Service Station in Washington D.C., and A.B.C. Australia. Lord Dacre announced to the press that he would be resigning and some weeks later, did; Sir Stephen Spender, his appetite aroused by an investigative reporter, enquired what time was breakfast served.

It was all great good fun, but it failed to take note of the fact that even in the past the "rule" had never been intended to create an Amyclaean silence. "I have a unique memory," says Patric Dickinson, "when my son at the age of twelve had to come up from Broadstairs to take the 3-day Challenge (the Westminster scholarship). It entailed one night in London. We couldn't fix. *Please* could he stay with me at the Savile? Rules were bent – and bless the committee – he could and did in the next room to me. In the morning Frank (the valet) came in beaming. 'He'll be alright, slept fine he says,' so I took him down to the silent breakfast behind those newspaper holders. A little boy of 12 at breakfast!!! I explained why and the newspapers were put aside. I remember how courteous and sweet these elderly men were to this nervous little boy – in particular Eddie Sackville-West (whose desk I had taken at the BBC). So David ate a good breakfast, talked away with them all, and we left for Dean's Yard not feeling sick. I can think of no more inspiriting truly friendly example of *sodalitas*. He got in."

And so much for the "Retreat from Mons".

If, from the first, as *The Times* of 1923 declared, the communal long table and the conversation it inspired was "the ark of the Savile covenant", the billiards-room was soon to become one of the most devotedly attended side-chapels for votaries to pursue its worship. There is, however, only a perfunctory reference in the Club records to a billiards table at Spring Gardens, and even this seems to have been installed as an afterthought in one or other of the public rooms. But after the move to Savile Row in 1871 a special room was set aside for devotees of the game and by the time the Club removed itself again to its more permanent premises at 107 Piccadilly in 1882 the billiards-room had become established as one of its foremost social centres. The annual accounts show that the table was by then always well occupied, though of necessity it was more of a spectator's sport as the room became a resort for many more members than could be accommodated in an actual game. The Savile's more liberal approach to convention than the normal run of London clubs allowed billiards to be played on Sundays, though without the attendance of the marker, who it was presumed would be more religiously observant than the members and was therefore allowed a day off on the Sabbath. It was this facility for Sunday billiards, unique among London clubs, that is said to have persuaded that abominator of conversation, Herbert Spencer, to swallow his prejudice, don his ear-plugs and seek membership of the Savile. It was in the billiards-room at Piccadilly also that the quotation recorded by Duncan in his *Life and Letters of Spencer* was reputedly first made: "It was remarked to me... that to play billiards was the sign of an ill-spent youth," and Club legend has it that the remark was made to him by Robert Louis Stevenson, but sadly it was in fact made by a Mr. Charles Roupell, who was not even a member, but a guest.

Stephen, however goes on to record that by 1883, after the move to Piccadilly:

> many members of the Club have reached degrees of proficiency [at billiards] of which they have felt no need to be ashamed, some particulars of which are sufficiently indicated by the book wherein are recorded scores of or above forty. Nor have the lesser variants of the game, such as pyramids or pool, been neglected. The billiards-room is adorned by a silver cup presented to the Club in memory of Arnold Glover, an exceedingly popular member of the Club, and an enthusiastic player whose early death was deeply lamented. It is utilised for recording the names of winners of the annual billiards handicap, a sporting event which has occurred annually since 1883, so far as the actions of the King's enemies have permitted, and seems year by year to evoke greater interest and excitement.

Being as much a social centre as a venue for serious play, the billiards-room tended to be a lively place at Piccadilly. Harry Plunket Greene's description of the antics which went on there has appeared elsewhere in this history but the late George Vaizey provides another more detailed account in his reminiscences of visits as a guest of his father just after the First World War. In 1918 George Vaizey senior was being introduced to the Club by Sir Archibald Hurd, a distinguished writer for the *Daily Telegraph*. As Vaizey himself remarks, "the focal points at Piccadilly were the billiards-room and the dining-room for it was in these settings that fun, wit and laughter abounded".

> One evening my father repaired to the charming house in Piccadilly and found Hurd waiting for him in the hall. In those days the billiards-room was the popular meeting place. True there was a card-room, a library at the top of the house and on the first floor a smoking-room with deep armchairs wherein learned professors used to sit and read, they hoped, disturbed only by subdued conversation. But the billiards-room, and of course the dining-room, was where bright, and often hilarious, talk flowed. The room itself was the shape of an L but reversed. The table was in the long part, flanked by cue cases on one side and raised seats on the other. The shorter part of

the room made a large alcove which stretched, with ample sitting space, to a vast fireplace. Logs were crackling there when Hurd took my father in and settled him near enough to the blaze but still with a view of the table. Around him in the alcove members were talking with enjoyment and animation, while on the benches, above the billiards table men talked together and heckled the players.

"Two to one on Smith."

"Taken, in post after dinner."

"Good Heavens! Fancy missing that, a sitter if ever there was one!"

"Can't think why you ever play billiards, Brown. Why not stick to draughts?" And so it went on, to my father's astonishment; badinage, railing, between jovial conversation and drinks.

"How can people play billiards with all this going on, Hurd? I always understood it was 'quiet on the stroke'."

"Not here," Archie chuckled. "This room is where we congregate before and after meals to meet each other and talk. We take no notice of billiards. If you play, good luck to you, but play in a light hearted manner – encouragement and the opposite are both part of the fun. And so amid a babel of conversation and criticism, the players soldiered on; my father at first shocked, then intrigued and finally reduced to laughter broke his lifelong rule, had another drink and sat back, mellow and delighted. He had never believed that such a happy atmosphere could be possible in a London club.

It is not quite clear when snooker overtook billiards as the more popular game at the Savile, though it was certainly established by the early 'thirties. The origin of snooker itself is wrapped in mystery, though Compton Mackenzie claimed to have established Sir Neville Chamberlain as its inventor. Be that as it may, *Savile* snooker has even less likely and more impenetrably remote origins. It is a peculiar form of volunteer snooker, played without the yellow and green balls and, so far as is known, played only at the Savile and in a pool room in Fiji where a keen exponent, an exile from Brook Street, was once a consular official. Stephen Potter codified its "rules" in the 1960s and imprinted himself upon the game forever by his use of it as an extension of his life-style. But like many another fashionable pastime the popularity of Savile snooker has ebbed and flowed. There have been periods, admittedly brief, when the billiards-room has been relatively deserted but enthusiasm has soon returned and restored it to its traditional place as one of the social hubs of Savile Club life. Perhaps its more recent locale at Brook Street with its restricted space for spectators has reduced some of its potential in this respect. On the other hand the greater intimacy induced by more confined quarters seems to be encouraging the sort of atmosphere which by all accounts obtained at Piccadilly and, whatever, the billiards-room and the social life to be found there has featured prominently in the memories of every generation of Savilians.

Stephen Potter, after whom the present room is named, memorialized it thus:

> On sunny summer afternoons the billiards-room is empty. This is a good time for Older Member, who may not have an excessively urgent business appointment that day, to try a few shots by himself. It doesn't matter if there is nobody to give him a game; because this is the least lonely room in the Club. The billiards-room is full of ghosts. Perhaps they emanate from the dust of the table, which still rises in clouds however hard we brush it. On the walls are the cartoons, on the marble shelf are the old break books, where any billiard break over 39 was carefully recorded. Let us look at the names. At first the artists seemed to be taking charge. Here is a good date – '1907, William Nicholson, 45.' This is 'Billy Nick', and if anybody represents the gayer spirit of the Savile it is he. All Old Members remember his airy and sprite-like presence in the 'thirties – his blue bow tie with large white spots, his white socks and his flowered shirt. He proudly words a 1911 entry thus:
>
> "Ben Nicholson (guest) 40. Sgnd. Nicholson *père*."
>
> But the most important entry of this year is "William Orpen, 40." "Orps", with his Irish accent of variable intensity, was a tremendous Club man of the extrovert kind. It was he who invented the rolling-the-pennies game down our splendid curved staircase. If his billiards opponent got in the break book, Orps would "do" him in the margin, perhaps adding a picture of the victim's closest female relative, in a hat looking like a one-sided concertina, designed for lady motorists in 1910.
>
> A new member, timidly entering the billiards-room on an afternoon in the mid-'thirties, would have found one of two contrasted atmospheres, both I think highly enjoyable. The quiet concentration of billiards, or the sociability of our own brilliantly successful invention, Savile Snooker. Playing billiards might be those two sound men, Jennings and Walter Danks. Walter, graceful and delicate, can still be seen in action, though I am sorry to see that at 92 he insists on "two games a day maximum". Or perhaps there would have been a small grey-haired figure practising alone. This was Dr Giles, of the perfect stance and copybook cue action, perfecting the nursery cannons which were the foundation of his many hundred breaks.
>
> But Giles would be not quite happy. The truth is that the room was still

full of the cigar smoke of the Late Lunch brigade. And their game even by 1935 – and this grieved Giles a little – was exclusively Savile Snooker. Even Billy Nick played it, and his otherwise not markedly decadent son Kit. So did "Boully" Boulenger of the Zoo Aquarium, whose fish-tank stare concealed an unimpressed sardonic humour which Giles may have found rather irritating. "As in Fig. B.", he would remark, when Giles brought the red back to precisely the correct position over the middle pocket: or "Good shot well shat" – and similar phrases which, when repeated to our wives, help them to understand, if only dimly, why the Savile Club has such a high reputation for intellectuality and wit.

So did Ivor Back. Ivor's defection from billiards was important because he was *the* club man, we felt. He was the "brilliant young" surgeon, and if neither of these adjectives perpetually suited him, he was a life-and-soul man above everything, a fine story-teller, a learned criminologist, and he certainly helped to make the snooker game amusing. It was Ivor who invented the splendid cry "corresponding angles" if he missed one pocket and fluked into another. He and Alison Russell played the game at a fast canter. Russell, the eminent partitioner of Palestine, literally ran round the table. Young Dr Leslie Lankester was just as quick, the greatest instinctive player of the game, a man who could pot a ball off the top of his nose into any pocket he wished, and the faster he played the more certain it was to go in.

Wartime memories of the billiards-room are rather confused. Giles continued to practise billiards in the afternoon. There was often an influx about midnight. People were keen. I remember that if I came in after 1 a.m. and found the Club in darkness I would hunt out the bedroom numbers of players like Howard Marshall – a master – or the less classical but more fiery Eric Linklater. It was taken for granted that, being wakened, they should dress, come down, and play.

Individualities of style seemed more marked in war time. Francis Meynell was perfecting the inadvertent miscue which ended in the absolute safety. A near-great player of this time was Joe Compton who, from a delightful excess of nervous keenness, lifted his head after every stroke as if his chin had been knocked back by an uppercut. Our current billiards chairman, Tom Martin, developed a different compulsion. Before playing a particularly difficult shot he would whistle the first bar of Mendelssohn's Spring Song. Opponents learned to dread the sound because it was always followed by the hollow "clop" of the ball falling into the pocket. Kiss-me Hardy frightened us at first with his trick of shutting one eye as he addressed the ball and opening it very wide immediately before he struck it, a habit which seemed to undermine the resistance of his opponent. Still haunting us are the ghosts of old regulars who are regulars no more. Francis Meynell is a bit of an absentee. Denys Kilham Roberts lives now in remotest Cornwall. As Byron said of Tom Moore, after producing a list of Moore's virtues, "he has one fault, he is not here". All are missed by Older Member who is delighted to welcome, however, with almost unqualified satisfaction, the talent and promise of the new generation.

That was written in 1968 when the billiards-room was still at the bottom of the ballroom stairs in what is now the morning-room.

Potter's name first appears in the "Breaks Book" on June 26, 1941, recording a break of 58. Though his heavy commitments at the BBC during the wartime years disrupted his devotion to games-playing his diaries are strewn with references to feats at the Savile snooker table such as:

> Nice little snooker after lunch – then at 4 a fine squash game with R. Richardson – 4-3 in his favour – best I have done.

And,

> I am playing good snooker these days. Somewhat exercised as to what my expression should be as I am now as it were and for the time being Master. Never look pleased? Then one tends to look pompous. Look pleased? Then one tends to look conceited. Rule: never appear not to be trying (e.g. always take coat off).

Nor was he averse to employing his own principles of gamesmanship to bolster his dominance at the table. In his memoirs *Not Prince Hamlet* Michael Meyer recalls a couple of such occasions.

> I was playing in a snooker doubles against him after lunch. He was by far the best player in the Club, and my task was never to leave him an opening. I was succeeding pretty well. Stephen began to glance at his watch, played several hurried strokes, and muttered to his partner that he had an appointment at three. The rest of us began to play more quickly, I made an error which let him in for a break of fifty and they won, whereupon Stephen sat down with a newspaper in the reading-room until tea-time. Once I had to play him in the final of the Club competition. It was the best of three frames; I had won the previous year and was twenty years his junior. Before we started, he said that he had promised to take his wife to dinner at the Garrick; should the match go the full distance, would I be his guest there and play the final frame afterwards? How could I refuse? At one all, he took me to the Garrick and dined and wined me well, then drove me back to the Savile, where I offered little resistance.

Potter, as can be seen, took the game extremely seriously and would have had no truck with the sort of heckling and badinage which George Vaizey recalled as being part and parcel of the Piccadilly experience. John Hadfield writes:

> I will never forget the courtesy and elegance with which Stephen Potter once shut me up when I was watching him at the snooker table with a fellow member, and we were talking a little too loudly. "Can you lower your voices a little, John," he said. "Your conversation is so fascinating that it's putting me off my stroke."

But Potter could be beaten, given opponents with sufficient iron determination. Brian Bliss recalls that,

> ... after the war I was initiated into the mysteries of Savile snooker by Chippy Kingham. This sport was then still a big feature in the life of the Club, and before the annual competition started there was a dinner followed by an auction-sweep of the entrants. Favoured "horses", such as Stephen Potter, might "go" for £20 or £30, a considerable sum in those days. Chippy Kingham specialized in training up unknown horses, who might be bought for as little as £1 and, he hoped, win him first prize which might come to two or three hundred pounds.
>
> He succeeded with me to the extent that I once defeated Stephen Potter, not, I think, in the final. Afterwards Stephen wrote me a note:–

> > Savile Club 23 Feb 1955:
> > Dear Brian, I don't think I ever thanked you properly for that game the other day – not only enjoyable and exciting but (here let me assume the manner proper to this solemn subject) never, in a long and painful history of being knocked out of this tournament, have I met more flawless end-game play. I don't know anyone else in the Club who could have done it . . ..

Needless to say this note is carefully preserved in my copy of Gamesmanship.

Francis Meynell was another keen snooker-player at that time, and reportedly a co-inventor with Stephen of the art or science of Gamesmanship. I was once playing a single against Francis when (whether or not in a feeble attempt at a gamesman's ploy) just before he was going to play a shot I made some remark about my admiration for the art of David Low (also a member of the Club and an occasional snooker-player) one of whose cartoons hung on the walls of the then snooker-room. I must have been successful in temporarily diverting Francis's attention, since he paused with his cue in the air and said in his light but penetrating tenor "Ah! But it isn't really art, it's just ephemeral journalism." At the same time I was aware of the door behind Francis having opened and Low's head, with the prominent eyebrows, peering in, rather as he sometimes depicted himself as an onlooker in his cartoons. He withdrew silently and Francis was quite unaware of what had occurred. Nor had I the sense or the guts to exploit this advantage-point in gamesmanship.

Gamesmanship as applied to Savile snooker certainly seemed to be contagious after Potter entered the scene for Tony Marr records a similar experience. In the mid-'fifties the annual snooker competition which had lapsed for a while was reinstated and Tony was entered for it.

> Hugh Stewart, who enlivened nearly all the Club's activities, urged me, an appallingly incompetent player, to take part. I was reluctant to but I did. Hugh went so far as to say that he would coach me into winning. Rumour had it that bets were laid. He sent me a note on the event of the first match I had to face and kept in touch subsequently by many encouraging telephone calls sizing up the strengths and weaknesses of any opponent. He enjoined me to consider the matter in hand seriously, by dinning into my mind "This is not a game; it is War". I did as I was told by Hugh and my nerve held.
>
> The outcome was: one opponent, a dogged and solid player who didn't care for being beaten at any time, became plain cross and lost quickly; another, an excitable Central-European film man, came near to hysteria when defeat seemed possible; his cue shook and his voice was shrill as he acknowledged the end in my favour. Finally I had to play Stephen Potter, the master. He may not have felt fit at the time or was perhaps just bored. I won.
>
> All this seemed to say a lot not only for Hugh but for Savile Snooker as a sporting invention. There was a cup, won a year or two previously by another Anthony I think; Witherby perhaps. He had mislaid it. When in time he found it again the cup sat lopsidedly above the billiards-room fireplace for a bit then vanished again.

Apropos: Guy Nicholson writes that "there is the story told by Anthony Marr, a friend of mine whom I miss now that he has gone to live in Scotland, about the Bishop who used to bite the ankles of anyone playing Savile snooker," adding, perhaps a shade ruefully, "But I have never had my ankles bitten."

Certainly the Savile billiards-room wherever it has been situated throughout the years has provided a marvellous observation post for the student of human quirkery, as is evidenced also by Winston Graham's memories:

> Denys Kilham Roberts, angular and devilish, never potting ball without a half inch of cigar ash hanging perilously over the green baize. And Chippy Kingham (never anything but sober) who, having lured his opponent into some false move, would always remark: "There's more ways of killing a cat than choking it with cream." And Lothar Mendes, whose

cue always wobbled agonisingly, not from drink but because he was trying to get his angles right, and who missing an easy one would mutter: "A shit-shot". Or who, to console himself and his partner when losing, would say: "It's only a game, Mulloy." (Dialogue, probably, from some early film he'd directed.) And Ernest Hardy, sighting a shot with one eye screwed up like a marksman, and putting a load of guilt upon his partner to play his very best, something which, in "Kiss Me"'s view, he never succeeded in doing. And Clifford Lawson-Reece with his splendid imitation of bird songs, so that linnets chirped when he potted the brown... All blown away in the wind.

Well... perhaps not altogether, for the billiards-room in its new quarters has its new and regular band of devotees with Jeremy Hornsby as the enthusiastic ring-master and, despite the Runyanesque undertones which can sometimes be detected in recent competitions, who is to say that future generations may not have cause to look back on this as yet another golden age?

Though there are no precise details extant, it is evident that play at cards was also a popular pastime in the early days of the Savile at Spring Gardens and at Savile Row, for Sir Herbert Stephen has written:

> By the time the Club moved to Piccadilly it had become definitely an institution where a rubber of whist could be played every day before and most days after dinner, and the general standard of good play was reasonably high. Whist was practically the only game played, with the exception that the card players had evolved an annual function which went by the name of the Club Birthday. This took place not, as might have been supposed, in May, but within a week or two of Christmas. It began with a dinner-party, for which the existence at Piccadilly of a guests' dining-room afforded special facilities. At this feast, evening-dress was not, as at the *table d'hôte,* "optional", and both the food and the wine had to be the best, quite regardless of expense, that the Club could provide. After dinner the company repaired – comparatively late – to the card-room, and for that night, with the connivance of the Committee, all rules were suspended, and those present indulged in gambling. Any game might be played except whist – and afterwards bridge – but the most popular was a form of loo introduced by Hood [the Club's honorary secretary], and capable of producing much excitement. In later years it was almost entirely superseded by poker. Between twelve and one o'clock large supplies of sandwiches appeared, and alcoholic drinks continued to be served as long as anyone stayed. The party never finally broke up until about 4 a.m., and

it is believed that once or twice the last revellers did not depart until something like 6 a.m. No one ever left without having made a substantial contribution to the fund which was eventually handed to such of the Club servants as had been kept up all night in attendance upon this festivity. The Birthday might be attended by about two dozen members, and though the gambling was fast and furious compared with whist at the shilling points prescribed by the rules of the Club, it would not have seemed worth sitting up for in one or two other institutions geographically situated at no very great distance. It is quite probable that no one ever won or lost more than twenty-five pounds at a Birthday. The institution was continued with slight modifications and variations for a great many years, but since the Club became, like others, not only a private gentlemen's house, but also a public-house, subject to the regulations and supervision of magistrates and policemen, it has obviously become impossible.

The only game played normally in the card-room was whist, with piquet as an adjunct for the temporarily unemployed, until 1896-7, when the orthodox players were constrained to vindicate their rights by means no less drastic than the alteration at an annual general meeting of one of the rules of the Club. Some enthusiasts began playing poker, with a limit of five shillings, and one or two modifications, agreed upon amongst themselves, of the ordinary rules of that game, in the card-room, and the older and more staid whist players found themselves much less sure of getting a rubber than they liked. Some of them, therefore, at the annual meeting of 1897, proposed to change Rule xxix, so as to make poker a forbidden game. They urged with pathetic insistence the sacred character of whist as a recreation, the foreign origin and profligate nature of the intruder, and the importance to the Savile of continuing to be one of the acknowledged homes of orthodox sportsmanship. The poker players pleaded that gambling was gambling, that if you gambled at all you ought to be allowed to choose your particular method of imperilling your soul and your property, and that if whist wasn't a good enough gambling game to take care of itself so much the worse for whist. Much the larger proportion of the meeting, not being personally concerned either way, voted for the alteration of the rule, which now runs:

"Gambling prohibited. – No Game which the Committee shall consider to be a gambling Game shall be played, nor shall dice be used in the Club, except for backgammon; and no whist points higher than one shilling nor bridge points higher than five shillings a hundred, shall be allowed."

The Committee promptly declared poker to be, in its opinion, a gambling game, and thereafter it has not been played in the Club except on "Birthdays", or under exceptional circumstances.

But in this world it is never safe to play very long odds on the permanence of any institution. A few months after whist had thus triumphantly vindicated its age-long supremacy, it changed into bridge at

371

the Savile, as it did everywhere else, in something between ten minutes and a week. The Club, however, proved much more conservative when "ordinary" bridge, seven or eight years later, gave way in its turn to "Royal Auction" bridge. For several years the two games were played side by side, and it was not very long before the war that the older game was entirely superseded.

Stephen was writing in 1923 and as he so wisely prophesised "... in this world it is never safe to lay odds on the permanence of any institution". Rule xxix which was altered in 1897 so as to prohibit gambling altogether has since become Rule 35, worded with all the ambiguity of a United Nations ultimatum: "No gambling game which the Committee *shall consider undesirable* shall be played."

As a result poker was reinstated and since the late 'fifties Tuesday evenings after dinner have become sacred to the game. Being perhaps the most anti-social of card games it is surprising that it has achieved such popularity at the Savile; that it has done so is a tribute to the Club's ethics and also to the several "masters of ceremonies" who have emerged at various times to impose Savilian moderation on a game where stakes can so easily multiply out of hand. The Savile game is played with chips, an agreed amount of which are purchased before play begins. Should a player lose his stake money he may, if he wishes, purchase more but it is equally open to him to quit the table without reproach. With a membership of such various financial resources this is an admirable if not essential rule.

A.D. Peters ("Pete") was for the years after the war until his death in 1971 the charming but commanding presence at the Tuesday night table. Despite his being most probably the richest man in the Club he would resist any attempt by others to raise the ante beyond the reach of other players present and more than once would "see" a reckless contestant rather than let him bet too extravagantly against his own unbeatable hand. After Pete died, Gordon Prince took on his mantle, thus posing the riddle for other members of whether psychiatrists have an unfair advantage at the poker table. It certainly seemed so to some when confronted with the like of Gordon or his colleague, Brian O'Connell. Gordon Prince's method of imposing restraint on his fellow players differed from A.D. Peters' Prussian stare; "Ah! Well, if my auntie had balls she'd be my uncle," was a typical warning to an over-ambitious opponent, and the message rarely had to be delivered twice. Since Gordon's death in 1985 Peter Aldersley has been the benign adjudicator, ruling the table with a firm and equitable hand, even if it does seem to the indigent to be too often the winning one.

Poker is but for once a week and always in the allotted card-room; bridge is played at many times (but always on a Thursday) and appears in many places. An earlier excerpt from Harry Plunket Greene's biography of Stanford has provided a picture of the card-room bridge-players at Piccadilly in the early part of the century. It is evident that while it "had no recognized customs it made up for it in its 'characters'." Foremost among them apparently was Stanford himself:

To Stanford after a long day's teaching at the Royal College the Savile card-room was like wine, but he was convinced that bad luck waited on the steps till he arrived, followed him up the stairs into the card-room and dogged him from table to table. He was a very good player and won oftener than he lost, but like other temperamental people of the sort he forgot the sheep in his indignation at the goats. His losses never amounted to much; Savile stakes were low, and he had forgotten all about it before he reached home, but it was his belief that at cards the gods had ticketed him as a loser. He was secretly ashamed of this weakness and when, as often happened, he had a run of really good luck he became miserably apologetic and disarmed everybody. It would not have mattered if he had kept these sinister beliefs to himself, but he could not help apostrophizing fate out loud, and tempers occasionally flared; but they generally blew up in laughter, as on the occasion when an opponent goaded to desperation, having asked him: "Why the blazes he didn't chuck the whole damned thing," he said: "What! give up me only recreation!", or the time when after a tragic statement of his immediate arrival at the workhouse door a small and irresponsible new member said in a quiet voice: "Dear me! Sir Charles. You'll have to write some more of your little tunes."

Such badinage was not uncommon for on another occasion the gargantuan Owen Lankester came to the bridge table to be greeted by Sidney Dark with: "Hullo time-honoured Lancaster! – Not Gaunt in being old."

When the Club moved to Brook Street in 1927 the bridge players installed themselves rather grandly in what had been Lord Harcourt's dining-room. It was only with the greatest reluctance that they were prised out of it after the war when the space was required to provide the Club with a proper bar. As a mite of compensation they were offered the equally spacious – if then rather dilapidated – ballroom in which to bid against one another. The ex-chairman of the Club and ex-trustee, Oliver Makower, recalls the scene when he first entered the Club in the late 'fifties:

> I used to come in with my father quite a while before I became a member of the Club, so by the time I was elected it was pretty familiar. Father played bridge fairly regularly and there was always a table, sometimes two, before dinner. In those days the card-room was the present ballroom and a very dingy sort of setting it was. The whole place had been painted brown, I think at the beginning of the war. I suspect this had originally been to preserve the decoration underneath, but by the 'fifties any such purpose had been forgotten and we were left with a large dreary ill-lit room. The card tables were grouped at the end of the far stair between it and the fireplace and were lit by standard lamps that over hung the tables. I used rather to like the lamps which gave adequate light for the players, but the rest of the room had a cathedral-like gloom. As a

youngster I viewed the Savile with a respect verging on awe so the card-room atmosphere was not in my eyes inappropriate.

I remember a few of the regulars in those days. Joe Compton, secretary I believe of the Poetry Book Society and a delightful man with the finest handwriting of any one I have ever met. He once wrote to me while I was still at school and the art-master pinned the letter on the board. Ernest Pooley was almost always there. A kindly, gentle man, for many years Clerk of the Drapers Company who incidentally have a very fine portrait of him. His nickname was "the headmaster". I do not think people used it much to his face, which suggests that it was apt. Billy Darwin (father of Philip and Raz) and Eric Hooper were also regulars as was Kiss Me Hardy, the dentist. Kiss Me was a magnificent dental craftsman even if in later years he was inclined to use his trousers to wipe the dust off his implements before putting them in your mouth.

Professor John Waterlow also has memories dating from the later 'forties when the card-players were still occupying the ballroom; not all of them, however, entirely happy.

> I used very much to enjoy a game of bridge, although I was, and still am, only a beginner. The stakes were for me quite high – a shilling a hundred – and if I lost I had to go without my dinner. Therefore one's partner was very important – we cut for partners, of course. There was one old gentleman called "the Doctor" – I never learnt his real name, who played every day. He was very poor and the convention was that if he won he collected his winnings but if he lost his partner paid up. Like me, he was not very good, and it was hazardous for me, equally poor and equally incompetent, to find myself paired with him. I remember one occasion when I found myself the partner of Sir Alan Barlow, then Permanent Secretary at the Treasury, and a first-rate player. We won handsomely and going back on the top of a bus I was reckoning up our winnings, when I realized that Sir Alan had added up the score wrongly and done me out of £3.

In the early 'sixties the Diaspora of the bridge-players was once again enacted and to the sounds of almost biblical lamentation they were removed from the ballroom so that it could be used more profitably as an annexe to the dining-room. In compensation they were awarded cozy premises in a spare room behind the bar leading out to the mews in Three Kings Yard. There they remained until 1988 when the massive rehabilitation of the building led to the old billiards-room becoming the new morning-room which, in turn necessitated the removal of the Savile snooker table to the then card-room. It seems almost too cruel to have to relate that the present, small but elegantly appointed, card-room which abuts the site of the Savile snooker table was, in the days of the Harcourts, the servants' lavatory; and though it is tempting to mutter *sic transit gloria ludorum* when reflecting on the descent from the spacious quarters of yesteryear to the converted lavatory of the present, one senses from the determined looks in bridge-players' eyes that their days of migration are not yet over, as some contemporary members wishing to use the library for its proper purpose can confirm.

The "Pennies Game" mentioned by Stephen Potter as an invention of Sir William Orpen has sadly fallen into disuse and there will be few members elected after the early 'seventies who will even have heard of it. Worse, the blame for this can firmly be laid within the Savile's own ranks for the Earl of Halsbury, who was chairman of the government committee overseeing the change to decimal currency with the consequential disappearance of the essential old penny piece, was a member of the Savile at the time. Even Orpen's claim to have been its inventor can be disputed for George Vaizey attributes its origin to that great Savilian eccentric, George Boulenger.

> ...this was an hilarious after-dinner game, invented by Boully in the Brook Street house. A silver coin was placed, as a jack, on the square of flat carpet upon which the two curved staircases from what is now the Card Room [i.e., the ballroom] converge. Standing above, competitors by now inspired by wine, port and brandy, placed copper coins in bannister grooves from which they leapt at the foot to fall near the jack. He whose missile fell nearest was the winner, took all and promptly, and generously, bought more brandy. Convivial competitors put thought into this game, some twisted their coin to give it running side, others the reverse way to give it check. But after port and brandy no decision could be made as to the efficiency of technique.

In the 'sixties, when the bronze bust of Sir Compton Mackenzie beamed down from the mezzanine landing of the ballroom stairs, some irreverent young members introduced an interesting new variant to the game. Any competitor who contrived to make his penny missile strike poor Monty's nose before hitting the floor received a bonus of a bottle of whatever he wished. For reasons possibly unconnected, that noble Scottish head has now been removed to a more pious situation outside the morning-room. After decimalization a thoughtful Savile member left a bagful of old pennies to the Club in his will so that the game could continue but they languish unused and valueless in the Club's vaults. As an afterthought, Vaizey produced an interesting example of how myth can persist in the face of real evidence:

> I shall never forget that after one or two sessions [of the penny game] a

comparatively new, and serious minded member took me aside and whispered "I am surprised, and shocked, to see you playing a game of chance on the very spot where Loulou Harcourt committed suicide". A sad event, true enough, but what did this young man expect us to do, rail off the area completely and make the staircases out of bounds?

No; no need at all for, as we have seen, all the evidence confirms that Harcourt died (by whatever means) elsewhere.

Mention of Lord Halsbury, incidentally, is a reminder that shortly after he became a member in 1947 when the smart set led by Princess Margaret and Herbert Agar's stepson, Billy Wallace, were in the habit of parting from one another with the benediction "See you later, Alligator" to which the reply was "In a while, Crocodile", Monja Danischewsky looked up from his book to speed Halsbury on his way from the Savile library to the House of Lords with a parting "See you later, hereditary legislator". The belted one paused for a moment and then replied, "In a while, bibliophile."

More cerebral than the penny game, chess has been played at the Savile proportionately to the fluctuating enthusiasms of its contemporary members. It received something of a shot in the arm when that great chess master and writer on the game, C.H.O'D. Alexander was elected to the Club in 1966. Colonel Hugh O'Donel Alexander – to give him his full denomination – was a genial and witty Irishman who was a distinguished mathematician and, in common with several other Savilians, had performed sterling work during the Second World War in breaking German naval codes at the Government Code and Cipher School at Bletchley Park. Since his early youth he had had an international reputation as a chess player and would have undoubtedly achieved an even greater position in the annals of the game had not his work for the government (which continued after the war and for which he was eventually awarded the C.B.E., and the C.M.G.) prevented him from participating in more major events. Nevertheless, at the Club he was always prepared to undertake "tutorials" for his "weaker brethren" while, at the same time, he was writing learned analyses of notable tournaments for the *Sunday Times, Financial Times, Evening News* and *Spectator*. After he died in 1974, the friendly and informal chess challenges against such opponents as the R.A.C., the City Livery Club, the National Liberal Club and the BBC, continued and in 1980 a transatlantic tournament was organized against the Metropolitan Club of Washington D.C. This had been arrranged between Captain Peter Belin, U.S. Navy, a member of the Metropolitan and, since 1946 an overseas member of the Savile, and Dennis Bertlin, who had been a member of the Savile since 1965. It has been a popular and occasional fixture ever since.

Dennis Bertlin is one of the several Savile members who have achieved distinction in the sailing world. From 1950-55 when he was in charge of building the Owen Falls Dam on the Nile he was Commodore of the local Sailing Club in Uganda and on his return to the United Kingdom determined to have his own yacht designed so as to continue his sporting diversions in home waters. The man he chose was Robert Clark, one of Britain's finest yacht designers, and since his election to the Club in 1962 one of its almost daily and most popular fixtures. Robert was a man of enormous charm, courtly manners and deeply held left-wing beliefs; in his later years when he was attempting to dismiss the recurring symptoms of leukaemia he could be occasionally irascible but his innate kindliness never failed to break through in the end. Without, apparently, any formal training in his chosen field, he possessed an intuitive genius which showed not only in the craft he designed but in his rather cavalier approach to the established methods and theories of the day. Having made his name with his first boat *Mystery*, launched in 1936, and her successors, such as *Ortac, John Dory* and *Lara,* which introduced revolutionary design methods to existing theories of yacht construction, he worked for the Admiralty during the war on small, fast boats for coastal forces. In this mode he was following in the footsteps of the only other naval architect known to have been a member of the Savile, Sir E.J. Reed, C.B., F.R.S., the famous and controversial constructor of ships to the Admiralty in the late Victorian era, who was a founder member in 1868. Afterwards Clark designed *British Steel,* in which Chay Blyth sailed round the world, and two of the *Gypsy Moths* with which Sir Francis Chichester achieved international fame by sailing single-handed around the world. As the magazine, *Yachting Monthly*, which set him on his career in 1934 when he won its design competition with *Mystery*, records:

> For Sir Francis Chichester, Robert Clark designed two *Gypsy Moths*. The boats stood him in excellent stead, and with them he achieved much. One of the few insights into Clark's character which come down through sea literature is to be found in Chichester's book *The Lonely Sea and the Sky*. Chichester describes an incident when he and Clark were walking down to *Gypsy Moth II* as she lay afloat on a bitter winter's day. At that time Chichester had been diagnosed as suffering from terminal cancer but, typically, was refusing to capitulate. As the freezing wind cut into his lungs Chichester suffered one coughing bout after another, each of which brought progress to a standstill. Clark became increasingly irritated by this state of affairs and instead of waiting sympathetically, he finally snapped, "Stop coughing *now*!" Chichester, to his own amazement, did stop and began to wonder if it were not, after all, a *malade imaginaire*. That was in 1960, and *Gypsy Moth III* went on to win O.S.T.A.R.

Robert adopted exactly the same attitude to his own physical ailments and, for a time, with similar success, so he could hardly be accused of lack of sympathy.

In its obituary *The Times* wrote of him:

He was at his best with the broad concept of lines plans, sail plans, and general arrangement drawings. Detail was not his forte. But the truth of his amazing natural feel for an overall concept can be seen in such lovely creations as the sail training yachts which he designed for the Ocean Youth Club, and the 300-ton three-masted schooner *Carita*, one of the largest yachts ever built.

Every craft to which Clark gave life possessed beauty, grace, and speed. And none more so than *Carita*, with its staterooms, study, and bathrooms. He was a good sailor himself, striking in his manner, and with great presence. His individualism made him not always the easiest person with whom to work... .

to which, Dennis Bertlin, would no doubt add, with the greatest of personal affection, a heartfelt "Amen". He describes his commission to Robert:

In 1960 I asked Robert Clark to design a yacht for me. It was to be in steel about 12m. long overall. I had been working on the details of my "dream ship" for some time and gave him my specification, which he put into a large book. I am convinced that he never looked at my specification again and designed for me a yacht he thought I ought to have – not one I thought I should have. The hull was built in Antwerp and the fitting out done in Breskens . . . When Robert showed me the lines, I had made a remark that they looked all right but said I thought it a pity that the length/beam ratio was not somewhat greater. Without discussing it with me he increased the length and then later explained that it would only increase the cost marginally. However, he forgot that it would entail another 2 tons ballast and I sailed a very tender ship indeed from Breskens to Cowes. On several occasions, Robert made me quite angry, usually by his slowness in processing equipment. I would go to his office in Albemarle Street, ready to be quite unpleasant. But Robert was so charming that one could not sustain any bitter feelings and in no time I would be eating out of his hand.

So was born *Ruanda*, an R.O.R.C. Class 2 yacht, in which I had many adventures and my friendship with Robert, whom I used to meet frequently in the Savile.

Indeed there was hardly a member of the Club who would not in his time have felt able to claim Robert as a sometimes difficult but always loyal and worthwhile friend. Dallas Bower, who proposed him for membership of the Savile, had himself qualified for membership of the Royal Ocean Racing Club by crewing for Robert Clark aboard *Ortac* in the 1949 Channel Race. Later, Dallas was to commission Robert as a naval adviser on a visit to Venice for a projected film of *Antony and Cleopatra* for Two Cities Films but which in the event was not produced.

As Dallas remarks, there were many occasions in Club history when the

R.O.R.C. might have press-ganged a well-qualified crew from the bar of the Savile. "Sammy Cook, Humphrey Hare and James Fisher had all earned the rather exacting qualifications for membership of the R.O.R.C. in my time when Robert Clark was one of its leading lights," says Dallas, "as, of course, had old 'Prod' and Kenneth Whitehead." Peter Rodd and Robert Clark apparently did not see eye to eye, perhaps because 'Prod' was as feckless a client as Robert was his cavalier adviser. Certainly there was a great falling-out between them, according to Dallas, who had to listen to both sides, when Prod, who maintained two boats in the Mediterranean, decided for some reason to swap their names and engaged Robert to oversee the matter with disastrous results at Lloyd's Register. Hugh Stewart remembers a typical piece of Prod *braggadocio* which might explain some of Robert Clark's not-so-well-suppressed rage:

> Peter Rodd was explaining to me about the various hazards he encountered sailing up and down the Mediterranean. I asked him if he ever got into trouble with the authorities. He said he didn't, and by way of illumination he produced from his pocket an ink-pad with a rubber stamp. The impressive wording on the stamp was 'PROD Mediterranean Area'. This legitimized all the documents he needed, he said.

Members of the Club with a particular association with sailing include the late Kenneth Whitehead, who, after a long military career and a spell at the BBC, spent much of his time in recent years living aboard his yacht and touring the Mediterranean. By pure coincidence, two of the Club's most enthusiastic yachtsmen have named their crafts after the wife of Zeus; Bill Beale Collins in the Greek mode, with *Hera*; and Michael Peacock in the Roman, with *Juno*, the IIIrd of which won the 1987 Fastnet Bowl and the IVth is, at the time of writing, contesting the Admiral's Cup.

Golf and Real Tennis have had their devotees within the Club for many years. In the early 1980s, in common with a number of the Club's "lost" or forgotten treasures, some silver cups were discovered in the vaults which seemed to show that golf had been played by Savilians at least from 1929 until 1938 and then revived again in 1971. The cups had been awarded annually to members recording the best scratch and handicap scores. The Savile programme now usually consists of three annual meetings: at St George's Hill, Weybridge, in May; Rye in June; and Royal Wimbledon in October.

Real Tennis is played regularly at Lord's, but occasionally the Club's team goes travelling; it has carried its colours as far afield as the United States and on a famous occasion in 1980, avowedly to avenge the French Dauphin's insult to King Henry V, took on a Real Tennis team from Bordeaux in a series of fixtures at

Lord's, Hampton Court and Hatfield. Sadly the result was less satisfactory than that at Agincourt. Ralph Richardson was a keen player of Real Tennis and, after his death, Michael Estorick, a member of the Savile team, presented on their behalf a silver challenge cup in his memory.

Richardson is, of course, well remembered at Lord's for his sociability and eccentricity if not for his skill at the game. Henry Johns, the Real Tennis professional there, now in his eighties, was once asked by an apprehensive Savile member how good was Richardson's game: "Oh, it's still as good as it's ever been," said Johns, "bloody awful!"

Surprisingly, the allure of horse-racing seems generally to have passed Savile members by. In the early days however there were one or two members who were well-known racehorse owners. Of these, perhaps the most famous was a man called Cloete, or, as Sir Herbert Stephen has it:

> It is likely enough that at the time [1884]... no other member of the Savile was known by name to so many of Her Majesty's subjects, or had it in his power to interest them so much, as William Brodrick Cloete... who was lineally descended from one of the founders of the Dutch colony at the Cape of Good Hope, and the grandson of the first High Commissioner of Natal.

Her Majesty's subjects were, no doubt, "interested" because they profited from his ownership of a horse called Paradox which, ridden by the great Fred Archer in 1884, won the Two Thousand Guineas; a week later was just pipped at the post in the Derby, and a few days after that, won the Grand Prix de Paris. Cloete later bred and trained a filly called Cherimoya who ran only one race but, as it was the Oaks and she won it, he must have been satisfied well enough. He owned large estates in northern Mexico which were overrun in the revolution of Pancho Villa and his brigands and in 1915, returning from America where he had been in an attempt to retrieve some of his losses, he was drowned in the *Lusitania*.

Another owner who was an early member of the Club was Sir John Thursby, who was to become senior steward of the Jockey Club during the war years and whose horse Kennymore won the Two Thousand Guineas in 1914. So far as can be discovered, the Club's only other (but less well-requited) flirtation with the Turf occurred in 1974 when a syndicate was formed to purchase a filly which was named Sodalitas. The project was masterminded by a then member, John Carrington, and optimistic bulletins were regularly issued which sadly and only too often contained such phrases as "It had been hoped... but...," and "Unfortunately, she has met with one or two minor training set-backs..." Sodalitas briefly revived her owners' drooping spirits when Willie Carson persuaded her into third place at Doncaster in

July 1974, but thereafter she faded once more into obscurity and could have been of interest only to the chef of that time whose sole accomplishment lay in producing rather dubious roasts.

But Club activities of most interest to members generally are those which take place within the house. During the past thirty years or so these have mainly consisted in "Discussion Dinners", Musical Evenings or Art Exhibitions – wherever possible with relevance to the work of a particular member. Although these have now become a regular feature of Savile Club life, the founding fathers took a less enthusiastic view. In June 1869 when the Savile was still known as the New Club, the minutes record that the Committee received:

> Dr Marsh's proposal to read a paper to the members of the New Club: *Considered. Agreed:* to allow him the use of the room at a convenient time, and so as not to interfere with the Club dinner – and to put up notice – The Committee cannot be responsible for anything further.

Evidently members at that time were more anxious for relaxation than instruction by Dr Marsh, but attitudes changed.

In the 'thirties, the Club held a series of House Dinners, at some of which a member read a paper followed by a discussion. The war, and staffing difficulties thereafter, caused them to be discontinued and it was not until the 'sixties that it was felt possible to revive them without interfering with the normal functioning of the Club.

Nowadays House Dinners and Discussion Dinners are separate occasions. House Dinners are held to coincide with General Committee meetings; no papers are read but members are encouraged to bring their candidates for election as guests so they may become acquainted with as many as possible of the Election Committee and other members. Discussions are confined to Festive Dinners which now occur six or eight times a year and have covered a range of topics as wide and as various as the membership itself, from learned papers by distinguished comtemporaries tugging a respectful forelock to their predecessors such as H.G. Wells, Henry James, Arthur Balfour and many others to musical evenings commemorating great Savilian composers of the past and present, Elgar, Walton, Alwyn and the rest.

One of the more spectacular of these events which attracted a record congregation on a Sunday, when the Club would normally have been shut, was staged by Alan Hill. Alan, professor of English language and literature at the University of London, editor of the letters of Dorothy and William Wordsworth and of two volumes on Cardinal Newman, chose as his subject for this occasion the former member, Henry James. His absorbing account of James's portly progress through London club life was further reinforced by the presentation of some of his text by members such as Edward Fox, Graham Crowden and Roger Braban, augmented by his lady guest, Eileen Atkins.

Art exhibitions in the bar and Sandpit have been a more recent innovation and have received, perhaps, a more mixed reception. Some have aroused fierce but differing passions in members' breasts; for being too banal, for being too *avant garde*, or for being there at all. But there have been some notable exceptions; George Aczel has had two popular displays of his work which have included also sculptures by his wife Suzy; the late Merlyn Evans had a retrospective of some of his more representative canvasses at the Club before they were dispersed to their more permanent resting places such as the National Museum of Wales, while an exhibition designed to lure the work of some of the Savile's 'Sunday painters' out of their artistic closets revealed some extremely fine work from the likes of Edgar Duchin, Brian Dowling, Michael Figgis and many others. Apart from arousing passions the Arts Committee's sometimes thankless endeavours have, on occasion, raised a few eyebrows. In 1980 Robert Lewin, who, with his wife Rena, ran the Brook Street gallery, had arranged several exhibitions at the Savile which included a notable display of John Piper's beautiful prints. Later, in 1981, this was followed by a collection of prints and landscapes by Piper's son Edward. These were extremely interesting and colourful concepts with a rather novel approach to eroticism; some of the "landscapes" appeared to be undeniably depictions of the female pudenda, on at least one of which meticulously drawn mechanical excavators seemed to be going about their business: "Reminiscent of the feverish imaginings of a Russian sex-maniac," was the comment of one member. The *Sunday Times* found the notion of "an exclusively male haunt playing host to a group of naked ladies" extremely funny, as indeed it was. Mrs Lewin was quoted as saying, "The gentlemen of the Savile Club haven't been exposed to this kind of painting before. I think they are looking with great interest at those girls." She was right; They hadn't and they were.

Of all the Club events which have been introduced in recent years none has proved so universally popular as the Friday night "candle-lit dinners" to which ladies may be invited. The word "events" is suitable as it is generally agreed (by most of the ladies as well as members) that to extend this innovation to other nights in the week would remove some of the *éclat* from what has become a series of very special occasions.

The question of admitting ladies to clubs generally, either as guests or full members, has been a perennial one for as long as anyone can remember, gaining greater force with the rise of the feminist movement in recent years. So far as the Savile in particular is concerned the matter seems to have been contemplated as long ago as 1868, the year of the Club's foundation, and Sir Herbert Stephen, writing on this subject in 1923, attributes this to "the very great preponderance of men who could be characterised as Liberals and... uncompromising Radicals" among the first list of members. However the subject was put aside until the move to Savile Row in 1871 when it was again proposed at the first general meeting at the new house and, in what seems to have been a lack-lustre debate, narrowly defeated. It appears that the general feeling was that the Albemarle Club, which had recently been founded for the express purpose of admitting members of both sexes, was a sufficient gesture to equality by clubland, thus relieving the Savile of any responsibility for further radicalism.

It is interesting, incidentally, that having been "deferred" from membership of the Savile, Oscar Wilde joined the Albemarle so the Club was spared the opprobrium of furnishing the address wherefrom he was to receive that notorious misspelt letter from the Marquess of Queensberry: "To Oscar Wilde, posing as a somdomite", from which was to spring all his later tragedy.

Changes of address seemed to re-inspire the notion of admitting ladies to the Savile premises. At the second committee held at 107 Piccadilly after the Club moved there in 1882 a proposal was made "in reference to the admission of ladies at the Review of the Troops on Nov. 18, '82", but the consideration of it "was postponed". As the Review of the Troops (who had taken part in the Afghan wars) was to take place on the day following the committee meeting the decision was tantamount to a rebuff for those in favour of occasional lady guests. However, the committee – one suspects, for commercial reasons – was soon to see the error of its ways when exploiting the Club's unique position in Piccadilly as a vantage point for viewing historic occasions, and ladies were subsequently admitted to the Savile grandstand for all the many royal and military processions which were to file past the clubhouse during the ensuing years.

Then in 1928 when the Club moved to Brook Street there was a "house-warming" to which members' wives were admitted and again in 1953 there was a similar reception to celebrate its twenty-fifth anniversary and Peter Ustinov provided the entertainment.

In 1949, 1954 and 1969 again – one suspects – for commercial reasons, the committee considered the question of admitting ladies as guests and even as members. As in 1869 and 1871 feelings, though fierce, were mixed and no positive decision for change was made. However, a thin end of the wedge had appeared when the exigencies of the post-war years led to the appearance of waitresses in the dining-room; also the staff used to have an annual dance at Christmas time to which their wives were welcome together with a few invited members and their ladies.

The debate on whether such visitations should become more regular provided its own amusing moments. "For years and years it was a subject of great controversy," says Monja Danischewsky,

> Traditionalists threatened to resign if they lost the day. They clung to their strongest argument — "Where could the ladies go to 'powder their noses'?" Gip Wells, a member of the committee, putting it bluntly, said: "We always seem to get bogged down at this point."

Then came the day the problem was solved, with the aid of an eminent architect member; notice was issued that on such and such a date members might bring their wives to a Midsummer Ball. A member countered: "May members bring their mistresses?" The committee went into session, and emerged having sentence given, with a memorable example of the English genius for compromise – "Members may bring their mistresses if they are the wives of other members."

Even after the Friday night candle-lit dinners had become so well established, further unexpected hazards appeared to haunt both members and their lady guests. Peter Green on one of his rare visits from the University of Texas took advantage of one to entertain his daughter:

> This occasion certainly had its own odd side: Sarah is a Cambridge social anthropologist finishing off a dissertation on, of all things, the lesbian communes of North London, so that – a little before the official stroke of midnight – the elegant dinner-companion was metamorphosed into an old-shirt-and-grotty-jeans academic Cinderella, anything more social being liable to arouse severe suspicions in the house where she was living.

But every attempt to make *membership* available to both sexes has been resisted and, to use the words of Sir Herbert Stephen in 1923: "... the Club as a whole wished to be a Club for men only, and to leave the development of epicene establishments of this character to other and more ardent reformers". Reasons for this all-male preference are complicated and have been debated endlessly elsewhere as well as in the Savile. J.B. Priestley was all for having ladies in: "I like to see the girls lighting up the place," he said once, adding that there was "something faintly silly about an all-masculine society". In the same article, however, he asked himself: "Would I go oftener [to the Savile] if this were a mixed Club?" and his answer was, a rather guarded, "Perhaps not." The psychiatrist Anthony Storr takes a more considered view:

> It is an odd but undoubted fact that women hate clubs and men love them. Although there are such institutions as women's clubs, very few women seem to enjoy them, and those that do are not generally the kind of women who inspire enthusiasm in the masculine breast. This is a difference between the sexes as real as the anatomical one with which most Savilians are familiar; and it has led me to reflect upon what it is that men actually enjoy about club life, and upon why they are so different from women in this respect.

His conclusions can roughly be summarized as these:

That it is satisfying, morale-boosting and stretching to mix on equal terms with men in one's own or other fields of activity of whom some may be of great distinction; that it is pleasant occasionally to escape from domesticity; that the Savile provides as "peculiar form of relationship... not often to be found between women . . . less than intimate friendship and more than mere acquaintance . . . a form of conversation which is both relaxing and stimulating simultaneously." Moreover, "men, much more than women need self-validation . . . Club life is, at one level, a gigantic reassurance system. We recognize, and pay tribute to, each other's achievements. We gossip just as much as women; but our gossip is more concerned with our work than with our love life or our children . . . We compete with and reassure each other at the same time; and this is something which only men can given each other."

The debate about the admission of ladies to membership will, no doubt, continue, but whether the views represented by J.B. Priestley or those of Anthony Storr prevail, one certain verdict is that if ladies are admitted to membership "the place will never be the same" and to this conclusion, feminist or otherwise, most ladies who have been to the Savile would probably have to agree.

The most important constituent of a club consists in its members; but almost equally important is the staff. As herbs and spices in a culinary dish they add flavour to the main ingredient and can enhance or detract from the characteristics of the whole. This essential contribution of the staff to club life will reflect the ability of the management as surely as the relative success of a gourmet meal will indicate the skill of the chef in choosing and juxtaposing the materials at his disposal. So it has been at the Savile. The years of prosperity and fair weather under competent management have been magnified by loyal and efficient servants; the occasional doldrums brought about by maladministration have been further exacerbated by demoralized, inadequate and ill-chosen staff. Fortunately, these latter periods have been relatively rare but whether in good times or bad the servants of the Club have provided material nearly as rich as that of the members for the Club history.

When the Club was founded in May/June 1868 at Spring Gardens it was part of the arrangement that the annual rent of £400 per annum would include the cost of "service" as well as "firing, lights, etc". "Service" seems to have consisted then in the attendance on the first few members of "Edwards", about whom nothing else is known except that he is costed along with the furniture in the first year's accounts in December 1869 at £31.0.0. Clearly his ministrations, no matter how diligent, were insufficient for the greater numbers who had hastened to join the Club by the end of its first year of existence, for when these accounts were presented, the committee discussed the "employment at higher wages of a servant under the exclusive control and for the separate use of the Club". This was agreed and from that moment it may be said that the Club took on the extra subtle flavour which only its staff could and would continue to give it.

No records exist of whomever this "exclusively controlled servant" (and presumably his fellows) turned out to be in those very early years. The rapid growth of the Club must have created the need for many more than one to supplement the efforts of Edwards and, in 1881, ten years after the move to Savile Row, when the committee took on direct responsibility for in-house catering rather than contracting it out as had been the original custom, the number of servants was further increased by the need to supply cooks and waiters, as well as footmen, page-boys, hall porters, clerks and all the other essential accoutrements of civilized Victorian club life which the burgeoning Savile now required.

And just as it has been impossible to provide a comprehensive portrayal of the numerically vast and infinitely various membership of the Savile since those early days, so it has proved difficult to delineate the particular (if not peculiar) features of all the staff who have served, suffered, cosseted, encouraged and sometimes refined it over the years. But there are some who have stood out as great personalities in their own right whether for their loyalty and long service or for their individual eccentricity.

Sir Herbert Stephen, writing in 1923, records that "the Savile has always... been admirably served by its staff" and notes that "as recently as 1914 'Sindon' was pensioned after more than thirty years' excellent service as Hall Porter."

Hall porters, by the very nature of their duties, provide the first impression of a club to guests entering it while also needing to preserve a certain imperturbability when assisting some of the entrances and exits of their members. In both these respects the Club has been well provided for over the years. Keene, who succeeded Sindon as guardian of the Savile hall-way and whose tenure of this post lasted even longer than Sindon's thirty years, possessed a certain *hauteur* which perhaps compensated for the lack of it elsewhere in the Club. This could be intimidating; Winston Graham recalls that, in 1950, "the first time I arrived on my own, Keene, the porter, looked me up and down as if he thought I should have tried the tradesman's entrance". However, his demeanour had its funny side. The distinguished French diplomat, Pierre Millet, *Officier de la Légion d'Honneur* and recipient of the *Médaille de la Résistance*, who was Ambassador to Laos from 1963 and to Libya from 1967-69, writes:

> I left London at the end of November 1938 to join the French Embassy in China as 'attaché d'Ambassade'. It was only at the beginning of February 1946 that I returned from the Far East on a British troopship... On my return to London I was longing, of course, to go to the Savile Club after so many years of absence, and what eventful years! I thought, on the doorstep of 69 Brook Street, that I had to introduce myself. I was about to do so when the hall porter looked at me and said, very quietly, as if I had never left England and the Club: "Good morning, Mr. Millet, there is a

letter for you". I must say I was rather amazed. When I told André Maurois that story, he was very amused and said it was one of the best "English stories" he knew.

The tradition continues. The post-war years saw the necessary introduction of lady receptionists to augment the male porters, and their presence perhaps softened the pangs of transition from the buffetings of the outside world to the welcoming anachronistic ambience of the Club rooms. Certainly the new formula has worked well, as contemporary members and guests who arrive at Brook Street to be greeted by the majestically charming Catriona, who presides over the contemplative and saintly Tom or the wittily ebullient Peter Fitzgerald, will testify.

Bar staff throughout the years have not only inspirited the members with their wares but have left a rich legacy of anecdote for them to mull over. Until 1940 there was no formal bar and all drinks were served individually by footmen and waiters. These were a highly individual band of servitors – either to the God Bacchus or the Demon Drink depending on the habits of the members or one's point of view. In 1923 Sir Herbert Stephen meaningfully wrote: "The longer the standing of members in the Club, the more certain it is that 'Cocks', 'Smith', 'Frank' and 'Godfrey' are numbered among their most constant friends." The use of the surname for "Cocks" and "Smith" perhaps hints at a more muted intimacy with their clientele than the more familiar "Frank" and "Godfrey". Of the latter it was written that during the time at Piccadilly when members regularly roistered until one or two o'clock in the morning: "Godfrey grew more and more sympathetic to man's need of alcohol as the night drew on." But it was Frank who stamped himself indelibly on the Club's psyche and so much so that he has necessarily made many appearances already in this Club narrative either as a valuable commentator on the surrounding motley or as a loyally devious witness for the defence of over-enthusiastic customers re-appearing at Bow Street magistrates court in the morning. In that earlier age servants were not expected to have a "private life" and nor, probably, if they had one, would they have wished it to be known: little can so be told of Frank outside of his existence at the Club. Nevertheless, the force of his personality, which he unconsciously bequeathed to the Club, is formidable. Certainly he must have served with gallantry during the First World War for he was festooned with medals as he went about his more peaceable business at Piccadilly and Brook Street. Just after the last war when waiter service was still operating in tandem with the newly instituted bar, the young Professor John Waterlow remembers the redoubtable Frank who, at some great age, was still impeccably performing:

> In those days you didn't have to go to the bar for drinks, but a waiter came round. He was an elderly man in breeches and silk stockings with a string of war ribbons. The second time that Oliver Kisch and I came into the Club I ordered 2 pints of beer and the waiter said "Mr Kisch only takes

half a pint, sir" – which was quite true. One cannot help feeling *"Quantum descensus ab illo"*.

Like all the great servants of the Club, Frank's memory for the idiosyncrasies of his members was vast and nearly always impeccable. His only recorded lapse is recalled by Monja Danischewsky:

> Francis Meynell told me of an incident in which, for once, the infallible Frank was rattled. Meynell's father had fallen out with the Savile and did not enter the Club for some twenty-five years. At last he allowed Francis to take him there for lunch. Frank showed no surprise. He greeted the old gentleman as he would a regular member. All went well until the time came for coffee and liqueurs. Frank looked distressed. He whispered to Francis. "I can't for the life of me remember if your father takes sugar with his coffee?"

Frank had been with the Savile since 1884 when he was first employed at Savile Row as a page-boy and he continued to be an eloquent source of information concerning what many later members must have considered a very distant past. His memories of the early days when such luminaries as Robert Louis Stevenson, Kipling and Sir Henry Irving were regular attenders gave members, until quite recently, the wondrous illusion of being in direct contact with another age.

In the mid-'forties when Frank would have been in his late eighties he tottered into the Sandpit in search of custom, to discover Dallas Bower meditating for once at the fender: "Ah! Good evening, Mr Stevenson," said Frank in his cheerful way. "What a lovely hot fire for you to warm yourself by." "Thank you, Frank," said Dallas, "But sadly I am not Mr Stevenson, who is dead, I am Mr Bower." "Just as well, sir," said the indestructible Frank, "else you would be in it rather than enjoying it."

In 1940, Frank's fame had extended far beyond the Savile and he was interviewed by the then leading London evening newspaper *The Star*. Discreet as always, he refused to name names but he consented to several innocent revelations of an anonymous nature. Among them was one which concerned a deeply superstitious member who would not leave the long table without hurling the left-over bones from his meal over his left shoulder; another who would eat a little of his lunch and then take out a large handkerchief, place the rest of the food into it and then walk out to finish the repast in Green Park. There was another on whom fell the analytical eye of Frank, who came to the Club on crutches yet never looked particularly lame. He was never seen without his crutches. One day, Frank looked out of the window and saw this member running like an athlete, with his crutches tucked underneath his arm, to catch a horse-bus which had just gone by.

He had also perfected his own methods of dealing with certain "difficult" members. "Dropping the tray" for instance, was the method he used to arouse one particular member who was in the habit of ringing the bell for service and then promptly falling asleep.

Only once did he meet his match. A "very testy professor" had ordered tea and boiled eggs to be served to him in the Smoking-Room at Piccadilly. Frank demurred:

> "I can bring you the tea, sir, but it's against the rules to serve eggs in the Smoking Room."
> "Where is the Rule? I have not seen it."
> "It's a verbal rule, sir."
> "Well, you must either bring me the Rule or the eggs."
> Frank brought the eggs.

The increasing popularity of the now well-established bar coupled with the inevitable but much mourned departure of the aged Frank in the mid-'forties inspired the committee to the daring innovation of employing bar-maids. Appropriately the first of these was called Eve who rapidly established herself as almost equal to Frank in her capacity for remembering the individual foibles of members in their drinking habits. She was occasionally assisted by a young pocket Venus whose low-cut dresses swelled also the takings though they threatened many a member with premature cardiac arrest. After many years of service Eve won a competition for which the first prize was a holiday in Spain and to the dismay of most of the members an over-zealous House Committee chairman dismissed her for taking it at an inconvenient time for the Club. Next came Barbara – "The Duchess of Portsmouth" – whose eventful and popular reign behind the bar has been chronicled in another chapter. She was succeeded by a glamorous blonde lady who was efficient enough but the atmosphere was never quite the same. One of her disadvantages was an extremely jealous husband who worked as a barman elsewhere. As well as being jealous, he was an enthusiastic consumer of his own wares with the natural result that he spent much of his time "between jobs". On these occasions he would station himself in the pantry behind the bar and glower threateningly at any member exchanging more than the few words necessary to purchase a drink from his wife. Even the grossly inefficient management of the time began to feel uneasy and felt it necessary to replace her. In doing so, they excelled themselves. Members arriving for an early drink one Monday morning were confronted with a lissome but moody-looking "cow-girl" in tight jeans with leather riding chaps, a bandolier about her shoulders and a holster containing two guns about her waist. It was a severe test of equanimity which the membership generally passed with flying colours. However there came one unfortunate exception; a member visiting the Club for the first time in several weeks and unaware of this development was, not unnaturally, surprised to find himself being served by this grotesque and, while attempting to establish by closer examination whether her guns were real or replica, discovered that among her other accomplishments she was also a black belt at Judo. So, with mixed feelings on both sides, "Two-Gun Annie" departed.

With the arrival of Peter Aldersley and the revival of good management at the Club the working of the bar was placed in more capable hands. The first sign of the new dispensation was the appearance of "Fred", who had been president of the

United Kingdom Bar Tenders Guild more times than anyone could remember. "Appearance" is the root word, for Fred would bustle in each morning at 10 a.m. to prepare the bar, dressed in pork-pie hat and a voluminous overcoat and, whatever the weather, carrying an eccentrically rolled umbrella. Having divested himself of these accoutrements he would emerge from the pantry with the air of a conductor about to ascend the podium to marshal his forces for the opening *tutti* on the dot of eleven. Fred was reputed to have at his finger-tips the precise recipes for well over a thousand cocktails but as the nearest he got to being able to demonstrate this accomplishment at the Savile was to fulfil the occasional request for a dry martini he must have lived in a constant state of frustration. Years of experience in the West End haunts of the rich had, moreover, left Fred with one unfortunate habit which he found it impossible to overcome; this was the intrusion of his thumb into the measure, and a prestidigitous way of operating the optics – now you see it, now you don't – which became the cynosure of a generally tolerant membership who regarded it as a kind of poll tax to set against his other more genial eccentricities. An exception was one Savilian who determined to demonstrate to Fred the error of his ways. One morning at eleven this member arrived at the bar armed with a measure he had purchased for the occasion and ordered a large neat gin. Having chatted without drinking for about ten minutes on the state of the stock-market – a subject of compelling interest to Fred and his life's accumulation from short measures – the member addressed himself to his glass:

"I think you'll agree, Fred, that a certain amount of the ice in this drink must have melted by now?"

"Yes, sir."

"Then in that case this measure I happen to have on me should overflow if I pour it in." Fred agreed, the experiment was made, and the measure remained half empty. A long silence ensued until the imperturbable Fred eventually blinked and said: "Good gracious, I've never seen that trick done before. Perhaps you'd better have a triple on me, sir", and thereafter returned to his old incorrigible ways. When he departed from the Club this member composed his epitaph:

"Gin and water sold I ever,

Proper measure gave I never;

So to the devil I must go,

Woe, woe, woe, woe!"

Professor Waterlow's dire foreboding that after the departure of Frank in the forties it would be a case of *"Quantum descensus ab illo"* was most convincingly and pleasurably dispelled by the arrival of Roy to replace Fred. Roy not only managed within his first week to index and file away in his head every member's individual tastes but, by an uncanny demonstration of what can only be extra-sensory perception, anticipate any deviation from the norm. A member approaching the bar would have been keenly observed on his way in from the Sandpit and having decided – say – on a gin instead of his more usual whisky find it waiting for him on arrival.

"Thought you'd ask for that today, sir," Roy would say, "Sorry for the delay."

Since 1988, Roy in semi-retirement, came in only in the morning his wonders to perform. Luckily, the versatile Richard, who came to the Savile from the Savoy Group in the nineteen eighties, was on hand to transfer his skills from the lunch-time dining-room to take charge of the bar in the evening and since Roy's retirement has created what must be one of the most civilized places in London to enjoy a drink.

Never has the equation of good and bad staff with the relative efficiency of the Club secretaries been so dramatically demonstrated as in the performance of the various dining-room managers. There have been, of course, the occasional exceptions but there was little they could do to overcome the incompetence of those above them during the bad times. In 1949 when the Club was struggling to compensate for the deprivations of the war years a new secretary was appointed whose lavish and irresponsible ways soon bid fair to bring the Savile to its knees. The dining-room manager at the time was one Goss, who did his best against almost insuperable odds. Keith Piercy remembers him as "one of the more excellent servants of those days... who presided over our domestic arrangements with urbane tact and efficiency." Goss had been valet to the sporting peer, Lord Lonsdale – there were some who suggested that he might also have been his illegitimate son – and was in the habit of justifying all of his own actions with the remark: "Oh, but this is the way his Lordship would have wished it done." On one occasion when Gilbert Harding was being helped into a taxi by another member, Goss came along to help, whereupon Harding shouted at him, "Get out of my way, you silly old man." The member felt he should apologize for this rudeness but Goss said, "Please don't worry, sir; I enjoy serving Mr Harding almost as much as his Lordship." Although he was an efficient dining-room manager within the scope of his own and others' limitations there were problems; Winston Graham remembers him as being:

> ... far more distinguished looking than even the most distinguished members of the Savile, unfortunately he was found the worse for drink on several occasions and was invited to leave. I spoke to the Chairman suggesting he might be given another chance. If taking too much to drink were the criterion people were judged by, where did many of the members of the Club stand? After all, I suggested, what was sauce for the Goss... But the committee remained adamant.

From the Savile, Goss went on to work at the Mansion House, where Keith Piercy again encountered him

> discreetly hovering in the background to see that everything was going smoothly and he greeted me warmly. During the evening I was talking to the Lady Mayoress, a charming and attractive Belgian woman, and she said how invaluable she found Goss in looking after the many functions which took place in the Mansion House.

Goss was succeeded by an equally distinguished-looking factotum whose superior ways terrorized even the most self-assured members. After some years' service he surmised that the Savile ship was indeed sinking and took his leave to become the manager of another "more gentlemanly and well-established West End Club" which some months later, admittedly through no fault of his, abruptly closed its doors forever. His departure coincided with perhaps the worst period of maladministration in the Savile's history. An abysmal procession of dining-room managers came and quickly went; "The White Rabbit," so named because he would scuttle off looking at his watch if anyone appeared to require service; the charming Russian lady, Maruska, who was occasionally efficient but never sober; "The Sicilian Bandit" with opaque glasses and a sinister air who only smiled when he was sharpening knives to cut the roast; and others too tedious to recall. Thankfully, for the past fifteen years under the direction of the present secretary, the dining-room has been more than ably managed by Alfredo and Omar who have built around themselves a loyal and long-serving staff such as must compare with the very best the Savile possessed in the pre-war years.

Even in the darkest days, however, there were the occasional bright exceptions. Winston Graham remembers a

> ... beautiful Irish waitress whom half the Club fell in love with, but none nearly so seriously as Denzil Batchelor, who would go to great lengths to be at the right table, and once said to me: "Doesn't it break your heart to see the way she serves the potatoes?" She married well, I'm glad to say, but not to a member of the Savile.

Then there was Norah. She had been with the Club since time immemorial, no one knew for how long because proper staff records do not go back so far; Certainly Norah did not care to say. When Peter Aldersley arrived to be the new Secretary he interviewed all the existing staff. When he asked Norah how long she had been with the Club she replied she could not remember. When asked how old she was she replied with some spirit, "Oh! I couldn't tell you that, sir." She was certainly well into her eighties and for the last five years before she was reluctantly forced, through illness, to retire in 1980 she was on "light duties" serving at breakfast and tea with a charm and old world courtesy which is still warmly remembered by those remaining members who knew her.

By coincidence the two of the Club servants who stand out most vividly from the past were called Frank. There was Frank the wine-waiter, as we have seen, but there was also Frank the valet who served from 1938 until he died in 1974. Patric Dickinson describes him admirably:

> To me he was the perfect "gentleman's gentleman", a stay of the Club. He somehow *gauged* one. Even the look as he brought one's tea implied that one's clothes hadn't been quite folded properly. But he was no Jeeves; he was never deferential; he had perfect manners, he was free, classless, the perfect free servant, as you will find in the comedies of Plautus – his own master.

392

Michael Figgis remembers his visits to the Savile in those dingier days after the war:

> Staying at the Savile in those days reminded me of many an Irish house of faded nobility. Bedroom carpets were worn, furniture was rickety, a catholic assortment of books lay on bedroom shelves. A vital member of the staff was the valet, Frank, also an Irishman who polished shoes with vigour, talked incessantly to himself and, whatever time one had indicated for a call, would invariably enter one's room several minutes late and even on the dreariest of days would fling back the curtains saying, "It's a grand day entirely. Ye've all the time in the world now and I'll have the bath full in a jiffey." With pride he laid the polished shoes at one's bedside and dashed off to attend the many "gintlemen" who required his services. His devotion and enthusiasm for his job was obvious. Even a fresh crease in one's trousers was a matter of seconds.

Frank was not *always* late with his early morning calls; sometimes he would arrive at a member's bedside at 6 a.m. when he came on duty to enquire cheerfully: "What is it you said the time was you wanted to be woken up?" He also proved the dictum that "no man is a hero to his valet" and made his disapproval obvious concerning members who offended his sense of decorum.

It was presumably Humphrey Hare's homosexuality that explains Winston Graham's recollection that:

> For some reason he did not much like Humphrey Hare, and Frank's greeting to me in the morning when he brought in my tea was almost invariably: 'Eight o'clock and ye're all right now. Hare's asleep.' It became such an accustomed greeting that I took the story home to my wife, who pictured Humphrey Hare as a stout, elderly, white haired old buffer, until one September she met the tall, good-looking old-Etonian in Venice.

But for the vast majority of the members, more congenial to Frank, nothing was too much trouble. William Barnes recalls that his proposer at the Club, the playwright St John Ervine, who had only one leg, "used to sing the praises of Frank the valet who was extra kind to him in helping him in and out of the bath".

When Frank died in 1974 he left a total estate of £1,000 out of which he left £500 to the Savile. With this money the committee purchased the elegant writing table which is now in the Sandpit, and though it has always been a rule that no brass plaques would be placed anywhere in the Club to commemorate past members – no matter how distinguished – an exception was made in this case, and one was affixed to the table in memory of this devoted and much loved servant.

Life at the Savile was informed and enriched for members by the likes of Frank and his wine-waiter namesake; Sindon and Keene, the hall porters; Norah, and all the many others who served at Piccadilly and Brook Street. It might have seemed at comparatively brief moments in the Club's history that personalities of their kind were gone, never to be found again. But the last fifteen years have shown this not to be so, and that the mutual affection between members and staff is now, in every respect, the equal of that which obtained during those golden pre-war years. That this is no pious exaggeration is indicated in Andrew Cooper's recent tribute:

> I had my 80th birthday party in the Morning Room, as it was then called, where everything was splendidly organized by the irreplaceable Peter Aldersley. The Club also gave me a separate birthday party kindly organized by Fred Kendall, another staunch Savilian. I still have the special menus signed not only by the guests but also by every member of the Club staff. Truly a family affair. But it is also evident that the "family" element is not confined to such festive gestures alone and it can have its more moving moments. Stelio Hourmouzios, a well-known and well-liked figure in diplomatic and journalistic circles had been a popular member of the Club from 1970 until his death in 1984. He had seen service as secretary to King George of Greece and subsequently to King Constantine, for which employment he suffered a period of imprisonment after the coup of April 1967. Thereafter he had worked for the Niarchos organisation in London which enabled him to become a regular attender at the Club, where his charm and his enthusiams – not least for a vast and undistinguished picture in the sandpit which he vainly averred was a Poussin – were much appreciated. When he was ill with cancer and spending his last days at St Joseph's Hospice it came to the ears of the staff that among the few creature comforts he was missing most was one of the Savile's special dishes, "Caramote Malaysienne" – a delicous confection of prawns in a creamy, spicy sauce. Alfredo the restaurant manager immediately made arrangements with the chef, Peter Lea, and the medical authorities at the hospice so that the dish was promptly prepared and served personally by those concerned.

"Truly", as Andrew Cooper has observed, "a family affair".

History, except for seers and the little sandwich-board man in Oxford Street, has no foreseeable end, but books, of necessity, must. This account of the Savile has proved to be longer than its author or his increasingly impatient publisher had intended. There are good reasons for this; the unexpected richness and diversity of the Club's members which was waiting to be discovered; the hitherto uncatalogued relationship between them and the massive movement of events in their time; and the various footnotes which the story of the Club provides to the social, political, artistic and scientific history of the last one and a quarter centuries – a period which has probably seen more revolutionary development in each of these fields then had occurred in the previous millennium. In most of these events Savile members have played their contributory part, though the guiding spirit of the Club has managed to accommodate the present while sustaining a respect for the civilized values which informed a less frenetic past. The unforeseeable future of the Savile's history is now in the hands of contemporary members and their successors; it is hoped that this glimpse of their inheritance may be of encouragement to them in their efforts to maintain an equally civilized future.

Honorary and Temporary Members; Reciprocal Memberships of other Clubs

From its earliest days the Club has made provision for "honorary" and "temporary" members. These terms have given rise to some confusion, particularly that relating to "honorary members" which is sometimes taken to refer to that device by which some other clubs invite an eminent person into their ranks to enjoy the privileges of memberhip without entrance fee, subscription or any of the usual preliminary vetting procedures. This does not happen at the Savile. The relevant clauses are contained in Rule 6, which states:

> The committee shall have power to admit any gentleman usually resident outside the British Isles as an honorary member, without payment, to the privileges of the Club for any period *not exceeding one month*, on the introduction of two members signified in the book provided for that purpose: provided that the total number of honorary members at any one time shall not exceed such limit as may from time to time be fixed by the committee... .

and Rule 7, which states:

> The committee shall have power, by unanimous vote of the Members present at any of its meetings, to elect any person, duly proposed and supported in the book provided for that purpose a Temporary Member of the Club upon the following terms... .

the terms being that the temporary membership can only be granted for periods of 3, 6, 9 or a maximum of 12 months, the current level of subscription to be paid *pro rata*.

To these rules were added a hand-written note on the frontispiece of the Temporary Members Book in 1871:

> *N.B. The committee requires information by letter or otherwise as to the fitness of all candidates before electing them.*

It will be seen from this that these two provisions offer no easy back door into membership of the Club and, in fact, they have been very rarely invoked, particularly in recent years. Nevertheless, the Candidates Books under each heading offer some interesting reading.

The earliest surviving book for honorary members dates from 1891; the first entry is on 9 September of that year for the Hon. Alfred Dobson, Solicitor General for Tasmania, who was proposed by Thomas Herbert Robertson, the honorary secretary of the Club from 1881-1890 and seconded by Henry John Hood who had shared that office with him during the years 1879-99. Those seeking honorary membership thereafter seemed to reflect the diversity of professions so greatly encouraged within the main body of the Club. In the three months which remained of 1891, among those elected under this heading were Augustus Daly, the manager of Daly's Theatre; an accountant from Bengal; a professor of Anatomy from Sydney University; a professor of American Folklore from Cambridge, Massachusetts; an analytical chemist from Barbados; a "rentier" from Chicago; and one of the Spring-Rice family visiting his Savilian relations from his ranch in Canada. The colonial branch of the Spring-Rice family were clearly welcome visitors to the Club, for both Bernard and Gerald who had extensive ranching interests in the North West Territories made regular appearances as honorary or temporary members at three or four year intervals over the ensuing forty years.

Many who used this facility during their brief visits from abroad were later to become full members of the Club when they were more permanently established in Britain. One of these, for instance, was the distinguished physician, Professor Sir William Osler, F.R.S., who used the Club as an honorary member during brief respites from lecturing in Canada and the United States in 1892, 1894 and 1898. In 1899 he became a temporary member for 12 months, and in 1900 when he took up his professorship at Oxford was elected a full member. Another was Frederick Courtney Selous – "Allan Quatermain" – who, in between his African exploits, was an honorary member in 1893 until settling in England in 1900 he became a full member. There were many others who followed the same path: George Haven Putnam, Litt.D., the American publisher, was a temporary member for a 12-months period in 1888, 3 months in 1891, an honorary member in 1892 and a full member from 1895 onwards; Sir William Nevill Montgomerie Geary, Attorney-General for the Gold Coast, was a temporary member in 1897, becoming a full member in 1898.

Those early years saw a procession of similarly distinguished government and administration figures on business or furlough from abroad making a bee-line for the Savile during their visits to London. Sir William Robinson, G.C.M.G., Governor of West Australia, came in 1895; Mynheer Van der Street, A.D.C. to the Queen of the Netherlands, in May 1897; followed two months later by Sir Henry Strong, Chief Justice of Canada. In 1902 came The Rt Hon. R.J. Seddon, Prime Minister of New Zealand, and in 1904, Sir Albert Hine, Prime Minister of Natal. In August and October of that year, R.J.B. Ross, the acting Attorney-

General of Lagos, availed himself of the four-week periods of honorary membership and in March 1907, Doctor Frederick Fitchett, Solicitor-General of New Zealand, did the same. His colleague the Hon. J.D. Findlay, K.C., Attorney-General of New Zealand followed after him in May, 1911, to find himself in the company of W.D. Davidson, C.M.G., the Governor of the Seychelles, who had arrived four days earlier and was to return for another four weeks' Convivium in September. On his return to England in 1912, Davidson, who was to become Sir Walter Davidson, K.C.M.G., was also elected to full membership.

A similar number of Government officials applied for temporary membership during this period so that they might stay longer than the one month prescribed for honorary members. Notable among them was Walter Goodall Bey, "Secretary to H.M. The Khedive of Egypt", who was elected for twelve months in June 1885. But one of the strangest revelations afforded by a browse through the relevant remaining documents is the attraction the Savile appeared to have for visitors from Japan. The first of these was a Mr S. Hayakura, Private Secretary to the Minister of Finance and Counsellor of the Treasury in Tokyo, who was granted honorary membership on the 31 October 1896. On the day before his month's membership expired he was joined by the enigmatic Mr M. Suzuki whose occupation is described as "Travelling for Pleasure". In December, Mr Hayakura was once again proposed and this time granted twelve months' temporary membership; nine weeks later, Mr Suzuki, still "travelling for pleasure", reappeared to be elected to six months' temporary membership, presumably so he could rest himself. Six months' after this expired, in January 1898, Mr Suzuki again appeared – this time on his own – and was proposed for another six months' temporary membership though no record of his subsequent election appears in the book. In June 1899, Mr Hayakura reappears (but now attached to the Japanese Embassy) and was granted six months' temporary membership. Reports back to Japan on *Sodalitas Convivium* must have been favourable for in 1906 there came as honorary members to the Savile a Professor Akyama and a Colonel Haga, legal advisers to the War Office in Tokyo, *en route* to Switzerland as delegates to the Geneva Convention. Three years later, in May 1909, Kengo Mori, assistant financial commissioner for Japan, was granted six months' temporary membership but the sun finally ceased to rise on this unlikely far-eastern Savile connection with the election to six months' membership of Joskio Jakamine, Doctor of Science at Kyoto University in 1920.

Word of mouth seems to have played as large a part in attracting honorary and temporary members to the Savile as it did for regular members. It must have been more than coincidence, for instance, that brought a procession of editors on leave from their jobs on *The Times of India* to the Savile during a period of more than forty years. Nor could it have been the presence at Piccadilly and later Brook Street of Rudyard Kipling that brought them there for he was only elected in 1895, two years after the influx began. The first to come was an H. Griven in 1883; he was followed by the assistant editor, Samuel Digby, in 1885. In 1888 came another editor, whose name is inscribed bluntly without initial "Curwen, editor, *The Times of India"*. In 1907 came yet another, Lovat Frazer, until the sequence came to an end with Sir Stanley Reed in 1919. Of these, Lovat Frazer went on to become a full member in 1909 as did Sir Stanley Reed in 1920.

Literary and artistic figures, as might be expected, abound in the records of honorary and temporary members, many of them also proceeding later to full membership. The painter James Tissot, as we have seen, arrived at the Savile by this method in January 1872. Francis Davis Millet, the American painter and writer who had served as a drummer boy with the Union forces and whose works appear in collections such as the Metropolitan Museum of Art in New York and the Tate Gallery, was a temporary member in 1879. He was drowned in the *Titanic* in 1912, the year that André Gide was elected an honorary member during his stay in London. In 1880, the year after Millet had appeared at the Savile, the American novelist Bret Harte was proposed for temporary membership by Thomas Hardy and Sir Walter Besant. Harte – also known as Francis Brett Harte – had with the aid of alcohol burnt himself out of a brilliant literary career in the States and in 1880 as part of perhaps the unlikeliest course of therapy in medical history, had been sent by his concerned friends in high places to be the American consul in Glasgow. His entry in the candidates book is amended "Entered here by mistake for Hon. Mem's book" and as this was lost in the great arson outrage of 1975 nothing can be told of his subsequent history at the Savile. In 1884 there arrived as temporary members of the Club three more great American figures of the time: A. Pulitzer, editor of the *New York Morning Journal* and son of the publisher and founder of the famous prize of that name, who was proposed by Sir Henry Irving and duly elected for twelve months; Brander Matthews, the essayist and drama critic, who was orginally elected for six months but became a full member in the same year; and in June, the most famous portraitist of this time, John Singer Sargent, who was introduced into the Club by his great admirer, Henry James, and was supported by Edmund Gosse. Sargent was duly elected for three months but there is an enigmatic note in the book against his entry in what appears to be Henry James's handwriting, "Transferred to Book of Introductions". What this is, or was, can only be surmised as it has disappeared – presumably with the other records destroyed in the blaze. It can be deduced, however, that his association with the Savile was more extensive than the remaining records show for, although a Paris address was given in the candidates book, he was constantly in London at the time and he had many more friends at the Savile in addition to Henry James and Edmund Gosse. Indeed, at least three of his great portraits were of contemporary Savile members, Robert Louis Stevenson, Sir Hubert Parry and Coventry Patmore – the latter being hung in the Sargent Gallery at the Tate.

In 1888 the novelist Henry Harland was proposed for six months' membership by Walter Besant, but for some reason the proposal seems to have been ignored. In 1889 he was again proposed – this time by Andrew Lang – and was accepted for three months. Later this was renewed for a further three months at the proposal once again of Walter Besant. It is odd that he did not go on to become a full member for he was to be professionally associated with so many of the Savile contingent of that day such as Kipling, Justin M'Carty, Alex and Robert Ross and Walter Besant at the Society of Authors, and with Henry James, Edmund Gosse, and Max Beerbohm through his editorship of *The Yellow Book*.

In 1896, the future Astronomer Royal, Sir William Christie, introduced David Gill, F.R.S., H.M. Astronomer at the Cape, into the Club as an honorary member and the publisher John Murray did the same for Augustus Lowell of the Lowell Institute at Baltimore. In 1897 there came two editors of influential American journals on a visit to London and hospitality at the Savile: Henry Loomis Nelson of *Harper's Weekly* and H.E. Scudder of *Atlantic Monthly*. They were later joined by Fletcher Harper himself, who took up temporary membership for twelve months.

In 1898 a young French "student", Elie Halévy, appears in the honorary members book. Within a few years he was to commence work on his *History of the English People in the Nineteenth Century* which even now remains probably the best, most detailed, impartial and brilliant account of that period. He was to continue using the Club in this way during his several visits to London over the next twenty years.

In 1898 also, amid all those members of "different" profession who congregated in the Club, none could have struck such a bizarre note as another Frenchman, the Comte Gilbert de Voisins, who declared his occupation to be that of "Euphuist". Whether he meant one of the two meanings of the term in English – "graceful and goodly" or "affected and bombastic", or whether the word carries some more esoteric meaning to the French aristocracy, we shall never know. As he was proposed by the rather dour Sir Peter Chalmers Mitchell whom Winston Graham (encountering him nearly fifty years later) remembers as "not exactly an apostle of lightness and joy", it is likely that the good Voisins's euphuism concealed a more acceptable *gravitas*. Such a flight of fancy in the candidates book was however immediately brought down to earth by the next entry, which was for the aptly named Arnold Clodd from Jamaica, whose occupation is given as "Planter".

In 1898 the composer Frederick Delius made his first appearance at the Club. As will have been seen in an earlier section he was to make use of honorary and temporary membership on five occasions during the next twenty years until his failing health prevented him leaving his home in France. However he remained on terms of great friendship with many musician members of the Savile such as Balfour Gardiner, Robin Legge and Roger Quilter, who visited him regularly in France.

No doubt because of the strong musical element which has always been a component of the Savile membership, a considerable number of visiting musicians feature in the honorary and temporary members books. Herr Rudolph Zwintscher, pianist at the Leipzig Conservatoire, was an honorary member in 1899 as was Giuseppe Aldo Raudigger, who was perhaps signifying his disapproval of the robust German school of performance by entering his occupation as *"piano-fortist"*. In 1906 the musician Victor Beigel was proposed for temporary membership by Robin Legge, Roger Quilter and Gervase Elwes and in the following year was elected to full membership. Two well-known singers of the time made ample use of the honorary membership provision: Clarence Whitehill of the Royal Opera at Covent Garden availed himself of it in May 1907, January 1909, and October 1910, being proposed an each occasion by Robin Legge; and Reinhold von Warlick in November 1907 on his return from St Petersburg, and in May and December 1908 on his return from Paris. In May 1909 von Warlick appears once more but gives his occupation this time as "Musician" rather than singer; by June 1911 he has returned from Paris and become a singer again; exactly a year later he returns to the Club from Paris – an *"Artist"*.

During these years some interesting figures from various other spheres appeared at the Savile as honorary or temporary members. Among them was "Capt. F. Whitworth Jones, late 51st King's Own Yorkshire Light Infantry", who was then Secretary to the English Committee for the Olympic Games. In March 1907 he was elected an honorary member and later that month granted twelve months' temporary membership. In July 1909 the name Pierre Loti appears in the honorary members book. This was the non-de-plume of the distinguished French naval officer, Captain Louis Viaud, who had served in the Tonking War and travelled widely before becoming one of the most original and talented French writers of the second half of the nineteenth century. At the time of his election he was a guest at the French Embassy and though he lived until 1923, the year 1909 when he was a visitor to the Savile coincided with his ceasing with authorship, and he was seen no more at Piccadilly.

The system of granting these limited periods of membership enabled the Savile to offer hospitality to visitors to international conferences and similar functions of interest to members. Thus in September 1892 we find two whole pages of the honorary members book filled with names of Arabic scholars from universities all over the world, and a few weeks previously, an entry for D. W. Gillman, President of the Johns Hopkins University, Baltimore, and P.E. Pavolini, Professor of Sanskrit at the University of Florence, who had presumably arrived to attend the same function. A similar gathering of international academics is elected *en bloc* at the behest of the committee on 18 May 1904, though the entry reveals no clue as to their purpose. The Imperial Education Conference in April 1911 saw the same courtesy being extended to its leading delegates and in July 1912 the principals of twenty universities and scientific institutes from all over Europe are inscribed into the book. An apparently identical function in April 1913 was less lavishly provided for with only nine academic heads being welcomed from America and Western Europe. In July 1917 the delegates to the Infant Mortality Conference held in London were elected *en masse* to honorary membership and in October, the French historian Halévy reappeared for one month.

In April 1914, Albert Coates, Conductor of the Imperial Opera at St Petersburg, made one of his regular applications for honorary membership but then political events occurring far away from the comfortable regime at 107 Piccadilly suddenly intruded upon the composition of the hospitality books. Entries after August 1914 ceased to be mainly academics, artists and "men of differing professions"; and of a sudden the proportion of colonels, brigadier-

400

generals, Red Cross commissioners, and their like began to dominate. Erstwhile academics are now intelligence officers or military attachés; artists tend to have the word "Rifles" appended to their designation; and the "men of differing professions" are either in the Army, the Navy or the Royal Flying Corps. Some entries reflect the course of the war; in March 1917, "Captain Norman Keith Hay Clark, Suffolk Regiment, invalided home after the Somme attack" was proposed by his father Theodore Clark and was elected to six months' temporary membership. When America came into the war all the senior officers at the U.S. Embassy were granted honorary membership. Nevertheless, the art critic Bernard Berenson, and one or two others such as the American journalist John Lloyd Balderston who were not in uniform relieved the warlike atmosphere in the smoking-room at Piccadilly when they were elected to honorary membership, while Edmund Gosse among others maintained his cultural contacts by proposing Henri Davray for six months' temporary membership as he was then attaché in London to the French Foreign Office. Balderston became a full member in 1918 and Frederick Delius made one of his rare forays into the Club in September, proposed, as usual, by Robin Legge but supported this time by "Boully" Boulenger. And then the end of the war is signalled with equal suddenness in the temporary members book. Lt. Col. Terence Keyes, C.I.E., was elected on 16 October 1918. A note in the margin adds, "Cancelled. 11/11", and a further entry by way of explanation reads: "left for Russia, Election cancelled, 11/XII/18."

A few months after leading the forces of King Faisal into Damascus and holding it until General Allenby could arrive to make it secure, Colonel T.E. Lawrence, C.B., D.S.O., arrived in London and sought honorary membership of the Savile, giving his occupation simply as "soldier". He was proposed by Lt. Col. Sir Arthur McMahon, K.C.I.E., C.S.I., G.C.M.G., G.C.V.O., seconded by D.G. Hogarth, C.M.G., F.B.A., and elected on 30 October 1918. D.G. Hogarth, a Savile member since 1889, was an old friend and admirer of Lawrence who had attracted his attention in 1911 for his interest in archaeology and his knowledge of colloquial Arabic which he had picked up while preparing a post-graduate thesis on Crusader architecture. Hogarth had invited Lawrence to join his expedition to Jerablus on the Euphrates to excavate the site of Carchemish for the British Museum; Lawrence accepted and spent the years 1911-14 working there under Hogarth's guidance, using the opportunity this afforded to explore Syria and Mesopotamia in native company – experience which was to prove invaluable in his subsequent emergence as "Lawrence of Arabia". His short membership of the Savile was presumably *en route* to the peace conference in which he was to play such a dominant part in the ensuing months.

Thereafter the candidates books for honorary and temporary members cease to be quite so exciting and gradually revert to normal, though their use is becoming significantly less frequent. In the immediate post-war years there is still a contingent bearing military titles but they seem to be engaged now in mopping-up operations. The great historian, Arnold Toynbee, became an honorary member in 1919, giving his occupation as "Peace Conference, Paris"; "Commander, Count

Robert de Belleregarde de St Lary, D.S.O., etc." was granted six months' temporary membership in April 1920, and the same facility was extended in July to Daniele Varè of the Italian Diplomatic Service who was attending the league of Nations. Varè became a full member in the following year and remained one until his death in 1940; his charming memoirs of a busy and rewarding diplomatic life are in the Monument. In May 1920, Count Camillo Springardt, "Official of the League of Nations" was elected for a three-month period, but from then on the effect of the war on the pattern of visiting membership fades away to almost nothing.

And then in 1921 there comes a whiff of scandal. On 20 June, Sinclair Lewis was in London in the course of restless travels which were to be a feature of his life. He was proposed for twelve months' temporary membership by Geoffrey Williams, the honorary secretary, and supported by Frederick Harcourt Kitchin. His entry in the book lies directly beneath that for "D.H. Kitchin, Sudan Civil Service, Singa, Anglo-Egyptian Sudan" who was proposed by his father Harcourt Kitchin and seconded by Geoffrey Williams. Lewis had just established himself as a major literary figure with *Main Street*, his satire on the narrowness of American provincial life which had appealed so powerfully to the spirit of introspection which settled on America after the First World War but he was yet to write those other major novels such as *Babbitt*, *Elmer Gantry* and the rest which were to gain for him the Nobel Prize in 1930. Nevertheless, at the time he was proposed for the Savile his achievement was already such that he should have made a most agreeable addition to the Sodality.

Both D.H. Kitchin and Sinclair Lewis were duly elected on 22 June but then, a month later, on 20 July is written with heavy hand across both entries, "WITHDRAWN, G.C." (General Committee). It certainly adds a delicious spice of mystery to an otherwise prosaically businesslike book. Could they, on the strength of finding themselves on the same page, have been tempted into what Winston Graham would call "a collusive malpractice"?

Sadly or not, such speculation must be wide of the mark for Kitchin was to be successfully proposed for temporary membership several times in future years during his visits from abroad. The discreetly written minutes of the committee meeting which led to their withdrawal cast no further light on the matter, but certain it is that Sinclair Lewis was seen no more at the Savile and it is probable that his hasty departure was due to the more prosaic reason which was eventually to lead to his physical as well as his social death – alcohol. As to Kitchin . . . maybe he had another urgent appointment.

In September 1921 came a writer of another kind, Stephen Leacock, the noted humorist whose *Nonsense Novels* and other writings were to have a great vogue, though he preferred to list his other occupation in the Savile register – "Professor of Economics, Montreal University". In 1922 Arnold Lunn became an honorary member. Though he listed his occupation (quite correctly) as "author" he was probably more famous in that year for having invented the modern ski slalom at Mürren and against great opposition gained international and Olympic recognition of both downhill and slalom racing.

From 1922 onwards, the custom of electing honorary and temporary members went into even sharper decline. Though the temporary members book covering the years 1923-46 is missing from the archives this falling-off is indicated by the fact that only one honorary members book has been required from 1913 to the present day, having been used only twenty times in the last thirty years; similarly the temporary members book was last used in June 1988 and in the ten years from 1981-1991 only eighteen members were elected by this method. Nevertheless there are some interesting figures contained within them, many of whom went on to become full members. There were the regulars like the singer Reinhold von Warlick who seemed to have made a second profession of being an honorary member of the Savile and, in July 1926, the Professor of Spanish at Trinity College, Dublin, Doctor Walter Starkie, who became an honorary member of the Club which had enjoyed in its early days the convivial and witty presence of his godfather, Sir John Mahaffey. In 1927, V.S. Pritchett put his toe in the water via honorary membership before becoming a full member on his return from Dublin the following year. In 1933, Pierre Millet appears, giving as his occupation "Reading for French Diplomatic Service", an occupation which was to lead to a distinguished career as ambassador in the years after he became a full member in 1934. Max Beerbohm continued to use the Club in which he had been such a presence in earlier days, and appears in the Honorary Members Book in 1935 during one of his visits to London: Edwin Beinecke, the banker and bibliophile put the process in reverse by graduating from honorary to full membership in that same year. In October 1937, Lyman Beecher Stowe, the less successful novelist son of the author of *Uncle Tom's Cabin*, spent a month at the Club.

The War of 1939-45 did not cause such an influx of transient military members as had its rehearsal in 1914. During the whole period of the war only nineteen honorary members were elected of whom eleven were in the armed services. The immediate post-war years yielded a smattering of officials concerned with creating the "peace" including a bloc of delegates to the Unesco conference in 1945. The pattern of membership generally had returned to normal by 1950 when Lothar Mendes, the eccentric but brilliant film director who unwittingly bequeathed the title of this book to the Savile, was elected to honorary membership before making his connection life-long in the same year. In 1952 the distinguished American novelist John P. Marquand became an honorary member and in 1956 the Club was treated to the presence of one Charles Spencer Chaplin who had forgone the more demotic "Charlie" no doubt in deference to his acquisition of a classic reputation and his staid proposer and seconder, Sir William Walton and the honorary secretary, Dick Kenderdine. Two years later, in 1958, another great American novelist, Robert Ardrey, was elected to one month's honorary membership of the Savile to provide him with congenial surroundings while he was in London and in 1959 Sidney Nolan, possibly the first and certainly the most outstanding of Australian artists, was proposed by C.P. Snow and Harry Hoff under the same rule, preparatory to being granted full membership in 1960. Similarly, Professor

Samuel Sambursky, professor of the history of science in Israel, was proposed by the ex-mayor of Jerusalem, Richard Graves, before becoming, as he still remains, an enthusiastic overseas member of the Club. "Jack Philip Cannon, composer" – now better known to members as plain Philip Cannon, appears first in the honorary members book in 1964 before becoming a full member later that year. In 1965 the tradition of hospitality to senior members of the American Embassy – particularly those concerned with cultural affairs – which had provided the Club with several stimulating companions for many years was continued with the election to temporary membership of Doctor Martin C. Carroll, Junior, the cultural attaché. The Club must have held its breath later that year when Robert Henriques introduced the Israeli Ambassador, Alaron Remez, to twelve months' temporary membership for, according to Tyrrell Burgess, the appearance of anyone from the Middle East at the Club in the company of Henriques presaged the immediate outbreak of war in that region. Perhaps coincidently a few months after his temporary membership expired the six-days' war broke out.

In June 1967, Eric Ambler anticipated his subsequent admission to full membership by embarking on three months as a temporary and was joined by the American author, John O'Hara, who returned to the States in September after his visit to London came to an end. George Movshon, an official of the United Nations, who was to be a popular member of the Club from 1970 until his death more than twelve years later, availed himself of three months' temporary membership in 1967 and Alistair Cooke appeared for a three-month period in the mid-summer of 1969.

But as we have seen, the pace of these memberships was becoming slower and slower and from 1959 onwards it ground almost to a total halt. Perhaps the only visitors after this date who have left – or continue to leave – their impressions on the Sodality have been the Rev. John Quinn, S.J., who anticipated Cyril Barrett by nine years in becoming the first Jesuit priest to take up membership of the Club, which he did for twelve months in 1969; Leo Rosten, the humorous chronicler of American Jewry who was a temporary member for three months in 1971; Andrew Davis, the conductor, for six months in 1978; and very nearly the end of the line, Donald Stearns, Legal Adviser to the U.S. Government, who made his first tentative appearance for three months in 1981 before becoming a full member later that year.

It has seemed worthwhile to deal at some length with the lists of honorary and temporary members for although so comparatively few have entered the Savile on this basis during the post-war years, the overall total since the Club was founded represents a significant percentage of the total membership even if, individually, their presence was often brief. They are interesting also in the consistency with which they have reflected the basic body of the membership in their distinction, their diversity of professions and opinions, and their classless devotion to *Sodalitas* and *Convivium*.

404

While the Savile, as we have just seen, has been enriched by the honorary and temporary members who have been invited at various times by the regular membership to join them during their brief sojourns in London, from its earliest days it has also benefited from the process of affiliation with other clubs of similar aims and principles at home and abroad.

By the 1870s exchanges of hospitality had become a commonplace between the Savile and the Burlington Fine Arts Club which was situated nearby Savile Row, and though many members belonged to both clubs they continued their separate ways, Savilians enjoying the occasional exhibitions at the Burlington and the Burlington's members enjoying hospitality at the Savile whenever holidays or renovations made it necessary for them temporarily to close.

In August 1876 the Savile began a relationship with the Arts Club which continues to the present day. Sir Herbert Stephen, writing in 1923, records how this began:

> It was in 1876 that another friendship began which now constitutes if not an alliance at least an extremely cordial *entente*. In August of that year there was communicated to the Committee "an offer from the Arts Club to receive members of the Savile in their house [in Hanover Square] whilst the Club was closed for the repairs on the understanding that members of the Arts Club should be received at the Savile while the Arts was closed." The bargain was struck. The Arts visited the Savile from the end of the August to the 10th of September, and the Savile was received at the Arts from the 11th to the 25th of September. This arrangement was continued for about ten years, after which it was found more convenient for the Savile to visit either the Oriental Club, in Hanover Square, or the Isthmian, then located in the building at the top of Arlington Street where the Ritz Hotel now stands. But at the close of the century the connection with the Arts was resumed, and of late years has become more firmly established than ever. Not long ago the Savile inflicted themselves upon the Arts for five consecutive weeks, and the kindness of the hosts gave no indication that the guests had outstayed their welcome. Since the Savile moved to Piccadilly, and the Arts, not very long after, to Dover Street, the advantage in available space has been with the Arts, but no members of the Savile can admit that the Dover Street site is as good as his own. The two Clubs are sufficiently near to each other in point of numbers to make the exchange work satisfactorily as a whole, and in days when modern habits require a somewhat longer period of annual closing for repairs and holidays than was usual forty years ago, the Club is fortunate to be so well suited in this particular.

In a later addendum to the Club's history written in 1958 there is the following paragraph:

Reference has been made to the Club's happy relations with the Arts Club and the exchange of hospitality during the Summer closing time. The practice was interrupted by severe bomb damage at the Arts. It has always been deeply regretted by those members of the Savile who know that, owing to war circumstances, there was, literally, no-one available at the Savile to realise what had happened and to offer to the Arts Club, our friend of 50 years, help and amenities which could have been made available. We are happy to see the Arts Club emerging so handsomely from the rubble, and to be again both host and guest.

In fact, the Arts Club had been a friend for 82 years not 50 but, this aside, amends were to be made. In 1973 the Arts Club had to close for three years while its clubhouse was being rebuilt. The Savile invited twenty of its members to be guests for the duration and to enjoy all the rights and privileges of full membership at Brook Street. On their return to the refurbished premises in 1976, the twenty Arts Club members made a substantial donation to the Savile cellars, accompanied by an appreciative letter and the following anonymously written verses:

SODALITAS CONVIVIUM

The day the Arts Club closed its doors
With the future still uncertain
Its members might have had good cause
To expect the final curtain.

They faced a dreary wilderness
A landscape without figures
An endless trail of distress
A life of club-less rigours.

But succour wasn't far away
A solution none would cavil
For twenty lucky members, they
were invited to the Savile.

The Savile gave them food and drink
Much friendly hospitality –
And for nearly three long years – I think,
A grand conviviality,

The lucky twenty oft opine
(There's little need to chivvy'em)
The days were happy at sixty-nine
and Sodalitas Convivium.

So back in Dover Street – it's nice
Among the artistic ladies!
(While some proclaim it's Paradise –
there's others think it Hades!)

So let us drink such fulsome toasts
As well deserves the Savile
And all our generous erstwhile hosts –
And the hindmost to the Devil!

The connection continues to the present day and "The Arts" is a popular venue for Savilians who wish to entertain a lady to week-day lunch when, contrary to Savile practice, it is *obligatory* to have a female companion before entering the premises.

The reciprocal arrangement with the Oriental Club continues as happily today as it did way back in the 1880s while limited hospitality is extended between both sides with the East India and Devonshire Club, the City University Club and the Gresham Club.

The summer closures which are now common to all the leading London Clubs see regular exchanges between the Savile and such other institutions as the Garrick, the "In and Out" and several others. This provides a welcome cross-fertilization of *mores* which can sometimes give rise to amusing collisions. One of the most enduring and joyous of Savile legends, for instance, dates from a summer closure when the Club was offered hospitality at the Guards Club. A Savilian tucked away unobtrusively in a dark corner of their bar overheard young Subaltern addressing his Colonel:

"I say, sir, fairly jolly chaps these Saviles, don't you think?"
"By Jove, rather," said another, "seem able to spout away about anything. Quite a treat, sometimes, listening to 'em."

"Quite so," said the Colonel, "but what a pity they seem to make their own trousers."

Whatever such minor sartorial or cultural clashes the Savile has maintained a happy and rewarding relationship with its sibling institutions and the intermingling has almost always been a fruitful one.

Other affiliations have been made over the years in Great Britain and abroad which are also of great mutual benefit. These include the major clubs in Scotland, Wales and Ireland; clubs in New York, Washington, Boston, and Philadelphia;

Canada, Sweden, Portugal, South Africa, France, Greece, New Zealand and Australia. Their members have enlivened the Savile at regular intervals, indeed, many of them such as the medical scientist, Paul Cranefield, and Ben Lucien Burman, the author of twenty-two books which included the delightful series of children's tales centred on the mythical Louisianna town of "Catfish Bend", were tempted into full membership in their own right after sampling Savile *Convivium* as reciprocal guests. Cranefield, happily, is still a regular visitor as was the indefatigable Ben Burman until he died in 1984 aged 88. Savilians in their turn will find themselves as equally welcome abroad as if they were coming through the doors at Brook Street.

INDEX

(Non-Savilians are in italic type)

Purcell, Henry, 195, 198, 202
Putnam, George Haven, 396
Pye-Smith, Dr Philip Henry, F.R.S., 10, 133

Quennell, Peter, 258
Quick, Diana, 305
Quiller-Couch, Sir Arthur, 21
Quilter, Roger, 84, 206, 207, 209, 399
Quinn, Rev. John, S.J., 404

Radford, Basil, 312
Ranalow, Frederick Baring, 208, 221
Rank, J. Arthur, (Lord), 279–80
Raphael, Frederic, 121–2
Rau, Anthony, 150
Rau, Dr Donald, 150
Rau, Dr Leo, 68, 150
Raudigger, Giuseppe Aldo, 203, 399
Ravel, Maurice, 212
Rawlins, William Donaldson, K.C., 185
Rayleigh, Lord *see* Strutt, Prof.
Raymond, John, 96, 327
Reagan, Nancy, 312
Redesdale, Lady (née Sydney Bowles), 176
Redgrave, Michael, 87
Reed, Carol, 309
Reed, Sir E.J., C.B., F.R.S., 10, 377
Reed, Henry, 89–90
Reed, Sir Stanley, 398
Reed, Tracy, 308
Reed, W.H., 214
Reeves, Amber, 324
Reeves, Pember, 324
Reilly, Paul (later Lord), 181
Reinhardt, Max, 94
Reith, Sir John (later Lord Reith), 276, 281
Reitlinger, Gerald Robert, 263–4
Remez, Alaron, 404

Reynolds, "Josh", 100
Reynolds, Stanley, 177, 251
Richard *see* Burleton, Richard
Richardson, Sir Ralph, 3, 89, 91, 93–4, 95, 99, 104, 226, 291, 300, 301, 302, 317–19, 332–3, 357, 367, 380
Richter, Hans, 210, 215
Riding, Laura, 258
Ritchie-Calder, Lord, 180, 181, 183
Roberts, Denys Kilham, 331, 366, 369
Roberts, Sir Wyn, 175
Robertson, Andrew, 348
Robinson, Rev. J., 8
Robertson, Thomas Herbert, 396
Robinson, Sir William, G.C.M.G., 396
Rockstro, William Smith, 198
Rodd, Peter Rennel ("Prod"), xi, 61–2, 83, 335, 341, 355, 379
Rodd, Sir Rennell (later Lord Rennell of Rodd), 61–2, 355
Rodway, Norman, 308
Rogers, Rev. W., 10
Romanes, George John, F.R.S., 128
Romero, George, 316
Ronald, Sir Landon, 240
Roosevelt, Franklin Delano, President, 278
Rosebery, Lord (5th Earl), 18–19, 23, 26, 69
Rosenthal, Tom, 265
Ross, Alec (Alex), 45, 322, 399
Ross, Robert, 45–6, 249, 256–7, 299, 399
Rossetti, Dante Gabriel, 59, 252, 262
Rosten, Leo, 404
Rothenstein, Lady Alice (née Kingsley), 262
Rothenstein, Sir William, D. Litt., 45, 66, 210, 217, 256, 259–62
Rothschild, Baron Meyer de, 18–19